The
Everything
Cookbook

Books by Betty Wason

The Art of German Cooking
The Art of Spanish Cooking
The Art of Vegetarian Cooking
Betty Wason's Greek Cookbook
Bride in the Kitchen
Cooking to Please Finicky Kids
Cooks, Gluttons, and Gourmets
Dinners That Wait
The Everything Cookbook
The Language of Cookery
A Salute to Cheese

The Everything Cookbook

by

Betty Wason

Illustrated
by
Leonard Cascioli

Hawthorn Books, Inc. / Publishers / New York

CONTENTS

Introduction—Read This First

The Best Cooking Is Simple

What meat is more succulently good than rare roast beef cooked to a turn, so tender it falls in limp slices from the carving knife?

What cook is more to be praised than the one who can produce fluffy-soft mashed potatoes every time, and top off the white fluff with gravy smooth and redolent of rich brown pan drippings? What better salad is there than thin-sliced cucumbers and sun-ripened tomatoes tossed lightly with an oil and vinegar dressing? What finer dessert than a home-baked fruit pie in flaky-crisp crust?

The cordon bleu cook may be admired extravagantly by her (or his) peers, but it's the home cook who can put beautifully prepared simple food on the table night after night who is most loved.

In today's American kitchens, food preparation is so easy that there's no excuse for anyone's not being able to produce good, simple food. The trouble is that in many ways it's *too* easy. The indifferent cook has only to put ready-to-heat frozen foods in the oven, or to add tap water to a package of dehydrated ingredients for what is euphemistically called a casserole, and her family will not starve.

At least hunger is met. But the shocking fact is that in affluent America thousands of children from well-to-do homes are malnourished, their appetites satisfied and their taste dulled with pizzas, frozen French fries, soft drinks, and chocolate bars.

Wonderful as the American supermarket is with its thou-

sands of convenience foods, its myriad counters of frozen products, and its year-round array of fresh vegetables and fruits,
good cooking is still, and always will be, the art of pointing up
the natural flavors of food, of knowing how to season lightly yet
deftly, and how not to oversauce.

We call it cooking, yet it is not any one dish alone that makes a
good meal. The art of the home cook is to produce a combination of foods that complement one another, whet the appetite,
and afterward leave the diners, whether they be family or
guests, content, well fed, with a feeling that this is the best of all
worlds.

A meal can be superb that includes not a single sauce, that
requires not one glance into a cookbook.

Buying wisely is the essential first step to cooking superbly,
for no dish is better than the ingredients that go into it.

Proper storage is important to preserve flavor and quality.

Understanding basic techniques not only makes it easier to
follow recipes, but when you have mastered the whys and
hows, you won't need to consult cookbooks nearly so often, and
that's when you become creative.

These are the reasons why this book deals first with food
selection and basic techniques, before presenting recipes.
Cooking is much more than recipes. It's the organization of an
art that begins with selection of ingredients and ends with a
composition of enticing aromas, colors, and taste sensations that
complement one another like details in a painting, or the music
of instruments in an orchestra.

No one ever sits down to read a cookbook from start to finish,
and it's not anticipated that this book will be so read. But the
material has nevertheless been arranged in logical sequence,
proceeding step by step to cover all a cook needs to know, so
that whatever question may be asked, the answer should be
found somewhere between these covers.

Do you want to know why a particular sauce curdled? Look it
up in the index, under *Sauces, how to prevent curdling*. Would
you like to serve your favorite spaghetti casserole, whose recipe
yield is only 6 servings, at a buffet supper for 16 people? Look
up *Recipes, how to multiply,* and perhaps *Recipes, how to figure serving portions.* Have you suddenly learned your husband
must go on a low-cholesterol diet? Look up *Special diets, low
cholesterol*.

Learn to use the index like a computer; let it help you locate
whatever information you seek.

For many homemakers, who must be responsible for putting meals on the table day after day, week after week, it's not new recipes that are needed nearly as much as inspiration, suggestions of what to have for dinner, how to break out of a culinary rut. For this reason, besides a separate section on meal planning, one-line menu suggestions are to be found with nearly every entree.

Above all, cooking should be a pleasure, an outlet for creative instincts. To this end, recipes are presented in a way that we hope makes them sound so delicious and easy to prepare that you'll go to the kitchen eager to try something new. For if you like to cook, you'll be a good cook. It's that simple.

A word about the way the recipes in this book were tested. For a number of years I served as consultant to food and wine firms, to whom I offered a home-kitchen recipe-testing service. I would develop recipes in my own elaborate test kitchen in Pleasantville, New York, a "laboratory" equipped with the best of labor-saving appliances, then I farmed out the recipes to housewives of different regional backgrounds and with different family situations for testing in their kitchens. Not only did these women report back whether or not each recipe was easy to understand and easy to prepare, but they gave me a family evaluation of each dish. Most of the recipes in this book came from files kept during those years; many still bear handwritten notations such as "Excellent!" or "All of us loved this."

But the book as a whole is far more than a collection of tested recipes. It is the fruit of a lifelong love of cooking, an insatiable curiosity about everything related to the table, and a genuine delight in receiving friends in my home. When I was a young art student, a teacher of mine liked to recount a tale about Whistler. When asked by a patron how much time he had spent on a certain painting, Whistler admitted candidly that he had finished it in just two days. The patron was outraged. How dared Whistler charge such a high price for two days' work? "Not for two days' work," the renowned painter replied. "For the knowledge of a lifetime."

And so it is with the information gathered between these pages: it represents not just a year's work, not just filing cases crammed full of recipes, but the essence of knowledge gained during a lifetime of cooking and enjoying it.

BOOK ONE

ABC's of Food Preparation

1 TO MARKET, TO MARKET

You're an efficient shopper who tries to take care of a week's marketing in a single morning. You may or may not have studied grocery ads on the lookout for specials, but you rely on the enticing displays of supermarket counters to inspire you in your selections. Yet the great hazard of impulsive supermarket shopping is that the shopping cart is quickly filled with unnecessary and extravagant "specials." At least try to be selective in your extravagance. And if you buy too much today, do store away the surplus in the freezer and/or pantry, and *next time*, make a list.

Before you leave home (or pick up the phone to order from a neighborhood grocer), check supplies on hand. Can't you make use of "bargains" in canned or packaged foods you bought two months ago? The jammed freezer: aren't there some cuts of meat buried beneath that heavy coating of frost that could be used this week?

And the staples: sugar, salt, flour, rice, breakfast cereals, onions, potatoes, catsup, and mustard. Are you sure you have enough of these always needed supplies to last through the week?

Now, if you are truly efficient you will jot down rough menus for the week ahead. *That's* the way to do it!

HOW TO BUY MEAT

One-fourth of the average American family's food expenditures goes into meat, and those who have meat more than once a day (as many families do) spend still more than this.

No matter how important your daily meat, you can reduce meat expenditures and still eat well. First, understand the various cuts of meat and how to use each most effectively. Second, learn the many ways of tenderizing "less tender" cuts and meats of less than choice quality.

Prepackaged meats offer the advantage of being already priced, so that you know exactly how much you are spending in advance, and so wrapped that you can pick them up for a close look. But the indications of quality are more difficult to spot. Often they have been so wrapped that you see only the prettier side: the bones and the fat are cleverly concealed.

When you buy something special, meat to be served to company, it is wisest to get it from a private butcher, or have the supermarket meat man cut it to order. In the end this will probably cost less per serving portion.

Judging Quality

Most, but not all, meat has been inspected in the packing plants for wholesomeness, and some of it has been *graded* as to quality by skilled federal inspectors. Unfortunately, the consumer rarely sees the blue-purple federal stamps any longer, because when meat is cut into consumer portions, the stamps are rarely visible.

Nevertheless, it is important to know what the terms mean. *Prime* means the finest quality, best for flavor, most tender. *Choice* is next best to prime. The other grades (rarely mentioned to the retail trade: are *good, standard, commercial,* and *utility.* Most meat sold in supermarkets is of either *good* or *standard* quality. The rest is used in making the cheaper sausages, for institutions, and for pet food.

BEEF. The best quality beef will be a bright-red color, the outside fat creamy-white and flaky, the bones reddish-pink and slightly porous. The lean of tender cuts should be well marbled with streaks of white fat. (Round steak is an exception: This has virtually no fat, and therefore often needs added fat for cooking.) Beef of poor quality will be darker in color, coarse-grained, and flabby; and if the bones are hard and white, it means the meat is from an older (and therefore tougher) animal. But the meat of even a young steer may be coarse-grained, tough, and less desirable in flavor, which is the reason for grading.

LAMB. For best quality look for meat that is lighter red than beef, fine-grained, almost velvety in texture, with clear white brittle fat. When darker in color it is from an older animal, with stronger flavor and not so tender.

Technically, the term "lamb" should be applied only to the meat of animals less than 1 year old. If 1 to 1½ years, the animal is called "yearling"; if more than 1½ years, the meat should be called "mutton." But since we almost never see "mutton" for sale in American markets, obviously some meat called "lamb" isn't. Suckling lamb, from an animal less than 2 months old, is occasionally found in cities with large Greek or Italian populations. This is the most tender and delicate of all. Genuine spring lamb has become a rather meaningless term, as the lambing season is now spread over the year. Size is some criterion. A smaller leg, even though it has less edible meat per pound, is likely to be more tender and delicate.

VEAL. The best-quality veal is pinkish-gray, velvety in texture, very fine grained, with soft, firm fat. Deeper pink veal is from an older animal; if light red, it will be more like beef (but not as tender). Milk-fed veal is from a calf butchered before it would have been weaned to grass. Veal has very little fat and should usually be cooked with additional fat and moisture.

PORK. The lean should be very light in color, pinkish-white, with a firm, creamy-white edging of fat and comparatively little fat through the lean. The lighter the color, the better the flavor. Freshness is very important, because pork is the most perishable of all meats and most subject to contamination. Also, it contains a larger proportion of fat per pound than any other meat. Examine precut portions carefully for position of bone; some roasts have bone running through the lean in such a way that it is very difficult to cut. All pork is tender, but needs to be cooked to well-done because of its perishability.

HAM. All ham (except *fresh ham*) is cured pork. *Country-cured hams* have been salted and slow-smoked. The meat of these is deep, dark red; the outside may be dark brown and heavily crusted with brown fat. Such hams must be parboiled, and consequently there is more waste, less edible meat per pound. *Tenderized hams* are a light, bright red in color: all have been cured chemically by injections deep into the meat, not just on the outside—and 90 percent of the hams in American markets are now of this type. The label *ready-to-cook* means the meat must be parboiled before baking, but there is proportionately less waste than with country-cured ham. *Ready-to-eat* means the meat could actually be eaten without cooking, but will have better flavor if baked, allowing 10 to 20 minutes per pound. *Picnic hams* are cured pork, but the meat is not taken from the leg. Most of it is from the shoulder, boned and rolled. All picnic hams should be precooked, unless the package label says "ready-to-eat." *Fresh ham* is the leg of fresh pork that has *not* been cured. This must be treated like all fresh pork.

Quality in ham is largely a question of how the meat has been processed in the plant, and therefore brand names are the best criterion. A higher price per pound generally (but not always) means more flavorful, succulent ham. If in doubt, ask the butcher to recommend a particular brand. Morrell and Boar's Head are two outstandingly good processors; Swift and Armour's, the two largest meat packers, each has several different types of ham to offer. All ham is tender: the differences lie in texture (the grain of the meat), flavor, and juiciness.

"Tender" versus "Less Tender"

"Tender" is the accepted term for those cuts of meat which can be cooked by direct heat—that is, by broiling or roasting. "Less tender" is the term applied to all other cuts. The less tender cuts generally should be cooked in liquid, or cooked covered so that the meat steams in its own juice—unless they can be satisfactorily tenderized by one means or another.

The chart on pages 8-9 shows how similar are cuts from the same part of the animal whether it is beef, veal, lamb, or pork. The tender cuts are mainly from rib, loin, upper leg (including ham), and, to a lesser extent, the shoulder. The lower ribs or stomach, foreshank, bonier parts of shoulder, neck, and hind-shank are less tender.

Names alone can be confusing, because the names for similar cuts vary from one part of the country to another and because fancy names are sometimes given to less desirable cuts to make them seem more attractive.

A Steak Isn't Always a Steak

Perhaps a rose by any other name would smell as sweet, but a tough piece of meat isn't rendered tender by being called "steak," even though some meat men would like us to think so.

Examples: a *skirt steak* is taken from the plate or brisket of beef and can only be braised or stewed, not broiled or pan-fried. *Chicken steaks* are cut from the blade section of chuck. If of choice quality, these might be broiled satisfactorily, but it's safer to braise them. *Flank steak* may be broiled, if of choice quality, but only to rare, and then sliced almost horizon-tally in very thin slices. Otherwise, flank should be stewed or pot-roasted. *Cube steaks* are thin fillets from the rump (a less tender portion) which have been made more tender by *scoring*, the muscular tendons severed by cutting into criss-cross waffle patterns with a special tool. These may be pan-fried, but will be tough if broiled.

The most tender steaks, and the most tender chops, are those from the rib and loin sections, and from shoulder sections ad-joining the rib.

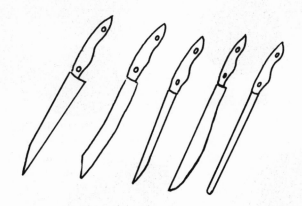

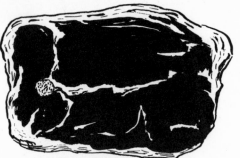

Beef Round Steak

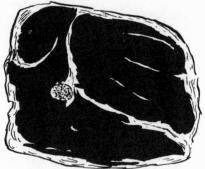

Veal Round Steak (Cutlet)

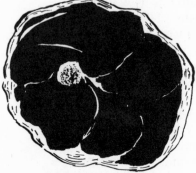

Pork Ham Slice

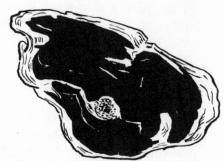

Lamb Leg Steak

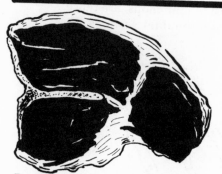

Beef Porterhouse or T-Bone Steak

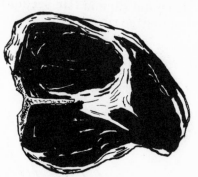

Veal Loin Chop

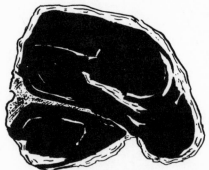

Pork Loin Chop

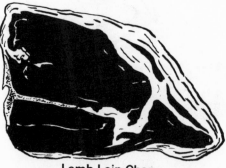

Lamb Loin Chop

Beef Rib Steak

Veal Rib Chop

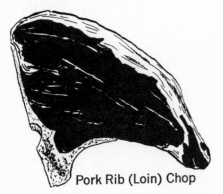

Pork Rib (Loin) Chop

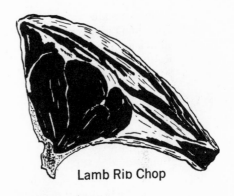

Lamb Rib Chop

Beef Brisket

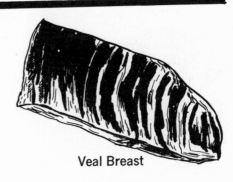

Veal Breast

Pork (Side Pork and Bacon)

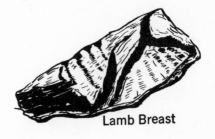

Lamb Breast

Braise, Stew, or Pot-roast *(Less Tender Cuts)*	Broil or Roast *(Tender Cuts)*
Bottom round	Top round
Heel of round	Eye round roast
Hind shank*	London broil
Rolled rump	Sirloin steak
Flank steak*	Porterhouse steak
Plate beef	T-bone steak
Short ribs	Club steak
Brisket	Delmonico steak
Corned beef	Filet mignon
Shank knuckle	Rib steak
Foreshank cross cut	Standing rib roast
Chuck pot roast	Rolled rib roast
Rolled chuck roast	Chuck steak (next to rib)
Arm pot roast	
Arm steak*	
Boneless neck*	
Oxtail	
Steer liver	
Beef kidney	
Tongue	

*May be broiled if previously tenderized, cooked to rare.

Boneless stewing meat is usually from chuck, rump, or bottom round.

Hamburger meat may be any combination of trimmings, put through food grinder.

Ground chuck is from shoulder, **ground round** from top round.

Beef Identification Chart

Top round

Eye round roast

Bottom round

ROUND

RUMP

Heel of round

Hind shank*

Sirloin steak

London broil

SIRLOIN

Porterhouse steak

Rolled rump

Flank steak*

FLANK

SHORT LOIN

T-bone steak

Plate beef

Delmonico steak

Short ribs

Club steak

Brisket

Corned beef

PLATE

RIB

Filet mignon

Shank knuckle

Rib steak

Foreshank cross cut

BRISKET

CHUCK

SHANK

Chuck pot roast

Standing rib roast

Rolled chuck roast

Arm pot roast

Arm steak*

Boneless neck

Rolled rib roast

Oxtail

Steer liver

Beef kidney

Tongue

Chuck steak (next to rib)

Braise, Stew or Pot-roast	*Fry, Broil, or Roast*
Scallopini	Scallopini†
Breast, for stew	Veal cutlet†
Heel of round	Leg roast (center cut)
Hind shank	Boned breast
Veal birds	Rump roast
Shoulder steak	Rump steak*
Boneless stew	Veal (sirloin) steak*
Foreshank, cut up	Loin chop*
Kidney	Rib chop*
Calf's brains	Rib roast (center cut)
Sweetbreads	Crown roast
Calf's liver*	Blade roast
Tongue	Rolled shoulder
	Arm roast

*Can be broiled if first marinated in oil; cook to well-done.
†Should first be pounded to soften tissues; may be breaded.

Veal Identification Chart

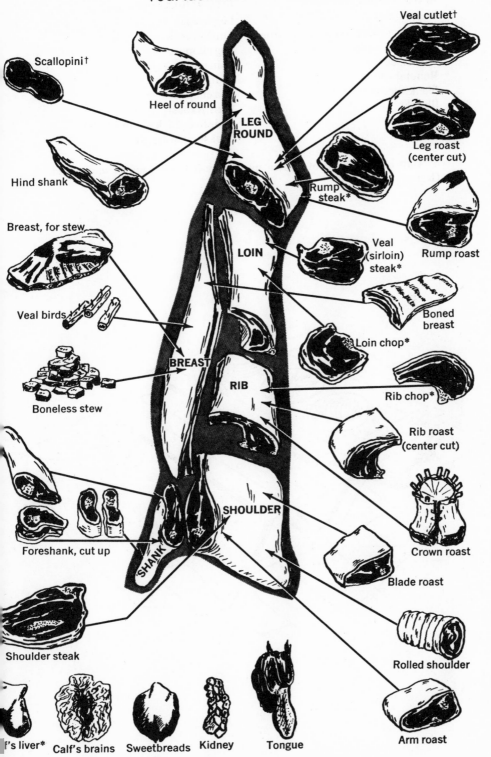

Scallopini†

Heel of round

Hind shank

Breast, for stew

Veal birds

Boneless stew

BREAST

Foreshank, cut up

SHANK

Shoulder steak

's liver* Calf's brains Sweetbreads Kidney Tongue

LEG ROUND

LOIN

RIB

SHOULDER

Veal cutlet†

Leg roast (center cut)

Rump steak*

Rump roast

Veal (sirloin) steak*

Boned breast

Loin chop*

Rib chop*

Rib roast (center cut)

Crown roast

Blade roast

Rolled shoulder

Arm roast

Braise or Stew
Shoulder chop*
Shoulder roast (bone-in or rolled)
Shoulder, cut up for stew
Breast, cut up for stew
Boneless stew
Neck slices
Shank*
Kidneys

Broil or Roast
Leg (roast)
Shish-kabob
Leg chop
Loin chop
Kidney chop
Rib chop
Crown roast
Saddle or rack of lamb
Breast (spareribs)

*Can be broiled if of choice quality or if tenderized or marinated first.

Lamb Identification Chart

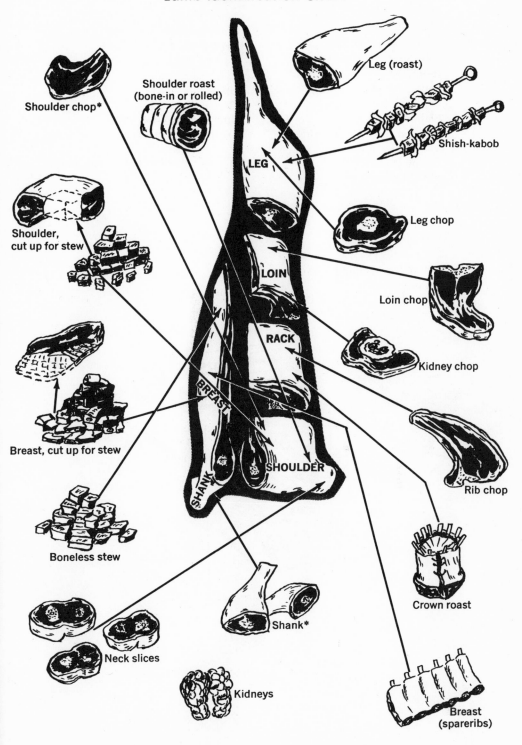

Shoulder chop*

Shoulder roast
(bone-in or rolled)

Leg (roast)

Shish-kabob

Shoulder,
cut up for stew

LEG

Leg chop

LOIN

Loin chop

RACK

Kidney chop

BREAST

Breast, cut up for stew

Rib chop

Boneless stew

SHANK

SHOULDER

Crown roast

Neck slices

Shank*

Kidneys

Breast
(spareribs)

Fry, Braise, or Stew

Ham, center slice
Canadian bacon
Loin chop*
Rib chop*
Butterfly chop*
Bacon
Salt pork
Fatback
Smoked shoulder (picnic)
Smoked shoulder butt
Boston butt
Shoulder hock
Hocks
Pig's feet
Jowl
Liver (for pâté)

Roast

Ham (butt half)
Ham (shank half)
Fresh ham (roast)
Pork tenderloin
Loin roast, center cut
Blade loin roast
Crown roast
Spareribs*
Fresh shoulder (bone-in or rolled)

*Can be broiled but must be cooked to well-done; baste during cooking to keep moist.

Pork Identification Chart

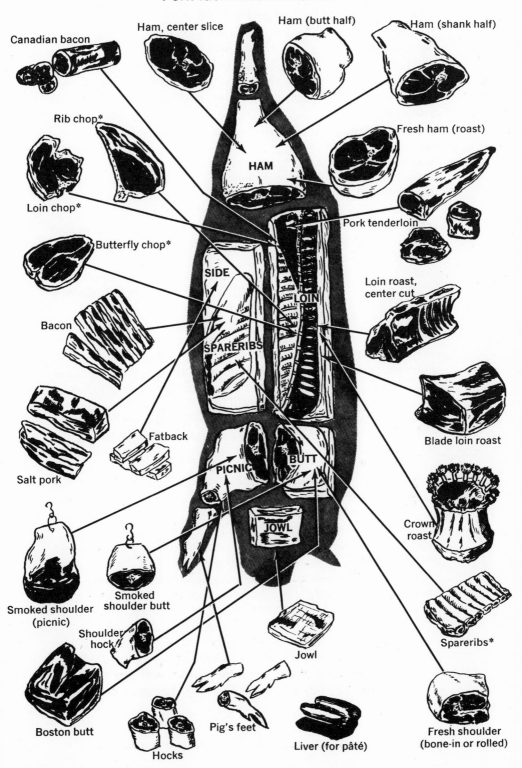

Canadian bacon

Ham, center slice

Ham (butt half)

Ham (shank half)

Rib chop*

Fresh ham (roast)

Loin chop*

HAM

Pork tenderloin

Butterfly chop*

SIDE

LOIN

Loin roast,
center cut

Bacon

SPARERIBS

Fatback

Blade loin roast

Salt pork

PICNIC

BUTT

JOWL

Crown
roast

Smoked shoulder
(picnic)

Smoked
shoulder butt

Shoulder
hock

Jowl

Spareribs*

Boston butt

Hocks

Pig's feet

Liver (for pâté)

Fresh shoulder
(bone-in or rolled)

What Is the Real Price Per Pound?

Judge the price by how many serving portions you can hope to get from a particular cut. How much are you paying for bones and fat? How much will the meat shrink with cooking?

A 5- or 6-pound roast with bone (purchased weight) may yield no more than 1½ pounds of edible cooked meat. Bones, fat, and extracted juice account for the rest. Even a *boned* rolled roast will shrink considerably with cooking, especially if it contains a large proportion of fat.

The shorter the cooking period, the less shrinkage. A 4-pound pot roast that must be cooked 3 or 4 hours will yield fewer servings than a 4-pound oven roast that requires only 1½ hours. *Meat that can be cooked rare* yields sometimes half again as many servings as that cooked to well done, because with longer cooking, more juice is extracted. (This is another way in which tenderizing can save money.)

The best buys are usually those meats with a small proportion of bone and fat (or no bone or fat) that can be cooked a relatively short time.

But flavor must also be considered. Both bones and fat contribute to flavor, which is why a standing rib of beef has better flavor than a rolled rib. And stewing meat, though it may not yield as many servings per pound as meat broiled for shish-kabob, may be more desirable because the meat juices in the stew contribute so importantly to the flavor of the sauce.

Remember quality, too. You get better flavor and often bigger yield with meats of choice or prime quality, and this may make the higher per-pound price worthwhile.

How to Estimate Servings Per Pound

Boneless meat that can be broiled or roasted rare: 4 to 6 servings per pound. Exception: sirloin or club steaks: allow ½ pound per serving—or more, if it is for steak-loving men.

Boneless meat to be stewed or pot-roasted: 2 to 3 servings per pound, depending on length of cooking time.

Meat with small amount of bone to be broiled or roasted: 3 to 4 servings per pound, depending on position of bone, amount of fat, and length of cooking time.

Meat with large amount of bone: 1 serving per pound.

Ground meat with small amount of fat, 4 to 6 servings per pound. With considerable fat, 3 to 4 servings per pound. If "extended" with added bread crumbs, liquid, and egg, a pound could make as many as 8 servings (meatballs or hamburgers).

Hamburger Hints

The above explains why ground meat is the best of all meat buys. But beware! Ground meat is perishable and should be purchased only 24 hours before use (unless frozen promptly); also, if it contains considerable fat, the meat will shrink greatly, and excess fat in a sauce can be ruinous.

It is always preferable to have meat ground to order: prepackaged ground meat or meat patties may contain a great deal of fat, and you can't know how much time has elapsed since the meat was put through the grinder. If ground to order, ask to see the meat before it is put through the grinder so you have some idea of the proportion of fat.

Ground round steak has the least fat. Ground chuck has slightly more, and is usually considered the best for hamburgers. What is called hamburger meat usually contains a great deal of fat, as do preshaped lamb patties (do not use these in a recipe calling for "lean lamb, ground" unless the excess fat is first drawn out).

Meatloaf mixture, prepackaged, usually consists of 2 parts beef, 1 part pork, 1 part veal. This can be used for either meatballs or meatloaf, but use it promptly and cook it to very well done. If you wish a different combination of meats, have meat ground to order.

Make Friends with the Butcher

A reliable butcher can save you money. When you find one you like and can depend on, patronize him regularly; let him know you appreciate quality. He will be able to select cuts that have less bone, or with the bone so positioned that the meat is easier to carve. A pork loin from a private butcher may cost 10 or 12 cents more per pound than one from the supermarket, yet yield so much more edible meat that its per-serving cost is considerably less. A top-quality chuck steak, broiled, may be better in flavor and more tender than a supermarket "bargain" sirloin.

Saving with Tenderizers

There are a number of different ways to tenderize meat (see index, under Tenderizing). The handiest is a commercial tenderizer; a number of different companies now manufacture tenderizers in both liquid and powder form. All are extracts of papain, a secretion from the rind of papaya fruit.

Tenderizing can actually turn a piece of stewing meat into

one that can be broiled or roasted. A hind shank of beef can be served as a miniature roast with the use of a tenderizer, and shish-kabob made with boneless beef stewing meat.

Tenderize meat *before freezing;* do not add salt—it's already in the tenderizer.

Plan-ahead Meat Buying

Use your freezer as a meat "bank": buy extra roasts, steaks, and chops when the price is attractive. If prepackaged, steaks can be placed in the freezer just as they are. So can some roasts; or ask the butcher to freezer-wrap a roast for you. Or, a roast may be cut up in one of the following ways to make several meals:

Whole loin of pork: Cut half into chops, keeping the remainder as a small roast. Or, bone the remainder, cut into small ¾- to ½-inch cubes, use in oriental dishes, Greek Pork and Celery Stew, Paella, for Székely Gulyás, or broil for Pork Satay.

Fresh ham: Ask butcher to bone it, use part rolled for small pork roast, remainder in cubes as above.

Leg of lamb: Cut off three or four leg chops, bone the rest. Cube, divide into meal-size portions for shish-kabob and/or curry. Chop up straggly pieces, use for Moussaka, Shepherd's Pie, or Greek Lamb Stew. *Shoulder of lamb* can be cut up in much the same way.

Eye round or rolled roast of beef: Have a number of very thin slices cut from one end by the butcher (on his slicing machine), package these separately for Steak Diane, Sukiyaki, or Chinese Pepper Steak.

Chopped meat can be purchased in 3-pound lots, divided into meal-sized portions, and placed in plastic bags for future use in hamburgers, meatloaf, or meatballs.

STORAGE OF MEAT

All meat should be refrigerated or frozen as soon as possible after purchase. If prepackaged, many cuts can be placed in freezer exactly as they are. But for storage in the *refrigerator,* the store wrapper should be removed, and meat loosely covered with plastic or foil.

Refrigerator Storage

The larger the cut, the longer it can be kept in the refrigerator before cooking: roasts up to a week (10 days for beef), chops 3 to 5 days, ground meats no more than 48 hours.

All refrigerated meat should be partially covered, but never completely covered. If placed in a plastic bag, leave one end open. If sealed tight, spoilage occurs more quickly, meat may become slimy. A good way is to place a sheet of plastic wrap over the top of the meat only.

What should you do if plans change and meat is not cooked as soon after purchase as expected? Should chops purchased a week ago now be placed in the freezer? No, not after this length of time. Bacterial action may already have begun and freezing will only temporarily delay it. Better to cook the chops immediately, then store them in the freezer in freezer containers, preferably covered by a sauce or marinade to keep the meat moist.

Freezer Storage

To be safe, store all meat in the freezer after purchase except that which you are reasonably sure will be used in less than a week.

Divide ground meat *immediately* into meal-sized portions, place in plastic bags to freeze. A sandwich-sized bag will hold enough chopped meat to make 4 hamburgers; the next size is sufficient for holding enough for meatloaf. The meat thaws much more quickly in smaller portions, and if not used as planned, there is less waste to be concerned about.

All meat stored in the freezer must be completely covered and sealed tight to exclude air. When ground meat is placed in a plastic bag, twist the top to push out air, and seal with a wire twister.

Solid pieces of meat, especially larger pieces, should be covered with sheets of plastic, foil, or freezer paper, folded and tucked at the ends, sealed with tape. If meat is to be stored for more than 2 months, glazed white freezer paper is best—and easiest to label, because you can write on it with magic marker. Identify cut, give date of freezing. It is inadvisable to keep meats (or any products) in the home freezer more than 6 months. They may not spoil (unless the power has been off at some time), but quality deteriorates in the intense, dry cold of the freezer.

RECOMMENDED STORAGE TIMES AT 0° F.

Ground meat, sausage, frankfurters, luncheon meat, 1 to 3 months.

Pork or ham, up to 4 months.

Lamb, veal, and beef in large or solid pieces, up to 6 months. (Chops, scallopini, stewing meat, up to 3 to 4 months.)

HOW TO BUY VEGETABLES AND FRUITS

Planning Ahead: Vitamins for Every Meal

Fresh, frozen, or canned, there should be vegetables or fruit or both in every meal. For convenience, the frozen and canned are great, but there is no substitute for local garden produce *in season*, and in many cases fresh vegetables cook just as quickly as the frozen and have far more flavor.

The criterion is *freshness*. Vegetables and fruits shipped from many miles away, no matter how effective the refrigeration, have already lost food value and flavor when they reach the supermarkets. In this case, the frozen or canned equivalent may be preferable.

Judging Freshness

Personal selection is the only way to buy fresh vegetables and fruit, and, for the most part, those piled loosely in display cases are easier to select than those in sealed or stapled plastic bags. Store managers prefer the bags because withering is postponed and the produce looks fresher than it is. But often when taken from their bags, the vegetables and fruit show signs of decay not evident before.

Don't hesitate to pick and choose produce. One brown spot on a yellow summer squash means it's past its prime. A very hard tomato will be lacking in flavor; a too-soft one may be mushy. The romaine lettuce stripped of all its outer leaves was probably so trimmed because the leaves were withered.

Preserving Garden Freshness

If fresh locally grown vegetables are to be used in the very next meal, there's no need to refrigerate them. On the other hand, those that will not be used for 24 hours or longer should be washed, trimmed, and, in most cases, stored in a tight-covered vegetable crisper or drawer in the refrigerator, or in a sealed plastic bag.

Salad greens, herbs, and all leafy green vegetables should be soaked in cold water for 15 minutes to wash away sand and grit *before* they are refrigerated. Simply place all the greens in a sinkful of water; most of the grit will soak away. Remove the greens from the water, shake well to toss off excess moisture, and drain off the water. If a great deal of sand and grit remains in the bottom of the sink, better repeat the process. Then place greens in vegetable freshener or other covered container or bag.

Parsley, dill, other fresh herbs should be similarly "freshened." Remove and discard stems, place leaves in glass container with tight-fitting top. They will keep fresh this way in the refrigerator a week to 10 days.

Selecting Full-flavored Fruits

Taking time out to shop in person for the best buys in fruit is even more important than in buying vegetables. First of all, frozen and canned fruit products are never the same as the fresh. Excepting frozen juices, the *only* frozen fruit product which is a better buy than the fresh is frozen raspberries—because fresh raspberries are so perishable, it is hard to find any completely free of mold.

Never hesitate to pick up fresh fruit from the display case and sniff it. With many fruits, this is the best test of ripeness. Some fruits retain flavor better if not refrigerated. Others are so perishable that they should be refrigerated immediately. With the exception of apples and citrus fruits, all other fresh fruits should be eaten as soon as possible after purchase or at peak of maturity (if still somewhat green when purchased).

How to Figure Servings

There is no rule to equate vegetable servings with pound weight, because the amount of waste and shrinkage varies so greatly, as the following partial list shows. This is something you must learn from experience.

Fresh Vegetable	Servings	Servings Per Frozen 10-ounce Box
Asparagus	2 - 3 per pound 7 - 10 per bunch	2 - 3
Broccoli spears	8 - 10 per bunch	2
Brussels sprouts	4 - 5 per pint	3
Cauliflower	7 - 8 per head	3
Green beans	4 - 5 per pound	4
Limas in pod	2 per pound	4
Peas in pod	2 per pound	4
Spinach	2 - 3 per pound	4 - 6

Watching for Specials

Canned goods should be purchased in quantity whenever there's a sale, especially *canned tomatoes*. Not only does the tomato retain its vitamin C and other nutrients during canning; good-quality canned tomatoes have more flavor and are more economical to use than the fresh, except in the peak of the local tomato season.

Other canned vegetables which retain flavor particularly well include kernel corn (especially the white variety), beets, sauerkraut, and pickled red cabbage. *Canned fruits* provide instant desserts whenever needed. Most popular are peaches, pears, pineapple, cherries, plums, and sliced apples.

Frozen vegetables and fruit juices are offered on sale at reduced price less often than canned goods, and when there is a sale, you should approach it cautiously. It could be prompted by an oversupply in the store, or the current could have been off in one of the frozen-food counters, permitting the frozen packages to thaw partially. Storage conditions in supermarket freezer displays are not always what they should be. Even if the electric current has not been off, packages at the top of the pile have not been at the same zero temperature as those nearer the bottom. Also, in unloading from trucks some frozen products are left on the sidewalk under a hot sun for too long. The foods may not have spoiled, but neither will they have the same keeping qualities or prime flavor as those kept solidly frozen all along.

Selection of frozen vegetables is largely a matter of personal preference. There are certain vegetables that come through especially well: artichoke hearts, lima beans, the tiny peas (which are best cooked in butter only). The only corn product which freezes well is the "corn-in-butter" pouch to be cooked unopened. Button mushrooms are good, but much more costly than the canned. Some of the combination frozen vegetables in sauce are good, but very expensive.

Frozen fruit juices are a great convenience, and if reconstituted in an electric blender (at low speed, for a few seconds only) are quite palatable. Not the same as fresh, but at breakfast time, much easier to whip up.

HOW TO BUY AND STORE POULTRY

CHICKENS

Broiler-fryers weighing 2½ to 3 pounds dressed (ready-to-cook) weight are the best meat buy in America, and a testimony to the miracle of modern poultry production. Today's chickens are plumper, more flavorful, and actually cheaper than those of twenty-five years ago. And because they are so young and tender, they can be cooked in half the time, reducing shrinkage, which means still more edible meat.

Chickens freeze well if frozen properly and kept at 0° F. storage until ready to use. So, when attractive plump chickens are on sale, it's wise to buy extras if you have sufficient freezer space to hold them.

Chicken parts are a good buy, and these, too, can be frozen for later use. (However, many of the commercially frozen chicken parts are tough and flavorless, especially the breaded chicken legs and breasts.) *Chicken breasts*, even though higher in price, offer more edible meat per pound than wings or legs and are especially useful in oriental recipes or for elegant dinners where one breast is served to each person. *Chicken wings and legs* are excellent broiled, fried or added to rice dishes or casseroles. *Chicken livers* can be turned into entrees, served as hot appetizers, or made into a pâté. *Chicken necks and backs* make excellent inexpensive soup or chicken stock.

Capons are cockerels (male chickens) which have been castrated. They grow larger, plumper, and more tender than roosters and provide the best of all roast chicken. Ready-to-cook capons are available from 7 to 9 pounds; for small families (2 or 3 persons) they are often a better buy than turkey, for a 9-pound capon will be more juicy and tender and may have more meat in proportion to bone than a 10-pound turkey.

Roasting chickens has become almost a rarity, because breeders find it better business to concentrate on the broiler-fryers ready for market in less than 2 months (and male chickens are not needed for egg production). Roasters when available average 4 to 5 pounds, a good size for spit-roasting.

Stewing chickens are hens, usually 2 years old, which no longer lay enough eggs to be worth their cost of upkeep. If these are Leghorn chickens (as most laying stock is), the meat is apt to be tough and stringy. If Plymouth Rock, White Rock, or Rhode Island Red hens, there will be more meat and more fat, and the resulting broth will be more flavorful. Such chickens purchased from a butcher will not carry any indication of breed; you can only judge from appearance: ample proportion of breast meat, light velvety pink or creamy yellow skin, firm yellow fat. If purchased direct from a farmer or at a farmer's market, try to find someone who sells hens of the breeds mentioned, for they make very fine chicken stews and soups (Brunswick Stew, Chicken and Dumplings, Chicken Pie, or Coq au Vin).

TURKEYS

The development of the American turkey to its present size is quite as miraculous as the breeding of chickens, and so successful have turkey breeders become in their mass-production methods, they've had to push a round-the-year turkey promotion to get rid of their abundant flocks.

Roast turkey is a fine economy dish for *large* families and deserves to be served throughout the year. There is far more meat in proportion to bone than in chickens; the price per pound of edible meat is therefore even more reasonable. For small families, however, the average 12-pound turkey is a lot of meat and may hang around a long time.

To meet the demands of smaller families, the so-called *Beltsville turkeys* were developed, named after the Agricultural Research Center at Beltsville, Maryland. These range from as little as 4 pounds up to 15, averaging 4 to 9 pounds for hens, 9 to 12 pounds for toms. The smaller turkeys, unfortunately, do not have the same flavor and succulence as the larger birds; a 9-pound capon is often a better buy than a 9-pound turkey—better for flavor and quality, that is, though the price of capons is much higher.

A *hen turkey* is considered by many to be more tender and juicy than a *tom* (male) and consequently usually costs a little more per pound.

Fresh-killed turkey is more succulent and flavorful than frozen because freezing dries out the flesh, but *frozen stuffed turkeys in a sealed self-basting bag* of polyester, now in distribution in many states, can be placed still solidly frozen in the oven (in the bag); they require only slightly more cooking time than fresh or defrosted turkeys, and the sealed bag retains moisture. The bird is really pressure-cooked and browns and bastes itself; at the right moment, the seal of the bag bursts at one end and the juices drain into the pan. A 10-pound frozen turkey will be cooked ready to serve in about 3½ hours. Directions and cooking times are given on the bag.

Turkey parts—separate breasts, legs, and boned "turkey rolls"—are now widely available, mostly frozen. They lack the succulence of whole fresh turkeys, and some turkey rolls even have an unpleasant flavor. But the boneless rolls are inexpensive and easy to use, and fulfill a need for quick and easy week-day meals.

DUCKS

Long Island ducklings account for about 90 percent of the ducks sold in American markets, and most are sold frozen. Ducklings from Massachusetts are beginning to appear. They are marketed after 8 to 9 weeks, weighing 4 to 5½ pounds. All are of the Peking duck variety, introduced from China in 1874. They are quite fat and even a 5½-pound duck will serve only 3 persons.

Occasionally **Muscovy ducks** are seen at farmer markets or in specialty shops. This is a gamy variety, difficult to raise because they fly and nest their young where they please, and fatalities are high. The Muscovy has very little fat and much more breast meat than the Peking but a stronger, gamier flavor.

Wild ducks, mallards or canvasbacks, are occasionally available (in season) at specialty markets, as are pheasants, partridges, grouse, and quail.

GEESE

Like ducks, most geese are sold frozen, the proportion of fat is very high, and there is comparatively little edible meat in proportion to weight. *Goslings*, marketed when less than 6 months of age, are the most tender. These run about 4 to 7 pounds. Mature geese, weighing 8 to 15 pounds, tend to be tough, and require long cooking in a self-basting roaster or in a bag punched with holes, allowing the fat to escape into the roasting pan.

CORNISH HENS

Supposedly a cross-breed between Cornish Rock chickens and game hens, the Cornish hens taste and look like miniature chickens but have a larger proportion of breast meat. The meat is delicate and tender, but it is not all white meat, as was once proclaimed. Once very high in price, Cornish hens may now frequently be found on special sale for less than a dollar each; they may or may not be frozen. They are less economical than chickens, but for company dinners can seem very special.

INSPECTION AND GRADING OF POULTRY

By law, all poultry which is shipped across state lines must be officially inspected for wholesomeness by federal supervisors.

This applies to chickens, turkeys, ducks, Cornish hens, and geese. The poultry itself and the plants where birds are slaughtered and packed are inspected to make sure all stipulated sanitary regulations are strictly observed and that the birds are healthy. But birds that are *not* shipped across state lines do not have to be so inspected. To be sure the chickens, turkeys, or ducks you buy are wholesome and healthy, look for a tag fastened to the skin of the bird bearing the seal of inspection.

A second tag may indicate *grade*.

Grading is an entirely different step, performed on a voluntary basis—it is not required by law. *Grade A*, of course, means top quality. *Grade B* may mean the chicken (or turkey, or duck) is of good quality, but the skin may be bruised or torn, bones may be disjointed or crooked, and, if frozen, there may be slight freezer burns. *Grade C* is applied to birds which are "poorly fleshed," to use the marketing term, and with a larger proportion of such defects as torn or bruised skin, broken or disjointed bones, or poor fat covering.

In addition, when buying *fresh* chickens or turkeys, there are certain signs you should look for. The skin should have a velvety look, the color clear and fresh (it may be pinkish, or it may be yellow—yellow skin reflects a larger proportion of corn in the diet). The flesh should be light in color and firm, the bones and gristle should be clean and pink-white (not red or dry-looking), and there should be a moderate amount of firm, clear yellow fat. (Excess fat is not good—the bird when cooked will be greasy, and there will be excessive shrinkage.) Beware when the skin has a dry, rough look, and the flesh is reddish and shrunken; such birds have probably come from the freezer, and were not properly frozen to begin with, or they may have been piled up in refrigerated warehouses for a long time. In either case, expect dry, flavorless flesh, or a taste reminiscent of wet feathers.

When purchasing *frozen* chicken, turkeys, or ducks, it is harder to judge quality because all you can see is the outer wrapping. Then the tag indicating grade becomes very important.

How to Figure Servings

Chickens and turkeys both yield from 1 to 1½ servings per pound. The larger the bird, the more meat in proportion to bone, and so proportionately more servings.

The way chickens are cut up makes a difference, however.

For example, a small (1½- to 2-pound) broiler split in half makes only 2 servings. A 2½-pound broiler in quarters makes 4 servings. A 2½- to 3-pound broiler-fryer cut into 10 to 12 pieces (if the bird is large and plump enough, the breast can be cut into 4 pieces, and so divided among more people) may serve as many as 5 persons, with 2 pieces to a person, and the backs for seconds. A 5-pound roaster will serve only 4 persons adequately; a big breasted 9-pound capon may serve 8 to 10.

An 8-pound Beltsville turkey is only enough for 4 to 6 persons; a 15-pound Butterball turkey with extra large breast may serve 18 to 20 persons. In buying turkey for roasting, some is usually wanted left over for sandwiches, and the big-breasted turkeys are far better for that.

Boned turkey goes even further; allow 3 to 4 servings per pound.

Ducks and geese: Allow 2 pounds for each serving. This means a 4-pound duckling will serve 2 persons, a 6-pound gosling will serve 3. The larger mature geese have more meat proportionately, but they require such long cooking, there is more waste. A 12-pound goose will serve no more than 6 persons, and that's scraping the bones.

Cornish hens: Normally 1 to a person, but those over 1 pound each may be split and broiled, for 2 servings each.

Storage

Fresh chickens to be used within 3 to 4 days should be *loosely* wrapped. If wrapped when purchased, remove the store wrapping and cover lightly with a sheet of plastic.

If meat is not to be used within 5 days, it's better to store in the freezer or freezing compartment, *tightly wrapped and sealed.* This applies to chicken parts quite as much as whole or cut up chickens. If stored in refrigerator freezing compartment, use within 7 to 10 days; for freezer storage, no more than 1 to 2 months. They won't spoil if kept longer, but they will be less flavorful.

The same general rule applies to other poultry, though frozen turkeys and ducks in sealed containers can be kept considerably longer at 0° F.

To defrost frozen poultry, smaller pieces, such as cut-up chicken, can be thawed in the refrigerator in 4 to 5 hours. Larger pieces, especially roasting birds, are better thawed at room temperature. Food processors advise thawing ducks and turkeys slowly in the refrigerator, but experience has taught me that this requires a good 48 hours or longer, and since frozen poultry takes up a lot of refrigerator space, this is a nuisance. (And besides, who plans that far ahead?) *To hasten thawing,* place the bird in an open roasting pan in oven set at 250° F. until soft enough to remove frozen giblets from cavity, then rinse the bird inside and out, and add stuffing (if desired). Return bird to oven, and increase temperature to 325° F. Or, if bird is to be spit-roasted, proceed with recipe directions.

HOW TO BUY SEAFOOD

Fresh and Frozen "Finny Fish"

To be good, fresh fish should be really *fresh*—that is, less than 24 hours out of the water. Unfortunately, the American marketing transportation system, marvelous as it is in other respects, is not geared to this. Even in our coastal cities, it is almost impossible to buy fish this fresh in retail markets.

Further, selecting truly fresh fish is rendered more difficult because of the way it is dressed. In other parts of the world, one looks at the eyes (they should be full and bright, not sunken or glazed), and at the gills inside the mouth (they should be bright red and moist). The odor—or lack of it, is another criterion. Truly fresh fish has no noticeable odor.

Most fish in American markets, however, are sold *drawn* (with entrails removed) and *pan-dressed,* with head, tail, and fins cut off. Smaller fish of the flounder family are sold *filleted,* while large fish are cut into *steaks* (cross sections).

Lacking the age-old criterion of freshness, the best alternative is to patronize a market specializing in fish where there is rapid turnover and let the fish man know you know the difference. If fish purchased has noticeable odor, or when cooked has an unpleasantly strong flavor, make a squawk. If more Americans did this, we would have better fish.

Nearly all fish (80 percent) is sold frozen. Freezing changes texture (makes it drier and coarser) and robs the fish of flavor, but frozen fish even so may be preferable to "fresh" fish that is not really fresh. Most commercially frozen fish is filleted (trout is the exception).

The principal fish varieties (frozen and fresh) sold in American markets include cod, trout, flounder (sole), perch, haddock, halibut, salmon, and swordfish.

HOW TO FIGURE SERVINGS

Fillets or steaks, fresh or frozen, 3 servings per pound.

Whole fish (pan-dressed), 1 pound per person.if small, ½ pound per person if large. Small fish are usually served 1 to each person.

HOME STORAGE

Always cook fresh fish the same day it is purchased. *Never freeze store-bought fish; deterioration may have already set in, and home freezing will only temporarily delay it. Fish fresh-caught by a member of the family or a friend may be successfully fast-frozen at 0° F. if processed a few hours after being hooked and kept solidly frozen until needed.*

To cook frozen fish most deliciously, either marinate in oil before cooking (after thawing) or cook with added liquid (poach, braise, or bake in sauce) rather than fry. The added liquid or oil (in a marinade) helps to replace depleted moisture.

If frying is preferred, defrost completely, dip in a batter or in milk or a mixture of beaten egg and milk, then in crumbs or flour.

Canned Fish

Tuna is consumed by more Americans than any other fish food, in any form. This is because canned tuna is *good*—better in flavor even than most fresh tuna—and inexpensive, and it can be kept on hand for use at any time. *Albacore* is the finest variety; this accounts for most of the "white-meat tuna." Other varieties (not usually identified on the can) are bluefin, skipjack, and yellowfin. *Bonito* is not tuna; it is from a related fish family, and is canned. Bonito is sometimes incorrectly called tuna (and is usually—or should be—considerably lower in price).

STYLES

Instead of being graded, tuna is described on the can according to the kind of *pack:*

Solid pack. The finest, consisting of almost solid meat with a few pieces added to fill the can. This is best for salads and hors d'oeuvres where appearance and fine flavor count.

Chunk style. Large meaty pieces combined with smaller pieces. Good for creamed dishes, salads, entrees.

Tuna flakes. The bits and pieces left over from other packs. Less desirable than the first two, but may be used satisfactorily for sandwich fillings or pâtés.

In oil. Most tuna is packed in vegetable oil, with salt added. Imported varieties (a very small portion of the tuna available) may be packed in olive oil. The oil greatly improves the tuna flavor.

Water-packed. For dietetic use (weight-control and low-sodium diets) some tuna is packed in water with little or no salt added. This is poorer in flavor, and the meat tends to be more coarse and tough.

SIZES

By far the most popular size is the 6½-ounce can, containing about ¾ cup. Some packers put out a 7-ounce can. There are small cans (3¼ and 3½ ounces, about 1/3 cup) and "family size" (12½ and 13 ounces, about 1½ cups), and a few 9¼-ounce cans (a little over 1 cup).

Canned Salmon, once a synonym for economy dishes, is now costly and in increasingly short supply. Brightest in color, most flavorful, and best for salads and entrees are the *red* varieties, including *sockeye, blueback,* and *silver.* These are also the most expensive. *Pink* salmons include *chinook* and *king.* The pink is not so attractive in appearance, but it is less expensive and where delicate flavor is wanted, as in certain salads and creamed dishes, perfectly satisfactory. Salmon is put up in 1-pound, 7¾-ounce sizes.

Sardines. One of several varieties of small fish with weak bones, canned in oil. *Maine sardines* are in reality herring, put up in cottonseed oil, some with tomato sauce. *Portuguese sardines,* a variety of pilchard, are canned in olive oil. *Norwegian sardines,* also pilchards, are put in peanut or soy oil.

Shellfish

Shrimp top the list of all seafood sales, and all but 5 percent of the catch is frozen right on the shrimp boats. This means that what is offered as "fresh shrimp" is usually simply frozen shrimp defrosted.

There are many varieties of the crustacean we call "shrimp" (it is known by other names elsewhere), differing in shell color and in size. In the wholesale market all uncooked shrimp are called "green," despite shell color, which ranges from pale gray to brownish, yellowish pink to deep red (the last particularly prized).

Shrimp in the shell contain only a little more than half as much edible meat as already shelled shrimp. (The larger the shrimp, the more edible meat per pound in proportion to shell, and the smaller the shrimp, vice versa.) If a recipe calls for "1 pound shrimp" it is very important to know whether this means shrimp in the shell, or already shelled.

The already shelled shrimp is a better buy if only edible volume is considered, but the shell contributes a great deal of flavor, and for some recipes in particular, the added flavor is an important consideration.

Shrimp is sold according to size, ranging from 30 to 40 per pound (the smallest) up to 12 to 15 per pound, which are sometimes (but incorrectly) called *prawns*. The average is about 20 shrimp (in the shell) to the pound. For cocktails, medium to small sizes are preferable.

Canned shrimp is available mainly in 6½-ounce sizes. A very small amount of *dried shrimp* is to be found in specialty markets, primarily those catering to Americans of oriental background.

Crabs and crabmeat are next to shrimp in volume of annual shellfish sales. There are four principal varieties: *blue crab*, native to the Chesapeake Bay area and New England; *Dungeness*, on the Pacific coast; *king crab* in Alaska; and *rock crab* (the least important commercially) off the New England coast.

Live hard-shell crab is available only in areas where it is caught, and even in these areas, *bulk crabmeat* (shelled) is more in demand. Such crabmeat, packed in 1-pound containers, is sold locally in fresh form, and is shipped frozen to markets all over the country. Some of it comes from Canada. The bulk crabmeat has not been cooked; it is sold in three styles: *lump*, the finest in solid chunks; *flake*, in bits and pieces; and *claw meat*, also in small pieces. *One pound of pure crabmeat will serve 4 to 6 persons.*

Soft-shell crabs are blue crabs caught during the molting season before new hard shells have formed. They are available fresh in the North Atlantic states during late spring and summer, and *frozen*, throughout the year in specialty markets. These are served *1 to a person.*

Canned crabmeat is not the same as the bulk crabmeat in cans. Most of it is taken from the claws of king crabs and packed in 6½-ounce cans, which contain about ¾ cup crabmeat. This, like other commercially canned products, has been processed under steam pressure so that the meat is thoroughly cooked.

Much of our supply comes from Japan. Some cans of crabmeat contain bits of gristle; in others the gristle has been removed. (The gristle is not edible and so must be carefully separated from the meat and discarded.)

Frozen Alaska king crab is available in two forms: leg sections, containing part of the gristle or bone, in 12-ounce packages; and chunks of meat in 6-ounce packages. Of the two, the leg sections seem to retain flavor better though neither product is comparable in flavor to bulk crabmeat in 1-pound containers; the meat is often watery and virtually tasteless. Frozen king crab need not be cooked before serving. The 12-ounce packages of crab leg provide 2 servings; the 6-ounce packages of crabmeat will make 4 servings for salad or in a sauce when combined with other ingredients.

Fresh crabmeat should be used immediately. *Frozen crabmeat* should be kept solidly frozen until needed, then thawed at room temperature. *Canned crabmeat*, of course, has no shelf age at all.

Lobster from northern waters, such as *Maine lobster*, is the tenderest and sweetest. (This is what the French call *homard.*) Unfortunately the supply is dwindling at such an alarming rate that most of those now available on the market even in the height of the season are rarely larger than 1 pound each, and the price keeps going up.

Not far behind in price are *rock lobster tails* from the variety properly called *spiny lobster* (in Europe, called *langouste.*) Most in our markets come from South Africa or New Zealand, a much smaller number from the Caribbean; all are frozen when caught. These range in size from 1½ ounces up to 13 or 14 ounces each. The smallest ones are suitable only for hors d'oeuvres, and, because of the large proportion of shell, they are the most costly in terms of edible meat. However, the meat of the very large lobster tails seems to be less tender than those of 6 or 7 ounces, the optimum size.

Serve Maine lobsters 1 to a person. They are usually purchased while still alive (they should be moving in the case), though the fish man will cook them for you if you so request. They lose flavor if they stand after cooking, so use the same day if possible.

Frozen bulk lobster meat in 1-pound containers is very high in price but is pure edible meat.

Barrels of live lobsters may be ordered direct from Maine, with or without a peck of clams, along with suitable cooking containers. These will be delivered by rail still alive to almost any point in the United States. Very expensive, but impressive for a feast.

Scallops are of two types: *sea scallops*, from deep waters in the North and Middle Atlantic (available both fresh and frozen), and smaller and more prized *bay scallops*, gathered in offshore waters from New England to the Gulf of Mexico, available only fresh. (The French call scallops *coquille St.-Jacques.*)

They have already been removed from their lovely fluted shells, and so are pure edible meat. Fresh scallops are in season from November to April. Cook and serve same day purchased—they are very perishable. Never cook ahead for later use; they toughen upon reheating.

One pound of scallops will serve 4 as an entree, 6 to 8 as an hors d'oeuvre.

CLAMS, OYSTERS, MUSSELS

Only in coastal areas can one buy any of these in the shell. Oysters in the shell should always be tightly closed when purchased (if shells are open, oysters are dead). *Clams and mussels*, if open slightly, are still alive, but shells should close when touched. All may be eaten raw if you are sure they are from unpolluted waters. (But it is no longer safe to dig your own on public beaches—unless in isolated areas far from public wastes.)

Clam varieties on the Atlantic coast include hard-shell (known in New England as *quahogs*, as *littlenecks* or *cherry-stones* in the New York area), and soft-shell clams known as *steamers*. Pacific clams include *razor, butter clams, pismo,* and *littleneck* (a different species from the Atlantic littleneck).

Season. Clams and oysters are in season from September to May (the R months); mussels have no season but demand for them is so slight (why, no one knows, because they are superb), they are hard to come by at any time.

Shucked clams and oysters are available frozen throughout the year, fresh in season. Fresh should be plump, with no noticeable odor, in clear liquid (no shell particles). Can be used up to 7 days after purchase if kept refrigerated at all times. Clams and oysters may be used interchangeably in recipes.

Canned clams are available in the shell (very costly), whole, chopped, and minced. The most common container is 6½ to 7 ounces; one packer puts up minced clams in a 10-ounce size. There are also a number of canned and frozen *clam chowders* in both New England and Manhattan styles, most in concentrated form in 10½-ounce sizes.

Canned oysters are usually sold in "No. 1" cans of 7½ to 8 ounces, to serve 3 or 4 persons.

Frozen oysters, thawed, can be used like fresh—but never refreeze after thawing.

Canned smoked oysters and clams, in oil, are widely available to serve as hors d'oeuvres.

How to figure servings. To serve any of these mollusks *in the shell*, allow ½ dozen per serving. *If shucked*, allow 1 quart for 6 servings; as an entree, 1 pint to serve 3. In soups, as hors d'oeuvres, or combined with other seafood, less, obviously, will be needed per serving. A 6½?ounce can of minced clams contains ¾ cup; use as directed in recipes.

HOW TO BUY AND STORE EGGS

Eggs vary in size from little pullet eggs up to extra large and jumbo. Most recipes, unless otherwise specified, have been tested with *medium to large* eggs. The latter must, by law, weigh at least 24 ounces per dozen. These are usually the most economical to buy. When serving the extra-large and jumbo size for fried, poached, or boiled eggs, you must still serve 1 or 2 eggs to each person. If you use extra-large eggs in a batter, you may end with too much egg, since the recipe was worked out with medium eggs. The little pullet eggs are of use chiefly for children's portions, or for boiled eggs (especially to be served as hors d'oeuvres).

Eggs are *graded* from AA to B and C. Grade AA means firm, high yolks and thick whites; they spread little when broken. Grade A eggs spread slightly more, are not quite so thick. Either of these are recommended for frying or poaching— whenever appearance is important. Grades B and C have the same nutritive value but the whites and yolks are thinner, spread out more. Recommended for use in batters, for breading, etc.

Shell color does not matter (brown and white eggs are the same), but *cleanliness* does. Open carton before purchase to make sure eggs are clean, not cracked or broken.

Storage: Eggshells are porous, other odors are easily absorbed. It's best to use them within 4 to 6 days after purchase. They may remain fresh (unspoiled) up to 2 weeks—but don't depend on it. *Leftover yolks* may be kept in a covered jar for a day or two; *leftover whites*, too, can be stored (if covered) for later use in cooking, but not to be used for meringues.

HOW TO BUY AND STORE CHEESE

The many wonderful kinds of cheese to be had in our markets will be more fully discussed in Book 3, Chapter 10, "Eggs and Cheese." Most cheese has excellent keeping qualities and may be stored in refrigerator, if tightly wrapped or covered, for many months. Only *fresh cheese* (cottage and cream) and the *soft dessert cheeses* (such as Brie and Camembert) are perishable and should be used within a short time after purchase.

Natural cheeses are those made from the drained curd of milk, ripened and aged. The firmer the cheese, the longer it keeps, though even a firm cheese like Cheddar or Swiss will dry out and lose flavor if not tightly wrapped at all times.

Pasteurized process cheese is made of natural cheese heated to molten pasteurizing temperatures, then poured into molds. It will keep almost indefinitely in the refrigerator if wrapped and sealed; but if wrap is broken, cheese dries up quickly.

Pasteurized cheese foods may contain only about 20 percent cheese plus milk solids and vegetable gum; the softer of these tend to go bad rather quickly once the jar has been opened.

For long storage cheese may be frozen, but this tends to dry it out.

Always remove natural cheese from the refrigerator at least 1 hour before serving to enjoy full flavor.

CONVENIENCE FOODS: WHEN ARE THEY WORTH THE PRICE?

American women have become so dependent on mixes and ready-to-use foods that they tend to think anything in a package is a time saver. It isn't necessarily so. Many frozen vegetables require as much cooking time as the fresh. One particular mix for popovers contains nothing but a leavening agent, salt, and flour—and for this the consumer pays about five times what the same ingredients would cost if purchased separately.

The packaged noodle mixes and rice mixes are far more expensive than the same ingredients purchased separately; they save little if any preparation time, and the chemicals added as preservatives are of dubious health value. It is claimed that the Food and Drug Administration has made sure the amount of chemical additives in any one product is not injurious to health. But when we think of how many of our everyday grocery products contain additives, we can't be sure that the aggregate effect on health is not adverse.

It would be hard, indeed, to do without convenience foods altogether. Consider how dependent we are now on packets of fruit-flavored gelatin, ready-to-cook noodles and spaghetti, canned and dehydrated soups, cocoa mix, dried yeast, and already sliced bacon. All these are "convenience foods" because they have been processed for immediate use and put up in sanitary containers.

The questions to consider are these:

•How much preparation time is saved?
•How does the cost compare with that of ingredients purchased separately (if the product contains a number of different ingredients)? If it costs three or four times as much, is the time saved worth the added cost?
•What about quality? Flavor? Does the finished product ready for the table compare favorably in flavor, texture, and appearance with a dish prepared the more laborious old-fashioned way?
•Does the product have a shelf life?

Many, many products do. Some breakfast cereals have been on the grocer's shelves a year or longer. Some packaged frozen foods have been in freezing counters over 6 months. Certain products deteriorate rather quickly, especially hot-roll and pizza mixes, yeast, and cake mixes.

Remember: the more labor that has gone into a convenience food, the higher the finished cost is bound to be. Those ready-to-heat-and-serve products which appear in greater and greater variety in frozen-food counters cost on the average three to four times as much as the same dish prepared at home from scratch. What is more, quality in many of the frozen ready-to-serve foods is shockingly poor; some are so unpalatable that it's a disgrace they are on the market.

Sales on convenience foods are worth watching for *if* you have proper and adequate storage facilities. But beware of unknown brands and of foods which may have been hanging around on shelves or in frozen-food cases for a long time. Also, avoid buying more than you can use within a reasonable length of time. It's never an economy to buy more than you need.

BE A LABEL READER

Every manufactured or processed food product must tell on the label what ingredients have been used, what the net measure or weight is, and whether artificial flavors or color or chemical preservatives have been added.

Some labels also specify style (whether a can of peaches is sliced or in halves, whether cherries are pitted, whether light or heavy syrup has been used, and so on). Some packaged products also indicate the number of servings.

If a recipe specifies a can of a certain size, use the closest container size; an ounce or two one way or the other will not matter. Cup measures for standard container sizes are indicated in the chart below.

Common Container Sizes

Product	Approximate Weight or Fluid Measure As Given on Label	Approximate Cups
Fruits, vegetables, tomato sauce	8 ounces	1
Tomato paste	6 ounces	¾
Condensed soups, some fish, meat specialties	10½ ounces	1¼
Vegetables, fish products, fruit	12 ounces	1¼-1½
Baked beans, cranberry sauce, meat products	14 - 16 ounces	1¾ - 2
Fruits, vegetables, ready-to-serve specialties	1 pound, or 16 - 17 ounces (No. 303)	2
Juices, ready-to-serve soups, specialties, pineapple	1 pound 4 ounces, or 1 pint 2 fluid ounces (No. 2)	2½
Tomatoes, fruits, sauerkraut, pumpkin	1 pound 13 ounces (No. 2½)	3½
Large-size fruit and vegetable juices, pork and beans, specialties; institutional-size soups	3 pounds 3 ounces, or 1 quart 14 fluid ounces	5¾
Institutional pack	6½-7 pounds (No. 10)	12 - 13

2 GENERIC TERMS: WHAT THEY MEAN

Ours is an ad-conscious society. Advertising jingles make brand names more familiar to us than the generic, or general, name of the product. But we must use generic names in recipes, since a number of manufacturers make similar products. If a generic term puzzles you, look for it in the following list.

The listing may also help to clarify what various products are to be used for, and why, and how they should be stored.

Butters, Fats, Oils

Butter is all made from sweet or sour cream, churned until smooth and solid, separated from the liquid (buttermilk). *Salted creamy butter* may or may not be made from sour cream, with a little salt added. *Sweet cream butter* is made with sweet cream, with added salt. *Sweet butter* contains no salt. *Whipped butter* has had air beaten in to increase volume and spreadability; usually unsalted. Use only at the table, not in cooking.

Store all butter in refrigerator, covered. Buy in limited quantities, for flavor goes strong quickly, or store in freezer. (The sad truth is that American dairy butter is not properly churned, and spoilage occurs more quickly than it should. If care were taken to get rid of every bit of liquid, it would remain fresh longer. Danish butter, which is churned to force out all liquid, keeps fresh and sweet for months in cold storage, without freezing.)

Margarine is made from refined vegetable oils with added artificial flavor and color (except in states where coloring is forbidden). Some, but not all, contains nonfat milk solids; some contains a small amount of butter. *Pure corn-oil margarine* may contain no milk solids; however, those on milk-free diets should check labels to make sure. *Whipped ("chiffon") margarine* has had air beaten in. *Diet margarine* is slightly lower in caloric content.

Both butter and margarine are put up in 1-pound packages containing four ¼-pound prints (except whipped butter and margarine, which are packaged in shallow containers). Any margarine may be used as a substitute for butter, but it is not recommended for sautéing or frying because it burns so easily. Refrigerate primarily to keep firm. (It will not go bad at room temperature, only soft.)

Vegetable shortening is also made of refined vegetable oils, bleached and hydrogenated to change from liquid to solid. It need not be refrigerated. Excellent for sautéing or frying, best fat for piecrust.

Lard is rendered pork fat, bleached, refined, and packed in 1-pound prints. Refrigerate at all times.

Vegetable oil is extracted under hydraulic pressure from corn, peanuts, soybeans, cottonseeds, or safflower seeds, then heavily refined and deodorized.

Salad oils are vegetable oils; they are best for frying because they are odor-free and do not spatter easily. They need not be refrigerated.

Olive oil is extracted from fully ripe (black) olives. Virgin olive oil, most prized by connoisseurs, is first extracted from the fruit; it is unrefined, pure, and somewhat more potent in flavor than what is called a "first pressing" of *refined olive oil*. Color, aroma, and quality of olive oils differ greatly; variable factors include care in processing, climate, soil, and olive variety. Olive oil is not recommended for deep-frying because of its high cost. It spatters easily, and once impurities get into the oil it turns rancid quickly. But top-quality virgin oil or a first pressing of refined oil will remain fresh and fragrant up to a year without refrigeration. Use for Mediterranean dishes, for salad dressings, and for sautéing.

Chocolate and Cocoa Products

Both are processed from cocoa beans (called cacao in Mexico, where the plant originated), but most of the fat has been removed from cocoa.

Unsweetened chocolate (also called "bitter chocolate") has no added sugar or flavoring; it is pressed into solid 1-ounce squares, which, wrapped individually, are sold in 8-ounce packages. The natural fat of beans explains the buttery content. Used primarily for baking; must be melted before combination with other ingredients.

Unsweetened chocolate-flavored baking product is a liquid mixture of cocoa, vegetable oil, and preservatives; it may be added to other ingredients without melting. Put up in 1-ounce packets.

Semisweet chocolate has some added sugar; it comes in both an 8-ounce package (with 1-ounce squares) and in small nuggets called *semisweet chocolate bits*, available in 6-ounce (1-cup) and 12-ounce (2-cup) packages.

Sweet chocolate has a larger proportion of sugar; it comes in 4-ounce bars marked in squares. For both cooking and eating.

Milk chocolate, with dried milk and sugar added, is primarily for eating.

Cocoa has had fat (cocoa butter) removed; it is processed into a powder which dissolves instantly. *Dutch cocoa* has been treated to darken color and reduce natural bitterness. *Instant cocoa mix* has been blended with sugar and, sometimes, instant dry milk, and will dissolve instantly in hot or cold liquids.

Dairy Products: Milk and Cream

Nearly all our milk and cream has been *pasteurized* (subjected to temperatures 145° F. or higher, then promptly cooled) and *enriched* with vitamin D. Most milk has been *homogenized* (processed to break up fat particles and distribute them through the milk to give it creamy consistency).

Grade A pasteurized (but not homogenized) milk will separate; that is, cream rises to the top, called *top milk*. **Skim milk** has had all or most of cream (butterfat) removed. **Buttermilk** used to be the residue left in the churn after butter had been made, but today most of it is simply pasteurized milk subjected to lactic acid culture. **Raw milk** has not been pasteurized. Unless it bears on the label the words *certified milk* (meaning the dairy where it was handled has passed rigid sanitary inspection), its use is not recommended.

Chocolate-flavored milk is whole or homogenized milk with cocoa and sugar added. If skim milk is used, it must be called *chocolate drink* or *chocolate-flavored drink*.

Special diet milks include *acidophilus* (skim milk treated with a lactic acid culture to give it a tart flavor and smooth consistency) and *low-sodium milk* (which has had 90 percent of the sodium removed).

Yogurt is also made by adding a culture to whole or partially skimmed milk to give it a thickened, custardlike consistency. **Diet yogurt** is made with skimmed or partially skimmed milk, and may or may not have nonfat dry milk solids added.

Instant nonfat dry milk has had nearly all butterfat and water removed, then is processed to dissolve easily in water or other liquids.

Canned milk products include **evaporated milk** (whole milk with 60 percent of water removed) and **sweetened condensed milk** (with 50 percent of the water removed and sugar added).

Cream products include **heavy cream**, containing 36 to 40 percent butterfat (the only cream that will whip), **light cream**, or "coffee cream," with 18 to 30 percent butterfat, **dairy half-and-half**, a mixture of milk and cream with not less than 10 percent butterfat (a favorite for breakfast cereal), and **dairy sour cream** (generally referred to simply as "sour cream"), light cream subjected to a lactic-acid culture for creamier consistency, usually containing 18 to 20 percent butterfat.

There is no equivalent in American markets of the European *double cream*, as thick as our sour cream but sweet and containing between 50 and 60 percent butterfat.

Refrigerate all fresh milk and cream, reconstituted instant nonfat dry milk, and canned milk that has been opened.

Flour

In this book, unless otherwise specified, "flour" means wheat flour, and **all-purpose flour** should be used. This is a selected blend of "hard" and "soft" wheats satisfactory for nearly all baking and general cooking.

Instant-type or instantized flours have been so milled and refined that the flour disperses instantly in cold liquid. They are fine for thickening gravies or sauces, but should not be substituted measure for measure for all-purpose flour. (At least this is true as this book is being written. It is possible that in the near future the milling industry will achieve a uniform product that can be so substituted. Meanwhile, it's best to stick to the manufacturer's directions when using the instant-type flour in preparing baked goods or batters.)

Cake flour is milled from "soft" wheat (lower in gluten content). This produces a softer product. Use only for cakes, not for piecrust or breads.

Bread flour is used mainly by commercial bakeries.

Bleached flour has been sifted repeatedly to remove all bits of grain, then bleached to whiten. **Unbleached flour** has not been quite so refined, and is consequently more nutritious.

Enriched flour has had vitamins and minerals added to replace in part the nutritive value removed during the refining process. It's an ironic comment on our overchemicalized society that we must first remove the natural goodness, then try to replace it by artificial means.

Whole-wheat or graham flour is milled from "hard" wheat with bits of the whole grain retained. This and **buckwheat, soy, rice, and rye flours** are sold mainly in health stores.

Self-rising flour has had baking powder and salt added; it may be used in recipes that call for baking powder (2 teaspoons baking powder have been added for each cup of flour). Do not use in making yeast breads.

Rice

Long-grain rice is the best type to use for general cooking. This is less glutinous (not so likely to be sticky or gummy) as *medium-* or *short-grain rice*. The best variety is called *Patna*. All *white rice* has had hulls, germ, and outer bran layer removed during the milling process. Some has been enriched to replace part of the food value removed in milling. **Brown rice** (available mainly in health stores) has had only the outer hull removed.

Converted rice, also called *parcooked*, is a long-grain rice cooked before milling by a special steam-pressure process which also preserves more vitamins and minerals. The yield is greater than that of packaged rice not so processed. (One cup uncooked converted rice makes 4 cups cooked; 1 cup uncooked regular rice yields only 3 cups cooked.)

Precooked rice is a different product entirely. It is milled long-grain rice that has been completely cooked, then dehydrated. When steeped in boiling water (reconstituted), it is ready to serve after just 5 minutes. It is higher in cost than other types and its yield is smaller (1 cup from the box makes only 2 cups cooked.

In addition to the above, there are dozens of packaged rice products, some of converted rice, others of precooked rice, nearly all containing packets of seasoning. The price is considerable more than that of the rice and seasonings purchased separately and the added convenience is debatable.

Wild rice is not a rice at all, but a reedlike plant, expensive because it cannot be grown commercially, but must be gathered in its wild state. Served mostly with game.

Corn Products

Corn meal is really a flour, milled from dried field corn. The color (yellow or white) is that of the corn variety used.

Cornstarch is the refined starch from the endosperm (the heart) of the kernel, used only for thickening sauces, puddings, or pie fillings. It dissolves more easily in cold liquids than does flour and gives a more translucent appearance. (Use half as much as flour for same thickening results).

Arrowroot, from a tuberous plant in the West Indies, and **potato flour** can be used measure for measure in a recipe calling for cornstarch—or vice versa.

Hominy is field corn with hull and germ removed from the kernels, soaked in a lye solution which swells and softens the kernel.

Pearl hominy has had hulls removed by machinery. **Hominy grits** (called simply "grits" in the South) have been ground into coarse, even particles for quicker cooking. The cooked product is similar to cooked short-grain rice, sticky and bland.

Other Grains

Oatmeal, or oats, is available in *quick-cooking, regular,* and *instant* forms. This has been "rolled" or milled to create flat, thin flakes. Even the "regular" oatmeal requires less than 10 minutes' cooking. It is used primarily as a breakfast cereal, though it can also be used to make bread and cookies. The "instant" requires no cooking at all, only the addition of boiling water, but like most such products, manages to taste distressingly like old-fashioned flour glue.

Bulgur (sometimes called "wheat pilaf") is whole wheat that has been cooked and dried with some of the bran removed, then cracked into coarse fragments. Somewhat like brown rice in flavor, it is used primarily in making couscous and other Arabic or Near Eastern dishes. **Cracked wheat** is similar but has not had the bran removed.

Kasha is milled buckwheat, very popular with those of Russian background. It, too, tastes a little like brown rice when cooked. In Jewish cookery, it is often prepared with onions and chicken fat.

Farina is a wheat product with the bran and most of the wheat germ removed, but is not as fine as wheat flour. It is used in this country mainly as a breakfast cereal, but Europeans use it in casseroles and for puddings and pastries. (It is packaged as "cream of farina.")

Wheat germ is the heart of the wheat kernel, high in protein, iron, and vitamins, with a nutlike flavor. It may be used as a breakfast cereal, or for breading croquettes, or in place of fine dry crumbs for topping casseroles. Especially recommended for its health value in diets of invalids or children who are poor eaters.

Storage of Flour and Other Grain Products

All grain products can be stored on cupboard or pantry shelves almost indefinitely, if kept dry and clean. Occasionally one may find tiny insects in a grain product. Usually these have been in the grain from the time it was milled. They are not injurious to health and no cause for panic, but to get rid of them you must throw away the product, then clean out and spray the entire cupboard, for they multiply rapidly and if not checked will turn up in many other packages.

Leavening Agents

The term is used to mean any product which by forming a gas causes breads, cakes, or other baked products to rise and expand.

Baking soda is pure sodium bicarbonate. Use, both as leavener and as antiacid, alone or in combination with baking powder, when a recipe includes sour cream, milk, buttermilk, molasses, or chocolate. It has other important uses in the home, too; dressing insect bites, whitening teeth (used like tooth powder), and, most important, *putting out grease fires.* For this purpose, keep a package always on hand close to the kitchen range.

A pinch of soda added to water for cooking green vegetables will keep the color bright green, but tends to destroy vitamins. Some cooks have been known to add a pinch of soda to stewed tomatoes to sweeten them, or to artichokes, to speed cooking, soften, and sweeten.

Baking powder is a mixture of baking soda with dry acids, acid salts, and starch. There are three main types. "Double-acting," also called SAS, reacts very slowly, releasing only a portion of the gas at room temperature, the rest after the product is in the oven. *Phosphate types* also react slowly, but about two-thirds of the leavening action may occur before the product is placed in the oven. *Tartrate* types react quickly, and the product should be placed in the oven at once. In most recipes, unless otherwise noted, double-acting types are recommended.

Cream of tartar is one of the ingredients in baking powder. It is used primarily with egg whites (meringues or angel-food cake batter) to increase volume and prevent cake or meringue falling after removal from oven. Can be used in combination with baking soda as a substitute for baking powder. (See *Food Equivalents.*)

Yeast is available as *active dry yeast* (granular, dehydrated, in 1-ounce envelopes) and *compressed yeast,* a moist mixture of yeast and starch in a firm cake which must be refrigerated. Both have shelf life; observe date printed on package before buying or using.

Meat Stock Concentrates and Bouillon Cubes

Bouillon cubes are a dehydrated product made from beef, chicken, onion-flavored, and vegetable stock. Use 1 cube for each cup liquid. Similar concentrates are available in envelopes (1 for each cup liquid) and in jars (1 teaspoon for each cup liquid).

Dehydrated soups may also be used in sauces and for seasoning if contents are well blended before measuring. **Canned soup concentrates** may, of course, be used similarly. (See *Food Equivalents.*)

Gelatin

Unflavored gelatin is a granulated, dehydrated meat by-product without added flavoring or sweetening, available in 1-ounce envelopes, each containing 1 tablespoon, enough for 2 cups' liquid.

Fruit-flavored gelatins are a blend of granular gelatin, sugar, and artificial flavors and colors, available in 3-ounce and 6-ounce packages. **Diet gelatins** are the same, but with a noncaloric sweetener in place of sugar. Do not substitute unflavored for fruit-flavored gelatin in any recipe.

Pudding Mixes

So many dessert mixes are now on the market that complete coverage here is impossible. One warning: *Instant pudding mixes* (requiring no cooking) must never be substituted for *pudding and pie filling*, which has a cornstarch base and must be cooked as directed. Always read package directions carefully, whatever the mix.

Sugars and Syrups

Granulated white sugar should be used in any recipe which calls merely for "sugar." This is refined beet or cane sugar, processed to pour easily.

Superfine sugar, equivalent to the English "castor sugar," has been screened into such small granules that it dissolves instantly in liquids.

Confectioners' sugar (sometimes called "powdered sugar") has been blended with a small amount of cornstarch. Use for frostings, candies, and over fresh fruit. Sift before measuring, unless an entire 1-pound box is required. (See *Food Equivalents.*)

(In antique cookbooks, "powdered sugar" meant a cone of sugar that had been crushed into granular form.)

Cube sugar, compressed into cubes of 1 teaspoon each, is for use in hot tea or coffee.

Brown sugar, available as *light* and *dark brown*, is a by-product of white sugar, containing some molasses; the dark contains more molasses than the light. Should be stored in tight-covered containers, in the refrigerator. If it cakes, place in a 250° F. oven until it softens, then beat in blender until smooth. *Granulated brown sugar* (sometimes called "brownulated") has been processed to flow freely, and never cakes; it is only for table use—do not substitute in recipes for regular brown sugar.

Molasses is liquid residue of cane sugar. Blackstrap molasses contains a higher proportion of ash (potassium). *Unsulphured molasses* has had sulphur removed for less bitter flavor. Store all molasses in a tight-covered jar in a cool, dry place.

Maple syrup is the concentrated sap of the maple tree. *Maple sugar* is extracted from maple sap, much as white sugar is extracted from molasses. **Maple-blended syrup** is a mixture of syrups from sugar or corn products plus a minute amount of maple sugar and artificial flavor.

Corn syrup is derived from cornstarch by hydrolysis. *Light corn syrup* has been clarified and bleached; *dark corn syrup* contains some refiners' syrup (a residue of cane sugar) for flavor and color. Both are used for candies, frostings, and glazes.

Honey is a natural product made by bees, extracted from the wax of the bee cone, strained, and clarified. (The cone, too, is edible). Most is *clover honey*; a few special honeys bear the flavors of other plants on which bees have feasted.

Vinegar

Cider vinegar, distilled from apple juice, is the most used and least expensive. **White vinegar**, distilled from corn, rye, or barley malt, is colorless and has very little aroma; it is used for pickling and preserving. **Malt vinegar**, russet in color, is distilled from barley malt, and has a distinctive flavor and aroma. **Pineapple vinegar** is similar to cider vinegar in color and fragrance.

For salads, most connoisseurs prefer **wine vinegar**—which is what all vinegars were originally: wine turned sour. Both red-wine vinegar and white-wine vinegar are now available in most supermarkets. *Sherry vinegar*, imported from Spain, is a gourmet product, better for seasoning hors d'oeuvres or gazpacho than salads.

Herb vinegars—distilled or wine vinegars in which herbs have been steeped—are also popular for salad dressings, especially *tarragon vinegar*.

3 POTS AND PANS

Choose pots and pans to last—cheap cooking utensils are rarely a bargain. For top-stove cookery, make sure all pans have fitted lids.

Aluminum utensils are especially good for oven use (roasting pans, muffin tins, cake pans) and for top-stove cookery (saucepans, a kettle for spaghetti and soup, a double boiler). A *heavy aluminum or cast-iron alloy,* such as Magnalite, is the best for "waterless cooking" (that is, using a minimum of water), for vegetables, rice, slow-cooking stews. For skillets, there is nothing as good as **cast iron**, unless it's *cast iron covered with porcelain.*

Teflon-coated utensils require little or no fat and are especially useful for omelets, muffins and pan-broiled meats, but the lining does not last, which means extra cost in relining or replacing utensils. For sautéing, a *well-seasoned* cast-iron skillet requires little more fat than a Teflon-coated skillet and will last many years longer.

Ovenproof glass and ceramic ware, especially the kind that can go from freezer to oven to table, is excellent for casseroles, baked puddings, custards, and pies. For top-stove cooking, the heatproof ceramic works well for vegetables, coffee makers, and slow-cooking stews, but is not as satisfactory for sautéing.

Copper utensils are beautiful for food photography and decorative effects, and the old ones, with solid heavy bottoms, made when metal was not so costly, are excellent for conducting and retaining heat, but today's copper utensils are too light and difficult to keep clean. (However, French cooks swear by them, so maybe I am unduly prejudiced.)

Earthenware casseroles are excellent for baking, especially for beans and certain kinds of stews, but they are fragile and must be used with care.

Enamel chips easily, heat distribution is uneven, and once the enamel is chipped dirt becomes imbedded in exposed parts. Not recommended.

Cast iron covered with porcelain is excellent for frying, top-stove casseroles or stews, and ovenware. Although they are heavy and cumbersome to handle, they can be taken to the table, and are especially recommended for buffet service because they retain heat so long.

"Seasoning" New Utensils

Certain metals need to be treated before first use to avoid sticking and, in some cases, to avoid rusting. This is especially true of *cast iron, omelet pans, woks, and paella pans.* First wash the utensil with soap or mild detergent, rinse and dry thoroughly, then coat the surface generously with *hot* oil; tilt so that all surface areas are moistened. Let stand this way for 24 hours, then wipe out thoroughly with paper towel. Do this after each use (do not wash with water) for 6 to 8 times. Should food stick during this time, do *not* scrape with abrasive cleaners, but add oil, let stand, then scrub with brush or dishcloth. After the metal is thoroughly seasoned, the utensil may again be washed, but *never* let it soak in water. Should the utensil begin to stick again, repeat the process. Some people never wash omelet pans, only rub them thoroughly with paper towel after each use. It may be harder to do this with an iron skillet, but if food has not stuck to the surface, the pan can be just as thoroughly cleaned with paper as with water, and if the surface is kept oil-smooth, sticking rarely occurs, and cleansing is therefore much easier.

Chart of Pan Sizes

Utensil	*Most Common Sizes*	*Description and "Uses"*
Baking dishes (casseroles)	4-inch diameter (1½ inches deep) 1-quart (2½ inches deep) 1½-quart (2½ inches deep) 2½-quart (3 inches deep)	Ovenproof glass, ceramic, or pottery; used for casseroles, baked pastas, scalloped entrees
Baking sheets (cookie sheets)	12 x 16 inches 14 x 9 inches 15½ x 12 inches	Aluminum or other metal; used for cookies, biscuits, pizzas, meringues
Pizza pans	14-inch diameter 16-inch diameter	Aluminum, round; used especially for pizzas
Bread or loaf pans	7½ x 4 x 2¼ inches 9 x 5 x 2½ inches 16 x 15 x 4 inches	The two smaller sizes are available in both aluminum and glass; used for baking yeast breads, fruitcakes, meat loaf, and sometimes for gelatin molds
Custard cups	3-inch diameter (2 inches deep) 3½-inch diameter (1¾ inches deep) 4½-inch diameter (1¾ inches deep)	Ovenproof glass or ovenproof ceramic china; used for baked custards and puddings, also as gelatin molds
Jelly-roll pans	15½ x 10½ x 1 inches	Thin sheet; used for jelly roll and cookies
Muffin tins	6-cup (2½ inches deep) 12-cup (2½ inches deep) 12-cup (1 inch deep)	Aluminum: used for muffins and cupcakes

Utensil	Most Common Sizes	Description and "Uses"
Pie pans	5-inch diameter (tart pan) 8-inch diameter 9-inch diameter 10-inch diameter	Aluminum or oven-proof glass; used primarily for pie and other pastries
Ring molds	1-quart (4 cups) 1½-quart (6 cups)	Aluminum; used for cakes, rice molds, gelatin molds
Gelatin molds	¾-cup 1-cup 6-cup 1-quart (8 cups) Turk's head (1½-quart)	Aluminum or copper; used primarily for gelatin molds, Turk's head for cake (has tube in center)

4 UNDERSTANDING BASIC TECHNIQUES: HOWS AND WHYS

A cook rarely lets foods actually *boil*. Many foods commonly called *fried* are not really fried at all. Some of the most important cooking techniques are not even known to many people who have been cooking for years.

On the following pages, food preparation techniques are grouped together according to similarity, so that the fine differences may be more easily explained. It is important to study these, because often the difference between success and failure in a recipe lies in such a little thing as not having cut the food into pieces of the proper size, or the water may not have been boiling hard enough when food was added, or it was allowed to boil too hard during the cooking process.

Even the experienced cook may learn something new by studying these instructions. There are seven or eight different ways of tenderizing meat; sauces can be thickened without a trace of flour or other starch; probably the most delicious way of preparing fish is to poach it gently in seasoned broth.

CHOPPING GUIDE

To **mince** food means to cut it into fine particles, almost but not quite as fine as if put through a food grinder (when it is **ground**).

To **chop** food is to cut it more coarsely than when mincing it. (Yet, to confuse everyone, the term *chopped chuck* means beef chuck put through a grinder.)

To **crush** means to reduce to much finer particles than when mincing or grinding. The term *crushed garlic* is not the same as *minced garlic*. To crush garlic, mash it until nothing but shreds remain; discard the shreds. For cold sauces this is easiest done with a mortar and pestle; for salads, in a wooden salad bowl, using the back of a spoon. In cooking, it's easier to sauté whole garlic cloves in fat until golden and soft, then mash with the tines of a fork. Putting a garlic clove through a garlic press is not crushing; that is mincing. When minced, garlic, still in fine particles, browns more quickly and has a more bitter, stronger flavor than when crushed. (The bitterness is in the fiber, the fragrance in the juice.) To *crush nuts* means reducing nut meats to fine, even particles, almost, but not quite, a powder. This can be done with mortar and pestle or in a blender. To *crush cracker crumbs*, a rolling pin is good, or do it in a blender, adding a few crackers at a time.

To **grate** food (lemon or orange rind, hard cheese, nutmeg, onion) means to rub it over the finest holes of a metal grater. These graters always have holes in several graduated sizes. To **shred** a firm but not hard cheese, you rub the cheese over medium to large holes of the grater, that is, cut the cheese in long thin shreds (carrots and cabbage are also shredded in this way).

Shredding, mincing, and chopping can all be done easily with a French knife on a butcher's block or chopping board. Hold the knife handle with your right hand, place the palm of your left hand over the thicker part of the blade, and use a quick, even up-and-down motion.

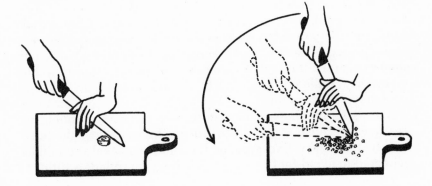

Mincing, chopping, and crushing can be done quickly in an electric blender—only take care not to let particles become too fine. (Turn motor on, off, on, off, several times.)

To **dice** means to cut food into cubes the size of poker dice. To **cube** means the food is in larger pieces, the size usually indicated in the recipe. To **slice** means to cut into thin wide slices, though if referring to certain vegetables (green beans, asparagus, celery) it may mean to cut lengthwise at an angle.

To **score** means to cut lines in square or diamond shapes with a small, sharp knife, not cutting all the way through. Lean, less tender meat is scored to cut muscular fibers (which shrink and toughen with application of heat). The fat over the top of a ham is scored in diamond shape so that as the fat shrinks with baking, an attractive pattern will be formed. Pastry is scored to form a pattern in the sugar glaze.

The fat edge of meat is sometimes **slashed**, that is, cut at regular intervals, because if not so cut the meat will curl up as the fat shrinks with cooking. Piecrust may be *slashed* (several vertical lines cut through the pastry) to allow steam to escape during baking.

PREPARING AND COOKING MEAT

Even those cuts of meat that have been precut and trimmed ready to cook frequently need additional attention at home. It may be necessary to remove excess fat, to tenderize the meat, or to truss it so that it will have a more attractive shape after cooking.

Removing Excess Fat

Most rolled roasts are sold with a thick layer of suet tied around the outside. This does not make the meat more tender (only fat inserted through the center of the lean does this), and may completely ruin the gravy. Gelatinous meat juices which brown in the pan give gravy its flavor. Excess fat will absorb these juices, make the gravy greasy and flavorless. To avoid this: 1) remove the layer of suet before cooking, and retie the meat; or, 2) ladle off the excess fat periodically during cooking, or remove with a syringe.

Excess fat on chops to be pan-broiled or sautéed should be removed because excess fat will ruin the sauce and the meat will be too greasy. Excess fat on the outside of steaks should be trimmed to avoid fat fires when the meat is broiled. A little fat is good—this adds to flavor, but in general the fat edging should be no thicker than ¼ inch.

Ways of Tenderizing Meat

Any one or a combination of the following methods will make less tender cuts, or meat of less than choice quality, more tender, and the length of cooking time will be reduced by tenderizing, which means less shrinkage, more edible meat.

1. **Tenderizing with wine**. Use leftover wine or any cheap table wine. Simply cover meat with wine, and soak 12 to 24 hours in refrigerator. Discard wine after it has done its tenderizing; do not use to make sauce or gravy. If meat is to be broiled or pan-fried after tenderizing, pat surface dry with paper towel.

2. **Tenderizing with olive oil**. Basically the same principle as "larding," but much easier. Punch deep holes in meat, and brush in olive oil so that it penetrates to center, first on one side, then on the other. Let meat soak in oil marinade *at room temperature* 2 to 4 hours. Before cooking, remove from marinade, pat off excess oil (using paper towel). Garlic lovers may want to rub the meat with garlic after oil has been worked in. (Olive oil is the most effective, probably because it contains more natural fruit acids, but corn, peanut, or soy oil may be used.)

3. **Larding**. Thin strips of suet or pork fat are inserted in lean of meat with a larding needle (available at shops carrying imported housewares). Suitable for roasts or pot roasts only.

4. **Marinades**. An acid (wine, vinegar, lemon or tomato juice) is usually the base, blended with herbs and other seasonings, and sometimes with oil. *Onion juice* also has a tenderizing effect.

5. **Yogurt or buttermilk**. The acid of the culture is the tenderizer in this case. Examples: a North German recipe for Sauerbraten calls for soaking the beef in buttermilk; in Turkey, lamb for shish-kabob is first soaked in yogurt; in South Carolina, chicken is sometimes soaked in buttermilk before being breaded and fried; and in Pakistan, chicken is marinated in yogurt before roasting. Meats marinated in yogurt or buttermilk become a ghoulish purplish color before cooking, but as they cook the outside becomes more brown than usual and the inside more tender. (Refrigeration is advised for meats or poultry so marinated.)

6. **Commercial tenderizers**. This is the easiest way to tender-

ize: keep the concentrate on the spice shelf at all times, and
apply it to the meat just before cooking. To use a combination of
commercial tenderizer and marinade (for more interesting flavor), apply commercial tenderizer first; then, after the 5-min-
ute application, add marinade.

7. **Scoring or pounding**. Scoring is done with a special utensil
or tool which cuts partially into surface to cut muscular fibers;
pounding is for the same purpose, but can be done with the
edge of a plate, or the heavy side of a cleaver. Working flour or
oil (or both) into the meat as it is pounded also helps to soften
tissues. This method can be used only for flat pieces of meat
(cutlets, thin steaks, or scallopini).

Trussing

A piece of meat may need trussing (tying up with cord, or fastening with skewers) for the sake of appearance. After it is
cooked, the meat will hold the trussed shape.

Sometimes meat is already trussed or tied when you buy it:
most boned rolled roasts today are sold tied ready for the oven.
But you may wish to remove excess fat from an already rolled
roast, or to place a filling inside the rolled roast, or to stuff a
boned breast of veal.

Trussing a roast is much like tying up a Christmas parcel.
Manipulate it into the shape you want, insert small skewers to
hold the shape while you tie *white butchers' cord* (available in
any hardware store) around the meat in several places. *Flank
steak* is trussed in the same way before braising or pot-roasting.

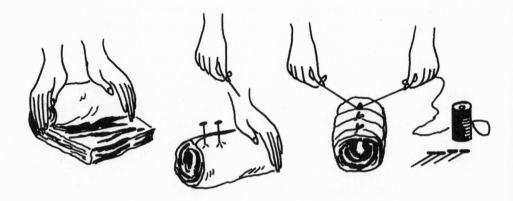

For *veal birds*, saltimbocca, or similar small meat roll-ups you may use only small skewers to hold the rolls together, or you may tie with heavy-duty thread borrowed from the sewing box. The opening of stuffed pork chops may be held together with either small poultry skewers or toothpicks.

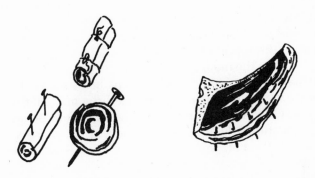

To truss *poultry* after it has been stuffed, pull the skin together by inserting small poultry skewers across the opening horizontally, then pull butcher's cord around the skewers in the same way you lace up ice skates.

It is helpful to have poultry skewers in two sizes, small and medium, for such trussing operations. These are sold by the card, three or four to a card, in housewares departments.

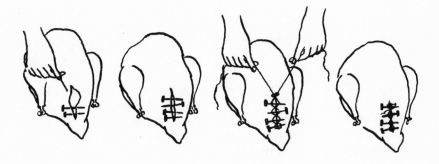

Cooking Less Tender Cuts

Cooking meat in liquid or steaming it in its own juice is another method of tenderizing—using moisture to soften tissues rather than acids. It is the preferred method for those less tender cuts of meat which acid tenderizers cannot penetrate sufficiently.

Braising means first *searing* the meat (browning it on the outside) in fat, then adding liquid, and cooking the meat, covered, until tender.

Stewing is a form of braising: the meat is usually browned, then liquid is added. However, the meat of some stews is added directly to the liquid (or the liquid added to the meat) without first browning the meat in fat.

Pot-roasting, too, may be a form of braising (if the meat is seared first); or, the meat may not be browned, merely cooked in liquid. Only a small amount of liquid should be added, and the pot should be kept tightly covered. A pot roast is always a solid piece of meat, whereas meat for stew is cut into cubes or small pieces.

"Boiling." This is a misnomer, for no meat should be really boiled. But what is called "boiled" (as in New England Boiled Dinner Corned Beef, the French Boeuf à la Mode, and German boiled beef) is in fact a process of simmering in a large quantity of liquid (much more than for pot roast) for several hours.

Broiling, Roasting, Spit-Roasting, Barbecuing

Only tender (or tenderized) meats can be cooked by these methods, all of which originally meant cooking by direct heat. **Roasting**, which used to be done on a turning spit over an open fire—what we now call **spit-roasting**—is really *baking*, since it is done in an oven. A shallow pan should always be used.

Barbecuing is from a Mexican word and meant originally cooking meat, fish, or poultry on a rack above an open fire. *Barbecue sauces* are the spicy-hot sauces of Mexican origin served over roasted or broiled foods. Today we use the term "barbecue" to mean all outdoor cooking, and also for indoor cooking over an open fire.

Cooking by direct heat tends to dry out meat. For this reason, many broiled, spit-roasted or barbecued meats are **basted** as they cook, either with fat or a basting sauce, to keep the meat more moist. A syringe is excellent for this.

Self-basting means that the natural fat of the meat performs the same function: meat turning on a spit is bathed by the natural fat oozing from it, which flows over the surface of the meat as it slowly revolves. Or, meat roasted in an oven may be partially covered so that the steam rising from the meat (from natural juices and fat) will be thrown back onto the surface.

Marinating meat before it is broiled, roasted, or barbecued is another way of keeping it moist: the meat is soaked in a flavored broth or a flavored oil and acid mixture in advance to absorb moisture. Hamburgers that are to be broiled or barbecued over an open fire will be far more succulent if marinated in advance, or basted as they cook.

A *well-larded* piece of meat will keep more succulent because the melting fat inside the lean bathes the meat as it cooks, from the inside out.

Breading, Frying, Sautéing

Since these methods are used for other foods besides meats, they are discussed under Cooking with Fats (which follows), but it may be pointed out that *breading* keeps meat more moist because the crust formed on the outside holds in natural juices. Breading does not in itself tenderize meat, but a breaded cutlet will often seem more tender because it is juicier.

COOKING WITH FATS

To **sauté** is to cook food in a small amount of fat, enough to cover the bottom of the pan noticeably. Usually foods are lightly browned (unless the recipe specifies otherwise), and the pan is not covered. If covered, the foods are actually braised.

To **fry** means to use more fat, usually to a depth of an inch. Food should sizzle when added to the hot fat and be cooked until crisply browned on all sides. (This method is sometimes called **pan-fried**.)

Stir-frying is a Chinese technique. A generous amount of fat is used, more than for sautéing, but food is cut in small pieces, kept from browning by being turned frequently and cooked until just barely tender.

Pan-broiled is a term applied only to meats. This means meat is cooked in a skillet without any fat, or with just enough to moisten the bottom of the pan and to prevent meat sticking until well browned on both sides. Salt is sometimes sprinkled over the surface of a hot skillet before chops are placed in the pan, in order to draw out the fat of the meat more quickly.

Deep-fried means foods are cooked in preheated fat deep enough to more than cover the food (1½ to 3 inches deep), hot

enough (365° to 375° F.) to seal the outside of the food instantly.

To **bread or batter-fry.** If foods are *breaded* they are dipped
first in beaten egg, then in fine crumbs (or sometimes in a
crumb-flour mixture). They may be fried in either shallow or
deep fat. If *batter-fried* the food is dipped in a batter made of
flour and egg, or flour, liquid and egg, then dropped into deep
hot fat.

Simmering in oil. Because this method is applied principally
to vegetables, it is discussed on page 64.

COOKING WITH LIQUIDS

When any liquid **boils**, the surface bubbles merrily and steam
can be seen to rise from the pot. When water boils in a teakettle,
steam comes from the spout in a white cloud. To **bring to a boil**
means that the liquid should reach the big-bubble stage, then
the heat should be lowered. A **rapid boil** is one with big uneven
bubbles. A **full, rolling boil** means the bubbles pop and break
with regularity. When food **simmers** the liquid forms small irregular bubbles, giving off only a small amount of steam. Sometimes a recipe will specify that the liquid should merely **smile**:
this means the surface should be like the sea on a calm day,
with only an occasional ripple or swell.

Poaching means the liquid should merely "smile," not simmer, *never* boil. It is a method used primarily for fish cookery
and for eggs.

Steaming means that food is cooked either on a rack above
boiling water (never touching the water) or in a very small
amount of liquid (perhaps its own natural juices), tightly covered.

When foods are cooked in liquid, even when steamed, the
liquid absorbs valuable nutrients. European cooks use cooking
water for soups. Americans, not given to soup making on such a
scale, should use the least possible amount of liquid in cooking,
so there's less to discard.

PREPARING AND COOKING
VEGETABLES

Most *fresh vegetables* should be used within a few days after
purchase. All should be cooked the shortest possible time in the
least possible amount of water.

Frozen vegetables should be kept solidly frozen until just before cooking, then cooked in the least possible amount of water. Some can be cooked in a pot without any liquid at all.

Peeling, Trimming, Cutting Up

Important nutrients are contained in the peel or rind of every vegetable, and often the dark green outer leaves are more nutritious than the insides. Scrape or peel off only the thinnest outer layer of potatoes, carrots, and other root vegetables, and onions.

Whenever possible, retain rind or peel. Zucchini, yellow summer squash, and locally grown eggplant all have edible rinds (though the rind of eggplant when shipped long distances may be bitter). When cooking fresh peas, add a few of the more crisp pods to the pan; "snow peas," available fresh on the West Coast, are edible, pods and all.

After peeling, vegetables should not be soaked—this only washes away flavor and food value, and may cause the cooked vegetable to be watery. If not to be cooked immediately, keep pared vegetables in plastic. *Potatoes*, however, turn black quickly after peeling (both sweet and white potatoes), and if not to be cooked at once, must be briefly *parboiled*—cooked in a small amount of water for 3 or 4 minutes, then drained. After this, they may be oven-browned and placed around a roast, or more water may be added later to complete cooking.

The leaves and tops of some vegetables may be cooked separately—beet and turnip greens, and the more tender leaves of cauliflower. Soak leaves, trim stems and coarser part of stalk, cook until limp; drain thoroughly.

Quick-cooking is important for flavor and food value. To speed cooking, discard all parts that are not edible or that require longer cooking. The most satisfactory way to cook *asparagus* is to bend the stalks so that they break at the point where the tougher portion begins, then *cook only the spears*. (I have tried peeling the lower portion of stalks, as the French do it, but find the stalk to be still fibrous, requiring longer cooking, so that the spears have less flavor.)

Broccoli should be cut into individual flowers, the stalks sliced or diced. Cauliflower, too, should be broken into individual buds or flowers.

How quick is "quickest possible"?

No rule can be established for the length of cooking time, because it depends on the freshness of the vegetable and the size of the pieces. Carrots, sliced or quartered, can sometimes be cooked in 3 minutes; sometimes they require 6 or 8 minutes. Asparagus generally takes about 6 minutes, green beans about 10, cauliflower and Brussels sprouts may be fork-tender in 4 minutes. "Fork-tender" is the best test: when a fork can be easily plunged through the center, the vegetable is cooked.

Remember: the less water used, the faster will be the cooking time and the least waste of vitamins. Also, smaller pieces cook more quickly.

This is the reason for slicing green beans "French style," for thinly slicing or quartering carrots, for slicing celery at an angle, for dicing squash.

When to cover, when not to cover the saucepan. For most vegetables, the saucepan should be tightly covered to keep in steam, prevent evaporation, and speed cooking. But steam robs certain green vegetables of their bright-green color, in particular broccoli, asparagus, and Brussels sprouts. The solution: place the lid on the pan so that some steam can escape but most of the pan is covered.

Blanching. Originally this term meant "to whiten," but now, applied to vegetables, it means to scald, or soften in boiling-hot water. Cabbage leaves, green peppers, and eggplants are blanched before stuffing. (Blanched brains and sweetbreads are whitened by parboiling; almonds, soaked in boiling water, are "blanched," i.e. whitened, when the brown skin is removed.)

Removing seeds. Seeds of most vegetables, green peppers and tomatoes in particular, are bitter. Carefully cut away all green-pepper seeds and the white inner membrane. Cut fresh tomatoes in half, hold cut side down, squeeze gently; most of the seeds will come out. Put canned whole tomatoes through a sieve or food mill to get rid of seeds, especially when tomatoes are to be used in making tomato sauce.

Cooking Vegetables in Oil or Butter

Oriental cooks rarely cook vegetables in water; instead they use peanut oil. Oil shortens cooking time because it softens the vegetables as much as does the heat; it also preserves color, and there's no water to throw away.

Mediterranean cooks slowly simmer onions and other vegetables together in olive oil with no added liquid except that of tomatoes (fresh or canned). The vegetables are not sautéed; they should cook at moderate to low heat, not brown at all.

What the Spanish call a *sofrito* and the French a *mirepoix* is the same basic technique. (See Sauce Techniques.)

To **"butter-boil"** is an American cookery method, first introduced by General Foods for the cooking of frozen vegetables; a very small amount of butter and water (usually 2 tablespoons each) are used for the cooking of the vegetables in a tightly covered saucepan. A number of fresh vegetables can be cooked the same way, notably carrots, tender young green beans, summer squash, celery, and green cabbage.

The technique in every case is basically the same: the vegetables *simmer* in oil or fat, which hastens cooking time and preserves all flavor and food value.

SAUCE TECHNIQUES: DO'S AND DON'TS

A detailed discussion of sauces per se will be found in Book 3, Chapter 2, "Sauces and Soups." Here we are concerned primarily with how to make a sauce with the cooking liquid of stews, pot roasts, chops, and casseroles.

How to Thicken Liquids

1. **With starch.** Add flour, cornstarch, potato flour, or arrowroot to liquid in one of three ways: 1) Stir flour into *melted fat* (the drawn-out fat of chops, melted butter, or oil), using 2 tablespoons flour and 2 tablespoons fat for each cup of liquid for a medium-thick sauce. This *roux*, as the French call it, should simmer several minutes before liquid (hot or cold) is added. 2) A small amount of cold water is stirred into flour, cornstarch, or other starch thickener, to make a thin paste; hot liquid is then stirred into the paste. 3) Flour is blended with softened butter in equal amounts and formed into small balls, then these are dropped into hot liquid (of stew or pot roast) during last 10 minutes of cooking. The sauce in this case thickens itself. *Do not add flavor or any starch direct to hot liquids* without first blending it with fat or cold water. It will lump immediately, and such lumps are hard to get rid of.

2. **With eggs.** This makes a rich, smooth, delicious sauce, but it's trickier to prepare than with flour. Especially recommended for chicken, veal, or fish sauces. *Egg yolks* are preferred, but whole egg or egg white (lightly beaten) can be used in the same way. *Do not add eggs directly to hot liquid:* add a very little hot liquid to well-beaten egg, stir until smooth, and add a very little

more hot liquid. Now combine the two, but turn off heat under pan. Hot liquid in pan will cook the egg sufficiently. *Do not add egg until 5 to 10 minutes before meal is to be served. Do not allow sauce to cook after egg has been stirred in.*

3. **With vegetables**. This is the *mirepoix* or *sofrito* technique. Minced vegetables—usually onion, carrots, and celery—are gently cooked in oil or butter in a skillet or saucepan until very soft, without browning. Minced ham may be added; crushed or minced garlic and minced parsley are usually added to a Spanish *sofrito*, as are chopped tomatoes, or tomato purée or paste. When the vegetables are cooked almost to a purée, broth is added; or, meat, fish, or poultry may be placed over the vegetables, then later broth or wine (or both) will be added. In a stew that cooks a long time, the vegetables may completely disintegrate without further attention. Or, if not, the liquid may be forced through a sieve or puréed in a blender for smooth consistency. *For curries, onion, garlic, squash, or pared apple is used for the thickening. A curry should never be thickened with flour or other starch. Do not allow vegetables to brown;* if onion, in particular, browns at all it must be removed from the pan. Slow, gentle cooking is the secret.

4. **By adding bread**. Diced plain bread may be added to a stew during last 10 to 15 minutes to thicken it; or, bread may first be fried in butter or oil before it is added (this is a Spanish method). Fried bread gives interesting flavor and texture to a stew, and will disintegrate completely in the liquid.

5. **By reducing volume**. This works well when there's a large quantity of sauce. Turn up the heat; cook *uncovered* so that liquid will evaporate rapidly; the reduced liquid will be thickened. *Watch pan carefully;* the danger is that it will cook down too much, or sauce may burn on bottom of pan.

6. **Using a blender**. Pour sauce into blender, beat covered at medium speed until thickened and very smooth. Even if sauce does not get as thick as gravy, appearance will be greatly improved. Or, first place an egg yolk in blender, beat egg until thick, then slowly add hot sauce with blender in motion.

7. **With heavy cream or sour cream**. By itself, cream does not thicken, though it gives a thin sauce smoother texture and flavor. If a thickened sauce is preferred, first blend cornstarch (or arrowroot) with small amount of liquid, simmer until sauce thickens, then turn off heat, stir in cream, beat *briskly* with whisk until smooth. *If using sour cream,* first add some of hot

liquid to cream, beat briskly, then combine the two. *Do not continue cooking over direct heat after cream is added.*

The Role of Fat in Sauces

In today's calorie-conscious society, there is a tendency to look upon the slightest measure of fat as too much. Yet it's fat that brings out other flavors. A small amount of fat is important, especially when meat is browned in fat, or onions are simmered in fat, or herbs reconstituted in fat.

In making a curry, herbs and spices should be added to the fat at the very beginning. This is true, too, in using paprika for Hungarian dishes.

Adding dried herbs and spices to fat restores the oils removed during the process of drying. (Fresh herbs, because they have not had natural oils removed, can be added at the end of the cooking.)

Pan drippings are the basis for meat gravies, the browned essence sticking to the bottom of the roasting pan or skillet. The clear liquid fat in the pan, however, will do nothing for gravy flavor and may ruin it. Pour or ladle off the clear fat; use only the brown essence with just enough fat to make a liquid mixture.

How much fat is too much? For flour-thickened gravies, always remember the rule of *2 tablespoons fat for each cup liquid.* For clear gravies, 1 teaspoon fat per cup of liquid is enough (and this should be entirely the brown essence, no clear fat).

To remove excess fat from stews or pot roasts. The easiest way is to cook the stew or pot roast a day ahead, then chill the broth. The fat rises to the top, forming a crust that is easy to remove. Or, if there isn't time for this, let the stew cool long enough for the fat to come to the top of the pan, then ladle off and discard the fat—it's of no use. Those bits of clear liquid fat that defy the ladle can be removed by wadding up a piece of paper towel, and dipping it just into the top of the liquid; the fat will cling to the paper.

The All-Important Broth or Stock

Whenever you are cooking meat or poultry from which bones have been removed, use the bones for making stock. This can make a world of difference in the sauce flavor. The stock (bones, water, salt) can simmer while the meat is cooking. (Use chicken necks and giblets for chicken gravy; the bones of a boned rolled roast for meat gravy; the bones of pork chops when you are using lean pork for an oriental dish or a casserole.) If possible, time the cooking of the broth so that it can stand for 5 to 10 minutes before the gravy is to be made, allowing fat to rise to the top. Then ladle off the fat, strain the broth, and add it directly to the pan drippings.

What to Do If Sauce Lumps

A sauce usually lumps because the starch was not thoroughly dissolved before adding to hot liquid, or because the heat is too high. In most cases, the lumps can be smoothed out by beating with a whisk. (This is true with cornstarch-thickened puddings, also.) If this doesn't work, the next best thing is to pour the sauce into a blender and beat *at low speed* until smooth. A third way is to force the sauce through a sieve or food mill. But this is a wasteful method (the lumps usually refuse to go through) and a lot of bother; so use it only out of pure desperation.

If a Sauce Curdles

Curdling is usually caused by one of three things: 1) a delicate protein food, such as cream (especially sour cream), eggs, or milk, is subjected too quickly to high heat; 2) an acid, such as wine, lemon juice, or tomato, fights with another ingredient—especially milk, butter, or cream; or 3) an *emulsified sauce* (mayonnaise or hollandaise) may curdle because fat (oil or butter) was added too quickly to the beaten egg.

To avoid curdling when preparing a hot sauce using egg or cream, first add a little hot liquid to well-beaten egg or cream in a bowl, turn off heat from under pan, then briskly beat the egg or cream mixture into the hot sauce. Do not cook further; keep warm over hot but not boiling water. *Do not add any concentrated acid to a sauce until it is already thickened and smooth,* and then beat briskly with a whisk.

If, despite these precautions, the sauce curdles, here are possible solutions:

•Pour sauce into blender, beat at low speed until smooth.
•Place an unbeaten egg yolk in blender, beat until thick, then slowly add curdled sauce with blender in motion. (If you don't have a blender, use a whisk, beating for all you're worth.) This is sometimes the only way to save curdled hollandaise.
•Force the sauce through a sieve.
•Pretend this is the way the sauce was supposed to look.

(Sometimes the sauce tastes perfectly all right—it only looks unpleasant. The Chinese dish Lobster Cantonese has such a curdled-looking sauce, and no one objects!)

When Should Sauces Be Strained?

Many European recipes specify that a sauce should be strained, so that it will be smooth and creamy, free of lumps, fine in texture. Often, beating the sauce in the blender will achieve almost the same result: the sauce will be puréed, rather than strained, but it will have a smooth texture and more attractive appearance. For simple family meals, this is usually all that matters—and all nutrients are preserved, an important consideration. However, for fancy cooking, straining is sometimes preferable—especially for *chaud-froid* sauce, or any sauce that should be completely free of small particles. Appearance must be the determining factor. You might try putting it in the blender first; if the sauce is still not as smooth as desired, *then* strain it.

SEASONING WITH HERBS, SPICES, AND OTHER CONDIMENTS

Fresh Herbs

Parsley should be kept on hand always; fresh parsley has a potency that dried parsley can never equal. There are two kinds: *curly* and *Italian* (large leaves). The former is best for garnish; the latter is the more pungent for use in sauces. Mince by chopping with a French knife or by snipping with scissors, as you prefer. Use as generously as you like, in either sauces or stews, or sprinkled over the tops of dishes ready to bring to the table. *To store:* wash well, discard stems, place leaves in tight-covered container in refrigerator. Can be frozen, but it loses its crispness.

Dill is nice with fish, tomatoes, carrots, all beans, in salads, and for seasoning Scandinavian meat dishes. Can be grown easily in any soil; *freezes well*. When fresh is not available, use dried dill.

Chives are useful chopped over soups, meat and fish sauces, many vegetables. Usually can be purchased in pots in spring, to keep in kitchen window. *Freeze-dried chives* are almost as good as fresh, and keep indefinitely in your spice rack.

Ginger root. Available in oriental groceries; tiny slivers of green ginger will do wonders for Chinese and Indonesian dishes. Keep tightly wrapped in plastic in refrigerator, or bury in moist soil in pot or window box where eventually it will sprout and reproduce itself.

Mint. Useful for summer drinks and for flavoring lamb, beans, and fruit compotes. Plant almost anywhere outdoors; it spreads like wildfire. *Dried mint* can be used as a substitute in hot sauces (not in drinks), but use sparingly.

Cilantro. Available in Spanish and oriental groceries. The English name is *coriander*, but the spice ground from coriander root has an entirely different flavor. Minced fresh cilantro is superb with pork, fish, and chicken, and over tomato soup. Store like parsley in covered container in refrigerator. (Also called Chinese parsley.)

Dried Herbs

Orégano is the most popular of all herbs in current use. Use with caution in tomato sauce, pizzas, meat sauces, stews. (Another name for orégano is *wild marjoram*; **marjoram** may be used in place of orégano, or vice versa.)

Thyme can be used as a substitute for orégano, or in combination with orégano. More delicate in flavor, but still must be used with caution.

Tarragon is best with fish, to flavor vinegar for salads, and over sliced tomatoes. Fragrant licorice-like flavor; use with caution.

Basil is used primarily with tomatoes and tomato sauces.

Laurel or **bay leaf** is very potent; use in meat stews—but with extreme caution.

Saffron is the world's most expensive herb, has a bitter tang, but does wonders for Bouillabaisse, Paella, and other Mediterranean specialties. Use in minuscule amounts.

Rosemary has a slight medicinal tang, is used by the Italians with lamb and for other meat sauces. Use with caution.

Sage is very strong; it is used to flavor commercial sausages, in poultry dressing, and for pork. Use sparingly.

Anise and **fennel** both have a slight licorice flavor, and may be used interchangeably. Powdered fennel will keep potent a long time, and is easier to use than the seeds or minced leaves.

Caraway is a seed, and therefore whether it should be classed as spice or herb is debatable. Used frequently in cuisines of Northern and Central Europe, in sauerkraut dishes and rye bread, and for flavoring meats, especially pork. Use in moderation.

Spices

Cinnamon is already a standby; use it not only to flavor apples, hot wine punches, and (with sugar) over buttered toast, but also in meat sauces, Near Eastern dishes, Indian and Indonesian specialties. Powdered cinnamon is the most useful; cinnamon sticks are used mainly for hot drinks.

Cloves. *Whole cloves* are useful for sticking into the fat side of ham, into oranges to be used in hot punches, and into onions to be used in stews, and for stocks. Use *powdered cloves* in much the same way as cinnamon, for both sweet sauces and desserts, and to season meats.

Allspice has a flavor similar to both cinnamon and cloves; use the same way. (The three are combined with ginger for *pumpkin pie spice.*)

Dry mustard is useful mostly for oriental sauces and peppery meat dishes or sauces.

Powdered ginger, too, is a must for oriental cookery; very good with cabbage, and useful (if used sparingly) in many, many sauces—fish, chicken, veal, vegetable, and even dessert sauces.

Peppercorns, both black and white, should be in every spice cabinet, to be ground as needed in a *pepper grinder*. The spice has infinitely more fragrance when freshly ground.

Coriander, dried, is useful mainly for Near Eastern dishes, but also for pickles and pastries.

Cumin is one of the loveliest of spices, with an inimitable aroma, excellent with chicken, fish, and pork. It is one of the ingredients in all curry powders and all chili powders. (Spanish name is *comino.*)

Paprika should be used for much more than giving color to otherwise pale dishes. For Hungarian cookery, use it by the tablespoonful. Also adds subtle flavor to all sour-cream sauces, to veal (pound it into the meat), and to Paella.

Nutmeg, like cinnamon, has more use in *meat cookery* than most Americans realize. A must for sprinkling over eggnog and baked custards.

Mace is from the outer husk of the nutmeg seed. Its flavor is more delicate and its use is primarily for meats and meat or fish sauces.

Cayenne is the hottest of all spices, must be used with extreme caution.

Cardamom is very flowery and fragrant, superb for fruit compotes; used much by the Scandinavians in pastries.

Salt, of course, is in every kitchen. Some gourmets insist that *sea salt* is much superior to ordinary salt; *iodized salt* that has been processed to flow freely is preferred by the vast majority of cooks. *Kosher salt* is very coarse, and is used to coat Salt-broiled Steak and for kosher cookery. For how much to use, see Salt Chart.

Monosodium glutamate, frequently called MSG for short, is used, like salt, chiefly to bring out other flavors. The American MSG is extracted from beets; in the orient, it is taken from seaweed. It has a very mild flavor of its own, but only those with very sensitive palates can detect it. Use generously over vegetables and for meat sauces and stews.

Curry powder. As this is a blend of many different spices, individual brands vary considerably. Most contain cumin, coriander, tumeric (very hot, bright yellow in color), mustard, ground fennel, and ground capsicums (peppers). Extremely useful: add the merest pinch for "what is this?" flavor to scrambled eggs, salad dressings, fish, chicken, sour-cream sauces, lima beans, mayonnaise, etc. For Indian curries, use by the tablespoon.

Chili powder. Also a blend of several spices and herbs, usually includes cumin, orégano, garlic powder, and cayenne. Used primarily for dishes of Mexican inspiration, such as Chili con Carne, though also can be used (sparingly) for scrambled eggs and in hamburgers.

Other Condiments

There is such a variety of commercial spice blends and sauces available that it would be impossible to cover them all. Here are the most important.

Tabasco sauce, a bottled sauce whose chief ingredient is cayenne pepper. The generic name is *liquid red pepper seasoning.*

How Much Salt to Use in Cooking

1½ teaspoons in water to cover
Stewed chicken

1 teaspoon per pound
Meat, no bone

1 teaspoon per quart water
Boiled potatoes

½ teaspoon per pound
Meat, large bone

½ teaspoon for 2 cups
Green vegetables

½ teaspoon per pound
Fish

½ teaspoon serving for 4
Fresh salad

1 teaspoon for 2½ pounds
Fried or broiled chicken

1 teaspoon per 3 quarts water
Spaghetti, macaroni, noodles

Soy sauce, of oriental origin, is a blend of caramelized sugar, salt, monosodium glutamate, and extract of soy beans. In the orient, several kinds of soy sauce are available, light and dark, but so far all American-manufactured soy sauces are the dark kind.

Worcestershire sauce is an English invention, a combination of soy sauce, spices, and vegetable extracts (carrots and onions chiefly).

A-1 Sauce is a bottled liquid sauce used chiefly over meats.

Prepared mustard is a blend of dry mustard, vinegar, and spices. *Dijon mustard* (French) is made with white wine, as is *Dusseldorf* (German).

Capers. The buds of a plant grown in the Mediterranean, put up in a vinegar brine. They give superb tang to certain sauces (especially fish sauces) and salads, and are useful for garnishing hors d'oeuvre mixtures.

Instant minced onion. Very handy for use in stews and sauces as a short cut.

Garlic powder. As above. (However, the commercial *garlic salt* tends to be bitter; it's better to make your own by crushing garlic with a mortar and pestle; work in as much salt as the garlic will take, about ½ cup salt to 1 or 2 garlic cloves. This can be stored, covered, in refrigerator, for instant use as a seasoner.)

BEATING AND BAKING TECHNIQUES

In preparing any baked goods (breads, pies, puddings, soufflés, and cakes), it is important to understand the meaning of the terms "stir," "beat," "whip," and "fold," because these refer to the amount of *air* that should (or should not) be incorporated into the food at a certain stage of preparation. If too much air is beaten in too soon, a cake may fall from lack of support. If too little air, it may never rise properly.

To stir means to move a spoon gently and slowly through a batter or mixture of food.

To beat is a brisker, faster motion, intended to make food very smooth or to beat in air, or both. It should always be steady and rhythmical, using a *cupping motion*, keeping the wrist constantly moving.

To whip is to beat very energetically so that a great deal of air is incorporated. To whip potatoes, for example, means to beat the cooked potatoes until they follow the fork or spoon in a light fluff. (To call them *mashed* potatoes is a very inadequate description.) To whip cream means to beat air in until the cream is doubled in volume, fluffy, yet stiff enough to hold its shape.

Stiffly beaten egg whites are really whipped. The test as to whether they have been beaten enough is to turn over the bowl: if the whites begin to slide out when the bowl is partially tipped, they need more beating. When sufficiently beaten, the egg whites will not fall out, even when the bowl is completely upside down.

When a recipe says egg yolks should be beaten *until thick and light in color* (or "lemon-colored"), it means that the yolks must be beaten very vigorously and steadily until as thick as heavy cream and considerably lighter in color than the whole yolks were when you started. A blender is excellent for this. If you don't have a blender, use a fork, a whisk, or a rotary beater.

To fold is a term used when a light, fluffy ingredient, like egg white or whipped cream, must be incorporated into a heavier batter. This is a gentle motion, which must always be done by hand—a figure 8, *under, up, over, under* movement of spoon through batter until all the fluffy ingredient is thoroughly mixed with the heavier mixture and all air retained.

A **batter** is a fluid mixture of flour with leavener, salt, and liquid. **Dough** is a mixture of flour, leavener, salt and liquid stiff enough to shape and roll out with a rolling pin. Most doughs are **kneaded**; that is, they are picked up from the bowl and worked with the hands and fingers until smooth. Dough for piecrust or biscuits is only lightly kneaded; bread dough is usually kneaded with vigorous punching until it is elastic.

Not all batters should be beaten. Muffin batter, especially, should be stirred just until all dry ingredients are moistened.

Leaveners cause flour products to expand in volume. Quick-acting leaveners (baking soda or baking powder) form a gas within seconds of being combined with liquid and flour; yeast, too, causes formation of a gas, though the yeast works more slowly, growing eventually to far greater volume. Eggs can be used in combination with either baking powder or yeast (never both); or, eggs alone may be the leavener.

Lightly floured board. Dough when rolled out tends to stick to a smooth surface, and the more glasslike the surface, the more readily the dough sticks. Conversely, dough does not stick as readily to a more porous surface, like the wood of a pastry board or of a chopping block. A little flour sprinkled over the surface also helps to prevent sticking—but it should be only a little, enough to dust the surface, or the additional flour will make the product too heavy and "doughy." Even better than plain flour is a little pancake mix (not biscuit mix, for this contains fat). The mix creates a kind of gritty surface which further discourages sticking.

When and how to **grease the pan**. To prevent food (especially baked products) from sticking to the pan when they come from the oven, a very thin film of fat (preferably vegetable shortening) is spread over the surface. Usually only the bottom is greased, not the sides, for cakes and breads pull away from the sides during baking, or a knife can be run around the sides. Muffin tins, however, should be greased both on bottom and on sides.

Some recipes specify that the pan should be "greased, then floured." This means that after greasing, flour is sprinkled over the surface, the pan shaken lightly, and turned over so the excess flour spills out. What flour remains stuck to the fat is sufficient.

Pans should *not* be greased for any of the following: sponge, angel food, chiffon, or genoise cakes; piecrust, baking-powder or soda biscuits; shortcake or pastry torte shells.

Lining the pan with paper is a substitute for greasing. This means that *waxed paper (not* plastic wrap) should be cut with scissors to fit exactly the bottom of the pan in which cake or bread is to be baked. For baking fruit bread (which is a very heavy batter), *heavy brown paper* (such as a nice clean shopping bag) is often used rather than waxed paper, then shortening is rubbed over *both sides* of the brown paper.

Cooling, chilling, freezing. To **cool** means to reduce the temperature from hot to room temperature. To **chill** means to put the food in the refrigerator. But hot food should never be put in the refrigerator without first cooling it to room temperature—this causes too much condensation and interferes with the efficiency of the refrigerator.

A quick way to chill foods (already cooled to room temperature) is to put them in the freezer or freezing compartment. A one-crust pie, so chilled, will hold its shape better during baking: the fat will not melt so readily, giving the flour more chance to firm with heat. After only 15 minutes at freezing temperature, even a regular Pyrex pie pan can go direct from freezer to oven.

To **freeze** means to place the food in a freezer at 0° F.

OTHER CULINARY TERMS YOU SHOULD UNDERSTAND

Brush. To apply liquid, fat, or a glaze in a thin film over the top of food. A pastry or barbecue brush should be used, but if you don't have one, use a spoon or syringe, applying very lightly.

Caramelize. To melt granulated sugar until it forms into a brown thick liquid; the best way is in a small iron skillet, over direct heat, watching carefully to avoid sugar's burning or forming a hard lump.

Clarify. To remove small particles (fat or scum) from clear broth, or scum from jelly, or to remove the white sediment from melted butter (when butter is melted, the white milk solids, being heavier, go to the bottom; the clear liquid fat can then be poured off). Boiled coffee is sometimes clarified of the grounds by adding egg shells or a single egg white, which captures and holds grounds in its adhesive film.

Coat, dredge, dust, flour. All of these refer to the same thing—covering the outside of a food lightly, usually with seasoned flour or other starch mixture, though cookies might be coated with crushed nuts, or cream cheese with crushed minced parsley. *Dredge* suggests a very heavy coating, *dust* a light one, and *flour* somewhere between the two.

Cream. As a verb this means to render a food as light and smooth as whipped cream.

Deglaze. See **Glaze**.

Dot, sprinkle. Fine ingredients or small particles are scattered over the top of a food, as a crumb topping may be dotted with butter, or grated cheese sprinkled over pizza sauce.

Flake. In reference to fish, it means the flesh of the fish should fall apart or break into flakes when touched with a fork. In reference to chocolate, coconut, or nuts, it means the food is slivered into wide but very thin particles.

Fork-tender. Food should be soft enough for a table fork to penetrate easily.

Fricassee. A term rapidly going out of use; it means a stew with thickened sauce or gravy.

Ghee. An Indian type of clarified butter.

Glaze. From an old English term, referring to a shiny surface, like glass reflecting light. In reference to pastries, it means a very thin frosting made of melted sugar; in reference to meats or sauces, it may mean to make the surface of the meat shiny, but more often refers to the gelatinous brown essence from the meat that gathers in the pan during cooking. To *deglaze* means to dissolve this gelatinous essence in liquid (water or stock). Vegetables are sometimes glazed with fat or sugar (or a combination of both) in a saucepan or skillet; this is the case with *glazed carrots* and *glazed onions*.

Marry. Used frequently in reference to ingredients combined in a sauce or marinade; it means the flavors are so perfectly blended that it is hard to distinguish one from the other.

Roux. The French term for a cooked blend of melted fat or butter and flour.

Spin a thread. In making a syrup, cook the syrup until it falls from the spoon in a long, thin thread.

Stock. Broth made by long simmering of meats (or poultry or fish) with herbs and vegetables in a large quantity of liquid; the broth is always clarified before it is used in sauce.

HOW TO MEASURE

There are three accepted methods of measuring foods in worldwide use.

1. **Level measurement.** Using standard measuring cups and spoons. This is our heritage from Fanny Merritt Farmer, the accepted American method.

2. **Measuring by weight**. The accepted European method.

3. **Measuring by look, "feel," and taste**. The way preferred by most creative cooks everywhere.

Level measurement are less trouble than using a scale to weigh every little ingredient (or is this only because it's what we are accustomed to?), but not quite as accurate as measurement by gram weight, the European way, especially when it comes to measuring ingredients for breads and pastries. Measuring by taste and feel is the least accurate and the riskiest—but it's far more fun.

The recipes in this book are all given in level measurements—except for pound and ounce measures of purchased products, which in most cases need not be weighed at home. However, it's a good idea to have a household scale handy for checking ready-to-cook weights of meats, or when you wish to use only part of a purchase, like ½ pound of a 3½-pound chuck roast, or ¼ pound ham, taken from half a ham. A scale is also useful in making preserves, when amounts may be given in pounds and you have purchased the fruit or vegetables in quart or peck containers.

Standard measuring spoons are available in every housewares department, every dime store, and every hardware store. They come in sets, ranging from ¼ teaspoon to ½ teaspoon, 1 teaspoon, and 1 tablespoon.

When a recipe calls for ⅛ teaspoon, fill the ¼ teaspoon measure and level off the top with a knife; then, with knife, divide the contents in half and discard one half.

When a recipe calls for 1/16 teaspoon, don't worry about measurement. This is simply a way of telling you the merest pinch is needed. A *pinch* is as much as you can hold between thumb and forefinger. A *dash* is much the same thing: for a "dash of salt," hold a salt shaker above the pan or bowl and shake in a little salt.

When a recipe calls for 3 teaspoons, you might as well use the 1-tablespoon measure, because it's the same thing. One-half tablespoon is equivalent to 1½ teaspoons; first measure 1 teaspoon, then use the ½ teaspoon measure. Or, you may fill the 1-tablespoon measure, level it off, and remove half.

What do you do when a recipe says 1 heaping tablespoon? This means you are measuring by the third method. A heaping tablespoon may be as much as 1½ tablespoons, or it could be as much as 2 tablespoons, if you heap the spoon very high. And suppose a recipe says "1 dessert spoon," a "soup spoon," or "1 coffee spoon" (terms sometimes found in Europe cookbooks)? A *dessert spoon* in England is approximately the same as our standard tablespoon measure (the English tablespoon is larger); a *coffee spoon* is smaller than our 1 teaspoon measure. A *soup spoon* is usually slightly smaller than our standard tablespoon. You still are using the third method.

Standard measuring cups are of two kinds. Nested cups, sometimes called Mary Ann cups, come in graduated sizes ranging from ¼ cup to 1/3 cup, ½ cup, and 1 cup. These are of metal or plastic, and are intended primarily for *dry measurement,* of such ingredients as flour, sugar, and rice. They may also be used for measuring chopped vegetables (onions, celery, or green peppers). Always fill the proper-sized cup to the top, then level off with a knife. For *liquid measure,* the glass container with measures marked on the outside is preferable, because the only accurate way to measure liquids is to hold the cup at eye level to see that the liquid is exactly at, say, the

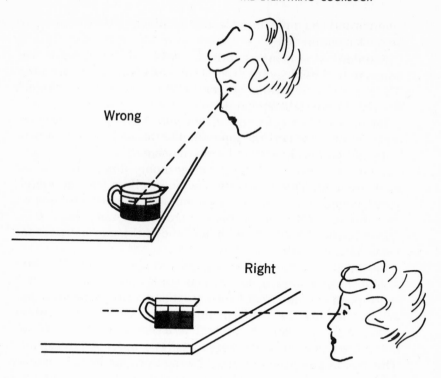

Wrong

Right

½-cup mark. Glass measures are available in 1-cup, 1-pint (2-cup), and 4-cup sizes. It is extremely helpful to have the 4-cup measure in your kitchen—when a recipe calls for 2 cups or more of an ingredient, it's far easier to use this than to fill a 1-cup measure several times.

The glass cup is also useful for measuring *oils, fats,* and *syrups.* Oils and syrups are measured like liquids. To measure solid fats: if a recipe calls for 2/3 cup shortening, place 1/3 cup water in the cup, add the shortening until the water has risen to the 2/3-cup line. And suppose a recipe calls for 1 cup shortening. You can use the 1-pint measure, placing 1 cup water in it, and adding shortening until the 2-cup level is reached.

Butter and margarine in stick form (4 sticks to a pound) have tablespoon measures marked on the paper wrapping. If the recipe calls for 1 tablespoon butter or margarine, it is usually safe enough to use the markings on the paper. True that this may not be an accurate measure—you may be adding in fact 1¼ or only ¾ tablespoon of butter, and in making delicate pastry the difference might alter the finished product. But in sauces and stews and for flavoring vegetables, a small difference is usually not important. Remember: ½ pound butter or margarine measures exactly 1 cup; ¼ pound (a stick) is ½ cup.

Using a household scale. American household scales are marked in ounces and pounds, the most typical being a 25-pound scale. For ounce measures, this is very hard to read and not very reliable, but it's better than nothing. As you can see in the Table of Weights and Measures, 4 ounces is ¼ pound. This means you will have to look closely at the first section on the scale to see that the needle does not go beyond the ¼ mark. A much more useful scale would be a 1-pounder with 16 sections, but as far as I know there is none such.

European kitchen scales are marked by gram weight, and designed especially for culinary use, so that it is much easier to measure small quantities by weight. Eventually gram measures will be a worldwide standard, and anticipating this I have given gram weights in comparison with pound and ounce weights in the Table of Weights and Measures. The table will be of use right now to those thousands of American cooks living overseas.

Checking Label Weights and Measures

Always check the labels and printed instructions on cans, packages, and frozen products to ascertain the weight and/or fluid measure. Sometimes this will make it possible for you to eliminate measuring at home. The Chart of Container Sizes on page 39 will be of help in gauging *approximate* cup measures. However, keep in mind that these were the weights *before* processing. Dry ingredients will have a smaller proportion of liquid than fresh or fresh-cooked equivalents. In case of doubt, measure again.

Why Some Dry Ingredients Should Be Sifted
Before Measuring

Most flours pack down on standing, so that what might measure 1 cup when freshly sifted would be only ⅞ cup if not sifted. Modern factory refining methods have reduced this variable, so that some American flour manufacturers claim that their products do not require presifting. Obviously it makes a difference as to what use is to be made of the flour. A ⅛-cup difference is not likely to matter as much in a bread batter as in a delicate, fluffy cake. Also, it matters how many cups are called for: what is a small variable in 1 cup becomes multiplied when 4 or 5 cups are used.

Sugars need to be presifted because of lumping: a few lumps here and there will alter the cup measure. Brown sugars are difficult to sift, and so must be *firmly packed* to get rid of the lumps.

Measuring by Taste and "Feel"

Neither level measurements nor gram weight can completely eliminate the need for measuring by taste—not even when recipes have been methodically kitchen-tested. This is because the ingredients themselves differ. Herbs that have been on the shelf a long time have lost much of their fragrance; some salts are saltier than others, some sugars sweeter than others, some canned tomatoes may be more watery than the canned tomatoes used for testing. Also, if a cut of meat contains more fat than the meat used in the test, there may be more waste and shrinkage, and excess fat could alter considerably the consistency and flavor of the sauce, even of the meat itself.

There is still another variable. An experienced cook can often judge by the look of a product what it should be like, but the novice, or even the experienced cook trying a brand-new recipe, can get into trouble even when following instructions to the letter. I have seen the same recipe tried twice in a test kitchen, by two separate home economists, with completely different results. The same ingredients were used, and the testers were professionals—yet the results differed.

And what does this mean? That common sense, or, if you will, instinct, must often be applied, and the recipe adapted accordingly.

I'm inclined to think we've carried our emphasis on level measurements too far, for good cooking is not so much a science as an art. One needs a light hand and a light heart, a spirit of adventure, and a sensual delight in lovely odors and flavors that excite the taste buds. There's more pleasure in improvising than in following a recipe to the letter. If your version is ever so slightly better than the one in the cookbook, you feel very proud of yourself. (And if it's worse? Better luck next time. Your little brush with adventure at least got you out of the rut, didn't it?)

The Art of Substituting

With all the thousands of items for sale in supermarkets, it is still not always possible to get exactly what a recipe calls for. Or, perhaps you have started a recipe and discover that certain necessary ingredients are missing. The Table of Food Equivalents and/or the Substitution Chart may save the day. In addition, use your own taste buds, imagination, and initiative in making substitutions.

CARVING: THERE'S NOTHING LIKE A GOOD SHARP KNIFE

Certain golden rules apply to the carver's art.

1. The carving knife must be *sharp*.

2. A carving fork is needed to hold the meat or bird in place.

3. Use a large, flat platter, or, even better, a board. If the carving is done at the table, remove all those pretty garnishes before the operation begins.

4. *Let the roast or bird cool* for 15 minutes after it has been removed from the oven. It will be much easier to carve when juices have started to coagulate: the slices are not so likely to fall in pieces, and you can cut thinner slices. A large roast will stay warm up to 30 minutes after it is removed from the oven.

5. Besides the long carving knife, a smaller knife is helpful for cutting around the knuckles and joints, and *poultry shears* may be helpful in separating joints or cutting through fine bones.

6. A knowledge of anatomy is essential to circumnavigate the bones successfully. Study the Meat Identification Charts and the sketches that follow.

7. A plate for holding carved slices should be handy.

How to Sharpen Knives

The best type of knife sharpener is a **carborundum sharpening stone**. It takes skill to sharpen a knife this way: the blade must be drawn towards you across the stone in rapid, even strokes, first on the coarse half, then the fine half of the stone. Then, for a smooth finish, draw the knife blade over a **steel**, preferably a magnetized steel, holding the steel at an angle with the left hand, pulling down the blade *toward you* with the right hand, *with very light pressure*. Some carving sets come complete with steel; or, a steel may be purchased separately at a

Finishing with a stone

Sharpening with a steel

hardware store. Eight to ten strokes on the steel is about right. *This method of sharpening may be used for all kitchen knives.*

Sharpening with both stone and steel is necessary only now and then. In between, a few strokes on the steel alone are enough to renew the edge. Stainless-steel knives, made of an alloy with softer steel, do not take as fine an edge or retain a sharp edge as long as blades of high-carbon steel. The type of knife called a "waverly," which has a beveled edge on one side and a scalloped edge on the other, holds up better than the regular stainless-steel knife, but this should be sharpened on the beveled side only. **Mechanical sharpeners**, operated by electric motor, don't do as good a job as the stone-and-steel method. They sharpen quickly, but cut too deep into the metal, and the knife edge in time becomes dulled beyond repair. Knives with scalloped or serrated edges should never be sharpened mechanically.

Electric carving knives are fine for slicing boned roasts and big-breasted turkeys, but for getting around the bones, nothing beats the hand method. And for cutting up steaks and smaller bone-in roasts, the electric knife is no good at all.

Keep Your Knives Sharp

Treat your knives with respect, and they won't be dull.

- Store in special knife holders, or on a magnetized rack.
- Do *not* throw into a utensil drawer, where they lie jumbled with other utensils; this dulls the cutting edge.
- Do all chopping, and as much slicing as possible, on a *wooden* surface. A hard surface (tile, ceramics, marble, formica) also dulls the cutting edge.
- Wash knives by hand; do not put in the dishwasher or soak in water. Very hot water causes handles to warp, and the alkali in soap and detergents will eat into the metal. The high-carbon steel blades (the best kind) will rust if not dried immediately with a cloth or paper towel.
- Now and then, like once a year, have your best knives sharpened and reground by a professional grinder. A good knife, so respected, will last a lifetime.

Carving a Rolled Roast

Carving any boned rolled roast is easy. Simply place the roast, with the flat side down, on a platter, and insert carving fork in left side, slice horizontally with knife from right to left. (These, of course, are the instructions for right-handed people.) The fork must be moved downward as the roast dwindles, and the last slices of the almost flat remainder are considerably more difficult to negotiate. Take care that your left hand is not directly in front of the knife blade; use the fork handle as a foil. (See Fig. 1.)

Fig. 1. Rolled roast

Bone-in Roasts: Know Your Anatomy

The main cuts used for roasting (whatever the animal) are the ribs, the legs and rump (together called ham in pork), and the shoulder. Today most rump and shoulder roasts are boned and rolled—this is the more economical buy, because negotiating the bones of rump and shoulder is quite difficult.

Rib roasts include *standing ribs of beef, rib roast of veal, pork loin (center cut),* and *rack of lamb.*

Standing ribs of beef are the largest, most sumptuous, and easiest to carve. As with a rolled roast, the meat should be flat side down with curved rib bones to the left. Insert carving fork between bones; slice horizontally from right to left. (See Fig. 2.) To facilitate removal of slices, first sever meat from rib bones. (See Fig. 3.) If desired, this can be done by the meat man at time of purchase, but the meat seems more succulent if still attached to the bones during cooking.

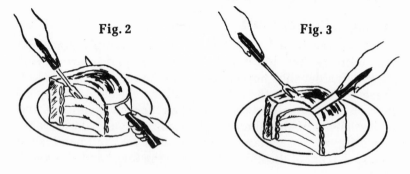

Fig. 2   **Fig. 3**

The rib roasts of veal, lamb, and pork are, of course, smaller. Instead of thin slices, these are cut into chop-sized pieces, severed between the rib bones. To facilitate carving, the *back-bone* should first be severed from the ribs; then, at table, the roast may be placed on its side so that the carver can see the lay of the rib bones and dissect accordingly. (See Figs. 4, 5.)

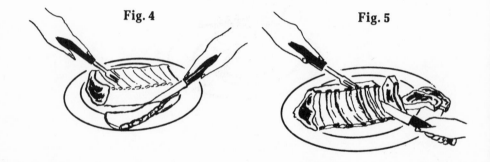

Fig. 4   **Fig. 5**

Crown roasts are quite easy to carve: simply cut down between the rib bones (easy to locate because they form the crown) into chop-sized pieces. These roasts may be of veal, lamb, or pork. (See Fig. 6.)

Fig. 6

Leg roasts include leg of lamb, center-cut leg of veal, and ham (fresh pork leg is called "fresh ham"). Figs. 7, 8, and 9 show how similar the bone structure is in these three meat animals. Fig. 10 shows how you cut the center slices of leg of lamb, and Fig. 11 how similarly you remove the center slices of a ham. To keep these awkwardly shaped roasts flat on the platter (or board), cut a thin slice from the bottom before bringing to the table.

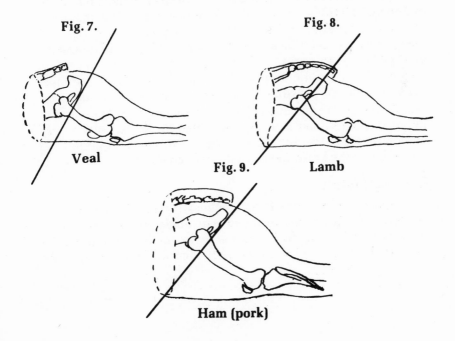

Fig. 7.

Veal

Fig. 8.

Lamb

Fig. 9.

Ham (pork)

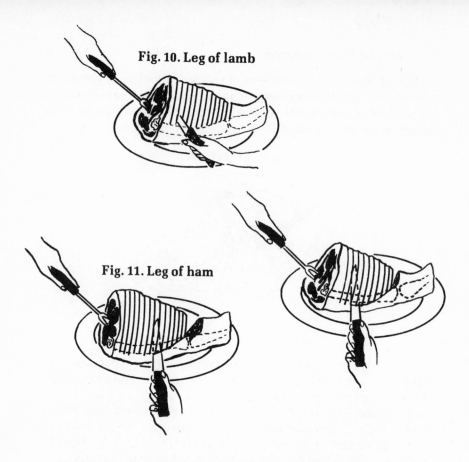

Fig. 10. Leg of lamb

Fig. 11. Leg of ham

The hard part of carving leg or ham roasts is when you tackle the bonier sections. There are two things to do: first, cut away the meatiest parts, and slice these across the grain; second, those parts that can't be so easily severed from the bone should be sliced off at an angle.

Cutting against (or across) the grain is advisable for most meat, whenever possible, for this cuts through tendons and muscle fibers. When you can't cut horizontally across the grain, the next best method is to slice at a 20 to 25° angle. Only a very tender roast can be sliced with the grain; you will be able to judge this as the knife goes into the cooked meat.

Carving Steaks

A thick boneless steak (2 to 3 inches), such as Chateaubriand or London Broil, should be sliced *at an angle* (Fig. 12). When the steak has a bone (or two), first cut away the bone, then cut the steak into sections (Figs. 13, 14). When cutting *chuck steak,* you will find some sections more tender than others, so serve two or three small pieces from different sections of the steak to each person. A shorter knife (about 8 inches) is better for cutting steak than a long carving knife, but it must be just as sharp.

Fig. 12. Thick steak

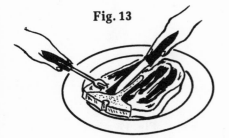

Fig. 13

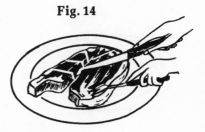

Fig. 14

Carving Turkey or Chicken

A good sharp long-bladed knife is just as important for carving poultry as for meat. In addition, you should have a shorter, broader knife for dissecting bones, and poultry shears for cutting through joints.

First, remove one leg. To do this easily, insert carving fork in the leg, slice down between thigh and breast, then give a tug with your left hand, fingers on the protruding bone (Fig. 15). If

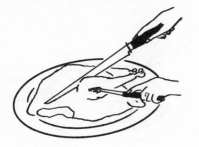

Fig. 15

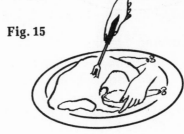

the bird is well-done, the hip joint ball-and-socket will come right apart. If not, force it away with the shorter knife. Remove the leg to a side plate, cut off the thigh (Fig. 16), and slice off some of the dark meat (if the leg is large enough).

Next, remove the wing on the same side (Fig. 17). This, too, should be easy to sever, but if not, poultry shears will do the job quickly.

With the breast fully exposed, start slicing *across the front* from the peak of the breast bone down, in wide slices (Fig. 18). This will probably expose some of the dressing. When the front has been finished, turn to the side where the leg was; remove as many slices from the side as possible.

Do not carve more than one side in the beginning, for once the bird has been cut up the flesh dries out quickly.

Fig. 16

Fig. 17

Fig. 18

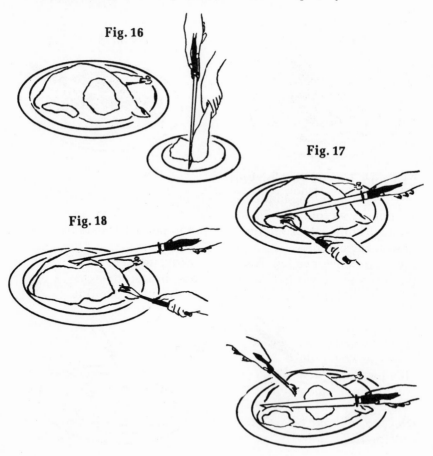

5 KITCHEN ARITHMETIC

It helps in the kitchen if you're a mathematical whiz. Just converting tablespoons to cups, ounces to cups, and cups to serving portions requires a basic command of arithmetic. And when it's necessary to multiply or divide recipe ingredients, or to decide how much food is necessary to feed 20 people, a course in bookkeeping is useful background.

Multiplication and Division: Do's and Don'ts

Theoretically, any recipe can be multiplied: to turn a recipe with servings for 4 into quantities to serve 20 should mean simply multiplying all ingredients by 5. Sometimes it works, sometimes it doesn't.

- *First, examine the list of ingredients critically.* How easily can each be multiplied? If a recipe calls for 1 egg, presumably one can use 5 eggs. But 3 eggs, in a larger recipe, might be enough. It's far easier to multiply such ingredients as rice, vegetables, and chopped meat: there you know that simple arithmetic will work.
- *Second, do you have facilities* for preparing that particular recipe in quantity? If a recipe calls for 1 cut-up chicken, be-

fore you buy 5 cut-up chickens, consider how long it will take you to sauté all those chicken pieces. Might not a roast turkey be better?

•As a general rule, *do not try to multiply a recipe by more than 4*. Doubling it is safer.

•*Seasonings* must be tasted as you go. Sometimes it's a simple question of multiplying: ½ teaspoon salt in a tripled recipe would become 1½ teaspoons. But keep in mind that if the original recipe was just a bit too salty for your taste, when tripled it could be very much too salty. Conversely, if ½ teaspoon of salt is divided into ¼ teaspoon for a recipe to be cut in half, it might be too little salt.

•*Dividing a recipe is often more difficult than multiplying.* How can you divide an egg in half? What do you do with a recipe for gelatin that calls for a 3-ounce package? Or a yeast-raised bread, cake, or pizza that requires a single envelope of active dry yeast? When dividing, as when multiplying, you should first examine ingredients critically to see how easily each can be adapted. For a small family, it is often better to make the original recipe as given, then to freeze half for another time, *if* the dish will freeze satisfactorily.

•Once you have decided a recipe does lend itself to enlarging or dividing, *sit down with pencil and paper and rewrite the recipe from start to finish.* It isn't enough just to write double quantities in the margin (or half quantities, as the case may be). Often within the method references are made to an ingredient in a specific quantity, and if you don't change the recipe all the way through you may find yourself in trouble. If it's a recipe you like very much, it's worth the trouble of first making all the mathematical changes, each calculated carefully, then rewriting it in permanent form, to be used now and filed away for future use.

Cooking for One or Two

Most recipes are given in quantities to serve 4 or 6 persons. Since it is often impossible to divide a recipe exactly in half, making the recipe as given, and freezing half, is the easiest solution. But few 2-person households boast a freezer, and the freezing compartment of an apartment-sized refrigerator is usually too small for this kind of storage.

Even more difficult than preparing food in small quantities is buying in small quantities—difficult for women who once had big households to feed, and difficult, too, for the young brides dazzled by supermarket bargains.

Meats: Best Buys

Chops, small steaks, and scallopini are the best. These can be purchased in small quantity (don't be shy about buying a single chop if that's all you need), such cuts keep better than ground meat, and can be cooked quickly. Veal scallopini is costly per pound, but 2 thin slices make a serving, so the per-portion serving is not so extravagant, and scallopini can be prepared in half a dozen interesting ways.

Chopped meat should be purchased only ½ pound at a time for immediate use, unless you have a freezer. Or, buy 1 pound and keep half of it in the freezing compartment for another meal. Always wrap in small portions, in plastic bags; the meat will defrost more quickly this way, and if you need double the quantity, just defrost two bags of ground meat. But once defrosted, the chopped meat should be used within 24 hours—never refrozen. If plans change and you do not cook it as soon as expected, make up the patties or meatballs and cover with wine marinade. This will delay spoilage and give the meat interesting flavor when cooked. Chopped meat can be kept in a marinade in the refrigerator for up to 72 hours—but no longer—and always, after such a delay, cook the meat to well done.

Roasts are possible now and then. A 3-pound rolled roast may be served hot the first time around, slices reheated in gravy for the next meal, and the remainder used for sandwiches or turned into a stew. Hind shank of beef makes a fine miniature roast if tenderized; a small leg of lamb can be cut up by your meat man so that it makes 3 chops and a very small roast. Double pork chops when baked taste much like roast pork.

Stews are fine; 1 pound of boneless stewing meat makes 3 average portions, and many stews improve with flavor if made ahead; they are often better on the second appearance than the first.

Luncheon meats (*including most sausages*) keep well, especially if purchased in sealed packets—except all-pork sausages. These should be used soon after purchase. Others, including frankfurters, sliced ham, bologna, and pastrami, can be kept in the refrigerator as long as the packet is sealed, but once the packet is opened, all but the amount needed for the first meal should be stored in the freezer or freezing compartment, wrapped separately in meal-sized portions (like 2 frankfurters per portion).

Vegetables must be purchased in small quantities. Most of the time it's best to buy frozen vegetables.

Egg dishes are always in order. Eggs keep a long time, are always there when you need them, and are even easier to prepare in small quantity than in large; no other basic ingredient is so versatile. They are as useful for supper as for brunch, for lunch, or for midnight snack. (See Eggs à la Flamenco, Skillet Eggs and Cheese, Omelets, Eggs à la King.)

Canned tuna, clams, and crabmeat solve many a quick-supper problem. Tuna is good cold on warm nights, sprinkled with lemon juice, accompanied by potato salad. Combine any of these or other canned seafood items with condensed cream soups for quick entrees. (Tuna à la King, Quick Curried Shrimp, and Crabmeat à la Russe are a few possibilities.)

Rice can always be turned into Pilaf or Spanish Rice, making use of leftovers, or such things as the meat of a single chop, a single chicken breast, or the last remains of baked ham. (See Basic Pilaf for Two.)

Oriental dishes are perfect for 2, and can be made of almost anything you have in the refrigerator—as long as you keep onions, celery, and soy sauce on hand for emergencies.

For desserts, canned fruits are the best "on hand" solution. Ice cream is fine if you have a freezer, but in a freezing compartment, it tends to get too soft. Fresh fruits can be cut up into imaginative compotes, alone or combined with canned fruits, sparked with brandy, wine, or a bit of liqueur.

Suitable Entrees for Two

To locate the following recipes, consult the index. Most should be divided in half; some recipes give instructions for preparing for 2 servings.

Hamburger 52 Ways	Any recipe for Pork Chops
Any recipe for Meatballs	Minute Steaks
Tournedos	Steak Diane
Minute Steaks Amontillado	Sukiyaki
Broiled Ham Steak Hawaiian	Chinese Pepper Steak
Economy Beef Kabobs	Ginger Beef
Gypsy Kabobs	Veal Scallopini (any variation)
Pork and Peppers Teriyaki	Wiener or Pork Schnitzel
Lamb Chops Riyanata	Veal Chops Caprice
Broiled Shoulder Lamb Chops	Roast Hind Shank of Beef

Sherried Ham Roast
  (use canned ham)
Pan-broiled Calf's Liver
Braised Liver
Calf's Liver with Bacon
Rognons au Fine Champagne
Kidneys and Mushrooms in Cream
Mixed English Grill
Sausages with Fried Apples
Luncheon Meat Picadilla
Pisto
Slumgullion
Chicken. See Economy Tips,
  Chicken Cookery
Any duck recipe
Shrimp Poached in Herb Bouillon
Shrimp Curry
Easy Seafood Scallop
Pan-fried Oysters
Fried Puffs of Sole
Poached Sole

Poached Cod
Tender Broiled Fish Fillets
Crabmeat à la Russe
Spanish Rice Pronto
  (or variations)
Fettucini Alfredo
Fettucini with Tuna Sauce
Spaghetti Bolognese
Noodle Casserole
Spaghetti Casserole
Family Paella
Chinese Fried Rice
Chop Suey
Pork and Cabbage Chow Mein
Creamed Tuna and Eggs
Eggs à la Cubana
Scrambled Eggs
Omelette au Fromage
Spanish Tortilla
Chinese Pork Omelet

COOKING FOR A CROWD

The problems involved in planning company meals for 20 to 40 persons are explored in Book 4, "Guide to Entertaining."

Two yardsticks must be used in selecting recipes for large-quantity service. First, do you have the proper utensils? Second, can the ingredients be handled easily in large quantity?

For the most part, large roasts and/or casseroles are best for the entrees. Chicken Pie is preferable to Fried Chicken, for example; casseroles of Macaroni and Cheese are easier to serve than mashed potatoes (which are hard to prepare in large quantity and lose flavor on standing).

For an outdoor barbecue, meats that can be cooked as needed are best—so that if an excess quantity has been purchased, what's left can be divided up for individual home dinners. Frankfurters, hamburger meat, and chicken in barbecue sauce ready to place over the open charcoal fire are good selections. Barbecued spareribs are not a good choice for a big affair; because a large quantity is needed (one must allow a minimum of ½ pound per serving), the ribs take up a great deal of space on the fire, and leftover pork spoils quickly.

The best *salads* are those that do not wilt easily: potato salad, cole slaw, mixed cooked vegetables, gelatin salads.

Desserts should consist primarily of cakes, pies or ice cream. Allow 6 servings for each pie, 10 servings for a 2-layer cake, and, using multiplication tables, make sure enough individual cakes and pies are prepared to meet the demand. Ice cream, of course, can be ladled out from gallon containers.

Coffee can be made with instant coffee with water kept boiling in preparation for refills (when made in large quantity starting with cold water, instant coffee has much more "coffee flavor" than when made by the cup). Or, rent a large coffee maker. *Tea* is better made on demand by the potful, for it grows bitter with standing. (To make *Iced Tea* in quantity, see page 787.) *Bottled drinks* require only refrigerator space and paper cups for serving.

Suitable Entrees for Serving a Crowd

Some of the following give yields of 10 to 12; the remaining ones may be multiplied easily to serve 12, 18, or more persons.

Swedish Meatballs
Danish Meatballs
Hungarian Meatballs
Kabob Smorgasbord
Baked Ham (any version)
Rolled Roast Beef
Tenderloin of Beef Wellington
Oriental Roast Lamb (boned)
Drunken Pig (use fresh ham
 instead of pork loin)
Garofalato al Roma
Catalán Pot Roast
Sauerbraten
Shrimp Curry
Capetown Chafing Dish
Mariscada

Salmon Poached
Bouillabaisse
Caldereta Asturiana
Carne Assada
Catalán Beef Stew
Carbonnade Flamande
Beef Stew in a Pumpkin
Ragout of Beef Manhattan
Beef Curry
Oven Fried Chicken
Barbecued Chicken
Chicken. *See* Increasing the
 Yield
Church Supper Turkey Pie
Chicken or Turkey à la King
Roast Turkey

ESTIMATING SERVING PORTIONS

Whether you are cooking for 2, 5, or 25, estimating how much food will be necessary to satisfy appetites requires as much instinct as mathematical precision. In this book, recipes are given in *average serving portions* in nearly every case. This means that if a recipe says "Makes 6 servings," it means just 1 serving apiece for 6 people, or 1½ servings for 4 people. If a dish is very good, the chances are someone will want seconds. Especially when you are serving guests, you should always have more than just enough.

Then there is always the unpredictable element of individual appetites. What is adequate for one 4-person household may be only half enough to satisfy appetites in another 4-person household. Children under five generally require only half as much food as adults; teenage boys need twice as much. Some men who lead sedentary, nerve-wracking lives only pick at their food. Men who spend a great deal of time outdoors, either as part of their work or in sports, will probably have robust appetites. Serving portions as given in recipes must be viewed accordingly.

In those cases where a recipe is more specific, saying "Serves 6," for example, it means that the particular dish can be served only in individual portions. If Cornish hens are the entree, for example, you would serve 1 to each person, so 6 Cornish hens would serve 6 persons. The same is true of Maine lobsters, or of split broiler chickens, or of stuffed double pork chops.

Another factor that must always be considered is the total quantity of food in a meal. If nothing is to be served for dinner except spaghetti, salad, and ice cream for dessert, you will want much more spaghetti than if you are serving a fish or soup course before the spaghetti, and a rich dessert afterward. At a buffet supper, when half a dozen different entrees may be set out, no one entree need provide as generous portions as if only one were offered.

When in doubt, it's always better to prepare too much rather than too little. Leftovers can be turned into interesting new entrees—or frozen for a later appearance.

ECONOMY IN THE KITCHEN

If your food expenditures have zoomed skyward, there are 6 possible courses of action:

1. **Stop buying more than you need.** Check supplies on hand. Why not use up those bargains you purchased two months ago? And take a list with you next time you go shopping!

2. **Keep grocery and supermarket receipts** in your kitchen "desk" for a few weeks, and look at receipts after you get home to see where the biggest expenditures are going.

3. **Try using less expensive cuts of meat**; learn to tenderize less tender cuts, to make kabobs out of stewing beef, fillets out of rump of beef (bottom round), and London Broil with top round (which goes further than steak because you can slice it so thin).

4. **Have meat less often,** maybe only five times a week instead of seven. On the other two days, try such entrees as Cheese Soufflé, Lasagne, a hearty Spanish Tortilla (potato and onion omelet), or Tuna and Macaroni Casserole.

5. **Use leftovers imaginatively**.

6. **Put a ceiling on carbonated drinks**. You can set a limit on the number of these beverages to be purchased each week; when that number has been exhausted, start creating less expensive punches to satisfy family thirst. (But don't cut down on fruit—this you need for health.)

7. **Instead of extravagant frozen entrees and dinners,** try new menu patterns. You'll find you needn't learn new recipes to do this—just put together easy-to-prepare foods in new combinations. This is one of the things explored in Book 2.

EQUIVALENT-MEASURE AND CONVERSION CHARTS

The following charts are designed to help you convert one measure to another, and, since most recipes list ingredients by cup or spoon measures rather than by weight or volume, to help you to estimate how many cups or servings you can count on from ounce, pound, gram, or liter measures.

If you cannot find the measure you are looking for in the left-hand column, try the center or the right column, then read backward to see how to convert.

Standard American Measures

Fluid ounces are used only for liquid measure; the equivalents in cup and spoon measurements are always the same.

Dry or solid ounces and *pounds* will vary in cup measurement according to the product. For the latter, look under Food Equivalents.

3 teaspoons	=	1 tablespoon		
2 tablespoons	=	1 jigger (small)	=	1 fluid ounce

1 jigger (large)	=	3 tablespoons	=	1½ fluid ounces
4 tablespoons	=	¼ cup	=	2 fluid ounces
5½ tablespoons	=	1/3 cup		
8 tablespoons	=	½ cup	=	4 fluid ounces
11 tablespoons	=	2/3 cup		
16 tablespoons	=	1 cup	=	8 fluid ounces
		1½ cups	=	12 fluid ounces
8 ounces (dry)	=	½ pound		
16 ounces (dry)	=	1 pound		
2 cups	=	1 pint	=	16 fluid ounces
2 pints (4 cups)	=	1 quart	=	32 fluid ounces
1 fifth of wine	=	1/5 gallon	=	25 fluid ounces
8 cups	=	½ gallon	=	64 fluid ounces
4 quarts (16 cups)	=	1 gallon	=	128 fluid ounces
8 quarts (dry)	=	1 peck	=	32 cups
4 pecks (dry)	=	1 bushel		

Gram-liter Tables

Dry-Solid Measures

1 gram	=	.035 ounce
1 ounce (dry)	=	28+ grams
100 grams	=	3½ ounces (a little under ¼ pound)
250 grams (¼ kilogram)	=	8¾ ounces (a little over ½ pound)
500 grams (½ kilogram)	=	17¼ ounces = 1 pound 1¾ ounces
1000 grams (1 kilogram)	=	34½ ounces
1 kilogram	=	2.21 pounds (just under 2¼ pounds)
2 kilograms	=	4.42 pounds (just under 4½ pounds)
1 pound	=	453.39 grams (about 450 grams)

Liters (Liquid Measure)

1 liter	=	1 quart 2 fluid ounces (4¼ cups)
1 demiliter (half-liter)	=	just over 2 cups
1 deciliter (1/10 liter)	=	scant ½ cup
2 liters	=	8½ cups = 2 quarts + 1 cup
4 liters	=	1 gallon plus 1 cup (136 fluid ounces) = 17 cups

British Measures

1 tablespoon English	=	4 teaspoons American (1 1/3 American tablespoons)
Dessertspoon (English)	=	1 tablespoon American

1 cup English (½ pint)	=	1¼ cups American
1 pint imperial	=	20 fluid ounces = 2½ cups American
1 gill	=	½ cup American + 2 American table-spoons
1 gallon imperial	=	160 fluid ounces = 5 quarts = 20 cups

Temperature Conversions

Description or Cookery Term	Fahrenheit	Centigrade
Frozen food storage	0°	−17°
Water freezes	32°	0°
"Room temperature"	72°	22°
Warm place free from drafts	85°	29°
Water simmers	115°	46°
Water boils (sea level)	212°	100°
"Soft-ball stage"	234-238°	112-114°
"Firm-ball stage"	240-242°	115-116°
"Hard-ball stage"	248-250°	120-121°
Slow oven	275-300°	135-150°
Moderate oven	350-375°	177-190°
Hot oven	400-425°	204-218°
Deep-fat frying	365-375°	185-190°

Food Equivalents

Bread	1 pound, regular slices	=	12-16 slices
	1 slice	=	About ½ cup soft crumbs
	1 slice, stale, grated	=	About ¼ cup fine dry crumbs
Butter and	2 tablespoons	=	1 ounce
margarine	¼ pound (stick)	=	1 cup
	½ pound (8 ounces)	=	1 cup

(Does not apply to whipped butter or chiffon margarine.)

Cheese,	8 ounces (½ pound)	=	1 cup
cottage,	3-ounce package	=	6 tablespoons (about 1/3 cup)
cream,	12 ounces	=	1½ cups
ricotta			
Cheese,	¼ pound (4 ounces)	=	1 cup, grated
firm or	½ pound (8 ounces)	=	2 cups, grated
hard			
Cream,	½ pint	=	1 cup
ice cream,	1 cup *heavy* cream	=	2 cups *whipped* cream
milk	1 pint	=	2 cups (4 servings ice cream)

	½ gallon	=	8 cups (16 servings ice cream)
	1 quart	=	4 cups (2 pints)
Evaporated	14½-ounce can	=	1 2/3 cups, undiluted
milk	6-ounce can	=	¾ cup
Sweetened	14-ounce can	=	1¼ cups
condensed			
Instant dry	3 tablespoons + 1 cup		
milk	water	=	1 cup skim milk
	¾ cup + 1 quart water	=	1 quart skim milk

Fruits

Apples	1 pound	= 3 medium	=	About 3 cups peeled, sliced
Berries	1 pint	= 2 cups	=	4 servings
Cherries	1 pint	= 2 cups whole, about 1 cup pitted	=	2-3 servings
Coconut, shredded, flaked	4-ounce package or can	= 1¼ cups		
	8-ounce bag	= 2½ cups		
	3½-ounce can	= 1 1/3 cups		
Dates	1 pound pitted	= 2½ cups chopped		
Lemons	1 medium	= 2-3 tablespoons juice	=	1 tablespoon grated rind
Oranges	1 medium (juice type)	= 1/3 cup juice	=	2 tablespoons grated rind
Raisins	1 pound seedless	= 2¾ cups		

Flour

All-purpose	1 pound	= 4 cups sifted
Cake	1 pound	= 4½ to 5 cups sifted

Nuts

Almonds	1 pound in shell	= 3½ cups shelled
	6 ounces shelled, whole	= 1 cup after blanching
	3¾ ounces, already blanched	= ¾ cup
Peanuts	1 pound in shell	= 2¼ cups shelled

	8 ounces already shelled	= 1¾ cups
Pecans	8 ounces shelled	= 2 cups
Walnuts	1 pound in shell	= 1 2/3 cups shelled
	2 ounces shelled	= ½ cup
	5 ounces shelled	= 1¼ cups
	16 ounces (1 pound) shelled	= 4 cups

Pastas

Macaroni and spaghetti	8 ounces (½ pound)	= 2 cups uncooked 4 cups - 4½ cups cooked (4 servings)
Noodles	8 ounces (½ pound)	= 3 cups uncooked 3¾ cups cooked (4 servings)

Rice

Long-grain (Carolina)	1 cup uncooked	= 3 cups cooked
Long-grain converted (parcooked)	1 cup uncooked	= 4 cups cooked
Precooked	1 cup from box	= 2 cups reconstituted

Sugars

Granulated (white)	1 pound	= 2¼-2½ cups
Superfine	1 pound	= 2 1/3 cups
Confectioners'	1 pound	= 4 cups unsifted, 4½-5 cups sifted
Brown, light or dark	1 pound	= 2¼-2 1/3 cups firmly packed
Brown granulated	1 pound	= 3¾ cups

Vegetables

Beets	1 bunch	= Trimmed, cooked without leaves (4-6 servings)
Broccoli	1 bunch	= Spears trimmed, cooked (6-8 servings)
Brussels sprouts	1 pint	= 2 cups (4 servings)
Cauliflower	1 medium head	= Trimmed, cut, leaves discarded (6-8 servings)

Green beans	1 pound	=	2 cups sliced or cut (4-5 servings)
Green peas	1 pound in pod	=	About 1 cup shelled (2-3 servings)
Lima beans	1 pound in pod	=	About 1 cup shelled (2-3 servings)
	10 ounces frozen shelled	=	2/3 cup
Onions			
Bermuda	1 pound	=	3 medium
Small white	1 pound	=	12-15 small
Spanish	1 pound	=	2 large
Yellow	2 pounds	=	12-15 assorted sizes
Potatoes			
White general-purpose	5 pounds	=	15 medium
Baking size (Idaho)	5 pounds	=	8-10
Sweet (yams)	2 pounds	=	6
Spinach	1 pound fresh	=	½-2/3 cup cooked (3 servings)
	10 ounces frozen chopped	=	¾ cup cooked
Tomatoes	1 pound	=	3 medium

Substitution Chart

The following contains suggestions of what to do when you do not have a specific ingredient called for in a recipe. Some work both ways: that is, if you do not have a 1-pound can of tomatoes, use 3 fresh tomatoes. If a recipe calls for dry mustard, and you have only the prepared, use prepared mustard, but triple the quantity.

If you don't have ...		Try using ...
Baking powder, per teaspoon	=	¼ teaspoon baking soda, ½ teaspoon cream of tartar; sometimes adding extra eggs (1 for each teaspoon b.p.) will do
Beef stock, per cup	=	1 teaspoon beef-flavored stock concentrate or 1 beef bouillon cube dissolved in 1 cup water; or canned beef bouillon
Biscuit mix, per cup	=	1 cup flour, 1½ teaspoons baking powder, ½ teaspoon salt, 1 tablespoon shortening

Buttermilk, *per cup*	= 1 cup lukewarm skim or reg. milk (or use instant dry milk reconstituted) + 1 tablespoon lemon juice; let stand 5 minutes, beat briskly.
Cake flour, *per cup*	= 1 cup all-purpose flour less 2 tablespoons
Chicken broth, *per cup*	= 1 teaspoon chicken stock concentrate or chicken bouillon cube + 1 cup water; or canned clear chicken broth
Chocolate, semisweet, 3 ounces	= 2 ounces unsweetened chocolate + 2 tablespoons sugar; or 1/3 cup cocoa mix + butter; or 1/3 cup unsweetened cocoa + 2 tablespoons sugar + 2 tablespoons butter or margarine
Chocolate, unsweetened, 1 ounce	= 3 tablespoons *unsweetened cocoa* (not cocoa mix) + 1 tablespoon butter or margarine
Cream sauce (Bechamel), 1½ cups	= 1 10-ounce can condensed cream of mushroom or celery soup + ¼ cup light cream
Corn syrup, *per cup*	= ¾ cup sugar + ¼ cup water
Cornstarch, *per tablespoon*	= 2 tablespoons flour; or 1 tablespoon arrowroot or potato flour
French dressing, per ¼ cup	= 3 tablespoons oil, 1 tablespoon vinegar, seasonings to taste
Gravy coloring (Kitchen Bouquet, Gravy Master), *per tablespoon*	= 1 teaspoon sugar, caramelized
Mustard, 1 tablespoon prepared	= 1 teaspoon dry mustard + 1 tablespoon white wine or vinegar
Onion, 1 medium, chopped	= 1 tablespoon instant minced onion, reconstituted
Self-rising flour, *per cup*	= 1 cup all-purpose flour + 1½ teaspoons baking powder + ¼ teaspoon salt
Sour cream, per ½ cup	= 3-ounce package cream cheese plus milk to make ½ cup; or, reconstitute packaged dry sour cream dip mix according to package directions, use ½ cup reconstituted dip

Soy sauce, per ¼ cup = 1 teaspoon sugar, caramelized, 1 teaspoon beef-flavored stock concentrate, + 3 tablespoons water; or, use 3 tablespoons Worcestershire, 1 tablespoon water

Spaghetti sauce, per cup = 1 cup (8-ounce can) tomato sauce + 2 tablespoons olive oil, 1 teaspoon instant minced onion, ¼ teaspoon oregano, minced parsley

Tomatoes, 3 medium ripe = 1 pound can peeled whole tomatoes, drained (use juice in sauce)

Tomato paste, 1 *tablespoon* = 1 tablespoons tomato catsup

Tomato purée, **per cup** = 2 tablespoons tomato paste + water to make 1 cup

Wine for marinades, per ½ cup = ¼ cup vinegar + 1 tablespoon sugar + ¼ cup water (do not use in sauce)

Worcestershire sauce, per tablespoon = 1 tablespoon soy sauce + dash liquid red-pepper seasoning

BOOK TWO

Menu Planning and Weight Control

Introduction

- It's never any one dish that makes the meal: it's the composition of the whole.
- Weight control and proper nutrition are partners: they should go hand in hand.
- Good nutrition is the best beauty treatment, for clear complexion, shining hair, bright eyes, proper distribution of weight.
- When you eat well, you feel well. Life looks brighter, things go better.

In many countries, it's the custom, just before sitting down at table, to wish everyone else "Good appetite!"

Appetites are enhanced if enticing aromas have been coming from the kitchen for some time and if, upon entering the dining area, one is greeted by an attractive array of food on a neatly set, softly lighted table. Often it takes no more than this to awaken smiles on faces that were grumpy or solemn moments before.

Good food can be an elixir. And if the food is good, appetites sharp, and the atmosphere congenial, digestion is improved. And if digestion is improved, so are dispositions.

Of course, it isn't all this easy, not in the tense, too-busy, trouble-ridden world we live in. But well-balanced nutrition is a goal worth striving for, and once you understand the basic principles, it can become a matter of habit.

1 THE CARDINAL RULES OF MENU-MAKING

Each individual menu needs to be well balanced *nutritionally*, *artistically*, and *in relation to other meals of the day*.

To show at a glance the easy way to do this, the following wheels are presented. In your mind's eye, place the daily menu wheel in juxtaposition to the others, and "spin" the wheels to help in determining the proper menu.

1. The Daily Menu Wheel

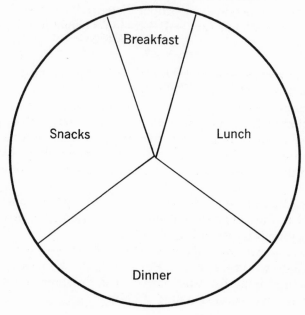

Think of four meals a day instead of three—for snacks often total as many calories as lunch or even dinner. When marketing, select snack foods that are nutritionally worth their price, and if overweight is a problem with anyone in your family (as it is in at least 60 percent of American households), look for low-calorie snacks.

If breakfast is a gulp and good-bye, lunch should be that much more substantial—and nutritious. If dinner is the main meal of the day, avoid snacks too close to dinnertime. This applies to adults who may indulge in cocktail hors d'oeuvres as much as to youngsters ruining their appetites with soft drinks and potato chips.

2. The Basic Four (Nutrition) Wheel

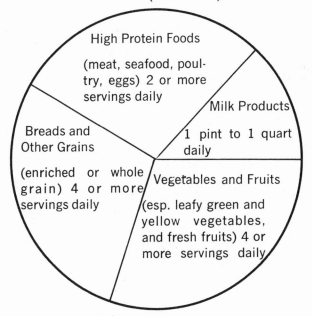

Nutritionists advise that all the foods shown here should be included in every *daily menu,* for every member of the family. *Milk products* include cheese, sour cream, ice cream, and instant nonfat dry milk. For children and teenagers, 3 to 4 glasses (1 quart) per day is recommended; for adults (especially young adults), 1 pint or its equivalent. Expectant mothers, of course, need more than this. The total may include whole, canned, or dry milk used in sauces, as an ingredient in baked goods, in puddings, and in other desserts, plus the dry milk in such commercial products as frankfurters, cookies, some margarines, packaged mixes, and so on. (Read labels to see which products contain milk.) Multiply pints (or quarts) according to the make-up of your household. If it's two children and two adults, you need 3 quarts a day; since part of this will be in ice cream or packaged products, 2 quarts from the milkman is probably sufficient.

3. The High-protein (Weight-control) Wheel

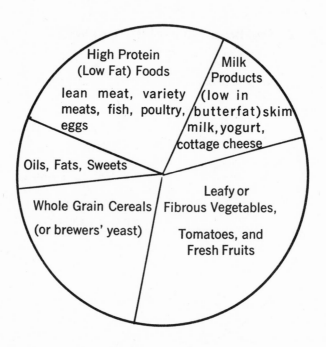

Note how similar this wheel is to the preceding one. All the Basic Four foods are here. The differences are primarily of emphasis and proportion. Protein foods include milk products low in fat; the vegetables are those low in starch; whole-grain cereals are included, though only a limited amount of fats and sweets are permitted. Starches, sweets, and fats, in general, are on the side of the enemy.

4. The Menu Pattern Wheel

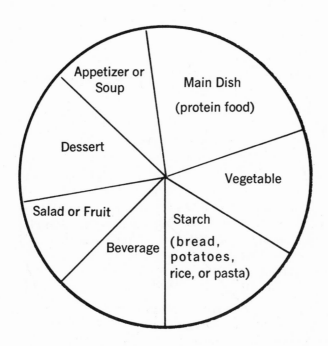

These are the component parts of the menu. Naturally not every item will appear in every meal. The breakfast main course may be toast, accompanied only by fruit juice and coffee; or it may be bacon and eggs plus bread, fruit, and beverage. For lunch, soup may be the main course followed by salad and dessert. Or a meat or chicken salad may be the main course (combining a protein food, salad, and vegetable in one).

When the appetizer is substantial, the main course should not be so hearty. When dessert is calorie-laden, keep the rest of the meal lighter. A first-course appetizer-salad eliminates the need for a salad course after the meat course; the dessert may be a fruit, combining the last two sections of the wheel.

5. The Good-eating Wheel

Use this wheel the way a painter uses his set of color tubes to select foods that complement one another in color, flavor, texture, and aroma.

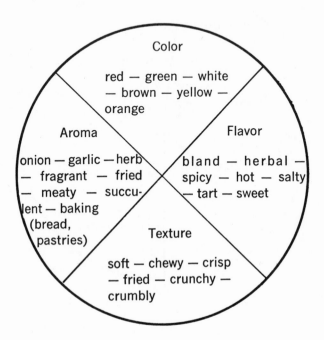

Avoid duplication in the same meal. No two fried foods, no two highly seasoned foods, no two starchy foods; offset soft vegetables (like mashed potatoes) with crisp ones (like broccoli or asparagus). Varied and complementary colors are important because this makes food look more tempting, and therefore whets the appetite. Aroma is doubly important, not only for anticipatory appetite, but because the flavor of individual foods is determined as much by the olfactory senses as by taste buds. Aromas, too, should be complementary. Too strong an odor of garlic can kill appetite; but the fragrance of a bubbling vegetable soup is a beautiful foil for roasting meat.

2 TIME FOR A SHORT COURSE IN NUTRITION

It would seem that all Americans, young and old, by now should know about good nutrition. It's taught in all the schools, and advertising slogans ring with nutrition clichés until such words as "protein," "vitamins," and even "polyunsaturated" are as common as "meat" and "potatoes."

Yet our nutritional habits are slipping badly. A United States Department of Agriculture comparison of family food purchases today with those of 1955 revealed that 20 percent of Americans are eating "nutritionally poor" diets (the proportion was only 15 percent in 1955), and in only half the households surveyed, including upper-income homes, were the family eating habits rated "good."

Where is the food money going? More for soft drinks, less for milk. More for meat, less for vegetables. More baked goods, especially cakes and cookies (starches and sweets, how we love you!), fewer fresh fruits.

Americans spend so much of their earnings on food that overweight has become a national problem. "Miracle" diets are followed by the gullible: diet pills threaten lives and offer young-sters who raid home medicine cabinets an easy way to become dope freaks.

Is there an easy way to *control* weight?

Yes—and no.

If you have the will power to stick to a sane pattern of eating day after day—yes. But if you are already considerably over-weight and are the type whose resistance to all temptation is low, it's bound to be uphill most of the way. But the results are well worth the effort. And if you have the determination to learn new eating habits, the time may come when weight con-trol is no longer a struggle.

Equate Good Nutrition with Weight Control

Eating is habit, and poor eating habits are the chief cause of overweight.

Those who have been indulging in fried foods and rich pas-tries all their lives will probably find relearning new eating habits a torture. They may never, in fact, wholly succeed. But youngsters can be taught good eating habits that will stay with them for a lifetime. This is one of the most valuable gifts a con-scientious mother can bestow on her offspring.

The good-for-you foods are also the best for weight control. *The fattening foods, for the most part, are not good for health.*

It is not necessary to count calories. Once you have a basic understanding of good nutrition, and learn to fill up on the "good-for-you" foods as a way of staying away from the fatten-ing ones, calories will take care of themselves.

Proteins, Carbohydrates, and Fats

There are no foods that are pure protein, pure carbohydrate, or pure fat. Nature intended us to have some of all of these three food components every day for sustenance. Yet it is im-portant to understand what the terms mean, and what role these food components play in diet.

Proteins are especially important for growth, for body main-tenance, and for lasting (as opposed to quick) energy. Protein foods contain a chain of amino acids of different types (22 types have been identified) and in different amounts. Of these, there are eight amino acids considered nutritionally essential. Foods that contain all eight of these particular amino acids are rated "high-quality" or "complete" protein foods—or simply "high-protein foods." These include meats, fish, poultry, eggs, milk, and cheese. Grains and nuts also contain protein, but these are "incomplete proteins," which means that by themselves they cannot supply essential nutritional needs.

Even a vegetarian diet must contain protein foods in abundance; when meat is eliminated, milk products (including cheese), eggs, and fish become that much more important.

Americans are meat eaters, and all meat is high in protein. Yet there are dangers in relying too heavily on meat for protein.

Foods highest in *carbohydrates* are the starches, sweets, fruits, and vegetables. We need carbohydrates to provide instant fuel (calories) for energy. All physical activity burns up calories. The less active and energetic we are, the smaller the proportion of high-carbohydrate foods we need. In an earlier age (and still today in some countries), when people did more walking, worked more in the open, performed more energetic household chores, such starches as bread and potatoes were needed in larger amounts. The liking for starches and sweets is a heritage from that time. Active children need a larger proportion of carbohydrates than adults, but American children of today are less active (parents of preschoolers may not believe this, but it's true), and so care must be taken not to let them fill up on starches and sweets and kill appetite for other more important foods.

We still need carbohydrates—they cannot be eliminated, but the wise thing is to concentrate on carbohydrate foods that provide other important elements in addition to quick energy—fruits, vegetables, and whole or enriched grain products. Those foods that provide little more than sugar and/or starch (candy, gum, carbonated drinks, most cookies, and many pastries) are often said to contain only "empty calories."

Fats (the generic term also includes oils) exist in nearly all foods to some degree, including high-protein and high-carbohydrate foods. Vegetables provide a chief source of oil; even the leanest meats contain a certain amount of fat. Fish and poultry are also fat sources.

Fats are important as carriers of vitamins to the bloodstream, for body lubrication, and as stored energy. *Fatty acids* are essential for growth and energy.

There is little danger of an American family's not having enough fat in the diet; the trouble is the opposite. Americans consume more fats than any other people in the world. But the kind of fat (or oil) consumed makes a difference.

Animal fats—fat meat, bacon drippings, chicken fat, butter, egg yolk, cream, and lard—are less desirable; in fact, they are often injurious to health when consumed in large quantities. They contain a high proportion of *saturated fats*, the fats that build up the cholesterol level in the bloodstream and so block or slow down the flow of blood to the heart muscle (and, in extreme cases, cause heart disease).

Older people, especially, need to cut down on consumption of animal fats, as do all men over forty. Those who do not already have a cholesterol problem may develop one if animal fats and fried foods are consumed with abandon. Besides raising the cholesterol level, animal fats are harder to digest, contribute to hardening of the arteries and tend to raise blood pressure.

Vegetable fats, especially the liquid fats called *oils*, are composed primarily of *unsaturated fats*. These are easier to digest, perform their functions more quickly, and, as body lubricators, give elasticity to the skin and oil to the hair and ease elimination of body wastes. An excess of vegetable fats or oils will, of course, result in excess body fat, but *in moderate amounts*, vegetable oils play a very important role in nutrition. This is why oil-dressed salads are so important in the daily diet. (Vegetable fats include all those extracted from corn, soy beans, cottonseeds, peanuts, safflower seeds, and olives.)

Fish oils (fats) are also unsaturated. This is why doctors recommend that people whose blood cholesterol level is high should have fish several times a week, in place of meat.

Too Much Meat Can Be Bad

The importance of high-protein foods having been established, it is necessary to point out why it is not desirable to consume meat (the most popular of protein foods) in excess.

An excess of meat, even lean meat, is known to contribute to high blood pressure and hardening of the arteries, and to put a strain on the heart.

Instead of a regular diet of hamburgers and steak (even if you can afford it), why not have poultry and fish more often? Or omelets, or macaroni and cheese, or soufflés?

The *variety meats*, on the other hand, liver, kidneys, brains, and sweetbreads, should be rediscovered. These have fallen so low in popularity with most American families that they are rarely displayed in meat counters, and must usually be purchased in frozen form. Yet they contain so many more vitamins and minerals in proportion to weight than other cuts of meat that they can rightly be looked upon as "health foods." And they are also comparatively low in calories.

Vitamins and Minerals

The importance of vitamins and minerals in the diet has been almost oversold to the American public—at least in the sense that vitamin pills are taken by young and old as a cure-all, and foods that have been "enriched" by the injection of vitamin and mineral concentrates are looked upon as being more important in the diet than those naturally good to begin with.

A daily meal pattern that includes all the Basic Four in the quantities suggested should furnish sufficient vitamins and minerals *in natural form*, making additives and pills superfluous. Here are a few nuggets of wisdom worth memorizing:

- Raw fruits and tomatoes are the best sources of vitamin C (ascorbic acid). Include fruits, tomatoes, or both on the menu at least once a day. (The tomato retains vitamin C even when subjected to the high temperature of canning.)
- Most yellow (or yellow-orange) foods (carrots, sweet potatoes, cantaloupe, apricots, egg, butter) are good sources of vitamin A.
- Whole-grain and enriched cereals are the best sources of vitamin B complex, the "nerve vitamin" (this includes riboflavin, niacin, and thiamin). Before cutting out all bread on your weight-reducing diet, think about this. If bread is eliminated, it would be well to take tablets of brewer's yeast, a natural source of vitamin B complex, as a supplement.
- The darker the green of green leafy vegetables, the more valuable to the diet. The outer leaves of cabbage and lettuce are richer in minerals (especially calcium) than the blanched inner leaves.
- Green *leafy* vegetables have properties not necessarily found in such green vegetables as peas and lima beans. Green peas and limas are also high in calories; peas are almost as high as white potatoes; lima beans contain *more* starch than white potatoes.
- Fish with edible bones (canned sardines and salmon) is as good a source of calcium as milk.
- Fish is the best of all weight-reducing foods; it is lower in calories than any other high-protein foods, packed to the gills with vitamins (A, B complex, D, and K) and minerals (iodine, iron, potassium, copper, calcium, and phosphorus).

•One of the best of all natural sources of vitamin A is liver, which is also valuable for phosphorus, iron, thiamine (B^1), riboflavin (B^2), niacin (B^3), and vitamin C.

Vitamin-Mineral Chart

Study this chart to learn natural sources of vitamins and minerals, and what role each of these mysterious substances plays in health.

Vitamin	*Source*	*Importance in Diet*
A	Carrots Spinach Turnip greens Sweet potatoes Beet greens Pumpkin Parsley Squash Cantaloupe Liver Liverwurst Kidneys Butter and margarine Egg yolk Fish	Good for eyes (especially in adjustment to light changes), for skin and complexion, helps to resist infection 

B complex	Liver
	Kidneys
	Whole-grain
	  cereals
	Enriched or
	  fortified
	  breads and
	  flours
	Fish
	Oysters
	Milk
	Peanuts
	Egg yolk
	Parsley
	Brewer's yeast
		Needed for steady nerves and alert mind, to help appetite and digestion, to resist infection, and to convert carbohydrates and fats to body use 

Vitamin	Source	Importance in Diet
C	Citrus fruits Tomatoes Oranges Strawberries Sweet potatoes Liver Most raw vegetables and fruits Parsley	Necessary for sound teeth and gums; helps prevent easy bleeding
D	Sunlight (outdoors) Egg yolk Fortified milk Fish-liver oil Oily-type fish (tuna, sardines, mackerel)	Helps in absorption and utilization of calcium, for strong bones and teeth
E	Butter and margarine Vegetable oils Beans and peas Wheat germ Egg yolk Nuts Green leafy vegetables	Needed for reproduction and growth
K	Green leafy vegetables Root vegetables Fruits Vegetable oils Fish	Needed for normal blood clotting

Mineral	*Source*	*Importance in Diet*
Calcium	Milk Cheese Green leafy vegetables Egg yolk Carrots Salmon Sardines Broccoli Whole-grain or enriched bread and cereals Dried beans Nuts	Needed for building bones and teeth; helps regulate nerve and muscle action and blood clotting 
Phosphorus	Milk Cheese Egg yolk Lean meats Legumes (beans and peas) Carrots Potatoes Fish (esp. sardines, clams)	Needed for building bones and teeth and for utilizing proteins, fats, and carbohydrates 
Iron	Liver Turkey Meats Eggs Legumes Nuts Green leafy vegetables Prunes Green peas	Helps provide energy; carries oxygen from lungs to rest of body
Sodium	Salt Corned beef Cheese Bread and cereals	Helps maintain water balance in body; needed for muscle contraction 

Green *leafy vegetables* include spinach, kale, beet greens, turnip greens, Swiss chard, broccoli, Brussels sprouts, green cabbage, watercress, all salad greens. and parsley.

Root vegetables include white potatoes, carrots, beets, parsnips, turnips, rutabaga, radishes, and horseradish.

Herbs for Health

It has long been a cliché that highly seasoned foods are not good for health. This is sometimes true of highly *spiced* foods, that is, foods containing large amounts of black or red pepper. salt, and mustard or turmeric. But *herbs* are extremely important for health. Note how frequently parsley appears in the Vitamin-Mineral Chart. The easiest way of all to sprinkle extra vitamins over food just before bringing it to the table is to add fresh (not dried) parsley. This should be a staple in every household.

The Importance of Breakfast

The day will go better if you start it right. Breakfast may be nothing more than juice, toast, and a beverage, but even that little is important. For the weight-conscious, it's well to remember that appetite at lunch can be better controlled if one has breakfast under the belt. For those who need to do "brain work" during the morning (students, office workers, executives), the brain works better with something to feed it, and protein at breakfast (meaning egg) is more sustaining than a sweet bun or Danish.

Children especially need protein at breakfast. A vanilla-flavored eggnog may be the easiest solution, providing both egg and milk in quick drinkable form. Or, you can sneak extra nutrition into breakfast pancakes by adding instant nonfat dry milk as well as whole milk and egg to the mix. A bacon sandwich may be easier for youngsters to eat when they are clock-watching than a sit-down plate of bacon and eggs.

Add Nutrition to Lunchbox and Picnic Meals

Be sure to include all the Basic Four in the lunch box: a meat or cheese sandwich (protein and grain), fruit, milk to drink. Vending machines dispense milk in cartons at schools, factories, many offices, and roadside service stations. Ice cream can be purchased in cones or cups from the machine, too. For school lunchboxes, with peanut butter and jelly as the standby, a hard-boiled or deviled egg might be added for extra protein. A few nuts, such as peanuts in the shell, serve the same purpose.

Apples, bananas, blue plums ("fresh prunes"), pears, and tangerines are the easiest fruits to eat. Or, instead of fruit, slip in carrot sticks or celery in moistureproof packets.

Remember that *frozen sandwiches* prepared the night before or even several days before (for a week's supply), if removed from the freezer at breakfast time, will be completely thawed by lunch.

For dessert, oatmeal and fruit-filled cookies are nutritionally preferable to plain sugar cookies.

What not to pack in a bag or lunchbox. Avoid overjuicy fruits, tomatoes, or salad mixtures that are likely to spill. (A bun is better for salad mixtures than bread slices.) Also, wedges of pie, or any soft mixtures which are likely to run or dribble. If a lunchbox is to be kept in a locker near heat, avoid perishable meats (pork, meat loaf) in sandwiches. Lettuce wilts easily; add it only if sandwich is to be eaten within 1 or 2 hours or unless bag or lunchbox can be kept in a cool place. Plan lunch so there's nothing to carry home—if that's possible.

The Snack Syndrome

Children will snack between meals, whether you approve or not. Even if you lock up pantry doors and cabinets, there will be generous neighbors who offer them cookies, candy, "sodas," and other "empty-caloried" goodies after school.

Since eating between meals, and perhaps before bed, is inevitable, plan it that way. Buy snack foods that are nutritious, such as individual boxes of raisins, dried apricots, nuts (in limited quantities), pickles, olives, yogurt, cheese spreads. Keep carrots and celery sticks cut, ready to eat, wrapped in plastic in the refrigerator.

Certain types of salted nibbles are more desirable than others. Triscuits, of shredded whole wheat, are preferable to potato chips, which are mostly fat and salt.

Ice cream, though high in calories, is also high in milk content. Canned applesauce makes a fine pick-me-up after school. And what better nightcap could there be for a teenager than a milk shake beaten to a froth in the blender?

Teenage Nutrition

Most of today's American teenagers are eating nutritionally inadequate diets, especially the girls because they want to have figures like skinny fashion models, yet this is a period of life when proper nutrition is particularly important, probably more so than at any other time. The complexion will be improved by an abundance of carrots and leafy vegetables, by salads dressed with oil (especially olive oil), plenty of fruit, and eggs. Complexions are made worse by fried foods, pizzas, candy, and nuts.

Hair will be more shiny and less oily if the diet is properly balanced; eyes will be more sparkling with an abundance of vitamin A foods. It's nuts, chocolate bars, soft drinks, potato chips, sour-cream dips, and pastries that cause hips and thighs to spread out and waistlines to bulge—not breakfast cereal and milk, or a morning eggnog.

Special Diets

Anyone who for reasons of health must observe a special diet should be under medical supervision. This includes those suffering from allergies and, perhaps even more important, those who must be on a low-cholesterol, ulcer, diabetic, or low-sodium diet. Medical supervision is necessary to know what foods will be harmful and why.

However, here are a few tips:

- Herbs can do wonders to improve the flavor of salt-free dishes, and for those suddenly on a bland diet after a lifetime of enjoying spicy foods, herbs can help to make bland foods more palatable.
- Chopped celery and dill are recommended seasoners in both diabetic and low-salt diets—not only because they make the food taste better, but because they have useful medicinal qualities.
- For a "soft diet," skillfully flavored broths consumed several times during the day will soothe irritated "GI" passages and help allay the pangs of hunger. These can be made with stock concentrates to save time (with the doctor's permission—otherwise make broth with chicken necks and backs), but add herbs and julienne-cut vegetables (green beans and carrots) for flavor. The vegetables will have to be cooked to soft, and the broth may have to be strained (if the doctor so orders), but food and flavor value will already have been added.
- Five *small* meals a day are better than three large for both heart and ulcer patients. A mid-morning and mid-afternoon

snack will do it; just keep lunch and dinner correspondingly lighter.

•For those who feel the meal is incomplete without dessert, fruit compotes are the answer. If raw fruit is forbidden (for those on ulcer diets), dietetic-pack canned fruits can be obtained in colorful assortments, and, if the doctor allows, a little wine or a dash of brandy will do wonders for flavor. Fresh fruits, or a combination of fresh and canned fruits marinated in orange juice, can make a luscious ending to any dinner.

•A blender is a must for those on special diets, for puréeing vegetables, for making sauces and soups without butter, for beating up quick fruit punches to replace forbidden beverages, and for adding herbal flavor to otherwise distressingly insipid foods.

•The following are forbidden on nearly all special diets: fried foods, pastries, highly spiced foods, animal fats and fat meats.

•Many serious illnesses (such as coronary disease, high blood pressure, liver complaints, and many cases of diabetes) have been traced to bad eating habits—a lifetime of overindulgence in fat-rich foods. It's not too late for you to change!

3 CALORIE INTELLIGENCE

•Calories count, but some count more than others.
•There's no way to eat your cake and not have it (as a bulging memento on your midriff).
•The best reducing exercise is pushing away your plate.
•Habit is the enemy. Temptation is his brother.

Do You Really Want to Lose Weight?

There is no quick way to get rid of excess weight once you've acquired it. Dieting successfully requires a strong will, and not just the first week, but the fourth and fifth weeks and thereafter. If you try to rush things in the hope of taking off five pounds or more a week, you may injure your health; and even if you escape that hazard, a crash diet is not one you can live with. In other words, you may lose five pounds the first week, and perhaps another the second week, but habit and temptation will soon take over once more, and the pounds will be back more quickly than they left.

A successful reducing diet is one you can stick to week after week without feeling nasty, irritable, and ready to commit mayhem, or so starved there's nothing to do but kick the traces and go on a big eating binge.

The Best Reducing Diet

The **high-protein diet**, *as long as it includes all the Basic Four foods daily*, has been proved over a long period of time to be the best and easiest to live with.

To follow this is much easier than counting calories; besides, calories are not the only criterion. Most high-protein foods have a fairly high caloric count, yet they do not contribute to obesity in the same degree as do the high-carbohydrate and high-fat foods.

Fats in some degree—especially the liquid fats or vegetable oils—are essential in the most rigorous reducing diet to provide *sustained* energy and body lubrication and to assist the proteins in their functions. But they must be limited in quantity, and foods naturally rich in fats must be avoided. Above all, avoid fried foods and pastries like the plague.

The most successful weight-reducing regimen is one that 1) fits into a family menu pattern without too much difficulty, 2) can be adapted to dining out, and 3) is flexible enough to offer endless variety.

The following chart shows how you can concentrate on certain "safe" or "friendly" foods without being concerned with calorie count—as long as you just as carefully avoid the enemies.

The Know-your-friends Reducing Chart

Friends (Foods You May Eat in Abundance)

Appetizers and Snacks
Cottage cheese
Fruits and fruit juices
Seafood
Tomato juice
Vegetable relishes
Meatballs, broiled

Soups
Clear broth
Tomato soup (fresh)
Gazpacho
Jellied consommé

Entrees
Fish and shellfish
Boiled meats
Broiled meats (no fat)
Roast meats (no fat)
Chinese entrees

Sukiyaki
Stews (unthickened sauces)
Vegetable plates

Vegetables

Artichokes
Asparagus
Broccoli
Brussels sprouts
Cabbage
Carrots
Cauliflower
Celery
Green or wax beans
Green leafy vegetables
Radishes
Sauerkraut
Squash
Tomatoes (any way but fried)
Turnips

Salads

Cucumbers
Lettuce of all kinds
Raw vegetable mixtures
Spinach
Tomatoes
Watercress

Desserts and Sweets

Canned fruits, unsweetened or
    dietetic pack
Compotes laced with wine
Fruit ices and dietetic sherbets
Fruited dietetic gelatin
Raw fruits (no sugar)

Milk and Milk Products

Buttermilk (low-fat type)
Cottage cheese
Diet yogurt
Farmer's cheese
Instant nonfat dry milk
Skim milk

Other Beverages

Black coffee
Club soda
Fruit juices (unsweetened)
Sangría
Table wine
Tea
Tomato juice
Unflavored gelatin as quick-energy
    drink
Wine spritzer

Enemies (Avoid at All Times)

Appetizers and Snacks

Fried appetizers
Mayonnaise dips or sauces
Most cheeses
Nuts
Salted chips and crackers

Soups

Bean, pea, and lentil soups
Chowders
Cream soups
Pastas in soups
Potato soups (Vichyssoise)

Entrees

Bean dishes
Bread stuffings
Fried foods
Meats with rich sauces
Pastas
Sausage and bacon
Stews with rich sauces

Vegetables

Corn
Dried legumes (split peas, gar-
    banzos, beans, black-eyed
    peas, etc.)

Fried vegetables (corn fritters, fried eggplant, tomatoes, onions, etc.)

Lima beans

Sweet potatoes or yams

Salads

Avocados

Commercial salad dressings

Fruit salads with sweet or cream dressings

Mayonnaise (except low-calorie)

Salads containing cheese, meat, potatoes, or lima beans

Desserts and Sweets

Baked or fried bananas

Candied fruits and maraschino cherries

Candy

Chocolate cake, frosting, mousse, sauce, etc.

Fruit salads with sweet or cream dressing

Ice cream

Pastries

Puddings

Starches

Pastas

Potatoes (except as specified)

Fats and oils

All rich gravies

Milk and Milk Products

Chocolate milk

Cream and whipped cream

Homogenized milk

Ice cream

Most cheese, especially soft dessert cheese and cream cheese

Sour cream

Other Beverages

Ale

Artificial fruit-flavored drinks

Beer

Brandy

Liqueurs

Manhattans

Martinis

Sweet and fortified wines

Putting a Ceiling on Calories

In order to lose weight, you must consume less than you have been habitually eating (and drinking).

If you study the foregoing chart and exclaim, "But this is the way I eat already!" the answer must be, "Then eat still less of the 'friendly' foods."

This is where counting calories comes in. The total caloric intake must be lower than it has been. Check the Calorie Computers to see which foods and beverages are higher, which ones are lower in calories of the "friendly" foods. Skip appetizers before dinner. Refuse second helpings (that plate-pushing exercise). Insist on smaller helpings of everything. Avoid all fried foods and high-carbohydrate foods. But keep your meal pattern balanced.

Limiting Fats, Oils, Starches

Keep to a daily limit of 1 tablespoon oil and 3 teaspoons (1 tablespoon) solid shortening (butter, margarine, vegetable shortening). This could mean 2 pats (1 teaspoon) of butter per day, 1 pat on the breakfast toast, the other to flavor vegetables. The other 2 teaspoons of solid fat (butter, margarine, or vegetable shortening) could be used in sautéing. In a recipe whose yield is 6 servings, if 2 tablespoons butter or other fat is used to sauté the veal chops, for example, that would be 1 teaspoon per serving.

For salad dressing, 1 tablespoon oil per person would be about 1/3 cup for 6 persons—the normal quantity in classic Vinaigrette dressing. If less than this is used for salad, proportionately more could be used for cooking.

Meal Skipping

Eating is habit, and so is hunger. You have to teach your body to expect less food. What works for one person does not necessarily work well for others. For some, skipping lunch entirely is effective. At the usual hour for lunch, at first, you will be ravenous and weak, but after a week of lunch-skipping, you may no longer be hungry at all. Skipping breakfast does *not* help to reduce weight, because this is the time of day when you are most likely to burn up the calories you have consumed. The best meal to skip is dinner, since most of us have little if any exercise following the evening meal. Snacks consumed just before bedtime are the worst of all.

A business executive who must frequently turn lunch into a business engagement, and whose lunch therefore becomes a "main meal," may try skipping dinner entirely, or may have nothing for dinner but soup and fruit. The difficulty is that those who return home after a tense day often need a cocktail or two to relax, and to drink alcoholic beverages without food is not advisable. Then the insidious cycle begins—and the weight-reducing regime totters.

Snacking to Lose Weight

A number of small meals throughout the day will be easier on the heart and digestion than three large meals, if the total caloric intake is kept under control. Snacks may consist of celery, radishes, raw apples, and unsalted unsweetened wafers, with an occasional hard-cooked egg or a carton of diet yogurt or a glass of gelatin drink.

Keep the fruit bowl always filled. And if snacks alone are not satisfying, have a high-protein broiled hamburger (no bun) to stave off hunger.

Whichever dieting method is easiest for the individual to follow is the best one—as long as the Basic Four are included in each day's diet, and a feeling of well-being can be maintained.

Drinking Do's and Don'ts

There is no question that highballs and cocktails contribute to overweight. Part of this is because alcohol overstimulates the appetite, so food is consumed along with the beverages. But also alcohol converts to sugar in the bloodstream. *Beer* and *ale* are both fattening because of the malt content.

Fortified sweet wines are as bad as distilled spirits, and liqueurs are worse (because they contain brandy and are high in sugar content).

Drinking is as much a habit as is eating, and the tired executive's need for a cocktail is primarily psychological. A drink in the hand has extraordinary "unwinding" powers, even when the drink consists only of a little light wine and soda. The best compromise for the dieter is to turn to wine drinks or dry (rather than sweet) vermouth at the cocktail hour, and to nibble on vegetable relishes along with the drinks, instead of potato chips, nuts, or cheese. Or, drink tea (hot or iced), which is soothing and only mildly stimulating.

Coffee and tea by themselves are virtually free of calories. It's the sugar and milk (or cream) that do the damage. Yet black coffee in excessive quantities is bad for the nerves, and the dieter whose nerves are already taking a beating is usually much better off having a little milk in the breakfast coffee than drinking it black. A mere teaspoon of milk adds only 4 calories; a tablespoon of milk is 12 calories, less than half as many as in a small glass of tomato juice.

Note that both quinine water (tonic) and ginger ale are quite high in calories. So is lemonade, because of the sugar.

The Insidious Lure of Sweets

For those who have a compulsive desire for sweets, giving up desserts is the cruelest part of a weight-reducing diet. For such people, the noncaloric sweeteners and the dietetic desserts (low-calorie gelatin and pudding mixes, dietetic-pack fruits, dietetic jams and jellies, and dietetic sherbets) serve an important function.

But it's no good living under the illusion that you may indulge in as many desserts as you like, just because you are using these noncaloric sweeteners as a crutch. Even though the number of calories has been somewhat reduced, the calories have not been eliminated, and the more desserts you consume, the more you are falling from grace.

Exercise and Weight Control

Calories are fuel. The more you exercise, the more calories you consume. Exercise *by itself*, however, rarely takes off excess pounds. The following chart shows that even an hour on the tennis court burns up only 426 calories, and the normal daily calorie intake is around 2000. If you played tennis for an hour *every day, without a change in diet*, you could not hope to lose more than a pound a week.

Dieting and exercise must go together. Walk more, eat less. Do your morning push-ups (or, even better, do push-ups just before bedtime), but also push away those pastries and chips.

CALORIES BURNED UP IN EXERCISE

Normal walking. An hour's walk at a leisurely pace requires 216 calories, or 3.6 per minute.

Bowling. You use 4.5 calories per time up, or 4.5 per minute.

Normal cycling. A half-hour's pedaling burns up 135 calories, or 4.5 per minute.

Golfing. If you walk around the course, 18 holes consumes 900 calories (about 3 hours), or 5 calories per minute.

Swimming. Twice the length of a 60-foot pool burns 10 calories.

Rowing. In an hour's leisurely row, you burn up 300 calories.

Fast walking. At a brisk pace (3.75 mph) you burn up 168 calories in a half-hour, or 5.6 per minute.

Skating. Ice skating or roller skating for an hour uses up to 360 calories, or 6 per minute.

Tennis. Two sets (1 hour) burns up 426 calories, or 7.1 per minute.

Water skiing. A half-hour consumes 240 calories, or 8 per minute.

Skiing. An hour uses 594 calories, or 9.9 per minute.

Running. A half-hour at 10 mph loses 450 calories, or 15 per minute.

When to Enjoy a Splurge

Dieters are human beings, and it isn't human to be perfect all the time. So, now and then, let yourself go. One lovely dinner in a fortnight will not put back all those discarded pounds. Such a splurge may, in fact, do you so much good psychologically that it will be easier to return to the dieting regime for another disciplined two weeks. It's the day-after-day food consumption that puts on the pounds, not an occasional extra 300 or 400 calories in a single evening.

Calorie Computer

Estimating the caloric content of any food is largely guesswork. No one can know for a certainty how much fat a piece of meat contains, and the slightest difference of fat used in cooking the food will alter the total caloric content. However, the following estimates give an idea of which of the foods highest in protein are the lowest in calories. Note the difference in caloric content between boiled shrimp and fried shrimp, and between broiled and fried chicken.

High-Protein Entrees

The following are average entree servings; 3 to 4 ounces per edible portion, or as noted.

Clams, canned or cooked, ½ cup, no fat	50
Crabmeat, ½ cup	60
Shrimp, boiled, 4 to 6	70
Cod or flounder, poached	80
Omelet, plain, or scrambled egg (1 egg per serving)	105
Lobster (1-pound Maine, or 4-ounce lobster tail), boiled	108
Liver, braised	140
Salmon, canned or boiled, ½ cup	145
Haddock or cod, broiled	160
Chicken, ¼ small broiler, broiled	160
Roast chicken or turkey, average serving	165
Tuna, canned, well drained	170
London broil	190
Hamburger patties from ground top round	200
Veal roast, 1 slice	200
Veal scallopini, braised in wine	210
Broiled halibut or swordfish steak	220
Roast leg of lamb, 1 slice, no fat	230
Fried chicken, ½ breast	230
Fried chicken, drumstick and thigh	245
Hamburger patties from ground chuck	245
Fried shrimp, 4 to 6	260
Loin lamb chops, 2, no fat	280
Pork chop, no fat	285

Roast beef, 1 slice, no fat   285
Porterhouse steak, 4-ounce portion (¼ pound), no fat   290
Frankfurters, 2, no bread   300
Baked ham, 1 slice (¼ inch), no fat   300
Steak, 4 ounces, with some fat   330
Roast loin of pork, 1 thick slice   400

Estimates of pot roast or beef stew cannot be given with any accuracy because of varieties in the richness of the gravy, the fat of the meat used, and which vegetables are cooked with the meat (and included in the serving portion).

Snack Foods

Radishes, each   1
Hot bouillon (made with bouillon cube)   2
Celery, each stalk   2
Cucumber sticks, each   3
Carrot sticks, each (¼ inch)   5
Green olives, each   6
Black olives, each   8
Dill pickle, ½   8
Apricots, dried, each   10
Sweet gherkin pickles, each   11
Shrimps, boiled, each (no sauce)   15
Clam-cottage cheese dip, 1 tablespoon   16
Saltines, each   16
Rye-Krisp, each   16
Prunes, each   19
Plain vanilla wafers, each   21
Pretzels, 5 thin sticks or 2 round   20
Graham crackers, each   27
Blue plums, each, raw   29
Prosciutto ham, 1 paper-thin slice   32
Peaches, each, raw   35
Tangerines, 1 medium   35
Almonds, 6 to 8, toasted, no fat   50
Fig newtons, each   55
Yogurt, ½ cup   60
Peanuts, 6 to 8   65
Bologna, 1 slice   66
Apple, 1 medium   70
Orange, 1 navel   75
Watermelon, 1 slice (¾ inch thick)   90
Banana, 1 medium   100
Potato chips, 8 to 10   100

Cheese nibbles or crackers, 3   100
Popcorn, 1 cup lightly buttered   100
Cheese, Swiss or Roquefort, 1 ounce   105
Cheese, Cheddar, Edam, or American, 1 ounce   115
Oatmeal cookies, each   115
Salami, 1 slice   130
Doughnuts, each   135
Chocolate bar, 1 inch square   145
Vanilla ice cream, 1 scoop   145
Brownies, each   165
Homogenized milk, 1 cup   165
Chocolate ice cream, 1 scoop   185
Chocolate-flavored milk drink (skim milk)   190
Peanut butter sandwich, each, no jelly   220
Cocoa, 1 cup   232
Chocolate cake, 2 inches square, with frosting   356
Chocolate malted milk   502

Beverages

Tea (no sugar or milk)   0
Black coffee (no sugar)   2
Club soda (seltzer water)   5
Coffee (1 tablespoon milk, no sugar)   12
Tea (1 teaspoon sugar)   16
Tomato juice, 4-ounce glass   25
Dry white wine, 3½ ounces   60-70
White wine spritzer, 8 ounces   65-75
Dry red wine (claret, Burgundy, Pinot Noir), 3½ ounces   65-75
Ginger ale, 7 ounces   70
Sauterne (domestic)   75
Quinine water (tonic), 7 ounces   75
Skim milk or buttermilk, no fat, 8 ounces   85
Beer, 8 ounces   100
Cola, 6 ounces   105
Orange juice, 6 ounces   110
Vermouth, dry, 3½ ounces   110
Sherry, dry, 3½ ounces   115-140
Scotch on the rocks, 1½ ounces   115
Rye or bourbon on the rocks, 1½ ounces   125
Bloody Mary   130
Bock beer, 8 ounces   135
Old fashioned, 4 ounces   135
Whiskey sour   140
Daiquiri   140
Milk, homogenized, 8 ounces   165
Gin and tonic   180

Manhattan	226
Martini (3 parts gin, 1 part dry vermouth)	260
Eggnog, 3½ ounces	335

Vegetables and Other Accessory Foods

The following estimates are for average servings of ½ cup each, no butter or margarine unless otherwise noted. Add 33 calories for each teaspoon (16 calories for ½ teaspoon) butter or margarine.

Sliced cucumber, 6 slices, salted	6
Green pepper, raw	8
Lettuce, raw	11
Raw cabbage	12
Celery, braised with tomato	12
Green beans	13
Cauliflower	15
Tomato, raw, 2 slices	15
Mushrooms	15
Mustard or turnip greens	15
Squash, yellow summer	18
Asparagus, 6 spears	20
Turnips	21
Cabbage, braised	22
Carrots	22
Spinach	23
Tomatoes, stewed or baked	23
Kale	23
Rutabaga	26
Broccoli, 2 spears or 1 large spear	26
Okra, ½ cup	28
Brussels sprouts	30
Beets	34
Onions, baked or stewed	40
Peas, green	55
Hominy grits	60
Potato, 1 small, boiled	65
Lima beans	75
Corn on cob	84
Potatoes mashed (milk and butter added)	90
Baked Idaho potato (no butter)	95
Rice	100
Noodles	100
Boston brown bread, 1 slice	100
Macaroni or spaghetti (no sauce or butter)	107

Rolls, each (plain)	115
Onions, fried	120
Corn muffins, each	155
French fried potatoes (10)	155
Sweet roll, each	178
Sweet potato, 1 medium	183
Avocado, ½ (no dressing)	185
Spaghetti with tomato sauce	210
Macaroni and cheese, ½ cup (as an entree, 1 cup serving, 475 calories)	237

Desserts

The following are estimates of average servings.

Strawberries (no sugar), ½ cup	27
Cherries, raw, ½ cup	33
Cantaloupe, ½	40
Watermelon, 1 slice	45
Compote of raspberries, blueberries, and peaches	45
Minted fresh pineapple	45
Peaches in cognac	70

Ambrosia (oranges, bananas, coconut)	75
Plain gelatin	78
Fruited gelatin	85
Angel food cake (no frosting)	110
Sherbet, 1 scoop	120
Cup custard	140
Vanilla ice cream, plain, 1 scoop	147
Pound cake, 1 slice	130
Cupcake, no frosting	130
Vanilla pudding	138
Gingerbread	180
Chocolate ice cream, 1 scoop	180
Strawberry ice cream	200
Baked apple (no cream)	200
Raspberry sundae (frozen raspberries)	215
Pumpkin or custard pie	265
Lemon meringue pie	300
Fruit pie, 2-crust (apple or cherry)	330
Chocolate chiffon pie	330
Hot fudge sundae	360
Layer cake (yellow) with chocolate frosting	365
Pecan pie	418
Banana split with chocolate sauce and whipped cream	600

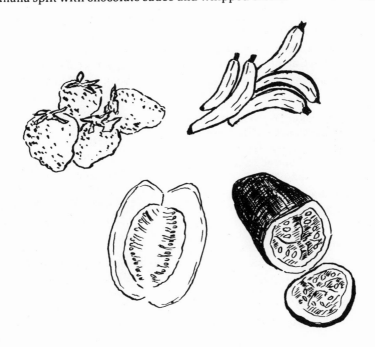

MENUS TO GO BY

For most of us, determining what to have for dinner night after night is more of a challenge than searching for new recipes. Of the menus that follow, the first group, *Menus Without Recipes*, illustrates how it is possible to have interesting and varied meals without having to learn new recipes.

The second group, *Week-at-a-Glance Menus*, suggests an easy way to plan seven meals ahead, adding vegetables and desserts when the time comes, according to what's available.

The third shows how the dieter may enjoy essentially the same menu as the rest of the family, with certain deletions.

Using Leftovers contains no actual menu suggestions, but suggests ways of turning leftover foods (meats, vegetables, starch foods) into appetizing second appearance dishes.

Freezer Bank Menus illustrates ways to make use of the freezer for plan-ahead meals. *Go-withs for Barbecue Meals* suggests what foods to serve as accompaniments to the standard meats prepared over the outdoor charcoal grill.

Menus Without Recipes

1

Cream of Tomato Soup,
Parsley Garnish

Broiled Lamb Chops

Buttered Carrots   Broccoli

Strawberries over Ice Cream

2

Roast Chicken, Herb Stuffing
(using packaged stuffing mix)

Mashed Potatoes   Green Peas

Tossed Lettuce and
Tomato Salad

Apple Pie (use canned apples
and piecrust mix)

3

Broiled Hamburgers with
Mushrooms

Potato Patties (frozen)

Brussels Sprouts

Sliced Tomatoes

Chocolate Pudding

4

Chicken and Noodles Amandine
(use leftover chicken,
packaged noodles amandine)

Spinach   Cauliflower

Lima Bean and Romaine Salad

Lemon Chiffon Pie
(using mixes)

5

London Broil

Parsleyed Potatoes

Asparagus

Celery and Black Olives

Canned Peaches

6

Fried Sole with Tartar Sauce

Italian Beans (frozen)

Beets (canned)

Cole Slaw

Lemon Sherbet

7

Barbecued Chicken
Lima Beans   Summer Squash
Tossed Lettuce and Radishes
Chocolate Cake, Ice Cream

8

Eye Round (Beef) Roast
Browned Potatoes
Whipped Squash (frozen)
Tomato-Cucumber Salad

Fruit Pie

9

Parsley Omelet
Frenched Green Beans
Broiled Tomatoes
Garlic Bread

Gingerbread (mix)

10

Fish Sticks with Barbecue Sauce
(use commercial sauce)
Corn-in-Butter (frozen)
Chopped Spinach (frozen)
Butterflake Rolls
(heat-and-serve)
Raspberry Sundae (frozen
raspberries over vanilla ice
cream)

11

Sliced Roast Beef, heated in
gravy
Noodles Artichoke Hearts
(frozen)
Green Pepper, Carrot, and
Cabbage Salad
Sliced Bananas and Cream

12

Pork Chops
Parsley Rice
Braised Zucchini
Radishes and Carrot Sticks
Blueberry Muffins
Chocolate Mint Ice Cream

13

Minute Steaks, topped with
Garlic or Herb Butter
Corn on Cob
Green Peas and Onions (frozen)
Watercress-Tomato Salad
Refrigerator Cake
(commercial)

14

Frankfurters and Sauerkraut
Boiled Potatoes
Green Pepper and Cottage
Cheese Salad
Fruit Crisp (use mix)

Week-at-a-Glance Menus

It's the entree that establishes the menu, so plan seven entrees for the week, add vegetables according to what you have on hand.

Recipes for all the entrees listed will be found in the recipe section of the book; consult the index to locate them.

Week 1

Fri: Beef Bourguignonne (stewing beef)
Sat: Spaghetti Bolognese (ground meat)
Sun: Roast Capon with Orange Sauce
Mon: Spanish Potato Omelet

Tue: Chicken Tetrazzini (use leftover capon)
Wed: Shrimp Curry
Thu: Veal Cutlet

Week 2

Fri: Sole Meunière
Sat: Economy Shish-kabob (use stewing beef)
Sun: Viennese Meatloaf
Mon: Greek Lamb Stew with Green Beans
Tue: Ham and Eggs
Wed: Spanish Rice with Chicken Wings
Thu: Pork Chops Neapolitan

Week 3

Fri: Swordfish Steak
Sat: Roast Loin of Pork with Prunes
Sun: Frikadeller (meatballs made with meatloaf mixture)
Mon: Pork Chow Mein (with leftover pork)
Tue: Lasagne (use ground meatloaf mixture or leftover Frika-
    deller in sauce)
Wed: Steak Diane
Thu: Fried Chicken

Week 4

Fri: Shrimp Neapolitano
Sat: Parmesan-stuffed Veal Roast
Sun: Broiled Chicken Indienne
Mon: Creamed Tuna and Eggs
Tue: Roast Veal reheated in gravy
Wed: Hamburgers in Red Wine Sauce
Thu: Noodle Casserole (making use of remaining veal, if any, or
    other leftovers)

Week 5

Fri: Zarzuela (seafood casserole)
Sat: Pork Satay
Sun: Meatloaf
Mon: Salmon and Crabmeat Casserole
Tue: Reheat meatloaf in gravy
Wed: Eggs à la Flamenca
Thu: Spaghetti with Tuna Sauce

Weeknight Family Menus

For weeknight dinners, plan meals that will wait for latecomers. Some entrees should be of the kind that can be reheated without undue loss of flavor; others that can be cooked after everyone is at home; or, part of the food might be cooked for an early supper, the remainder cooked later.

1
Beef Stew with Vegetables*
Buttered Noodles
Tossed Salad†
Ice Cream

2
Pork Chops with Orange Sauce*
Rice*
Brussels sprouts †
Cottage Pudding (pound cake with hot Lemon Sauce)

3
Chinese Noodle Soup*
Chicken Chop Suey†
Rice*
Tomato, sliced water chestnut, and watercress salad
Vanilla pudding with raisins

4
Spaghetti, Lima Bean, and Ham Casserole*
Lettuce salad
Apple Brown Betty
(good hot or cold)

5
Pork Fried Rice*
Fried Bananas †
Green or Italian beans †
Sliced tomatoes
Fruited blackberry gelatin, whipped topping

6
Tuna à la King*
Rice*
Broccoli †
Cucumber salad
Peach Cobbler
(good hot or cold)

7
Braised Shoulder Lamb Chops,*
with Cranberry-Orange Relish
Cauliflower
Cottage-fried Potatoes†
Green salad with Roquefort Dressing
Citrus fruit salad

8
Center ham slice†
Braised Celery *
Sweet Potatoes *
Melon (in season)

Weeknight Menus for One or Two

These are all quick and easy dinners that can be prepared within 30 minutes from start to finish. Some may be prepared in

*Can be kept warm in oven or can be reheated.
†Finish preparation after family is assembled.

double quantities, to be reheated for a second meal. Note how rice and noodles are used on successive nights. Consult index to find recipes.

1

Scallopini au Marsala
Buttered linguine
Green peas (frozen)
Lettuce salad
Canned fruit

2

Hamburgers in Vermouth
Italian beans (frozen)
Corn on cob
Raw apples and Roquefort
cheese

3

Curried Scrambled Eggs and
Bacon
Frenched green beans (frozen)
Beets (canned) with Mustard
Sauce
Ice Cream topped with peaches
(canned or fresh)

4

Sukiyaki (cook at table)
Almond Rice
Canned apricots laced with
Grand Marnier
(or other liqueur)

5

Broiled Sole (use frozen sole)
Green peas and mushrooms
(frozen)
Toasted corn muffins (frozen)
Strawberries in Orange Juice

6

Chinese Pepper Steak
Rice
Braised Celery and Tomatoes
Diced Oranges and Walnuts

7

Quick Beef Stroganoff
(use top round cut in slivers)
Rice (reheated from previous
night)
Dilled carrots and peas (frozen
carrots and peas,
cooked in butter with dill)
Sliced tomatoes and cucumbers
Fresh fruit in season

8

Veal Chops Caprice
Spinach (fresh or frozen)
Corn in butter (frozen)
Radishes and celery
Peach ice cream
laced with white rum

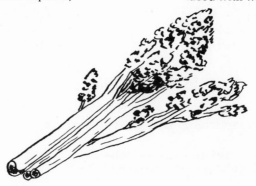

Fitting Reducing Diet into Family Meals

The following menus for a week do not include bread or milk, nor are snack meals listed.

1st Day

Breakfast

Tomato juice
Scrambled eggs
Cinnamon toast (1 piece
for dieter)
Beverage
(coffee with milk for dieter)

Lunch

Chicken noodle soup
(dieter leaves noodles in bowl)
Tuna fish salad sandwiches
(tuna salad on lettuce
for dieter, no bread)
Canned (dietetic pack) or fresh
peaches
Cottage cheese

Dinner

Broiled chicken
Broccoli
Parsley rice
Sliced tomatoes
Ambrosia (dieter skips coconut)

2nd Day

Breakfast

Half grapefruit
Breakfast cereal (dieter skips)
Poached egg on toast
Beverage

Lunch

Cottage cheese-green
pepper salad
Ham-on-rye sandwiches
(dieter has
1 thin slice ham, no bread)
Beverage (dieter has iced tea
with

noncaloric sweetener)

Dinner

Broiled halibut steak,
Lemon Butter
(dieter skips butter or
has only ½ teaspoon)
Spinach
Buttered carrots
Hot rolls (dieter skips)
Ice cream with fudge sauce
(dieter has sherbet, no sauce)

3rd Day

Breakfast

Orange juice
Boiled egg (hard or soft)
Frozen Corn Toasties (dieter has
one with jam, no butter)
Beverage

Lunch

Hamburgers (dieter skips the
bun and catsup)
Carrot sticks with stuffed
green olives
Potato chips (dieter skips)
Baked apple (dieter has
raw apple)
Milk or tea (dieter has skim milk)

Dinner

Wonton soup (dieter has only
the clear broth)
Shrimp egg rolls (frozen)
(dieter skips)
Chicken Chow Mein, or Moo Goo
Gai Pan
Rice
Ice cream topped with berries
(dieter has only the berries)

4th Day

Breakfast

Melon
Eggnog (dieter's is made
with skim milk)
Cinnamon rolls (dieter skips
Beverage

Lunch

Tomato-rice soup
Grilled cheese sandwiches
(dieter has open-faced sandwich,
1 slice Swiss cheese, not grilled)
Fresh fruit
Beverage (dieter has tea
with skim milk)

Dinner

Broiled lamb chops
Asparagus
Yellow squash
Yogurt with raspberry jam
(dieter uses dietetic jam)

5th Day

Breakfast

Juice
Bacon sandwich with
whole-wheat toast
(dieter skips bacon,
may have cottage
cheese with 1 slice toast)
Beverage

Lunch

Mixed vegetable soup
Western sandwich
(dieter skips the bread,
has only a Western omelet)
Fresh fruit

Dinner

Boiled Beef with Horseradish
Cream
(dieter allowed 1 teaspoon

sour cream)
Noodles
Swiss chard or beet greens
Lettuce and cucumber salad
Watermelon

6th Day

Breakfast

Melon
Steamed Skillet Eggs
Gluten bread toast with dietetic
jam
Beverage

Lunch

Corned beef on rye sandwiches,
mustard pickles
(dieter has open sandwich)
Ice cream or milk sherbet
Beverage

Dinner

Chicken and rice Casserole
Spanish artichoke hearts
(packed in brine),
French dressing (dieter skips)
Radishes and celery
Fruited gelatin with whipped
cream
(dieter skips cream)

7th Day (Sunday)

Breakfast

Fresh fruit of season
Breakfast cereal
Toast, jam
(dietetic pack)
Beverage

Dinner (Mid-day)

Tomato juice cocktail,
or clams on half shell
Roast beef, browned potatoes
(dieter has 1 slice beef, no fat;
1 potato, no gravy)

Green beans
Salad Valenciana
Berry shortcake (dieter has
only the berries)

Supper
Vegetable relishes

Hot dogs or hamburgers (dieter
skips the bread)
Tossed salad
Instant chocolate pudding
(dieter skips, has yogurt or
raw fruit instead)

Using Leftovers

The following are suggestions for ways of turning leftover
meats, poultry, fish, vegetables, or grain foods into dishes for
future meals. Use the Menu Wheels for guidance in building
menus around the suggested dishes. Consult the index to locate
recipes.

Baked Ham

Sliced: Ham and Eggs sur le Plat
Macaroni and Ham
Spaghetti-Lima-Ham Casserole
Escalloped Potatoes and Ham
Saltimbocca
Ham Sandwiches

Bits and pieces: Cassoulet
Lentil Soup
Yankee Bean Soup
Spanish Rice
Jambalaya
Veal and Ham in Patty Shells
Scrambled Eggs, Ham and Avocado
Ham Stuffing for Cabbage
Ham Salad (for Sandwiches)
Chef's Salad
Ham and Chicken a la King

Roast Beef

Sliced: Sandwiches, hot or cold
Reheated in gravy
Reheated in Red Wine Sauce

Bits and pieces: Roast Beef Hash
Curried Beef Stew
Stuffing for vegetables
Chef's Salad
Beef and Potato Salad
Beef Stroganoff

Roast Leg of Lamb

Lamb in Plum Sauce
Lamb Curry
Greek Lamb Stew
Moussaka (chop or mince the meat)
Stuffed Baked Tomatoes

Roast Veal

Reheat in gravy, Sour Cream Sauce, or
   Mushroom and Sherry Sauce
Roast veal sandwiches, with green pepper or lettuce
Veal Stew Viennoise
Veal and Ham in Patty Shells
Veal and Mushrooms in White Wine
Curried Veal
Veal in Sauce Supreme
Veal and Green Peas in Tomato-Cream Sauce

Roast Pork

Sliced: In sandwiches, with lettuce and mustard
Reheat in gravy, Sour Cream Sauce, or Sauce Robert
Bits and pieces: Pork Stroganoff
Pork Chow Mein
Pork Fried Rice
Spanish Rice, Jambalaya, or Paella
In scrambled eggs
With mushrooms in Sour Cream Sauce

Chicken or Turkey (cooked turkey can be used in any recipe specifying chicken)

Sliced: Sandwiches, hot or cold
Reheat in gravy
Reheat in Sauce Supreme
Reheat in Mushroom-Wine Sauce
Chicken (or Turkey) Divan
Bits and pieces: Stuffing for raw tomatoes (salad)
Stuffing for baked tomatoes
Luncheon salad
Chef's Salad
Chicken salad for sandwiches
Chicken (or Turkey) Tetrazzini
Chicken and Ham in Patty Shells
Chicken and Mushrooms in Tomato Cream Sauce

Chicken and Chicken Livers in Noodles
Chicken Chow Mein
Chicken Fried Rice

Fish

In salad, with mayonnaise
Filling for Piroshki
Creamed, with green peppers, hard-cooked
egg, and pimiento
In Curry-Cream Sauce
Pâté (for cocktail appetizer)

Vegetables

Beets: Serve cold, with oil-vinegar dressing, or with sour cream
Use as garnish for potato salad

Broccoli: Add oil-vinegar dressing, serve as salad (do not reheat cooked broccoli)

Brussels sprouts: Same as above

Corn on cob: Slice off kernels, add lima or green beans, reheat in butter, serve as Succotash
Reheat sliced kernels in butter and cream
Make into Corn Fritters
Add chopped ham, onion, and green peppers, sauté in butter
Add sliced kernels to pancake batter

Green beans: Reheat with mushrooms or canned small white onions, in butter
Serve cold, dressed with oil and vinegar
Add to salads; especially good with hard-cooked eggs

Lima beans: Add to kernel corn for Succotash
Use in salads
Add to creamed veal, chicken or ham
Use in spaghetti casserole
Use in Spanish rice, or any rice casseroles

Mushrooms: Add *at last minute* to stews or sauces (do not cook further)
Use in chicken or tuna salad mixture for sandwiches
Mince, add to liver pâté or other appetizer mixtures

Potatoes, boiled: Make potato salad, adding green peppers, green beans, or hard-cooked egg; use either oil-vinegar dressing or mayonnaise
Use in Roast Beef Hash
Add to stew, just long enough to reheat

Potatoes,

mashed: If a large amount is left over, use as topping for
Shepherd's Pie
Or, make Potato Cakes
If only a small amount is leftover, use to thicken
stews, or as part of the stuffing for baked whole
tomatoes or other baked stuffed vegetables

Spinach: Reheat in cream sauce
Purée in blender with *hot* cream, serve as Creamed
Spinach
Serve cold with oil-vinegar dressing, as salad

Tomatoes,

sliced: Use in stew
Add to tomato sauce, cook down

Tomatoes,

stewed: Add to tomato or spaghetti sauce
Use in meatloaf for part of liquid
Add to Baked Stuffed Green Peppers as sauce
Add to pot roast

Turnip: Purée in blender with leftover potatoes and *hot*
cream; reheat in top of double boiler or in oven
(covered)

Grain Foods

Macaroni or
spaghetti: Turn into a casserole, add meat or chicken, tomato
sauce, parsley, cheese, and crumb topping
Make a salad, adding green peppers, onion, and
mayonnaise
Reheat in tomato sauce
Chop, add to soup

Noodles: Add meat or chicken and gravy, turn into a casserole,
with or without almond topping
Reheat in gravy or Sour Cream Sauce, serve garnished with almonds or minced parsley
Chop, add to soup

Rice: Reheat in butter to serve again
Make Fried Rice (with pork, shrimp, ham, or chick-
en)
Make Spanish Rice
Use as stuffing for tomatoes (salad or baked)
Use as stuffing for cabbage, eggplant, squash, green
peppers
Make Viennese or Andalusian Rice Salad

Stale bread: Make French toast
Cut in cubes or dice, sauté for croutons

Cut in rounds, fry, use for canapes
Use as stuffing in vegetables, poultry, meat, or fish
Soak in liquid, squeeze dry, use to extend meatloaf,
meatballs, or hamburgers

Corn bread or
muffins: Use as stuffing for chicken or turkey
Slice, sauté in butter or margarine, serve under asparagus spears

Gravy, soups,
broth: Add leftover gravy to soup or other sauces
Use leftover broth to make gravy
Purée soups, use in sauces (often good in spaghetti
sauce)

Freezer-bank Meals

There are three main ways to use the freezer for plan-ahead meals. One is to buy meats that can be cut into portions for multiple meals, freeze them already trimmed and ready to cook. The second is to cook foods in double quantities, serve half immediately, and freeze the remainder for later. The third method is to cook foods (casseroles, stews, breads, pies, and cakes) in a marathon food-preparation spree, so that for weeks to come there are foods ready to take from freezer to oven as needed.

A fourth major use of the freezer as a bank is for storing leftovers. Almost any leftovers can be frozen, if properly wrapped to exclude all air, and they are likely to be far more interesting if a few weeks elapse between the first and second appearance on the table.

Buying Meats and Poultry in Multiple-meal Portions

Fresh Ham (7 to 8 pounds)

Ask butcher to bone the leg of pork and tie one half into a rolled roast. Cut up the remainder to use in any of the following ways:

• In 1-inch cubes for Pork Satay, Greek Pork and Celery Stew, or Székelys Gulyás.
• Into ½-inch pieces for Pork Fried Rice, oriental soups, Paella, Cassoulet.
• Large slices for Pork Schnitzel.

Leg of Lamb (7 pounds)

The entire leg may be boned and cut into meal-size portions; or, a little less than half may be cut into a roast (retaining the bone), 3 or 4 chops may be cut off, and the remainder cut into cubes for Shish Kabob.

In summer, when Shish Kabob is served more frequently, the entire leg may be cut into cubes, dividing it into meal portions (allow three 1½-inch cubes per serving), each portion to be wrapped and sealed separately. Bits and pieces that do not cut well into cubes may be cut with scissors into very small pieces to be used in:

• Turkish Pilaf with Prunes
• Greek Lamb Stew
• Moussaka

Unless the above are to be cooked before freezing, place the meat in a plastic bag, seal tight, label.

Whole Smoked Ham
Ask the butcher to cut the whole ham in the following four pieces:

• Butt end to roast
• 2 center slices
• Cut off the bony part of the shank end for Lentil Soup
• Use the remaining shank end for baked ham

Or, have the shank end boned, and cut up in the following ways:
• Cut half in 1-inch cubes for Ham en Brochette.
• Dice the rest for use in Jambalaya, ham salad, or Cassoulet, wrap in 1-cup portions.

Boned or Eye Round Roast of Beef (6 to 7 pounds)
Retain 4 pounds in one piece for roasting; ask butcher to tie it for you.

Ask butcher to cut off 4 to 8 very thin slices (using his ham slicer machine) to use for Sukiyaki or Steak Diane.

Any remaining ends or pieces, cut into slivers and wrap separately to use in making Beef Stroganoff or Chinese Pepper Steak.

Lamb or Veal Stew
Buy boned stewing meat for freezing: it's more compact to package and store. Allow 1½ pounds boned meat for 4 servings

of cooked stew; divide into meal-sized portions, wrap and label. Or, cook ahead and freeze for later use. Blanquette de Veau, Viennese Veal Stew, Veal Marengo, and English Veal Pie are a few of the delicacies that can be made with stewing veal. Use lamb for Moussaka, Greek Lamb Stew, Cochifrito, Irish Lamb Stew, Lamb Curry, or Minted Lamb Stew—all of which, if cooked ahead, improve with freezing.

Ground Chuck (3 pounds)

Use approximately 1 pound immediately for hamburgers or meatballs; freeze the remainder in two or more of the following ways, wrapping and sealing each in small plastic bags:

- Season 1 pound of the meat with 1 teaspoon salt, form into 4 to 6 hamburger patties, place the shaped patties on a baking sheet, put into freezer just until patties are frozen enough to be stiff, then remove, stack on top of each other in plastic bag, and seal tight. They will come apart easily later, and can be cooked as needed without previous thawing.
- Divide remaining ground meat into thirds, place each third of loose meat in a plastic bag; seal tight. The meat can be used as needed to make hamburgers, or combined with ground pork (or pork and veal) to make meatballs, or can be used with crumbs as stuffing for vegetables.
- Or, make up part of the meat now into meatballs, cook, cover with sauce or gravy, place in container, seal, freeze for later use.

Ground meatloaf mixture can be handled in exactly the same way and is ideal for Swedish Meatballs or Viennese Meatloaf.

Veal, Lamb, or Pork Chops

Buy extra chops when the price is attractive, place on baking sheet, freeze quickly; when frozen stiff, put chops together in meal-sized portions (according to the size of household); wrap, seal, and label. If frozen like this, the chops come apart instantly when needed and can be cooked with thawing.

Excellent for such dishes as Pork Chops in Orange Sauce, Veal Chops Caprice, Veal Chops Paprika, Mixed English Grill.

Chicken Breasts (12 Halves)

- Wrap 4 halves in one package (for 4 servings) to be broiled, fried, or braised later.

•Bone 4 halves (use bones for stock), cut in 1-inch pieces, use for Moo Goo Gai Pan or other Chinese dishes.

•Wrap remaining halves in 2 separate packages (2 halves each), boned or not as you please. These can be used for nights when someone arrives home late, or used in combination with other foods (as in Chicken and Lobster Costa Brava, or Pork and Chicken Adobo).

•Or, bone 6 halves, prepare for Chicken Kiev but do not cook before freezing. The outside will be more crisp and the butter inside will not escape if the breaded chicken breast is solidly frozen before frying.

Prepare Double Portions; Freeze Half

All the following freeze well and can go from freezer to oven without additional attention. Curries and stews actually improve in flavor if frozen before serving.

Lamb or Beef Curry
Lasagne
Chicken Tetrazzini
Beef Bourguignonne
Quiche Lorraine
Chicken Pie
Beef and Vegetable Pie
Veal Marengo
Noodles Romanoff
Macaroni and Cheese
Fruit Pies
Cakes of all kinds, including Cheesecake
Breads of all kinds

Cooked chicken does not freeze as well as raw chicken; only when it is enclosed in a crust, as in Chicken Pie, or Chicken Kiev, is the texture firm (otherwise it shreds, as does a reheated chicken stew, or canned chicken).

Go-Withs For Barbecue Menus

When meals are cooked outdoors, it is wise always to have a first course which can be enjoyed while the meat (or poultry or fish) is being cooked. This may be a cold soup, vegetable relishes, seafood cocktail, or assorted hors d'oeuvres.

Vegetables to accompany the meat may be cooked in the

coals of the fire (wrapped in foil), or cooked ahead and served from a casserole. Salads, of course, are always good with outdoor meals and may replace other vegetables.

The following menus do not include beverages or bread (except where special breads are suggested). Add these according to family tastes.

1

Green Goddess Salad
Steak
Potatoes Anna (baked in foil)
Ratatouille (cold casserole)
Bing cherries in kirsch

2

Chlodnik (cold soup)
Spicy Spareribs
Corn on cob (baked in husks)
Sliced tomatoes and cucumbers
Orange Cake with Fudge Frosting

3

Carrot sticks and olives
Hamburgers on onion buns
Potato chips
Eggplant Kabobs
Macaroni Salad (cold), or Baked
Beans (hot)
Watermelon

4

Shrimp with Green Mayonnaise
London Broil
Garlic bread
Green bean and egg salad
Blueberry whirl ice cream,
coconut topping

5

Antipasto
Broiled Flank Steak

Potato Salad
Zucchini
Rhubarb Pie

6

Vichyssoise
Chicken Teriyaki
White Bean Salad
Tomato Aspic
Cantaloupe with ice cream

7

Avocado halves
Salmon Steak au Vermouth
Garbanzo Salad
Yellow Squash Pisto
Mimosa Salad
Blackberries on ice cream

8

Gazpacho
Shish Kabob
Potato and Pea Salad
Olives and radishes
Cheesecake

9

Cold consommé
Spit-roasted Chicken,
Tomato Glaze
Fasslia Fresca (green beans,
Greek style)
Jellied Beet Ring, Cottage Cheese
Dressing
Blueberry Pie

BOOK THREE

Recipes

1 APPETIZERS AND SNACKS

The role of appetizers in the American cuisine has changed drastically. As recently as fifty years ago, it was considered proper to start every formal dinner with soup; a banquet "from soup to nuts" was likely to be at least five courses long.

Today the first "course" is usually eaten in the living room, with fingers instead of forks, the second course is meat or fish, and the final course a dessert which can be served without fuss at table.

The disappearance of servants is the principal reason for the change, but increasing awareness of calories and waistlines has had its influence, too. Not only are five courses too many; if there are only two courses they are both simple.

Ironically, the appetizer course is the only one that has grown increasingly larger, until now some overzealous hosts offer so many tempting tidbits before dinner that the entree course becomes almost an anticlimax. Appetizers should be interesting and varied, but they should be light—unless it's a cocktail buffet, a smorgasbord, or an open house, when the appetizers become in effect the meal.

The custom of offering cocktails before dinner has also had its influence on our meal patterns. By no means all adult Americans drink cocktails; yet so general is the custom that it is now good manners to offer drinks even if host and hostess do not indulge. If drinks are served, there must be something to nibble on, and the nibble foods might as well serve as a first course.

Because everything French is in fashion where food is concerned, the term "hors d'oeuvre" has come to be synonymous with appetizer, though actually the French hors d'oeuvre is meant to be served at the table, and typically consists of pickles or salad mixtures.

In adapting the appetizers of other countries to our needs, we have changed them into finger foods whether they began that way or not, because who can handle a plate and fork with one hand while holding a drink in the other?

At their simplest, appetizers may be nothing more than vegetable relishes, raw or pickled, accompanied perhaps by a dip and salted nibblers. But when a formal meal is planned, regard appetizers as the introductory course, even if a formal first course, such as soup, seafood cocktail, or stuffed avocado is to be served at table.

Use the Good Eating Wheel as a guide in planning an elaborate hors d'oeuvre spread; when selecting appetizer foods, think of color, texture, and contrasts of flavor and seasoning. Avoid two very rich or two fried appetizers; if one is very highly seasoned, offer others more delicately flavored; one hot appetizer makes the chilled ones more interesting. Three kinds of appetizer are about right as a prelude to dinner; for example, a tray or bowl of vegetable relishes, a pâté with crackers, and shrimp.

Canapes are difficult for a servantless home, because bread becomes soggy with standing. There are ways to overcome this: use fried bread, which will stand up better than plain bread or toast, or spread butter on bread very thickly before adding other ingredients, or cover the decorated canapes with clear aspic. These are all time-consuming operations. The easiest way, which is perfectly proper in an American home, is to set out a pâté with a knife for spreading and a selection of crackers or chips so that guests can help themselves, in effect making their own canapes.

Snacks are by definition the foods eaten between meals or before bed, but many of the same foods that serve as before-dinner appetizers are equally good as snacks. The difference is primarily in the way they are served: often only the makings are put out, so that snackers may put together whatever combinations they like.

Some snacks are substantial enough to be little meals. Should Swiss Fondue, for example, be classed as a snack or an entree? It's hearty enough to be considered a meal, yet depending on the way it is served, it can be more like a snack. The same is true of Quiche Lorraine, pizzas, and Welsh Rarebit. Each of these, in turn, may be served at a cocktail party. Even sandwiches in dainty form qualify as appetizers; a canape could be called a cameo version of an open-faced sandwich.

VEGETABLE RELISHES

At least one kind of vegetable relish belongs with every hors d'oeuvre spread. An assortment is more attractive. Some may be raw, some cooked or canned, some pickled.

Raw vegetables, especially celery, carrots, and radishes, will be more crisp and flavorful if soaked in iced salted water for half an hour, then well drained and kept covered in the refrigerator until shortly before time to serve.

ARTICHOKE HEARTS. Unless artichokes are grown locally, the frozen or canned hearts are less expensive than the fresh, and they are available throughout the year. For ways to cook, see Book 3, Chapter 8, "Vegetables."

AVOCADO BALLS OR CUBES. Cut a ripe avocado in cubes or balls (using a melon cutter), keep completely covered by oil-vinegar sauce until time to serve, then remove from marinade, roll in minced parsely, and serve with cocktail picks. Attractive with radishes and cauliflower buds.

BEETS. Canned whole beets are the easiest to serve; spear each with a cocktail pick and dip in sour cream. Or, marinate in oil-vinegar sauce with a bit of dry mustard added.

CARROT SLIVERS. Cut carrots in half lengthwise, lay on counter or chopping board with flat side down, and cut each half in three or more sections lengthwise. Soak in salted iced water ½ hour; drain; keep covered in refrigerator until shortly before time to serve.

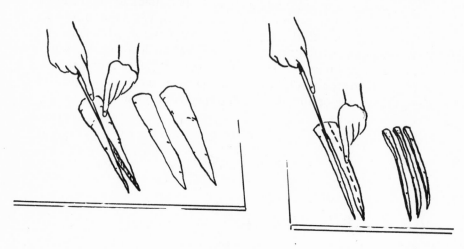

CARROT CURLS. Large, thick carrots are best for these. With a vegetable parer, cut wide slice down the length of carrot. Roll slice around index finger, fasten with a toothpick. Place in salted iced water for ½ hour; remove from water, and take out toothpick. Curl will remain in shape. Keep chilled, covered, until shortly before time to serve.

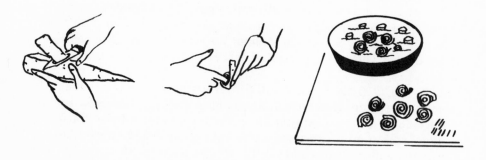

CAULIFLOWER BUDS. Separate a head of cauliflower into buds, and cut larger ones in halves or quarters. Soak in salted ice water 15 minutes; drain; keep wrapped in plastic in refrigerator until time to serve. Especially good with Curry Mayonnaise as a dip.

CELERY CURLS. Cut celery stalks in 2½-inch lengths. With a small sharp knife, cut each end in slivers, then place in salted water until ends curl up. Remove from water; drain; keep covered in refrigerator until time to set out on platter.

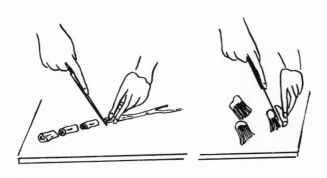

CHERRY TOMATOES. Wash, serve as is (with green caps, if any, left on). Or, cut a slit in the top of each, and fill with smoked oysters, cream cheese, Camembert, Liederkranz cheese, canned tiny Danish shrimp, or liver pâté

CUCUMBER STICKS. Peel a thick cucumber, cut in half lengthwise (as for carrot slivers), then, laying halves flat on board or counter, cut each in as many pieces as possible, lengthwise. Soak in salted iced water 15 minutes; drain. Roll in minced parsley. Keep chilled, covered, until shortly before time to serve.

GREEN PEPPER STICKS. Seed crisp, fresh green peppers, trim away all white membrane, cut into sticks lengthwise. Serve in bundles; especially good with a sour cream-onion dip.

MUSHROOMS. Canned button mushrooms may be served just as they come from the can; or, drain and cover with commercial Italian dressing and a little minced parsley. Serve with cocktail picks.

Pickled Fresh Mushrooms

1 pound fresh button mushrooms	1/8 teaspoon crushed cumin
1/2 cup olive oil	1/2 teaspoon paprika
1 teaspoon salt	2 teaspoons minced parsley
1 tablespoon sugar	2/3 cup white wine vinegar
1/4 teaspoon orégano	Rings from 1 large onion slice

Select fresh white mushrooms. Wash thoroughly, but do not peel; only trim off ends of stems. Combine remaining ingredients, pour over mushrooms; let stand 12 to 24 hours at room temperature. Remove from sauce; drain well; serve with cocktail picks. No cooking necessary. *Makes 18 to 20 servings.*

OLIVES. Both green and black olives may be served just as they come from jar or delicatessen counter. Or, for variety, spike the brine in one of the following ways:

Garlic Olives. Place a slivered garlic bud in a jar of green olives for 24 hours before serving.

Vermouth Olives. Pour off half the brine from a jar of green olives, add dry vermouth. Marinate several hours before serving.

Sherried Black Olives. Drain liquid from 1-pound can pitted California black olives, saving juice. Combine 1/2 cup of juice with 1/2 cup sherry, 1 teaspoon cider or sherry vinegar, and 1/4 teaspoon thyme. Cover olives with mixture; marinate several hours. Drain before serving. *Makes about 12 servings.*

PIMIENTO. Drain canned pimientos, cut in 2-inch squares, sauté in olive oil with 2 or 3 peeled garlic cloves until delicately browned. Remove garlic; discard. Sprinkle pimiento squares with salt. Serve cold as an hors d'oeuvre, sprinkled with minced fresh parsley. Very nice with artichoke hearts and green olives.

RADISHES. If small and well shaped, simply soak whole radishes in salted iced water for 1/2 hour, drain, keep chilled until shortly before time to serve. Or, for a fancier effect, make *Rad-*

ish Roses. With small sharp knife, cut part way through each radish in vertical slivers. Or, remove top, cut partway down the sides of each radish. Soak in salted iced water to make radishes curl. Serve chilled. For *Radis au Beurre*, a French favorite, serve sweet butter with the radishes.

TURNIP STICKS. Peel white turnips, cut in sticks or slivers. Sprinkle with salt. Serve in bundles. Sweet and crunchy, need no sauce or dip. (Also very low in calories.)

Dilled Vegetables

Carrots, green beans, cherry tomatoes, celery, and mushrooms can all be dilled this easy way. Simply save the brine (liquid) from a can of dill pickles; add the brine to saucepan containing the vegetable along with ¼ teaspoon salt and a sprig of fresh or frozen dill (or 1 teaspoon dried dill weed). Bring to a boil, cook raw carrot sticks, whole green beans, or celery sticks about 6 minutes, until partially cooked but still crisp. Keep in liquid in refrigerator until time to serve.

Cherry tomatoes and fresh mushrooms need not be actually cooked in the dill mixture; simply bring to a boil, turn off heat, let stand until liquid is cooled, then refrigerate.

Canned button mushrooms can be marinated in a mixture of equal parts dill brine and red wine vinegar, plus a dash of powdered cumin and sugar to taste.

Wrap-ups

A quick, easy way to prepare attractive hors d'oeuvres is to wrap very thin slices of ham (prosciutto or Westphalian), smoked salmon, or salami around chunks of fruit or vegetables. Or, wrap pimiento squares or strips around chunks of sardines, or a mixture of caviar and cottage cheese.

ARTICHOKE HEARTS IN HAM. Roll each cooked or canned artichoke in a slice of prosciutto cut to fit; fasten with a pick. Serve plain, or dribble Italian dressing over the wrap-up.

RADISHES IN HAM. Use either very tiny radishes or larger radishes cut in quarters; wrap strips of prosciutto around each; fasten with pick.

GHERKINS IN SALAMI. Roll tiny sweet gherkins in very thin slices of salami; fasten each with a pick.

CUCUMBER CUBES IN SALMON. Peel cucumber, cut in small cubes, sprinkle lightly with salt, vinegar, and oil, let stand ½ hour. Drain. Roll in minced parsley, then wrap with strips of smoked salmon. Fasten with pick.

HONEYDEW IN PROSCIUTTO. Cut honeydew melon in small cubes, wrap each with a slice of prosciutto, fasten with pick.

PINEAPPLE IN PROSCIUTTO. Cut fresh pineapple in cubes or wedges, sweeten if necessary, wrap with strips of prosciutto or Westphalian ham, fasten with pick.

SALAMI AND PIMIENTO. Cut strips of thin-sliced salami and strips of canned pimiento to fit. Roll up, fasten with picks. Marinate in a mixture of 3 parts oil, 1 part vinegar, and a dash of salt. Drain well before serving. Serve garnished with parsley sprigs, accompanied by black olives.

Stuffed Celery

Celery is a universal favorite, and almost any pâté, cheese spread, or salad mixture may be used to stuff it (omitting, minced celery from salad mixtures). Cut stalks into 2- or 2½-inch lengths, using the wider part for stuffing.

Oriental Stuffed Mushrooms

15 to 20 large mushrooms	½ cup minced cooked pork
2 tablespoons butter	¼ cup fine soft bread crumbs
¼ cup minced celery	1 tablespoon soy sauce
2 tablespoons chopped onion	1 teaspoon lemon juice

Remove stems from mushrooms; mince stems. Sauté caps in 1 tablespoon of the butter until lightly browned. Remove. Melt remaining butter, add minced mushroom stems, celery, and onion; cook until soft. Add pork, bread crumbs, soy sauce, and lemon juice; stir until well blended. Stuff caps with mixture. Place on broiler pan. Shortly before serving, place under broiler until filling is lightly browned. Serve hot. *Makes 15 to 20.*

Stuffed Cucumbers

Core cucumbers first. Select fairly thin cucumbers, averaging 6 inches in length. Partially peel (leaving lengthwise strips), cut slices from ends of each so that they will stand upright. Scoop out centers, leaving a hollow core. Sprinkle cucumbers with salt, sugar, and vinegar; let stand ½ hour. Place upright on counter, over waxed paper; force filling inside, packing as tightly as possible. Chill until filling is firm, then slice thickly.

SALMON STUFFING (for 3 Cucumbers)

1 1-pound can red salmon, drained	cottage cheese
2 tablespoons cream cheese or	2 tablespoons softened butter
	1 tablespoon minced parsley

Combine stuffing ingredients, beat until smooth. Divide in thirds, pack into centers of cucumbers. Chill until filling is firm, then cut in slices ¼ to ½ inch wide. Sprinkle additional minced parsley over tops of each slice. Keep chilled until time to serve. *Makes about 18 slices.*

BLUE CHEESE STUFFING (for 2 Cucumbers)

1 cup creamed cottage cheese	1 tablespoon minced green onion
1 4-ounce wedge blue cheese, crumbled	2 tablespoons minced parsley
2 tablespoons softened butter	Salt

Combine all ingredients, beat until smooth. Force filling into hollowed cucumbers, packing tightly. Chill until filling is firm, then slice thickly. Sprinkle additional minced parsley over tops. *Makes about 12 slices.*

Dolmadakia (Stuffed Grape Leaves)

1 medium onion, chopped	2 slices bread, soaked in water, squeezed dry, or ½ cup rice (uncooked)
1 pound lean lamb or beef	
2 cloves garlic, crushed	
3 tablespoons olive oil	1 12-ounce jar vine (grape) leaves in brine*
½ cup chopped parsley	
¾ teaspoon salt	½ cup boiling water
¼ teaspoon thyme	½ cup tomato juice
2 tablespoons pine nuts	½ cup olive oil

Sauté onion, meat, and garlic in olive oil until onion is soft. Add parsley, salt, thyme, pine nuts, and bread or rice. Cool mixture slightly.

Remove vine leaves from jar, lay out on board in overlapping pairs. Into each pair, spoon a little of the filling. Fold over sides, roll up. Place in skillet, overlapping sides down. Add boiling water, tomato juice, and olive oil. Weight down with plate. Simmer 30 to 40 minutes until tender. Serve cold. *Makes 25 to 30.*

*Available in Greek delicatessens, or you can blanch freshly picked smooth leaves by covering them with boiling salted water; allow to stand in water 10 minutes.

PÂTÉS, SPREADS, AND DIPS

A *pâté* is any paste of minced foods, usually beaten until smooth. A *spread* is also made of minced ingredients, but is not so smooth. A *dip* is thinner in consistency, so that other foods can be dipped into it—some dips are pure liquid, others are creamy. In addition to the dips listed here, there are a number of sauce recipes which can be used as dips to be found in Book 3, Chapter 2, "Sauces and Soups."

Potted Cheese

Use bits and pieces of cheese that have become dried up to make this zesty spread.

1½ to 2 cups grated or shredded cheese (any kind, firm or soft)
2 tablespoons butter or olive oil
Dash cayenne pepper, or powdered cloves
2 tablespoons bourbon, cognac, aquavit, beer, or ale mixture

Beat all ingredients together by hand or in blender until smooth. Age in a covered jar or crock at least 2 days. Before serving, allow to soften at room temperature. *Makes about 1 cup.*

CHEESE AND CHUTNEY SPREAD. To above mixture add 3 tablespoons minced chutney.

Guacamole

2 ripe avocados
1 clove garlic, crushed*
1 to 2 tablespoons olive oil
1 teaspoon lemon juice
2 dashes Tabasco, or ⅛ teaspoon cayenne
¼ teaspoon salt, or to taste

Make sure avocados are fully ripe before peeling; the skin must yield easily to pressure. If the avocados turn out to be overripe when peeled, cut away all discolored sections. Crush garlic to juice in small mixing bowl; discard any remaining shreds. Add avocado, mash with back of spoon to blend with garlic. Stir in olive oil, lemon juice, Tabasco (or cayenne) and salt. Beat until light and fluffy. Sprinkle additional lemon juice over top. Keep covered with waxed paper until time to serve. Serve with corn chips as a dip, or as a sauce for cooked shrimp. *Makes 1 cup.*

*Instead of garlic, 1 teaspoon grated onion may be used.

Potted Ham

¾ cup chopped ham
2 teaspoons Worcestershire sauce
2 tablespoons butter
2 teaspoons grated onion

1 to 2 teaspoons horseradish
1 tablespoon bourbon or brandy
2 tablespoons tomato catsup

Place all ingredients in blender, beat until smooth. Place in small crock or bowl. Improves in flavor if allowed to marinate 24 hours before serving. *Makes about 1/2 cup.*

Potted Shrimp

1 teaspoon lemon juice
2 tablespoons medium sherry
2 tablespoons shrimp liquid
Dash Tabasco
2 tablespoons butter

1 tablespoon freeze-dried chives
Salt, pepper
6 ounces shelled shrimp,
    cooked, or 6 ½-ounce can
    shrimp, drained

Place all ingredients but shrimp in blender, cover, beat until well blended. Add shrimp a few at a time until coarsely chopped. Stop blender occasionally, push down mixture with rubber spatula. Continue beating until fairly smooth. Transfer to bowl; cover with waxed paper, chill until time to serve. Serve garnished with capers and pimiento strips. *Makes 1 1/4 cups.*

Curried Tuna Pâté

1 envelope unflavored gelatin
¼ cup cold water
1 7-ounce can chunk tuna, drained
½ cup chopped celery
½ lemon, seeded, quartered

1 small onion, quartered
1 teaspoon curry powder
½ teaspoon salt
½ cup boiling water

Soften gelatin in cold water. Place with all remaining ingredients in blender; beat until fairly smooth. If necessary, stop blender occasionally to push down mixture around blades. Turn mixture into mold; chill until firm. Unmold. Serve with thin Finn-Crisp wafers for a delicious low-calorie appetizer. *Makes 1¾ cups.*

Quick Tuna Pâté

1 7-ounce can chunk tuna, drained	1 tablespoon capers, chopped
¼ teaspoon curry powder	1 tablespoon minced parsley
1 teaspoon garlic salad dressing	1 tablespoon olive oil
mix*	1 tablespoon mayonnaise

Combine all ingredients in bowl, mix lightly until well blended. Serve garnished with minced parsley and pimiento strips. *Makes 1 cup.*

*Or use ½ teaspoon garlic powder, a pinch of salt, and ¼ teaspoon crushed orégano.

Crab-Almond Pâté

1 6 ½-ounce can crabmeat	2 tablespoons minced parsley
¼ cup blanched almonds	¼ teaspoon salt
1 tablespoon oil	2 tablespoons dry sherry

Drain crabmeat, remove any bits of gristle. Sauté the almonds in oil until lightly browned. If you have a blender, crush the almonds with the oil in the blender, then add crabmeat, a little at a time, parsley, salt, and sherry; beat until fairly smooth. Or, to prepare by hand, chop nuts fine, mix in bowl with remaining ingredients, beat until fairly smooth. *Makes 3/4 cup.*

Potted Bubbly-Jock

"Roasted Bubbly-Jock" was the old Scots name for roast turkey with sausage-liver stuffing.

1½ cups chopped cooked turkey	1 turkey liver, fried until crisp
1 tablespoon grated onion	¼ cup diced cooked pork
1 tablespoon butter	sausage, well drained

Add chopped bits of turkey gradually to blender until turkey is beaten to shreds, then add remaining ingredients in the order given: beat until puréed. Transfer to small crock or earthenware casserole. Spread top with additional softened butter Chill. *Makes 2 cups.*

If you do not have a blender, put turkey, a quarter of an onion, liver, and sausage through a food grinder, blend with butter and cream.

Herb Butter

Allow ¼ pound butter to soften at room temperature, then work in 2 tablespoons fresh herbs (parsley, dill, tarragon, basil, orégano, or thyme) or 1 teaspoon dried herbs.

Picante de Huevos (Mexican Appetizer)

6 hard-cooked eggs, chopped
2 ripe avocados, peeled,
  chopped
3 tablespoons minced parsley
¼ teaspoon ground dried hot
  chili peppers, or ⅛

teaspoon cayenne
1 teaspoon grated onion
2 tablespoons vinegar
½ teaspoon salt, or to
  taste

Combine all ingredients; chop fine but do not beat. Chill. Serve from a bowl with corn chips or on toast rounds for a canape, or use as stuffing for celery. *Makes 1¾ cups.*

Chopped Chicken Livers

1 pound chicken livers
3 tablespoons sweet butter or
  chicken fat
½ cup chopped onion

1 teaspoon salt
½ cup dry white wine
Sieved cooked egg yolk
  for garnish

Sauté the chicken livers in butter or chicken fat until well browned. Add onion after livers are partially cooked; cook until onion is soft. Season with salt. Transfer to blender, add wine, beat until smooth. Place in a serving bowl; sprinkle egg yolk over the top. Chill. *Makes 2 cups.*

Molded Shrimp Pâté

2½ cups cooked shrimp (12
  ounces already shelled frozen
  shrimp)
½ cup dry sherry
1 envelope unflavored gelatin
¼ cup cold water
½ cup boiling water

Pimiento-stuffed olives for garnish
1 tablespoon instant minced onion
2 cups mayonnaise
1 teaspoon lemon juice
¼ teaspoon salt

For best flavor, cook the shrimp gently in herb-and-wine-flavored broth (see "Boiled" Shrimp). Let cool in broth, then remove; place in blender with sherry and beat until puréed. Soften gelatin in ¼ cup cold water; add ½ cup boiling water, stir to dissolve. Pour a small amount of this clear gelatin in bottom of 1-quart mold (preferably a fish-shaped mold). Place slice of olive over spot for eye of fish in fish mold, place carrot slivers where fins belong. Chill until garnishes are firmly held in place.

    Meantime, add instant onion to remaining gelatin, then combine gelatin mixture with shrimp, mayonnaise, lemon juice and salt, beating until mixture is smooth. Pour into mold, filling to top. Chill until aspic is very firm—at least 4 hours. Unmold on long platter; keep chilled until time to serve. *Makes enough to serve 25 to 30 persons for a formal cocktail buffet.*

Liptauer Cheese Cone

1 8-ounce package cream cheese, softened
2 tablespoons butter, softened
1 anchovy fillet, chopped
1 teaspoon mustard

1 teaspoon caraway seeds, crushed
½ teaspoon paprika
Capers for garnish

Blend all ingredients but capers. With spatula, form into tall cone. With back of spoon, make indentation down sides of cone, in a swirl. Press capers along the indentation in lines. Chill. Serve with Rye-Krisp or pumpernickel slices. *Makes 1 cup.*

Classic Cocktail Sauce

¾ cup tomato catsup
1 to 2 tablespoons horseradish
2 tablespoons lemon juice

Dash of Tabasco or cayenne (optional)

Blend ingredients well. Serve immediately, or keep sauce in refrigerator to use as needed (it will keep fresh almost indefinitely). Good with shrimp, lobster, crabmeat, mixed seafood, or as a dip for cocktail frankfurters or meatballs. *Makes less than 1 cup sauce.*

Mustard-Cream Sauce

Blend 2 tablespoons very hot prepared mustard into ½ cup sour cream. Add Tabasco or cayenne and salt to taste. Use as a dip for meat sticks or seafood.

Chinese Mustard

Use either dry English mustard or powdered Chinese mustard from an oriental grocery. Blend with white wine or vinegar to consistency of thin cream.

Yogurt Dip

1 cup thick yogurt
1 teaspoon grated onion or 1 large clove garlic, crushed
¼ teaspoon curry powder, or

powdered ginger
1 tablespoon minced parsley or cucumber
Salt

Combine ingredients, blend well. Serve as a dip for vegetable relishes or seafood, or as a sauce for seafood. *Makes 1 cup.*

The Duke's Dip

6 hard-cooked eggs, peeled
1 tablespoon olive oil
2 anchovy fillets, chopped
2 thin slices onion
1 stalk celery
¼ cup chopped green pepper

¼ cup chopped pimiento
¼ cup mayonnaise
1 teaspoon red wine vinegar
Salt, pepper
1 tablespoon minced parsley

Add eggs to blender one at a time; beat until chopped fine. Add oil, anchovy, onion, and celery to blender; keep blender in motion until chopped fine. Add all remaining ingredients but parsley; beat until fairly smooth. Place in bowl. Garnish with minced parsley. *Makes a little under 1 cup.*

Caponatina (Italian Eggplant Relish)

2 cups diced celery
½ cup olive oil
6 cups unpeeled eggplant, cut in
   cubes
1 large onion, chopped
1/3 cup red wine vinegar
1 teaspoon sugar

2 tablespoons tomato paste
1 cup water
1 tablespoon capers, drained
¼ cup chopped green olives
1 tablespoon minced parsley
Salt

Cook celery in olive oil until golden; remove. Add eggplant to oil; cook until soft and lightly browned. Add onion; cook until soft, but do not allow to brown. Remove eggplant and onion; drain on absorbent paper. Pour off oil from pan; add vinegar, sugar, tomato paste, and water. Simmer, uncovered, for 15 minutes. Replace vegetables, add capers, olives, parsley, and salt; simmer 10 minutes. Cool. Serve at room temperature as an hors d'oeuvre relish, accompanied by crusty bread. *Makes 6 to 10 servings.*

Hot Shrimp Dip

1 10½-ounce can frozen
   cream of shrimp soup
¼ cup dry vermouth

½ teaspoon curry
Few drops lemon juice

Heat soup with vermouth and curry, stirring until smooth. Add lemon juice just before serving. Serve from chafing dish, or keep warm in casserole over candle burner. Dunk vegetable relishes or meat sticks (ham, luncheon meat, or roast beef) into dip. *Makes 1 3/4 cups.*

COLD SHRIMP PASTE. Omit vermouth from above recipe, using 1 3-ounce package cream cheese instead. Add a bit of garlic powder, if desired. Heat to blend, then chill. Serve as a spread for crackers.

Bagne Caude (Italian Hot Garlic Dip)

4 tablespoons butter	A few fresh basil leaves, or
4 tablespoons olive oil	⅛ teaspoon dried basil
3 or 4 cloves garlic, slit	1 cup heavy cream
8 anchovy fillets, rinsed, chopped	Vegetable Relishes

Place butter and oil in a heavy skillet over moderate heat; add garlic, cook until garlic is golden, but take care that neither garlic nor butter turns brown. When garlic is soft, press with tines of fork to release juices into oil, then remove and discard garlic. Remove pan from heat. Add anchovy (rinsed with warm water to remove excess salt) and basil; beat vigorously until anchovy is blended and mixture is smooth. Separately place the cream over moderate heat in an enameled saucepan, bring to a boil but beat constantly with a whisk to prevent actual boiling, cook until cream is reduced and thickened. Carefully stir cream into anchovy mixture, beating with whisk to blend thoroughly. Serve the hot dip at once (it may curdle if reheated; if this should happen, beat vigorously with a whisk or in the blender). Offer with it assorted vegetable relishes, which may include celery sticks, strips of crisp green or red sweet peppers, carrot sticks, turnip sticks, cucumber sticks, scallions. These should have been soaked in salted ice water, then drained and kept chilled until time to serve. *Makes 1 cup dip, very rich but marvelous.*

Red-Hot Indonesian Dip

2 tablespoons soy sauce	1 tablespoon brown sugar or honey
1 medium onion, minced	
¼ cup lemon juice	⅛ teaspoon ginger
½ teaspoon dried hot red pepper flakes	¼ cup water

Combine all ingredients in small pan, bring to a boil, simmer 5 minutes. Strain. Serve as clear dip for shrimp, meatballs, or cocktail franks. *Makes 1/2 cup.*

Taramasalata (Greek Red Caviar Appetizer)

2/3 cup red caviar (from salmon
or red mullet)
2 thick onion slices
1 clove garlic, crushed
1 teaspoon minced parsley

2 tablespoons lemon juice
2 slices white bread, crusts
trimmed
1 cup olive oil

Place caviar in blender, add onion, garlic, parsley, and lemon juice; turn blender on, off, on, off until mixture is smooth. Add part of the bread, broken in pieces, and part of the olive oil with blender in motion, continuing to add bread and oil until mixture is as stiff as mayonnaise. Chill. Serve cold with crackers or toast fingers. *Makes 1 3/4 cups.*

Green Caviar (Eggplant Dip)

1 large very fresh eggplant
1 small onion, quartered
2 cloves garlic, crushed
¼ cup minced parsley
½ green pepper, seeded, minced

(optional)
2 to 3 tablespoons olive oil
1 teaspoon vinegar
½ cup yogurt or sour cream
(optional)

Roast eggplant in oven or over charcoal fire until skin is wrinkled. Peel off skin; press out excess liquid from pulp. Place in blender with remaining ingredients, beat until smooth. (If adding yogurt or sour cream, stir mixture after removing from blender.) Serve chilled on lettuce with additional minced parsley for garnish. *Makes about 2 cups.*

APPETIZER SALADS

These may be served as part of buffet spread, to be eaten with forks, or may be offered as help-yourself canape toppings. Often the most delicious salad mixtures are those made with bits of leftovers, combined with just enough dressing to hold the mixture together, seasoned imaginatively with such unusual flavors as caraway, cumin, ginger, horseradish, or dill.

The following basic recipe with variations may be used as your general guide, but try adding other things, such as raw turnip, chopped apple, diced oranges, or leftover cooked vegetables (peas, green beans, limas, beets, or asparagus). Everything must be minced—and always go light on the dressing.

Basic Appetizer Salad

1 cup minced meat, poultry, or seafood

1 teaspoon grated onion, or 1 clove garlic, crushed

¼ cup minced celery

2 tablespoons minced green pepper

2 tablespoons chopped pimiento

1 to 2 tablespoons oil

1 to ½ tablespoon vinegar

1 tablespoon minced parsley

1 to 2 tablespoons mayonnaise or sour cream

Salt

Combine all ingredients, blend well; chill. Serve on lettuce; sprinkle minced parsley over top, or garnish with pimiento slivers. *Makes 1 1/2 cups.*

LOBSTER APPLE SALAD. Prepare as above, using 1 cup cooked or canned lobster; add ½ cup diced tart apple, and use a combination of sour cream and mayonnaise. Add curry powder to taste (about ¼ teaspoon).

SHRIMP OR CRABMEAT SALAD. Prepare basic recipe, using 1 cup minced shrimp or flaked crabmeat.

CORNED BEEF SALAD. Use 1 cup chopped corned beef (cooked or canned); instead of green pepper, add chopped gherkin pickles; add 1 tablespoon catsup.

CHICKEN AND PEA SALAD. Use 1 cup chopped cooked chicken (or turkey), omit pimiento, add ½ cup cooked green peas. Omit green pepper, oil and vinegar. Season with a pinch of cumin.

HAM-MUSHROOM SALAD. Use 1 cup diced cooked ham, add 1 cup chopped raw mushrooms and ¼ teaspoon cumin.

CARIBBEAN CLAM OR CONCH SALAD. Use chopped conch, or 1 can chopped sea clams, well-drained. Use very thinly sliced rather than grated onion; omit green pepper and mayonnaise.

PORK AND TOMATO SALAD. Use 1 cup cooked minced pork; omit pimiento and celery, add ¼ cup diced raw turnip; add ¼ teaspoon cumin or powdered ginger. Garnish with cherry tomatoes or tomato wedges and sprinkle sieved egg yolk over top.

MUSHROOM-EGG SALAD. Instead of meat, use ½ cup (4-ounce can) mushroom bits and pieces, well drained, and 2 hard-cooked eggs, chopped. If desired, add 1 tomato, chopped. Use sour cream rather than mayonnaise.

TUNA-PICKLE SALAD. Use 7-ounce can tuna, well drained; instead of green pepper, use minced dill pickle or sweet gherkins; add ½ teaspoon prepared mustard. Use thinly sliced rather than grated onion.

HERRING SALAD. Chop pickled herring to make 1 cup; add ¼ cup diced tart apple and 1 orange, diced and seeded. Use sour cream rather than mayonnaise, omit oil and vinegar.

LUNCHEON MEAT SALAD. Use a mixture of chopped bologna or frankfurters, chopped salami, and ham. Use chopped pickles instead of green pepper (either gherkins or mustard pickles); omit oil. Season with a generous amount of freshly ground black pepper.

Salpicon de Mariscos

2 3½-ounce cans small California shrimp, or 2 jars tiny Danish shrimp, or 1 6½-ounce can shrimp, well drained
2 small white onions, sliced paper-thin
1 carrot, cooked until tender-crisp, cut into tiny cubes
1 cup cooked peas
¼ cup diced pimiento
¼ cup olive oil
½ cup wine vinegar
Salt

Mince shrimp, combine with remaining ingredients, marinate at least 1 hour before serving. *Makes about 10 appetizer servings.*

SPANISH TUNA SALAD. Drain canned white-meat or chunk-style tuna, toss the tuna with fresh olive oil and a little red wine vinegar or lemon juice. Add a small onion, very thinly sliced, and a generous amount of minced parsley. Serve as an hors d'oeuvre salad or part of an antipasto. For a cocktail spread, beat the tuna with a fork until all the pieces are well broken up.

Egg and Sardine Salad

1 can Portuguese sardines
Few drops vinegar or lemon juice
2 hard-cooked eggs
¼ cup minced pimiento
1 teaspoon capers

3 tablespoons olive oil
1 tablespoon vinegar
½ teaspoon orégano
¼ teaspoon salt, or to taste
Freshly ground black pepper

Drain sardines on absorbent paper; in a bowl, sprinkle with vinegar or lemon juice. Mash lightly with fork (if desired, remove skin and bones). Combine with remaining ingredients, tossing lightly. Serve over thin slices of pumpernickel. *Makes 1 cup.*

Salade Russe

1 cup finely diced cooked carrots
1 cup cooked green peas
¼ cup minced celery
1 tablespoon minced parsley

2 to 3 tablespoons mayonnaise
Salt, pepper
Pimiento slivers

Combine all ingredients but pimiento; blend well. Serve over lettuce, or use as a canape topping. Garnish with pimiento. *Makes 2 1/4 cups.*

Fried Bread Circles

To turn any of the foregoing salad mixtures into party canapes, cut day-old bread in circles (use a biscuit cutter), fry in butter or olive oil until crisp on each side. Drain well. Top with salad mixture during last hour before guests are due, (Bread must be stale; when fresh, it absorbs more fat.)

Vorschmack (Russian Herring Salad)

2 salt herrings
2 cups milk
1 medium onion, quartered
1 tart apple, peeled, chopped
2 slices dark rye bread, crumbled
3 tablespoons olive oil

2 tablespoons vinegar
1 1-pound can small whole
   beets, drained
1 1-pound can black olives,
   drained
1 lemon, thinly sliced

Soak herring in milk 24 hours. Remove from milk and discard milk; bone and skin herrings. Place onion in blender, beat until finely minced. Add herring fillets, cut in cubes, apple, bread, and oil. Beat until fairly smooth, then stir in vinegar. Remove from blender; shape into mound on round platter or plate with beets and black olives as garnish. Arrange lemon slices on top. Serve with thin-sliced pumpernickel. *Makes 2 cups.*

Rhinelander Herring Salad

1 jar pickled herring, drained
½ cup diced cooked or canned
  beets. well drained
½ cup peeled chopped apple
2 medium potatoes, cooked, diced
1 small onion, minced
½ cup chopped walnuts (optional)

½ cup sour cream
½ cup mayonnaise
1 teaspoon sugar, or to taste
1 hard-cooked egg, sliced
6 to 8 small whole beets
1 tablespoon minced parsley
  or dill

Combine herring with diced beets, apple, potatoes, onion, and nuts. Toss with sour cream, mayonnaise, and sugar. Arrange in a bowl or on a platter; place egg slices over top and whole beets around the edges for garnish. Sprinkle with minced parsley or dill. Serve with sliced pumpernickel and sweet butter. *Makes 6 to 8 appetizer servings.*

Garbanzo Salad

1 1-pound can chick-peas
  (garbanzos), drained
3 green onions (scallions),
  minced
1 or 2 cloves garlic, crushed
1 large tomato, chopped, or

¼ cup chopped pimiento
¼ cup minced parsley
6 tablespoons olive oil
2 tablespoons wine vinegar
½ teaspoon salt
Freshly ground black pepper

Combine all ingredients, blend well. Marinate several hours. Serve at room temperature. *Makes 8 appetizer servings.*

Gigantes (Greek Bean Salad)

1 1-pound can dried white beans
1 tablespoon olive oil
1 teaspoon grated onion

2 tablespoons chopped parsley
1 to 2 tablespoons vinegar

Heat the beans in their own liquid; when hot, drain well, then immediately add remaining ingredients. Let stand at room temperature several hours before serving. Serve cold (but not chilled). *Makes 8 hors d'oeuvre servings.*

Deviled Eggs (Basic Recipe)

6 small hard-cooked eggs
1 teaspoon prepared mustard
1 teaspoon grated onion (optional)

Salt, pepper
2 to 3 tablespoons mayonnaise

Let hard-cooked eggs cool completely before removing shells. Cut in half lengthwise, remove yolks. Mash yolks lightly with tines of fork, add remaining ingredients, beat until fluffy. Pile mixture in whites. Sprinkle minced parsley, paprika, or chopped pimiento over tops. *Makes 12 stuffed halves.*

SHRIMP-STUFFED EGGS. Add a little minced shrimp to sieved egg yolk, season with curry powder (¼ teaspoon) instead of mustard, use half mayonnaise, half chili sauce. Garnish with capers.

ANCHOVY-STUFFED EGGS. Add a little minced anchovy, use 1 teaspoon horseradish instead of mustard, and use half mayonnaise, half sour cream. Garnish with pimiento strips.

HAM-STUFFED EGGS. Add minced ham to egg yolk mixture (½ cup for 6 egg yolks, ¼ cup for 3 egg yolks.)

PÂTÉ-STUFFED EGGS. Add ¼ cup liver pâté to 6 egg yolks (or half this much for 3 egg yolks), use sour cream instead of mayonnaise, omit mustard, sprinkle minced parsley or chopped green pepper over top.

DEVILED EGG PLATTER. Vary the basic recipe by adding a little minced shrimp, chopped ham, liver pâté, grated Cheddar or crumbled Roquefort to the yolk mixture; some may contain shrimp, others cheese, and so on. Garnish with caviar, pimiento, or green pepper strips, or even nut halves.

EGG SLICES ON POTATO CHIPS. Hard-cook eggs; when cold, remove the shells. Slice with an egg-slicer. Serve egg slices on large firm potato chips as an appetizer.

CANAPES

Anchovy-Pimiento Canapes

Cut stale (2-day-old) bread into well-trimmed squares or circles. Fry lightly in oil or butter until crisp on each side. Cut pimientos to fit the bread; place a slice of pimiento on each. Place a curled anchovy (with caper in center) over each. Keep at room temperature until time to serve.

ON TOAST. Instead of fried bread, toast circles or squares may be used if preferred; pimiento base prevents juice from soaking into bread.

Anchovy and Egg Canapes

Slice hard-cooked eggs; place 1 slice on each buttered toast round (Melba toast may be used, or make your own). On each slice of egg, place a small square of anchovy.

Spicy Cheese Dreams

1 tablespoon minced onion
1 teaspoon beef-flavored stock base concentrate
1 3-ounce package cream cheese,

softened
½ cup grated Cheddar cheese
1 teaspoon prepared mustard
6 slices bread, crusts trimmed

Blend onion and stock concentrate with the two cheeses and mustard. Toast bread; cool. Spread cheese over toast. Cut slice of toast in 4 pieces. When ready to serve, place under broiler until cheese melts and is bubbly. *Makes 24 canapes.*

Louisiana Crab Canapes

These are *not* easy to make, but they are so delicious that the effort is worthwhile. Very rich!

CRABMEAT MIXTURE

2 tablespoons butter
1 small white onion or shallot, minced
1 tablespoon flour

½ cup chicken broth or white wine
1 6½-ounce can crabmeat

Melt butter, add onion, cook until onion is soft but not browned. Stir in flour, cook until mixture bubbles, then stir in broth, cook until smooth. Remove all gristle from crabmeat; flake. Stir crabmeat into broth. Cool.

CHEESE TOPPING

2 tablespoons butter
2 tablespoons flour
4 ounces (1 cup) grated Parmesan

cheese
4 ounces (1 cup) grated Swiss or Gruyère cheese

Melt butter, stir in flour, cook until mixture bubbles. Add cheeses, blend well. Cook, then form into firm round balls.

TO COMPLETE CANAPES

Cut an unsliced loaf of white bread lengthwise in slices ¼ inch thick. Cut into 1½-inch squares, fry in butter or oil until crisp. Drain well. Spread each square with crabmeat, then place cheese ball over each. Just before serving, place in hot oven (425° F.) for 5 minutes until melted and bubbly. *Makes about 50.*

Homemade Melba Toast

Freshly made Melba toast is infinitely better than the packaged commercial product, which is usually stale after being on the shelf for months. Simply buy unsliced white bread; when 1 day old, slice it quite thin, cut into circles with a biscuit cutter (or into squares, if that's easier), and toast slowly in an oven set at 300° F. until pale gold. Use the same day.

CHEESE FANCIES

Gorgonzola Balls

¼ pound (4 ounces) Gorgonzola cheese

¼ pound (1 stick) sweet butter
½ cup minced parsley

Blend cheese and butter together, beat until smooth. Form into 1-inch balls, refrigerate until firm, then roll each in parsley Chill until ready to serve. *Makes about 25.*

Pecan-crusted Cheese Balls

1 8-ounce package cream cheese
¼ cup milk
¼ cup grated Cheddar cheese

¼ cup minced onion
Dash of salt
¼ cup shelled pecans, crushed

Blend all ingredients but nuts until smooth. Shape into 1-inch balls, refrigerate until firm. Crush nuts in blender or with mortar and pestle; roll balls in nuts. Chill again until ready to serve. *Makes about 25.*

SESAME CHEESE BALLS. Instead of crushed pecans, roll cheese balls in toasted sesame seeds.

Shrimp-Cheese Balls

1 8-ounce package cream cheese, softened
1 tablespoon lemon juice
Dash of Tabasco
1 teaspoon onion juice or grated

onion
1 cup cooked or canned shrimp, minced
Chopped parsley or toasted sesame seeds

Combine all ingredients but parsley or sesame seeds; blend until smooth. Chill until mixture can be handled easily, then shape into small balls; roll balls in parsley or sesame seeds. Chill again until needed. *Makes about 35 ½-inch balls.*

SHRIMP-STUFFED CELERY. Use the above mixture as celery stuffing, but instead of Tabasco add a dash of curry powder.

Käsestangen (Cheese Twists)

2 cups sifted all-purpose flour
½ teaspoon salt
2 tablespoons vegetable shortening
½ pound (2 sticks) cold firm butter

6 tablespoons ice water
1 to 1½ cups shredded Swiss, Cheddar, or Cheshire cheese

Combine flour and salt, cut in vegetable shortening, work with fingers to blend well, then chop 1 stick of the butter in flour until pieces are the size of peas. Add the ice water 1 tablespoon at a time; blend to form firm dough. Roll out half at a time: dot each roll of pastry with butter in tiny pieces and spread the cheese over each, dividing evenly. Fold again in thirds, let stand 10 minutes, then roll out again. Repeat, this time chilling in refrigerator 10 minutes. Roll out the third time between sheets of waxed paper to prevent sticking. Cut in strips ½ x 2 inches, twist, then chill. Bake in oven preheated to 425° F. until crisp and golden, about 15 minutes. *Makes about 60.*

DANISH BLUE TWISTS. Instead of shredded firm cheese, sprinkle 1 cup crumbled Danish Blue Cheese over rolled pastry, in above recipe.

CURRIED CHEESE TWISTS. Add 1 teaspoon curry powder to basic recipe.

Nun's Beads

1 3-ounce package cream cheese, softened
⅛ teaspoon salt
2 egg yolks

Pastry for 2-crust pie, or 1 package piecrust mix
2 to 3 tablespoons milk

Beat together cream cheese, salt, and egg yolks until smooth. Roll out pastry, half at a time, to ⅛ inch thick. Cut into 2-inch rounds. Place a bit of cheese mixture in center of half the pastry rounds, cover with remaining rounds; seal by moistening edges, then pressing together with tines of fork. Brush tops with milk. Bake in oven preheated to 400° F. for 15 to 18 minutes, or until golden. Serve hot. (To prepare ahead, place pastries on baking sheet, freeze until firm, then transfer to plastic, wrap, and seal. Replace on baking sheet to bake when needed, allowing an extra 5 minutes' baking time.) *Makes 25 to 28 appetizer pastries.*

PETITS CHASSONS AU ROQUEFORT. Instead of cream cheese, use a 3- or 4-ounce wedge (or ¾ cup) crumbled Roquefort cheese; omit salt; add a little minced green onion or chives.

BOUREKAKIA. Use feta cheese (rather than cream cheese) and beaten egg; cut the pastry in squares, then fold over with the cheese inside. Brush melted butter, rather than milk, over the tops before baking.

CHEESE PROFITEROLES. Prepare Choux Paste, form into cocktail-size profiteroles. When baked, fill with cheese spread from pressure tube by inserting tube directly into the little pastries.

HAM PROFITEROLES. Use a mixture of equal amounts deviled ham and cream cheese, or use Ham Pâté, to fill profiterole cases.

Walnut-Cheese Sticks

Pastry for 1-crust pie, or ½ package piecrust mix
½ cup shredded sharp cheese

½ cup chopped nut meats (walnuts, almonds, or peanuts)

Prepare piecrust in the usual way, working in the cheese. Roll thin, sprinkle with the nuts, press nuts into the pastry with heel of palms or with a rolling pin. Cut into strips ½ inch x 2 inches. (May be frozen at this stage, for baking when needed.) Bake on baking sheet in oven preheated to 450° F. for about 6 minutes, or until golden. *Makes about 18.*

SEAFOOD APPETIZERS
Shrimp in Cocktail Sauce

Cook shrimp in simmering (not boiling) salted water for 2 minutes; turn off heat, let stand in liquid until cold. If not to be served immediately, store in the liquid, covered, until shortly before time to serve, then arrange shrimp around edge of a bowl containing Classic Cocktail Sauce.

SHRIMP WITH DIPS. Serve cooked shrimp with Guacamole, Green Mayonnaise, Curry Mayonnaise, or Soy-Horseradish Dip.

Sherried Shrimp

This is a two-in-one recipe. Either cook the shrimp first, then marinate in the remaining ingredients and serve cold, or marinate the raw shrimp in the remaining ingredients, and just before serving place the shrimp under the broiler, cooking until bright orange, and serve very hot.

1 pound shelled shrimp

2 to 3 tablespoons olive oil

2 tablespoons minced parsley   1/3 cup dry sherry
1 tablespoon wine vinegar   ½ teaspoon salt

If shrimp are to be cooked first, then marinated, take care to cook them gently—do not allow water to boil, only simmer.

If to be broiled, marinate raw shrimp in remaining ingredients for at least 1 hour (preferably 2), then remove from marinade to place under broiler, cook only until shrimp turn bright color, serve hot on cocktail picks with the reserved marinade as a dip. *Makes about 30 to 35 (depending on size of shrimp).*

Shrimp Vinagreta

1½ pounds shrimp in shells, cooked
3 tablespoons olive oil
1 teaspoon lemon juice
1 teaspoon vinegar

¼ teaspoon salt
1 teaspoon prepared mustard
1 tablespoon capers
1 tablespoon grated onion
1 hard-cooked egg

Shell shrimp, leaving tails intact. Combine all remaining ingredients but egg; blend well; pour over shrimp in bowl, tossing to mix ingredients. Marinate 1 hour or longer. Serve sprinkled with chopped egg as garnish. *Makes 25 to 30 appetizer servings.*

Shrimp Toast

6 ounces shelled shrimp, or ¾ pound shrimp in shell
5 canned water chestnuts, minced, or ¼ cup minced celery
1 teaspoon minced fresh ginger root, or ⅛ teaspoon powdered ginger
1 teaspoon grated onion

2 eggs, beaten
1½ teaspoons cornstarch
1 tablespoon sherry, beer, or gin
½ teaspoon salt
8 slices stale white bread, crusts trimmed
Oil for deep-frying

Shell, then mince shrimp without cooking. Combine shrimp with water chestnuts, ginger, onion, eggs, cornstarch, sherry, and salt. Beat (in blender if you have one) until very smooth. Spread mixture evenly over bread; cut each slice into 4 sections. Heat oil to 356° F. Place 1 piece at a time in slotted spoon, lower gently into hot oil. Repeat until as many "toasts" have been added to oil as it will hold without crowding. Turn over pieces to brown on the other side. Remove from oil; drain in absorbent paper. Repeat until all are fried.

These may be frozen *after frying* to be reheated and served later: place fried "toasts" on baking sheet, freeze until stiff, then transfer to freezer container. Cover tightly. Reheat without thawing in 350° F. oven shortly before serving. Serve hot. *Makes 32.*

Shrimp Baked in Foil

This method preserves the delicate flavor of shrimp, and some people find it easier than cooking them in water.

1 pound shelled shrimp	Juice of ½ lemon
½ teaspoon salt	2 tablespoons slivered lemon peel
3 green onions (scallions), minced	

Place *uncooked* shrimp in center of large sheet of foil (about 12 inches square). Sprinkle with salt, onion, and lemon juice. Add lemon peel; fold over foil, twist ends to secure. If not to be cooked immediately, refrigerate. Shortly before shrimp are to be served, bake in oven preheated to 450° F. for 10 minutes, or until shrimp are delicately pink. Serve hot like this, or with Soy-Horseradish Dip or Green Mayonnaise. *Makes about 30, depending on size of shrimp.*

SHRIMP TEMPURA is often served as a hot appetizer with dips. (See index.)

BABY LOBSTER TAILS, cooked delicately until the flesh is opaque and snowy white, make the most sumptuous of all before-dinner appetizers. Remove the meat from the shells, cut in thick slices, and serve on picks with almost any dip. These will go fast!

DEVILED CRAB BALLS can be prepared by the same recipe as for Deviled Crab Cakes Maryland—just form bite-size balls and deep-fry them to be served hot. Or, deep-fry ahead of time, freeze, reheat when needed. (The frozen miniature crab balls, ready to heat, are also good, one of the better frozen food products. Prepare according to package directions.)

BABY CODFISH BALLS also make fine hot hors d'oeuvres. Use the same recipe as for New England Codfish Cakes, but form into bite-sized balls, fry in deep fat. Like the crab balls, these can be prepared ahead and frozen, to be reheated in the oven when needed.

Caviar

True caviar, the roe of sturgeon, is the most costly of all hors d'oeuvre items—and, for those who like caviar, the most sumptuous. It need only be served ice-cold (usually in a bowl placed over cracked ice) with lemon wedges on the side, and freshly made Melba toast served with it. Beluga caviar (large gray eggs) is the most costly and the most delicate in flavor. Pressed black caviar is the cheapest, and much more "fishy" in flavor. "Red caviar" is not truly a caviar at all; it is salmon roe. Nor is lumpfish, which is black, caviar: It is the roe of a deep-water fish from the North Atlantic.

A few caviar eggs can be very effective used as a garnish on stuffed eggs, canapes, or smørrebrød, or over appetizer salads. Used in this way, caviar adds piquancy even for those who are not caviar lovers. But for decoration, one of the less costly types of caviar will do just as well.

Smoked Salmon Appetizer

Arrange slices of smoked salmon on a platter, cut in wide strips or rolled up, as you please. Garnish with capers and black olives; brush with olive oil. Serve with lemon wedges, the juice to be sprinkled over the salmon, and have a cruet of olive oil nearby for those who like their salmon generously doused with oil.

Instant Antipasto

Arrange attractively on a platter, or on individual plates, five or more of the following:

Sardines
Salami slices in rolls
Solid pack tuna
Pickled beets
Watercress
Green or black olives

Tomato slices sprinkled with parsley
Pimiento squares sprinkled with olive oil and capers
Artichoke hearts

Instant Hors d'Oeuvre Variées

Set out at least six of the following, each in individual dishes:

Sardines
Mackerel in white wine
Radishes
Very thinly sliced cucumber in Italian dressing
Herring in wine sauce (Scandinavian style)
Canned button mushrooms (marinated in dill pickle liquid)
Canned or cooked whole green

beans, marinated in Italian dressing
Smoked oysters or clams
Hard-cooked eggs, cut in halves
Tomato slices sprinkled with oil and tarragon
Ham slivers (canned or leftover) with capers and French dressing

If you have time, add to the above one or two salad mixtures, making use of any bits of leftovers in the refrigerator.

Sardine Hors d'Oeuvre

Serve Portuguese or Norwegian sardines just as they come from the can, sprinkled with minced parsley and lemon juice or sherry vinegar. Garnish with very thinly sliced onion rings and wedges of hard-cooked egg and cherry tomatoes (or tomato wedges).

Oysters

Fresh raw oysters served on the half-shell with lemon wedges and Tabasco sauce make a fine first course for a gourmet dinner, but oysters, like caviar, have limited appeal for many Americans, and since they are very costly it is wise to purchase them only when you are reasonably sure they will be appreciated.

At least 3 oysters should be served to each person.

Frozen or bulk oysters may be used in preparing the following appetizer. They are admittedly of poorer flavor than the fresh oysters right from the shell, but they are easier to prepare and probably, for most people, quite as acceptable.

Angels on Horseback

12 large, plump oysters
6 strips lean bacon
Minced chives or parsley

Juice of 1 lemon
12 circles fried bread

Drain oysters thoroughly. Partially cook the bacon strips to draw out excess fat, but bacon should still be limp. Cut strips in half: over each ½ strip of bacon, place an oyster, sprinkle oyster with minced chives or parsley and lemon juice; fasten bacon around oyster with toothpick. Shortly before they are to be served, place angels under broiler; cook until bacon is crisp, turning once. Reheat fried bread at same time. Serve on the hot fried bread. *Makes 12 appetizers.*

WITH CLAMS. Use canned whole clams or fresh shelled clams instead of oysters for the angels. Lemon juice and Tabasco are the only necessary condiments, though Classic Cocktail Sauce is also frequently served as a dip.

Steamed Clams

These are preferred by most people to raw clams, and the only trick is to brush the shells *thoroughly* in advance to get rid of all sand and grit, then rinse them through several waters. After this place the clams in a saucepan, add water to cover and salt (1 teaspoon salt for each 2 cups water), bring to a boil, simmer just until shells open—about 3 minutes. Discard clams whose shells do not open. Serve right from the shells (well drained) just as they are or with Butter Sauce, Caldo Bagne, or Soy-Sherry Dip. Another way is to steam the clams in part water and in part white wine; or, add a little oil and a clove of garlic to the water in which they cook.

Scallops

As appetizers, bay scallops are preferable to sea scallops, but they are only available fresh, whereas sea scallops can be found in frozen seafood counters in many large supermarkets. Fresh bay scallops can be served raw (like oysters or clams) sprinkled with lemon juice, salt, and pepper.

FRIED SCALLOPS can also be served as appetizers, with Tartar Sauce as a dip.

Scallops Vinaigrette

1 pound scallops
1 cup white wine
1 small onion
1 sprig parsley
1 pinch thyme
½ teaspoon salt

1 cup Vinaigrette Sauce
Lettuce
Sliced onion rings
Capers
Wedges of hard-cooked eggs

Cook the scallops for 10 minutes in white wine with onion, parsley, thyme, and salt. Cool in liquid; when cold, drain thoroughly and cut larger scallops in half. Marinate in Vinaigrette Sauce for 2 hours. Serve on picks over lettuce, garnished with onion rings, capers, and egg wedges. *Makes about 20 appetizer servings.*

Lomi-Lomi

1½ pounds fresh salmon or tuna,
  or fresh or frozen halibut
4 teaspoons lime or lemon juice
8 scallions, chopped

4 ripe tomatoes, peeled,
  seeded, chopped
1 teaspoon sugar
1 teaspoon salt

Bone fish and cut in cubes. Sprinkle liberally with salt and 2 teaspoons of the juice; let stand in refrigerator overnight. Put remaining ingredients, including remaining 2 teaspoons juice, in blender; beat until smooth. Spread paste over fish. Cover bowl containing fish; chill 1 to 1½ hours longer. *Makes 15 to 20 appetizer servings.*

Stuffed Mussels

2 quarts fresh mussels (about 48)
½ cup cold water
½ cup dry wine
½ teaspoon salt
1 large onion, chopped
2 tablespoons olive oil

½ cup uncooked rice
¼ cup pine nuts, or slivered
   blanched almonds
¼ cup yogurt or sour cream
Freshly ground black pepper
Minced chives or parsley

Wash mussels under running water, scrub thoroughly, remove beards. Place in kettle with cold water, wine, and salt. Bring to a boil, cook until shells open (discard any with unopened shells). Cool in broth. Remove from broth, saving broth. Remove mussels from shells (saving shells); chop the meat. Cook onion in olive oil until soft and yellow; add rice and 1 cup of the liquid in which mussels cooked (but strain liquid very carefully to be sure all sand or grit is removed). Cook rice, covered, until all liquid is absorbed; add *chopped* mussels, nuts, yogurt or cream, and black pepper. Blend well. Use this as stuffing, piling in shells. Sprinkle minced parsley or chives over top for garnish. *Makes 48 to 50 appetizer servings.*

Pescado Exquisito

2 pounds red snapper,
   swordfish, or halibut fillets
1 tablespoon lime juice
2 teaspoons salt
¼ cup water

½ cup orange juice
½ teaspoon chili powder
1 small onion, thinly sliced
1 pimiento, chopped
1 teaspoon olive oil

This is a Latin American version of pickled raw fish. As in Lomi-Lomi, the fish is cut in cubes, then sprinkled with lime juice and salt, but for only 10 minutes; then it is covered with ice water to stand for 10 minutes longer. Drain, pat dry, place in a serving platter, and cover with mixture of remaining ingredients. Refrigerate at least 1 hour or until time to serve. Serve cold; or, if preferred, place under preheated broiler for 4 or 5 minutes and serve hot. *Makes 20 to 25 servings.*

Mackerel in White Wine

1½ pounds mackerel fillets
Salt, pepper
1 small onion, thinly sliced
2 or 3 sprigs parsley, minced

⅛ teaspoon thyme
1 cup dry white wine
Juice of ½ lemon
Minced chives or parsley

Place fish in shallow top-of-stove casserole. Sprinkle with salt and pepper. Cover with onion, parsley, and thyme. Add wine and lemon juice, cover casserole, bring just to a boil; lower heat, simmer 4 minutes or until fish is firm and translucent. Cool in broth. When cold, remove onion slices, pour off and strain broth. Cut mackerel into serving pieces. Separately reduce broth to ½ cup; pour over fish. Sprinkle fish with chives or parsley and garnish with onion rings. Serve cold. *Makes 12 to 15 appetizer servings.*

MEAT APPETIZERS

Dogs in Blankets

Prepare Cheese Pastry, working ¼ cup grated Cheddar cheese into 1 recipe piecrust dough or 1 package mix. Roll out in the usual way, cut in strips 2 inches x 3 inches, roll each strip around a cocktail frankfurter, seal the ends by moistening and pressing with fingers. Bake in over preheated to 425° F. for 30 minutes, or until pastry is crisp and golden. Serve hot.

PIGS IN BLANKETS. Prepare like Dogs in Blankets, but use brown-'n'-serve sausage links, roll in strips of plain pastry (made with piecrust mix or your favorite recipe). Bake in oven preheated to 425° F. until pastry is golden and crisp.

DRUNKEN DOGS. Keep cocktail frankfurters hot in red wine, sherry, or sweet vermouth in the blazer of a chafing dish, or in a casserole over a candle warmer. Serve with picks.

SHERRIED SAUSAGES. Use canned Vienna sausages, well drained, or brown-'n'-serve pork sausage links; keep warm in hot sherry.

MAHOGANY SAUSAGES. Keep Vienna sausages warm in a sauce made of 2 tablespoons each soy sauce and sherry, and ¼ cup tomato catsup.

Flaming Sausages

Use either brown-'n'-serve sausage links or chorizo sausage; if the latter, cut into 1-inch lengths. Place sausage in chafing-dish blazer or shallow heatproof casserole with brandy, whiskey, or rum; heat the liquor, then set it aflame. When flame dies out, the hot sausages should be served immediately, or kept warm in hot liquor.

Appetizer Meat Sticks

Cut any solid luncheon meat, such as unsliced salami or bologna, or Spam, Taylor ham, or canned ham, into sticks approximately ½ inch by 2 inches. Marinate before serving in Red Wine Marinade, or serve cold with Soy-Horseradish Sauce.

Meat Roll-ups

Any thin-sliced luncheon meat looks more attractive if the slices are rolled up and fastened with picks, arranged on a platter with radishes, black olives, and squares of cheese. Ham is delicious when filled before rolling with curried cream cheese (add curry powder to taste to softened cream cheese) or sour cream spiced with curry. Salami is good filled with cream cheese or cottage cheese and minced chives. Bologna becomes interesting with a filling of Danish Blue Butter. Pastrami slices may be filled with ricotta cheese or Danish Blue Butter.

Ham in Cheese Biscuits

Make Cheese Biscuits 1 inch in diameter, split, butter while hot, and place squares of ham inside. If biscuits are made ahead, reheat (wrapped in foil) in oven just before serving.

Appetizer Meatballs

Use any favorite meatball recipe, form small meatballs (approximately ½ inch in diameter). Sauté or broil until well browned on all sides. Serve hot on cocktail picks, plain, or with Sherry-Soy Sauce, Cocktail Sauce, or Chinese mustard.

Tipsy Meatballs

Make meatballs by any favorite recipe, shape into appetizer-size balls, broil or sauté in fat until well browned. Drain well on absorbent paper. Keep warm in blazer of chafing dish with enough sweet vermouth or sherry to come halfway up sides of meatballs. Serve with cocktail picks.

Meatballs Manhattan

Prepare appetizer-size meatballs, using 1½ pounds ground meat. Brown on all sides. Marinate in the following sauce for 24 hours before serving, then reheat balls in the sauce. Serve with cocktail picks.

2 tablespoons minced onion	¼ teaspoon orégano
1 clove garlic, crushed	1 teaspoon flour
2 tablespoons fat	1 cup beef broth
¼ teaspoon salt	1 teaspoon dry mustard

1 dash Angostura bitters   3 tablespoons sweet vermouth
1/3 cup whiskey (rye or bourbon)

Sauté onion and garlic in fat; add salt and orégano, and stir in flour. Slowly add beef broth; when mixture is bubbling, add remaining ingredients. Cook until reduced and slightly thickened. Add meatballs to sauce; marinate in refrigerator until next day. (Do not serve immediately.) Reheat shortly before serving. *Makes about 50 appetizer servings.*

Pu-Pus

This is the Polynesian name for bite-size bits of meat, liver, chicken, or seafood broiled over charcoal on small skewers. Usually a selection of at least three dips are offered with the pu-pus. These are particularly appropriate for a patio meal, for they can be cooked on a small hibachi at the table, or on the outer edge of a big charcoal grill at the same time the main-course meat is being cooked.

Usually a selection is offered of, say, chicken livers, small pieces of lean pork, and shrimp. Or, the combination might consist of squares of breast of chicken, small chunks of ham, and brown-'n'-serve pork sausage links, each cut in half. Spear on 6-inch bamboo skewers, 3 or 4 pieces on each skewer, marinate in Teriyaki Sauce or the following Curry Fruit Sauce, then grill at table just before eating. Serve with several dips, such as Chinese mustard, a clear soy dip, and the marinating sauce.

CURRY FRUIT SAUCE

2 apples, peeled, diced   ⅛ teaspoon cinnamon
1 cup chicken broth   ⅛ teaspoon nutmeg
1 teaspoon instant minced onior   ⅛ teaspoon garlic powder
2 to 3 teaspoons curry powder   ¼ cup port wine, or cherry
1 teaspoon dry mustard   wine or liqueur

Combine all ingredients in saucepan. Simmer until apples are very soft and sauce is thickened. Beat in blender until smooth. *Makes 1¼ cups.*

Rumaki

For these you need chicken livers, water chestnuts, and bacon. Cut chicken livers into quarters, cut water chestnuts into thick slices, and put a piece of chicken liver and a piece of water chestnut together inside ½ slice bacon. Fasten each with a pick, marinate 1 hour in a mixture of soy sauce and port, cherry wine, or rum. Remove from marinade, place in broiler pan 5 inches from heat and broil, turning once, until bacon is crisp. Serve hot.

Chicken in Packets

1 whole chicken breast, skinned, boned	2 tablespoons dry sherry
	1 tablespoon soy sauce
2 scallions, chopped	½ teaspoon salt
2 thin slices fresh ginger root, or ¼ teaspoon ground ginger	½ teaspoon sugar
	20 6-inch squares foil

Cut chicken into 20 pieces about 1 inch square. Combine remaining ingredients (except foil); marinate chicken pieces about ½ hour. In each square of foil, place 1 piece chicken and 1 piece scallion; fold over and twist ends to seal. Just before time to serve, place packets in oven preheated to 450° F. or in coals of charcoal fire; bake 5 minutes. Serve hot in foil packets, 1 for each person. Especially delicious as first course for a barbecue meal, preceding charcoal-grilled fish or barbecued ribs. *Makes 20 appetizer servings.*

APPETIZER PASTRIES

Empanadillas

Almost any meat, fish, or poultry mixture may be used to fill these—a good way to turn leftovers into interesting appetizers.

1 cup minced cooked meat, fish, chicken, or canned tuna, well drained	4 tablespoons olive oil
	¾ teaspoon salt
2 onions, minced	2 tablespoons sherry or Madeira
1 2-ounce can chopped pimientos, drained	2 packages piecrust mix

Sauté minced meat, fish, chicken, or tuna with onions and pimientos in olive oil until lightly browned. Sprinkle with salt and wine.

Prepare piecrust dough in the usual way; divide in 4 parts. Roll out each part to ⅛ inch thick, cut with 2-inch biscuit cutter into circles. Over half the circles, place a heaping teaspoon of filling. Moisten edges, cover with remaining circles, press edges together with tines of fork to seal. Prick tops with fork. Bake in oven preheated to 400° F. for 25 minutes or until crisp and golden. Serve hot. *Makes about 20.*

To freeze: Prepare as above but do not bake. Place on baking sheet, freeze until hard, then remove to freezer container and cover tightly. To bake when needed, place frozen empanadillas on baking sheet, bake at 400° F. for 30 minutes or until crisply browned.

Piroshki

Piroshki may be made with Puff Paste or yeast-raised dough, but the easiest way is to use piecrust mix or a standard piecrust recipe. It is nice to offer an assortment: 3 different fillings—one of meat, one of fish or chicken, the third of cabbage (very Russian).

FISH FILLING

½ cup cooked fish (sole,   1 hard-cooked egg, chopped
   whiting, halibut, or cod)   1 tablespoon sour cream
Salt, pepper

Combine ingredients. *Makes about 3/4 cup.*

BEEF FILLING

1 cup chopped cooked meat (pot   2 tablespoons sour cream
   roast, stew, any cooked beef)   1 tablespoon catsup
1 teaspoon instant minced onion   1 tablespoon sherry

Combine ingredients. *Makes about 1 cup.*

CABBAGE FILLING

1 cup shredded cabbage   2 tablespoons sour cream
1 tablespoon shortening   1 pinch ginger
½ teaspoon salt

Sauté cabbage in shortening until soft; add remaining ingredients. Be sure to leave sufficient edge around filling and to seal edges of pastry completely to avoid leakage.

PASTRY

Prepare 2 packages piecrust mix in the usual way, but divide dough in 3 parts, roll out each to ⅛ inch thick. Cut in 4-inch squares or in rectangles 3 x 6 inches. Place a spoonful of filling on each, roll up, seal the edges and ends. Bake in oven preheated to 400° F. for 20 to 25 minutes, until crisp and brown. Serve hot. *Makes about 20.*

To freeze: Prepare in advance but do not bake; freeze on baking sheet until firm, transfer to freezer container. To bake when needed, allow an extra 5 minutes' baking time.

Quiche Lorraine

Quiche Lorraine and Swiss Flan are members of the same family. Pastry is used to hold a custard mixture which may contain cheese, bacon, onions, anchovies, even sauerkraut. Quiche Lorraine is served in France as a luncheon dish, but in America it is popular as an appetizer, cut into thin wedges.

Pastry for 1-crust pie (or 1 stick piecrust mix)
1 egg white
6 slices bacon
1 cup (¼ pound) shredded Swiss or natural Gruyére cheese
½ cup grated Parmesan cheese
2 cups light cream or dairy half-and-half
2 eggs, well beaten
1 teaspoon salt
Pinch of cayenne (optional)

Prepare pastry in the usual way; line a 9-inch pie pan with the pastry, fluting edges. Brush unbeaten egg white over bottom of pastry. Chill in freezer while preparing filling.

Cook bacon slices until crisp; drain on absorbent paper. Break into small pieces. Combine remaining ingredients, add cooked bacon, pour into chilled pastry shell. Bake in oven preheated to 425° F. for 10 minutes, then lower heat to 325° F., bake 30 minutes, or until a knife inserted in center comes out clean. Cut in 10 wedges for 10 appetizer servings.

To freeze: Prepare as directed but bake only a total of 30 (instead of 40) minutes. Cool, wrap and seal, label, and freeze. Complete baking when needed, starting in cold oven set at 325° F., for 20 to 25 minutes, or until knife inserted comes out clean.

SHRIMP QUICHE. Instead of bacon, use ¾ to 1 cup minced cooked shrimp in recipe; reduce Parmesan to ¼ cup; instead of cayenne, add a pinch of curry powder.

CRABMEAT QUICHE. Instead of bacon, use ¾ to 1 cup flaked crabmeat in basic recipe; omit Parmesan cheese, add 1 teaspoon minced chives or green onion (scallions).

INDIVIDUAL QUICHE. Instead of a 9-inch pie pan, make individual pastry tarts: cut rolled pastry in 4½-inch circles, shape with fingers into small cup, press aluminum foil around dough to hold in shape. Or, press inside individual tart pans or inside small muffin tins. You will need twice the amount of pastry (2 sticks piecrust mix). Brush the shells with egg white; chill in freezer, then divide custard filling among the shells. *Makes 10 to 12.*

Swiss Flan

PASTRY

1 cup flour
1 teaspoon baking powder
¼ teaspoon salt

1/3 cup butter
1 egg, beaten

Combine flour, baking powder, and salt; chop in butter until fine; add egg, form stiff dough. Press dough into 9-inch pie pan with fingers and heel of palm, so that it extends up above rim of pan.

FILLING

1 large onion, sliced or chopped
2 tablespoons butter
2 eggs, beaten

2 cups (½ pound) shredded
    natural Gruyère cheese
¼ teaspoon salt

Cook onion in butter until soft; cool slightly. Combine beaten eggs, cheese, and salt; stir in onion. Pour mixture into pastry. (This is a firmer mixture than that in a quiche.) Bake in oven preheated to 425° F. for 15 minutes, reduce heat to 350° F., and continue baking 25 to 30 minutes, or until a knife inserted in center comes out clean. Cut into 10 wedges.

To freeze: Follow instructions for freezing Quiche Lorraine.

PIZZAS

Basic Pizza Dough

1 envelope active dry yeast
1 cup warm (not hot) water
1 teaspoon salt

2 tablespoons olive oil
3½ cups sifted flour
½ teaspoon sugar (optional)

Dissolve yeast in water. Stir in salt and olive oil; gradually add flour and sugar, if desired. Beat until smooth, then turn out dough on lightly floured board and knead until dough is elastic. Place dough in deep bowl; brush top with olive oil, cover lightly, let rise in warm place (85° F.) until doubled. Divide dough in half, roll each into a ball; then, with fingers, press to fit 2 14-inch pizza pans or rectangular baking sheets, making edges thicker and slightly higher than center. Brush with additional olive oil. Add desired filling. Bake in oven preheated to 450° F. for 20 to 25 minutes, or until crust is golden. *Makes enough dough for 2 pizzas, each serving 6 to 8 persons.*

To freeze: Before baking, place on pizza pan, freeze until hard, then wrap in plastic, return to freezer until needed, then bake as directed.

Pizza Sauce (Basic Recipe)

2 to 3 tablespoons olive oil
1 or 2 cloves garlic
½ cup chopped onion
¼ teaspoon orégano

2 tablespoons chopped parsley
2 cups tomato sauce (or 15-ounce can)

Place split garlic cloves in olive oil in skillet; cook until golden; press garlic into oil with tines of fork, then remove and discard shreds. Add onion, cook over low heat until soft; add orégano, parsley, and tomato sauce. Cook until very well blended. Beat in blender or force through food mill. *Makes 2 cups, enough sauce for 2 pizzas.*

CLASSIC PIZZA. Cover each 14-inch pizza with 1 cup Pizza Sauce. Place thin slices of Mozzarella cheese over the sauce; sprinkle with Parmesan cheese.

MUSHROOM PIZZA. For each pizza, sauté ½ pound sliced mushrooms in butter until lightly browned; add to 1 cup Pizza Sauce.

SAUSAGE PIZZA. Add sliced Italian sweet or hot sausage to Pizza Sauce; sprinkle generously with chopped parsley; place Mozzarella slices between sausage slices.

PIZZA BOLOGNESE. Sauté ¼ pound ground hamburger meat in 1 tablespoon olive oil until meat loses its pink color; add ¼ cup chopped onion, cook until soft. Add 2 cups Pizza Sauce. *Enough for 2 pizzas.*

SAUSAGE GRINDER PIZZA. Brown ½ pound chopped Italian sweet sausage in 1 tablespoon olive oil; or, cook 8 small pork sausage links and drain off excess fat. Add green pepper and pimiento cut in strips, and 1 onion, sliced. Cook until onion is tender. Spread over 2 pizzas; top each with 1 cup Pizza Sauce and ½ cup Parmesan cheese.

PISSALADINA. For pizza filling, slice 6 to 8 onions, cook slowly in olive oil until very soft. Season with salt; place on pizza dough, garnish with pimiento strips and pitted black olives. Bake until dough is golden.

Hot Fingers

Use refrigerated oven-ready rolls, separate as directed on package, then press each with heel of hand to ¼ inch thick. Cut with sharp knife into "fingers" about 1 inch wide. Press any of the following mixtures into the dough, then bake in oven pre-heated to 400° F. for 10 to 12 minutes until dough is golden and topping bubbles. Serve at once. *One package of rolls makes about 20 appetizer servings.*

CLAM TOPPING. Drain a 7-ounce can of minced clams, add ¼ cup chopped onion and 2 tablespoons chopped pimiento. Sauté mixture in 1 tablespoon oil until onions are soft. Add salt to taste. Press a spoonful of mixture over top of each finger of dough. (Or, use instant minced onion, chopped pimiento, and a little chopped green pepper; blend with oil; do not cook mixture before placing on dough.)

CLAM-BACON TOPPING. For topping, combine well-drained minced clams (1 7-ounce can) with 3 slices cooked bacon, crumbled, and 2 tablespoons chopped almonds.

TUNA TOPPING. Drain a 7-ounce can white meat of tuna, add 1 tablespoon minced capers and 2 tablespoons chopped pimiento; blend well. Press into dough, bake as directed.

HAM TOPPING. Sauté ¾ cup minced cooked ham in 1 tablespoon oil or butter with 2 tablespoons chopped onion and 2 tablespoons minced parsley. Press into dough, bake as directed.

Anchoïade

1 long loaf French or Italian bread, or 1 round loaf	2 or 3 cloves garlic, minced
	3 tablespoons olive oil
6 anchovy fillets	Few basil leaves
3 large tomatoes, sliced	Few drops of vinegar

Slice bread in half lengthwise. Soak anchovy fillets in luke-warm water a few minutes, then drain, to get rid of excess salt. Cook the sliced tomatoes, garlic, and basil leaves in olive oil until tomatoes are soft but have not yet completely lost their shape. Add tomatoes to anchovies, mash to a paste; spread mixture over the cut side of bread. Cut the bread in 2-inch pieces; place under broiler, 3 inches from heat, until lightly toasted. Serve with red wine or beer. *Makes 12 servings.*

HOT PEASANT SANDWICH. For each serving, cut a crusty roll in half, brush cut side of one half generously with olive oil, rub with a split garlic clove, cover with sliced tomatoes. Sprinkle tomatoes with salt, or with salt and minced parsley. Cover with the other half of the roll, press together. Sesame-seed or poppy-seed rolls are good if very crisp. Marvelous for a picnic or patio supper.

Pan Bania

1 long loaf French or Italian bread	1 2-ounce can anchovy fillets, drained, diced
1 clove garlic, split	Black Greek or Italian olives, pitted
1 cucumber, peeled, sliced	
1 tomato, thinly sliced	Olive oil
3 pimientos, cut in squares	Wine vinegar

Slice bread in half lengthwise. Rub cut side with garlic. Over half the loaf, arrange cucumber, tomato, pimiento, anchovy, and olives. Sprinkle generously with olive oil, lightly with vinegar. Top with the other half of the loaf. Press tightly together. Cut in 2-inch lengths for individual sandwiches. *Makes 6 servings.*

Hero Sandwiches

The American hero sandwich is in reality a slightly altered version of the Anchoïade and Pan Bania. Into these giant sandwiches almost anything goes. Split Italian bread or hero buns in half horizontally, brush with Garlic Butter or oil, add sliced meat (cold cuts), tomatoes, cheese, pickles, relishes, sliced beets, or what have you. Sometimes the cut loaf is spread with liverwurst; sometimes pimientos or green peppers are added, or raw onion.

Other possible additions: Sliced hard-cooked egg, cole slaw, potato salad, or fried onions. French or Italian dressing is sprinkled over all. A *hot hero* is the same except that it is wrapped in foil and heated in the oven or in the coals of a charcoal fire.

Peacemaker Sandwich

A New Orleans specialty. Loaves of French bread are split lengthwise and the soft insides scooped out to allow room for creamed oysters; then the top is put back on. Presumably the name was bestowed on the hot sandwiches by husbands returning home from a night of carousing: they would buy the delicious oyster-filled loaves on the way home to placate wives bound to be angry by their late return.

FONDUES AND THEIR COUSINS

Swiss Fondue

1 clove garlic, split
2 cups dry white wine
1 pound natural Gruyère or Swiss
  Emmentaler cheese, shredded
  (4 cups)
1½ tablespoons flour

3 tablespoons kirsch or cognac
Grated nutmeg or freshly ground
  black pepper
Italian or French bread, cut in
  1-inch cubes

A round casserole, chafing dish, or fondue pot is needed. Rub insides with the split clove of garlic; discard garlic. Add wine; heat until bubbles form. Toss the shredded cheese with flour; add a handful of cheese at a time to the wine, stirring after each addition until cheese is melted, keeping heat low. Add kirsch or cognac and nutmeg or pepper. When cheese is bubbling slightly and is deliciously gooey, spear cubes of bread with fondue forks, twirl the bread in the cheese, quickly lift to the mouth, and try not to let the cheese stream out between mouth and table. When all of the cheese has been consumed, the brown crust remaining on the bottom is considered a special prize. *Makes 4 to 8 supper servings, or 10 to 12 appetizer servings.*

Welsh Rarebit

2 tablespoons butter
¾ teaspoon salt
½ teaspoon dry mustard
Freshly ground black pepper

3 cups shredded sharp Cheddar
  cheese
¾ cup beer or ale
1 egg, well beaten

Melt butter in casserole or chafing dish. Add seasonings, cheese, and beer or ale. Stir constantly over low heat until cheese is melted. Just before serving, quickly beat in egg. Serve over toast triangles as a hot snack or supper dish. *Makes 4 to 6 servings.*

Rum Tum Diddy

1 10½-ounce can condensed tomato soup
1 ½-pound package quick-melting

process cheese, such as Velvee-
  ta
½ teaspoon dry mustard

Combine all ingredients; heat, stirring, until cheese is melted. Serve over toast triangles as a luncheon dish or hearty after-school snack. *Makes 4 to 6 servings.*

202

Fondue Bourguignonne

2 pounds choice sirloin or fillet
  of beef, cut in ½-inch cubes
¼ pound butter

1 cup olive oil
Assorted dips
Pickles and relishes

A fondue pot is essential in preparing this Swiss specialty, one with a narrow top. Preheat the butter-oil mixture to 375° F.; keep hot over an alcohol flame or by thermostatic control.

Pieces of steak arranged on a platter are speared by the guests, plunged into the oil, and left in the oil 3 minutes (for rare) or longer for medium to well-done. When cooked as desired, the meat is dipped into one of several sauces, then popped into the mouth.

Appropriate sauces are: Béarnaise Sauce, Classic Cocktail Sauce, Hot Chinese Mustard, and Barbecue Sauce. Makes enough for 12 persons as an appetizer, or 6 persons as a supper dish. For a supper menu, add tossed mixed salad, garlic bread, and hot coffee.

Karibabyaki

1 whole chicken breast, skinned,
  boned, cut in 1-inch pieces
1 pound shelled raw shrimp

8 green onions, sliced
4 to 6 cups chicken broth
Soy Horseradish Sauce

Arrange raw chicken and raw shrimp on platter. Provide long bamboo skewers or fondue forks. Garnish platter with watercress. Heat onions and chicken broth in deep pot (a deep fondue pot is perfect). Broth must be simmering at all times. Place chicken or shrimp in broth until cooked: chicken will be completely white; shrimp should be delicately pink. Dip in sauce, pop into mouth. *Makes 20 appetizer servings.*

Chinese Hot Pot

½ pound lean pork, cut in ½-inch
  pieces
½-pound sirloin steak or fillet of
  beef, cut in ½-inch pieces
1 whole chicken breast, skinned,

boned, cut in 1-inch pieces
6 tablespoons minced onion or
  scallion
6 cups chicken broth
Assorted dips

The pork, beef, and chicken should be cut into pieces of more or less uniform size, though the chicken pieces may be larger as the chicken cooks more quickly. Like Karibayaki, the meats are speared on long bamboo skewers or on fondue forks, placed in bubbling chicken broth until cooked, dipped in sauce, then popped into the mouth. Add the minced onion or scallion to the broth, keep the broth bubbling all the time. For dips, Curry Fruit Sauce, Oriental Plum Sauce, Hot Chinese Mustard, and Soy-Horseradish Sauce (or Soy-Sherry Sauce) are all appropriate. *Makes about 20 appetizer servings, or enough to serve 4 to 6 persons as a supper dish.*

SMØRREBRØD

These are really miniature meals atop a single piece of bread, and nothing else is needed for lunch but beer or coffee and a simple dessert.

When they are to be made ahead, the open sandwiches can be kept fresh in the refrigerator for several hours if the bread is buttered very thickly (to prevent seepage into the soft bread) and the pan holding them is covered very tightly with plastic wrap.

Another way is to cover each smørrebrød with clear aspic. This keeps them fresh-looking for hours, though only certain combinations are suitable for such treatment.

Smørrebrød sandwiches are particularly attractive when tomato, cucumber, or lemon slices are placed on the bread so that they stand up, "legs" apart, looking like dancing figures. The slice is cut halfway across, to the center, then spread out or twisted.

Danish Blue Cheese and Egg

Place a thin slice of Danish blue cheese over a thickly buttered slice of bread, preferably pumpernickel. (To slice without crumbling, use a thin-bladed knife, cover the knife blade with plastic wrap. The cheese clings to the plastic rather than the knife blade and so is easier to place directly onto the bread without falling apart.) Make a hole in the center of the cheese and place a raw egg yolk in the hole. Or, make a tomato ring, as in the preceding recipe, and place the tomato ring on the cheese with the egg yolk inside. Lay a few capers over the egg yolk; pass the pepper grinder.

Smoked Salmon and Egg

Thickly butter thin slices of rye or white bread. Over the butter, place slices of smoked salmon; cut to fit the bread exactly. Remove the center from a slice of tomato to form a ring. Place the tomato ring in the center of the open sandwich. Carefully separate an egg without allowing the yolk to break, then slip the egg yolk into the tomato ring. Over the egg yolk, arrange several well-drained capers. At the table, pass a pepper grinder.

Smoked Salmon with Scrambled Eggs

Lay a slice of smoked salmon over a slice of thickly buttered rye bread. Scramble an egg lightly, season it with a pinch of curry powder. Arrange the scrambled egg diagonally across the salmon, and put borders of minced parsley or minced fresh dill on either side of the scrambled egg. Or, border the egg with red caviar. Serve with a lemon wedge. (Yes, a drop or two of lemon juice is very good on scrambled eggs.) Serve with a cucumber salad.

HAM WITH SCRAMBLED EGG. Exactly the same, but use a slice of ham instead of smoked salmon.

Roast Beef and Potato Smørrebrød

Thickly butter thin slices of dark rye or white bread. On each place a very thin slice of roast beef; curl up one end of the slice of beef so that meat does not lie flat on the bread. Under the curled-up part of the beef, place a curl of iceberg lettuce to hold the meat in place. On top of the beef, place a spoonful of potato salad (made according to your favorite recipe, or purchased from the delicatessen if you are in a hurry). On either side of the potato salad, arrange tomato twists or cucumber twists. Place slivers of green pepper over the potato salad. If desired, put dabs of mayonnaise around the edges.

Hans Christian Andersen

Spread butter thin over a piece of white bread, then over the butter spread a thick layer of liver pâté. Arrange crisp cooked crumbled bacon all across the liver pâté, and put a tomato twist over the bacon. Sprinkle with minced parsley.

Sardine and Egg

Thickly butter a slice of white bread trimmed to form an exact square. Place a sardine diagonally across the bread. On either side of the sardine, place rows of hard-cooked sieved egg yolk; next to the egg yolk, place rows of minced green pepper. Pipe mayonnaise around the edges. This may be covered with Clear Wine Aspic.

Tartare Smørrebrød

For this you need freshly ground beef, either sirloin or top round, put through the grinder twice. (The purists insist that the beef must be *scraped* with a very sharp knife, rather than put through the grinder—a good idea if you have the time and patience.) Season the meat with salt to taste and plenty of black pepper. Spread the meat over thickly buttered bread, to the very edges, then, in the center, make a well. In the well place a raw onion ring, and inside the onion ring, carefully slip a raw egg yolk. Place a few capers over the egg yolk. Serve with chopped onion; pass the pepper grinder.

Three-in-One

Place a thin slice of breast meat of chicken (or turkey) over a thickly buttered slice of white bread. Trim edges to fit. Lay crumbled cooked bacon in a diagonal row across the chicken, and rows of overlapped baby shrimp on either side of the bacon. This may be glazed, if desired, with Clear Wine Aspic.

Shrimp on Tarragon Butter

Blend dried tarragon with softened butter (using ¼ teaspoon tarragon to 1 stick butter). Spread over trimmed slices of white bread to the very edge. Arrange 3 medium shrimp (cooked, shelled, and deveined) in center, overlapping so that they do not lie flat. Around the shrimp, place crumbled cooked bacon. Over the shrimp, scatter a few eggs of black or red caviar. Cover with Clear Wine Aspic.

These can be made into canapes: cut bread in quarters, cover first with butter, then with crumbled bacon, then place 1 shrimp in center of each. Sprinkle capers over shrimp.

SANDWICHES, PLAIN AND FANCY

It's no wonder sandwiches are so popular with young and old alike. There aren't any rules, so you may do as you please, indulging in wildly incongruous combinations. In fact, the best kind of sandwich party is one where the makings are set out on a counter or table and each person selects his own combinations.

For lunchboxes or picnics, or any occasion when the sandwiches need to be made ahead for later eating, freezing is a good idea. The bread defrosts slowly en route and the sandwiches are ready to eat when the time is ripe. Just about the only ingredients that should not be put into sandwiches headed for the freezer are lettuce, tomatoes, and mayonnaise.

Wrapping sandwiches is much easier than it used to be, too, thanks to those handy little sandwich-size plastic bags that are available in every supermarket. These keep the bread fresh and the fillings moist, and can be thrown away when lunch is finished.

Basic Sandwich Salad Filling

¾ to 1 cup chopped cooked meat or poultry, or flaked cooked or canned fish

½ cup minced celery
2 to 3 tablespoons mayonnaise
Salt, pepper

Mix all ingredients; add condiments or seasonings to taste. If it's tuna salad, a little minced parsley and a few drops of lemon juice add important flavor. Ham salad will be improved with a little mustard, and you may want to add chopped green pepper or chopped hard-cooked eggs. A teaspoon of catsup tastes good with chicken salad. Roast beef salad (made with leftover roast beef) is improved with just a bit of horseradish.

This makes approximately 1½ cups of filling, enough for 6 sandwiches, perhaps more, depending on how thickly the filling is spread.

EGG SALAD SANDWICHES. Use 4 hard-cooked eggs, shelled and chopped, with ½ cup minced celery, 1 teaspoon minced parsley (optional), ¼ teaspoon prepared mustard, and 2 tablespoons mayonnaise.

Grilled Cheese Sandwiches

Any kind of cheese may be used, but the easiest kinds are those firm enough to slice thinly. Swiss, Cheddar, Munster, American cheese, brick, Jack, and caraway cheese are all good choices. Place between unbuttered bread slices; spread softened butter or margarine on the outside; cook in a sandwich grill or hot skillet until golden on each side and cheese is melted.

Besides plain cheese sandwiches, ham, salami, tomato, or pickles may be added to the filling before grilling.

Croque Monsieur

This is a grilled cheese and ham sandwich made like French Toast: a slice of Swiss or Gruyère cheese and a slice of ham are placed between 2 pieces of white bread, then the entire sandwich is soaked in a mixture of beaten egg and milk. For easier handling, the sandwich should be cut in quarters (which makes it a perfect size for hot appetizers). Fry in hot fat until golden on each side; serve immediately.

Western Sandwich

Make a Western Omelet, and serve between toast as a sandwich.

Hot Roquefort-Nut Sandwich

Cover slices of toast with slices of Roque.ort or other blue cheese. Dust with cayenne pepper. Place under broiler 5 inches from heat until cheese starts to melt, then sprinkle with slivered almonds until almonds are lightly browned. Serve at once.

For canapes, cut the open sandwich in quarters while hot, making 4 bite-size canapes.

Camembert and Onion on Pumpernickel

This makes a very fine sandwich to go with beer; or, it can be cut in quarters to serve as appetizers. Spread Camembert cheese (softened to room temperature) over pumpernickel bread; top cheese with a thick slice of onion, or chopped onion. Cover with another slice of bread, buttered or not, as you prefer.

Tea Sandwiches

The reason they are called "tea sandwiches" is that they are dainty and therefore appropriate to serve at a ladies' tea. But they can be served with cocktails. To keep moist, place in a shallow pan and cover tightly with plastic wrap; or cover with a moist towel until time to serve.

CUCUMBER SANDWICHES. Place thin slices of cucumber between thinly sliced buttered white bread. Cut in squares, or use a biscuit cutter to cut in circles; roll the edges in mayonnaise and then in minced parsley.

WATERCRESS SANDWICHES. Place chopped watercress between thin slices of buttered white bread; cut in squares or triangles.

RIBBON SANDWICHES. Use an unsliced sandwich loaf, plus an unsliced loaf of whole or cracked wheat. Cut bread lengthwise, ¼ inch thick, using a long bread knife with serrated edges. Cut away all crusts and trim the slices to uniform size. First spread white bread with pimiento-cheese spread (or another yellow cheese); top with whole- or cracked-wheat bread, spread this with minced watercress blended with softened butter. Cover with another slice of white bread, spread this with still another filling, such as crumbled cooked bacon blended with cream cheese. Finally, top with a second slice of whole- or cracked-wheat bread. Still another filling and another slice of bread (white this time) may be used, if desired—as long as the filling is made with either butter or a soft cheese. Chill the loaf until the fillings are firm, then cut into squares, triangles, or rectangles, so that the fillings show up like ribbons.

PINWHEELS. Trim crusts from an unsliced sandwich loaf; slice lengthwise. Spread with an herb butter or soft cheese mixture. Roll up the bread; keep moist inside a damp towel in the refrigerator. When filling is firm, cut across the roll in ¼-inch slices.

BUFFET ASPICS

For a cocktail buffet or smorgasbord, baked ham and/or roast turkey is always in order. For most occasions, just cook in the usual way and cut slices as needed. For a more elaborate and pretentious occasion, the bird or the roast may be covered with glaze or Chaud-Froid Sauce. This is not as difficult as it looks, especially for those who are clever with garnishes, and, best of all, the pièce de résistance so glazed continues to look elegant until the evening's end.

Ham Chaud-Froid

A canned ham is excellent for this, for it is already boned, cooked, and the fat removed. A 10-pound ham is best, though a 5-pound ham could be served for a smaller gathering. Trim the ham to shape it, cutting away uneven spots and making the outside as uniform as possible. Prepare Chaud-Froid Sauce. Coat the outside of the ham completely with the sauce; chill until the sauce is set but not hard. Remove ham from refrigerator, place on cake rack over shallow roasting pan. Arrange any desired garnishes in the sauce: carrot slices cut to look like daisies, thinly cut slices of cauliflower, "ribbons" of pimiento slivers, thinly sliced mushrooms, sliced stuffed olives, green pepper strips, sliced hard-cooked eggs, capers, sliced radishes.

After the garnishes have been placed in the Chaud-Froid, brush Aspic Glaze over the top. Chill until firm, then add a second coat of Aspic Glaze. Repeat with 2 more layers of the glaze. Keep ham in refrigerator until time to serve.

Clam-Tomato Glaze

2 cups blended clam-tomato juice
1 envelope unflavored gelatin

Heat juice, add gelatin, stir until dissolved. Cool slightly, then spoon a thin covering over canapes. Chill until partially set, add a second layer of aspic. Keep canapes chilled until time to serve. The color is bright red, which is attractive over any canapes made with shrimp, sliced hard-cooked egg, or ham. *Makes 2 cups glaze.* (If less is needed, use ½ tablespoon gelatin with 1 cup clam-tomato juice or tomato juice.)

Aspic Glaze

2 envelopes unflavored gelatin   1 cup hot water or clear broth
½ cup cold water

Soften gelatin in cold water; dissolve in hot water. Use as directed. If aspic begins to solidify, heat until completely liquid once more. At least 2 layers of aspic are needed for a smooth appearance. *Makes 1 1/2 cups glaze.* (If less glaze is needed, halve ingredients.)

Salmon en Gêlée

1 5-pound fresh salmon   2 teaspoons salt
4 cups water   6 peppercorns
4 slices onion   1 envelope unflavored gelatin
1 stalk celery   ¼ cup cold water
2 sprigs parsley   Vegetable garnishes

Wrap salmon in cheesecloth; place on rack in large kettle. Combine water with onion, celery, parsley, salt, and peppercorns; add to kettle. Simmer gently, covered, without allowing to boil, for about 50 minutes, or until fish is firm to the touch. Carefully remove salmon without allowing to break. Remove skin and bones; reshape. Strain the stock, measure 1 cup, heat this to boiling. Soften the gelatin in the ¼ cup cold water, then add the stock; stir to dissolve. Brush a little gelatin over the fish; chill until partially set. Add vegetable garnishes as desired. Cover with glaze. Repeat with 2 more layers. *Serves 30 to 35 persons for a cocktail buffet.* Serve with homemade Mayonnaise or Caper Mayonnaise.

Clear Wine Aspic

1 envelope unflavored gelatin   1 green onion, chopped
½ cup dry white wine   ¼ teaspoon thyme
½ cup water or clarified broth

Soften gelatin in wine. Heat water or broth with onion and thyme to boiling; strain over gelatin, stir until dissolved. *Makes 3/4 cup.*

Sültze

4 pigs' knuckles (about 3 pounds)   ½ cup vinegar
1½ pounds veal breast or shank,   1 teaspoon sugar
  with bones   1 envelope unflavored gelatin
8 cups water   ¼ cup cold water
1 tablespoon salt   1 10-ounce package frozen broc-
8 peppercorns   coli spears, sliced lengthwise
1 bay leaf   2 hard-cooked eggs, sliced
¼ teaspoon allspice   Slivers of green pepper and pi-
1 onion, stuck with 2 cloves   miento

Place pigs' knuckles, veal, and veal bones in water with salt, peppercorns, bay, allspice, onion, vinegar, and sugar. Cover, bring to a boil; simmer 3 hours, or until veal is very tender. Remove meat and bones; discard bones, chop lean meat into fine pieces. Strain the stock through cheesecloth or a very fine sieve. Chill so that fat will come to top and can be completely removed. Heat stock again; add gelatin softened in cold water, stir until dissolved. Cool, then chill stock until it becomes the consistency of unbeaten egg white.

  In the bottom of a mold (a small roasting pan may be used), arrange the sliced broccoli spears, egg slices, and green pepper and pimiento strips to look like flowers. Add a thin layer of the meat stock; chill until set. Add chopped veal to remaining meat stock. Pour this over the garnishes. Chill until very firm. Unmold; keep chilled until time to serve.

  Serve garnished with radishes, stuffed green olives, and carrot curls, with ribbons of mayonnaise, or horseradish-flavored mayonnaise, around the base of the mold. (Use 1 tablespoon horseradish for 1 cup commercial mayonnaise.) *Makes about 36 appetizer servings.*

2 SAUCES AND SOUPS

It is important to understand the principles of saucemaking, because this is the secret of turning a simple basic recipe into a dozen quite different and often exotic dishes. Sauces are added for flavor—for excitingly provocative flavor. Some (the marinades) are used for soaking the food before cooking; some become an integral part of the dish. Others are basted over food while it cooks; and finally there are the sauces that are served alone, as embellishment to the food. Most sauces are quite easy to make, especially today, when there are so many respectable short cuts available for reducing preparation time.

Sauces and soups are cousins. Nearly every category of sauce has its counterpart in a soup or soups. This is why canned condensed soups and dehydrated soup concentrates can be used successfully in making many sauces.

Utensils Needed for Sauce Making

You need not go out to buy special equipment for preparing sauces, but certain utensils are especially important.

If you don't have a *whisk* already, march yourself down to the nearest hardware store to buy one. Many a curdled or lumpy sauce has been saved by this simple and inexpensive instrument.

Double boiler: Essential for all custard-type and chocolate sauces.

Blender or food mill: For puréeing vegetables and sauces.

Stirring spoons, a *slotted spoon,* and a *wooden spoon* are other inexpensive helps. A *sieve* is necessary for straining some sauces. A *mortar and pestle* are extremely useful for making pastes of herbs and garlic, or for crushing nuts.

A Quick Way to Make Stock

To make stock in the manner of a French chef requires more time than most American cooks can spare. But if you are buying meat for a roast, by all means ask for bones. A simple stock may be prepared while the meat roasts. Chicken stock can be made with the neck, gizzards, and the bonier parts of the back while the chicken is frying or roasting, or with chicken necks purchased by the pound.

Place bones in a deep saucepan or kettle, add water, salt, an onion, a few celery leaves, or a chunk of carrot. No need to measure ingredients. If chicken parts are placed in a 2-quart saucepan, add water to the halfway mark. If bones are placed in a kettle, add enough water to cover the bones. Add ½ teaspoon salt (no more) for each 2 cups water (you can always add more later).

Meat broth (from bones) should simmer at least an hour. Dump the bones in a kettle as soon as you return from marketing, and make the broth immediately—the broth requires less space in the refrigerator than the bones. If you cook the broth in advance, then chill it, the fat will rise to the top, forming a crust, easy to remove with a spoon. If you have made more stock than you need immediately, put the remainder in a jar or bowl and refrigerate it once more. It will keep fresh at least a week and probably 2 weeks for use in other sauce and gravies.

Chicken broth requires only 30 minutes' simmering, and there is less fat to worry about. In fact, to make the sauce you can strain the chicken broth right into the skillet or roasting pan in which chicken was fried or roasted.

Any broth will cook down considerably with boiling, but don't let this worry you. If what started out as 3 cups cooks down to ½ cup, you have a very concentrated broth, one to which you can add water without loss of flavor. Just be careful that the broth does not cook down to less than ½ cup, or you have so little that there's nothing much to add to.

Broth made in this way has a flavor superior to that of any soup concentrate, and it really is very little trouble.

Homemade Consommé

When you want a really full-flavored broth for a special sauce, or a consommé to serve as a first course for dinner, here is an easy recipe.

2 pounds chicken necks and backs	1 onion, stuck with cloves
2 quarts water	1 sprig celery leaves
4 teaspoons beef-flavored stock concentrate	1 sprig parsley
	⅛ teaspoon thyme

Place everything together in a kettle; bring to a boil, simmer uncovered over very low heat for 2 hours. Cool liquid. Remove chicken parts with slotted spoon. Strain liquid through fine sieve. Chill. After fat has risen to top and congealed, remove carefully; reheat liquid, add salt to taste if needed. If it is to be served as a soup, strain once more, preferably through cheesecloth. Serve hot with or without garnishes; or serve chilled as cold consommé. Or use in any recipe calling for beef broth or meat stock. *Makes about 1 quart (4 cups).*

To Clarify Homemade Stock or Consommé

If straining through a fine sieve still leaves bits of sediment from vegetables or bones, add an egg white and/or egg shells to the broth, bring to a boil, and stir constantly for 2 minutes. Turn off heat; add an ice cube; let broth cool. Strain a second time, through cheesecloth. This produces a beautiful clear broth.

Cream Sauces

Béchamel, White, and Cream Sauces are the same thing.

THICK WHITE SAUCE is a Béchamel with a larger proportion of butter and flour: 3 tablespoons butter and 3 tablespoons flour to 1 cup liquid. This is used as a thickening ingredient (as for croquettes or batters).

THIN WHITE SAUCE, used mainly in making cream soups, has only 1 tablespoon each butter and flour to each cup liquid. Any of the following methods may be used for preparing a medium, thick, or thin white sauce.

Béchamel or Medium White Sauce (Classic Method)

2 tablespoons butter

2 tablespoons flour

¼ teaspoon salt

⅛ teaspoon nutmeg or freshly

ground black pepper (optional)

1 cup milk

1 egg, beaten (optional)

Melt butter in saucepan, stir in flour, cook over low heat until flour bubbles; do not allow flour to brown. Add salt and nutmeg or pepper, gradually add milk, stirring with a whisk. If sauce is to be used in a casserole or soufflé or as the basis for another sauce, 3 to 5 minutes' simmering is sufficient. If to be served on its own as a sauce, simmer 20 to 30 minutes over very low heat or hot water, stirring occasionally.

Add egg only if master recipe so specifies, or if especially rich sauce is desired. To add egg, first blend a little hot sauce with beaten egg, stir briskly to blend well, then add egg to remaining sauce. Cook over lowest heat, stirring, for 1 or 2 minutes longer. *Makes 1 cup sauce.*

For 1½ cups sauce, use 3 tablespoons each butter and flour, 1½ cups milk.

For 2 cups sauce, use 4 tablespoons each butter and flour, 2 cups milk.

BÉCHAMEL OR MEDIUM WHITE SAUCE, BLENDER METHOD. Place in blender 2 tablespoons each butter and flour, ½ teaspoon salt, and 1 cup hot milk. Beat, covered, at high speed until smooth. Pour into saucepan (the same pan used for heating the milk), cook over low heat 3 to 5 minutes, stirring occasionally.

MEDIUM WHITE SAUCE WITH INSTANT-TYPE FLOUR. Combine in a small saucepan 1 cup *cold* milk, 2 tablespoons flour, ¼ teaspoon salt, and a dash of pepper; stir until smooth. Cook 1 minute. This is recommended primarily as a basis for other sauces or in recipes calling for Medium White Sauce.

CHEDDAR CHEESE SAUCE. Instead of butter, add ½ cup grated or cubed Cheddar cheese; stir over heat until cheese is completely melted. If a spicier sauce is desired, add ¼ teaspoon dry mustard or 1 teaspoon prepared mustard and a dash of Tabasco.

CURRY-CREAM SAUCE. Add 1 teaspoon curry powder to basic recipe.

CREAM OF MUSHROOM SAUCE. Sauté ¼ pound sliced or chopped fresh mushrooms in 3 tablespoons butter until lightly browned; stir in 2 tablespoons flour, salt, and pepper or nutmeg. Slowly stir in 1 cup milk (or ½ cup milk and ½ cup cream). Use to reheat leftover chicken, turkey, or beef; or use as the basis for a casserole (such as tuna or a mixture of leftovers), or as a filling for crepes. *Makes about 1¾ cups.*

MUSTARD CREAM SAUCE. Add 1 to 2 teaspoons prepared mustard to basic recipe. Good with beef, pork, tongue, fish, or meatballs.

Sour Cream-Mushroom Sauce

¼ pound fresh mushrooms, sliced
3 tablespoons butter
¼ teaspoon salt
Dash of nutmeg or cumin
1 can condensed cream of mushroom soup
½ cup sour cream

Sauté mushrooms in butter until lightly browned; add salt and nutmeg or cumin. Add canned soup, stir until heated thoroughly and well blended. Turn off heat; add sour cream. Let stand 5 minutes before serving. *Makes about 1¾ cups.*

Velouté Sauce

2 tablespoons butter
2 tablespoons flour
1 to 1½ cups chicken broth, or veal or fish stocks

Melt butter, stir in flour, cook over low heat until flour bubbles (do not allow to brown). Slowly add broth or stock; simmer, stirring occasionally, until smooth and thickened. Amount of liquid depends on use to which sauce is to be put. If it's to be an ingredient in a casserole, or the base for another sauce, 1 cup broth is probably sufficient. If to be served as a separate sauce, 1½ cups liquid is better. *Makes 1 to 1½ cups sauce, depending on amount of liquid used.*

BLENDER METHOD. Place flour, butter and hot broth in blender, beat until smooth. Return to saucepan in which broth was heated, cook, stirring, until smooth, thickened and velvety.

QUICK VELOUTÉ SAUCE. Add ¼ cup cream or white wine to 1 can condensed cream of chicken soup.

Mornay Sauce

To basic recipe for Béchamel or Velouté Sauce, add 2 tablespoons each shredded Swiss or Gruyère and grated Parmesan;

or add 4 tablespoons Swiss cheese. Stir until cheese is completely melted. *Makes 1 cup sauce.*

An egg is often added to Mornay Sauce. (See how in classic method for preparing Béchamel.)

If recipe calls for 1½ cups sauce, use 3 tablespoons each butter and flour, 1½ cups liquid, and 6 tablespoons cheese.

For 2 cups sauce, use 4 tablespoons each butter and flour, 2 cups liquid, and 8 tablespoons cheese.

Sauce Soubise (White Onion Sauce)

Use this to reheat leftover veal or pork, or as a sauce for shrimp, or as the base for a vegetable casserole.

2 tablespoons butter	¾ cup milk or chicken broth
1 cup chopped onion	¼ cup light cream
½ teaspoon salt	⅛ teaspoon nutmeg
2 tablespoons flour	

Melt butter without permitting it to brown; add onion, cook until onion is very soft, without browning. Add salt and flour, stir to blend. Slowly add milk or broth; cook, stirring, until smooth and thickened—about 3 minutes. Add cream and nutmeg. If a very smooth sauce is preferred, purée in blender or force through sieve or food mill. *Makes 1 cup.*

INSTANT SAUCE SOUBISE. Soften 2 tablespoons instant minced onion in 2 tablespoons water; add to ¾ cup condensed cream of chicken soup plus ¼ cup light cream; simmer 10 minutes. *To make 2 cups, double all ingredients.*

Cream-Caper Sauce

Add 1 tablespoon capers and 1 teaspoon grated onion to basic recipe. Delicious over vegetables (cauliflower especially), to reheat cold roast lamb, over fish, or with meatballs.

Chaud-Froid Sauce

1 recipe Velouté Sauce	2 tablespoons cold water or broth
1 envelope unflavored gelatin	

Prepare Velouté Sauce by either the classic or the blender method. Soften the gelatin in the cold water or broth while sauce cooks, then stir the softened gelatin into the hot sauce. Use to mask cold meats, poultry, or fish prepared for a cold buffet. The sauce should be cold (room temperature) before it is spooned over the chilled food, then it is chilled until partially set, when garnishes are placed in the sauce. When these are firmly in place, a layer of Clear Aspic is brushed over the entire bird (or whatever). *Makes 1 cup. To make 2 cups chaud-froid, double all ingredients.*

Sauce Supreme

Excellent with chicken, hard-cooked eggs, or pork. For a delicious entree, add cubed leftover roast pork to the sauce, and serve over rice.

2 tablespoons butter	¼ cup heavy cream
2 tablespoons flour	Few drops lemon juice
Salt, pepper	Canned button mushrooms,
1½ cups *homemade* chicken broth	drained (optional)

This is virtually the same as a Velouté, but richer and of lighter (thinner) consistency. Make a *roux* of the butter and the flour, being careful not to let flour brown in the slightest. Add salt, pepper, and the broth. (The excellence of the sauce depends on the flavor of the broth.) Cook over very low heat, stirring occasionally, for 15 minutes. Stir in heavy cream and, just before serving, the lemon juice. (Canned button mushrooms, well drained, may also be added to the sauce, if desired.) *Makes a little more than 1½ cups.*

SAUCE ALLEMANDE. Exactly the same as Sauce Supreme, except that 2 egg yolks are added, after sauce is thickened and smooth, but before the lemon juice.

QUICK SAUCE ALLEMANDE. Combine 1 can condensed cream of chicken soup, ½ cup well-flavored homemade chicken broth, ¼ cup heavy cream, and 1 egg yolk. Beat in blender until smooth; transfer to saucepan. cook, stirring with whisk, just until heated through and smooth. Sprinkle in a few drops of lemon juice.

Avgholemono Sauce

Use as a sauce for lamb, meatballs, chicken, or vegetable if made with chicken broth; for shrimp or fish, use fish stock.

3 egg yolks	1 cup hot chicken broth or fish
2 tablespoons lemon juice	stock

Beat egg yolks until very thick; add the lemon juice slowly, beating all the while, then very slowly add the boiling hot chicken broth, beating constantly. Stir over very low heat or over hot water until creamy-smooth. *Makes 1 cup.*

Boiled Dressing

A tangy old-fashioned salad dressing that is superb for cole slaw or potato salad. May also be served as a separate sauce for ham or cold roast beef.

1½ teaspoon salt	2 egg yolks
1 teaspoon dry mustard	1½ tablespoons butter
1½ tablespoons sugar	¾ cup milk
Pinch of cayenne	½ cup vinegar
½ tablespoon flour	

Combine salt, mustard, sugar, cayenne, and flour; blend well. Add egg yolks to flour mixture, one at a time, beating after each addition. In top of double boiler, melt butter, add egg yolk-flour mixture; stir to blend thoroughly. Slowly add milk, cook over hot water, stirring occasionally with whisk, until it starts to thicken, then add vinegar. Cook until smooth and thickened. Remove from heat; cool. If only part is used immediately, store the rest in refrigerator, covered with waxed paper to prevent formation of skin. *Makes 1 cup.*

Celery-Horseradish Sauce

Serve as a sauce with fried oysters or clams, fried fish, corned beef or tongue.

1 10½-ounce can condensed cream of celery soup	horseradish, well drained
	¼ cup light cream
1 to 2 tablespoons prepared	

Combine all ingredients in saucepan; stir over moderate heat until smooth. *Makes about 1 cup.*

Quick Cheese Sauce

Use this in recipes in which Cheese Sauce is an ingredient, or to top waffles as a supper dish, or over rolled filled crepes.

1 10½-ounce can condensed Cheddar cheese soup	wine, or sherry
	Dash of Tabasco (optional)
¼ cup light cream, beer, dry	1 tablespoon butter

Combine all ingredients; stir over moderate heat until thoroughly heated and smooth. *Makes a little under 1 cup.*

Cheese-Celery Sauce

This may be used as a topping for escalloped dishes to be browned under the broiler, or as a substitute for Mornay Sauce.

1 10½-ounce can condensed cream of celery soup
¼ cup light cream
4 tablespoons shredded Swiss

cheese, or 2 tablespoons each Swiss and grated Parmesan cheese
½ teaspoon freeze-dried chives

Combine all ingredients; stir over moderate heat until well blended, hot, and smooth. *Makes about 1 cup.*

Double-quick Mushroom Sauce

Use in casserole recipes or to reheat leftover meat, poultry, or vegetables.

1 10½-ounce can condensed cream of mushroom soup
1 2-ounce can (¼ cup) mushroom bits and pieces, with liquid

¼ cup light cream or milk
1 tablespoon butter
1 tablespoon sherry or cognac

Combine ingredients; simmer 10 minutes over very low heat, stirring occasionally. *Makes a little over 1 cup.*

Always save trimmings of fresh mushrooms to use in stock or broth. It's in the peel that the mushroom flavor is concentrated. In making the above Double-quick Mushroom Sauce, if you simmer mushroom trimmings in cream first, then strain, the canned mushrooms may be omitted.

Basic Meat Gravy

Meat gravies are the best known, the most served, and perhaps the most difficult to prepare of all the brown sauces. Meat gravies are difficult for one overriding reason: pan drippings are used for the fat, and in more cases than not, there is excess fat in the drippings. If the excess fat is not removed, the gravy will be ruined.

Yet the brown gelatinous essence which is mixed with the fat is what gives the gravy its distinctive and succulent flavor.

For the inexperienced cook, or the cook who has always been timid about making gravy, the safe way is to pour off *all* the fat, measure it, and use *only 2 tablespoons fat for each cup of liquid.* The fat to use is that containing the brown essence; all clear fat should be discarded.

This brown-essence is then returned to the same pan (skillet or roaster), and an equal quantity of flour—2 tablespoons for each cup of liquid—is stirred into the fat. As in making the roux for Béchamel, the flour and fat must cook together several minutes so that the starch granules in the flour will cook thoroughly before liquid is added. Also, if there is excess fat in the mixture it will be noticeable, and can still be corrected by pouring off all fat not absorbed by the flour. Liquid is now added, slowly, no more than ¼ cup at a time, and stirred after each addition so that the sauce is smooth and free from lumps.

For the best, most delicious gravy, the meat stock (made with the bones while the meat cooks) is far preferable to water. Yet water can be used successfully *if* there is sufficient quantity of gelatinous extract from the meat.

After all liquid has been added, the sauce should simmer at least 10 minutes. Taste for salt; if meat stock has been added, perhaps no additional salt is needed.

To thicken meat sauces with cornstarch or arrowroot, use the proportion of 1 tablespoon to each cup liquid. Cornstarch is advisable for thickening the sauce of a stew or pot roast, for it dissolves in liquid more readily than flour and produces a shiny smooth texture: blend a little liquid with the cornstarch, add to the hot sauce, simmer until thickened. Arrowroot is used the same way and is preferred by many cooks because it is less gelatinous.

Clear Pan Gravy

In making an unthickened gravy, it is even more important than in making a thickened gravy to remove all excess fat. If there is time, the best method is to pour off all pan drippings into a small bowl, then place this in the freezer so that the fat will rise to the top and congeal. The congealed fat is easier to remove than liquid fat, and the brown essence, being heavier, will remain on the bottom of the bowl.

Return the brown essence to the pan in which the meat cooked (for there may be more gelatinous bits still clinging to the pan); add water or meat stock slowly over *high* heat, stirring constantly to loosen all gelatinous bits from the bottom of the pan, and to dissolve the brown essence in the liquid.

Taste for seasoning; add salt cautiously. Serve in a French-type sauce boat, if you have one (one with a pouring spout halfway up the side, so that if there is some fat left in the gravy, it will remain on top and the fat-free essence comes out from the bottom).

The flavor of such gravies depends equally on the gelatinous essence, the absence of fat, and the richness of the meat stock.

To Give Gravy a Browner Color

Everyone expects gravy to be a deep brown in color, and when it's not, even if the flavor is good, the diners are likely to be offended. The easiest solution is to add a little gravy coloring (Kitchen Bouquet and Gravy Master are the two best-known brands). These contain caramelized sugar for the color, plus a little concentrated beef stock base (as in beef bouillon cubes). Just be careful not to overdo it: a little of the gravy coloring goes a long way.

Another way is to caramelize sugar yourself (see How to Caramelize Sugar). Place about 1 tablespoon sugar in pan, melt until golden; this is ample for 1 to 1½ cups gravy.

Still another method is to add a little catsup or tomato paste—which darkens the color, but also alters the flavor, which may or may not be desirable.

Using Gravy Mix

Most commercial gravy mixes contain a mixture of flour, salt, caramel for dark color, and the same beef-flavored stock concentrate (with artificial flavoring) as contained in bouillon cubes and sold in jars. Such a mix is a big help in making any of the following brown sauces. But if a mix is used to make simple meat gravy, the cook must still be sure to remove all excess fat from the drippings, and salvage as much of the brown essence as possible.

Beef-flavored stock concentrate by itself has an artificial flavor with a chemical aftertaste. Canned beef bouillon, and canned beef gravy have this same undesirable taste. But for all of us, emergencies arise occasionally when making gravy the right way is not possible; and for such occasions, the following are short-cut recipes which anyone can serve with pride. (In any recipe that calls for 1 can beef gravy, gravy mix may be used instead: use proportions given on label to make 1 cup gravy.)

Wine Gravy

1 can beef gravy	2 tablespoons chopped parsley
¾ cup white wine	1 tablespoon butter

Combine all ingredients; cook, stirring occasionally, until sauce is reduced to desired consistency. (If by chance there is fat-free brown essence in the roasting pan or skillet to which this can be added, the gravy will be even better.) *Makes about 1½ cups.*

Rich Brown Gravy

1 can beef gravy, or gravy mix plus water to make 1 cup gravy	¼ cup medium sherry or Madeira
	1 teaspoon instant minced onion
1 tablespoon tomato paste	1 to 2 tablespoons butter

Combine all ingredients; simmer 10 minutes. *Makes 1 to 1¼ cups gravy. To make 2 to 2½ cups, double all ingredients.*

Easy Sauce Espagnole

Sauce Espagnole is one of the great classic sauces; as made by master chefs, it requires 3 or 4 days to prepare. Escoffier would not have approved of this short-cut version, but then Escoffier never had to supervise a household of children or meet the commuter train every night. Excellent for reheating game or roast meat.

1 small onion, chopped	1 tablespoon tomato paste
About ¼ cup grated carrot	1 cup beef broth
1 tablespoon minced parsley	1 can beef gravy
2 tablespoons butter	½ cup red wine
1 tablespoon flour	

Simmer onion, carrot and parsley in butter until soft. Stir in flour; cook 2 minutes. Add tomato paste; purée in blender at high speed, adding the beef broth a little at a time. Add mixture to beef gravy and wine; simmer, stirring occasionally, until sauce has cooked down to desired consistency. *Makes about 2 cups.*

SAUCE DIAVOLO. To ½ recipe Sauce Espagnole, add 1 tablespoon Worcestershire, ½ teaspoon dry mustard, and a dash of Tabasco. Excellent with hamburgers or to warm up leftover pot roast cut into slices or chunks.

SAUCE CHASSEUR. Sauté ¼ pound mushrooms, sliced, in 2 tablespoons butter. Add 1 cup Sauce Espagnole. Serve over sautéed veal scallopini.

MADEIRA SAUCE. To 1 cup Sauce Espagnole, add 2 to 3 tablespoons Madeira wine. Excellent with any meat.

Brown Steak Sauce

1 can condensed beef consommé	1 tablespoon catsup
¼ cup medium dry sherry	1 teaspoon instant minced onion
2 tablespoons soy sauce	1 tablespoon minced parsley

Combine all ingredients but parsley. Boil 5 minutes; add parsley. Serve as a thin sauce over steak. *Makes 1½ cups.*

Hot Currant Sauce

To 1 cup hot beef gravy, add ½ cup currant jelly and ½ teaspoon dry mustard. Stir until jelly is melted. Very good with game, ham, or cold roast pork.

Sauce Robert

Excellent with pork chops or to reheat any cooked pork.

2 large onions, sliced	made with mix
2 tablespoons butter	¼ cup red or white wine
1 can beef gravy, or 1 cup gravy	2 tablespoons heavy cream

Cook onions slowly in butter until soft. Add beef gravy and wine; cook until reduced to desired consistency. Turn off heat; stir in cream. *Makes a little over 1 cup.*

QUICK SAUCE ROBERT. Add 2 tablespoons instant minced onion, ¼ cup wine, and 2 tablespoons cream to beef gravy; simmer 10 minutes.

Yogurt and Sour Cream Sauces

When yogurt or sour cream is added to a warm sauce, the heat should be turned off completely, or at least turned very low, and the sauce beaten briskly with a whisk until smooth. If not to be served at once, keep warm over hot water.

Cold yogurt and sour cream sauces are easier. Often nothing more is needed to make a sauce of the basic ingredient but to add seasonings.

Hungarian Sour Cream Sauce

Delicious over cauliflower, meatballs, or fish.

2 egg yolks, slightly beaten	½ teaspoon salt
1 cup (½ pint) thick sour cream	1 teaspoon paprika
2 teaspoons lemon juice	¼ teaspoon black pepper

Combine ingredients in top of double boiler; cook, stirring constantly, over hot water for 3 to 5 minutes, or until sauce is thoroughly heated. Keep warm, covered, until needed. *Makes 1 cup.*

Polish Dill Sauce

Very good with cold pork or beef, over noodles or meatballs. Combine 1 can beef gravy (or 1 cup gravy made with mix), ½ cup sour cream, and 1 tablespoon chopped fresh dill (or 1 teaspoon crumbled dill weed). Heat over very low heat or hot water, stirring constantly, until thoroughly hot. Serve garnished with sieved egg yolk. *Makes 1½ cups.*

Yogurt and Cucumber Sauce
Use as a salad dressing, or a sauce with shrimp or fish.

½ cup cucumber, chopped
½ teaspoon salt
1 teaspoon sugar
1 cup (½ pint) plain yogurt

½ teaspoon freshly ground
black pepper
1 teaspoon dried mint, crumbled

Sprinkle cucumber with salt and sugar; let stand 15 minutes; drain. Add remaining ingredients. *Makes 1½ cups.*

SOUR CREAM-HORSERADISH SAUCE
Blend 1 tablespoon prepared horseradish (well drained) with ½ cup sour cream. Serve as a sauce with cold roast beef, cold ham, pork, or poached fish.

SOUR CREAM-DILL SAUCE
Add 2 tablespoons chopped fresh dill to ½ cup sour cream. Serve over sliced cucumbers, pickled beets, or cold meat, or as a topping for borscht or other soups (hot or cold).

SOUR CREAM TOPPING FOR POTATOES
Crush a garlic clove in a small bowl; discard shreds. Add ½ cup thick sour cream, salt to taste, and about a tablespoon of freeze-dried chives. Blend well. Pass in a sauce boat.

SOUR CREAM-MAYONNAISE SALAD DRESSING
To equal parts mayonnaise and sour cream, add a few drops lemon juice, plus salt, pepper, and paprika to taste. Serve over salad greens.

Blue Cheese-Cream Dressing

1 cup sour cream, or ½ cup each
sour cream and mayonnaise

½ cup crumbled blue cheese
Salt, pepper

Combine ingredients; beat to blend well. Serve over crisp salad greens. *Makes 1½ cups, enough for 6 servings of salad.*

BLUE-CHEESE-YOGURT DRESSING.
Use 1 cup yogurt instead of sour cream.

Yogurt-Mint Dressing

1 cup plain yogurt
½ teaspoon crushed dried mint
1 pinch cayenne

½ teaspoon freshly ground
  black pepper
Salt

Combine ingredients. Serve over crisp salad greens or with seafood. *Makes 1 cup, enough for 4 to 6 servings.*

Basic Sofrito

1 medium onion, chopped
1 clove garlic, split
1 small carrot, peeled, grated
¼ cup minced parsley
2 to 3 tablespoons olive oil, or 1
  tablespoon olive oil and 2 table-

spoons butter
1 small tomato, peeled, seeded,
  chopped
¼ teaspoon salt
1 cup clear chicken broth
½ cup dry white wine

Gently cook onion, garlic, carrot, and parsley in oil (or a blend of oil and butter) until very soft—about 15 minutes. When garlic is soft, mash into oil with tines of fork. After 10 minutes add the chopped tomato; sprinkle salt over vegetables. Add chicken broth and wine; continue cooking until liquid is reduced to 1 cup. Taste for seasoning; add more salt if needed. For a smooth sauce, force through sieve or purée by beating in blender. *Makes 1 cup.*

For 1½ *cups sauce,* increase amount of chicken broth to 1½ cups. If sauce is not as thick as desired, thicken with ½ tablespoon cornstarch dissolved in small amount of sauce, then added to remaining sauce.

Basic Mirepoix

2 leeks, chopped, or 4 shallots,
  chopped, or 2 small white onions, sliced
1 small carrot, peeled, grated
1 stalk celery, chopped
1 teaspoon minced parsley
2 tablespoons butter

2 tablespoons minced ham
  (optional)
1 medium tomato, peeled, seeded, chopped or 2 tablespoons
  catsup
2 cups clear chicken broth or
  meat stock

Cook leek or onion, carrot, celery, and parsley in butter until very soft. If ham is to be added, cook the ham with the vegetable until lightly browned. Add the tomato or catsup; cook until very soft. Purée mixture, or force through sieve. Blend with chicken broth; simmer until liquid is reduced and thickened. Taste for salt; add more if needed. (This should be more delicate in flavor than the Sofrito.) *Makes about 1½ cups.*

Homemade Tomato Sauce (Basic Recipe)

1 ½ to 2 cups chopped onion
2 cloves garlic, minced
¼ cup olive oil
2 teaspoons salt
6 to 8 tomatoes, peeled, chopped,
  or 1 large (1-pound 12-ounce)
  can peeled tomatoes

1 6-ounce can tomato paste
1 teaspoon orégano or blended
  spaghetti sauce seasoning, or ½
  teaspoon each thyme and
  orégano
½ teaspoon sugar

Simmer onions and garlic in oil until soft and golden but not browned. Add salt and tomatoes; cook until tomatoes are very soft—about ½ hour. Force through sieve or food mill, return to pan, add tomato paste, orégano, sugar and any other desired seasonings to taste. Continue cooking over very low heat until thickened to purée consistency. *Makes about 2 cups.*

GREEK TOMATO SAUCE. After straining tomato mixture, add, with tomato paste and orégano, ½ cup minced parsley and ½ teaspoon cinnamon.

SPANISH TOMATO SAUCE. Along with the chopped onion and garlic, cook about ¼ cup chopped pimiento. Omit sugar, add ¼ cup minced parsley.

CAPER TOMATO SAUCE. After straining tomato sauce, add 2 tablespoons drained capers and 1 teaspoon lemon juice.

WITH SALT PORK. Instead of ¼ cup olive oil in basic recipe, use 1 tablespoon oil or butter and 2 ounces diced salt pork. Draw out fat from pork; discard remaining cubes of pork. Add ¼ teaspoon basil to sauce in last step.

WITH WINE. Add ¼ cup medium sherry or sweet vermouth; omit sugar; cook until reduced to desired consistency.

BOLOGNESE SAUCE. Sauté ½ pound chopped beef in olive oil before adding onion; cook until meat loses pink color. Proceed as in basic recipe.

MARINARA SAUCE. Essentially the same as Homemade Tomato Sauce. Any difference is pretty much at the whim of the cook. Some add chopped green pepper; some thin it with dry red or white wine.

Quick Spaghetti Sauce

1 15-ounce can tomato sauce, or 2
  8-ounce cans
¼ cup minced parsley
1 tablespoon instant minced onion
1 clove garlic, minced, or ½ teaspoon garlic powder
2 to 3 tablespoons olive oil

Combine all ingredients; simmer 10 minutes. *Makes a little under 2 cups.*

Tomato Glaze

A basting sauce for spit-roasted chickens, pork, or beef.

½ cup minced onion
1 small clove garlic, minced
½ cup minced celery
¼ cup olive oil
2 tablespoons tomato paste
2 teaspoons beef stock base, or 2
beef bouillon cubes
1 tablespoon cornstarch
1 teaspoon gravy coloring
½ cup medium dry sherry
1 cup water
½ teaspoon mixed herbs

Simmer onion, garlic, and celery in olive oil until soft; add tomato paste, beef stock base or bouillon cube, and cornstarch, stirring to blend cornstarch. Cook, stirring, 3 minutes. Add sherry, water, and herbs. Simmer 15 minutes. Strain through sieve. *Makes about 1½ cups.*

French Tomato Sauce

¼ pound salt pork, diced
4 shallots, chopped, or 2 small
  white onions, chopped
1 carrot, peeled, grated
⅛ teaspoon thyme
½ bay leaf (optional)
1 teaspoon minced parsley
2 tablespoons butter
1 tablespoon flour
6 medium fully ripe tomatoes,
  peeled, seeded
1 cup broth
1 teaspoon sugar
Salt

Draw out the fat from the salt pork until cubes are reduced to very small size; remove and discard them. Add the shallots or onion, carrot, and herbs; cook until soft. Stir in flour, cook until it bubbles. Add tomatoes, beef broth, and sugar. Simmer until sauce is reduced and thickened. Purée in blender or force through food mill. Adjust seasonings to taste. *Makes about 2 cups.*

WITH CANNED TOMATOES. Instead of fresh tomatoes, use 1 large (1-pound 12-ounce) can peeled tomatoes, force through sieve or food mill to remove seeds.

TOMATO SAUCE PROVENÇAL. Prepare as for French Tomato Sauce, but add 1 teaspoon capers, 6 pitted black olives, and 1 tablespoon Madeira wine or brandy.

Basic Curry Sauce

Make the sauce this way to use for reheating leftover roast lamb, beef, or turkey; or, first sauté raw meat, shrimp, or other seafood in oil, then add remaining ingredients.

2 or 3 medium onions, minced
2 or 3 cloves garlic, minced
3 tablespoons oil
1 tablespoon curry powder, or mixed blended spices to taste
½ green pepper, chopped
2 tart apples, peeled, seeded, chopped*

2 tablespoons seedless raisins or currants
1 to 1½ cups chicken or meat broth
1 tablespoon catsup or tomato paste (optional)
Salt

Cook onions and garlic slowly in oil until soft; after 5 minutes, add curry powder. Add green pepper and apples, continue cooking until almost like a purée. Add remaining ingredients, simmer until sauce is of desired consistency. *Makes about 3 cups.*

*Instead of the apples, 1 yellow squash, peeled and chopped, may be used.

Fruit Sauces for Meat

Most of these are sweet-sour; some are sweet-sour-spicy combinations. They are to be found in the cuisines of many different countries.

Cumberland Sauce

½ cup currant jelly
2 tablespoons dry mustard
1/16 teaspoon cayenne
¼ teaspoon powdered ginger

2 tablespoons lemon juice
1 tablespoon grated lemon rind
1 tablespoon grated orange rind
1/3 cup port wine

In a small saucepan, melt jelly over low heat. Separately, combine spices with lemon juice and grated rind; stir in the port. Add this to the melted jelly. Brush over poultry, serve with cold beef, or game as a glaze. *Makes about 1 cup.*

Curried Plum Sauce

Especially delicious with lamb; a good way to turn leftover roast lamb into a new entree.

1 large can blue plums	¼ teaspoon curry powder
1 tablespoon instant minced onion	1 pinch ginger
1 teaspoon gravy mix	1 teaspoon grated lemon rind
1 tablespoon soy sauce	1 teaspoon lemon juice

Pit 8 of the plums; place in blender with 1 cup of the syrup. Add remaining ingredients; beat until smooth. Heat, stirring. (If leftover roast lamb or pork is to be heated in the sauce, simply add meat mixture, and heat in skillet until thoroughly hot.) *Makes 1 cup.*

Raisin Sauce

A classic German sauce for tongue, ham, or cold game.

2 tablespoons butter	Grated rind of ½ lemon
2 tablespoons flour	Few drops lemon juice
1½ cups meat stock	Salt, sugar
½ cup white wine	1 tablespoon Kitchen Bouquet
1/3 cup seedless raisins	or Gravy Master

Make a roux of butter and flour; cook until flour bubbles. Slowly add meat stock or beef broth; cook until thickened. Add wine, raisins, rind, lemon juice, and salt and sugar to taste. Stir in gravy coloring for more attractive appearance. *Makes 2 cups.*

QUICK RAISIN SAUCE. Combine 1 can beef gravy, 1/3 cup raisins, 2 tablespoons currant jelly, 1 tablespoon vinegar, freshly ground black pepper, and 1/3 cup white wine or 2 tablespoons rum or brandy. Heat until well blended. *Makes 1 to 1 1/3 cups.*

Teriyaki Sauce

¼ cup Japanese soy sauce	1 tablespoon oil
¼ cup dry sherry or gin	⅛ teaspoon ginger
1 tablespoon brown sugar or	½ cup chicken broth,
honey	or ½ cup orange juice

Combine all ingredients. A basic sauce in Japanese cuisine. Used primarily as a marinade for pork, beef, chicken, shrimp, or fish, but also as a dip or sauce for fried shrimp or vegetables Tempura. *Makes 1 cup.*

Sherry, soy sauce, and orange juice are used together in various combinations. Sometimes it's pineapple juice instead of orange juice; sometimes white wine is used rather than sherry, but these really are variations on the same theme.

Chinese Sweet and Pungent Sauce

Use this sauce for Chinese-style spareribs, fish, meatballs, pork, or chicken livers and ham.

2 tablespoons oil
1 large clove garlic, minced
¼ cup chopped onion
¼ cup sliced bamboo shoots or water chestnuts
1 green pepper, chopped
1/3 cup pineapple juice
½ cup vinegar

2 to 4 tablespoons brown sugar, or 1 tablespoon molasses
2 tablespoons cornstarch
2 tablespoons soy sauce
1 cup water or chicken broth
Salt
10 to 12 chunks canned pineapple

Heat oil; add garlic, onion, and bamboo shoots or water chestnuts. Cook 2 to 3 minutes. Add green pepper; cook 1 minute. Separately, combine pineapple juice, vinegar, brown sugar or molasses, cornstarch, and soy sauce; stir to dissolve cornstarch. Add water or broth; add this mixture to vegetables. Simmer until thickened and translucent. Add salt to taste, then the pineapple. Cook 3 minutes longer. *Makes 1¾ cups.*

Basic Oriental Brown Sauce

2 teaspoons cornstarch
1 tablespoon cold water
1 cup chicken broth
2 tablespoons soy sauce

1 tablespoon brown sugar, or 1 teaspoon molasses
¼ teaspoon dry mustard (optional)

Dissolve cornstarch in water; add to chicken broth, bring to a boil. Blend together soy sauce, molasses, and mustard; stir into chicken broth. Simmer until thickened and translucent. Used over Foo Yong, or as the sauce to thicken many Chinese entrees. *Makes a little over 1 cup.*

Sherry-Soy Sauce

½ cup medium sherry
¼ cup soy sauce

Dash of Tabasco or cayenne

Combine all ingredients. Use as dip or marinade. *Makes ¾ cup.*

Pineapple-Soy Marinade

½ cup canned pineapple juice
¼ cup Japanese soy sauce
2 tablespoons vinegar
2 tablespoons honey

¼ cup dry sherry or white wine
½ teaspoon salt
Dash of Tabasco

Combine all ingredients. Use as marinade or barbecue sauce. Especially good with pork or ham. *Makes 1¼ cups.*

Curried Orange and Soy Sauce

1 cup orange juice
2 tablespoons soy sauce
¼ teaspoon curry powder

½ teaspoon salt
1 tablespoon oil
1 small onion, grated

Combine all ingredients. A good marinade for chicken, pork, duck, ham, or fruit. Also an excellent basting sauce for spit-roasted chicken or spareribs. *Makes 1½ cups.*

Soy-Horseradish Sauce

¼ cup soy sauce
1 to 2 teaspoons horseradish

½ cup dry sherry or white wine

Combine all ingredients. Use to marinate fish or beef or as a dip for broiled appetizers (shrimp, pork, or beef bites especially). *Makes ¾ cup.*

Peach Sparerib Sauce

½ cup syrup from canned peaches
Dash of Tabasco or cayenne
2 tablespoons soy sauce

½ cup dry sherry or
  white wine
1 teaspoon vinegar

Combine ingredients. Brush generously over spareribs during last 15 minutes of cooking. *Makes a little over 1 cup.*

Red-hot Indonesian Sauce

2 tablespoons Japanese soy sauce
1 medium onion, minced
2 bay leaves
½ teaspoon dried hot red pepper

flakes
¼ cup lemon juice
¼ cup water

Combine all ingredients in saucepan, bring to a boil, simmer 5 minutes. Strain. Serve as clear sauce or dip for broiled appetizers or over broiled fish, chicken, or beef. *Makes ½ cup.*

Satay Marinade

A thick sauce to be served as a relish over barbecued skewered beef, pork, or chicken.

1 large clove garlic
1 small onion, quartered
2 tablespoons shelled peanuts
2 green chili peppers, seeded,
  chopped
¼ teaspoon crushed hot red
  pepper

1 teaspoon brown sugar
2 tablespoons lemon juice
¼ cup water
¼ cup shredded coconut
¾ cup milk
1 tablespoon Japanese soy
  sauce

Place all ingredients in blender, beat at high speed until

crushed. Transfer to saucepan, bring to a boil, cook 2 minutes.
Cool to room temperature: refrigerate 24 hours before using.
Serve as a relish. *Makes about 1 cup.*

Satay Sauce

2 cloves garlic, crushed
4 tablespoons peanut butter
1 tablespoon vinegar or lemon
  juice

3 tablespoons soy sauce
¼ teaspoon cayenne
4 tablespoons hot water (¼ cup)

Combine all ingredients, beat to blend. *Makes about ¾ cups.*

Coconut Milk

This is best made with fresh grated coconut, unsweetened,
but as a short cut, canned coconut (shredded or flaked) is acceptable.

1¼ cups fresh grated coconut, or
  1 4-ounce can shredded coconut, or 1 3½-ounce can flaked

coconut
1 cup hot milk

Place coconut in bowl; cover with milk, let stand 30 minutes.
Drain through a sieve, forcing through as much of the coconut
as possible. Or, place coconut and milk in blender, beat until
coconut is soft and pulpy, then strain. Discard the coconut; the
milk will have coconut flavor. *Makes 1 cup.*

Flavored Butters

Exact measurements are not important in preparing any of
the following. They are convenient when kept in the refrigerator for quick seasoning of vegetables, to brush over French
bread, or as a sauce for broiled steak.

Maître d'Hôtel Butter

½ cup (1 stick) butter, softened   A few drops lemon juice
About 2 teaspoons chopped parsley

Blend all ingredients. Chill until firm. Cut into squares or
shape into balls (using a melon cutter or a small spoon) or curls
(using a butter paddle—available at gourmet bazaars). Place
firm cold butter pats or balls on each serving of hot grilled
steak. *Makes 10 to 16 servings.*

Herb Butters

The following are good all-purpose combinations, which may
be used for vegetables, chicken, fish, or meat, or a little may

even be added to hot sauces (such as Velouté made with canned cream of chicken soup and cream) for stepped-up flavor. Use approximately 1 teaspoon dried herbs or 1 tablespoon chopped fresh herbs to ½ cup softened butter. Or, use a combination of dried and fresh herbs.

For each ½ cup butter, use

- ¼ teaspoon each thyme and orégano and ½ to 1 tablespoon chopped parsley
- ½ teaspoon tarragon and ½ teaspoon thyme
- 1 teaspoon tarragon and ½ teaspoon thyme
- 1 teaspoon minced fresh dill and 1 teaspoon minced parsley,
- ½ teaspoon freeze-dried chives
- ¼ teaspoon dried basil, ¼ teaspoon thyme, and ¼ teaspoon marjoram
- 1 tablespoon chopped fresh cilantro (especially good over broiled pork chops or tomato soup)

Chill before using.

CARAWAY BUTTER. Crush ½ teaspoon caraway seeds in a mortar; work in ½ cup butter to a paste. Remove to small bowl; chill. Use over fish, broiled or fried, or over a grilled slice of ham.

TARRAGON BUTTER. Work dried or chopped fresh tarragon into softened butter; add a few drops of lemon juice. Use over broiled chicken or fish.

CURRY BUTTER. Work ½ to 1 teaspoon curry powder (according to taste) into ½ cup butter. Excellent with lima or green beans.

Drawn Butter Sauce

Clarify butter by melting it in a small sauce pan or skillet over low heat; strain off the clear golden liquid (so that none of the casein particles remain in the butter). Add a few drops of lemon juice. Serve immediately over hot boiled lobster, hot cooked shrimp, or poached fish, or with steamed clams.

Garlic Butter

MELTED GARLIC BUTTER. Place whole garlic cloves in melted butter in a small skillet, cook until garlic is golden (but do not allow to brown). When golden and soft, press with tines of fork to release juices. Discard garlic. Brush butter over cut slices of French bread for Garlic Bread.

COLD GARLIC BUTTER. Crush garlic in a small bowl, then work in softened butter. Chill. Use pats over hot grilled steak.

Lemon Butter

Cut a fresh lemon into quarters; sauté in butter until peel is lightly browned; squeeze with tines of fork to release some of lemon juice. Pour hot butter over grilled fish, chicken, or pork chops, or over boiled lobster.

Mustard Steak Sauce

4 tablespoons butter	1 teaspoon Dijon mustard
1 large or 2 medium cloves garlic	

Melt butter in small skillet; peel garlic, split in half, place garlic in butter and cook until lightly browned. Press garlic with tines of fork to release juices. Remove and discard garlic, if desired. Add mustard, stir to blend. Pour into small bowl or sauce boat, pass as hot sauce for steak. *Makes ½ cup.*

Emulsified Sauces

Mayonnaise and Hollandaise are made according to the same basic principle: as fat is beaten into egg (or, better, egg yolk), the mixture thickens into cream and finally becomes stiff and creamy. When made by hand, the mixture must be beaten with great vigor and the fat (oil or butter) added very, very slowly. With a blender or even an electric mixer, it is far easier: the machine does the beating, and your only job is to add the oil (or hot melted butter) in a thin, steady stream. If the fat is added too quickly, the mixture may fail to thicken, or if the weather is too hot and humid, or the utensils (or the oil) too cold, you may never achieve anything more than a sauce the consistency of cream. Or, worse, the sauce may thicken beautifully—but before it can be served, it has broken down again into its component parts.

Making mayonnaise by the original, centuries-old method is not difficult once one has learned the trick of beating quickly and rhythmically with a supple turn of the wrist. The sauce acquires a beautiful shiny gloss; its color is a brighter yellow, too, and even the flavor seems different. But there is a trick to making it this way, and not everyone has the patience or determination to master it. Commercial mayonnaise is so available and so much easier to use!

Of all the emulsified sauces, Hollandaise is the trickiest, because it must be beaten over warm (not hot) water, or with warm melted butter, and because egg is so sensitive to heat, curdling may occur despite the greatest care. Using a blender is the safest way, and also the easiest—and this sauce is so very delicious that it's worth mastering.

Homemade Mayonnaise (Classic Method)

2 egg yolks
½ teaspoon salt
1 cup oil (all olive, all vegetable oil, or ½ cup each olive and vegetable oil)

1½ tablespoons vinegar
A few drops lemon juice
½ teaspoon prepared mustard (optional)

Beat egg yolks until very thick and very light in color. Add salt. Continue beating egg yolk (now very creamy and thickened), adding oil in a very thin stream; or, add about ½ teaspoon oil to the eggs at a time, beating briskly after each addition until smooth and slightly thickened. After half the oil has been added, and mixture begins to thicken visibly, oil may be added in a thicker stream or 1 teaspoon at a time, alternately with the vinegar (1 teaspoon at a time). When mixture is quite stiff, add the lemon juice and mustard, if desired. Keep refrigerated between servings. *Makes about 2 cups (1 pint).*

BLENDER METHOD. The recipe is the same, except that the beating is done in the blender instead of by hand. Set at *low speed.* A whole egg may be used instead of 2 egg yolks, if preferred.

MIXER METHOD. Just like the blender method, except that electric mixer is set at *high speed.* Use the small mixing bowl.

IF MAYONNAISE CURDLES. Put another egg yolk in a clean bowl (or remove the curdled mayonnaise from the blender and wash out the blender). Start all over, beating the egg yolk until thick, then add the curdled mayonnaise about ¼ cup at a time, beating after each addition until very smooth.

Quick Mayonnaise Variations

CURRY MAYONNAISE. Add 1 teaspoon curry powder to ½ cup commercial mayonnaise. A nice sauce for fish or seafood salad.

RUSSIAN DRESSING. Blend together ¼ cup chili sauce or cat-sup with 1 cup mayonnaise. If desired, add a little grated onion and a few dashes of Worcestershire sauce. *Makes 1¼ cups.*

THOUSAND ISLAND DRESSING. Basically the same as Russian Dressing, but with 1 hard-cooked egg, chopped, a little grated or minced onion, some minced parsley, and chopped pimiento.

SOUR CREAM-RUSSIAN DRESSING. Combine equal quantities commercial sour cream and commercial mayonnaise, plus a little catsup (1 tablespoon to 1 cup sauce). A good dressing for fruit salads.

CHUTNEY MAYONNAISE. Chop commercial chutney in fine pieces, about 1 to 2 tablespoons to a cup of mayonnaise (or, use half mayonnaise, half sour cream). Delicious with fruit.

COLD RAVIGOTE SAUCE. Crush 1 anchovy fillet with 1 tablespoon chopped parsley; add 1 cup commercial or homemade mayonnaise and 1 hard-cooked egg, chopped.

TARRAGON MAYONNAISE. Use tarragon vinegar in making Homemade Mayonnaise.

Tartar Sauce

1 cup mayonnaise	1 tablespoon minced parsley
2 tablespoons minced sweet gherkins	3 pimiento-stuffed green olives, chopped
1 tablespoon grated or minced onion, or 1 teaspoon instant minced onion	1 teaspoon vinegar, or ½ teaspoon lemon juice

To mayonnaise, add remaining ingredients in order given. Serve as a sauce for fish, or, mixed with tuna, as a sandwich filling. *Makes about 1¼ cups.*

Caper Mayonnaise

1 or 2 cloves garlic	1 tablespoon minced fresh basil, or ½ teaspoon dried basil, crushed
1 cup mayonnaise	
1 tablespoon capers, drained	
1 teaspoon Dijon mustard	1 tablespoon minced parsley

Crush garlic cloves in small bowl; discard shreds. Add remaining ingredients, blend well. Serve as a dip with vegetable relishes, shrimp, or luncheon meat, or as a sauce for cold cuts. *Makes 1 cup.*

Green Mayonnaise

6 to 8 fresh spinach leaves,
  or 6 sprigs watercress
¼ cup chopped parsley

2 tablespoons chopped fresh dill
¼ teaspoon dried tarragon
1 cup mayonnaise

Remove stems from spinach and watercress; mash in mortar and pestle or in blender with parsley, dill, and tarragon; add mayonnaise; beat until mayonnaise is an even green color. *Makes 1¼ cups.* Serve as a dip for shrimp, a dressing for sliced tomatoes, or as a filling for smoked salmon roll-ups.

Sauce Rémoulade

1 cup mayonnaise
1 tablespoon Dijon mustard
2 tablespoons chopped gherkin
  pickles
2 tablespoons chopped, drained
  capers

1 teaspoon grated or minced onion
1 tablespoon chopped parsley
¼ teaspoon dried tarragon
1 anchovy fillet, mashed, or 1 teaspoon anchovy paste

Combine all ingredients; beat to blend thoroughly. Serve as a separate sauce at a cold buffet, for cold meat, turkey or seafood. *Makes 1¼ cups.*

Aioli (Ailloli) Sauce

This may have preceded mayonnaise historically; it has been made in Spain, the Balearics, and southern France for as long as anyone can remember, and it is essentially the same as mayonnaise, but with garlic—lots of garlic. Served with grilled lamb chops, over fish (it's a favorite with bacalao in the Mediterranean), hard-cooked eggs, and/or boiled potatoes.

4 or 5 cloves garlic
1 cup olive oil
1 egg

1 tablespoon lemon juice
¼ to ½ teaspoon salt, or to
  taste

Crush garlic in mortar or narrow bowl, work in ¼ cup olive oil a little at a time until thickened, then add egg, beat vigorously until smooth, and start adding remaining ¾ cup oil just as for mayonnaise: a thin stream at first, until sauce is consistency of thick mayonnaise. Add lemon juice and salt at the end. *Makes about 2 cups.*

BLENDER METHOD. Chop garlic in large pieces, place in blender with ¼ cup of the oil, beat until thick and smooth. Add egg, beat until thoroughly blended with oil. Add remaining oil in thin stream, as for mayonnaise, beating until blended.

Tapenade

A spicy, sharp, garlicky caper sauce which may be used as a dip for vegetable relishes or shrimp or a sauce for seafood appetizers. The name is from the Provençal word meaning "capers."

2 tablespoons capers, well blended
1 or 2 cloves garlic
6 anchovy fillets

Freshly ground black pepper
½ cup olive oil
1 to 2 tablespoons lemon juice, or to taste

In a mortar, crush the capers and garlic into a paste, then add the anchovies, one at a time, mashing into a paste. Transfer the paste to a bowl (or to blender or small bowl of electric mixer) and slowly beat in the olive oil, a very little at a time at first, adding more as the mixture becomes creamy and thick. Add black pepper and lemon juice at the end. (Do not add salt.) *Makes about 1 cup.*

Hollandaise (Classic Recipe)

½ cup (1 stick) butter
2 or 3 egg yolks
1 tablespoon lemon juice

1 tablespoon water
¼ teaspoon salt

BLENDER METHOD. Melt the butter just until liquid; do not allow to brown in the least. Remove from heat. In blender place egg yolks (2 for normal sauce, 3 if thicker sauce is desired), lemon juice, water, and salt. Beat at low speed until somewhat thickened; then, with blender in motion, slowly add the melted butter (clear liquid only, not the white particles), pouring through hole in cover, until mixture is thick and creamy. *Makes 2/3 to 3/4 cup.*

CLASSIC METHOD. Cut butter into fourths. In top of double boiler, place lemon juice, water, and salt; heat until lukewarm. Make sure water in lower part of double boiler does not touch upper part, and while it should be hot, it must never come to the boil. Add egg yolks to warm lemon juice mixture; beat constantly until thickened, then add first fourth of the butter; beat steadily until blended thoroughly. Repeat with remaining butter. Remove from heat; stir in a few drops additional lemon juice, if desired. Keep pan covered and in warm place, but do not reheat. *Makes 3/4 cup.*

SAUCE BÉARNAISE. Prepare Hollandaise by either blender or classic method. Separately, simmer 2 tablespoons chopped shallot, scallion, or small white onion and ½ teaspoon dried tarragon in 2 tablespoons dry white wine for 2 to 3 minutes, until wine is evaporated. Add to *warm* stiff Hollandaise along with a generous amount of freshly ground black pepper. Stir to blend. A favorite sauce for grilled, poached, or fried fish, and for Steak Chateaubriand.

SAUCE MOUSSELINE. Prepare Hollandaise by either blender or classic method. Stir in 1 cup whipped cream (½ cup heavy cream before whipping) and a few drops lemon juice. May be served as a dessert sauce, or with cold fish (such as salmon) or a buffet aspic. *Makes 2 cups.*

SAUCE MALTAISE. Prepare Hollandaise by either blender or classic method. Add 1 tablespoon grated orange rind and 1 tablespoon orange juice. A tablespoon of heavy sweet cream or sour cream may also be added, if desired. Beautiful with pheasant, turkey, or ham.

WHAT TO DO IF HOLLANDAISE CURDLES. Place 1 raw egg yolk in blender, add a little of the curdled sauce at a time with blender in motion. Or, if you don't have a blender, place the fresh yolk in top of double boiler over warm (not hot) water; beat with whisk, adding curdled sauce bit by bit.

German Hollandaise

6 tablespoons butter	broth
1 tablespoon flour	4 egg yolks
1½ cups fish, chicken, or veal stock, or 1½ cups clear chicken	2 tablespoons lemon juice

Melt 1 tablespoon of the butter in saucepan, stir in flour, cook until mixture bubbles. Slowly add stock or broth, cook 3 to 5 minutes until smooth and thickened. Place egg yolks in top of double boiler; beat over hot (not boiling) water until thickened. (Water must not touch top of pan.) Add a little of the warm sauce and 1 tablespoon butter; beat until smooth. Add rest of hot sauce about one-fourth at a time, adding 1 tablespoon butter

with each addition, until all sauce and butter have been added. When creamy and thick, add the lemon juice. Remove from heat; keep covered in a warm place until needed. *Makes 1¾ cups sauce.*

Curry Mousseline Sauce

¼ cup shredded coconut
½ cup light cream or dairy half-and-half, heated
¼ cup shredded coconut
1 can condensed cream of chicken soup

3 egg yolks
1 teaspoon to 1 tablespoon lemon juice
2 tablespoons heavy cream or sour cream

Add coconut to cream or half-and-half; heat in saucepan until steaming, but do not allow to boil. Let stand 15 minutes, then force through sieve (discarding coconut, keeping cream) or beat in blender until coconut is completely puréed. Stir coconut-cream into soup; blend well. Place egg yolks in top of double boiler, add soup mixture a little at a time, beating thoroughly over hot (not boiling) water until smooth and thickened. Add 1 tablespoon lemon juice if using sweet cream, only 1 teaspoon if using sour cream; blend thoroughly. Then add cream. Superb as a sauce for shrimp or chicken. Or, serve over rice, as an accompaniment to cold turkey or cold ham. *Makes 1¾ cups.*

Mock Hollandaise

2 egg yolks
1 cup commercial mayonnaise

1 teaspoon lemon juice
2 tablespoons butter

Beat egg yolks in blender until very light and thick. Add ¼ cup mayonnaise at a time, beating until very stiff. Add lemon juice. Transfer to top of double boiler over hot (not boiling) water. Add butter, beat constantly until smooth. Remove from heat; keep pan covered in warm place. *Makes 1¼ cups.*

Vinaigrette Sauce (French Dressing)

¼ teaspoon salt
⅛ teaspoon dry mustard (optional)
3 tablespoons olive or other salad

oil
1 tablespoon vinegar
Freshly ground pepper (optional)

This is the classic recipe for salad dressing, as used throughout most of the civilized world. When used as salad dressing, it is not necessary to mix the ingredients in advance; simply sprinkle over the greens in the order given, then toss the greens to coat with the dressing. It is best not to mix more than will be used at a time, even when it is to be served as a sauce (besides its use as a salad dressing, it is frequently passed as a sauce for fish, grilled, poached, or baked). *Makes ¼ cup, enough to dress 4 cups of salad greens, or 4 to 6 servings. For ½ cup (8 to 10 servings), double all ingredients.*

VINAIGRETTE MARINADE. Double ingredients in basic recipe to use as a marinade for steak, hamburgers (to be charcoal-broiled), fish, or vegetables to be broiled *en brochette.*

TOMATO DRESSING (LORENZO SAUCE). To basic recipe, add 1 tablespoon tomato catsup or chili sauce and 1 tablespoon chopped watercress or parsley. Use to dress mixed-vegetable salad or as a sauce for broiled or fried fish; double ingredients to use as a marinade.

ROQUEFORT VINAIGRETTE DRESSING. Crumble about a tablespoon of Roquefort or other blue cheese into (¼ cup) basic Vinaigrette Sauce; use to dress tossed salads.

TARRAGON VINAIGRETTE. Use tarragon vinegar in making Vinaigrette Sauce.

SHERRY VINAIGRETTE. Use sherry vinegar in making Vinaigrette, or add 2 tablespoons dry sherry to basic Vinaigrette recipe. *Use as a salad dressing, or as a marinade for meat or chicken.*

HERB VINAIGRETTE. Add any desired chopped fresh herbs to Vinaigrette Sauce: basil, orégano, thyme, marjoram, or chives. Or, use mixed herb vinegar in making the sauce.

Spanish Dressing

1 small onion, very thinly sliced
½ teaspoon salt
1 teaspoon paprika
2 tablespoons red wine vinegar
2 tablespoons olive oil
¼ cup orange juice
1 orange, peeled, chopped, seeded
2 tablespoons minced parsley

Combine all ingredients; let stand 1 hour before serving as a dressing for salad or as a marinade for chicken or pork to be barbecued. *Makes about ½ cup.*

Low-calorie Vinaigrette

¼ teaspoon salt
¼ teaspoon orégano or thyme
¼ teaspoon mustard

2 tablespoons warm water
2 tablespoons oil
1 tablespoon vinegar

Dissolve salt in warm water, add orégano and pepper; add oil, shake to blend, then add vinegar. (If sweetened dressing is preferred, add noncaloric sweetener to taste.) *Makes a little more than ¼ cup,* enough for 4 to 6 servings as a salad dressing.

Italian Dressing (American Style)

½ teaspoon salt
¼ teaspoon pepper
½ teaspoon dry mustard
¼ teaspoon thyme
½ to 1 teaspoon sugar, or to taste

¼ cup water
2 tablespoons vinegar
4 to 6 tablespoons oil, or to taste
2 tablespoons minced parsley (optional)

Combine first 7 ingredients; shake until sugar is dissolved. Add remaining ingredients, shake again. *Makes about ¾ cup.*

Commercial Salad Dressings

These come bottled, in all flavors and styles, besides the packages of mixes to which you add your own oil and vinegar. The following are suggested variations for commercial dressings:

CURRIED DRESSING. Add ¼ to ½ teaspoon curry powder to each cup dressing (any kind).

PARMESAN. Shake in 2 tablespoons grated Parmesan cheese to 1 cup prepared dressing.

ANCHOVY-GARLIC. In blender, or using mortar and pestle, crush 1 anchovy fillet and 1 garlic clove together to form a paste; slowly add 1 cup prepared dressing.

HERB DRESSING. Add minced fresh parsley, dill, chives, or cilantro to 1 cup prepared dressing.

FRUIT DRESSING. Add 1 tablespoon honey, 1 teaspoon grated orange rind, and 1 tablespoon orange juice to 1 cup commercial

French dressing, to dress citrus or mixed fruit (for a first-course salad).

Hot Salsa Verde

¼ cup olive oil
2 cloves garlic
½ cup Italian parsley, minced
2 tablespoons flour
½ teaspoon salt

¼ teaspoon ground ginger
Few grains freshly ground pepper
2 tablespoons milk or light cream
½ cup water
¼ cup white wine

Pour olive oil in skillet; add garlic cloves, sauté until golden and soft. Remove garlic, mash in mortar with parsley to form a smooth paste. Add flour, salt, ginger, and pepper to garlic-parsley paste; blend well. Return to pan over moderate heat, slowly add milk or cream, then the water; shake pan occasionally as sauce cooks. After it has thickened, stir in wine; continue cooking 30 seconds to 1 minute until smooth. An excellent sauce for seafood, chicken, and vegetables. Especially delicious over boiled potatoes, accompanied by hard-cooked eggs for a vegetable dinner. *Makes about 1 cup.*

Pesto Genovese

A delicious Italian sauce for spaghetti or other pastas, or to serve over broiled tomatoes, or with baked or fried eggplant. It should always be made with *fresh* basil. If this is not available, increase parsley to ½ cup.

½ cup olive oil
¼ cup chopped fresh basil
¼ cup chopped Italian parsley

2 cloves garlic
½ teaspoon salt
¼ teaspoon black pepper

Place all ingredients in blender; beat at high speed (covered) until very smooth. If you do not have a blender, first mash the herbs in mortar with pestle, then work in olive oil, beating until smooth. *Makes ½ cup thick sauce.*

Marinades and Barbecue Sauces

The purpose of a marinade is primarily to flavor the meat, poultry, fish, or vegetables which soak in the sauce, sometimes also to tenderize the food. Some marinades may be used as basting sauces. Besides those on the following pages, almost all variations of Vinaigrette Sauce may be used as marinades, as may many of the soy-based sauces.

Barbecue sauces are of Mexican origin and are traditionally very hot and spicy. But the American-style barbecue has developed into a unique cookery technique until now any sauce spooned or brushed over food as it broils may be classified as a barbecue sauce.

Red Wine Marinade

¼ cup minced onion
2 tablespoons olive oil
¼ cup chopped Italian parsley
1 tablespoon dry mustard
½ teaspoon sugar
¾ teaspoon salt

¼ teaspoon freshly ground
  pepper, or dash of cayenne
1 teaspoon grated lemon rind
1 cup red wine
  or bourbon

Combine all ingredients. Use as a marinade for hamburgers or chicken. *Makes 1½ cups.*

Tarragon Marinade

2 teaspoons tarragon
1 cup white wine
1 teaspoon salt

½ teaspoon thyme
1 tablespoon minced parsley

Combine all ingredients. Pour over uncooked chicken or fish to marinate at least 30 minutes before broiling. *Makes 1 cup*

Madeira Marinade

¼ cup Madeira wine
½ cup orange juice
¼ cup chicken broth

Pinch of cumin
Salt, pepper

Combine ingredients. Use to marinate any seafood, duck, chicken, beef, or pork before cooking. *Makes 1 cup.*

Orange Marinade

½ cup orange juice
½ cup olive oil
1 tablespoon wine vinegar

¼ teaspoon ginger or cumin
1 teaspoon salt
1 teaspoon instant chopped
  onion

Combine all ingredients. Use to baste chicken after it has been turning on rotisserie spit for 10 minutes, and periodically until chicken is done. *Makes 1 cup.*

Orange Barbecue Sauce

4 cloves garlic, crushed
¾ cup chopped onions
½ cup olive oil
1 cup canned tomatoes or peeled,
  chopped fresh tomatoes

¼ cup chopped pitted black olives (preferably Italian)
1 tablespoon Worcestershire or
  soy sauce
1 cup orange juice

¼ cup brown sugar
1 teaspoon grated orange rind
1 teaspoon grated lemon rind

1 tablespoon sherry, bourbon, or
  brandy
¼ cup chopped parsley

Sauté garlic and onion in olive oil until very soft. Add tomatoes; cook until reduced and well blended with onions. Add remaining ingredients, simmer 20 minutes. Use as a marinade; or, strain or purée sauce in blender, and pass as a sauce to serve over any charcoal-grilled meat or poultry. *Makes about 2 ½ cups.*

Tomato Barbecue Sauce

1 cup chopped onion
1 clove garlic, minced
½ cup olive oil
3 cups canned tomatoes
1 6-ounce can tomato paste
½ teaspoon crushed hot
  red peppers

4 tablespoons vinegar
1 tablespoon lemon juice
2 teaspoons sugar
½ teaspoon Tabasco, or
  ¼ teaspoon cayenne
1 teaspoon dry mustard

Cook onion and garlic in olive oil until soft and golden; add tomato and tomato paste; stir to blend. Add crushed peppers, simmer 5 minutes. Add remaining ingredients, simmer 20 minutes. Force through a sieve or food mill, or, purée in blender. Cool. Serve cold as a sauce or relish (excellent with hamburgers), or keep in refrigerator to use as needed as a spicy (very spicy) barbecue sauce. *Makes 2½ to 3 cups.*

SOUPS

Clear soups depend for their goodness on the flavor of the broth that is their base. Chicken broth is used for some, meat broth for others. The instructions for making stock (p. 212) apply to soups as much as to sauces. The recipe for Homemade Consommé is basically a soup recipe which can also be used in the making of sauces. When soup concentrates (canned or dehydrated) are used to make soups, flavor will be greatly improved if herbs, slivers of meat, or thin-sliced or julienne-cut vegetables are added to the broth and simmered 5 to 10 minutes before serving.

Egg Drop Soup

3 cups homemade chicken broth
1 egg, unbeaten

Heat broth to boiling. Beat the egg lightly with a fork just to break the yolk, then add to the boiling broth, stirring constantly until egg is separated into thin strands. *Makes 4 servings.*

MADE WITH STOCK CONCENTRATE. Combine 3 teaspoons stock concentrate with 3 cups water. Add 2 tablespoons minced green onions or chives and 1 teaspoon sherry; simmer 5 minutes. Add egg, stir quickly until in shreds.

THICKENED EGG DROP SOUP. If soup with a more glutinous consistency is preferred, blend 1 tablespoon cornstarch with a little cold water, add to 3 cups chicken or beef broth (homemade or from concentrate), bring to the boil, simmer until thickened. Stir in the egg; sprinkle top with minced freeze-dried chives.

WITH SOY SAUCE. Some cooks like a bit of soy sauce added to the broth. Use 1 to 1½ teaspoons for 3 cups liquid.

Oriental Soup with Vegetables

3 cups Homemade Consommé or clear chicken or beef broth

About 2 tablespoons very thinly sliced or julienne-cut carrots

2 tablespoons white turnip,* cut in thin slivers

1 tablespoon minced chives or scallions

3 or 4 fresh spinach leaves, coarsely chopped, or 2 sprigs watercress, stems removed

Bring consommé or broth to a boil, add the vegetables, simmer 3 or 4 minutes. Serve in oriental bowls. *Makes 4 servings.*

*Slivers of water chestnut may be used in place of turnip, but the turnip improves the flavor of the broth.

Japanese Pork and Spinach Soup

5 cups water

4 teaspoons chicken or beef stock concentrate

1 pork chop, or ¼ cup slivered lean pork

2 tablespoons julienne-cut carrots

2 scallions, minced

6 fresh spinach leaves, stems removed

1 teaspoon soy sauce, or to taste

Add stock concentrate to water, bring to a boil, stir until concentrate is dissolved. If pork chop is used, carefully remove all fat, cut meat into very thin slivers. Trim all fat from bone; add bone and meat to the broth, simmer 10 minutes. During last 3 or 4 minutes, add vegetables and soy sauce. Remove and discard bone. Serve soup in oriental bowls. *Makes 6 servings.*

NOTE. The bone of the pork chop adds decided flavor to the broth, but it may also tend to make the broth greasy, despite efforts to remove all fat. For this reason, lean pork (cut from a roast, perhaps) may be better—but it should be *raw* pork, not cooked. It is the pork flavor that makes the broth so delicious. When the meat is cut in such fine slivers, 10 minutes' simmering is quite enough.

Chinese Pork and Broccoli Soup

¼ cup slivered lean raw pork
5 cups water
4 teaspoons chicken stock
concentrate

2 frozen broccoli spears,
defrosted*
1 teaspoon soy sauce

Place the slivers of raw pork in water with the stock concentrate; bring to a boil, cook 5 minutes. Slice the broccoli as thin as possible and cut in small pieces. Add to the bubbling broth, cook 3 minutes longer (broccoli should still be crisp). Season with soy sauce Serve in small oriental bowls. *Makes 6 servings.*

*Remaining broccoli may be cut up and added to Chow Mein.

Wonton Soup

6 cups chicken or beef broth
2 scallions, minced

1 recipe Wonton
6 fresh spinach leaves

Prepare the wonton first (see index for recipe). Heat the broth, adding scallions. When broth is boiling rapidly, add the wonton; cook until the filled squares of dough rise to the top of the soup. Add spinach; cook just until limp. Serve in oriental bowls or soup plates. *Makes 6 to 8 servings.*

French Onion Soup

6 medium onions, thinly sliced
2 tablespoons butter
1 tablespoon olive oil
1 teaspoon sugar
6 cups beef broth or consommé
Salt, pepper
½ teaspoon Dijon mustard·

(optional)
6 thick slices French bread, toasted
6 tablespoons shredded natural Gruyère or Swiss cheese, or grated Parmesan cheese

Cook onions in butter and olive oil over moderate heat for about 20 minutes, until very soft. Add sugar during last 10 minutes; allow onions to brown slightly, turning with spatula to prevent burning. Add broth; cover pot, simmer 1 hour. Taste for seasoning; add salt, pepper, and mustard if needed. Toast bread under broiler. Place a slice of bread in each of 6 individual heatproof casseroles. Sprinkle 1 tablespoon cheese over top of each. Place under preheated broiler until cheese melts and top is lightly browned. *Makes 6 servings.*

Chicken Soup with Kreplach

6 cups homemade chicken broth,   1 recipe Kreplach
  clarified   1 tablespoon minced parsley

Make chicken broth with necks and backs of chicken, or with a stewing chicken. Strain; reheat to boiling. Add kreplach (see index for recipe); cook until noodle triangles rise to top of soup. Serve in bowls or soup plates with parsley scattered over top of each serving. *Makes 6 servings.*

Prinz Orloff Soup

Dumplings   1 scallion, minced
6 cups beef or chicken broth   1 teaspoon minced parsley
1 small tomato, peeled, chopped

First prepare parsley or Quick Liver Dumplings; form with spoon into ¾-inch balls. Heat broth with tomato, scallion, and parsley; when boiling rapidly, add the dumplings a few at a time. As the dumplings rise to the top of the soup, remove with slotted spoon and set aside. When all are cooked, serve the soup in soup plates, adding 3 or 4 dumplings to each serving. *Makes 6 servings.*

PARSLEY DUMPLINGS

1 cup biscuit mix   ½ cup milk
2 eggs, separated   2 tablespoons minced parsley

Combine biscuit mix, egg yolk, milk, and parsley, forming a dough. Beat egg whites until stiff; fold in. Form 24 small balls.

QUICK LIVER DUMPLINGS. Add ¼ cup canned liver pate to Parsley Dumplings before adding the egg whites.

Sopa Castilla la Vieja

8 cups beef consommé   2 cups toasted croutons
¼ cup olive oil   ½ cup toasted almond slivers
1/3 cup crushed almonds   ¼ cup Parmesan cheese
Salt

Heat consommé. Work olive oil into the crushed almonds, forming a paste. Add to the consommé, stirring to blend well. Add salt to taste, if needed. Pour soup into 6 earthenware bowls. Top each serving with some of the toasted croutons and cheese. Place under broiler until cheese is lightly browned. Remove, sprinkle toasted slivered almonds over top. *Makes 6 servings.*

German Bread Soup

6 slices stale pumpernickel or
  dark rye
8 cups beef broth
1 medium onion, chopped

1 or 2 tablespoons meat drippings
  or butter
2 or 3 tablespoons leftover gravy
  (preferably pork gravy)

Break bread into cubes; place in bowl, cover with boiling hot beef broth. Let stand until bread is soft. Separately sauté onion in meat drippings or butter until soft and yellow. Combine with bread and broth; simmer ½ hour. Taste for seasoning; add salt if needed. Stir in gravy. *Makes 8 servings.*

Easy Tricks with Beef Bouillon

Beef bouillon from a can or made with concentrate will become far more interesting with any of these variations.

WITH AVOCADO. Cut ripe avocado into tiny cubes or thin slices; float over bowls of hot bouillon.

ORANGE ZEST. Add grated orange rind and a dash of Angostura bitters to each serving of bouillon.

SOUR CREAM TOPPING. Blend minced chives or minced dill in sour cream, top each serving with a dollop of the cream.

TOMATO BOUILLON. Blend ½ cup tomato sauce with 3 cups beef bouillon; add a tablespoon of sherry or Madeira. Heat to boiling; serve with very thin lemon slices in each bowl.

WITH FRIED CROUTONS. Cut stale bread in cubes, fry in olive oil (along with a garlic clove, if desired) until bread is browned on all sides. Drain on absorbent paper. Add while warm to hot consommé or bouillon.

Cock-a-Leekie Soup

6 leeks, thinly sliced (only a little
  of green part)
2 tablespoons butter
6 cups homemade chicken broth

¼ cup rice
4 to 5 pitted prunes, snipped
  (optional)

Cook leeks in butter until soft; add chicken broth and rice, simmer 20 minutes until leeks are completely soft and more or less disintegrated in soup. Add prunes; cook until softened but not mushy. *Makes 8 servings.*

Avgholemono Soup (Greek Egg and Lemon Soup)

5 cups homemade chicken broth   3 tablespoons lemon juice
1/3 cup rice, uncooked   Grated lemon rind
3 egg yolks

Place chicken broth and rice in kettle, bring to a boil, simmer 20 to 25 minutes (rice should be very soft). Beat egg yolks until light in color and very thick. Add a little of the hot broth to egg yolks to blend well, then add egg slowly to soup, stirring constantly over very low heat until broth is slightly thickened. Turn off heat, add lemon juice, blending thoroughly. Cover, let stand 6 minutes. *Makes 6 servings.*

WITH BLENDER. Cook rice in broth, as above, but beat the egg yolks in a blender, slowly adding hot chicken broth with blender in motion. When slightly thickened, add lemon juice, beat 2 seconds; serve at once.

SHORT-CUT VERSION. Heat to boiling a can of condensed chicken with rice soup and 1 soup can water. Beat 2 egg yolks or 2 whole eggs until smooth and thick (not foamy), beat in 2 tablespoons lemon juice, slowly add hot soup to beaten egg-lemon mixture, beating constantly. Serve at once. *Makes 4 servings.*

Royal Soup

½ chicken breast, boned,   spoons chicken stock concen-
  chopped   trate
2 tablespoons lean ham, chopped   6 cups water
1 tablespoon butter   ¼ cup medium sherry
1 tablespoon olive oil   2 hard-cooked eggs
Salt   Croutons fried in olive oil or but-
2 thin slices onion   ter
4 chicken bouillon cubes, or 4 tea-

Sauté raw chicken and the ham in butter and oil until chicken meat is opaquely white and ham lightly browned. Sprinkle lightly with salt from shaker. Add onion, cook until yellow and soft. Add bouillon cubes or stock concentrate, water, and sherry. Bring to a boil, stirring to dissolve bouillon cubes. Simmer, uncovered, 15 to 20 minutes. During last 5 minutes, add some of hot broth to yolks of eggs, return to pot, simmer until slightly thickened. Taste for salt. Serve topped with chopped egg white and croutons. *Makes 6 to 8 servings.*

The King's Soup

4 medium onions, very thinly sliced
3 to 4 tablespoons butter
Pinch of mace
Salt
1 tablespoon cornstarch
½ cup water

1 quart milk
2 cups chicken broth
2 egg yolks, beaten
1 tablespoon minced parsley
1 cup toasted croutons

Cook onions in butter over moderate heat until very soft; do not allow onions to brown. Sprinkle with mace and salt from shaker. Dissolve cornstarch in ½ cup water, add to onions. Slowly add milk, cooking until slightly thickened. Add chicken broth; taste for seasoning; add more salt if needed. Shortly before serving, add some of hot broth to beaten egg yolks, blending well, then add egg yolks to remaining soup. Turn off heat; keep soup warm. Serve in soup bowls, sprinkling parsley and croutons over each serving. *Makes 10 rich, beautiful servings.*

Cream of Onion Soup

4 medium onions, sliced
¼ pound (1 stick) butter
⅛ teaspoon mace
4 tablespoons flour
1 quart milk
2 cups chicken broth or vegetable

stock
Salt
1 egg yolk
1 tablespoon minced parsley
½ cup toasted croutons

Simmer onions in butter until soft and golden but not brown. Sprinkle with mace. Stir in flour, cook until it bubbles. Slowly add milk, stirring gently. Cook until slightly thickened—about 10 minutes. Add the broth or stock, simmer 5 minutes longer. Blend some of the hot soup with egg yolk, add to remaining soup, cook, stirring, about 1 minute. Serve topped with minced parsley and croutons. *Makes 8 servings.*

WITH INSTANT-TYPE FLOUR. Use same measure of instant-type flour, but dissolve in *cold* milk before adding to onions.

SHORT-CUT VERSION. Use a 1-pound can whole onions; purée onions and liquid in blender. Add 2 cans condensed cream of chicken or cream of celery soup, 1 cup cream or homogenized milk, and 1 egg yolk, beat in blender until smooth. Transfer to saucepan, heat, stirring, until smooth and somewhat thickened. Serve topped with parsley and croutons.

Cream of Shrimp Soup

4 tablespoons butter
4 tablespoons flour
1 cup milk or dairy half-and-half
3 cups shrimp broth (saved from boiling shrimp), heated

Dash of cayenne
Salt (optional)
3 shrimp
1 tablespoon minced parsley, dill, or chives

Place butter, flour, and milk in blender, beat at low speed, slowly adding *hot* shrimp broth. Add cayenne and shrimp, beat until shrimp are minced. When thoroughly blended, transfer to saucepan, stir until smooth. Taste for seasoning; add cayenne and salt if needed. Serve topped with fresh minced herbs. *Makes 5 to 6 servings.*

WITH INSTANT-TYPE FLOUR. Use same ingredients, but blend flour with *cold* milk and shrimp broth, stir until mixture starts to thicken, then add butter, cayenne, salt (if needed), and minced shrimp. Cook over low heat about 10 minutes.

Crema de Pipian

1 can condensed split pea soup
1 can clear chicken broth
1 can water
2 tablespoons medium sherry

¼ cup cream
Crumbled cooked bacon, or toasted slivered almonds

Combine the two soups, water, and sherry. Bring to a boil, stirring until well blended. Stir in cream. Serve hot topped with bacon, or chill and serve cold topped with almonds. *Makes 6 servings.*

Shrimp and Celery Soup

1 can condensed cream of celery soup
½ teaspoon salt
Dash of cayenne
1 ripe avocado, thinly sliced

½ cup sliced pitted ripe olives
1 can frozen cream of shrimp soup
2 cups milk
¾ cup light cream

Combine soups, milk, cream, salt, and cayenne. Heat to simmering, until well blended (do not allow to boil). Serve topped with avocado and olive slices. *Makes 8 servings.*

Cream of Asparagus Soup

Simple and inexpensive: just save the liquid in which asparagus cooked and put aside a couple of spears for the soup. Nice for a summer luncheon, preceding Chef's Salad.

3 tablespoons butter
3 tablespoons flour
2 cups liquid in which asparagus cooked
1 cup dairy half-and-half, or ½

cup milk and ½ cup cream
Pinch of cayenne
2 stalks asparagus, cooked, chopped
2 hard-cooked eggs, chopped

Melt butter, stir in flour, cook until it bubbles; slowly add asparagus liquid, cook, stirring, until smooth and thickened. Add dairy half-and-half, cayenne, and chopped asparagus; simmer over low heat 5 minutes longer. Serve with chopped egg. *Makes 4 servings.*

Classic Shrimp Bisque

6 ounces shrimp, in shell
6 cups water
1 teaspoon salt
3 tablespoons butter
1 small onion, minced
¼ cup grated carrot
1 medium tomato, peeled,

chopped, or 1 teaspoon tomato paste
Dash of cayenne
¼ teaspoon black pepper
2 tablespoons sherry or Madeira
2 tablespoons heavy cream
Fried or toasted croutons

Cook shrimp in water with salt for 2 minutes; turn off heat, let shrimp stand in liquid 10 minutes. Remove shrimp; shell. Return shells to liquid and cook, covered, 15 minutes. Strain, saving liquid. Mince shrimp; put aside.

Melt butter, add onion, carrot, and tomato; cook until very soft. Add cayenne and black pepper and half the shrimp. Cook 5 minutes longer, then place in blender with the strained shrimp liquid, sherry, and cream. Beat until slightly thickened and very smooth. Transfer to saucepan, add remaining minced shrimp; cook, stirring, over low heat another 5 minutes. Serve topped with croutons. *Makes 6 servings.*

QUICK SHRIMP BISQUE. Combine 1 can frozen cream of shrimp soup, 1 can condensed tomato soup, 1 soup can water, and ½ cup medium sherry or white wine; heat, stirring, just until mixture starts to bubble. *Makes 8 servings.*

Tomato Bisque

1 can condensed tomato soup
½ cup milk

¼ cup grated Parmesan cheese
1/3 cup sherry

Stir in cold milk into tomato soup; blend thoroughly. Stir sherry into mixture with equal care. Add cheese. Stir over low heat until soup is steaming, but do not allow to come to boil. *Makes 3 to 4 servings.*

Garden Tomato Soup

8 large vine-ripened tomatoes
2 tablespoons butter
2 slices onion
1 tablespoon cornstarch, or 2
 tablespoons flour
½ bay leaf

Few leaves of thyme
2 whole cloves
2 cups water
Salt
1 teaspoon sugar (optional)
Grated Parmesan cheese

Immerse tomatoes in boiling hot water so that skins can be easily removed. Cut in half, hold cut side down over strainer, and squeeze gently to remove seeds. Chop tomatoes. Melt butter in deep heavy saucepan, add onion, cook until soft; stir in cornstarch or flour; cook until it bubbles. Add chopped tomatoes, bay, thyme, and cloves; simmer until tomato is soft. Add water, salt, and sugar if desired; cook 20 minutes. Force through strainer or food mill. Serve topped with cheese. *Makes about 6 servings.*

WITH CANNED TOMATOES. When local tomatoes are not in season, use 1 large can (1 pound 12 to 14 ounces) best quality canned peeled tomatoes. Add herbs, onion, butter, and cloves as above, simmer 10 to 15 minutes, and force through sieve. Add water, sugar, and salt or 3 beef bouillon cubes; simmer 15 minutes longer. Serve topped with cheese or dollops of sour cream.

TOMATO SOUP WITH CILANTRO Serve soup topped with whipped cream (or sour cream) and chopped fresh cilantro—a deliciously different flavor.

Vegetable Beef Soup

1 marrow bone
¼ pound soup meat (beef plate
 or bargain stewing beef)
2 onions, stuck with cloves
1 sprig celery
1 sprig parsley
2½ quarts (10 cups) water

1 tablespoon salt
1 tomato, peeled, chopped
1 carrot, scraped, sliced
1 white turnip, peeled, slivered
½ pound green beans
6 to 8 fresh spinach leaves,
 or 6 watercress sprigs

Place soup bone, meat, onions, celery, and parsley in soup kettle; add water and salt. Bring to a boil; cook 2 hours, skimming occasionally. (Liquid will reduce with cooking.) Remove meat and bone; when cool enough, strain stock. Chop meat, return to soup kettle with strained broth. Add tomato, carrot, turnip, and green beans cut into ½-inch pieces. Bring to a boil, simmer 10 minutes. Add spinach or watercress (trimmed of stems); cook 2 or 3 minutes longer. Serve in soup plates. *Makes about 8 servings.*

Green Cabbage Soup

2 tablespoons butter
2 cups shredded green cabbage
½ teaspoon salt, or to taste
1 teaspoon paprika
6 cups beef, chicken, or vegetable
broth
1 ripe tomato, peeled, chopped, or 2 tablespoons tomato sauce
Sour cream

Melt butter in large pot or kettle, add cabbage, cook just until wilted. Sprinkle with salt and paprika. Add broth and tomato; bring to a boil; cook just until cabbage is tender but still a little crisp. Taste for seasoning; add more salt if needed. Serve topped with dollops of sour cream. *Makes 6 to 8 servings.*

Chinese Cabbage and Pork Soup

1 tablespoon oil
¼ pound lean pork, cut in slivers
1 small onion, thinly sliced
¼ teaspoon powdered ginger
2 cups Chinese cabbage (celery
cabbage), thinly sliced
6 cups chicken broth
1 teaspoon soy sauce
Salt

Heat the oil in a heavy pot, add the pork, cook until lightly browned. Add the onion and ginger; cook 2 minutes. Add the Chinese cabbage and broth; cook 10 minutes. Add soy sauce and salt to taste. *Makes 8 servings.*

WITH GREEN GINGER. Thinly sliced green ginger root, added with the onion, is even better than powdered ginger.

WITH GREEN CABBAGE. When Chinese cabbage is not available, fresh green cabbage, shredded, can be used instead.

Russian Borscht

2½ quarts (10 cups) water
2 tablespoons salt
8 peppercorns
2 pounds soup meat with bones
2 large carrots, scraped, sliced
2 stalks celery, sliced
2 onions, sliced
8 large beets, peeled, cut in slivers
2 tablespoons butter
1 tablespoon vinegar
4 cups shredded cabbage
2 cups canned tomatoes
Sour cream

Place water, salt, and peppercorns, and meat in soup kettle; bring to boil; simmer 2 hours, or until meat is ready to fall from bones. Remove meat and bones; cut meat in small pieces; discard bones. Strain broth. Reheat broth, adding carrots, celery, and onions; simmer 20 minutes. Separately, cook the slivered beets in butter and vinegar, with just enough water to barely cover beets, for 10 minutes, covered. To soup, meanwhile, add cabbage, tomatoes, and cut-up meat; cook 10 minutes. Add beets; heat thoroughly. Serve in large soup plates with sour cream over each serving. *Makes 8 servings.*

WITH POTATOES. Potatoes, peeled and cubed, are often added to a Russian Borscht, and fresh dill may be used in place of bay leaf.

POLISH SAUERKRAUT SOUP. Instead of cabbage, add 1 pound sauerkraut to Russian Borscht.

Jewish Borscht

3 quarts (12 cups) water	2 cloves garlic, minced
2 pounds brisket of beef	1 tablespoon salt
Beef marrow bone	3 tablespoons brown sugar
8 large beets, peeled, grated	1/3 cup lemon juice
2 onions, chopped	2 eggs beaten

Place water, beef, and bone in soup kettle. Bring to a boil, cook ½ hour, skimming occasionally. Add beets, onions, garlic, and salt. Cover, lower heat, cook 2 hours. Remove meat and bones. Strain stock or force through food mill. Add brown sugar and lemon juice, stir to dissolve sugar. Meat may be chopped and returned to soup, or it may be used in some other way, if a clear soup is preferred. Add a little hot broth at a time to the beaten eggs until well blended, then return egg mixture to rest of soup. Serve hot with bits of meat in the soup, or chill and serve cold topped with sour cream. Will keep well in refrigerator. *Makes about 10 servings.*

Quick Cold Borscht

5 cups beef bouillon	½ tablespoon minced fresh dill,
1 1-pound can sliced beets	or ½ teaspoon dried dill weed
1 cup (8-ounce can) sauerkraut	½ cup thick yogurt or sour cream
1 small potato, peeled, diced	1 tablespoon minced parsley

For the bouillon, use bouillon cubes or powdered concentrate with water, or use condensed canned bouillon, reconstituted. Add beets, sauerkraut with juice, diced raw potato, and dill. Cook 20 minutes. Purée by forcing through sieve or food mill or beating in electric blender. Chill. Combine yogurt or sour cream and parsley, serve dollops of the sour cream on each serving. (If preferred, sour cream may be beaten into the beet broth, to make a pink soup.) *Makes 6 servings.*

Vegetable Soup Provençal

2 leeks, chopped
2 medium onions, chopped
1 tablespoon butter
1 tablespoon olive oil
1 stalk celery (including leaves), chopped
1 tablespoon minced parsley

1 carrot, scraped, grated
3 tomatoes, peeled, diced, or 1-pound can peeled tomatoes
2 medium potatoes, diced
6 cups water or bouillon
Salt

(Leeks are expensive in our markets and may be omitted. But they give a flavor that onions alone cannot impart.)

Cut off only the rather withered tops of the leeks; carefully separate upper part of the leaves to remove all sand and grit, then slice thinly, mincing the green part. Put this in a large heavy pot with the onions, butter, and olive oil. Simmer over moderate heat until onions are soft. Add the celery, parsley, and grated carrot; simmer 5 minutes longer. Add the tomatoes, the diced raw potatoes, and the bouillon (which may be made with chicken, beef, or vegetable stock, or bouillon concentrate). Salt to taste. Bring to a boil, lower heat, simmer until potatoes are soft. Serve this way or purée in an electric blender. The puréed soup will be more attractive with croutons over the top. Equally good reheated. *Makes 6 to 8 servings.*

Spanish Onion Soup

2 large Spanish onions, or 4 large yellow onions
½ cup olive oil
6 cups boiling water or bouillon
2 teaspoons salt,* or to taste
Freshly ground pepper
Pinch of mace

Pinch of powdered cloves
1 teaspoon wine vinegar
2 tablespoons minced parsley
6 eggs
6 slices toast
Grated cheese (optional)

Slice the onions, simmer gently in the olive oil until soft and golden, almost puréed. Add the water or bouillon, salt, spices, vinegar, and parsley. Bring to a boil, lower heat, simmer gently for 15 to 20 minutes. Carefully break eggs one by one into custard cups, then slip egg into gently simmering broth (liquid must not be boiling). Cook until eggs are poached. Place a slice of toast in each serving dish, spoon an egg over each piece of toast, add soup to each dish. Pass grated cheese if desired. *Serves 6.*

*If using bouillon cubes or stock concentrate, salt may not be needed.

Spanish Potato Soup

1 or 2 medium onions, chopped fine
¼ cup olive oil or butter
6 cups chicken or beef stock
¼ cup dry sherry
6 potatoes, peeled, diced
Salt

Sauté onions in oil or butter until yellow. Add stock and wine, bring to a boil, add the potatoes, cook 20 to 30 minutes until very tender. When served, potatoes are mashed in the broth, giving it a thick consistency. *Makes 6 to 8 servings.*

Vichyssoise

An American original created by Louis Diat, a French chef, while in charge of the kitchens at the old Ritz-Carlton Hotel in New York City. The name is in honor of Diat's native town of Vichy, France, where his mother had made a similar soup, but always served it hot.

4 leeks
3 tablespoons butter
4 medium potatoes, peeled, quartered
3 cups homemade chicken broth
Salt, pepper
Dash of nutmeg
1 cup heavy or light cream
Minced chives

Discard most of the green part of the leeks; trim off the "beard." Cut in 1-inch lengths, examining carefully to make sure no sand is caught in the sworls. Cook gently in butter, not allowing leeks to brown at all. Add potatoes and broth; bring to a boil, simmer until potatoes are very soft. Taste for seasoning and add salt and pepper as needed, plus a dash of nutmeg. Purée in blender or force through sieve or food mill. Add cream (or milk and cream); blend well. Chill for several hours. Serve cold, with minced chives over each serving. *Makes 6 servings.*

Caldo Verde

4 to 6 medium potatoes, peeled, quartered
2 onions, peeled, quartered
2 quarts (8 cups) water
2 teaspoons salt, or to taste
2 tablespoons olive oil
1 cup shredded turnip greens*
¼ cup slices chorizo sausage or diced ham (optional)

Cook potatoes and onions in salted water until tender. Add olive oil; purée in blender or force through food mill. Return to pot, add turnip greens (which should be very finely shredded, like threads) and the sausage or ham (if used). Cook 10 minutes. Serve hot. *Makes 6 to 8 servings.*

*Or, use shredded broccoli or cauliflower leaves.

Creole Vegetable Soup

A thick, hearty, delicious soup for a supper entree, to be followed by salad and dessert.

3 large carrots, peeled, sliced
3 or 4 medium onions, sliced
4 white turnips, peeled, sliced
1 large sweet potato, peeled, sliced
1 stalk celery, with leaves, minced
2 tablespoons minced parsley
6 tablespoons butter
9 cups water

1 cup split peas*
Pinch of cayenne
2 teaspoons salt
¼ teaspoon freshly ground black pepper
½ cup light cream
Croutons

Place carrots, onions, turnips, celery, parsley, butter, and ¾ cup of the water in a kettle. Cook, uncovered, over moderate heat until water is evaporated. Add peas, remaining water, and seasonings. Simmer 2 hours. Force through strainer or food mill (or, strain in collander, saving broth, then purée the vegetables in electric blender). Return puréed vegetables to broth with cream, stir to blend well, reheat slowly. Serve topped with croutons. *Makes 6 servings.*

*Quick-cooking peas do not need previous soaking, but regular split peas should be soaked the preceding day.

Greek Bean Soup

1 pound dried navy beans
2 large onions, sliced or chopped
2 cloves garlic, crushed
½ cup olive oil
¼ teaspoon thyme
1 tablespoon tomato paste

2 teaspoons salt
Freshly ground black pepper
Boiling water to cover—about 4 quarts
Juice of ½ lemon
2 tablespoons minced parsley

Soak the beans overnight; drain. Cook the onions and crushed garlic in olive oil until transparent; add thyme and tomato paste. Add the drained beans, salt, pepper, and enough water to stand at least 2 inches above top of beans. Cook slowly, covered, until beans are very soft—2 to 3 hours. Shortly before serving, add lemon juice and parsley. *Makes 8 servings.*

Lentil Soup Madrilena

1 large onion, chopped
1 green pepper, seeded, diced
1 pimiento, drained, diced
4 tablespoons olive oil
2 tablespoons flour

1 1-pound can peeled tomatoes
4 large carrots, scraped, cubed
1 tablespoon salt, or to taste
1 pound lentils
2 quarts (8 cups) water

Cook onion, green pepper, and pimiento in the olive oil over moderate heat until onion is soft and golden. Stir in flour. Cook until mixture bubbles, but do not allow it to brown. Stir in juice from can of tomatoes, then add whole tomatoes and remaining ingredients. No need to soak lentils—use just as they come from the package. Cook, covered, over very low heat for 2 hours. Stir occasionally to prevent possible sticking. Add more water during cooking if needed. *Makes 6 to 8 servings.*

Lentil Soup with Rice and Cheese

½ pound (1 cup) lentils
2 medium onions, chopped
2 cloves garlic, crushed
Leftover ham bone with meat, or
 ½ cup finely diced ham
2 teaspoons salt

Water to cover—about 3 quarts
½ cup long grain rice
1 large carrot, cut in thin strips
1 cup shredded Swiss cheese
1 tablespoon minced parsley
1 hard-cooked egg, minced

Wash lentils thoroughly; combine with onions, ham bone, salt, and water to cover. Simmer over low heat until lentils are soft—1½ to 2 hours. Add rice and carrots; cook 20 minutes longer. Place cheese in soup bowls; add soup. Serve topped with minced parsley and egg. Hearty enough for a supper entree, and marvelously good. *Makes 6 to 8 servings.*

Yankee Bean Soup

1 pound (2 cups) navy beans
3 quarts (12 cups) water
2 to 3 teaspoons salt

1 ham hock
1 medium onion, thinly sliced
Minced parsley (optional)

Soak the beans overnight (unless they are the quick-cooking kind, which do not require presoaking). Drain thoroughly, place in soup kettle with 3 quarts cold water and 2 teaspoons salt to start. Add ham hock (trimmed, but with meat clinging to bone) and onion. Simmer, covered, about 3 hours. Remove ham, cut away the meat, dice the meat and return to the soup. Taste for seasoning. Add minced parsley, if desired. *Makes 8 to 10 hearty servings.*

Minestrone

1 cup (½ pound) dried marrow
  beans
2 quarts (8 cups) water
1 medium onion, chopped
1 tablespoon minced Italian
  parsley
1 small clove garlic, minced
½ green pepper, diced (optional)

¼ cup olive oil
¼ teaspoon orégano
2 cups (1-pound can) tomatoes
1 cup shredded green or Savoy
  cabbage
1 cup uncooked elbow macaroni
Grated Parmesan cheese

Soak beans in water overnight; drain. Add water, bring to a
boil. Meanwhile, sauté onion, parsley, garlic, and green pepper
in olive oil until soft but not browned. Add to beans in soup kettle with thyme, orégano, and tomatoes. Cook until beans are
soft—about 2 hours. Add macaroni during last 20 minutes,
shredded cabbage during last 10 minutes. Serve in soup plates
topped with Parmesan cheese. *Makes 6 to 8 hearty servings.*

INSTANT MINESTRONE. Combine in a large saucepan 1 can
condensed vegetable soup, 1 can condensed chicken noodle
soup, 2 soup cans of water, 1 cup canned white or kidney beans,
well drained, and 2 or 3 tablespoons minced parsley. Bring to a
boil, simmer 3 or 4 minutes until heated through, then serve
topped with grated Parmesan cheese. *Makes 6 servings.*

Mulligatawny Soup

4 chicken backs, or 2 chicken legs
7 cups chicken broth
3 tablespoons butter
¼ cup chopped onion
¼ cup chopped celery
¼ cup finely chopped or grated
  carrots
2 tart apples, peeled, diced

1 tablespoon curry powder
¼ teaspoon powdered fennel
Pinch of ground cloves
½ green pepper, diced
Salt
1 cup tomato juice or sieved
  canned tomato
½ cup uncooked rice

Place chicken parts in broth (made with bouillon cubes or
stock concentrate); simmer until chicken is very tender. Remove chicken; cut away meat and return meat to broth.
(Discard bones and skin.)

    Meanwhile, melt butter, add vegetables, simmer until soft
but not browned. Add apples, curry powder, fennel, cloves, and
green pepper. Cook until apple is mushy. Add tomato juice, the
chicken broth with bits of chicken, and rice. Simmer 20 minutes. *Makes 8 hearty servings.*

WITH LAMB OR MUTTON. Use 1 lamb shank or any inexpensive cut of mutton instead of chicken in above recipe.

Split Pea Soup

1 pound split peas (yellow or green)	(or both)
¼ pound salt pork, cubed	1 ham bone, with meat clinging to bone
2 onions, chopped	3 quarts water
1 clove garlic, minced (optional)	Salt
½ cup chopped celery or carrots	Toasted croutons (optional)

Soak peas overnight (unless they are the quick-cooking kind, which need no presoaking). Brown salt pork in heavy skillet to draw out fat, turning until pork cubes are nicely browned; remove browned pork with slotted spoon and set aside for garnish.

Cook onions, garlic, and celery or carrots in drawn-out pork fat until soft. Place in kettle with split peas, ham, water, and 2 teaspoons salt. Bring to a boil; simmer, covered, until peas are soft—about 2 hours. Remove ham bone and cut off all usable bits of meat. If a puréed soup is preferred, beat in blender or force through food mill. Or, serve the soup as is, with its bits of vegetables. Replace bits of ham in the soup (whether puréed or not) and serve with the fried pork and toasted croutons over the top. *Makes 8 hearty servings.*

WITH FRANKFURTERS. Add 3 thickly sliced frankfurters to puréed soup, reheat, simmer 10 minutes.

New England Clam Chowder

¼ pound salt pork, cubed	Salt, pepper
1 large or 2 small onions, chopped	1 quart water, heated to boiling
1 quart shucked quahogs (hard-shell clams), with their liquor	¼ teaspoon thyme (optional)
4 to 6 medium potatoes, peeled, thickly sliced	1 quart milk
	1 tablespoon butter
1 tablespoon flour	Ship's crackers or oyster crackers (unsalted)

Place pork in heavy skillet, heat until fat has been drawn out and pork is golden. Remove pork with slotted spoon and discard. Add onions, simmer in fat until golden and soft. Pick over the quahogs; chop fine, removing any bits of shell. Place in a soup kettle layers of onion, quahogs, and potatoes, sprinkling salt from a shaker over onions and potatoes. Sprinkle flour over layers of onion. Add the reserved strained quahog liquid and boiling hot water; cover, bring to a boil, lower heat, cook until potatoes are soft—about 15 minutes. Add milk and butter; heat until milk steams, but do not allow to boil. Serve chowder in soup plates with the crackers. *Makes 8 servings.*

FISH CHOWDER. Instead of quahogs, use 3 to 3½ pounds fresh haddock. Cook fish in 1 quart salted water for 10 minutes; remove bones, place haddock in layers in kettle with onion (sautéed in the pork fat), potatoes, salt, pepper, and flour, as in above recipe, using the fish broth as the liquid. Add milk and cream, as above.

Corn Chowder

¼ pound salt pork, cubed
1 large onion, chopped
2 potatoes, peeled, diced
1 green pepper, seeded, chopped
1½ cups corn kernels scraped from the cob, or 1 12-ounce can kernel corn, drained
2 teaspoons salt, or to taste
Freshly ground black pepper
1 quart milk
¼ teaspoon paprika

Draw out the fat from the salt pork as in preceding chowder recipes; remove and save browned pork. Sauté onion and potatoes in pork fat until golden. Add green pepper, corn, salt, and pepper; cook 1 minute. Add milk and paprika. Cook over low heat (do not allow to boil) until vegetables are tender. Serve topped with fried pork cubes. *Makes 6 servings.*

QUICK CORN CHOWDER. Sauté cubed potatoes in butter or margarine instead of pork fat, use 1 tablespoon instant onion instead of chopped fresh onion, and canned cream-style corn. Top with crumbled cooked bacon.

Quick Clam and Corn Chowder

4 strips bacon
1 small onion, sliced thin
1 can New England-style clam chowder
2 cups milk
1 12-ounce can whole-kernel corn, drained
⅛ teaspoon thyme
Salt, pepper

Fry bacon until brown and crisp. Drain on absorbent paper; when cold, crumble into bits. Pour off all but 2 tablespoons bacon fat. Cook onion in fat until tender and lightly browned.

Separately, combine clam chowder, milk, corn, and thyme. Add sautéed onions. Heat thoroughly until mixture steams, but *do not allow to boil.* Serve garnished with the cooked crumbled bacon. *Makes 4 hearty entree servings.*

Tuna Chowder

2½ cups milk
1 can cream of celery or cream
of mushroom soup
1 can New England-style clam
chowder

1 7-ounce can tuna fish, well
drained, flaked
1 tablespoon minced parsley, or 1
hard-cooked egg, minced

If you have a blender, put 1 cup of the milk in blender with the two soups; beat until smooth. (If you don't have a blender, place soups first in saucepan, stir in milk, then add tuna.) Transfer mixture from blender to saucepan, add remaining milk and the tuna; simmer, stirring, until thoroughly heated—about 10 minutes. Serve garnished with parsley or egg. *Makes 6 to 8 servings.*

Manhattan Clam Chowder

1 quart shucked quahogs (hard-
shell clams), with their liquor
¼ pound salt pork, cubed
1 large onion, chopped
2 tablespoons flour
2 medium potatoes, peeled,

finely diced
3 cups canned tomatoes
¼ teaspoon thyme
1 sprig celery leaves, minced
5 cups water
Oyster crackers

Sort over the clams, carefully removing any bits of shell. Chop the clams, removing the hard part and saving the liquor. Draw out the fat from the salt pork until pork is golden and crisp; remove pork with slotted spoon; set aside. Cook onion in pork fat until soft and golden. Sprinkle flour over onion. Add potatoes, tomatoes, chopped clams, thyme, celery, reserved clam liquor, and water. Bring to a boil; cook until potatoes are soft. Serve in soup bowls, with oyster crackers. *Makes 8 servings.*

VARIATIONS. Instead of celery leaves, ½ cup chopped celery may be cooked with the onion. Tomato juice may be used instead of canned peeled tomatoes (which makes a slightly thinner soup). Besides thyme, some cooks add a dash of cayenne or a bit of dried sage.

WITH CANNED CLAMS. Instead of fresh clams, 3 7-ounce cans minced or chopped sea clams may be used with their liquor.

QUICK MANHATTAN CHOWDER. Combine 2 7-ounce cans chopped or minced sea clams with their liquor, 2 cans tomato sauce, 1 teaspoon instant minced onion, ¼ teaspoon thyme, 1 tablespoon butter, and 1 teaspoon minced parsley or chives. Bring to a boil; simmer 3 minutes. *Makes 4 or 5 servings.*

Quarter-of-an-Hour Soup

1 pound fresh or frozen cod fillets
2 small rock lobster tails (3 ounces each)
6 cups water
2 teaspoons salt
1 medium onion, chopped fine
½ cup olive oil
1 medium (1-pound) can tomatoes

¼ cup blanched almonds
1 6- or 7-ounce can minced clams and liquor
Few shreds of saffron
1 cup shelled fresh or frozen peas
Toasted French bread

Poach cod and lobster in the salted water for 10 minutes after water comes to boil. Meanwhile, cook chopped onion in the olive oil until soft; add tomatoes and parsley; simmer until thickened. Crush almonds to a powder in a mortar and pestle or electric blender. Remove fish and lobster from stock, cut into serving pieces. Discard lobster shells. Combine fish stock, onions, clams, saffron, almonds, and peas; bring to a boil; cook until peas are wrinkled—3 to 8 minutes. Replace fish and lobster; simmer 2 minutes. Serve over toasted French bread in soup dishes. *Makes 8 servings.*

VARIATIONS. If desired, 2 or 3 chopped hard-cooked eggs and ¼ cup diced ham or 4 slices diced cooked bacon may be added to the soup. Instead of lobster tails, 2 cans lobster meat or 8 shelled shrimp may be used, added with the peas, but cook shrimp only 2 minutes.

Oyster Stew

2 quarts oysters
About 5 cups milk
1/3 cup minced onion
4 tablespoons butter
Pinch of mace

3 tablespoons flour
Salt
Freshly ground black pepper
½ pint (1 cup) heavy cream

Strain oysters; measure liquor. Add milk to oyster liquor to make 6 cups altogether. Cover minced onion with water, bring just to a boil, drain. Add the butter to the blanched onions; cook over low heat until onions are tender. Add the mace and flour; stir until smooth. Add oyster liquor and milk; cook slowly until thickened slightly. Add salt and pepper to taste. Add oysters; cook until edges begin to curl. Just before serving, add the cream. *Makes 6 to 8 servings.*

Shrimp Gumbo

1 pound shrimp in shells
2 quarts water, or water plus
  1-pound can tomatoes to make 2
  quarts
2 teaspoons salt
1 medium onion, thinly sliced
1 clove garlic, minced
2 stalks celery, chopped
2 or 3 tablespoons butter

1 bay leaf
1 tablespoon chopped parsley
½ teaspoon dried thyme
¼ teaspoon cayenne, or 1 teaspoon crushed red pepper
2 tablespoons cornstarch
1 package frozen sliced okra
1 pint oysters (optional)
1 tablespoon filé powder

Shell shrimp; add shells to water or water and tomato, with salt. Boil shells 10 minutes; strain, saving stock. Separately, cook onion, garlic, and celery in butter until soft; add bay, parsley, thyme, and cayenne or crushed red pepper. Dissolve cornstarch in some of the shrimp stock; add to remaining stock with onion mixture and okra. Bring to a boil; simmer 15 minutes. Add shrimp; cook 2 minutes. Add oysters, if desired; cook just until edges curl. Stir in filé powder just before serving (it thickens the liquid). Do not cook after adding filé powder. *Makes 10 servings.*

CRAB GUMBO. Instead of shrimp, use 1½ cups crabmeat (fresh, frozen, or canned).

Oxtail Soup

1 oxtail, cut up
2 quarts (8 cups) water
2 teaspoons salt, or to taste
4 peppercorns
1 sprig celery
2 sprigs parsley
½ carrot, scraped, cubed

1 medium onion, sliced
1 clove garlic, minced (optional)
2 tablespoons butter
1 1-pound can peeled tomatoes
½ cup red table wine, or ¼ cup
  medium sherry
1 tablespoon gravy mix

The preceding day, place the oxtail in salted water with peppercorns, celery, parsley, and carrot. Simmer, uncovered, skimming occasionally, until meat is very tender—about 3 hours. Remove meat with slotted spoon. Strain stock. Cut meat from bones and chop it; replace meat in stock; discard bones.

Cook onion and garlic in butter until soft; add tomatoes, forcing through sieve to remove seeds. Combine stock, meat, and wine with tomato mixture. Store in refrigerator overnight.

Next day, remove congealed fat from top of soup. Reheat soup; adjust seasonings, adding more salt as needed. Thicken the soup with gravy mix, adding a little of the broth to gravy mix at a time until smooth. Simmer 5 to 10 minutes after gravy mix is added. *Makes 7 or 8 servings.*

Gazpacho

There are so many ways of preparing this Spanish cold soup, according to the province or the whim of the cook, that almost anything goes. The following is my favorite recipe, out of dozens I have tried.

1 large or 2 small cloves garlic
2 slices white bread, broken in
   pieces
½ cup water
¼ cup olive oil
Salt, pepper
2 pounds fully ripe fresh tomatoes, peeled, chopped, or 1 large

(1-pound 12-ounce) tomatoes,
   sieved
¼ cup grated or finely minced
   onions
2 pimientos, chopped
2 cups ice water
2 tablespoons wine vinegar
   (preferably sherry vinegar)

Crush garlic in bowl (or mince through garlic press). Add bread, water, oil, salt, and pepper. Let stand several hours or overnight. Add tomatoes, onions, and pimiento; beat in electric blender or mixer until puréed. Keep chilled until ready to serve, then add ice water, vinegar, and more salt and pepper, if needed. *Makes 6 servings.*

GARNISHES. Pass, in small bowls, chopped onions, chopped green pepper, chopped cucumber, hard-cooked egg, and fried croutons.

ANOTHER WAY. Omit bread; beat together in blender 8 peeled tomatoes, 1 green pepper seeded, chopped, 1 small onion, and 2 cucumbers peeled, chopped. Add ¼ cup olive oil, 6 tablespoons vinegar, and 2 teaspoons salt. Chill this mixture overnight. Beat again in blender with 3 cups ice water. Serve with assorted garnishes.

Gazpacho with Almonds

3 cups homemade chicken
   broth, clarified
1 large (1-pound 14-ounce) can
   tomatoes, sieved
24 blanched almonds, finely
   ground
1 tablespoon minced parsley
1 clove garlic

1 green pepper, seeded, chopped
1 cucumber, peeled, cubed
1/3 cup olive oil
1 teaspoon salt
⅛ teaspoon cumin (optional)
1 8-ounce can blended vegetable
   juice
Sour cream

Combine chicken broth with tomatoes. Crush together to a paste (in mortar and pestle or blender) the almonds, parsley, and garlic. Add pepper and cucumber; beat until finely chopped. Slowly add olive oil, salt, cumin (if desired), and then part of the chicken broth-tomato mixture. Remove from blender; add remaining broth and tomato and the vegetable juice. Chill thoroughly. Serve topped with sour cream (this is strictly American touch, but delicious). *Makes 10 servings.*

Tzatziki (Yogurt and Cucumber Soup)

½ cup raisins
3 cups yogurt
½ cup heavy sweet cream
1 hard-cooked egg, minced
1 cucumber, peeled, minced
¼ cup minced scallions

2 teaspoons salt
¼ teaspoon freshly ground black pepper
1 tablespoon minced parsley
1 teaspoon minced fresh dill, or
  ½ teaspoon dried dill weed

Soak raisins in cold water to cover until plump and soft; drain off water. Beat yogurt and cream together until foamy; add remaining ingredients. Chill in refrigerator 24 hours. Beat again just before serving. Garnish each serving with a little minced parsley, or dill. *Makes 6 to 8 servings.*

Chlodnik

2 cups buttermilk or yogurt
2 cups sour cream
1 cup diced cooked veal or
  chicken
1 cup cooked beet tops, well
  drained, minced, or ½ cup
  chopped pickled beets

2 cucumbers, peeled, diced
3 tablespoons chopped fresh dill
1 cup dill pickle juice
3 hard-cooked eggs, chopped
1 4½-ounce can large shrimp,
  drained, minced

Combine buttermilk or yogurt and sour cream; beat until foamy. Add remaining ingredients, keeping aside 1 egg for garnish. Chill several hours. Serve topped with egg slices. *Makes 8 to 10 servings.*

Mexican Pumpkin Soup

4 cups chicken broth
¼ cup minced onion
3 scallions, minced
1 1-pound can unseasoned
  pumpkin

1 cup light cream
½ teaspoon salt, or to taste
2 medium tomatoes, thinly sliced
¼ cup heavy cream, whipped, or
  ¼ cup sour cream

To the broth add onion and the white part of the scallions (saving the green tops for garnish). Bring to a boil; simmer 15 minutes. Add pumpkin; blend well; simmer 5 minutes longer after it comes again to a boil. Purée in electric blender until smooth. Cool. When cool, add light cream and salt. Place in cups; chill thoroughly. Gently place a thin slice of tomato on each cup. Decorate each tomato slice with a rosette of whipped or sour cream. Garnish with minced green tops of scallions. *Makes 6 to 8 servings.*

Senegalese Soup

6 cups homemade chicken broth
1 cup yogurt
½ cup sweet cream
1 teaspoon curry powder
2 egg yolks

Salt
½ cucumber, peeled, minced
¼ cup chopped peanuts
¼ cup shredded coconut

Heat clarified broth; stir in yogurt, cream, and curry powder over low heat until mixture steams—do not allow to boil. Add some of the hot broth to egg yolks, then combine mixtures and simmer, stirring, 2 or 3 minutes. Season to taste. Chill once more. Pass bowls of minced cucumber, peanuts, and coconut for garnish. *Makes 8 to 10 servings.*

Consommé Madrilène

2 cups tomato juice
½ teaspoon grated onion
2 cups clear chicken broth

(preferably homemade)
1 teaspoon grated lemon rind
Sour cream

Combine tomato juice, onion, broth, and lemon rind; heat to boiling. Cool; chill. Serve cold topped with dollops of sour cream. *Makes 6 servings.*

JELLIED MADRILENE. Soften 1 envelope unflavored gelatin in tomato juice; add *hot* broth; stir to dissolve. Add onion and lemon rind; chill. Omit sour cream.

Polish Blueberry Soup

1 15-ounce can wild blueberries
1½ cups water or white wine
Juice of ½ lemon

1 tablespoon cornstarch
1 cup sour cream

Purée canned blueberries with their syrup; add water or wine and lemon juice. Blend cornstarch with a little of the liquid, add to remaining purée, and bring just to a boil; cook 1 minute. Chill. Blend with sour cream; serve cold with dollop of sour cream on each serving. *Serves 4.*

3 MEATS

Americans are a nation of beefeaters. Other meats are available, and occasionally served, but beef tops them all. And, in truth, chopped beef (or ground beef, as it more properly should be called) is the best meat bargain to be found anywhere.

I have classified meat recipes according to cookery method rather than kind of meat, because it is often possible to substitute one kind of meat for another. Lamb, for example, can be used in almost every recipe calling for beef—and vice versa. For those who do not care for the flavor of lamb, it's good to know that shish-kabob can be made just as well with cubes of beef, or that moussaka can be made with ground beef instead of ground lean lamb.

Lean pork can often be used in recipes calling for veal—and vice versa. I have made blanquette de veau with lean pork, and it was perfectly delicious. My friend Helen Feingold once told me that her Austrian mother found that the best American approximation to wiener schnitzel as made in Vienna was with pork fillet, pounded thin as veal cutlet would be pounded. When pork is less expensive than veal, try this switch. Conversely, if veal can be purchased at a good price, why not try it with a sauce suggested for pork?

Because barbecuing is no longer limited to warm-weather months, meats for the barbecue are included in this chapter. Steaks and hamburgers will continue to dominate the barbecue scene, because of the propensity for anything as long as it's beef, but lamb, pork, and veal can all be barbecued successfully and deliciously. Pork needs to be cooked to well-done (and should be cut in small pieces to make sure it cooks all the way through), and veal needs to be marinated in an oil mixture before barbecuing, because it lacks fat—but with such precautions, these meats can be substituted in certain recipes calling for beef. As for lamb, it was the first of all meats to be barbecued, by those ancient Greeks and Persians who stuck the meat on their swords, or suspended it on pronged sticks above a fire of twigs.

Review the Buying and Storage guides for meat and the sections on basic techniques of meat cookery, in Book 1. And remember that many of the sauces and marinades given in the preceding chapter may be used to vary the meats in your meals.

GROUND MEATS

Chopped chuck is usually the best and most economical buy in ground meat. What is called *hamburger meat* contains much more fat, and the fat will drain away with cooking, causing considerable shrinkage. *Chopped round steak* has less fat than chopped chuck, but not a great deal less, the price is higher per pound, and in flavor it is no better. *Meat loaf mixture* is a combination of beef, pork, and veal, and is excellent for certain dishes, but must be used or frozen immediately, because ground pork is the most perishable of meats. *Lamb patties*, often available on special sale, made with scraps and trimmings from more expensive lamb cuts, are often a very good buy—but it is best to cook the meat first, to draw out excess fat, before adding a sauce.

It is always better to have meat ground to order, whether it's beef, pork, veal, or lamb, so that you can see what is going into the grinder.

Hamburgers 52 Ways

It is entirely possible to have hamburgers once every week for an entire year and never repeat the same recipe. And this is not including meatballs, or many, many other dishes to be made with ground meats.

Basic Hamburger Recipe

For each pound of ground beef, add ¾ to 1 teaspoon salt. Work salt into meat, handling as lightly as possible. Shape into patties. For thick hamburgers, make 4 patties to a pound. For medium hamburgers, 6 to a pound. For very thin hamburgers, 8 to a pound (this makes hamburgers of about the same size as those sold at most roadside stands and is often adequate for serving younger children).

TO PAN-BROIL. Place a very small piece (about ½ teaspoon) of butter or vegetable shortening in a hot skillet, just enough to moisten the surface of the skillet. Brush or rub over entire surface until it glistens. Or, sprinkle salt over a hot skillet, add the patties, loosen with a spatula before they can stick. (The salt brings out the fat from the meat.) *For medium or thin hamburgers,* cook over high heat, turn as soon as well browned on one side, brown on the other, allowing a total of 6 minutes cooking time for well-done, 3 to 4 minutes for medium rare. *For thick hamburgers,* cook over moderate to low heat for a total oı 10 to 15 minutes for well-done, a total of 8 minutes for medium rare; truly rare burgers must be thick, cooked over high heat until well browned on each side—a total of about 6 minutes.

TO PAN-FRY. Place 1 to 2 tablespoons fat (butter, bacon drippings, or vegetable shortening) in hot skillet. When fat is sizzling, add patties, brown quickly.

TO BROIL IN BROILER OVEN. Remove rack, preheat oven to 500° F. (very hot). Rub rack lightly with just enough fat or oil to prevent sticking. (Remove excess fat with paper towel). Make *thick* patties; place on rack, broil 2 inches from unit until well browned on each side, allowing a total of 8 to 10 minutes for well-done (4 to 5 minutes each side); or a total of 5 to 6 minutes for rare to medium rare. (Broiled hamburger patties will be jucier if marinated before cooking.)

TO BROIL OVER CHARCOAL. Be sure to marinate first, because the direct heat of a charcoal fire dries out the meat. Soak in Vinaigrette Sauce, a barbecue sauce, or a wine marinade for at least an hour before placing over fire. Cook 2 to 3 inches from fire (depending on intensity of heat) until well browned on each side; test for doneness by pricking center with a fork.

VARIATIONS. Add to each pound of ground beef one or more of the following:

- *Ice water.* 2 tablespoons for juicier texture.
- *A few dashes of Angostura bitters.*
- *¼ teaspoon garlic salt.*
- *1 teaspoon grated onion.*
- *1 tablespoon minced parsley.*
- *¼ teaspoon dried orégano.*
- *2 tablespoons catsup.*

Economy Hamburgers

1 pound ground chuck or hamburger meat

½ cup soft white bread crumbs,   Freshly ground pepper
  soaked in 1/3 cup milk   (optional)
1 teaspoon salt

Soak bread until very soft, then work into meat with seasonings until thoroughly blended, handling lightly. Shape into 6 to 8
patties (depending on thickness desired). Chill for 30 minutes;
remove to room temperature 15 minutes before cooking.
Pan-broil or pan-fry to desired degree of doneness. *Makes 6 to 8
hamburgers.*

ENRICHED HAMBURGERS. Work 3 tablespoons instant dry
milk into basic recipe before shaping patties. (A good way to
sneak nutrition into meals of children who are poor eaters.)

WITH EGG. For 1½ pounds meat (and ¾ cup bread crumbs
soaked in ½ cup milk), add 1 beaten egg to mixture, plus 1½
teaspoons salt. *Makes 9 to 12 hamburgers.*

Soyburgers

Prepare basic hamburger recipe, but use 1 teaspoon
beef-flavored stock concentrate instead of ¾ teaspoon salt and
add 1 tablespoon soy sauce. Pan-broil hamburgers; when
cooked, add ¼ cup soy sauce and ¼ cup orange juice to pan
drippings; spoon this sauce over the meat.

Cheeseburgers

Pan-broil hamburgers; as soon as they are browned on both
sices, place a slice of American cheese on each, cover pan, keep
over heat about 1 minute or until cheese is partially melted.
With spatula, transfer hamburgers to buns. Serve with piccalilli
or India relish.

CHEESE-TOMATO BURGERS. Pan-broil or broil hamburgers;
place a slice of tomato on each hamburger, dust tomato slice
with salt, cover with a slice of American cheese. If pan-broiled,
cover pan, cook over low heat until cheese is partially melted. If
broiled, leave under broiler unit until cheese starts to melt.
Transfer to buns with spatula.

HAMBURGERS WITH CHEESE SAUCE. Instead of serving
hamburgers in buns with a slice of cheese, serve on toast
topped with Quick Cheese Sauce or Rum-Tum-Diddy.

ROQUEFORT BURGERS. Place sizzling-hot hamburgers in
buns; crumble about a tablespoon of Roquefort or other blue
cheese over the tops of each. Cheese will partially melt from
heat of meat.

SWISS BURGERS. Prepare as for Cheeseburgers, but use sliced Swiss cheese and add a little chopped onion or chopped green pepper.

Potato Chip Burgers

Place sizzling hamburgers in buns. Over each hamburger place 2 or 3 potato chips and, if desired, a little chopped onion. Close the bun, crush together slightly with fingers. This causes the potato chips to crumble with the onion.

Steakburgers

1 pound round steak, ground, or 1 pound sirloin, ground	1 tablespoon butter, melted
¾ to 1 teaspoon salt	1 tablespoon meat stock, or ½ teaspoon gravy coloring

Place meat and salt in bowl; add butter and meat stock or gravy coloring. Blend with fork, then shape into *thick* patties. Marinate 15 to 20 minutes in Vinaigrette Sauce, Steak Marinade, or Garlic Barbecue Sauce. Broil under preheated broiler or over charcoal, allowing a total of 6 to 8 minutes for rare (3 to 4 minutes each side), 10 minutes for well-done. *Makes 4.*

STEAKBURGERS AND ONIONS. Pan-fry rather than broil Steakburgers. Remove from skillet; keep warm. Add to pan drippings 1 to 2 tablespoons butter or margarine, heat to sizzling, add 1 cup sliced onions. Fry onions, turning occasionally with spatula, until soft and lightly browned. Serve steakburgers topped with onions.

MUFFINBURGERS. Split English muffins with a fork, toast in pop-up toaster or under broiler unit. Butter while hot. Place a sizzling hamburger inside each.

HAMBURGERS IN ONION BUNS. These are smaller than regular hamburger buns, so the patties to go into them should be made smaller. Heat buns in oven while making hamburgers. Kosher dill pickles are marvelous as a garnish.

CORNBURGERS. Use frozen corn muffins or corn toasties. Heat in a pop-up toaster. Place sizzling hamburgers on the hot muffins; serve with chili sauce and piccalilli.

Hamburger Relishes

Besides the standard relishes, try one or more of the following:

Escoffier Sauce	Pesto Genovese
A-1 Sauce	Green Relish

Tapenade
Homemade Chili Sauce
Mustard Pickles
Cranberry-Orange Relish
Oriental Relish
Tabasco Sauce

Chutney
Sauerkraut
Potato Salad
Cole Slaw
Tomato Chutney

Hamburgers in Vermouth

Prepare thick hamburgers; pan-broil or pan-fry; when cooked as desired, add ½ cup dry or sweet vermouth to the pan, let burgers simmer in vermouth 2 minutes. Remove burgers; scrape up pan drippings, pour over burgers. Serve as an entree with broccoli, parsley potatoes, and salad.

Hamburgers in Red Wine

Pan-fry hamburgers; add 1 cup red wine, 1 tablespoon Worcestershire or soy sauce, and 1 teaspoon prepared mustard to pan. Simmer 2 minutes. Remove hamburgers. Boil sauce to reduce to ½ cup, scraping up pan drippings. Serve sauce over hamburgers.

SUGGESTED GO-WITHS. Crisp French fries (homemade), carrots with Herb Butter, Roquefort salad.

Hamburgers Maître d'Hôtel

Serve each hamburger topped by a pat of Butter Maître d'-Hôtel (with lemon juice and parsley).

Hamburgers with Mushrooms

Pan-fry 6 hamburger patties in butter, remove from pan; keep warm. Add 2 tablespoons butter and ½ pound sliced mushrooms, cook mushrooms until lightly browned. Turn off heat. Add 1 tablespoon sour cream and 1 tablespoon catsup; stir to blend. Serve as sauce over hamburgers, accompanied by braised celery, and Green Beans Vinaigrette.

Hamburgers Teriyaki

Marinate hamburgers in Teriyaki Sauce for at least 30 minutes. Broil; serve with sweet potatoes and green beans.

Sherried Hamburgers

Pan-broil hamburgers; when browned on both sides, add ¼ cup medium sherry, 1 tablespoon soy sauce, and ½ cup chicken broth (use 1 teaspoon chicken stock concentrate dissolved in ½ cup water). Do not add salt. Simmer hamburgers in sauce 2 or 3 minutes. Serve with cauliflower and carrots with minced dill (or parsley), and Greek Salad.

Tomato-glazed Hamburgers

Prepare *thick* hamburgers; broil over charcoal, brushing frequently with Tomato Glaze. Serve with Zucchini Italienne, radishes, Caesar Salad.

Hamburgers Indonesian

Broil hamburgers over charcoal, basting as they cook with Red-hot Indonesian Sauce. Serve with chutney, Almond Rice, and curried lima beans.

HAMBURGERS WITH GARLIC BUTTER. Serve each hamburger topped with a pat of Cold Garlic Butter.

HAMBURGERS HOLLANDAISE. Top broiled hamburgers with Hollandaise Sauce.

HAMBURGERS RAVIGOTE

Serve hamburgers in buns topped with Ravigote Sauce.

PINEAPPLE HAMBURGERS. Pan-broil thick hamburgers; in same pan sauté pineapple slices. Serve in buns; top each burger with pineapple, spooning a little pan essence over the fruit. Serve with choice of mustard, Worcestershire, India relish, or shredded coconut.

Chuletas (Mexican Hamburgers)

2 pounds ground chuck	2 eggs
½ cup minced onion	Freshly ground black pepper (lots
½ cup minced parsley	of it)
2 teaspoons salt	1 cup fine dry herb-seasoned
Pinch of cayenne or dash of	crumbs
Tabasco	

In a bowl combine meat with onions, parsley, salt, cayenne or Tabasco, and eggs; blend well. Form into 1-inch balls. Sprinkle half the crumbs over a pastry board at a time, press the meatballs into *thin* patties over the crumbs so that the crumbs form a thin crust on each side. Chill the patties. Grill over charcoal or under the broiler until crusty-brown, about 3 minutes to each side. Serve in buns or as an entree. *Makes 10 to 12 servings.*

SUGGESTED GO-WITHS. Barbecue sauce, tortillas, enchiladas, avocado salad.

Barbecued Hamburgers in Red Wine Marinade

Prepare medium or thick patties, marinate in Red Wine Marinade 12 to 24 hours before cooking. (If plans are changed, and hamburgers will not be cooked until a day later, the marinade helps to preserve the meat; also, the longer marinating gives the meat interesting flavor.) Broil burgers over charcoal; baste with sauce as they cook. For a patio meal, serve with Garbanzo Salad, tomato aspic ring filled with cottage cheese, carrot sticks, and potato chips.

Hamburgers in Orange Barbecue Sauce

Marinate medium to thick hamburger patties 1 hour or longer in Orange Barbecue Sauce. Remove from marinade, broil over charcoal; heat marinade, purée in blender, pass as a hot sauce for the burgers.

SUGGESTED GO-WITHS. Succotash, sliced tomatoes, artichoke hearts.

Hamburgers Hawaiian

Marinate thick or medium hamburger patties in Sherry-Soy Sauce ½ to 1 hour, broil over charcoal or in the oven. Serve with Curried Fried Bananas, broiled pineapple slices (broil alongside the hamburger patties in the oven, or marinate in the soy mixture and broil on the barbecue grill), and bowls of shredded coconut and chopped peanuts as garnishes. A tossed green salad and cantaloupe for dessert make this a perfect summertime meal.

Hamburgers Stroganoff

Pan-fry 8 medium or thick hamburgers until nicely browned on each side. Remove; keep warm. To pan drippings, add commercial gravy mix blended with water to make 1 cup gravy, 1 tablespoon instant minced onion, and ¼ cup tomato sauce. Cook until smooth and thickened. Turn off heat. Add some of the hot gravy to ½ cup sour cream; when well blended, add sour cream to remaining gravy. Replace hamburgers in sauce, simmer 2 to 3 minutes.

SUGGESTED GO-WITHS. Noodles, Brussels sprouts, tossed green salad, Cherry Crisp for dessert.

Hamburgers Provençal

Pan-fry thick hamburgers. When browned on both sides, remove, keep warm. Add to pan Tomato Sauce Provençal. Return hamburgers to sauce, simmer in sauce 2 to 3 minutes. Serve over steamed rice with fried eggplant and Salade Niçoise.

Deutsches Beefsteak

This is the original hamburger, as made in Hamburg, Germany.

1 cup crumbled stale white bread	1 tablespoon minced parsley
¼ cup milk	(optional)
1 pound ground beef, or mixture	1 small onion, minced
of beef, pork, and veal	(optional)
¾ teaspoon salt	6 tablespoons fat
1 egg, beaten	

Soak bread in milk until soft. Add meat, salt, egg, parsley, and onion. Blend with fingers until fairly smooth and compact, forming 6 thick patties. Heat fat to sizzling; add patties; cook until crisply browned on each side. *Makes 6 servings.*

BEEFSTEAK À LA MAYER. Prepare Deutsches Beefsteak, serve on fried bread or toast, top each meat patty with a fried or poached egg.

Bremer Beefsteak

1 pound ground beef	1 teaspoon minced parsley
½ cup mashed potatoes (leftover)	(optional)
¾ teaspoon salt, or to taste	2 tablespoons sour cream
Freshly ground black pepper	6 tablespoons fat

Combine beef, potatoes, salt, pepper, and parsley. Blend well. Work in sour cream with fork. Shape into 4 to 6 patties. Heat fat to sizzling and brown patties in it until crisply browned on both sides. Serve with gherkins or dill pickles, steamed salted potatoes, and celery salad. *Makes 4 to 6 servings.*

Stuffed Hamburgers

Of each pound seasoned chopped beef, make 8 thin patties. In the center of half of the patties, place one of the following fillings. Top with remaining patties, press edges together to seal, so that filling is completely encased. Pan-fry with 2 to 3 tablespoons fat until well browned on each side, allowing 5 minutes per side. (These must be cooked well-done so that filling is heated thoroughly.)

CHEESE-STUFFED BURGERS. Put about 2 teaspoons grated or shredded cheese inside each patty.

MUSHROOM-STUFFED BURGERS. Sauté chopped fresh or canned mushrooms lightly in butter before cooking the hamburgers. For 4 stuffed hamburgers, ¼ cup chopped mushrooms is about right.

ONION-STUFFED BURGERS. Sauté 1 medium onion in butter or margarine before cooking hamburgers; place about 1½ tablespoons fried onion inside each of the patties.

HAMBURGERS GENOVESE. In fat, fry 2 cloves garlic, whole or split, with ¼ cup minced parsley until garlic is golden; mash to a paste. Place a teaspoon of the paste inside each patty.

SAVORY STUFFED BURGERS. Use packaged commercial bread stuffing, moistened with water according to directions; or add herbs, salt, and pepper (to taste) to stale bread broken into fine pieces. Place a tablespoon bread stuffing inside each patty, along with about ½ teaspoon butter.

Flaming Hamburgers

1½ pounds round steak, ground
¾ teaspoon salt
1 tablespoon water
1 teaspoon beef-flavored
   stock concentrate
1 teaspoon grated onion

(optional)
6 tablespoons butter
¼ cup brandy, bourbon, or rum
Grated rind of 1 lemon
1 teaspoon lemon juice (optional)

Have meat ground to order, run through the grinder twice. Blend with salt first, then add the water to stock concentrate and work this into meat, blending thoroughly but handling with a light touch. Add grated onion with the stock concentrate, if desired. Form into 6 patties. Melt butter in a large heavy skillet, until sizzling but not browned. Add meat patties, cook over high heat until well browned on each side, allowing 3 minutes on each side for rare (but test one of patties by peeking inside with a knife to be sure it is not *too* rare). Place 1 tablespoon brandy in a spoon or ladle, lower into pan, hold it there so brandy will be warmed, then set aflame. (After match has been lighted, let it burn until sulphur fumes have disappeared). Spoon up pan drippings to keep brandy burning; add remaining brandy 1 tablespoon at a time. When flame has burned out, add grated lemon rind and juice, let sauce simmer about 1 minute longer. Serve at once. *Makes 6 servings.*

SUGGESTED GO-WITHS. Artichoke hearts, glazed baby carrots, Orange and Avocado Salad.

Hamburger Heroes

Instead of hamburger buns, use French or Italian bread sliced in half lengthwise, or hero buns. Shape patties so that they will fit into the bread. Pan-fry meat in butter; brush cut side of bread with pan drippings. Have a big selection of relishes ready plus cheese, sliced tomatoes, sliced onion, and bottled French or Italian dressing. As for a Sandwich Smorgasbord, each person selects his own hero ingredients.

Hamburger Peacemaker

2 loaves French bread
1 pound chopped chuck
¾ teaspoon salt
1 tablespoon butter

1 can frozen oyster stew
½ soup can light cream
⅛ teaspoon nutmeg

Cut a thin slice lengthwise from top of each loaf of bread. Remove part of soft bread from inside, leaving each with a shell about ½ inch thick. (Keep bread crumbs for other use, such as in meat loaf.) Add salt to meat; form into meatballs, sauté in butter until well browned on all sides. Place meatballs inside the hollowed loaves, dividing in half. Heat oyster stew with cream until thoroughly hot; season with nutmeg. Pour oyster stew over meatballs. Replace cover. Serve hot as a luncheon entree with a crisp green salad. *Makes 4 to 6 servings.*

Hamburger Steak

2 beef bouillon cubes (or beef-
  flavored stock concentrate)
¾ cup boiling water
1½ pounds top round of beef,
  ground
¾ teaspoon salt

¼ teaspoon thyme
¼ teaspoon basil
2 teaspoons Worcestershire sauce
1 egg
½ cup tomato sauce

Dissolve bouillon cubes or stock concentrate in boiling water. Cool slightly. Add beef, seasonings, and egg; mix thoroughly. Shape into 1 steak, 1 inch thick. Place steak in lightly greased shallow pan, spread tomato sauce over top. Preheat oven to 450° F. Cook steak 15 minutes until browned. *Makes 4 to 6 servings.*

Hamburgers Diane

1½ pounds top round of beef,
  ground
1½ teaspoons salt
1 teaspoon butter
2 tablespoons brandy

¼ cup red wine
Dash of Tabasco
1 tablespoon catsup
½ cup water
Salt

Lightly blend meat with salt; shape into 6 thick patties. Melt butter in heavy saucepan, turning pan to moisten surface completely. Cook hamburgers over *medium*, not high, heat, until well browned on each side. Remove; keep warm. Add brandy to pan; stir up browned bits in bottom of pan. Add wine and Tabasco; let sauce boil, stirring. Add catsup and water, boil until sauce is reduced about one-third. Add salt as needed. This makes a thin sauce to spoon over tops of burgers. *Makes 6 servings.*

SUGGESTED GO-WITHS. Very thin noodles tossed with butter and Parmesan cheese, asparagus, and watercress salad. For dessert, Cherries au Kirsch.

Portuguese Hamburgers

¾ pound ground beef
¼ cup minced chorizo*
½ cup fine dry bread crumbs
2 tablespoons minced parsley
2 tablespoons minced onion

2 eggs
½ teaspoon salt
¼ teaspoon black pepper
1 tablespoon oil or butter
Cream of Tomato Sauce

Combine beef and sausage, bread crumbs, parsley, onion, eggs, salt, and pepper; blend well, form into patties. Heat oil or butter in skillet, brown the patties until crisp on both sides. Remove to platter; keep warm. *Makes 7 or 8 servings.*

*If chorizo sausage is not locally available, use chopped cooked ham or salami and ¼ teaspoon garlic powder or garlic salt.

CREAM OF TOMATO SAUCE. To pan drippings add 1 cup tomato juice blended with ¼ cup milk and 1 tablespoon heavy cream or sour cream; stir briskly over low heat to prevent curdling, just until heated through. Add salt and pepper to taste. *Makes 1¼ cups sauce.*

SUGGESTED GO-WITHS. Steamed rice, cauliflower, black olives, and radishes; Apple Brown Betty for dessert.

Danish Steakburgers with Onions

2 pounds lean chuck steak,
  coarsely ground
1 teaspoon salt
3 tablespoons flour
3 large onions, sliced

5 or 6 tablespoons butter or margarine
1½ cups milk
Kitchen Bouquet or Gravy Master

Form chopped meat into small individual steaks, about 1½ inches square, 1 inch high. Pound with flat side of knife until smooth and firm. Combine salt and flour; roll steaks in mixture. Meantime fry onions in butter or margarine until tender; remove, drain on absorbent paper. Keep warm until ready to serve (these can be fried in advance and kept in readiness in a warming oven). Shortly before they are to be served, brown steaks in fat remaining in pan, over moderately high heat, allowing 5 minutes on each side. Remove. Top each steak with a spoonful of fried onions. (Steaks will have crusty outside, will be rare in center.)

Make gravy by adding remaining flour mixture to fat in pan, and if necessary, add additional flour to make a smooth *roux* with the fat. Slowly add milk and a few drops of the gravy coloring. Cook, stirring, until smooth and thickened. Season to taste with additional salt. Arrange steaks on platter, surrounded with the gravy. *Makes 8 to 12 servings.*

SUGGESTED GO-WITHS. Mashed potatoes, corn on the cob, Pineapple Cole Slaw.

Steak Tartare

1½ pounds top round of beef or sirloin	1 raw egg yolk
1½ teaspoons salt	Capers
1 teaspoon grated onion	Minced parsley
1 small onion, chopped	Freshly ground black pepper

The proper way to make this northern European favorite is to scrape the solid lean cut of meat with a very sharp knife until all the meat has been transformed into very fine particles—the fat and gristle, of course, discarded. The lazier way is to have your meat man put it through the grinder, twice or even three times—but be sure he first trims off every bit of fat and gives you choice quality meat. It must be ground to order the same day it is served.

Blend salt and grated onion into the meat, shape it on a round plate into a low mound, then make a depression in the center, and in this depression place the egg yolk. This is all that is done in advance. At the table, place chopped onion, capers, and minced parsley in small bowls around the meat, and a pepper grinder should be prominently displayed. The host (for this is a man's dish, usually prepared by men) traditionally is the one to mix the steak, and he may add the chopped onions, capers, parsley, and black pepper (lots of freshly ground black pepper) to the meat, or he may only mix the egg yolk and black pepper with the meat and let the others add onion, capers, and parsley to taste. The meat is served raw, chilled, accompanied by crusty bread or pumpernickel and a salad. The beverage should be beer, ale, or schnapps, followed by black coffee. *Makes 4 servings.*

Other condiments sometimes offered include Worcestershire, A-1 Sauce, hot prepared mustard, and mixed pickles.

Meatballs 25 Ways

Meatballs are basically the same as hamburgers, except that they are formed into round balls instead of patties. To serve as appetizers or in soups, make tiny meatballs (about ½ inch in diameter). As an entrée, they may be 1 to 1½ inches in diameter. Some meatballs are sautéed; some are dropped in bubbling broth. Learn to prepare meatballs by the following basic recipes: then, simply by changing the sauce, you can create countless dishes.

Meatballs I

¾ to 1 teaspoon salt
1 pound ground meat (all the same kind, or a mixture)

Work salt into meat; shape into balls by rolling between palms of hands. Fry, sauté, broil, or boil in broth as specified in recipe. Makes about 30 appetizer-size balls (½ inch each), 15 1-inch balls, or 10 1½-inch balls.

Meatballs II

1½ pounds ground or minced meat (all the same kind, or a mixture)
1 egg, well beaten
1½ teaspoons salt

1 slice white bread soaked in ¼ cup water, milk, or other liquid, or ¼ cup fine dry crumbs plus ¼ cup liquid

Blend all ingredients well, knead and form with fingers into smooth round balls of desired size. Fry, broil, or cook in broth or sauce according to recipe. Makes about 50 appetizer-size balls, about 25 1-inch balls, or 16 1½-inch balls.

Meatballs III

Like Meatballs II, but with an additional egg and twice as much bread (2 slices bread soaked in 1/3 cup liquid or ½ cup fine crumbs). This makes about 70 appetizer-size balls, about 35 1-inch balls, or 25 1½-inch balls.

Spaghetti and Meatballs

Prepare either Meatballs I or II; shape balls 1 inch in diameter. Sauté in fat or oil until well browned on all sides. Add spaghetti sauce (homemade or commercial). Simmer meatballs in sauce for 10 minutes, while cooking spaghetti separately in rapidly boiling water. Drain cooked spaghetti thoroughly; serve topped with meatballs and sauce. Pass grated Parmesan cheese. For 4 average servings, you will need 1 recipe meatballs, 2 cups sauce, and 1 pound thin spaghetti.

SUGGESTED GO-WITHS. Green salad, garlic bread, ice cream with fruit topping for dessert.

Sherried Meatballs

Prepare Meatballs I or II, fry in butter until well browned, add ¼ cup sherry and 2 tablespoons tomato sauce or purée; simmer 5 minutes. Serve over steamed rice. Sprinkle minced parsley over top.

SUGGESTED GO-WITHS: Asparagus or broccoli, and broiled tomatoes.

Meatball Casserole

1 recipe Meatballs II
¼ teaspoon each thyme and
  orégano
4 slices bacon
1 medium onion, thinly sliced
2 tablespoons catsup

1 4-ounce can sliced mushrooms,
  with liquid
½ pound noodles, cooked
1 10-ounce can cream of mushroom soup
2 tablespoons medium sherry

Prepare meatballs, working herbs into the meatball mixture. Fry bacon slices until crisp; remove from pan. Sauté meatballs in bacon fat until browned on all sides; remove. Add sliced onion to fat in pan; cook until soft and lightly browned. Drain mushrooms (saving liquid); add mushrooms to onions. Cook the noodles in boiling salted water; drain well. Arrange noodles, onion-mushroom mixture, and meatballs in layers in 1½-quart casserole. Combine mushroom liquid with cream of mushroom soup, sherry, catsup, and salt to taste. Pour over other ingredients. Crumble bacon; sprinkle over top. (All this may be prepared ahead.) Cover casserole, bake in oven preheated to 375° F. (moderate) until sauce is bubbling—about 45 minutes. *Makes 4 to 6 servings.*

SUGGESTED GO-WITHS. Butterfly rolls, Golden Glow Salad (gelatin mold) on lettuce: coffee ice cream topped with sliced bananas and chopped peanuts for dessert.

Albondigas (Spanish Meatballs)

1 recipe Meatballs II, using beef or veal and pork
¼ teaspoon white pepper
¼ teaspoon nutmeg
1 tablespoon minced parsley
3 to 4 tablespoons olive oil
¾ cup chopped onion
1 clove garlic, chopped

2 pimientos, chopped
1 tomato, chopped
1½ cups water
1 tablespoon brandy
Salt
1 cup (½ package) frozen tiny peas

Prepare meatballs, adding pepper, nutmeg, and minced parsley to basic recipe. Shape into 18 balls. Sauté in oil until browned on all sides. Remove meatballs; add to pan drippings the onion, garlic, and pimiento. Cook until very soft. Add tomato: cook 2 minutes longer. Add water, brandy, and salt to taste. Replace meatballs in sauce; simmer another 15 minutes. Or, if prepared ahead for later serving, store meatballs in sauce in refrigerator, reheat, simmering until sauce is somewhat thickened. Add frozen peas; cook until peas are tender—about 7 minutes. *Makes 6 servings (3 meatballs each).*

ANOTHER WAY. Use same meat mixture as for Portuguese Hamburgers, but shape into 1-inch balls. Sauté in oil until well browned; add 1 cup Homemade or Quick Tomato Sauce, or red wine; simmer 5 to 10 minutes longer.

Greek Meatballs Avgholemono

1 recipe Meatballs II, using ground lean lamb only
¼ cup minced parsley
¼ cup minced onion
⅛ teaspoon cinnamon
¼ teaspoon black pepper

1 or 2 tablespoons olive oil
1 teaspoon chicken stock concentrate
1 cup water
4 egg yolks
4 tablespoons lemon juice

Prepare meatballs, adding parsley, onion, cinnamon, and black pepper to basic recipe. Form meatballs 1 inch in diameter; sauté in oil until browned on all sides. Remove; keep warm. Add chicken stock concentrate and water to skillet; stir, loosening browned bits; bring to a boil, stir until dissolved.

Separately, beat egg yolks until thick; beat in lemon juice 1 tablespoon at a time. Add the hot pan broth to the egg mixture a little at a time, beating with whisk. Return to skillet; cook over low heat, stirring constantly, until smooth and thickened. Serve sauce over meatballs. Or, if not to be served at once, place meatballs and sauce in covered casserole, keep warm in oven set at 275° F. *Makes 4 to 6 servings.*

SUGGESTED GO-WITHS. Rice, artichokes, Greek Salad, Raspberry Yogurt for dessert.

QUICK MEATBALLS AVGHOLEMONO. Make the sauce with condensed cream of chicken soup, ½ cup water, 3 whole eggs, and 2 tablespoons lemon juice, beaten together in blender. Add to pan in which meatballs were sautéed, stirring with whisk until smooth. Replace meatballs in sauce.

Koefte (Turkish Meatballs)

1 recipe Meatballs III	2 fully ripe tomatoes, peeled, chopped
1 medium onion, minced fine	
1 tablespoon tomato catsup, or 1 teaspoon lemon juice	1 green pepper, seeded, chopped
	1 small onion, thinly sliced
¼ cup seasoned flour	Pinch of dried mint
¼ cup salad oil or olive oil	Salt, pepper

Prepare meatballs, adding minced onion and catsup or lemon juice to basic recipe. Knead until smooth and compact. Shape into 1-inch balls, dredge with seasoned flour (salt and pepper added). Fry in hot oil until a brown crust has formed over outside of balls. Add tomatoes, green pepper, onion, and mint, and shake salt and pepper over vegetables. Cover pan. Cook at very low heat 15 minutes. *Makes 4 to 6 servings.*

SUGGESTED GO-WITHS. Rice, fried eggplant, green salad dressed with oil and lemon juice, or with Yogurt Mint Dressing.

FRIKADELLER (Danish Meatballs). Prepare like Koefte; but use beef and pork; omit tomatoes, green pepper, and mint. Fry in butter or margarine instead of oil. Make gravy with pan drippings.

Ladies' Thighs (Kadinbudu Koefte)

Prepare the basic recipe for Meatballs III with all lamb, but use 2 eggs, and instead of bread crumbs, use ½ cup cooked rice, and add ¼ cup minced onion; put mixture through food grinder or purée in blender until smooth and compact. Form into

oval-shaped rolls (the ladies' thighs); chill until firm. Dip these
croquettes in egg, then roll in fine dry crumbs. Fry in hot fat or
oil until crisply browned on all sides. Serve with Fried Parsley.
Makes 6 servings.

SUGGESTED GO-WITHS. Ratatouille, crusty bread, green salad with black olives, red wine.

Swedish Meatballs I

1 recipe Meatballs II, using
  mixture of veal and pork
¼ teaspoon nutmeg
4 tablespoons butter
¼ pound sliced mushrooms

2 tablespoons flour
1 cup beef broth (made
  with concentrate)
½ cup sour cream

Prepare meatballs as in basic recipe, but increase milk to ½
cup and add nutmeg. Mixture will be moist. Shape into small
balls (¾ to 1 inch) with spoon. Chill balls for at least 30 minutes.
Melt butter in skillet; when it is sizzling (but not brown), sauté
meatballs until browned on all sides, adding only as many as
pan will hold without crowding. Remove as meatballs are finished; keep warm. Add mushrooms to pan; sauté until lightly
browned. Stir in flour, then slowly add beef broth. Simmer 5
minutes. Turn off heat; add some of sauce to sour cream, beating until well blended. Add sour cream to warm sauce in skillet.
Replace meatballs in sauce. Serve immediately, or transfer to
casserole and keep warm in 275° F. oven until time to
serve—up to 1 hour. Or, freeze to be reheated on another day.
(To reheat frozen meatballs, place casserole in *cold* oven, set
oven at 325° F., allow 45 minutes to 1 hour. If heat is too high,
sauce will curdle). *Makes 6 servings.*

    Serve as part of a smorgasbord, or as an entree, accompanied
by boiled potatoes and green peas.

Swedish Meatballs II

1 pound ground meatloaf mixture, or ½ pound beef, ¼ pound
  each ground pork and veal
2 eggs
1 teaspoon salt
Pinch of nutmeg
½ cup soft bread crumbs, soaked

in ½ cup milk
1 tablespoon minced onion
  or parsley
3 cups beef or chicken broth
1½ tablespoons cornstarch
½ cup sour cream

Combine ground meat, eggs, salt, nutmeg, and bread crumbs
soaked in milk. Add onion or parsley, if desired. Knead or beat

until very well blended; chill until it can be handled more easily, then shape into small round balls.

Heat broth (can be made with concentrate) to boiling; drop
meatballs into broth without crowding pan; cook about 15 minutes. Broth must continue at a simmer but should not boil hard.
Remove meatballs as they are cooked, adding more until all are
cooked.

Blend sour cream and cornstarch. Add a little of the hot broth
to the sour cream, then add sour cream to broth over low heat,
beating constantly with whisk until well blended and smooth.
Return meatballs to sauce. Serve at once, or keep warm in casserole in oven up to an hour, or freeze to reheat later. *Makes 4
to 6 servings.*

Königsberger Klopse

1 recipe Meatballs III, using beef
and pork
1 green onion, minced
½ teaspoon grated lemon rind
1 teaspoon lemon juice
2 anchovy fillets, minced
6 cups beef broth
1 stalk celery

1 small carrot, scraped, cubed
1 onion, quartered
3 egg yolks
2 tablespoons cornstarch
Few drops lemon juice
1 tablespoon capers
Minced chives or parsley

Prepare meatballs according to basic recipe, using 2 parts
beef and 1 part pork, but reduce salt to ½ teaspoon. Add to meat
mixture the onion, lemon rind, lemon juice, and anchovy.
Knead to blend well. Shape into 1½-inch balls. Chill for 30
minutes. In a large pot place beef broth (can be made with concentrate), celery, carrot, and onion; bring to a boil; simmer 15 to
20 minutes. Remove vegetables with slotted spoon. Add meatballs to bubbling broth, without crowding pot. Simmer 20 minutes; as balls rise to top, remove with slotted spoon; keep warm.
Blend together egg yolks and cornstarch. When all meatballs
have been cooked, boil broth to reduce to 2½ cups. Add a little
of the hot broth to egg yolk mixture, then add egg mixture to
broth; beat with whisk over *low* heat until smooth and somewhat thickened. Add lemon juice and capers. Pour sauce over
meatballs in casserole. Sprinkle minced chives or parsley over
top. *Makes 6 servings.*

SUGGESTED GO-WITHS. Saltzkartoffeln or mashed potatoes,
red cabbage, salad of cooked green beans and onion slices.

QUICK KÖNIGSBERGER KLOPSE. Prepare Meatballs II, using ground meatloaf mixture. Cook in 4 cups beef broth (can be made with concentrate), to which instant minced onion has been added. Combine ¾ cup of this broth with 1 can condensed cream of celery soup, 1 whole egg, well beaten, and 1 tablespoon capers, well drained. Add meatballs; sprinkle grated lemon rind over top. (Save remainder for use in other sauces.)

Viennese Meatballs

1 recipe Meatballs II, using veal and pork	2 egg yolks
6 cups beef or chicken broth	2 tablespoons cornstarch
1 onion, cut in quarters	½ cup heavy cream
1 stalk celery (including leaves), chopped	Grated rind of ½ lemon
	1 teaspoon minced parsley (or the chopped celery leaves)

Prepare meatballs according to basic recipe, using 1 part veal and 1 part pork. Shape into 1½-inch balls. Heat broth (can be made with concentrate) to boiling with onion and celery; simmer 15 minutes; remove onion and celery. Add half the meatballs at a time; simmer 20 minutes, removing when meatballs rise to top of broth. Keep warm. Beat egg yolks, cornstarch, and cream together; add lemon rind and parsley or chopped celery leaves. When all of meatballs have been cooked, add a little of the hot broth to the egg yolk mixture, then add remaining egg mixture to broth over *low* heat, beating briskly with whisk until smooth and somewhat thickened. Pour sauce over meatballs in casserole. *Makes 6 servings.*

SUGGESTED GO-WITHS. Buttered noodles, green peas or asparagus, tomato and lettuce salad, white wine. Linzer Torte for dessert.

Chinese Meatballs (Lion's Head)

1 pound ground pork	½ teaspoon salt
1 tablespoon dry sherry	½ teaspoon sugar
1 tablespoon soy sauce	1 egg, beaten
1 tablespoon cornstarch	

The pork should contain some fat in proportions of 1 part fat to 3 parts lean. Mix meat lightly with remaining ingredients; shape into 1½-inch balls. Deep-fry in oil (1 inch deep), until crisply browned on all sides. Serve with Sherry-Soy Sauce as part of a Chinese family dinner. *Makes 8 servings.*

CHINESE MEATBALLS WITH CELERY CABBAGE. Prepare Chinese Meatballs, but instead of frying cook them with sliced celery cabbage in 1 cup chicken broth and 1 tablespoon soy sauce, covered, for 10 minutes. Add 1 tablespoon cornstarch blended with 1 teaspoon sugar to the sauce; simmer, uncovered, 5 minutes longer.

CHINESE MEATBALLS IN ORIENTAL BROWN SAUCE. Prepare Chinese Meatballs, but add to mixture a few slices minced green ginger or ¼ teaspoon powdered ginger; shape into 1-inch balls. Fry until brown on all sides. Add Basic Oriental Brown Sauce; simmer 5 minutes longer.

Midwestern Meatballs

1 pound ground chuck	Pinch of thyme
2 tablespoons flour	¼ cup minced onion
½ teaspoon freshly ground black	¾ cup undiluted evaporated milk
pepper	¾ cup water
1 teaspoon salt	Oil for deep-frying

Place meat in blender with flour, seasonings, and onion; beat until very smooth. With blender in motion at low speed, add milk mixed with water, until all has been absorbed. Transfer to bowl, cover, store in refrigerator at least 3 or 4 hours. Drop by tablespoons in hot oil (1 inch deep); cook until well browned on all sides. Outside will be crusty, inside quite soft and fluffy. *Makes 4 servings.*

Curried Meatballs

1 recipe Meatballs I or II, using	1 tablespoon minced parsley
beef or lamb	2 tablespoons oil
¼ teaspoon freshly ground	1 recipe Basic Curry Sauce
black pepper	

Prepare meatballs, adding pepper and parsley. Shape into 1-inch balls; sauté in oil until well browned. Remove meatballs; in same pan prepare Basic Curry Sauce. Return meatballs to sauce; simmer 20 minutes. Serve as part of an Indian dinner, with rice and assorted condiments. *Makes 4 to 6 servings.*

MEATBALLS IN CURRY SAUCE. Prepare meatballs by any preferred recipe; sauté in fat until browned; serve in Curry-Cream Sauce, made with condensed soup, sour cream, and curry powder.

Luleh Kebab

1½ pounds ground lamb or beef
1 large onion, grated
2 eggs
1 teaspoon salt

½ teaspoon freshly ground pepper
¼ teaspoon cinnamon
Olive oil

Flatten ground meat on waxed paper. Cover surface with grated onion. Allow to stand 15 to 20 minutes or longer. Scrape onion from meat and discard. Place meat in large mixing bowl, add eggs, salt, pepper, and cinnamon. Knead with hands until meat is very smooth. Form into oblong or round patties. Brush with olive oil. Refrigerate until ready to use. Place on barbecue grill or in broiler, 2 inches from heat; cook until well browned, turning once. *Makes 6 to 8 patties.*

Hungarian Meatballs

1 recipe Meatballs II
3 tablespoons fat
1 clove garlic, minced
1 medium onion, sliced
½ green pepper, chopped

1 tablespoon paprika
2 tablespoons flour
1 cup beef broth
1 tablespoon catsup
½ cup sour cream

Use any desired combination of ground meat, or all beef, as preferred. Shape in 1-inch balls; sauté in fat until well browned. Remove. In same pan, sauté garlic, onion, and green pepper for 1 minute. Add paprika; cook until vegetables are soft. Stir in flour, then add the beef broth (can be made with concentrate). Add catsup; return meatballs to sauce. Simmer, covered, 15 minutes. Turn off heat. Blend some of sauce with sour cream, then add remaining sour cream to sauce. *Makes 4 to 6 servings.*

SUGGESTED GO-WITHS. Noodles, braised green cabbage, hot rolls, pickled beets.

Baked Meat Patties in Bacon

1½ pounds chopped chuck
1 cup canned tomatoes
1 cup fine dry crumbs
1½ teaspoons salt
Dash of freshly ground pepper

1 teaspoon minced parsley
 (optional)
1 egg, beaten
9 strips bacon

Combine meat, tomatoes, crumbs, salt, pepper, egg, and parsley. Blend well with fingers; shape into 9 patties or meatballs. Wrap each with a strip of bacon. Place in a 9 x 9-inch baking pan or dish so that one wrapped meatball (or patty) has bacon around it horizontally, the next vertically. Bake in oven preheated to 375° F. until bacon is crisp and meat browned— about 45 minutes. Serve from the baking dish, or remove to platter. *Makes 9 patties.*

SUGGESTED GO-WITHS. Baked or creamed potatoes, parsleyed carrots, cole slaw.

Meatloaf

Meatloaf is basically the same as meatballs, only larger; a mixture of meats is usually preferable to all beef. Some of the same sauces and relishes traditionally served with hamburgers may be served with meatloaf: catsup, mustard pickles, tomato chutney, and barbecue sauce, to name a few. Flavoring ingredients may be varied according to the whim of the cook. Many people add a bit of soy sauce to the meat mixture; others like horseradish. Lemon juice tenderizes and brings out flavor.

If you like meatloaf to have a crusty exterior, it's better to bake it in a shallow roasting pan; placing the mixture in a loaf pan may seem easier, but only the top browns, and the sides remain soft.

Yankee Meatloaf

1½ pounds meatloaf mixture or ground beef
1 cup fine dry crumbs
½ cup minced onion (optional)
¼ cup tomato catsup
¾ cup milk (or undiluted evaporated milk)

2 eggs
1½ teaspoons salt
¼ teaspoon pepper
Pinch of cayenne (optional)
Pinch of thyme (optional)
1 to 2 tablespoons oil or melted butter (optional)

In a bowl, combine all ingredients but oil or butter; blend well. Place mixture in greased shallow roasting pan; shape into rounded loaf. For a crisp exterior, brush oil or melted butter over top. Bake in oven preheated to 375° F. until outside of loaf is crisply browned—1 to 1½ hours. Cool in pan 10 minutes, then remove to platter by slipping a spatula under the loaf to loosen. Make gravy with the pan drippings (see Basic Meat Gravy). *Makes 6 to 8 servings.*

MIDWESTERN MEATLOAF. Instead of catsup and milk, use 1 cup (8-ounce can) tomato sauce. Add ¼ cup minced green pepper, or, instead of thyme, add ½ bay leaf, crumbled. Crushed cracker crumbs may be used instead of fine bread crumbs.

QUICK MEATLOAF. Combine 1½ pounds ground meat, 1 cup packaged herb-seasoned bread stuffing, 1 8-ounce can tomato sauce, 1 egg, beaten, salt, and pepper. Blend well; place mixture in shallow pan and form into loaf shape, or bake in greased loaf pan.

SUGGESTED GO-WITHS. Baked Potatoes (baked in oven at same time), Escalloped Tomatoes, Carrot Cole Slaw, hot rolls.

Extra-tender Meatloaf

1 pound ground beef, chuck or
   top round
1 pound lean pork, ground
2 eggs
1 teaspoon grated lemon rind
1 cup fine dry crumbs
¼ cup tomato catsup

1 tablespoon lemon juice
½ cup milk or water
1 small onion, minced
1 tablespoon minced parsley
1 tablespoon olive oil or melted
   butter

Combine all ingredients but olive oil or butter; knead to blend well; place meat in greased shallow roasting pan and form into loaf shape. Brush oil or butter over top. Bake in oven preheated to 350° F. for 1½ hours. Parboil potatoes at same time; during last half-hour, place potatoes around meat in pan, turning to brown. Remove meatloaf from pan with spatula; remove browned potatoes and arrange on same platter. Make gravy with the pan drippings, either a sour cream gravy as for the Viennese Meatloaf, or a standard brown gravy, or a mixture of canned beef gravy and ½ cup tomato sauce, simmered in pan until well blended and smooth. *Makes 8 to 10 servings.* (Very good cold for sandwiches.)

SUGGESTED GO-WITHS. Mashed potatoes, whipped rutabagas, Winter Salad, Peach Cobbler (baked in oven at same time as meatloaf).

Mushroom Meatloaf

1½ pounds ground top round of
   beef
1 can condensed cream of
   mushroom soup
1 tablespoon minced parsley

1 teaspoon freeze-dried chives
1 teaspoon salt
½ cup fine dry crumbs
1 egg

Place all ingredients in bowl; mix with fork and/or fingers until well blended. Place in greased shallow pan and shape into loaf; or place in greased loaf pan. Bake in oven preheated to 350° F. for 1 hour. Serve with gravy made of pan drippings. *Makes 6 to 8 servings.*

Viennese Meatloaf

1 pound ground veal
½ pound ground pork
¼ teaspoon ground nutmeg
1½ teaspoons salt
1 cup soft bread crumbs, soaked in
1/3 cup water
2 eggs, beaten

1 small tomato, peeled, chopped,
   seeded
2 tablespoons butter, melted
2 tablespoons flour
1 cup veal or chicken broth
½ cup sour cream

Combine meats, nutmeg, salt, soaked crumbs, eggs, and tomato. Blend well. Place mixture in greased shallow roasting pan; shape into loaf. Brush melted butter over top. Bake in oven preheated to 375° F. until top is very brown and crusty—1 to 1¼ hours. Remove from oven, let cool in pan 10 minutes, then slip spatula under meatloaf and slip out onto platter. Return to oven to keep warm.

To pan drippings, add flour; stir over moderate heat; cook 2 minutes. Slowly add broth; cook until smooth and thickened, stirring occasionally. Turn off heat. Blend some of hot sauce with cream, then add cream to sauce in pan. Serve the meatloaf with the sour cream gravy, with noodles and baked acorn squash. *Makes 6 to 8 servings.*

Meatloaf Ring

Prepare meatloaf by any of the preceding recipes; place meat mixture in well-buttered 1½-quart ring mold. Bake in oven preheated to 350° F. until top is crusty brown—about 45 minutes. Turn out on heatproof platter; return to oven until what is now the top is browned. Serve with Creamed Potatoes in the center of the ring, accompanied by Brussels sprouts (or another green vegetable) and a salad. *Makes 6 to 8 servings.*

Homemade Sausage

If you feel nostalgic about real smoked country sausage, try making your own with ground pork.

Old-fashioned Pork Sausages

1½ pounds lean pork
½ pound pork with some fat
2 teaspoons salt*
½ teaspoon coarsely ground
   black pepper

¼ teaspoon cayenne or ginger
½ teaspoon sage, crumbled
½ teaspoon marjoram, crumbled
Sausage casings (optional)

The meat must be put through the grinder at least twice. If you don't have a home grinder, ask your meat man to do this for you—but look at the pork before he grinds it to make sure it does not have too much fat. Add seasonings; blend with fingers until thoroughly mixed.

Shape into patties, or force into sausage casings (available from many butchers). Season in refrigerator for 24 hours before cooking. If not to be cooked for several days, freeze, carefully wrapped, sealed, and labeled. Makes 2 pounds, enough for 12 breakfast sausages.

*Use hickory-smoked salt rather than ordinary salt, if you prefer. Presumably this gives it the same flavor as if it were smoked in a smokehouse, but that's something of an exaggeration.

PORK SAUSAGE APPETIZERS. Use all lean pork, no fat; shape into miniature meatballs. Pan-broil until well browned on all sides. Makes about 50 little balls.

SAUSAGEBURGERS. Use all lean pork; shape into patties; wrap each individually in foil. Cook in ashes of charcoal fire for 20 to 25 minutes. Serve in hamburger buns with assorted condiments.

Homemade Chorizo

This Spanish sausage has a flavor all its own. If you have a smoke oven, the links can be smoked slowly to develop their inimitable spicy flavor; they will then keep for several weeks.

2 pounds coarsely ground pork, containing some fat
¼ cup vinegar
¼ cup olive oil
4 cloves garlic, minced
2 tablespoons paprika
3 teaspoons salt
½ teaspoon freshly ground black pepper
¼ teaspoon sage
¼ teaspoon cumin
Sausage casings

Combine pork with vinegar, oil, garlic, and seasonings. Blend thoroughly. Force into sausage casings, pressing as tight as possible. Hang suspended in a smoke oven for 24 hours over low heat. Use in recipes calling for chorizo. *Makes 2 pounds.*

STEAKS, CHOPS, KABOBS, AND CUTLETS

The most important thing to know about cooking steaks and chops is how to select the meat. If you have good or choice meat to begin with, cooking it is simple. If the meat is of poor quality, it takes real skill to make it juicy, tender, and flavorful.

Review the sections on buying meats (Judging Quality, Tender Versus Less Tender, and A Steak Isn't Always a Steak) in Book 1. Also read those parts of Understanding Basic Tech-

MEAT BROILING TIMETABLE

Cut of meat	Thickness (Inches)	Marinate?	Approximate Cooking Time for Each Side (Minutes)			Comments
			Rare	Medium	Well-done	
Porterhouse, sirloin, Delmonico, rib	1 1½ 2 2½	Not necessary; recommended if over charcoal	4-6 5-7 8-10 10-15	7-8 8-10 10-15 18-22	10+ 12+ 20+ 25+	Most tender cuts
Chuck	1 2 2½	Tenderizing recommended unless choice quality	Same cooking times as above			Excellent flavor when choice quality
Flank		Soak 1 hour in oil marinade	3-5			Tender only when rare
Top round	½ 1	Soak ½ hour in oil marinade	3-5 4-6	5-7 7-8	8+ 10+	
London broil	1½ 2	Soak ½ hour in oil marinade	5-7 10-15	8-10		Slice at angle; serve rare
Hamburgers	Thin Thick	Will be juicier if marinated, esp. over charcoal	2-3 3-4	4-5 5-6	6+ 8+	Use low heat, longer cooking for extra juiciness
Lamb chops	½ 1	Not necessary Not necessary	3-4 4-5	4-5 6-7	6+ 7	
Shish kabob (lamb or beef)	1-inch cubes 1½-inch cubes	Recommended Recommended	4-5 5-6	6-7 7-8	7+ 8+	Tenderizing may shorten cooking time
Veal chops Veal steaks	½ 1 1½	Soak ½-1 hour in oil marinade			7-8 9-10 12-15	Must be cooked to well-done
Pork chops	½	Wine marinade recommended			7-8	
Pork chops	1	Wine marinade recommended			12-15	Must be cooked to well-done
Pork teriyaki	¾-inch cubes	Soy-wine marinade			12-15	Total cooking time
Ham steak	1 1½	Fruit-soy marinade Fruit-soy marinade			15-18 20-22	6 inches from heat 6 inches from heat

niques having to do with meat cookery, especially Ways of Tenderizing Meat.

Steaks

Any meat that is to be *broiled*, whether in a broiling oven or over charcoal, should have excess fat trimmed from it to prevent fat fires. Yet it needs fat *through the lean* for tenderness. If the meat is not well marbled, punch holes in it and brush in oil or a marinade. But before putting the oil-treated steak over the fire, pat the meat with absorbent paper to remove excess oil—or the dripping oil will cause smoking.

But not all steaks are broiled. *Pan-broiling* is better for certain cuts, especially when the sauce is as important as the meat itself. *Pan-frying* is recommended for minute steaks. And a less tender steak may even be braised (like the Bullfighter's Beefsteak).

If steaks have been frozen, *defrost completely* before cooking. Otherwise, they may turn out to be still raw (not rare) inside when nearly burned on the outside. The only exception: *very thin* steaks that you want to be rare inside and well browned on the outside. These need be only partially defrosted.

Remember that cooking over or under direct heat tends to dry out meat, and the longer it cooks, the more dry it will be, unless measures are taken to retain or restore juices.

Oven-broiled Steak (Basic Recipe)

If the steak needs no marinating—if it is of choice or prime quality, well marbled, and a tender cut, the only advance preparation needed is to trim excess fat from the edges, and this may already have been done by the meat man. Remove broiler pan from oven; rub grids with just enough oil or fat to prevent sticking. Preheat oven to broil position, or 550° F. Place 1-inch-thick (the normal size) steak on broiler rack 2 to 3 inches from heat. A thicker steak should be placed farther away from the heat, so that it will have a chance to cook through before it is sizzling on the outside. A thin steak (less than 1 inch) must still be placed 2 inches from the heat, but must be well chilled, or partially frozen, if preferred rare yet browned on the outside.

In an electric oven, the door must be left ajar. In a gas oven, it may be closed. Watch for fat fires; keep a syringe filled with water handy to douse out small flames—and have a box of baking soda nearby if the fire should get out of hand. (Baking soda quenches the flames immediately, but the soda will also destroy the flavor of the meat, so use only in dire emergencies.) Even when broiling in a thermostatically controlled oven, and with careful timing (see Broiling Timetable on next two pages), it's wise to cut a small slash in the center of the steak to determine when it is cooked to the degree you prefer. Sprinkle steak with salt when it is almost ready to take from the oven, while the juices are sizzling. Serve at once, cutting into serving pieces with a well-sharpened knife, with individual steak knives at each place setting. Steak lovers will want the meat this way, no fancy trimmings. Crisp French fries, garlic bread, and a Roquefort salad are the most popular go-withs.

Charcoal-broiled Steak (Basic Rules)

Just as for oven-broiled steaks, the steak for the charcoal fire must be well trimmed of fat. Otherwise, the fat melts into the fire and burning grease tends to coat the meat with cindery, greasy ash. Before starting the fire, remove the grid and rub it *lightly* with oil or fat to prevent meat from sticking.

Next to the meat itself, the fire is the most important element. Every American supermarket today carries hardwood charcoal briquets; so do hardware stores and even delicatessens. There are dozens of kinds of fire starters available. The best and safest kind is treated paper, in squares that can be torn from a sheet one or more at a time. These leave no odor and are not explosive. There are also electric units which, held next to the charcoal, cause it to ignite, as well as various jellies and liquids. The latter must be used with extreme caution; many a tragedy has occurred when such a liquid has been doused over briquets that looked dead but were not.

After the charcoal has taken, let it burn for at least 30 minutes, fanning occasionally with a bellows. When the charcoal is covered with large areas of gray, but not yet reduced to red-glowing ash, it is time to place the meat over the fire.

Steaks no more than 1 inch thick should be cooked 2 to 3 inches above the fire, until sizzling and well browned on each side. Thicker steaks should be higher above the heat (the thicker the higher). Cut a small slash in the center when steak is approaching this description to see how red (or gray) the meat inside has become. Charcoal broiling requires an adventurous spirit. There are no hard and fast rules. Sprinkle meat with salt just before removing from fire. (But add no salt if steak has been tenderized in advance with commercial meat tenderizer.)

To Marinate or Not to Marinate

Three things can be accomplished by marinating a steak before broiling: it may serve to tenderize the meat (depending on the ingredients in the marinade), it will impart a different flavor (if that's what you want), and it will help to keep the meat juicy. For charcoal broiling, the third is the most important reason. A vinaigrette-type sauce is best for this—a mixture of oil and vinegar, or oil and lemon juice, or oil and dry wine, lightly seasoned (salt and pepper only). The meat should be punched full of holes and the mixture brushed in.

If the tenderness of the meat is in question (because of either quality or cut), sprinkle with commercial tenderizer, according to package directions, before adding a marinade.

Any meat that contains a considerable amount of fat (pork, ham, steaks with considerable fat) is better marinated in a wine mixture or a tomato mixture, rather than oil. Or, the marinade may contain a small amount of oil, but mostly wine or tomato.

If the marinade contains any sugar, or a sweetened ingredient such as soy sauce, catsup, or molasses, remember that sugar burns readily and the meat so soaked may burn on the outside before it is cooked through. It is wise to pat off excess marinade before placing the meat over the fire.

Slow-broiled Steak

There are some who insist that a steak will be more succulent and tender, and have a crisper, browner exterior, if it is broiled 6 inches from the heat. According to this theory, more of the juices are retained when the meat is not subjected to intense heat so close to the surface. The meat should be brushed on both sides with olive oil or melted butter before it is placed on the broiling rack (or over the charcoal fire). Cooking times will be longer; 20 minutes on each side (a total of 40 minutes) is usually about right for a 1½-inch-thick Delmonico or rib steak cooked to rare. For a 1-inch steak, cook 12 to 15 minutes on each side. Make a slit in center of meat after it has cooked 10 minutes on the second side to test it for doneness.

When done, remove meat; add to the pan drippings butter and minced chives or parsley (if cooked in the broiling oven), and a bit of lemon juice or brandy. Swirl until butter is melted; pour over the hot steak. Serve garnished with watercress, accompanied by grilled mushroom caps and fried tomatoes.

Salt-broiled Steak

This method of cooking steak involves forming a thick coat of moistened salt on both sides of the meat. The salt hardens into a crust; it does not penetrate the meat.

For a 3-pound sirloin, use ½ cup salt moistened with enough water to form a paste. Spread half the paste on one side of the meat; lay a piece of moistened brown paper over the salt. Place the meat in a hinged steak holder, paper side down. Spread remaining salt over the other side. Cover this with moistened brown paper.

Cook steak over a charcoal fire, or pan-broil in a heavy iron skillet, 3 inches from the heat. The fire should be very hot. Don't be concerned if the paper burns; the salt coating will protect the meat. By the time the steak is turned, even the top coating of salt will be firm enough to adhere. For a 1½- to 2-inch-thick steak, allow 15 to 20 minutes for each side; turn frequently if cooked over charcoal, only once if pan-broiled.

The salt crust will be easy to scrape off when the steak is finished. Then spoon ½ cup melted butter over the meat. Test for doneness. If it is not cooked as much as desired, return to fire for a few minutes longer on each side. Slice meat thinly at an angle and spoon over the slices a sauce of melted butter and meat juices. A few drops of lemon juice or a tablespoon of brandy may be added. The steak will not be browned outside, but the pink meat inside will be especially juicy and flavorful.

SUGGESTED MENU. Gazpacho first, then (with the steak) broccoli Hollandaise, garlic bread, crisp red radishes; watermelon for dessert.

Chateaubriand

Today's Chateaubriand is a 2½- to 3-inch-thick steak, slow-broiled until the outside is very brown, almost charred, the inside quite rare. Sirloin and top round are the best cuts, but get the meat from a butcher from whom you can be sure of quality, choice or prime. Serve rare. Chateaubriand needs no embellishment, although Sauce Béarnaise is sometimes passed. Slice at an angle, very thin.

London Broil

When top round of beef is used, London Broil is much like a Chateaubriand: the meat is cut 2 inches thick, cooked to rare, and sliced at an angle across the grain in very thin slices. But very often *flank steak* is used for London Broil. This is a thin piece, all lean, but it must be of top quality if it is to be broiled, and it can only be served rare; if cooked to medium or well done, the meat will be tough. Slice broiled flank steak almost horizontally, in the thinnest slices possible.

LONDON BROIL TERIYAKI. Marinate either round steak or flank steak in Teriyaki Sauce for 30 minutes to 1 hour before broiling. Especially delicious when charcoal broiled.

FLANK STEAK NEAPOLITANO. Rub a split clove of garlic over both sides of flank steak to be broiled; punch holes in the meat, douse with olive oil. Marinate in oil 30 minutes to 1 hour before broiling over charcoal.

Charcoal-broiled Steak Variations

BRANDIED STEAK. Douse both sides of steak generously with brandy, let stand 15 minutes before broiling. Brandy lends interesting flavor variation and also helps to tenderize.

DEVILED STEAK. Combine prepared mustard with softened butter (1 tablespoon mustard to 4 tablespoons butter), a dash of Worcestershire, and a few drops of lemon juice. Dot over steak that has been broiled on one side, while sizzling, so that melted butter will penetrate.

STEAK (OR ENTRECÔTE) MAÎTRE d'HÔTEL. Place "nuts" of chilled Maître d'Hôtel Butter (with parsley and lemon juice) over hot steak at table. (*Entrecôte* is the French word for steak cut from between the ribs.)

ROQUEFORT-FLAVORED STEAK. Combine equal parts blue cheese and softened butter, work in a little minced parsley, spread thinly over broiled side of steak while the underside is cooking.

LEMON STEAK. Serve lemon wedges with steak; sprinkle fresh lemon juice over meat at table.

HERBED STEAK. Rub mixture of 1 teaspoon soy sauce or Worcestershire, ¼ teaspoon orégano, ½ teaspoon garlic powder, and 2 tablespoons olive oil into steak 1 to 2 hours before broiling. Especially good with round steak (London broil).

Broiled Veal Steaks Basque Style

The best cut is rump of veal, cut 1½ inches thick, but this you must get from a private butcher; you will never find it in the supermarket. Thick veal chops may also be broiled, but they must be at least 1 inch thick. Crush 1 or 2 cloves garlic with minced parsley, work in olive oil. Rub this over veal, punching holes in meat with heavy skewer so oil will penetrate through meat. Marinate several hours at room temperature. Slow-broil over charcoal until well browned on outside and all pink is gone from inside of meat (cut slit in center with sharp knife to test doneness). When the veal itself is good, this is utterly delicious. Serve with a big salad, potatoes baked in the coals, and a cool ice cream dessert with fruit topping.

Tournedos

True tournedos are small individual boneless steaks cut from the end of the tenderloin, the filet mignon. In Europe, these are the best steaks obtainable. But a poor man's tournedos can be made from top round of choice quality, if the meat is tenderized before broiling by marinating in olive oil. The meat should be 1½ inches thick, but only about 3 inches in diameter. From 1½ pounds of round steak, count on 4 individual steaks, or 6 steaks from 2 to 2¼ pounds of top round.

These may be broiled in oven or over charcoal, or pan-broiled in a heavy skillet; the latter is preferable when the pan essence is important. Cook 3 minutes over high heat on each side for rare.

TOURNEDOS ROSSINI. Marinate 6 individual steaks in mixture of ¼ cup each olive oil and sherry or Madeira for 1 hour. Pierce meat so mixture will penetrate. Remove from marinade, saving the sauce. Pan-fry in heavy skillet in mixture of 2 tablespoons each olive oil and butter until well browned on each side. At same time, sauté 6 thick slices of French bread in olive oil until browned on each side. Spread bread with liver pâté (or pâté de fois gras). Place steaks over the liver pâté. To pan drippings, add the reserved marinade with ½ cup water and ½ teaspoon salt; bring to a boil, reduce to half. Pour this clear sauce over the steaks. *Serves 6.*

TOURNEDOS À LA PROVENÇALE. Marinate 6 steaks in a mixture of equal parts red wine and olive oil. Broil or pan-fry in mixture of olive oil and butter until well browned on each side but rare in center. Serve with Aioli Sauce, accompanied by broiled tomato slices.

TOURNEDOS HENRI IV. Marinate the individual steaks in mixture of 2 parts olive oil and 1 part lemon juice. Pan-fry in butter. Serve on fried bread garnished with artichoke hearts and Sauce Béarnaise.

TOURNEDOS TERIYAKI. Marinate the steaks in a mixture of ¼ cup each soy sauce, sherry, and oil. Broil in oven or over charcoal; serve with thin slices of lemon; press lemon into meat with tines of fork at table.

OTHER TOURNEDO VARIATIONS. Broiled mushroom caps are often served on top of each steak. Fried eggplant, broiled tomatoes, and creamed spinach are favorite go-withs. Popular sauces besides Béarnaise include almost any of the flavored butters, Hollandaise, or commercial steak sauces such as Escoffier, A-1, or Worcestershire.

Steak au Poivre (Pepper Steak)

1 tablespoon coarsely ground black pepper	½ teaspoon salt
3 pounds sirloin steak. 2 inches thick	5 tablespoons butter
	3 tablespoons cognac or dark rum
	¼ cup water

Press pepper into both sides of steak with heel of hand. Let stand 1 hour at room temperature. Sprinkle salt over bottom of large iron skillet; let salt brown slightly over high heat. Add 4 tablespoons of the butter. As soon as butter is melted (do not let it brown), add the steak; sear quickly on both sides. Then cook 8 minutes on each side for rare. When steak is turned, add the remaining tablespoon butter to skillet. When steak is finished, add cognac or rum, set aflame. Because of the butter, this will make a high flame, so make sure nothing flammable is nearby. Spoon up pan drippings until flame dies out. Serve steak with pan gravy made with drippings and ¼ cup water. *Makes 8 to 10 servings.*

WITH BONELESS CHUCK STEAK. Choice-quality chuck steak can be used instead of sirloin. When cooked to desired degree, slice at an angle.

SUGGESTED GO-WITHS. Asparagus, crusty rolls (to absorb the sauce), curried rice salad; strawberries in orange juice for dessert.

Minute Steaks O'Brien

Minute steaks are improved if tenderized, and this is a good way to do it: Blend together a tablespoon of grated onion, 2 tablespoons of olive oil, and a few drops lemon juice. Spread mixture over the steaks (1 for each person); let stand at least 15 minutes before cooking. (Both the onion and the oil help to tenderize the meat.) Pan-fry over moderate (not high) heat in additional oil (or a mixture of oil and butter) just until delicately browned on each side. Serve with cottage-fried potatoes and parsleyed carrots.

Bullfighter's Beefsteak

3 pounds chuck steak, 1¼ inches thick	2 cloves garlic
1 lemon, quartered	2 whole cloves
½ orange, quartered	1 bay leaf
	½ cup olive oil

Almost any reasonably tender chuck steak will do. Heat lemon, orange, garlic, cloves, and bay leaf in olive oil until the rind of the fruit is browned. Pour while hot over the meat in a bowl or roasting pan. Marinate meat for 4 hours at room temperature, turning several times. Pierce meat so that marinade will penetrate. Cook in a large heavy skillet over *very low* heat for 20 minutes on each side for rare, 25 to 30 minutes on each side for medium. Can also be cooked over charcoal, same cooking time, but place at least 6 inches from heat. Meat should be butter-tender when done. Serve with choice of condiments, such as Worcestershire, seasoned salt, any favorite barbecue sauce, prepared mustard, commercial or homemade steak sauce. *Makes 8 to 10 servings.*

SUGGESTED MENU. Saffron rice, braised zucchini, avocado salad; melon.

Minute Steaks Amontillado

6 minute steaks or thin top round fillets	mushrooms, with liquid
Salt	¼ teaspoon powdered cumin
2 tablespoons butter	¼ cup amontillado (medium) sherry
1 3- or 4-ounce can button	

Pound meat with side of saucer or with cleaver until very flat. Sprinkle salt over heated heavy skillet; brown the salt. Add butter; as soon as it is melted, quickly fry the steaks, over *moderate* heat, just until lightly browned on each side. Add remaining ingredients; simmer until liquid is reduced, scraping up browned bits from pan. Serve sauce over the meat. *Makes 6 servings.*

Venison Steak

6 individual venison steaks, well trimmed
½ cup coarsely cracked black pepper
2 teaspoons salt

8 tablespoons butter
1/3 cup brandy
1 cup cream
1 tablespoon A-1 or Escoffier Diablo Sauce

Venison steaks may or may not need tenderizing. If these are furnished by a hunter friend, the hunter will probably tell you how, or if, the venison need be treated before cooking. Press the pepper into the steaks on both sides with heel of hand; sprinkle with salt. Melt butter in a large heavy skillet (or divide butter in half and melt in two skillets, if you haven't one large enough). Add the steaks; cook quickly in butter until seared on both sides. Lower heat; cook slowly to desired degree of doneness. Remove steaks to hot platters. Pour off most (but not all) of the butter (keep butter for other cooking use). Add brandy, set aflame. When flame has died down, add the cream and sauce, simmer, stirring, 2 minutes. Serve the sauce over the steaks. *Makes 6 servings.*

SUGGESTED MENU. Crisply browned rissole potatoes, cauliflower, artichoke and black olive salad; Raspberry Parfait for dessert.

Broiled Chuck Steak

The inner part of the chuck, as cut by most American butchers, is the most tender. When chuck is on special sale, buy extras and cut the tender steak section from 2 or more steaks (allow ½ steak per serving); use the remaining part for stew.

Sprinkle both sides of steak with commercial meat tenderizer according to label directions. Do not add salt. Broil in preheated broiler oven or over a hot charcoal fire for 5 minutes on each side for rare (if 1 inch thick). Consult Broiling Timetable for thicker cuts, or for cooking steak to medium or well-done. Brush with basting sauce as it cooks for flavor variation; or top with Maître d'Hôtel Butter or other flavored butter while still sizzling.

SUGGESTED GO-WITHS. Broiled tomato slices, hashed brown potatoes, Mimosa Salad; for dessert, apple pie.

Broiled Ham Steaks Hawaiian

For broiling, a center slice of ham should be used, but it should be cut at least 1 inch thick, because otherwise the meat will be much too dry after cooking. For the same reason, it is well to marinate the ham before cooking—in a wine or fruit-juice mixture, *not* with oil.

1 center slice of ham, 1¼ inches thick	pineapple juice
¼ cup soy sauce	1 tablespoon wine vinegar
1 cup orange juice, or ½ cup orange and ½ cup	2 tablespoons brown sugar
	1 teaspoon prepared mustard (optional)

Marinate the ham 30 minutes to 1 hour before cooking in mixture of soy sauce, fruit juice, vinegar, sugar, and mustard. Slow-broil ham 5 or 6 inches from heat until lightly browned on each side, basting frequently with marinade. Makes 4 servings.

SUGGESTED GO-WITHS. Sweet potatoes, parsleyed limas, romaine and watercress salad. For dessert, lime sherbet topped with coconut.

DEVILED HAM STEAK. For the marinade, use a mixture of 1 cup syrup from canned peaches, 3 teaspoons prepared mustard, a pinch of ginger, and lemon juice (or vinegar) to taste. This is a delightful sweet-sour combination.

Kabobs

The word *kabob* is from the ancient Persian, and originally it meant simply "meat." Shish kabob was meat cooked on a skewer (the *shish* was a sword). In the Near East today the word, spelled in various ways (kabob, kebob, kabab, kibby), still means meat, and may even refer to ground meat baked in loaf form in the oven. But in the contemporary American language, kabob means any food cooked on a skewer, and so we use it here.

Skewered meats are to be found in the cuisines of most countries of the world, known by different names everywhere. In

Indonesia, the word is *satay*. In France, the term is *en bro-chette*. On the island of Madeira, I found *espadinhas*—the Portuguese word for "little sword"—to mean chunks of beef strung on long skewers, hung suspended before an open fire. In Germany, the word is *spiess*, and many German restaurants feature a special *spiesskarten*. The *souvlakia* of Greece differ little if at all from the *shaslik* of Armenia.

Meat cut in cubes cooks more quickly than steak, and usually kabobs are also more economical, because the meat can be "extended" by combination with vegetables and other ingredients, and often quite inexpensive meats may be used.

In summer, it's a good trick to buy an entire boned leg of lamb for shish kabob: cut the meat into cubes, divide into meal-size portions, and freeze all but the amount needed for the first meal. The kabobs defrost more quickly than steak, and the lamb can be served up in different combinations each time, as the following recipes indicate.

Shish Kabob (Basic Recipe)

1½ pounds lean lamb (from leg or shoulder), cut in 1- to 1½-inch cubes
1 green pepper, cut in 1-inch squares
2 small (4-inch) yellow squash, thickly sliced, or 12 large mushroom caps
1 onion, thickly sliced (optional)
¼ teaspoon freshly ground black pepper
1 teaspoon salt or onion salt
1 or 2 cloves garlic, crushed (optional)
1/3 cup olive oil
1/3 cup white wine
About 10 cherry tomatoes
Lemon wedges

Marinate meat and vegetables (except tomatoes) in mixture of seasonings, garlic, oil, and wine for at least 2 hours at room temperature, or overnight in refrigerator. Remove from marinade, arrange meat on skewers alternately with vegetables. Broil 3 inches from heat over charcoal or on rotisserie spit for approximately 7 to 10 minutes, turning frequently or continuously. (Vegetables soaked in oil mixture need no previous cooking.) Serve with lemon wedges, the lemon to be squeezed over the meat. *Serves 4 to 6.*

SUGGESTED MENU. Big bowl of tossed vegetable salad, garlic bread, potato salad; banana split for dessert.

STEAK KABOBS. Exactly like Shish Kabob, but use sirloin or top round of beef instead of lamb.

ECONOMY BEEF KABOBS. Use boneless stewing beef (chuck) cut in chunks for the meat in Shish Kabob; tenderize meat with commercial meat tenderizer before adding the marinade. Any combination of vegetables may be used—or omit the vegetables altogether, if preferred. Instead of wine, use 2 tablespoons vinegar, ¼ cup orange juice, and onion slices in the marinade.

Turkish Yogurt Kabobs

2 pounds boned lamb, cut in 1½-inch cubes	1 tablespoon minced onion
1 cup yogurt	2 cloves garlic, crushed
1 teaspoon dried mint	½ teaspoon salt
	Bay leaves

Marinate lamb in mixture of yogurt, mint, onion, garlic, and salt for 1 hour before cooking. Remove from marinade (ignore revolting color of meat—the outside will be crisply browned and the inside especially delicate and tender when cooked). Place cubes of meat on skewers with bay leaves between cubes. Cook over glowing coals of charcoal fire, turning frequently until crisply browned. *Makes 6 servings.*

SUGGESTED MENU. Pine Nut Pilaf, Eggplant Caviar, Greek Salad; peach compote for dessert.

SHASLIK. Like Shish Kabob, but omit wine, use 2 tablespoons lemon juice, increase black pepper to ½ teaspoon.

PERSIAN KABOBS. Like Shish Kabob, but omit wine, use 2 tablespoons lemon juice, and in addition to black pepper, use ¼ teaspoon cinnamon in marinade. Use any vegetable combination desired, or omit vegetables.

SOUVLAKIA (Greek Kabobs). Like Shish Kabob, but marinate in a mixture of ¾ cup red wine, ½ cup olive oil, ½ teaspoon orégano, and 1 teaspoon salt. Arrange on skewers alternately with slices of zucchini or eggplant which have been marinated with the meat.

Souvlakia Lefkas

1 pound lean pork, cut in ¾-inch cubes	Olive oil
¾ teaspoon salt	Cooked rice
¼ teaspoon crushed dried sage	Lemon wedges

Rub salt and sage into meat, then brush with oil. Impale on skewers; cook over charcoal, turning frequently, until meat is crisply browned. Serve over a bed of cooked rice, with lemon wedges: the lemon juice should be sprinkled over the pork at table. *Makes 3 servings.*

SUGGESTED MENU. Ratatouille, black olives and cherry tomatoes, deviled eggs.

ABBACHIO AI FERRI (Italian Kabobs). Use lamb, beef, or pork as preferred. Marinate in a mixture of ½ teaspoon crushed rosemary, ½ cup white or red wine, 1 garlic clove, crushed, 1 tablespoon tomato paste, 1 teaspoon salt, and ¼ cup olive oil. Broil over charcoal or on rotisserie skewers, turning frequently until meat is crisply browned.

Cordero à la Valenciana (Spanish Lamb Kabobs)

1½ pounds lean boneless lamb, cut in cubes	1 tablespoon lemon juice
½ cup olive oil	½ teaspoon cumin
¼ cup orange juice	¼ teaspoon orégano
	1 teaspoon salt

Marinate meat in mixture of remaining ingredients for 1 hour before cooking. Arrange on skewers alternately with any desired vegetables; broil, turning frequently, until meat is crisply browned. *Makes 4 to 6 servings.*

SUGGESTED MENU. Fried eggplant, Garbanzo Salad, sliced tomatoes; for dessert, Orange Custard.

Beef Satay

1½ pounds beef sirloin tip or top round, cut in 1-inch cubes	black pepper
2 cloves garlic, crushed	1 teaspoon sugar
1 teaspoon salt	2 tablespoons lemon juice
½ teaspoon freshly ground	1 tablespoon Japanese soy sauce

Rub beef with garlic, pressing garlic into meat. Sprinkle with salt, pepper, and sugar. Cut beef into 1-inch pieces; thread on skewers. Set aside. Combine lemon juice and soy sauce; brush over meat. Grill or broil 3 to 4 inches from heat until browned on all sides. Serve with Satay Sauce. *Makes 4 to 6 servings.*

SUGGESTED MENU. Saffron rice with tomatoes, braised celery; for dessert, cantaloupe balls over lime sherbet.

PORK SATAY. Use lean pork instead of beef; season with ⅛ teaspoon powdered ginger and ¼ teaspoon cinnamon in addition to pepper. Serve with Satay Sauce. Or, marinate pork in Satay Marinade.

Gypsy Kabobs

Cut frankfurters into 1-inch pieces; combine on skewers with chunks of canned ham and chicken livers, with squares of green pepper and canned onions between the pieces of meat. Brush with Vinaigrette Sauce or bottled Italian dressing. Broil over charcoal, turning frequently, until meat is lightly browned. Serve with Curry Rice and tomato and lettuce salad.

Ham-Pineapple Teriyaki

Combine cubes of ham and wedges of fresh or canned pineapple on skewers with squares of green pepper; marinate in Teriyaki Sauce. Broil until ham is lightly browned. Serve with green peas, cauliflower, hot butterfly rolls.

HAM-PEACH KABOBS. Use cubes of peeled fresh or canned peaches instead of pineapple wedges, marinate in Soy-Sherry or Soy-Horseradish Sauce.

Pork and Peppers Teriyaki

1 pound lean pork, cut in ¾-inch cubes

2 green peppers, cut in 1-inch squares

8 cubes fresh or canned pineapple

Teriyaki Sauce

Arrange pork, green pepper, and pineapple alternately on bamboo skewers. Marinate in Teriyaki Sauce ½ hour; broil on hibachi over charcoal, turning until well browned. Serve on rice accompanied by cucumber salad and artichoke hearts. *Makes 4 servings.*

Steak Strips Teriyaki

1 pound top round of beef, in one piece

Teriyaki Sauce

1 1-pound can whole onions

Slice meat very thin across the grain, then cut in strips about 1 inch wide. Marinate steak strips in Teriyaki Sauce for 1 hour. Weave meat on skewers (preferably bamboo skewers) with onions between (see illustration). Grill over charcoal, turning frequently. *Makes 4 servings.*

Spareribs

To most Americans, this word has come to mean the breast or thinly meated ribs of pork. Yet the ribs of other meats can be cooked the same way. Those who observe Jewish dietary laws frequently cook *veal spareribs* (breast of veal), using the same basic recipes. *Lamb spareribs* can also be prepared from breast of lamb, though lamb requires a different type of marinade. Parboiling of both lamb and pork spareribs is advisable to get rid of excess fat. Veal contains little fat to begin with, and so can be slow-broiled without parboiling.

Barbecued Spareribs (Basic Recipe to Serve 6)

4 pounds lean spareribs (pork or veal)
1 to 1½ cups marinade or basting sauce

The meat should be partially cut through the ribs and cracked by the butcher for easier separation after cooking. Allow ½ to ¾ pound per serving. There are two accepted methods of cooking.

1. *PARBOILING AND MARINATING.* Cook ribs in salted water 20 to 30 minutes; drain well. Cover with marinade, soak in sauce 30 minutes at room temperature, or several hours in refrigerator, turning frequently. Broil 4 or 5 inches from heat over charcoal or in broiler oven, turning once, until crisply browned— a total of about 30 minutes. Or, bake on rack in oven preheated to 450° F. for 45 minutes, turning once.

2. *SLOW-BROILING.* Omit parboiling, broil 6 or 7 inches from heat over slow charcoal fire or in broiler oven set at 375° F., for about 1 hour, turning several times. During last 20 minutes, start brushing with sauce, first on one side, then the other. *For 8 servings* you will need 6 pounds spareribs but the same amount of sauce. *For 4 servings*, 3 pounds spareribs will do and ¾ cup sauce will probably be ample.

SUGGESTED GO-WITHS. Macaroni salad, assorted vegetable relishes, toasted herb bread; cake à la mode for dessert.

PEACH MARINADE

¼ cup brown sugar	½ cup syrup from canned peaches
1 tablespoon salt	¼ cup vinegar
1 tablespoon chili powder	Dash of powdered cloves
½ cup catsup	½ cup water
1 or 2 cloves garlic, crushed	

Combine all ingredients; bring to a boil. Pour over parboiled ribs. Let stand several hours. Remove meat from marinade; place 5 to 6 inches from heat, turning frequently, until well browned on both sides—about 30 minutes' total cooking time. *Makes 1¾ cups marinade.*

HAWAIIAN MARINADE

1 cup canned pineapple juice	½ teaspoon cumin
2 tablespoons lemon juice	½ teaspoon curry powder
1 tablespoon soy sauce	Few thin slices onion

Combine all ingredients; pour over parboiled spareribs; let stand 15 to 30 minutes. Broil 5 to 6 inches from heat until well browned, about 30 minutes altogether. *Makes about 1½ cups sauce.*

BEER AND HONEY MARINADE

1½ cups beer	1 teaspoon sage, crumbled fine
½ cup honey	2 tablespoons horseradish
¾ teaspoon dry mustard	2 teaspoons salt
1 teaspoon chili powder	1 tablespoon lemon juice

Combine all ingredients; pour over ribs in large shallow pan; let stand several hours or overnight. *Makes 2 cups sauce.*

Fruited Lamb Spareribs

Have lamb breast cut partially through ribs and cracked for easy separation. Parboil in salted water for 20 minutes; drain. Marinate in a mixture of 1 cup orange juice, ¼ cup lemon juice, 2 tablespoons soy sauce, 1 teaspoon crushed mint, and ½ teaspoon cumin. Bake in oven or slow-broil over charcoal until well browned—a total of 45 minutes.

Spareribs, breast, and flank steak—all cuts which may on occasion be barbecued—are also suitable for roasting, but when roasted they must be cooked at low heat and with added liquid—in other words, braised. For stuffed breast of veal or lamb, or for rolled stuffed flank, an ordinary bread stuffing may be used, with perhaps a bit of celery or onion added. A fruit stuffing is still more interesting. Boned shoulder of veal, lamb, or pork may also be stuffed. The same stuffing recipe may be used for any of these.

Fruit-stuffed Breast of Veal

1 boned veal breast (about 2½ pounds after boning)	1 cup dried apricots, chopped
	2 cups stale bread crumbs
1 small onion, sliced or chopped	½ teaspoon salt
1 pimiento, chopped	¼ teaspoon thyme
1 clove garlic, minced (optional)	Oil or melted butter
	Salt
2 tablespoons butter or margarine	½ cup red wine or orange juice

Lay the boned breast out flat; trim edges to make uniform shape. Mince the trimmings. Sauté the minced meat, onion, pimiento, and garlic in butter until lightly browned. Combine with chopped apricots, bread crumbs, salt, and thyme. Blend well. Place over meat. Roll up and tie with cord (see sketch). Brush outside of meat with oil or melted butter; dust with salt. Place in shallow roasting pan and roast at 300° F. for about 3½ hours, basting occasionally with wine or orange juice. Serve with rice and artichoke hearts (or Italian beans). *Makes about 6 servings.*

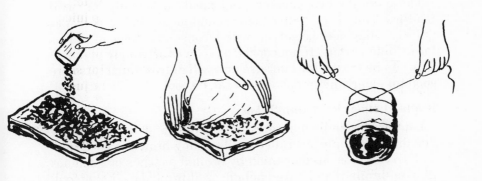

FRUIT-STUFFED SHOULDER OF VEAL. The same, except that the shoulder of veal is boned, with a pocket left in the meat by the boning.

FRUIT-STUFFED LAMB SHOULDER ROAST. Lamb shoulder is boned, with a pocket left for stuffing. Use the same stuffing as given above, or use pitted prunes, chopped, in place of apricots, and green pepper in place of pimiento. Baste with a mixture of sherry, soy sauce, and orange juice.

FRUIT-STUFFED PORK SHOULDER ROAST. Fill a boned shoulder with either stuffing given above, or, for the fruit, use a mixture of raisins and peeled chopped apples. Increase bread crumbs to 3 cups and salt to ¾ teaspoon.

SUGGESTED GO-WITHS. Baked or mashed potatoes, flat Italian beans, raw spinach, and Boston lettuce salad.

Celery-stuffed Flank Steak

Lay flank steak out flat; fill with packaged seasoned bread crumbs mixed with 1 cup minced celery and 2 tablespoons melted butter or margarine. Roll up meat; tie with cord. Sear on all sides in hot oil or melted fat. Place in a casserole; add 1 cup water; cover; bake in 325° oven for 3 hours; or add 2 cups water and simmer, covered, on top of stove over lowest heat for approximately the same length of time, until meat is tender when pierced with fork. Serve with a gravy made of the juices, or with Raisin Sauce.

Chops, Cutlets, Fillets

These are the best cuts for quick meals, especially for small families. They keep better than ground meats and cook just as quickly. They may be served with a constant change of sauces for infinite variety. If not cooked as soon as originally planned, they can be frozen for later use and will defrost quickly, so are good for emergency meals. Many can be cooked at the table.

Broiled Loin or Rib Lamb Chops

Loin or rib lamb chops are so delicious (and so expensive!) that they need only be broiled until sizzling-brown on each side, and served as is, accompanied by broiled peaches or tomatoes (if oven-broiled) and baked potato; or, if broiled over charcoal, serve with sprigs of watercress, marinated artichoke hearts, and crisp French fries.

The Greek way is to rub lamb chops with a bit of thyme or orégano before broiling, then serve sprinkled with lemon juice—a superb flavor twist.

Pan-broiled chops may be embellished with clear pan gravy (*au jus*). First sprinkle a heated skillet with salt, add the chops, move the meat around to prevent its sticking to the pan as the fat is drawn out, then cook until browned on each side. Remove the chops if desired, then add about ½ cup water or red or white wine to the pan; boil up, scraping the brown gelatinous bits to dissolve in the liquid; pour this essence over the meat. Or, leave the chops in the pan; add the water or wine; simmer the meat in the wine for 2 or 3 minutes. With lamb chops cooked this way, serve broccoli or asparagus or Pine Nut Pilaf, a simple green salad, and a pastry (such as cherry tarts) for dessert.

Lamb Chops Riyanata

4 loin or 8 rib lamb chops
1 tablespoon butter or olive oil
1 teaspoon orégano
2 tablespoons lemon juice
1 medium tomato, peeled,
seeded, chopped
½ cup water
1 bouillon cube, or 1 teaspoon beef-flavored stock concentrate

Trim the chops of excess fat; with small skewers, fasten the "tail" around the meaty section of each; melt butter or oil in heavy skillet; add the chops; sear quickly over high heat until well browned on each side. Remove chops. Add orégano, lemon juice, and tomato to skillet; cook until tomato is soft. Add water and bouillon cube; simmer, stirring, until dissolved. Return chops to sauce; simmer 10 minutes. Serve with rice, spinach, and lima beans, with red table wine as the beverage. *Makes 4 servings.*

For 2 servings, exactly the same, but use only 2 loin or 4 rib chops. The sauce is not excessive for 2 servings.

For a small family, it is wise when buying a leg of lamb to have chops cut from the upper part of the leg; use the remainder as a small roast. Leg chops are the meatiest of all, like steaks. These may be prepared in any of the ways suggested for loin or rib chops—just as loin or rib chops may be prepared by the following recipe. The difference is primarily in size: leg chops are larger.

Pungent Broiled Lamb Chops

Homemade Garlic Salt*
4 lamb chops cut from leg
1 large onion, thinly sliced
1 lemon, thinly sliced
Paprika

Rub about 1 teaspoon Homemade Garlic Salt over the top of

Homemade Garlic Salt. Mash 1 or 2 cloves garlic in a mortar; work in about ¼ cup salt, mashing into a paste. This can be kept, tightly covered, in a jar in the refrigerator to be used as needed.

each chop. Line the bottom of a bowl with sliced onion; place the garlic-rubbed chops over the onion; cover with the lemon slices and finally the remaining onion slices. Cover; chill in refrigerator overnight. Remove chops and scrape off salt. Sprinkle generously on both sides with paprika. Broil over charcoal or in the oven until crisply browned on both sides. *Makes 4 servings.*

SUGGESTED GO-WITHS. Braised zucchini, baked potatoes, black olive and cucumber salad.

Shoulder lamb chops are considerably less expensive than chops from leg, loin, or ribs, and, if marinated in advance, can be very delicious. The flavor of the meat is not quite as good as that of the more tender cuts, and longer, slower cooking is generally advisable—though if the lamb is of choice quality, the shoulder chops may be delicious if simply pan-broiled and braised in wine.

Broiled Shoulder Lamb Chops

4 shoulder lamb chops, ½ inch thick	½ teaspoon freshly ground black pepper
2 tablespoons olive oil	1 tablespoon grated onion
2 tablespoons lemon juice	1 clove garlic, crushed
1 teaspoon salt	

Cover chops with marinade composed of remaining ingredients; soak in mixture at least 2 hours at room temperature or longer in refrigerator, turning once or twice. Remove from marinade; pat dry. Broil 3 inches from heat in preheated broiler or over charcoal until browned on both sides, basting chops with marinating sauce after turning. *Makes 4 servings.*

For 2 servings, use 2 chops; remaining ingredients are the same.

BRAISED SHOULDER LAMB CHOPS. Marinate chops, but instead of broiling, moisten a skillet with a teaspoon of butter or oil and pan-broil meat until browned on both sides. Add 1 cup water or table wine, simmer uncovered over moderate heat for 20 minutes. Serve chops with unthickened pan gravy.

These can be cooked at table in electric skillet.

SUGGESTED GO-WITHS. Hashed-brown potatoes, buttered beets, green salad.

Pork Chops Neapolitan

4 green peppers, or 1 small jar
  roasted sweet red peppers
  (pimientos)
3 tablespoons olive oil
1 large clove garlic
2 slices onion
4 large lean pork chops, well

trimmed
1 8-ounce can tomato sauce
½ cup dry red or white wine
¾ teaspoon salt
½ teaspoon sugar
2 tablespoons grated Parmesan
  cheese

If fresh peppers are used, burn outside by holding with fork directly over flame of gas burner, or place close to broiler until blackened. Skin off blackened portion, seed, and cut remaining pepper into thin strips. (*If canned sweet peppers are used,* simply drain, cut in strips.)

Sauté the pepper strips in the olive oil with the whole garlic clove and onion slices. When garlic is browned, remove and discard. Remove pepper strips and onion to large shallow casserole. Sauté the pork chops in oil remaining in skillet until lightly browned on both sides. Remove to casserole. Pour off oil from skillet. Add tomato sauce to skillet, also the wine, salt, and sugar. Boil up, scraping all browned bits in pan. Pour sauce over chops. Bake, uncovered, at 350° F. for 30 to 40 minutes. During last 10 minutes, sprinkle cheese over chops. Serve from casserole with rice or noodles. *Makes 4 servings.**

   *Leftover chops may be stored in refrigerator or freezer to be reheated in the sauce.

Pork Chops à l'Orange

4 pork chops, well trimmed
1 tablespoon butter or oil
1 small navel orange, sliced
2 tablespoons flour
1/3 cup orange juice

1 to 1½ teaspoons salt
1 cup water
2 tablespoons heavy sweet cream
  or sour cream

Sauté pork chops in butter or oil until nicely browned on each side. Cover pan; braise chops over low heat for about 20 minutes. When chops are tender, remove, place orange slices in pan drippings just to brown lightly, then remove orange slices. Add flour to pan drippings, stirring to blend. Add orange juice, salt, and water; simmer until smooth and thickened. Turn off heat. Stir in sweet or sour cream, beating with whisk to prevent curdling. Serve chops with Celery Rice; top each chop with an orange slice. Pass sauce separately. *Makes 4 servings.*

Spanish Pork Chops with Spinach

½ teaspoon salt
4 tablespoons flour
4 large pork chops, well trimmed
2 tablespoons olive oil
1 or 2 cloves garlic, minced
2 tablespoons minced parsley
1 tablespoon chopped onion

½ cup dry white wine
½ teaspoon prepared mustard
1 package frozen chopped spinach,
  thawed
¼ teaspoon salt
½ cup bread croutons, fried
  in olive oil

Rub mixture of ½ teaspoon salt and 4 tablespoons flour into pork chops. Brown the chops in olive oil on both sides; cover; cook over low heat 10 to 15 minutes. Remove to shallow casserole or heatproof platter; keep warm in oven. Add garlic, parsley, and onion to oil in pan; cook until soft. Add wine, mustard, spinach, and ¼ teaspoon salt. Cook, covered, for 4 minutes; drain off excess liquid. Beat in blender or with spoon until puréed. Pile spinach over chops. Top with small cubes of bread (croutons) which have been fried until golden in olive oil. Serve at once, or cover, keep warm in oven up to 40 minutes. *Makes 4 servings.*

Baked Stuffed Pork Chops Kijafa

4 double pork chops
¼ cup raisins
1 teaspoon brown sugar
¼ teaspoon curry powder
⅛ teaspoon cinnamon

2 tablespoons minced onion
1 teaspoon salt
½ cup Cherry Kijafa or port wine
1 tablespoon Angostura bitters
½ cup water

Cut pocket in center of each pork chop (see sketch). Combine raisins, sugar, curry powder, cinnamon, and onion; divide into 4 parts and insert as stuffing in pork chops. Rub salt over chops. Place chops in shallow roasting pan and bake at 450° F. until chops begin to brown. Pour or spoon off excess fat in pan. Add half the wine mixed with the bitters, spooning over top of

chops. Bake 15 minutes longer; add remaining wine; bake until deep golden brown—about 10 minutes longer. Remove chops from pan; skim off excess fat. Add ½ cup water to pan and boil until reduced and slightly thickened, scraping up residue from bottom of pan. Serve this as sauce over pork chops. Serve with baked potatoes (baked in same oven at same time) and a salad. *Makes 4 servings.*

For 2 servings, use 2 double pork chops, divide all other ingredients in half but wine. (With less wine, you will have too little sauce.)

Pork Chops Charcutière

4 thick pork chops	1 medium tomato, peeled, seeded, chopped
¼ cup flour	1 teaspoon minced parsley
Salt, pepper	1 teaspoon salt
3 tablespoons butter, or half butter, half oil	1 cup dry white wine, or ½ cup wine, ½ cup water
4 to 6 shallots, chopped, or 3 small white onions, thinly sliced	1 teaspoon gravy coloring

Dust the chops with flour seasoned with salt and a generous amount of freshly ground black pepper. Sauté over high heat in melted butter until golden on each side. Remove. Add shallots or onion and tomato; simmer in pan juices until soft. Replace chops; add parsley, salt, wine, and gravy coloring. Simmer, covered, for about 25 minutes. Or, place in a casserole and bake in oven preheated to 350° F. for ½ hour. *Makes 4 servings.*

For 2 servings, use 2 pork chops, 2 tablespoons each seasoned flour and butter, 2 small onions, 1 tablespoon catsup, ½ teaspoon salt, ¼ cup wine, ½ cup water.

SUGGESTED GO-WITHS. Steamed rice, Petits Pois à la Française, tossed salad; peach tarts for dessert.

PORK CHOPS FORESTIÈRE. Prepare as for Pork Chops Charcutière, but add to onion 1 clove garlic, minced, and ½ green pepper, chopped, and, if desired, canned sliced or button mushrooms (use mushroom liquid instead of water in sauce).

PORK CHOPS PROVENÇALE. Sauté pork chops in olive oil until well browned on each side. Add Tomato Sauce Provençal, 1 tablespoon capers, and ¼ cup pitted black olives. Simmer uncovered in sauce for 25 to 30 minutes. Serve with rice and green bean salad.

Lomo Trufado

4 double loin pork chops	2 tablespoons flour
¼ cup minced mushrooms	½ to ¾ teaspoon salt
1 tablespoon minced onion	About 2 tablespoons olive oil
2 tablespoons minced green pep-	2 tablespoons brandy
per	1 cup chicken broth
Pinch of cumin	¼ cup raisins
¼ teaspoon salt	

Cut a pocket in the center of each pork chop. Combine mush-rooms, onion, green pepper, cumin, and ¼ teaspoon salt; insert a little of mixture into each chop. Dust chops with flour and salt; sauté in olive oil until crisply brown. Drain off all fat, add brandy, set aflame. When flame has died out, add broth and raisins; simmer, covered, until chops are tender—about 35 minutes. Or, transfer to casserole and bake, covered, in moderate (350° F.) oven for 45 minutes. *Makes 4 servings.*

For 2 servings, divide all ingredients in half.

SUGGESTED GO-WITHS. Saffron rice, baked or broiled tomatoes, green salad with olives and thin-sliced onions; for dessert, cheese and grapes.

Pork Chops in Cream

4 loin pork chops	1 tablespoon flour
1 tablespoon butter	1 teaspoon chicken stock
4 shallots, minced, or 2 green	concentrate
onions, chopped	½ cup water
½ green pepper, seeded, chopped	1 tablespoon catsup
1 pimiento, chopped	½ cup light cream or sour cream

Sear the pork chops in butter until golden on each side. Remove. Add shallots or onions, green pepper, and pimiento; sauté until soft without browning. Stir in flour, then add chicken stock concentrate and water. Simmer, stirring, until chicken stock concentrate is dissolved. Stir in catsup. Replace chops; simmer, covered, about 20 minutes. Add light cream; or, add some of broth to sour cream, turn off heat, stir cream into remaining sauce. *Makes 4 servings.*

SUGGESTED GO-WITHS. Thin noodles tossed with butter and poppy seeds, Beets in Mustard Sauce, and tossed salad. For dessert, Peach Cobbler.

HAM STEAK IN CREAM. Use 1 center slice of ham instead of pork chops in preceding recipe; cut ham in 4 serving pieces.

Ham Steak a l'Orange

1 center slice ham, ¾ inch thick	1 medium orange, peeled, sliced
2 tablespoons butter	½ cup Château La Salle wine

Brown the ham in butter over moderately high heat; push ham to one side of pan. Add orange slices; cook about 1 minute in the butter. Add wine, turn heat low, braise ham in the wine for 10 minutes. If wine cooks away, add just a little water, enough to capture essence in the pan. Remove ham; arrange on platter with orange slices; scrape up gelatinous bits in pan; simmer until sauce is well blended—about 30 seconds. Ordinarily no salt is needed in sauce, but taste to make sure. Pour unthickened sauce over ham. *Makes 4 servings.*

SUGGESTED GO-WITHS. Sweet potatoes, green cabbage in cream, marinated artichoke hearts.

Bourbon-glazed Ham

1 center slice ham, 1 inch thick	⅛ teaspoon ground cloves
3 tablespoons brown sugar	2 tablespoons melted butter
⅛ teaspoon curry powder	2 tablespoons bourbon
1 teaspoon prepared mustard	

If ham slice has rim of white fat, slash fat at 1-inch intervals and stick with whole cloves.

Place ham in shallow casserole or baking dish. Combine sugar, curry powder, mustard, cloves, butter and bourbon; blend well; spread over ham. Place 4 inches from heat in broiler oven; broil about 25 minutes until nicely browned (do not turn). Superb with buttered sweet potatoes (or baked white potatoes), lima beans, and salad. *Makes 4 to 6 servings.*

Ham in Sherry Sauce

1 center slice of ham, ½ inch thick	2 or 3 thin slices onion
1 tablespoon butter	½ cup dry sherry

Sauté the ham in butter until golden on each side. Add onion to pan after ham has been turned over. Cover pan; cook 10 minutes over low heat. Add sherry; cook about 10 minutes, stirring to loosen gelatinous browned bits from pan. Serve ham with the pan essence. *Makes 3 to 4 servings.*

SUGGESTED GO-WITHS. Parsleyed rice, carrots, and cauliflower; for dessert, flan.

WITH CANNED HAM. Cut canned ham in thick slices; prepare as above.

Minute Steaks Provençal

4 individual minute steaks
3 tablespoons olive oil
1 clove garlic, crushed
Salt, pepper
1 8-ounce can tomato sauce
1 teaspoon instant minced onion

8 to 10 pimiento-stuffed green
olives or pitted black olives
1 tablespoon capers, well drained
(optional)
1 tablespoon sherry or Madeira

Combine olive oil and garlic; pour over the meat; pound meat with edge of plate so that oil is worked into the meat and the muscle fibers softened at the same time. Let meat marinate in the oil and garlic for 30 minutes to 1 hour, then sauté in a heated skillet over *low* heat until browned on each side. Sprinkle with salt and pepper. Add remaining ingredients; simmer, covered, until meat is very tender, about 25 minutes. *Makes 4 servings.*

For 2 servings, use 2 steaks, the same amount of oil and garlic, and divide remaining ingredients in half.

SUGGESTED GO-WITHS. Baked potatoes with sour cream, buttered spinach; for dessert, strawberries in orange juice.

Very thin slices can be cut from top round of beef for any of the following group of recipes. Or, when buying a rolled boned roast of beef, ask the meat man to cut off 6 or 8 thin slices with his ham slicer; use these as fillets, the rest as a roast.

Steak Diane

4 to 8 thin slices top round, or
slices cut from boned roast of
beef
Salt or meat tenderizer
2 tablespoons butter
4 very thin slices onion
2 tablespoons brandy

2 tablespoons minced parsley
1 tablespoon catsup
½ teaspoon prepared mustard, or
dash of Tabasco
Freshly ground black pepper
¼ cup red wine

The number of slices needed depends on the size: if very large slices, serve one to each person; for smaller slices, make it two. If the beef is choice-quality top round, or cut from choice eye round or rolled rib roast, merely sprinkle it with salt from shaker before adding to pan. If there is any question about its tenderness, it is wise to sprinkle it with commercial meat tenderizer before cooking, following label directions.

Melt butter; sauté meat over moderate heat until *lightly* browned—about 2 minutes on each side. Add onion slices to the pan around the meat; cook 1 minute longer. Add brandy, set aflame. When flame has died out, add remaining ingredients, simmer until well blended, about 3 minutes. *Makes 4 servings.*

For 2 servings, use half as many slices of beef, but otherwise the same ingredients for sauce.

Sukiyaki

Exotic in name only, this is so easy to prepare that it should become a family dish.

8 paper-thin slices (½ to ¾ pound) top round of beef
¼ cup (4 tablespoons) dry sherry
4 tablespoons brown sugar
4 tablespoons Japanese soy sauce
⅛ teaspoon powdered ginger
6 green onions (scallions), minced

4 tablespoons butter or salad oil
2 stalks celery, sliced diagonally
1 can (5 ounces) water chestnuts, sliced, or 1 turnip, cut in julienne sticks
8 large mushrooms, thinly sliced
8 to 10 spinach leaves, washed, trimmed

Prepare all ingredients in advance. Marinate the beef for 1 hour in a mixture of sherry, sugar, soy sauce, and ginger. Cut vegetables; arrange artistically on a platter or tray. Shortly before meal is to be served, remove meat slices from marinade; arrange on a platter. Pour the marinade into a pitcher.

At table, heat butter or oil to sizzling in electric skillet or chafing dish. Add a few slices of meat at a time; brown *lightly*. Push to one side of pan. Add remaining meat slices. When all meat has been cooked, add remaining ingredients except spinach. Sauté briefly. Add the marinade and the spinach leaves; cook 5 minutes. Serve with rice and tea. (Nothing else is needed.) *Makes 4 servings.*

For 2 servings, halve all ingredients. Allow 2 slices meat per serving.

Chinese Pepper Steak

1 pound round steak, sliced thin crosswise, then cut in strips	1 green pepper, seeded, cut in squares
2 tablespoons soy sauce	2 celery stalks, diced or sliced at angle
⅛ teaspoon ginger	
2 tablespoons dry sherry (optional)	2 teaspoons cornstarch
4 tablespoons oil	½ cup water
3 or 4 scallions, minced	

Marinate the meat in mixture of soy sauce, ginger, and sherry for 15 to 30 minutes. Heat oil in skillet or wok until it sizzles; add meat, lifting it from marinade with slotted spoon; cook quickly until lightly browned. Lower heat; add vegetables; cook, stirring, about 5 minutes. Blend cornstarch and water; add to reserved marinade; add to meat-vegetable mixture; cook until vegetables are tender but still crisp—about 5 minutes. *Makes 4 servings.*

For 2 servings, halve all ingredients.

Fillet of Beef with Mushrooms

8 very thin slices top round of beef or cut from rolled roast	1 cup beef stock
	2 to 3 tablespoons fat
4 tablespoons flour seasoned with salt and pepper	2 tablespoons brandy or Madeira
	Minced parsley
½ pound mushrooms	

Pound the meat with the edge of a plate, working in the flour and flattening the meat until it is wider and thinner than the original pieces. Trim and slice the mushrooms; add the trimmings to beef stock made with concentrate and water. (While sautéing the meat, simmer the beef stock with the mushroom trimmings.)

Heat fat in skillet (an electric skillet may be used, set at 360° F.); when it sizzles, add the meat without crowding the pan. Cook until browned on each side; remove. Add the mushrooms; sauté until lightly browned. Replace the meat and add the *strained* beef stock and the brandy or Madeira. Simmer 5 minutes. Add parsley. *Makes 4 servings.*

SUGGESTED GO-WITHS. Rice, green peas with onions, carrot cole slaw; for dessert, Cottage Pudding.

Veal scallopini, or scallops, or escalopes, as they are variously called, are one of the most versatile of all meat cuts. They are very thin small slices cut from the leg. They are not the same as *veal cutlet*, which is one large thicker slice, similar to a center slice of ham, cut from the upper part of the leg.

The price of veal scallopini per pound is astronomical, but since the normal serving is 2 thin slices per person, the per-serving portion price is not as high as that of chops.

Braised Scallopini (Basic Recipe)

8 scallopini	3 or 4 tablespoons butter or oil,
2 tablespoons flour	or a mixture of the two
1 teaspoon salt	1 cup liquid or sauce, as specified
½ teaspoon paprika	Salt, pepper

Thin as scallopini are when purchased, they must be pounded with the edge of a plate to break down and soften tissue. Work in a mixture of flour, salt, and paprika (or other spice as specified) as you pound. Melt butter or butter and oil in large skillet; when fat is sizzling, add scallopini, without crowding skillet. When browned on each side, remove. When all are browned, add liquid or sauce; simmer, stirring, until browned bits are loosened from pan. Replace meat in sauce; add salt and pepper to taste; simmer 5 minutes. *Makes 4 servings.*

SCALLOPINI AU MARSALA. Instead of paprika, use ¼ teaspoon nutmeg in flour mixture, and for liquid use ¼ cup Marsala wine or cream sherry plus water to make 1 cup. Simmer covered until meat is tender. Serve with fettucini and a green salad.

SCALLOPINI WITH MUSHROOMS. After meat has been cooked, remove, add ½ pound sliced or button mushrooms to pan with 1 additional tablespoon butter, cook until lightly browned (or use canned sliced or button mushrooms with their liquid, omit extra butter). Replace meat; add ¼ cup medium sherry plus water or chicken broth to make 1 cup. If desired, stir in 2 tablespoons heavy cream or sour cream just before removing from stove.

SCALLOPINI ROMANO. Prepare as in basic recipe, but for liquid add 1 cup well-seasoned tomato or spaghetti sauce plus 2 tablespoons minced Italian parsley. Simmer 10 minutes. Serve with spaghetti or rice and Caesar Salad.

VEAL SCALLOPS OPORTO. Use ¼ teaspoon nutmeg instead of paprika, and for liquid use ½ cup port wine and ¼ cup water. Simmer 5 minutes; stir in ½ cup light cream. Stir and cook until sauce is smooth and slightly thickened. Serve with rice and watercress and tomato salad.

VEAL SCALLOPS AU JEREZ. Prepare meat as in basic recipe; remove meat, add to pan 1 cup sliced onions. Cook onions until soft (add additional oil or butter if needed). Add 1 cup chicken broth for the liquid, plus 1 bay leaf, crushed, 2 tablespoons cream sherry, and 1 teaspoon minced parsley. Replace meat; simmer, covered, 30 to 45 minutes. Serve over or with rice topped with toasted slivered almonds. Artichoke hearts are a perfect accompaniment.

Breaded Veal Scallopini

4 to 8 slices scallopini, depending on size*
Salt
Paprika
2 eggs, beaten until light
3 tablespoons milk or water

1 cup crushed cracker crumbs or herb-flavored fine bread crumbs
Oil for frying
Lemon wedges

Pound meat with edge of plate or with mallet until very thin and half again its original circumference, sprinkling with salt and paprika as you pound. Dip each slice in egg mixed with 3 tablespoons milk or water, then in crumbs, then repeat, dipping a second time in beaten egg and crumbs. (For 8 slices, it may be necessary to use another egg and more crumbs.) Chill at least 1 hour before cooking. Oil should be ¼ inch deep in skillet. Fry until crisply browned on each side. Serve hot, with lemon wedges, mashed or Duchess Potatoes, and broccoli or asparagus. *Makes 4 servings.*

For 2 servings, divide all ingredients by half.

*Some scallopini as sold in supermarkets will be so small that two are needed per serving; if purchased from a private butcher, the slices may be large enough so that one per serving is ample.

VEAL PARMIGIANA. Prepare Breaded Veal Scallopini; place in a shallow casserole or individual casseroles, cover with well-seasoned tomato or spaghetti sauce, then with sliced Mozzarella; cover with more sauce and top with grated Parmesan cheese. Bake in hot oven or under broiler until cheese is melted and top lightly browned. Serve with rice or noodles and a green salad.

SCOTCH COLLOPS. Essentially the same as Breaded Veal Scallopini, except that the slices of scallopini are cut small (about 2 inches in diameter) and are dipped in a mixture of beaten egg, minced parsley, and finely minced mushroom pieces, while the crumb mixture consists of ¾ cup fine crumbs, ¼ cup grated Parmesan cheese. Chill, then fry as for Breaded Veal Scallopini.

SCALLOPINI GRANADINA. Essentially the same as Breaded Veal Scallopini, but for 12 small scallopini (6 servings) pound into the veal slices a mixture of ¼ teaspoon cinnamon, ⅛ teaspoon cumin or curry powder, ⅛ teaspoon black or white pepper, ½ teaspoon salt, and ½ cup flour. Dip in egg, then in crumbs as for basic recipe; fry in mixture of olive oil and butter.

TO FREEZE ANY OF ABOVE. Prepare as directed, freeze, then wrap and seal securely. Reheat in preheated 350° F. oven until crisp and sizzling—about 40 minutes.

Wiener Schnitzel

1 large veal cutlet	milk, or cream
About 2 tablespoons flour	1 to 1½ cups fine crumbs*
½ teaspoon salt	Oil or vegetable shortening for
⅛ to ¼ teaspoon freshly	frying
ground black pepper	4 lemon slices
2 or 3 eggs, beaten until light	4 curled anchovies
3 tablespoons water,	4 capers

Slash the edges of the cutlet to prevent curling. Pound with edge of plate, working in a mixture of flour, salt, and pepper. Dip cutlet in egg mixed with 3 tablespoons water, milk, or cream, then in crumbs, in egg and crumbs a second time. (Start with 2 eggs and 1 cup crumbs; amount needed depends on size of cutlet.) Chill at least 1 hour. Heat oil or shortening to sizzling, add cutlet, fry until crisply browned on each side. Serve at once, topped with lemon slices, and over each lemon slice, place a curled anchovy (with caper in center). Cut into 4 portions to serve, with a lemon slice on each portion. Lemon should be pressed into meat at table, so that a little lemon juice flavors the meat. *Makes 3 or 4 servings, depending on size of cutlet.*

*Either use fresh (not stale) cracker crumbs, or make your own bread crumbs by slow-toasting (in oven) thinly sliced day-old bread until golden. Crush this in blender until very fine. The freshness of the crumbs is important in the success of the schnitzel.

PORK SCHNITZEL. Instead of veal cutlet, use pork cut from the upper part of a fresh ham, from pork shoulder to tenderloin. If the latter, the pieces will be approximately the size of scallopini. Pound the meat exactly as for Wiener Schnitzel, and dip in eggs and crumbs the same way. Garnish with lemon slices or lemon wedges and serve with crisp Fried Parsley, baked potatoes, and broiled tomatoes.

Saltimbocca

12 veal scallopini
12 thin slices ham
½ teaspoon sage

4 tablespoons olive oil, or a mixture of oil and butter

Top each piece of veal with a slice of ham. Pound edges together with mallet or heavy end of hammer, with a sprinkling of sage in the center of each "sandwich" of veal and ham. Heat oil in large skillet; brown the saltimbocca on each side until golden. *Makes 6 servings.*

SUGGESTED GO-WITHS. Parsleyed rice, Swiss chard with Vinaigrette Sauce, tomato and lettuce salad; for dessert, Gorgonzola cheese and crisp apples.

Veal Scallops Cordon Bleu

8 veal scallopini
½ teaspoon salt
About ¼ teaspoon freshly ground
   black pepper
4 slices Swiss or natural
   Gruyère cheese
4 thin slices ham

1 egg, beaten
4 tablespoons flour
½ cup fine bread or cracker
   crumbs
3 tablespoons butter
1 tablespoon oil

Pound scallopini with edge of plate, working in salt and pepper. Place 1 slice cheese and 1 slice ham over four of them, trimming to fit evenly. Brush edges with beaten egg. Place remaining veal slices over top of each. Pound edges to seal. Dust each with flour, then dip in beaten egg, then in crumbs. Sauté in mixture of oil and butter until well browned on both sides. Transfer to shallow casserole, bake in oven preheated to 375° F. for 25 to 30 minutes. *Makes 4 servings.*

For 6 servings, use 12 slices veal, 6 slices each cheese and ham, and thin the egg with 2 tablespoons milk. Increase amount of crumbs as needed.

For 2 servings, use half as much veal, cheese, and ham, same amount of egg, and crumbs as needed.

SUGGESTED GO-WITHS. Lima beans, spinach, broiled tomatoes.

Veal Chops Viennoise

4 loin veal chops, trimmed	1 or 2 tablespoons butter
1 teaspoon paprika	¾ cup water
Salt, pepper	¼ cup sour cream

Rub paprika into chops on both sides; dust with salt and pepper. Melt butter in skillet to sizzling; quickly sear the chops on
both sides. Lower heat; cover pan. Simmer for 15 minutes in
juice extracted from meat. Add water; simmer, uncovered, until chops are tender—about 10 minutes longer. Remove chops.
Stir to loosen all browned bits from bottom. Turn off heat. Add
some of sauce to cream, blend well, then add cream to sauce in
pan. Serve chops covered with the sauce. *Makes 4 servings.*

For 6 servings, use 6 veal chops, but brown only half at a time;
return to pan and simmer, covered, as above. Increase sauce by
one-half.

For 2 servings, use 2 veal chops, only 1 tablespoon butter;
decrease water to ½ cup, sour cream to 2 tablespoons.

SUGGESTED GO-WITHS. Mashed potatoes, lima beans, and
salad of cucumbers, green olives, and lettuce; Blackberry Pie
for dessert.

Veal Chops Caprice

4 loin veal chops, trimmed	4 thin slices Swiss or natural
Salt	Gruyère cheese
Paprika	Lemon wedges
3 tablespoons olive oil	Fried Parsley

Fasten tails of chops to meaty part with skewers. Dust on both
sides with salt and paprika. Heat olive oil in skillet; add chops;
cook over *moderate* heat until well browned on each side. Place
a slice of cheese on each chop; keep warm. Just before serving,
place 4 inches under broiler until cheese is melted. Serve at
once with lemon wedges and Fried Parsley. *Makes 4 servings.*

For 2 servings, divide all ingredients in half.

SUGGESTED GO-WITHS. Asparagus, cauliflower, crusty rolls;
peaches and cream for dessert.

Veal Chops à l'Orange

Prepare like Pork Chops à l'Orange, but use veal loin chops
instead of pork chops.

ROASTS

For a family of four or more, a roast is generally the most economical of meats to buy. It is also the easiest of meats to cook, especially when it's a tender cut.

Roasts of beef, veal, and pork should be purchased with an eye to leftovers. All can be used sliced cold in sandwiches, or reheated in gravy, and when the roast is reduced to bits and pieces, it can be used in hash, stew, or oriental dishes, or with rice or pasta. Lamb is not as good cold as hot; it is best when purchasing a roast of lamb to get one of a size suitable for one meal, or have it cut up in advance to be cooked in several different ways (some as chops, some as kabobs, ends and pieces for curries or other stews).

When roasts are offered on sale, it is wise to purchase extras for future meals—if you have sufficient freezer space. But defrost completely before roasting for dependable results. In fact, it's best to cut roasts for freezing into smaller portions in *advance*. Smaller pieces of meat will thaw more quickly and thus be usable on shorter notice.

Boneless, or boned, roasts are easier to carve and in most cases more economical than roasts with bone in. However, the bone contributes flavor, and if the location of the bone is such that carving is not too difficult, the bone-in roast is sometimes preferable. When a boned roast is purchased, ask for the bones to use in making stock (see A Quick Way to Make Stock, Book 1).

A *meat thermometer* is worth many times its purchase price; only by using a thermometer inserted into the center of the meat can you be sure whether it has cooked to the degree of doneness you prefer—and if you like beef rare, only with a thermometer can you avoid over- (or under-) cooking the roast. Use cooking times per pound on the chart opposite as a gauge for anticipating approximately when meat will be ready.

Spit-roasting cooking times are approximately the same as those given for oven-roasting, but the use of a meat thermometer is even more important than for oven roasts because the heat of the fire is less reliable, and outdoor temperature, drafts, and the shape and size of the meat also affect total cooking time.

When planning a meal, you of course need some idea of when the meat can be served. Multiply the estimated cooking time per pound by the number of pounds, and to this add 15 to 30 minutes' "cooling off" time, because all meat is easier to slice, and more slices per pound can be obtained, if the roast has been allowed to cool after it has been removed from the oven.

Meat Roasting Timetable

Cut	Oven Temperature	Meat Thermometer	Approximate Time Per Pound (Minutes)
Beef			
Standing rib	450° F.	140° (rare)	10-12
	325°	140° (rare)	18-20
		160° (medium)	22-25
		170° (well)	27-30
Rolled boneless	400°	140° (rare)	12-15
rib, eye round,	325°	140° (rare)	30
chuck, rump,		160° (medium)	35
shoulder, sirloin		170° (well)	40
Tenderloin (filet mignon)	450°, then 325°	140° (rare)	10-12
Lamb			
Leg with bone	400°	140-145° (rare)	15-18
	325°	145° (pink)	20-25
		170° (medium)	30
		180° (well)	35
Boned rolled leg	400°	140-145° (rare)	25-30
or shoulder	325°	140-145° (rare)	30-35
		170° (medium)	40
		180° (well)	45-50
Crown roast	450°, then 325°	140-145° (rare)	10-12
		170° (medium)	20-25
Veal			
Rib, loin or kidney roast, or rump (with bone)	325°	175-180°	35-40
Rolled boned rump, shoulder, breast, or arm roast	325°	175-180°	45-50
Crown roast	325°	175-180°	35-40
Pork			
Loin (with bone)	325°	180-185°	35-40
Fresh ham (with bone)	325°	180-185°	45-50
Boned shoulder	325°	180-185°	45-50
Crown roast	325°	180-185°	35-40

(For baking ham, see page 343.)

Roast Beef with Yorkshire Pudding

3-rib standing rib roast of beef,   roast or eye round roast of beef
  trimmed, or 6-pound rolled rib

OVEN METHOD. Place standing roast in large shallow roasting
pan, preferably on a rack, and place in oven preheated to
450°F. Roast meat 10 minutes at this temperature, then reduce
heat to 325° until meat thermometer registers 140° for rare,
150° for medium—approximately 3 hours. For a rolled roast,
insist that the butcher *not* add a covering of suet; only roll and
tie the roast with its attached fat. When roast is done, remove to
platter, keep in warm place, loosely covered with foil. Fat in
pan should be no more than ¼ inch deep; if more than this,
drain off excess.

YORKSHIRE PUDDING

3 eggs   1 teaspoon salt
1½ cups milk   Pan drippings
1½ cups sifted flour

Combine eggs, milk, flour, and salt, beat with rotary beater
until smooth. This may be mixed when roast first goes into
oven; it will thicken slightly as it stands, but only needs to be
stirred once or twice before pouring into roasting pan. Pour
pudding batter in pan containing meat drippings, return to
oven, raise oven temperature to 375°, and bake until puffed
and golden—25 to 30 minutes. *Serves 6 to 8.*

ROTISSERIE METHOD. Only a rolled roast can be used for
the rotisserie. Make sure the roast is not wrapped with a covering of suet. This is important, for too much fat will ruin the
Yorkshire pudding. Insert thermometer in meat so that it does
not touch metal of spit, preheat rotisserie at "bake" position for
10 minutes, then place meat on spit, turn to "rotisserie" position.

Place large roasting pan under meat to catch drippings. Watch thermometer, and when indicator is within 5° of desired temperature, pour off excess fat, leaving 3 to 4 tablespoons in pan. Add pudding batter to drip pan. When meat is done, remove to warm place; keep loosely covered with foil. Change oven back to "bake" position; finish cooking the pudding. Yorkshire pudding made this way is less puffy than when baked in an oven, but has a richer, more custardy consistency. *Serves 8 to 10 generously.*

Rolled Roast of Beef with Browned Potatoes

If this is a tender cut (rolled rib, eye round, Delmonico, or sirloin tip), all you need do is place it in a shallow roasting pan, insert a meat thermometer in the center, and roast it according to the Meat Roasting Timetable. Parboil peeled potatoes (1 medium potato for each serving) for 5 minutes; drain well. Place around meat in pan after enough fat has been drawn out to moisten the bottom of the pan; turn potatoes in fat. Allow 30 to 45 minutes to bake potatoes, turning once so that they will be golden and crusty on all sides. If you see that a considerable amount of fat has collected in the pan, use a syringe to draw it off, and discard it. Fat should not be more than ¼ inch deep at any time. Excess fat not only makes the potatoes greasy, but it makes it impossible to have rich brown gravy. You get those delicious browned bits in the pan only with moderate fat.

When meat has reached desired doneness, and potatoes are crusty, remove both to a platter. Make gravy with the pan drippings (see How to Make Gravy, Book 1).

If rolled chuck or rump is to be roasted, it is wise to tenderize it before cooking, by one of the ways suggested under Ways to Tenderize Meat, Book 1.

To spit-roast, balance on rotisserie spit, insert meat thermometer, cook to desired doneness according to Meat Roasting Timetable.

Roast Hind Shank of Beef

At least two butchers told me this couldn't be done—but I've done it.

Choose a cut of hind shank with a good proportion of meat around the marrow bone, so that it is possible to insert a meat thermometer in the lean without touching the bone. Simply punch the meat with a blunt skewer and work olive oil into the holes with a pastry brush; let meat stand several hours, preferably overnight. If it is to be frozen, marinate with oil *before* freezing.

Roast to rare (140° F.) in an oven preheated to 350° for a miniature roast to serve 1 or 2. (If cooked to medium or well-done, the roast will be tough.) The gravy is superb, because of the marrow that comes from the bone. Slice meat as thin as possible, diagonally, across the grain.

Filet Mignon

This is rarely sold in American markets, and usually only on special order. It is boneless, long and thin in shape, and very high in price. Tuck the narrow ends under, fasten with small skewers (remove the skewers before serving). Place on a rack in a shallow roasting pan. Brush olive oil or melted butter (olive oil is preferable) over the outside. Grate pepper over the top with a pepper grinder. Insert a meat thermometer in thickest part. Preheat oven to 450° F. (very hot), place meat in oven, reduce heat to 375°, roast about 50 minutes (10 minutes per pound) until outside is crusty brown and meat thermometer registers barely 140°. Sprinkle with salt just before or just as you remove meat from oven. Slice at an angle ¾ to 1 inch thick. Allow 6 ounces per serving: a 5-pound filet serves 12.

SUGGESTED GO-WITHS. Potatoes baked in same oven (but allow 1 hour for potatoes), sautéed mushrooms, and artichoke hearts or petits pois. This is so special that a vintage French Burgundy or Bordeaux should be served with it, the cork pulled a good 2 hours before the wine is poured.

Tenderloin of Beef Wellington

1 4-pound beef tenderloin
  or filet mignon
1 cup minced mushrooms
1 tablespoon chopped onion
1 tablespoon each butter
  and olive oil
1 teaspoon minced parsley

½ cup liver pâté (canned or
  homemade)
2 recipes Flaky Piecrust,
  or 2 packages piecrust mix
1 egg, lightly beaten
3 teaspoons water

Tenderloin should be formed into even shape. Place fat side up in rack in shallow pan; bake in oven preheated to 450° until meat thermometer registers 130°—about 25 minutes. Remove from heat; let stand until meat is cool enough to handle easily.

Sauté the chopped mushrooms and onion in butter and oil until lightly browned; blend with parsley and liver pâté. Prepare the piecrust dough; roll out to form a rectangle 12 x 18 inches. (The dough should be thicker than for piecrust.) Brush the mushroom mixture over the dough, leaving a 1-inch margin all the way around. Press mixture into the dough. Place the meat in the center of pastry, cover completely, sealing securely at ends and where pastry overlaps: moisten edges of pastry with water; press together with fingers. Place seam side down in shallow baking pan. Decorate top of pastry with shapes cut from any leftover pieces of the pie dough, pressed onto the dough in a pattern.

Brush top of pastry with mixture of egg and water. If meat is not to be served within the hour, refrigerate, tightly covered with plastic wrap. Remove from refrigerator 1 hour before baking. Bake in oven preheated to 400° F. until pastry is golden and crisp—about 40 minutes. Serve to an elegant gathering with Béarnaise Sauce or Madeira Sauce. *Serves 10.*

SUGGESTED GO-WITHS. Cheese-topped baked tomatoes, asparagus or cauliflower, avocado salad, Parker House rolls; Crêpes Suzette for dessert, prepare in a chafing dish at table.

Roast Lamb (Basic Recipe)

Lamb is the only meat besides beef that can be served rare, and for most Americans rare lamb is still a rarity; most standard cookbooks give instructions only for cooking it to well-done. But rare (or "pink") lamb has more delicate flavor and greater tenderness, and because it is cooked a shorter time there is less waste from shrinkage.

Leg of lamb is the most popular cut for roasting, but lamb shoulder is just as tender, and if boned and rolled makes an excellent roast. Lamb shanks may also be roasted and served one to a person (like roasting a hind shank of beef); however, the flavor of the shank meat is stronger and less tender than leg or shoulder meat.

Crown roast of lamb is a gala offering: these are rib chops, uncut, formed into a crown. They should not be cooked to more than medium (170° F.), and are better if rare or at least pink.

There are three methods of roasting lamb to rare:

•Preheat the oven to 400° F., roast the meat for approximately 15 minutes to the pound (1½ hours for a 6-pound leg of lamb) or until the thermometer registers 140°. If the meat is preferred more done, roast it to 145° to 150°.

•Another way is to preheat the oven to 450° (very hot), sear the meat for 15 minutes, then reduce heat to 325°. For this, allow 20 to 25 minutes to the pound.

•Keep the oven at 325° the entire time. Presumably there is less shrinkage when the lamb is slow-roasted, but the meat does not get quite so brown on the outside.

Spit-roasting is another good way to roast lamb. A leg of lamb must be well trimmed, most of the shank bone removed, and carefully balanced on the rotisserie spit. A rolled roast is easier to balance on the spit, and easier to slice when cooked (it can be sliced right from the spit, if preferred).

In any case, and however you like the meat cooked, be sure to use a thermometer.

Oven-browned potatoes may be cooked around the roast, as for roast beef, if desired. Mint jelly is the traditional garnish with lamb, especially in households of British ancestry.

Gigot Bretonne (Leg of Lamb Brittany Style)

1 pound dried white marrow beans	paste
Salt	1 6- to 7-pound leg of lamb
3 cloves garlic	2 tablespoons butter, melted, or olive oil
2 medium onions	Freshly ground black pepper
1 medium tomato, peeled and chopped, or 1 teaspoon tomato	Minced parsley

If beans are the quick-cooking type, presoaking is not necessary. Otherwise, they should be soaked in cold water overnight. Drain well, cover with fresh water, add salt to taste, a garlic clove, the onions, and the tomato. Cook, covered, until tender but not mushy—about 2 hours (these must be started before the meat).

The lamb may be roasted in an open pan in the oven, or spit-roasted on the rotisserie. Insert 2 cloves garlic, split down the center (making 4 halves) around the bone of the meat. If meat is to be spit-roasted, place spit so that it is well balanced. Brush outside with melted butter or olive oil. Pepper. Roast to rare (140° to 145° F.), allowing 15 to 18 minutes to the pound in oven preheated to 400°, or by one of the other methods suggested in the basic recipe.

When meat is nearly cooked (thermometer reading approaching 130°), drain beans, removing garlic and onions. Remove meat to platter. Drain off excess fat; add drained onions to the pan drippings; cook, mashing the onions, until sauce is reduced and creamy in appearance. Add this to the beans with the parsley. Serve the beans with the roast lamb, carving the lamb in thin slices across the grain. *Makes 8 to 10 servings.*

Reheat leftover lamb with any leftover beans.

Lamb al Vino

1 6- to 7-pound leg of lamb	1 clove garlic, crushed
1 cup red wine	Grated peel of ½ lemon
¼ cup grated onion	½ teaspoon rosemary

Marinate meat in refrigerator in mixture of remaining ingredients for 24 hours before cooking. Remove from marinade; roast in oven or on rotisserie according to any of the methods described in the basic recipe. Baste with the *strained* marinade during roasting. Make gravy with the pan drippings. *Makes 8 to 10 servings.*

SUGGESTED GO-WITHS. Spring vegetable soup, as first course; mashed potatoes, dandelion greens, celery, and olives; rhubarb pie for dessert.

Swedish Lamb with Dill Sauce

1 6-pound leg of lamb	2 tablespoons butter
Soup vegetables (celery, parsley, onion, carrot)	2 tablespoons sugar
	4 tablespoons minced fresh or
10 to 12 small white onions, peeled	frozen dill, or 2 teaspoons dill weed
10 to 12 new potatoes, peeled	

Have lamb boned, rolled, and tied; use bones for making stock the day before. Place bones in kettle with salted water to cover; add vegetables; simmer 2 to 3 hours. Strain; chill. When fat rises to top and congeals, remove carefully.

Roast boned lamb either in oven or on rotisserie spit according to one of methods described in basic recipe. Cook onions and potatoes in strained stock until tender; drain, saving stock. Glaze onions in mixture of butter and sugar until lightly browned; place with potatoes around roast in pan, or in drip pan under rotisserie. Cook meat until well browned on all sides and thermometer registers desired temperature. Remove meat and vegetables to platter. Make gravy with reserved stock and pan drippings. *Makes 8 to 10 servings.*

Oriental Roast Lamb

Rub the outside of lamb ready for roasting (leg of lamb or boned rolled leg or shoulder) with the following mixture.

½ teaspoon cinnamon
½ teaspoon coarsely ground
  black pepper
2 teaspoons lemon juice

2 tablespoons oil
1 tablespoon grated onion
1 to 1½ teaspoons salt

Roast according to any of the methods described in basic recipe.

Lamb with Caper Sauce

1 6- to 7-pound leg of lamb,
  boned
1 sprig celery
Parsley
1 onion, stuck with cloves
4 tablespoons softened butter
1 clove garlic, crushed

1 teaspoon salt
¼ teaspoon cayenne
About 2 cups lamb broth
¼ teaspoon saffron (optional)
¼ cup capers, drained
½ cup cream
1 tablespoon cornstarch

Make broth with bones from lamb preceding day, adding celery, parsley, and onion; simmer 2 hours; strain; chill so fat will congeal on top.

Spread out boned meat; make a paste of butter, garlic, salt, and cayenne. Spread this over meat; roll up; tie with cord into even shape. Roast on rack in roasting pan or on rotisserie spit, according to one of methods described in basic recipe, to desired doneness.

Make caper sauce with pan drippings: Pour off excess fat, saving only the brown essence. Heat 2 cups of the reserved lamb broth with saffron; strain broth into pan containing drippings; bring to a boil, stirring up browned bits to dissolve. Add capers; reduce heat, stir in cream. Thicken by adding a thin paste made of cornstarch thinned with water; simmer until smooth. Serve as a gravy with the roast lamb. *Makes 8 to 10 servings.*

SUGGESTED GO-WITHS. Risi-Bisi, cold Zucchini Vinaigrette, hot yeast rolls; for dessert, pineapple sherbet drizzled with creme de menthe.

Roast Veal (Basic Rules)

Because veal has little natural fat, it needs added fat in some form. This may be done by inserting fat in a rolled roast, before rolling; or by larding; or by punching holes and working in olive oil; or by brushing oil or melted butter over the outside; or by laying strips of bacon over the veal.

Rump of veal is the best bone-in cut for roasting. A roast loin of veal is delicious, but costly. A kidney roast is also very special; the kidney is left attached to the ribs, and cooks to tenderness bathed by the meat juices. All of these need only be brushed with melted butter or oil on the outside before being placed in a roasting pan.

Oven-roasting is the preferred method, with the oven set at 325° F., and the meat should be cooked to well-done. A rolled veal roast can be spit-roasted on a rotisserie with thermostatic control, but it is not wise to do so over a charcoal fire with its variable temperature.

Basting the meat as it cooks is also advisable, to keep the meat juicy and succulent. It may be basted with melted butter, with wine, or with a wine marinade.

Wine-basted Roast of Veal

1 5- to 6-pound rump of veal
1 slice suet
1 teaspoon salt
½ teaspoon paprika
½ teaspoon powdered cumin
1 tablespoon flour

About 3 tablespoons olive oil
1 cup red wine
1½ tablespoons cornstarch or arrowroot, or instant-type flour
1½ cups water

Ask butcher to bone and roll the meat for you, but with the suet on the *inside*, not the outside. No suet should be on the outside at all. Combine salt, paprika, cumin, and flour; rub mixture into outside of meat. Brush olive oil over the flour mixture so that it is completely moistened.

Preheat oven to 325° F.; place meat in shallow roasting pan; roast approximately 3 hours, or until meat thermometer registers 175°. Baste frequently with the wine. After first hour, cover meat with tent of aluminum foil. (If desired, place potatoes around meat to bake in pan during last 1½ hours.)

When meat is done, remove meat and potatoes from pan, pour off excess fat, leaving approximately 2 tablespoons drippings in pan. Add cornstarch blended with a little of the water; stir into pan drippings with remaining water. Simmer until smooth and thickened. Serve as gravy with the meat. *Makes 12 to 14 servings;* also excellent sliced and served cold with currant jelly or Cumberland Sauce.

Roast Veal à l'Orange

1 4- to 5-pound rump of veal,
  rolled, tied
1 teaspoon salt
2 tablespoons flour
3 tablespoons olive oil
½ cup chopped onion

1 clove garlic (optional)
1/3 cup orange juice
Grated rind of 1 orange
  (about 3 tablespoons)
½ cup water
½ cup sweet sherry

Make sure the veal has no suet on the outside. Rub salt and flour into meat; brown on all sides in olive oil. Remove meat to casserole. Cook onion in pan drippings until soft and yellow; add garlic, if desired; cook until soft, then crush into drippings with tines of fork. Add orange juice, rind, water, and sherry. Bring just to a boil; lower heat; cook 2 minutes. Pour over veal in casserole. Cover; bake in 300° F. oven for 2 hours. Remove cover, increase oven heat to 375°, bake 45 minutes longer, basting with juices in baking dish. Remove veal to serving platter; skim off excess fat from remaining liquid. Heat sauce to boiling, strain if desired, serve in a sauce boat with the veal. (This is delicious both hot and cold.) *Makes 8 to 10 servings.*

SUGGESTED GO-WITHS. Rice, braised zucchini, cherry tomatoes, lettuce and onion salad.

Parmesan-stuffed Veal Shoulder

1 4- to 5-pound boned veal
  shoulder, with pocket for
  stuffing
2 cups bread crumbs
¼ cup milk
½ pound lean pork,
  finely ground
6 tablespoons grated Parmesan
  cheese

¼ teaspoon salt
⅛ teaspoon freshly ground
  black pepper
1 tablespoon minced parsley
4 or 5 slices bacon
1 cup red table wine
½ cup water
3 tablespoons flour

Be sure to ask butcher to give you bones removed from veal. Place these in 2 cups salted water; bring to a boil; simmer 1 hour to make stock; strain and set aside. Soak bread in milk until soft. Combine soaked bread with pork, cheese, salt, pepper, and parsley. Stuff pocket of roast with this mixture. Secure pocket opening with poultry skewers, arrange bacon strips over top, and place in roasting pan. Roast at 325° for 3 hours or until meat thermometer registers 180°. Baste occasionally with the wine and water; add more water if pan is dry at any time. When meat is done, remove. Pour off any excess fat; thicken remaining pan drippings with 3 tablespoons flour, stirring to blend. Slowly stir in 2½ cups strained stock; cook until thickened and smooth. Add salt to taste if needed. Serve meat accompanied by small parsley potatoes and buttered spinach, with Chianti wine. *Makes 10 to 12 servings.*

Roast Pork (Basic Recipe)

Loin of pork is the most popular cut, and the butt end is the easiest to carve and slice. But a fresh ham is also excellent, especially for a large family; have the fresh ham cut in half when purchased, and freeze half for later use. A boned pork shoulder also makes a fine roast, but a shoulder cut with bone in is extremely hard to carve, and there is a great deal of waste.

Pork has ample fat and is naturally tender. It must, however, be cooked to well-done because of its perishability. Roast in an open pan in the oven, with potatoes browning around the meat (as for Roast Beef with Browned Potatoes), until meat thermometer registers 185° F. (see Roasting Timetable). Remove meat and potatoes to platter, pour off excess fat, make gravy of the remaining pan drippings. If there is a good amount of brown gelatinous essence, the gravy will be brown and flavorful. Applesauce is the traditional accompaniment, though orange-cranberry relish is also delicious with roast pork. And some prefer sweet to white potatoes.

Loin of Pork Florentine

1 4- to 6-pound loin of pork
1 or 2 cloves garlic
1½ teaspoons salt
1 tablespoon flour
¼ teaspoon rosemary

6 to 8 whole cloves
½ cup red table wine,
 or ¼ cup orange juice and 2
 tablespoons lemon juice

Cut garlic cloves in thin slivers; insert in meat along cracked bones. Cut fat over the top of the roast into squares; combine salt, flour, and rosemary and rub into fat. Insert whole cloves in center of squares. Place meat in open shallow pan, bake at 325° F. until thermometer registers 185°, or allowing 30 to 35 minutes per pound. Baste occasionally with wine or juice. When done, remove meat from pan, let stand 15 minutes before serving. Meantime, make gravy with pan drippings. *Makes 7 to 10 servings,* depending on amount of bone.

SUGGESTED GO-WITHS. Mashed potatoes, parsleyed carrots, tossed salad; Prune Compote au Rhum for dessert.

Drunken Pig

1 4- to 6-pound loin of pork
1 clove garlic
Salt, pepper
1 tablespoon oil

2 to 4 cups inexpensive red wine
1 tablespoon tomato paste
   (optional)

Insert slivers of garlic next to bone of meat; rub meat with salt and pepper. Brush oil over meat, place in casserole, cover with wine. Roast uncovered in 325° F. oven for 2½ hours, or until meat thermometer registers 185°. Wine should reduce to half. Baste occasionally with wine; if too much evaporates, add a little water. During last half-hour a tablespoon of tomato paste thinned with water may be added, if desired. Remove meat to platter; skim off fat from liquid in pan; taste for salt and add more if needed. Serve meat with unthickened sauce. *Makes 7 to 10 servings.*

SUGGESTED GO-WITHS. Braised Savoy cabbage, yams; for dessert, berry shortcake.

Roast Pork Greek Style

Insert slits of garlic around the bone of a pork roast (loin, shoulder, or ham). Rub meat all over with cut side of lemon; sprinkle with salt. Roast according to timetable. Serve with Pilaf, broiled or baked tomatoes, and salad of black olives, thin-sliced onion, and lettuce.

Chinese Roast Pork

1 1- to 1½-pound pork fillet,
   or 4-pound loin of pork,
   boned, trimmed
¼ cup soy sauce
3 tablespoons tomato paste

2 tablespoons dry sherry
2 cloves garlic, crushed
4 slices fresh ginger, minced,
   or ¼ teaspoon ground ginger
½ teaspoon salt

Trim all fat from pork; cut off ends squarely and tie if necessary to make roll uniform in shape. Marinate in mixture of remaining ingredients for 2 hours, turning several times. Remove pork from marinade: place *on rack* in roasting pan. Preheat oven to 350° F. Roast pork for 30 minutes or until meat thermometer inserted in center registers 160°. Baste with marinade. Increase heat to 450° and roast until thermometer registers 185°—15 to 20 minutes longer. Remove from oven; cool 15 to 20 minutes, cut diagonally in very thin slices. Serve as part of a Chinese family dinner. *Makes 4 to 6 servings.*

Mexican Pork Roast

1 pork shoulder, boned, rolled, about 4 pounds *after* boning	⅛ teaspoon sage
	1 clove garlic, crushed
2 tablespoons chili powder	1 teaspoon salt
⅛ teaspoon coriander	1 small can tomatoes, sieved

Punch holes in pork with skewer; rub mixture of chili powder, coriander, sage, garlic, and salt into meat. Brown in oven preheated to 450° F. for 15 minutes; reduce heat to 325°, add sieved tomato, and roast until thermometer registers 180°, allowing 35 minutes per pound. Baste occasionally with tomato in pan. When meat is done, remove from pan and skim off excess fat; make gravy with pan drippings. *Makes 8 to 10 servings.*

SUGGESTED GO-WITHS. Baked sweet potatoes, turnip or beet greens, green salad; mixed fruit compote for dessert.

Crown Roast of Pork

This is formed of uncut rib chops, the most tender and succulent part of the pig, fastened together in crown shape. Usually must be ordered in advance, shaped and fastened by the butcher. Roast slowly according to Meat Roasting Timetable, basting with pan juices and cider, red wine, or beer. To serve, fill the center of the crown with rice to which slivered almonds and/or raisins have been added. Serve with baked acorn squash (or whipped frozen squash), salad, and individual fruit tarts.

Baked Ham

There are now so many types of ham on the market, it is virtually impossible to give a basic recipe which applies to all. Something like 90 percent of all hams now sold are *tenderized*, which means they have been cured by an injection of chemicals rather than salted and smoked the old-fashioned way.

Many hams come with baking instructions printed on the wrapper. If not, follow these general rules.

1. *Country hams,* including Smithfield and Old Kentucky hams, must be soaked in water 12 hours, then parboiled in fresh boiling water, allowing 25 minutes per pound. When cool enough to handle, the rind must be removed, then the fat should be scored and a whole clove stuck in each square. If desired, brush a sweet glaze over top. The ham is then baked for a *total* of 30 minutes at 375° F. (moderately hot) until the top is glistening brown.

2. *Ready-to-cook tenderized hams.* These need no parboiling, but rind should be removed first, and this may be easier if the ham is soaked in *hot* water for ½ hour. This also gets rid of excess salt. Then score the top, cover with any desired glaze, and bake in 325° oven until meat thermometer registers 160°, allowing about 25 minutes per pound.

3. *Ready-to-eat tenderized hams.* If these are to be baked and served hot, the rind must be removed, the fat scored, and a glaze rubbed over the top. Bake in 325° oven, allowing 10 to 15 minutes to the pound, until meat thermometer registers 130° (only warmed through).

4. *Canned hams.* Chill before opening can; scrape off gelatin. Add a glaze (if the ham is to be served hot); bake at 325°, allowing 10 minutes to the pound, until meat thermometer registers 130°

Ham Glazes

MUSTARD GLAZE. Combine 1 tablespoon prepared mustard with ¼ cup brown sugar; spread over the top of ham *before baking*. Stick whole cloves in scored squares in ham fat. Enough for ½ ham, or a 5-pound canned or boned ham; double for whole ham.

CURRANT GLAZE. Combine 1 cup currant jelly, ⅛ teaspoon allspice, and 1 teaspoon horseradish. Spread over top of ham during last 15 minutes. Sprinkle slivered almonds over top. Enough for ½ ham or 5-pound canned or boned ham.

PICKLED PEACH GLAZE. Combine 1 cup peach jam, 4 tablespoons vinegar, ¼ teaspoon powdered cloves, ½ teaspoon cinnamon, and 1 tablespoon brown sugar. Spread half the mixture over ham before placing it in oven; add remaining glaze 15 minutes before ham should be done. Enough for ½ ham or 5-pound boned or canned ham. Double for whole ham or 10-pound canned ham.

Baked Ham with Barbecue Sauce

A delicious way to prepare canned or boned rolled ready-to-eat ham: the sauce makes the meat juicier, adds delightful flavor.

½ cup tomato sauce
⅛ teaspoon powdered cloves
⅛ teaspoon allspice
1 tablespoon soy sauce

1 tablespoon prepared
  horseradish
¼ cup sweet cider or syrup
  from canned peaches or pears

Combine all ingredients. Marinate ham in mixture before baking. Transfer meat to shallow baking pan or casserole. Bake at 325° F., allowing 10 minutes per pound, or until meat thermometer registers 130°. Baste occasionally with marinade.

Sherried Ham Roast

Marinate a canned or boned ham in an entire bottle of inexpensive domestic sherry for 24 hours. Remove from sherry, brush melted butter over top, sprinkle top with sugar, and bake as in preceding recipe, basting occasionally with the sherry.

POT ROASTS AND BOILED DINNERS

Basically a pot roast is a solid piece of meat not tender enough to roast in an oven or over direct heat, so it must be slow-cooked in liquid. Most are cooked on the top of the stove in a heavy pot or kettle, but there are also "oven pot roasts" wrapped in foil and baked at low heat in the oven, or a pot roast may be cooked in a covered casserole or earthenware pot in the oven. There will be considerable waste of meat from shrinkage, but since the meat juices go into the sauce, what is lost in number of serving portions is regained in the sublimity of the sauce—that is, if care is taken in removing all fat from the sauce before serving.

A pot roast differs from *boiled beef* primarily in the amount of liquid added to the pot; the latter must simmer in a large quantity of liquid, though the liquid should merely simmer or "smile," not really boil. Also, a pot roast is usually (but not always) seared before liquid is added. The reason for searing is to draw out the gelatinous essence from the meat and brown it, to give deeper color and that special brown-gravy flavor to the sauce. The meat itself, after long cooking in liquid, will lose much of its brown crust, so if the sauce is attractive in color and delicious in flavor, searing is not really necessary.

Beef Pot Roast (Basic Recipe)

1 4- to 5-pound bottom round (rump) or chuck of beef, or beef brisket
2 tablespoons oil or shortening
2 medium onions, peeled (or 2 leeks)
2 carrots, scraped, cubed

1 celery stalk, diced
1 tablespoon salt
3 to 4 cups water or other liquid
Herbs and other seasonings
1 tablespoon catsup, or 1 teaspoon tomato paste (optional)
2 or 3 whole cloves

Wash meat thoroughly; trim off excess fat. Sear in hot oil or shortening in heavy pot until well browned on both sides. Add vegetables, liquid, and seasonings as desired. Bring to a boil; skim once or twice. Cover pot. Lower heat, simmer covered 3 to 3½ hours or until meat is very tender. (Test by piercing with fork.) Remove meat. Strain and measure broth. If time allows, cool liquid so fat will rise to top and can easily be skimmed off. Better, cook a day ahead and chill broth so fat will congeal on top and can be scraped off. Strain the stock, or purée by beating in blender (after such long cooking, the vegetables will have disintegrated.) Reheat meat by simmering in strained stock; add fresh vegetables, such as green beans, diced carrots, small whole onions, lima beans, mushroom caps or diced turnip. Simmer until meat is thoroughly hot and vegetables just tender—about ½ hour. Remove meat to a platter, vegetables to a serving dish. Thicken the sauce with flour, cornstarch, or fried bread (see Sauce Techniques, How to Thicken Liquids, Book 1), using 2 tablespoons flour or 1 tablespoon cornstarch per cup of liquid, or 1 slice fried bread for 4 cups. Simmer until thickened. Serve sauce separately. *Makes about 3 cups sauce; pot roast should make 8 to 10 servings, perhaps more.*

VARIATIONS. Seasonings: The most commonly used herbs are thyme, basil, marjoram, and/or bay leaf. A sprig of parsley never hurts. A little grated lemon rind gives nice piquancy. For spicier flavor, black pepper, mace, cayenne, or a pinch of ginger may be added to taste.

Liquids: Tomato, canned or fresh, is often added (in which case reduce amount of water). Table wine or sherry may be added to taste (but be careful about adding old table wine; it may have gone sour and could ruin the sauce). Sour cream or heavy sweet cream may be added to the sauce at the last moment: in this case, boil down the sauce to reduce in volume before adding the cream.

SUGGESTED GO-WITHS. Always serve mashed or boiled potatoes or noodles with pot roast as a foil for the rich gravy. If vegetables have been cooked with the meat, nothing else is needed but a green salad.

Tender Blade Roast

This method can be used to make an inexpensive cut of beef taste very good indeed.

About 4 pounds blade chuck
   roast
1 cup olive oil
1 shriveled lemon, quartered
1 clove garlic, crushed
2 tablespoons minced parsley

Vegetables
Canned tomato
½ cup dry sherry
Salt
Herbs

Prick meat all over with long-tined kitchen fork. Heat the olive oil with the lemon, garlic, and parsley until the lemon rind is well browned. Pour *while hot* over the meat. Marinate meat at room temperature for 1 hour. Remove meat from marinade, pat with absorbent paper to remove excess oil, then sear over high heat in heavy pot until well browned on all sides. Proceed as for basic recipe: Add soup vegetables (onion, carrot, celery), canned tomato and ½ cup dry sherry for the liquid, salt and herbs to taste. Simmer, covered, over very low heat for 3 hours. *Makes 6 or 7 servings*, depending on amount of bone in roast and degree of shrinkage.

Garofalato alla Roma

4 pounds rump of beef
2 cloves garlic
¼ cup minced Italian parsley
¼ cup olive oil
2 large onions, chopped

1 large (1-pound 12-ounce) can
   Italian tomatoes
2 teaspoons salt
¼ to ½ teaspoon orégano
⅛ teaspoon ground cloves

The meat should be in one solid piece, with little or no fat. Slit garlic cloves lengthwise, roll in the minced parsley, and insert these at several places in the meat, first cutting slits in meat with small sharp knife, then inserting garlic in the slits. Brown the meat on all sides in the olive oil; transfer to deep pot or Dutch oven. Simmer the chopped onion in the olive oil until soft, but not brown; add the canned tomatoes, salt, orégano, cloves, and remaining minced parsley. Simmer about 20 minutes until reduced and thickened; force through sieve or food mill, return to stove, and continue cooking until of purée consistency. Pour over meat in pot; cover pot tightly, cook over very low heat until meat is very tender—about 3 hours. *Makes 10 to 12 servings.*

MACARONI GAROFALATO. If any is left over—either meat, sauce, or both—turn it into a superb macaroni casserole: layer meat, cooked macaroni, and ricotta cheese with sauce, finishing with macaroni. Place thin slices of mozzarella cheese over top, bake at 350° F. until cheese is melted and lightly browned—about 35 minutes.

Catalan Pot Roast

1 3- to 4-pound boned, rolled rump of beef or chuck	1 1-pound can tomatoes
¼ teaspoon marjoram	1 tablespoon sugar
2 bay leaves, crushed	¼ teaspoon cinnamon
1 clove garlic, crushed	⅛ teaspoon cloves
4 tablespoons olive oil	1 cup red wine
1 green pepper, minced	1 tablespoon red wine vinegar
1 small onion, chopped	2 to 3 teaspoons salt

With a mortar and pestle, crush together the marjoram, bay leaf, and garlic with 1 teaspoon of the oil. Mix this with the green pepper and onion and rub over the meat. Let stand an hour. Place remaining olive oil in a deep heavy pot or Dutch oven, place the meat in it, sear in the oil over high heat, then add the tomatoes, sugar, cinnamon, cloves, wine, vinegar, and salt. Cover tightly; cook at lowest heat for 3 to 4 hours until meat is fork-tender. Skim off excess fat from sauce; transfer meat to platter. *Makes 8 to 10 servings.*

SUGGESTED GO-WITHS. Rice, green salad; fruit compote.

Boeuf à la Mode

A very elegant, sumptuous French pot roast whose secret of success is a combination of larding and marinating in wine before cooking. It should be started 2 days before serving.

1 4- to 5-pound boneless rump (bottom round) or brisket of beef	1 teaspoon thyme
Salt pork for larding	1 bay leaf (optional)
Minced parsley	4 whole cloves
2 large onions, sliced	2 cups red table wine
2 large carrots, scraped, cubed	¼ cup brandy
2 celery stalks with sprig of leaves, chopped	2 or 3 tablespoons oil or butter
	4 cups beef broth or stock
	1 split calf's foot (optional)

You may be able to get the butcher to lard the meat for you, but if not, and if you do not have a larding needle, cut deep narrow gashes in meat in several places, force strips of the pork fat into the meat as deep as possible. If you are doing this yourself, dip the pork in wine or brandy (the same to be used for the marinade) and roll in minced parsley before inserting in the meat.

Arrange in a deep bowl layers of the sliced vegetables mixed with the herbs and cloves. Place meat over half the vegetables; cover with remaining vegetables. Add wine and brandy. Marinate 6 hours at room temperature or 24 hours in refrigerator. Turn beef at least once.

Remove from marinade, wipe meat with absorbent paper. Sear meat in hot oil or butter until well browned on all sides. Pour off fat, add the vegetable-wine-brandy marinade and beef broth, and the calf's foot, if you can find one. Simmer covered until meat is very tender—2½ to 3 hours. Remove meat and calf's foot (discard calf's foot). Strain broth; chill so that fat will come to top and can be completely removed. Trim meat of all fat; cut in thick slices. To reheat meat for serving, boil sauce to reduce to 3 cups; taste and adjust seasoning (add salt if needed), then reheat sliced meat in the sauce. *Makes 8 to 10 servings.*

SUGGESTED GO-WITHS. Parsley potatoes, glazed carrots, watercress salad; for dessert, Clafotis Limousin.

Estufado Machado

This Spanish version of larded pot roast is less complicated to prepare, especially when baked in foil by the American technique, and it's superb.

1 3½- to 4-pound boned, rolled chuck roast	½ teaspoon grated lemon peel
	1 teaspoon paprika
¼ teaspoon freshly ground black pepper	1 or 2 cloves garlic, crushed
	2 tablespoons olive oil
¼ teaspoon tarragon	

Pierce meat with skewer or cut tiny slashes in surface with sharp knife. Combine seasonings with olive oil; force into slits in meat, pushing down with back of spoon. Sear meat under broiler until well browned on all sides. Place meat in center of large sheet of heavy-duty foil; close foil, sealing all edges with double fold to form airtight package. Do not add any liquid or salt. Place in shallow roasting pan in oven set at 250° F.; roast 4 hours. When unwrapped, about 1½ cups of sauce will have formed. Pour sauce into saucepan, skim off excess fat, strain, boil until reduced to half. Add salt as needed. Serve clear as Continental-type sauce, or thicken with flour if American-type gravy is preferred. Sauce is rich, spicy. *Makes 8 to 10 servings.*

Corned Beef and Cabbage

1 4- to 5-pound corned brisket of beef	1 medium green cabbage, cut in wedges
Water to cover	Prepared horseradish or mustard

Most corned beef today is sold in packages with cooking directions on the outside. The term "corned" means that it has been cured with salt or a chemical process. Therefore, never add salt to the water! Cook, covered, with water until meat is tender (easily pierced with fork)—about 3 hours. When meat is tender, add wedges of cabbage to the kettle, cook 10 to 15 minutes longer. Serve the corned beef on a platter with the cabbage. Pass horseradish or mustard (or both) as a sauce. Serve with boiled potatoes (which may also be cooked in the same pot, allowing 25 minutes, if desired). *Makes 10 to 12 servings.*

Leftover corned beef is excellent sliced for sandwiches, or for making hash, or for Red Flannel Hash.

New England Boiled Dinner

1 4-pound corned brisket of beef	6 potatoes, pared, quartered
6 to 8 small to medium yellow	½ green cabbage, cut in wedges
onions, peeled	Celery-Horseradish Sauce,
2 turnips, peeled, cubed	or Mustard-Cream Sauce
6 carrots, scraped, cubed	

Cook corned beef according to package directions. About 1 hour before it should be done, add the onions. Cook uncovered during final ½ hour. In last 30 minutes, add turnips, carrots, and potatoes. In last 15 minutes, add the cabbage. Serve corned beef on platter surrounded by vegetables. Pass the hot sauce in a gravy boat. *Makes 10 to 12 servings.*

ANOTHER WAY. Instead of corned beef, use a picnic ham butt. Remove meat before serving, scrape away the rind, cut in slices to serve surrounded with the vegetables.

Boiled Beef with Horseradish Sauce

This fine German dish is especially good for those on reducing diets (who should skip the horseradish blended with cream, and content themselves with plain prepared horseradish as a sauce, or with a blend of applesauce and horseradish).

1 4- to 5-pound rump or	2 sprigs parsley
brisket of beef	1 bay leaf
Beef marrow bones	1 stalk celery
2 medium carrots, scraped, cubed	4 peppercorns
2 medium onions, stuck with	6 cups water
whole cloves	

The day before, place all ingredients in a soup kettle; bring to a boil, lower heat, simmer 3 hours or until meat is very tender (fork pierces it easily). Remove meat from broth. Strain broth; discard vegetables and marrow bones. Chill broth so fat will rise to top; scrape off fat. Reheat meat next day in the strained broth. Serve hot with Horseradish Cream, or Celery Horseradish Sauce, or applesauce blended with a little horseradish, accompanied by Saltzkartoffeln and red cabbage. (Serve the strained broth separately as soup for the first course, with or without dumplings.) *Makes 10 to 12 servings.*

Pot-au-Feu

Basically this is a simple French family dish which differs from German Boiled Beef primarily in the way a stock is prepared first, then the beef cooked in the stock with vegetables. However, those French families who can afford it often make the stock of such lavish ingredients as a 5-pound stewing hen and shin bones. Gourmet versions of this country dish are sometimes very elaborate, indeed. The following is a shortened, more possible version—but in essence this is still as plebeian a dish as the New England Boiled Dinner.

1 1-pound hind shank of beef
1 chicken drumstick
Beef marrow bones or veal
  knuckle
1 leek
2 onions, stuck with
  whole cloves
Celery sprigs
½ teaspoon thyme
1 bay leaf
1 tablespoon beef stock con-

centrate, or 3 beef bouillon
  cubes
1 4- to 5- pound rump or
  brisket of beef
3 large carrots, scraped, cubed
10 to 12 small white onions
2 stalks celery, chopped
2 parsnips or white turnips,
  scraped, quartered
Melted butter
1 teaspoon minced parsley

The day before, combine in a soup kettle the hind shank of beef, chicken, marrow bones or veal knuckle, leek, onions, celery, thyme, bay leaf, and stock concentrate. Add 2 quarts cold water; bring slowly to a boil. When liquid is boiling hard, skim repeatedly until almost clear. Lower heat; simmer 3 hours. Turn off heat; cool liquid. Remove meat, chicken, and bones. When cool enough to handle, cut off and chop all edible pieces of meat; put these aside for the soup. Strain broth. Chill so fat will congeal on top and can be removed.

Next day, place rump or brisket of beef in strained broth; bring to a boil; simmer about 3 hours until meat is tender. During last ½ hour add remaining uncooked vegetables; cook until tender. Remove meat, cut in thick slices, place in casserole. Remove vegetables with slotted spoon, place around meat. Add a little of broth to keep moist. Keep warm in oven until needed.

Serve the broth as a first course as soup with the bits of chopped meat and marrow from marrow bones. Serve meat and vegetables as a second course, basted with melted butter and sprinkled with minced parsley. Nothing else is needed but good crisp bread, a simple red table wine, and fruit for dessert. *Makes 10 to 12 servings.*

EASY POT-AU-FEU. Simmer a rump of beef in beef bouillon made with stock concentrate plus a stalk of chopped celery, instant minced onion, and a pinch of thyme. During last ½ hour, add peeled quartered vegetables. Serve the soup first as a clear soup, the meat and vegetables as the main course, basted with melted butter and sprinkled with parsley.

Sauerbraten

1 4- to 5-pound rump of beef

VINEGAR MARINADE

2 cups red wine vinegar	1 bay leaf
4 cups water	¼ teaspoon thyme
1 large onion, sliced	2 whole cloves
4 peppercorns	Parsley sprigs

SAUCE

¼ cup flour	(like gingerbread-man cookies)
4 tablespoons butter or	or crushed gingersnaps
other shortening	2 tablespoons gravy coloring
2 carrots, scraped, cubed	½ cup red wine
2 whole onions	1 cup currants or raisins
1 tablespoon tomato catsup	½ cup slivered toasted almonds
½ cup grated dry gingerbread	Cranberry-Orange Relish

Place beef in bowl. Combine ingredients for marinade, bring to a boil, pour boiling hot over meat. Marinate meat in cool place for 3 days, turning several times. Remove from marinade (saving the marinade); wipe dry. Dredge with flour; sear in butter in heavy pot. Add vegetables, catsup, and 1 cup of strained marinade. Cover; simmer until very tender—2½ to 3 hours. Remove meat to platter; skim fat from top of sauce, strain or purée sauce in blender. Measure liquid and add water if necessary to make 2 cups. Add grated gingerbread or gingersnaps, gravy coloring, wine, and currants or raisins; bring to a boil; cook until thickened. Serve the meat sliced, covered with the sauce, with almonds sprinkled over the top. Pass the cranberry relish. (In Germany, lingonberry sauce is served with Sauerbraten, but Cranberry-Orange Relish is a good substitute.) Should be accompanied by mashed potatoes, noodles, or potato dumplings. *Makes 10 to 12 servings.*

BAVARIAN STYLE. Instead of vinegar marinade, soak beef for 24 hours in mixture of 4 cups beer, 2 cups water, 1 lemon, sliced, peppercorns, onion, and bay leaf. Remove meat from marinade, and as in previous version, simmer in broth to which part of strained marinade has been added, until tender. Strain and skim fat from sauce; thicken with butter-flour roux and stir in ½ cup sour cream just before serving.

NORTH GERMAN SAUERBRATEN. Instead of beef, use boned shoulder of pork or fresh ham, and instead of vinegar marinade, use a quart of buttermilk; marinate 24 hours in refrigerator. Sear meat in fat, cook like any pot roast in water, but add ½ cup red wine and 1 tablespoon vinegar for part of the liquid.

Cocido, or Olla Podrida

This is the Spanish version of pot-au-feu. It is also sometimes called *puchero.* The name *olla podrida* means literally "putrid pot" and refers to the way the soup or pot roast may be the receptacle for countless leftovers added from day to day each time it is reheated.

2 pounds rump or brisket of beef	1 pound garbanzos, previously soaked
1 large chicken leg, or ½ stewing chicken	4 onions, peeled, whole
Beef marrow bone or veal knuckle	2 carrots, scraped, cubed
¼ pound lean ham	1 turnip, peeled, quartered
¼ pound chorizo sausage	2 or 3 sprigs parsley
Water to cover	Turnip greens or shredded cabbage
Salt	Olive oil
	Vinegar

Place beef, chicken, marrow bone or veal knuckle, ham, and sausage in kettle. Add water, 1 tablespoon salt to begin with, and the garbanzos, which should have been soaking since the day before. Bring to a boil, skim repeatedly for about 15 minutes, then lower heat; cook, covered, for 2 hours. Add vegetables (except turnip greens); continue to cook until vegetables and garbanzos are tender. Add turnip greens during last 15 minutes. Remove meat and vegetables to platter with slotted spoon. Sprinkle best-quality olive oil and a few drops of vinegar over the meat from cruets. Serve the broth as a first-course soup, followed by meat and vegetables. *This makes 8 to 10 servings.* It is even better when reheated the second (or third, or fourth) time.

Oven Pot Roast (Basic Recipe)

This is an American original for which we can be duly proud. It is easy, the sauce is luscious, and there is less waste from shrinkage than with other methods of cooking meats classified as "pot roasts."

Place a 4-pound rump of beef in the center of a very large sheet of heavy-duty aluminum foil (or, better, use 2 sheets of foil). Sprinkle the meat with salt. Add a little sliced onion, if desired. Wrap and seal securely. Place in shallow baking pan; bake in 250° F. oven ("cool") for 4 hours. When the packet is opened, about 1½ cups of liquid will be found. Remove meat to platter. Pour liquid into a tall narrow receptacle (like a 4-quart Pyrex pitcher) and skim off fat. Season the unthickened sauce to taste; serve as a clear sauce over the sliced meat.

VARIATIONS. Besides sliced onion, add sliced mushrooms, diced carrot, a garlic clove, and grated lemon rind (or slivers of lemon peel). Or place a tomato, peeled, chopped, over the meat. Vegetables cooked with the meat will disintegrate, so consider them as primarily sauce ingredients. A little brandy (1 or 2 tablespoons) will add interesting flavor to the sauce; or try adding sherry or vermouth (about ¼ cup). For a sauce of deeper color, add a little gravy coloring or tomato paste.

Veal in Fruit Sauce

Place a boned rolled shoulder of veal (about 4 pounds after boning) in the center of a double thickness of aluminum foil. Dot the meat with butter; add mixture of 4 scallions, sliced, ¼ cup raisins, ¼ cup orange juice, ¼ teaspoon cinnamon, and 2 teaspoons salt (for a 4-pound roast). Seal securely by crimping edges of foil; bake 4 to 5 hours in oven set at 275° F. Serve meat with unthickened sauce, or thicken with cornstarch. *Makes about 10 servings.*

Swiss Steak

1 2-pound chuck steak or roast, 1½ inches thick
½ cup flour
1 teaspoon salt
Freshly ground black pepper
4 to 6 tablespoons shortening
2 large onions, sliced
3 cups beef broth

This can be a bargain steak or roast, a less tender cut. Dredge the outside with flour blended with salt and plenty of pepper. Heat the shortening to sizzling in a heavy deep skillet or top-of-stove casserole. Sear the meat over high heat until brown-crusted on both sides. Remove meat. Lower heat; add onions, cook until golden and soft. Remove onions; replace meat in pan, top with the onions. Add beef broth (which may be made with concentrate). Cook, covered, over low heat until meat is very tender, about 2 hours. Serve from the casserole, with mashed or baked potatoes, spinach or kale, and carrot sticks. *Makes 6 to 8 servings.*

WITH TOMATO SAUCE. Use only 2 cups beef broth, and add 2 cups tomato sauce to meat.

STEWS

Nothing else in cookery offers such creative opportunity as a stew. You can make a stew of any kind of meat, and the entire spectrum of vegetables, herbs, and sauce combinations awaits your bidding. Most stews taste better when reheated. They freeze beautifully. They can be inexpensive and simple for family meals, or exotic and glamorous for company. Learn to make a stew properly, and you've found the secret of dozens of different fun dishes.

Stew (Basic Recipe)

1½ pounds boneless meat (beef, veal, lamb, or pork), or 2½ pounds meat with bone, or 1½ to 2 cups cubed leftover meat
Flour
Salt and other seasonings, as desired
2 to 3 tablespoons fat

Onions, leeks, or shallots, sliced
Garlic (optional)
Fresh or dried herbs (thyme, bay leaf, celery, parsley, marjoram, etc.)
2 to 3 cups liquid
1 or 2 cups other vegetables*

Sear *raw* meat in fat until browned on all sides. *For a crisper surface,* dredge meat in seasoned flour before browning in fat. (Omit this step when using cooked leftover meat for stew.) Add onions and garlic to the fat, cook until soft. Mash garlic into the fat with tines of fork. Add herbs or spices, stir to blend with fat. (Leftover cooked meat is added at this stage.)

The liquid may be almost anything but pure water: tomato

Suggested Vegetables. Carrots, green beans, green peas, celery, green peppers, mushrooms, kernel corn, limas, white or sweet potatoes.

juice, wine, fruit juice, broth, or a combination of any two or
three of these. The broth, of course, may be made with bouillon
cubes or stock concentrate, and in this case use less salt. (For
choice of wine, see Using Wine in Cooking, Book 5.) Sometimes
a little of the syrup from canned fruit can also be added with
astonishingly good results (and the sweetness will not be noticeable). Sometimes, too, condensed soups may be added, as in
Beef à la Jensen, or Beef Stew Lyonnaise.

Onions should always be cooked *with* the meat, as should
such vegetables as turnips, celery, and parsnips. Carrots are
also sometimes added at the beginning, but will have better flavor if added only during the last ½ hour. Other vegetables,
fresh or frozen, should be added only toward the end of the
cooking period, including potatoes.

For various ways to thicken the sauce for the stew, see How to
Thicken Sauces, in Book 1.

Yields. Amounts in this basic recipe make *4 or 5 servings. For
6 servings,* use 2 pounds boneless meat, or 3 to 3½ pounds meat
with bone; increase liquid to 3 cups. *For 2 servings,* use ¾ to 1
pound boneless meat, or 1½ to 2 pounds meat with bone, and
1½ cups liquid (or, better, make the full recipe, refrigerate or
freeze for a second appearance).

For a *Weight Watchers' Stew,* eliminate browning of meat
and onions in fat (see Irish Stew), serve with a thin sauce, using
only 1 tablespoon cornstarch for 2 to 2½ cups liquid. Do not add
green peas, limas, or potatoes, instead use such low-calorie vegetables as celery, carrots, tomatoes, green beans.

Ragout Niçoise

Prepare stew according to basic recipe, using either boneless
beef or pork as the meat. With the sliced onion, cook 2 garlic
cloves, add ¼ teaspoon allspice, 1 teaspoon paprika, and ½ teaspoon thyme. Use 1 cup white wine or 1 cup tomato juice for
part of liquid. During last half-hour add diced carrot, seeded
and chopped red or green sweet pepper, and ½ cup pitted black
olives or pimiento-stuffed green olives.

Beef Stew Lyonnaise

Prepare stew according to basic recipe, using boneless beef
for stew; omit onions, but add 1 envelope onion soup mix with 3
cups liquid, 2 tablespoons catsup, and 1 tablespoon vinegar.

Omit salt. Simmer until meat is tender. Serve topped with minced parsley.

Lamb Stew al Jerez

Make lamb stew according to basic recipe, using 4 pounds lamb for stew (with bone); sauté meat in olive oil. Add 1 teaspoon powdered cumin, 1 teaspoon cinnamon, and ¼ teaspoon cloves to fat, and cook 2 tomatoes (peeled, chopped) with the onions and garlic. For liquid, add 1 cup dry sherry and 2 cups water; salt to taste. During last 15 minutes of cooking, add 1 package frozen limas. Serve with saffron rice. *Makes 10 servings.*

Swedish Lamb Stew

Make lamb stew according to basic recipe for stew, using boned lamb from leg or should r. Instead of sliced onions, add 12 small whole onions; for liquid, use 1 can (1 pound) peeled tomatoes and 1 cup chicken broth made with concentrate. Add 1 tablespoon chopped fresh or frozen dill for seasoning. Thicken as desired. Serve with noodles or boiled potatoes.

Beef à la Jensen

Prepare beef stew according to basic recipe for stew, adding 1 4-ounce can pimientos, drained and diced, with onions. For liquid, first add 1 cup water, then, after meat has simmered about 1 hour, tightly covered, add 1 can condensed tomato soup (undiluted). Stir to blend, cook until meat is tender—about ½ hour longer. Just before serving, turn off heat, stir in 1 cup sour cream. Serve with mashed or baked potatoes; sprinkle minced chives over top.

Hungarian Beef Gulyás

1½ pounds beef for stew, cut in cubes
2 to 3 tablespoons shortening
1 tablespoon imported paprika
½ teaspoon salt
1 green pepper, seeded, cut in squares
2 large onions, sliced
1 or 2 carrots, scraped, cubed
¼ cup tomato sauce
2 cups beef broth (made with concentrate)
1 tablespoon cornstarch, or 2 tablespoons instant-type flour

Heat 2 tablespoons shortening to sizzling in heavy pot; add meat; brown on all sides over high heat. Add paprika and salt; stir so that meat is covered with paprika. Add green pepper, sauté until slightly browned; remove pepper. Add onions and carrot and an additional tablespoon shortening if needed. Cook over moderate heat until lightly browned. Remove carrots; set aside with green pepper. Add tomato sauce and beef broth to pan; simmer, covered, over very low heat until meat is very tender—2 to 2½ hours. Replace green pepper and carrot in sauce about 10 minutes before serving. Thicken sauce with cornstarch or flour dissolved in a little cold water; cook until sauce is thickened and smooth. *Makes 4 or 5 servings.*

SUGGESTED GO-WITHS. Mashed or boiled potatoes, green salad, hot rolls; for dessert, cherry pie.

Boeuf Bourguignonne (French Beef Stew)

3 pounds stewing beef, cut in large cubes
About ¼ cup flour
2 teaspoons salt, or to taste
Freshly ground black pepper
¼ cup (2 ounces) diced salt pork
2 tablespoons olive oil
2 medium onions, chopped
1 clove garlic, minced (optional)
1 tomato, peeled, seeded, chopped, or 1 teaspoon tomato paste
2 cups red wine
¼ cup brandy
1 cup beef broth
1 bay leaf
10 to 12 small white onions, peeled
¼ pound button mushrooms
2 tablespoons butter
1 tablespoon sugar
Minced parsley for garnish

Dredge the beef with flour blended with salt and pepper. Place salt pork in skillet, heat until most of fat has been drawn out and cubes of pork are crisply browned. Remove pork cubes; save for garnish. Add olive oil to fat in pan; heat to sizzling, add beef, quickly sear until well browned on all sides. Remove meat temporarily; add onions, garlic, and tomato; cook until onion is soft. Pour off fat and oil. Replace meat; add wine, brandy, beef broth, and bay leaf. Cook, tightly covered, for 2½ to 3 hours over very low heat.

During last hour, parboil the onions until tender; drain. Sauté mushrooms in butter until lightly browned. Remove mushrooms with slotted spoon; add to meat. Add sugar to butter in skillet, add the onions, and glaze, turning until golden on all sides. Remove onions; add to meat. Stir 1 tablespoon flour into butter, cook until brown and bubbling; add fat skimmed from top of sauce in which meat has been cooking, then another tablespoon flour, cook until mixture bubbles. Add more sauce from casserole, stir to blend, then return this sauce to casserole and cook 10 minutes over moderate heat. (If sauce is not a rich deep brown in color, add a tablespoon of gravy coloring.) Serve stew from the casserole, sprinkled with parsley and with reserved salt pork for garnish. *Makes 8 servings.*

SUGGESTED GO-WITHS. Mashed or parsleyed potatoes, Brussels sprouts or carrots, green salad; for dessert, Camembert cheese and grapes.

Carbonnade Flamande

This is basically the same as Boeuf Bourguignonne, except that beer is used for the liquid (instead of red wine and brandy) Also, a *bouquet garni* of herbs (thyme, bay leaf, and marjoram) is used for seasoning in place of bay leaf (though some recipes for Boeuf Bourguignonne also call for a *bouquet garni*).

Beef Bourbonnaise (Bourbon-flavored Beef Stew)

Prepare as for Boeuf Bourguignonne, but for the liquid, use 3 cups beef broth (made with stock concentrate). ½ cup bourbon, and 1 tablespoon red wine vinegar. Instead of mushrooms, add 1 10-ounce package frozen tiny peas during last 15 minutes of cooking.

Catalán Beef Stew

2 ounces salt pork, cubed	chopped
2 tablespoons olive oil	½ cup red or white table wine
2 slices stale bread	1 bay leaf
2 pounds stewing beef, cubed	Salt, pepper
2 medium onions, chopped	1 cup beef broth
1 clove garlic, minced	¼ cup brandy or sherry
1 medium tomato, peeled,	

Cook salt pork in olive oil until cubes are crisp; remove. Add bread to fat; fry until crisp on both sides; remove. Add beef; sear until well browned on all sides. Remove. Add onion and garlic; cook until soft; add tomato, simmer 5 minutes. Pour off excess fat. Return meat to pan. Cook, tightly covered over lowest heat, for 1 hour. Soften the fried bread in the wine, add to the meat with bay leaf, salt, pepper, broth, and brandy. Simmer until meat is tender—about 1 hour longer. Serve garnished with crisp pork. *Makes 6 servings.*

Carne con Chili

1 pound stewing beef, cut in
   small cubes
3 to 4 tablespoons shortening
2 to 3 tablespoons chili powder,
   or to taste
4 large onions, sliced (2 cups)
2 or 3 garlic cloves, minced
4 green tomatoes, quartered, or

1 1-pound can peeled
   whole tomatoes
1 cup water or beef broth
Salt
1 tablespoon brown sugar
1 tablespoon vinegar
1 slice stale bread
1 1-pound can red kidney beans

Sauté the beef in hot shortening until well browned on all sides. Add the chili powder; stir until meat is well coated with the spice. Add onions and garlic; cook until soft. Add salt, tomatoes, water or beef broth, brown sugar, and vinegar. (If using beef broth, reduce amount of salt.) Simmer, covered, over very low heat until meat is tender—about 2 hours. Rub stale bread with a cut clove of garlic; add to stew; add kidney beans; cook until stew is thickened. Serve from the casserole in which it cooked, with rice and a citrus salad. *Makes 4 to 5 servings.*

Chili con Carne

2 tablespoons shortening
2 cloves garlic
2 or 3 large onions, sliced
½ green pepper, seeded, chopped
1 tablespoon chili powder
½ teaspoon cumin
½ teaspoon orégano

1 pound ground meat
1 1-pound can peeled tomatoes,
   or 1 8-ounce can tomato sauce
1 1-pound can red kidney beans,
   with liquid
1 cup water or broth
Salt

Heat shortening to sizzling, add split garlic cloves and onions; cook until soft. Mash garlic into fat with tines of fork. Add green pepper, chili powder, cumin, and orégano; cook 2 minutes. Add ground meat; cook, stirring, until it loses its pink color. Add tomatoes (or sauce) and kidney beans with liquid. Add water or beef broth made with stock concentrate, and salt to taste. (If broth is used, salt may not be necessary.) Simmer, covered, about 40 minutes. Serve with rice and a green salad. *Makes 6 servings.*

For 2 or 3 servings, prepare full recipe, freeze the rest for another time—it will taste still better when reheated.

Beef Stroganoff

2 pounds boneless beef,
   top or bottom round

2 tablespoons flour
2 tablespoons shortening

1 teaspoon paprika
4 medium onions, sliced
1 tablespoon tomato paste,
  or 2 tablespoons tomato catsup
2 cups beef broth (made with

concentrate)
Salt
1 tablespoon cornstarch
1 cup sour cream

The original Beef Stroganoff was made with fillet of beef, cut in thin slivers, briefly cooked. Top round of beef (round steak) can be so prepared, and cooking time will be shorter. But a very delicious Stroganoff can also be made with bottom round or chuck, and the longer, slower cooking produces a richer-flavored sauce. Cut bottom round in 1- or 1½-inch cubes.

Dredge meat with flour; sear in hot fat. Add paprika; stir so meat is colored. Remove meat. Add onions, cook over moderate heat until soft. Add tomato paste. Replace meat. Add beef broth. Cook, covered, until meat is tender. If slivers of top round are used, ½ hour may be enough cooking time. If less tender beef is used, cut in larger pieces, allow 2 to 2½ hours. Taste for seasoning; add salt if needed. Thicken with cornstarch thinned with a little cold water; simmer until sauce is smooth and thickened.

Turn off heat. Add some of hot sauce to sour cream, then stir sour cream into remaining sauce. Serve from a casserole, topped with minced chives for garnish, accompanied by mashed potatoes, broccoli, and tomato aspic on lettuce (or serve tomato soup as a first course); pear compote with crème de menthe would make a fine dessert. *Makes 6 servings.*

For 8 to 10 servings, use 3 pounds beef, increase remaining ingredients by one-half.

VEAL STROGANOFF. Use cubed veal instead of beef in above recipe.

PORK STROGANOFF. Use cubed shoulder of pork or fresh ham in basic recipe.

QUICK STROGANOFF. Buy round steak; cut into slivers; sauté quickly in fat. Add 1 can beef gravy, 2 tablespoons instant minced onion, 1 teaspoon tomato paste, and ¼ cup red wine. Simmer, uncovered, for 10 minutes. Turn off heat; stir in ½ cup sour cream.

Irish Stew

1½ pounds boned lamb or beef
for stew, or 2½ pounds
lamb for stew, with bone
2½ cups water
1½ teaspoons salt
2 medium onions, peeled,
quartered
2 large carrots, scraped, cubed
1 turnip, peeled, diced

1 bay leaf, or ¼ teaspoon
thyme
Sprig of celery leaves,
or ¼ teaspoon celery seed
1 peeled, chopped tomato or
1 tablespoon catsup (optional)
Freshly ground black pepper
6 small potatoes, peeled
(optional)

Place all ingredients but potatoes in heavy pot. Bring to a boil;
cook, tightly covered, over very low heat until meat is very
tender—2 to 3 hours. Add potatoes during last ½ hour. For a
low-calorie entree, omit potatoes, serve sauce unthickened, but
if calories need not be counted, thicken with 1 envelope gravy
mix for better appearance and flavor. Simmer 10 to 15 minutes
after thickening. This is a one-dish meal which needs nothing
else but a dessert (which should be raw fruit for weight watchers). *Makes 4 or 5 servings.*

Ragout of Beef Manhattan

This dish is a superb example of how a simple stew can be
turned into a sumptuous entree.

2 pounds beef for stew
Flour seasoned with salt and
pepper
2 tablespoons butter, or 1
tablespoon each butter and
olive oil
8 to 10 small white onions, peeled
2 carrots, scraped, cubed
½ teaspoon powdered fennel
1 tablespoon chopped fresh or

frozen dill, or 1 teaspoon dill
weed
1½ cups water
2 beef bouillon cubes, or 2 teaspoons beef stock concentrate
½ cup syrup from canned peaches
¼ cup cream sherry
1 4-ounce can button mushrooms

Dredge the meat with flour; sauté until well browned in butter
or butter and oil. Add onions, carrots, herbs, water, bouillon
cubes, peach syrup, and sherry. Bring to a boil; cover, simmer
over lowest heat until meat is tender, 1½ to 2 hours. Add mushrooms during last 20 minutes. Thicken with 1½ tablespoons
cornstarch or with balls of flour blended with softened butter (2
tablespoons flour with 1 tablespoon softened butter). *Makes 6
servings.*

Veal Paprika

2 pounds boneless veal, cubed
¼ cup flour
½ teaspoon salt
Freshly ground black pepper
2 tablespoons each butter and
　olive oil
1 tablespoon paprika

1 small white onion, thinly
　sliced
1½ cups chicken broth (made
　with concentrate)
½ cup sour cream
Minced chives or parsley

Dredge the meat with mixture of flour, salt, and pepper. Melt butter with olive oil; brown meat in the fat, adding paprika to the fat. Add the onion; cook until soft. Pour off excess fat. Add chicken broth, simmer tightly covered over low heat until meat is tender. Turn off heat; blend sour cream with some of hot sauce, then combine the two. Turn heat on again to very low; cook, stirring, about 5 minutes longer. Serve with chives or parsley sprinkled over the top, accompanied by noodles and Brussels sprouts. *Makes 6 servings.*

PORK CHOPS PAPRIKA can be made by the same recipe, but use 6 pork chops instead of veal, and only 1 tablespoon butter (no oil). Or, use 2 pounds lean pork, cubed, instead of veal. Serve accompanied by Escalloped Tomatoes and baked potatoes.

Beef Curry with Vegetables

2 to 3 pounds boneless chuck,
　cut in 1-inch cubes
2 tablespoons shortening
½ cup chopped onion
1 green pepper, seeded, minced
1 or 2 cloves garlic, minced
1½ tablespoons curry powder
½ cup seedless raisins

1 yellow summer squash,
　thickly sliced
3½ cups water
2 teaspoons salt
½ pound green beans, Frenched,
　or 1 package French-cut beans
1 package frozen lima beans
Shredded coconut

Brown the meat in the shortening in a skillet; transfer to top-of-stove 3-quart casserole or Dutch oven. Add onion, green pepper, garlic, and curry powder to fat; cook over moderate heat, stirring once or twice, until vegetables are soft but not brown. Add raisins, squash, water, and salt; simmer 2 or 3 minutes to blend well, then pour over meat in casserole. Cover; simmer until meat is tender—1½ to 2 hours. Let cool, then chill until ready to serve. (Preferably this part should be done preceding day.) Reheat when needed, add beans, simmer until vegetables are tender, about 20 minutes. Serve topped with shredded coconut accompanied by rice. *Makes 6 to 8 servings.*

Exotic Curry of Lamb

Instead of using commercial curry powder, try blending your own spices for curry. The combination given here produces a curry that is sweeter and spicier, not so biting hot as that made with a commercial blend.

1½ pounds boneless lamb, cubed	2 or 3 large onions, sliced
2 to 3 tablespoons vegetable shortening or clarified butter	2 or 3 garlic cloves, minced
1 teaspoon curry powder	1 tomato, peeled, seeded, chopped
¼ teaspoon nutmeg	1 tart apple, peeled, seeded, chopped
½ teaspoon cumin	
½ teaspoon ginger	¼ cup raisins or currants
¼ teaspoon powdered fennel or anise	2 cups chicken broth
	Salt
½ teaspoon cinnamon	Fresh cilantro or Italian parsley, minced
½ teaspoon freshly ground black pepper, or ¼ teaspoon dry mustard	Assorted condiments

Sauté the meat in hot shortening until well browned. Add all the ground spices; stir so meat is covered with the spices. Push meat to one side of pan, or remove. Add onions, garlic, and tomato; cook over lowered heat until soft. Spoon or pour off excess fat. Add apple and raisins and return meat to pan. Add half the chicken broth at a time, each time bringing to a boil. Lower heat; cover pan tightly; simmer until meat is very tender—about 2 hours. Taste for seasoning after first hour; add salt if needed. Improves in flavor if made a day ahead, then reheated. Serve in rice ring, sprinkled with minced fresh cilantro or parsley. Pass condiments. *Makes 6 servings.*

OTHER POSSIBLE CURRY SEASONINGS. Crushed cardamom seeds, powdered cloves, saffron, crushed red peppers (for a very hot curry), and paprika are frequently used in curry mixtures. Coriander, too, is a favorite Indian spice—unless fresh cilantro (*cilantro* is the Spanish word for coriander) is used as garnish. Herbs are also sometimes added, especially orégano (in small amounts), dill, and bay leaf. The use of commercial curry powder is not necessary, but I have found that it helps to use a little of the commercial blend along with other spices to achieve a subtle blend.

ASSORTED CONDIMENTS. Toasted slivered almonds, chopped pistachio nuts, shredded coconut, chutney (homemade or Major Grey's), chopped pitted dates, chopped peanuts, watermelon pickles, chopped pickled peaches, fried or plain sliced bananas, sliced raw onions in yogurt, thinly sliced cucumbers.

Korma Curry

2 pounds boneless lamb or top
  round of beef
2 medium onions, sliced
½ teaspoon powdered ginger
1 tablespoon crushed coriander
¼ teaspoon powdered cloves
2 or 3 cloves garlic
2 teaspoons salt
4 tablespoons clarified butter

  or shortening
3 carrots, quartered lengthwise,
  or 2 cups cubed eggplant
1 cup water
2 cups buttermilk or yogurt
1 teaspoon curry powder
Rice
Freshly ground black pepper
Lemon wedges

Buy the meat in one piece. Make a paste of about one-fourth of the sliced onion, the ginger, coriander, cloves, garlic, and salt, by crushing together with mortar and pestle or an electric blender. Rub this paste over the meat, working it well into the surface of the meat. Let stand 2 hours at room temperature. Slowly cook the remaining onion in the shortening until soft. Push to one side. Cut the meat in cubes, brown the meat slowly in the shortening, giving it plenty of time. Remove the meat and onions; add the carrots or eggplant; brown lightly. Replace the meat and onions; add the water; cook uncovered over very low heat until liquid is nearly evaporated, turning meat frequently. Add half the buttermilk or yogurt blended with curry powder; cook, uncovered, until reduced and thickened. Add remaining buttermilk; cover; cook until meat is tender. Or, transfer to casserole and complete cooking in oven set at 325° F. for 30 to 40 minutes. Serve with rice; grind black pepper over each serving at table, and serve with lemon wedges, the lemon to be sprinkled over the meat. *Makes 6 servings.*

Lamb Cochifrito

2 pounds boneless lamb, or 3½
  pounds lamb, with bone, cut for
  stew
Seasoned flour
1 clove garlic
3 to 4 tablespoons olive oil
1 tablespoon minced parsley

1 teaspoon paprika
Juice of ½ lemon (1 tablespoon)
1 cup water
1 tablespoon instant
  minced onion
1 package frozen artichoke
  hearts

Carefully cut away fat and muscle tissue; cut meat into cubes.
Roll in seasoned flour. Place whole garlic clove in oil, heat until
garlic is brown, then remove. Brown floured meat in oil until
brown on all sides; push to one side of pan. Add parsley and
paprika, cook a few seconds, then add lemon juice and water.
Cover, simmer until lamb is tender, about 1 hour. During last 10
minutes add artichoke hearts, cook until tender. Serve with
rice. *Makes 6 servings.*

Greek Lamb Stew with Okra

2 pounds boneless lamb, or 3
  pounds lamb cut for stew (hind
  shanks or shoulder)
¼ cup olive oil
¼ cup chopped yellow onion

2 cups tomato juice
¼ teaspoon thyme
1 teaspoon salt
1 package frozen okra
1 teaspoon lemon juice

Brown the meat in olive oil. Push to one side, cook onions until
soft. Add tomato juice, thyme, and salt. Bring to a boil; cook,
covered, until meat is tender—about 1½ hours. Add okra and
lemon juice during last 15 minutes. Serve with rice. *Makes 4
servings.*

GREEK LAMB STEW WITH GREEN BEANS. Instead of okra,
add ½ pound green beans.

Blanquette de Veau

3 to 3½ pounds boned veal* (from
  breast, shoulder, or rump), cubed
½ cup white wine
1 carrot, scraped, quartered
1 leek, sliced
Sprig of parsley
¼ teaspoon thyme
16 to 20 button mushrooms,
  trimmed
3 cups water

2 teaspoons salt
16 small white onions
2 tablespoons butter
2 tablespoons flour
2 egg yolks
2 tablespoons heavy cream
Juice of ½ lemon
Grated lemon rind
Minced parsley for garnish

  *Boned cubed pork can be used instead of veal for an equally deli-
cious entree.

ADVANCE PREPARATION

Marinate cubed veal in wine for 1 hour. Remove veal, saving wine. Place veal, carrot, leek, parsley, thyme, and mushroom trimmings in kettle or pot, add water and salt; cook, covered, 1½ hours, straining scum occasionally. Remove meat. Cool broth; strain and measure. Add reserved wine and enough water to make 3 cups.

Separately boil onions in salted water for 20 minutes or until fork-tender but still a little crisp; drain. Sauté trimmed mushrooms in butter until lightly browned; remove mushrooms, add to onions. Stir flour into butter, cook until mixture bubbles. Slowly stir in strained stock, bring to a boil, lower heat, cook 5 minutes, beating with whisk. Add meat; cook, covered, until meat is very tender. Add onions and mushrooms. (This part can be frozen for future use if desired.)

During last hour before dinner: Beat egg yolks until thick; stir in cream. Reheat veal in its sauce until steaming. Add hot sauce a little at a time to egg yolk mixture, beating constantly with whisk. When about 1 cup of hot sauce has been added, combine with remaining sauce in pot. Stir in lemon juice. Add mushrooms and onions. Transfer to ovenproof casserole. Sprinkle grated lemon rind and parsley over top. Keep in 200° F. oven until time to serve—up to 30 minutes. *Makes 8 to 10 servings.*

SUGGESTED GO-WITHS. Steamed rice, green peas or broccoli, tomato and lettuce salad; for dessert, peaches in port.

Veal de Naranja

2 pounds boneless veal, cubed	1 cup chicken broth
2 tablespoons flour	½ cup raisins
1 teaspoon salt	¼ cup ground almonds
4 tablespoons olive oil	¼ teaspoon cinnamon
1 small onion, chopped	⅛ teaspoon ground cloves
1 cup orange juice	

Dust veal with flour blended with salt. Brown in olive oil until crisp on all sides. Push to one side of pan, add onion, cook until soft. Add remaining ingredients, cover, simmer gently 1 hour. *Makes 6 to 8 servings.*

SUGGESTED GO-WITHS. Thin noodles, Italian beans, salad; for dessert, Brie and crackers, or cheesecake.

Porco Alentejana (Portuguese Pork and Clams)

1½ pounds lean pork tenderloin, cubed
1 tablespoon lemon juice
2 tablespoons flour blended with 1 teaspoon salt
3 tablespoons olive oil
1 small onion, chopped
1 or 2 cloves garlic, crushed
½ green pepper, seeded, chopped
(optional)
1 tomato, peeled, chopped
2 dashes Tabasco
½ cup dry white wine
½ cup water
1 pint clams, in shells, or 1 7-ounce can chopped sea clams
Minced parsley or fresh cilantro

Sprinkle pork with lemon juice, let stand 1 hour. Dust meat with flour and salt, sauté in olive oil until browned on all sides. Push to one side of pan; add onion, garlic, and green pepper, cook until onion is soft. Add tomato; cook 2 minutes. Add Tabasco, wine and water, cover, cook until meat is tender—about 30 minutes. Add clams during last 5 minutes, cook covered until shells open. Serve sprinkled with parsley or cilantro. *Makes 4 to 6 servings.*

SUGGESTED GO-WITHS. Saffron rice, Frenched green beans, black olives and celery. For dessert, caramel custard (flan).

Osso Buco

3 veal shanks, or 3 pounds veal knuckle
1/3 cup flour
1 teaspoon salt
½ teaspoon freshly ground black pepper
2 tablespoons olive oil
2 tablespoons butter
½ teaspoon sage
1 teaspoon rosemary
1 medium onion, chopped
1 or 2 cloves garlic, crushed (optional)
1 cup dry white wine
2 cups chicken broth
1 tablespoon tomato paste
2 tablespoons minced parsley
1 tablespoon grated lemon peel, or very thin slivers of lemon peel

The veal should be sawn by the butcher into pieces 2 inches thick so that marrow is exposed. Dredge the meat with mixture of flour, salt, and pepper. Heat olive oil and butter to sizzling (do not allow to brown); add meat; brown a few pieces at a time quickly on both sides, without crowding the pan. Remove meat; add herbs, onion, and garlic. Simmer until soft; crush garlic into fat. Pour off excess fat. Replace meat, add wine, chicken broth, and tomato paste. Simmer, tightly covered, until meat is very tender—about 2 hours. Add parsley and lemon peel during last 5 minutes. Taste for seasoning; add salt if needed. Serve from casserole with hot buttered noodles and a tossed green salad, accompanied by red wine, with fruit pastry for dessert. *Makes 6 to 8 servings.*

Pork and Celery Avgholemono

2 to 3 pounds lean pork, cubed	1 cup water or chicken broth
6 tablespoons butter	1 tablespoon minced parsley
2 medium onions, sliced	1 bunch celery, including most
1½ teaspoons salt,	of leaves, or 1 large celery
or to taste	knob (celeriac)
2 tablespoons flour	4 egg yolks
½ cup dry white wine	4 tablespoons lemon juice

Brown pork in butter, push to one side of pan. Add onions; cook until soft. Add salt and flour, cook until flour is lightly browned. Add wine slowly, then water or broth, and cook until smooth. Add parsley. Simmer covered 1½ hours. Chop celery or slice stalks diagonally and mince the leaves. (If celery knob is used, peel root and cut into slivers.) Place over meat; cook, covered, 20 to 25 minutes. Beat egg yolks until thick; beat in lemon juice 1 tablespoon at a time, then add 2 or 3 tablespoons of the broth from the meat. Pour egg mixture over celery and meat, stir to blend with sauce in pan. Leave covered 5 minutes with heat turned off. *Makes 8 servings.*

SUGGESTED GO-WITHS. Rice, Greek Salad, garlic bread; seasonal melon for dessert.

VARIETY MEATS AND SAUSAGES

How strange are some of the generic terms which have been applied to meats. "Variety meats" include all the "innards," such as kidneys, liver, sweetbreads, brains, heart, tongue, and tripe.

"Sausage" is a term technically applied to all smoked or cured meats; it includes frankfurters, bologna, and salami in addition to the pork sausages that the word immediately suggests to most of us. "Luncheon meats" are also technically sausage.

Liver

The best and most expensive is calf's (veal) liver, but steer liver, which costs much less, can be almost as good if cooked at low heat, either marinated in advance, or simmered in a sauce.

"Beef liver" is tougher, requires longer cooking in liquid (braising). Pork and lamb livers can also be good if very fresh, but they are rarely offered in American markets.

Pan-broiled Calf's Liver

1 pound calf's liver, sliced ¼-inch thick	Salt, pepper
2 tablespoons butter	1 tablespoon minced parsley
2 tablespoons olive oil	Lemon wedges

Heat butter and oil together in heavy skillet just until butter is melted. Add slices of liver, cook over *low to moderate* heat until lightly browned on each side, about 10 minutes per side. (Slash in center to be sure liver is done; no red should show.) Sprinkle with salt from shaker and parsley just before removing from pan. Serve with pan essence spooned over meat, with lemcn wedges, the lemon to be sprinkled over meat at table. *Makes 4 servings.*

SUGGESTED GO-WITHS. Steamed potatoes, Harvard beets. Mixed compote for dessert.

Braised Liver

1 pound steer or beef liver, cut in ½-inch slices	1 medium onion, minced
3 tablespoons flour	2 cups beef or vegetable broth
½ teaspoon salt	½ teaspoon gravy coloring
4 or 5 tablespoons olive oil	2 tablespoons lemon juice
	1 tablespoon sugar

Cut liver in pieces 1½ x 2 inches. Pound beef liver with edge of plate to soften tissues. Roll in flour blended with salt. Sauté in hot olive oil over moderate heat until delicately browned on both sides. Remove. Add onion, cook in oil until soft. Stir in any remaining flour. Replace liver over onions. Add remaining ingredients (blended together first), simmer over low heat, covered, until liver is tender. Even better if cooked a day in advance, then reheated in sauce. Serve with mashed potatoes, spinach, and tomatoes sprinkled with tarragon and oil. *Makes 4 servings.*

Calf's Liver with Bacon

4 slices bacon	Salt, pepper
2 large slices liver, ¼ inch thick	Minced parsley

Cook the bacon in a heavy skillet until crisp; remove. Add the slices of liver to the bacon fat, cook over moderate heat until lightly browned on each side and until, when slashed in center, no red appears; sprinkle with salt and pepper. Serve each slice of liver with 2 pieces of bacon; sprinkle parsley over top. *Makes 2 servings.*

SUGGESTED GO-WITHS. Spinach, baked tomatoes, corn muffins.

Steer's Liver with Onions

1 large or 2 medium onions, sliced
3 tablespoons shortening

4 slices liver, ¼ inch thick
Salt, pepper

Fry the onions in shortening until soft and lightly browned; sprinkle with salt and pepper; remove. Add the liver, cook over moderate heat until slightly browned on each side; sprinkle with salt and pepper. Serve liver topped with fried onions. *Makes 4 servings.*

For 2 servings, use 1 medium onion, 2 slices of liver, 2 tablespoons shortening.

SUGGESTED GO-WITHS. Baked potatoes with sour cream, cole slaw.

Kidney

Lamb and veal kidneys are tender enough to broil or braise with brief cooking—in fact, the flavor is more delicate if they are cooked very briefly, nor have I found it necessary to soak them first in acidulated water, as many cooks recommend. If cooked more than a total of 10 minutes, the kidneys toughen and then must be cooked an hour or longer.

Beef kidney, on the other hand, requires both marinating and long cooking—unless it is very fresh, of choice quality beef.

Kidney and Mushrooms in Cream

1 veal kidney, or 5 lamb kidneys
12 button mushrooms, trimmed
2 tablespoons butter
1 teaspoon prepared mustard

1 chicken bouillon cube. dissolved in ½ cup hot water
¼ cup heavy cream

Dice veal kidney or slice lamb kidneys. Sauté with mushrooms in butter until lightly browned. Add mustard; stir to blend. Add the chicken bouillon dissolved in hot water, simmer, covered, 4 or 5 minutes. Turn off heat, stir in cream. Serve at once with parsley rice and broiled tomatoes. *Makes 3 or 4 servings.*

Rognons au Fine Champagne

The first time I ever tasted kidneys was in a little restaurant on the Left Bank of Paris where this dish was the *spécialité de la maison*. They were being flamed at table, and the sight so fascinated me that I ordered the dish without even knowing what it was. I have been mad about kidneys ever since, having learned from this experience that the sauce of kidneys skillfully cooked can be superb.

6 lamb kidneys, thickly sliced
1 tablespoon butter
2 tablespoons cognac *(fine champagne)*
2 egg yolks, beaten until thick

1 tablespoon lemon juice
½ teaspoon salt
2 tablespoons heavy cream
   or sour cream

Everything should be ready beforehand, for this dish should be cooked at table, preferably in a chafing dish. Melt the butter in the blazer of the chafing dish; add the sliced kidneys; move around in the butter until they are lightly browned on each side—about 6 or 7 minutes. Add the brandy 1 tablespoon at a time, lowering it in a ladle into the pan so that it has a chance to warm slightly. Set aflame. Add the second tablespoon of brandy, set it aflame. Spoon up the sauce to keep the flame alive. When the flame has died, spoon some of pan essence into the beaten egg yolk; blend well. Mix the lemon juice and salt with the egg, then pour this mixture into chafing dish blazer (or skillet); turn off heat; beat briskly to blend the egg with the pan essence. The sauce will thicken with the heat left in the pan. Stir in the cream or sour cream. Serve at once, with steamed rice and Petits Pois a la Francaise. *Makes 3 or 4 servings.*

Veal Kidney with Mustard Sauce

1 veal kidney
2 tablespoons butter
1 teaspoon prepared mustard

½ teaspoon salt
1/3 cup rosé wine

Cut kidney in small cubes, cutting away membranes. Sauté in butter over moderate heat until lightly browned. Add mustard and salt; stir to blend. Add the wine, cover, simmer 4 or 5 minutes. Serve at once, with rice and asparagus or buttered cauliflower, with Ambrosia for dessert. *Makes 3 servings.*

Steak and Kidney Pie

2 cups biscuit mix
Pinch of baking soda
2/3 cup buttermilk
1 pound top round of beef, diced

4 or 5 lamb kidneys, or 1 very
   fresh beef kidney
1 teaspoon salt
½ cup shelled peas (fresh

or frozen)
1 large or 2 small potatoes,
  peeled, diced
1 small onion, minced

¼ cup red wine
2 cans or 3 cups beef gravy
1 tablespoon minced parsley

Combine biscuit mix with soda and buttermilk to make pastry dough. Roll out two-thirds of the dough to fit the bottom and sides of a square Pyrex baking dish (about 9 x 9 inches). Roll out remaining dough for top crust, to ¼ inch thick.

Arrange a layer of beef over bottom crust, then a layer of sliced kidneys, sprinkling each layer with salt. Add layers of peas and sliced raw potatoes and minced onion. Repeat, until all meat and vegetables are used. Blend wine with gravy, pour over meat and vegetables. Sprinkle parsley over all. Place top crust on pie, seal the edges. Cut out a circle or star from center of top crust. Bake in preheated 350° F. oven for 1½ hours. Serve from the baking dish. Nothing else needed to complete the menu but a big tossed salad and an ice cream dessert. *Makes 6 servings.*

Mixed English Grill

4 loin lamb chops
4 lamb kidneys, split
4 pork link sausages
1 medium onion, thickly sliced
¼ cup dry vermouth or white
  wine

2 tablespoons olive oil
¾ teaspoon salt
Freshly ground black pepper
¼ teaspoon orégano
2 tomatoes, thickly sliced

Place chops, kidneys, sausages, and onion in bowl, cover with mixture of vermouth or wine, oil, salt, pepper, and orégano. Marinate several hours. Lift from marinade, arrange in broiler pan with chops placed on top of onion slices. Place tomato slices around edge of broiler pan, spoon the marinade over each. Broil 3 inches from heat until chops, kidneys, and sausages are browned on each side. *Makes 4 servings.*

Brains and Sweetbreads

Both these "variety meats" are delicate and deliciously good if first parboiled in "acidulated water," which means water containing a little lemon juice, vinegar, or dry wine. *If frozen when purchased, they should be completely defrosted before cooking.* Take care to keep water at a gentle simmer, not boiling; cook 20 minutes; let brains or sweetbreads cool in broth. They will then be white and firm. Remove from water; cut away membrane; slice or chop the solid part.

Brains à la King

2 veal (calf's) brains	1 small white onion, thinly
Salted acidulated water	sliced
2 tablespoons butter	1 cup Velouté Sauce
1 pimiento, diced	4 patty shells
½ green pepper, seeded, chopped	

Precook brains gently in salted acidulated water (for 3 cups water, add 2 tablespoons vinegar, ½ teaspoon salt) for 20 minutes. Remove from water, cut away membrane, dice the brains. Melt butter in skillet, add pimiento, green pepper, and onion, cook about 2 minutes (onion should be yellow and soft but not browned). Add brains, cook 1 minute. Add Velouté Sauce; simmer until thoroughly hot. Serve in patty shells, accompanied by buttered broccoli and braised celery or summer squash. *Makes 4 servings.*

SWEETBREADS À LA KING. Parboil sweetbreads, use in place of brains in above recipe.

OTHER WAYS. Add cooked green peas, diced cooked ham, or hard-cooked egg (chopped) to sauce. Or, instead of serving in patty shells, serve sauce over a slice of baked or boiled ham.

Heart Fricassee

Use 1 beef heart or 2 veal hearts; cut in 1-inch cubes, discarding membrane and any hard parts (no hard-hearted sauce wanted). Prepare as in basic recipe for Stew, add carrots and green beans during last ½ hour. Thicken by adding canned beef gravy or gravy mix. Or, use 1 can condensed tomato soup for part of liquid, and add sour cream (as for Beef a la Jensen).

Boiled Tongue

1 beef tongue	chopped
Cold water	4 or 5 peppercorns
Salt	1 bay leaf
1 onion, stuck with 2 cloves	1 large carrot, cubed
2 stalks celery, with leaves,	2 or 3 sprigs parsley

Place tongue in kettle; cover with cold water, add 1 tablespoon salt for 6 cups cold water. Bring to a boil, reduce heat, and simmer 2½ to 3 hours, skimming now and then. After first hour, add onion, celery, peppercorns, and bay leaf. When tongue is almost done, add carrot and parsley. When tongue is very tender, remove, immediately pull off skin while meat is warm.

Remove carrots with slotted spoon, Strain broth; save for use in sauces. When meat is cool, slice at an angle. Serve cold with the cooked carrot marinated in Vinaigrette Sauce; or reheat in a sauce, such as Raisin Sauce, Madeira Sauce, Celery-Horseradish Sauce, or German Hollandaise (Sauce Allemande). Served cold, it is also good with Cumberland Sauce. A beef tongue makes about 12 slices.

Tripe

There are three kinds of tripe, honeycomb (the most tender and flavorful), smooth tripe, and pocket tripe (the least desirable). Most fresh tripe as sold in American markets has already been tenderized or partially cooked and so needs only short cooking—about ½ hour—but ask which type it is when you buy it. If not pretreated, it could require as much as 16 hours' cooking. Pickled tripe is usually already thoroughly cooked, put up in brine. It needs to be soaked before using.

Boiled Tripe

Prepare a stock of 6 cups water with 1 tablespoon salt, a celery stalk, onion stuck with cloves, and a diced carrot. Bring to a boil. Add tripe, cook until fork-tender. (See above.) Remove from stock; save stock to use in sauce recipes calling for either beef or veal stock.

Fried Tripe

Boil tripe until tender. Remove from stock; cut into serving portions. Dip in beaten egg, then in crumbs; or dip in a thick egg batter. Fry in sizzling-hot shortening or bacon fat (½ inch deep) until golden on each side. Serve with catsup and lemon wedges, or Celery-Horseradish Sauce, accompanied by boiled potatoes and mustard greens.

Tripe à la Creole

Cook 1 pound honeycomb tripe until tender; cut into serving portions. Prepare Homemade Tomato Sauce, adding chopped green peppers. Add the tripe, simmer 2 hours. Serve topped with minced parsley, accompanied by boiled potatoes (a one-dish meal).

Sausages with Fried Apples

Pan-fry pork sausage links, or sausage patties shaped from bulk pork sausage, until brown on both sides. Remove. Slice apples horizontally ¼ inch thick (do not peel); cut out core from center of slices. Fry apple slices in the sausage fat, until lightly browned on one side only. Serve apple slices with the sausage, along with sweet potatoes and cooked greens or spinach.

Scrapple

Cut prepared or commercial scrapple into thick (¼- to ½-inch) slices; dredge with flour. Fry in bacon drippings or shortening until brown on each side. Serve for breakfast with scrambled eggs, or top each serving with a fried egg as a supper dish.

Corned Beef Hash with Eggs

Chill canned corned beef hash in refrigerator before opening can; open can at both ends, slip out hash, slice thickly. Fry in bacon drippings or shortening until browned on each side. Serve each slice topped with a fried or poached egg. A good supper dish with spinach or carrots (or both).

Crisp Corned Beef Hash

Empty contents of can of corned beef hash, break up with fork. Heat 3 or 4 tablespoons shortening or olive oil in heavy skillet; add hash, moisten with 2 or 3 tablespoons water. Fry very slowly until a solid brown crust forms on bottom. Lift up gently with spatula as crust forms, fold over like an omelet. Slip out onto warmed platter; serve with stewed tomatoes and a green salad.

Luncheon Meat Picadillo

1 12-ounce can luncheon meat	1 tomato, peeled, seeded,
3 tablespoons olive oil	chopped, or 2 tablespoons catsup
1 large onion, chopped	¼ cup water
2 garlic cloves, minced	Salt, pepper
1 green pepper, seeded, chopped	

Open can of luncheon meat, cut into small cubes. Heat oil in skillet, add onion, garlic, green pepper and luncheon meat; cook, stirring, until lightly browned. Add tomato and water; sprinkle with salt and pepper. Cook about 10 minutes longer. Serve as a supper dish with mashed or baked potatoes and a green vegetable. *Makes about 4 servings.*

USING LEFTOVER MEAT

There is always some use to make of leftover meat. A section of roast or pot roast large enough to slice can be reheated in sauce (or gravy); or it can be cut into chunks and used to make a stew (see basic recipe for Stew). Smaller bits and pieces can be added to a pasta casserole (noodles, macaroni, or spaghetti) or a rice dish, or used in a Chinese entree. Minced cooked meat may be used to enrich spaghetti sauce or chili con carne, or as filling for Empanadas (or Empanadillas), or Piroshki, or to make hash.

Roast Beef Hash

1 to 1½ cups diced cooked roast beef	1 tablespoon minced parsley
	3 tablespoons shortening
3 or 4 medium potatoes, peeled, diced	Salt, pepper
	2 or 3 tablespoons gravy
2 medium onions, chopped	(optional)

The secret of success in this recipe is to cut both meat and potatoes in very small uniform pieces, the size of poker dice. The potatoes should not be cooked; the flavor will be far better if the hash is made with raw potatoes—unless you have leftover cooked potatoes and want to use them up. In this case, use a combination of cooked and raw potatoes.

Heat shortening to sizzling; add meat, potatoes, onions, and parsley. Cook over moderate heat, turning with a spatula as the mixture browns. Don't rush it. Don't let the onions burn. Chop with a small sharp knife as the mixture cooks, cutting into still smaller particles. Sprinkle with salt and pepper. Add the gravy only at the end—or you may prefer it without gravy. After the mixture is browned and a little crusty, cover; simmer over low heat until potatoes are fork-tender. Serve with catsup, accompanied by buttered beets and/or cauliflower for a fine family supper. *Makes 4 or 5 servings.*

Hash Stew

2 cups leftover meat	3 tablespoons olive oil
2 carrots, scraped	2 tablespoons flour
2 medium onions	½ teaspoon salt
2 tomatoes, peeled, seeded	2½ cups water

Any leftover meat may be used—beef, pork, veal, ham, lamb, or a combination. For best results, it should be put through a food grinder, but if you haven't a food grinder, cut in small pieces, add to electric blender with ½ cup of the water in the blender. (If you haven't either a blender or a food grinder, mince everything as fine as possible by chopping with a French-bladed knife.)

Heat olive oil in skillet. First add the minced meat, cook, stirring, until it starts to brown. Then push the meat to one side of pan, add carrots and onions, cook about 1 minute. Add tomatoes, cook until mushy, then blend in flour and salt. Stir until all ingredients are well mixed. Slowly add water. Cover; simmer over low heat 15 to 20 minutes. *Makes about 8 servings.*

Red Flannel Hash

This is an old New England dish, often made with what's left over from a New England Boiled Dinner. Other vegetables, such as cooked carrots and turnip, may also be added, chopped fine. Minced parsley may be added, too, if desired.

6 medium or 8 small cooked or canned beets	(cooked or canned)
	3 tablespoons fat
4 medium potatoes, cooked	Salt, pepper
1 cup chopped leftover beef, or 1 cup chopped corned beef	1 tablespoon cream

Chop beets and potatoes fine; mix with meat also chopped in very small pieces. Melt fat in heavy skillet, add the meat and vegetable mixture, moisten with a little hot water (2 or 3 tablespoons); sprinkle with salt and pepper. (If corned beef is used, go very light on the salt.) Cook slowly until a brown crust begins to form. Add cream toward the end. Lift up with spatula and fold over. Serve at once, with cole slaw and sliced tomatoes or carrot sticks. Pass both catsup and mustard. *Makes 4 servings.*

Pisto

This Spanish hash is sometimes made of vegetables only, sometimes of vegetables and meat. It's a good entree to make when you have only a little meat and need to extend it mightily.

¼ to ½ cup diced lean ham or pork	or 2 yellow squash, sliced
	1 package frozen artichoke hearts, or 1 package frozen Frenched green beans
¼ cup olive oil	
2 large onions, sliced	
1 pimiento or sweet red pepper, seeded, diced	1 1-pound can tomatoes
	Salt
2 cups eggplant, diced (not peeled), or 2 zucchini, sliced,	2 or 3 eggs, beaten, scrambled (optional)

Sauté the meat in olive oil until lightly browned. Add onion and pimiento, cook until lightly browned. Add eggplant or squash; brown lightly. Add the artichoke hearts or beans (partially defrosted), the tomatoes, and salt to taste. Simmer, covered, until vegetables are tender. Scramble eggs in another pan as the meat and vegetables cook. When cooked, cut the egg in slivers. Serve the hash topped with egg. *Makes 6 to 8 servings.*

Slumgullion

1 large onion, sliced	1 6-ounce can tomato paste
2 tablespoons fat	¾ cup water or broth
1½ to 2 cups minced	Salt, pepper
cooked meat*	1 pound spaghetti, cooked
1 package frozen peas	al dente
1 bay leaf	½ cup medium sherry
Pinch of powdered fennel	½ cup grated Romano cheese
½ teaspoon orégano	

Cook the onion in fat (bacon fat, shortening, butter, margarine, or oil) until soft and yellow. Add meat, peas, herbs, tomato paste, and water or broth. Add salt and pepper to taste. Simmer, covered, until peas are tender.

Separately cook spaghetti. When cooked, add to meat mixture; stir to blend well. Add sherry. Transfer to casserole; top with cheese. This can be done ahead. Bake in oven preheated to 350° F. for 30 minutes. *Makes 6 to 8 servings.*

*Any leftover meat can be used, but beef and pork are especially recommended. Or, the dish can be made with 1 pound hamburger meat. Instead of peas, use frozen lima beans. Instead of spaghetti, cook 2 cups rice (6 to 7 cups cooked rice). Vary seasoning to taste.

Picadillo

Use same recipe as for Luncheon Meat Picadillo, but use any diced leftover meat (beef, pork, ham, lamb, or veal).

Reheating Meat in Sauce or Gravy

When you have enough gravy left over for reheating sliced meat, that, of course, is the easiest way to do it. But when you haven't gravy enough, heat the meat in a Brown Sauce, or a Tomato Sauce, or even a Mustard-Cream Sauce or Sauce Soubise. Lamb is delicious in Curried Plum Sauce, and veal in Sauce Mornay. Other suggestions: ham in Cumberland Sauce, beef in Caper-Cream Sauce, and pork in Sauce Robert or Avgholemono Sauce.

Other meat recipes will be found in Book 3, Chapter 7, "Casseroles."

4 POULTRY

Of all the meat foods, there's none more versatile or inexpensive than chicken.

Advances in technology, breeding, and feeding, have resulted in chickens and turkeys that have more meat per pound and cook more quickly. Where once it required an hour to braise or fricassee chicken, now 25 minutes may be enough. Turkeys once had to be placed in the oven early in the morning to be ready for Thanksgiving dinner; now they bake in 3 to 4 hours. Also, turkeys and turkey parts are available throughout the year, to use for barbecuing and quick family dinners.

The same stuffings and the same sauces may be used for chicken, turkey, and Cornish hen.

Ducks, geese, and game birds play a much less important part in the American cuisine. They are less available (ducks can be found in most markets, but nearly always frozen), not quite so easy to prepare, and the edible meat per pound is considerably less. But for special occasions, these not-so-ordinary birds can be very festive. Duckling especially can be a real treat if properly prepared and served with a luscious sauce.

Economy Tips in Chicken Cookery

Chicken, one of the most economical of "meat foods" to begin with, can be stretched still further if cut up and separated before storing. Using a sharp knive and poultry shears, first cut away all those portions that do not make pretty eating: the wing tips, the tail, the neck, giblets, and awkward parts of the back. With these, make stock either for gravy or for soup. By adding a few julienne-cut slivers of vegetables to be cooked in the soup (and perhaps a few slivers of pork, if you happen to have some on hand), you may make a soup to be served as the first course. If the broth is not used immediately for either soup or gravy, save it, stored in a jar, for later use in other meals.

Cut the tender parts of the chicken into small pieces: the breast in 4 pieces (with poultry shears, remove protruding bones), and the legs in two pieces each; cut the neck from the back, pushing this down flat so that it will serve as an attractive portion. In this way, twelve serving portions can be cut from one chicken. In a small household, half of these can be put away in the freezer for another meal. Or, eight pieces can be used for one meal, the other four combined with other meats (pork or ham) or seafood for a rice dish (Paella, Jambalaya, Pilaf).

When serving a chicken dish to company, cutting up the chicken like this is wise, because then several people can enjoy the breast, the meatiest part of the chicken. Otherwise, the hostess seems to favor one or two guests above the others by serving the largest portion to them. This trick also makes it possible to offer more pieces per serving portion, and even if the pieces are smaller, it seems more equitable.

Poultry Roasting Timetable

All poultry should be cooked to an internal temperature (as registered on meat thermometer) of 180-185° F. When bird is stuffed, allow 15 to 30 minutes extra time. Stuffing is not recommended for birds cooked on rotisserie spit.

Bird	Pound Weight	Oven Temperature	Approximate Cooking Times Stuffed	Not Stuffed	Rotisserie
Chicken	1¾-2	375°	1-1¼ hours	45 minutes	45-60 minutes
	2½-3	375°	1½-1¾ hours	1¼ hours	1-1¼ hours
	5-6	325°	2-2½ hours	1¾ hours	2-2¼ hours
Capon	7-8	325°	2-2½ hours	2 hours	2-2¼ hours
Cornish hen	¾	400°	1 hour	45 minutes	45-60 minutes
	1	400°	1¼ hours	1 hour	1-1¼ hours
Duck	4-5	450°, then 325°	2-2½ hours	1½-2 hours	1½-2 hours
Turkey	8-9	325°	2½ hours	2 hours	2 hours
	10-12	325°	3 hours	2½ hours	2½ hours
	13-15	325°	3-3½ hours	3 hours	——
	16-20	325°	3¾-4½ hours	——	——
Goose	10-12	450°, then 325°	4-4½ hours	3½-4 hours	——
Pheasant	2	325°	1¼-2 hours	1-1½ hours	——
Partridge,	½-¾	450°		20-25 minutes	——
quail,		400°, then 300°	1-1¼ hours	45-60 minutes	——
squab		325°	1-1¼ hours	45 minutes	——

Crisp Fried Chicken (Basic Recipe)

1 broiler-fryer, about
  2½ pounds, cut up
¾ cup flour
2 teaspoons salt

¼ to ½ teaspoon freshly
  ground black pepper
½ cup shortening for frying

Separate the neck, giblets, wing tips, and less attractive pieces of back from rest of chicken. Make stock with these: cover with 2 cups water, add ½ teaspoon salt; simmer, covered, ½ hour; strain. Use the stock for making chicken gravy.

Combine flour, 2 teaspoons salt, and pepper; place in a clean paper bag. Add a few of remaining chicken pieces at a time; shake so that chicken is completely covered with flour mixture. Heat shortening to sizzling in a large heavy skillet or electric skillet set at 360° F. (the shortening should be about ½ inch deep). Add chicken pieces, but do not crowd skillet. Cook only part at a time over moderate heat until crisply browned on all sides. Remove pieces as they are cooked, to casserole in oven preheated to 350°. The liver should be cooked last, and briefly. Crisp chicken in oven for 15 to 20 minutes, while making gravy. *Makes 4 to 6 servings, allowing 2 pieces per person.*

TO MAKE GRAVY. Pour off all but 3 tablespoons fat from skillet. Add 3 tablespoons of flour mixture, stir and cook until it is lightly browned. Slowly stir in strained chicken stock (if it has cooked down considerably, add water to make 1½ cups). Simmer until smooth and thickened. Taste for seasoning; add salt if needed. *Makes 1½ cups gravy.*

SUGGESTED GO-WITHS. Mashed potatoes, Frenched green beans, cole slaw; ice cream and chocolate fudge cake for dessert.

NORTHWESTERN FRIED CHICKEN. Before shaking chicken pieces in flour, dip each in cream. Proceed as in basic recipe.

SOUTHERN FRIED CHICKEN. Soak chicken pieces in 1 cup buttermilk for 1 hour before dredging in flour mixture. Otherwise proceed as in basic recipe.

FRIED CHICKEN MARYLAND. Beat 2 eggs; blend with ¼ cup water or milk. First dredge chicken pieces in flour mixture, then dip in beaten egg, then in fine dry crumbs (you will need about 1½ cups crumbs). Fry in sizzling-hot vegetable shortening but at lowered heat so that chicken fries slowly; watch it carefully to prevent burning. When well browned, transfer to a casserole and bake, uncovered, in oven preheated to 350° F. for 30 minutes. Serve hot with Cream Gravy: make gravy as in basic recipe, but use only 1 cup chicken stock and add ½ cup milk or light cream. Simmer about 10 minutes, stirring with whisk until smooth.

Oven-fried Chicken

A ridiculous name, of course, because how can it be fried chicken if it's baked? But it looks like fried chicken, it can be eaten with the fingers, and it's very easy to prepare. Proceed as in the basic recipe for Crisp Fried Chicken: dredge the chicken pieces in the flour mixture, but instead of solid shortening, use corn or other vegetable oil. Pour one-fourth of the oil in the bottom of a shallow baking pan. Add the chicken pieces; turn until they are moistened with oil. Pour remaining oil over chicken pieces. Preheat oven to 450° F.; bake chicken until pieces are crisply browned, turning once. Remove chicken from pan; drain on absorbent paper; keep warm in turned-off oven. Pour off all fat and drippings into small bowl; discard clear fat, saving 3 table-spoons brown-streaked drippings; place in skillet. Add flour (as in basic recipe); cook and stir until browned, then slowly add 1½ cups chicken stock (made as in basic recipe) for gravy.

Chicken Parmesan

1 broiler-fryer, about 2½	1 teaspoon salt
pounds, cut up	1 cup fine dry crumbs
2 eggs, beaten	½ cup Parmesan cheese
¼ cup water or milk	¼ cup oil

Dip chicken pieces (one at a time) in mixture of beaten egg, water or milk, and salt. Roll in mixture of crumbs and cheese. Chill ½ hour. Pour half the oil in bottom of shallow roasting pan or casserole. Place chilled chicken pieces in oil, turning to moisten. Cover with remaining oil. Bake in oven preheated to 400° F. until chicken is crisp on all sides, turning once. Remove from pan; drain on absorbent paper. Serve with buttered noodles and avocado salad. *Makes 4 or 5 servings.*

Broiled Chicken (Basic Recipe)

1 broiler-fryer, cut up,	Paprika
quartered, or split	2 to 4 tablespoons butter or olive
Salt	oil, or a blend of the two

Line broiler pan with foil. Place chicken pieces in the foil; sprinkle each lightly with salt and paprika, turning to cover all surfaces. Dot with butter or brush with oil. Broil 6 inches from heat in preheated broiler oven, with reduced heat (400° F.). Turn as pieces brown. *Makes 2, 4, or 5 servings, depending on size of chicken and how it is cut up.*

PIQUANT BROILED CHICKEN. Prepare as in basic recipe, but use 2 tablespoons olive oil only; as chicken browns, sprinkle with lemon juice.

PEACH AND CHICKEN DINNER. Broil chicken pieces as in basic recipe; after pieces have been turned, place canned peach halves around the edge of broiler pan; baste peaches with pan drippings. As peaches start to brown, baste chicken with peach-flavored pan drippings. Serve with rice, with watercress sprigs for garnish.

CURRIED BROILED CHICKEN. Dust chicken with mixture of 1 tablespoon flour, ½ teaspoon salt, and 1 teaspoon curry powder. Proceed as in basic recipe. If desired, cover with 1 cup yogurt or sour cream during last 5 minutes. Serve with parsley rice, limas, broiled tomatoes (cooked around edges of broiler pan at same time as chicken), with chutney as a relish.

SAVORY BROILED CHICKEN. Instead of dusting outside of chicken with seasonings, force dabs of an Herb Butter under the skin of the chicken pieces. Place chicken pieces in broiler pan; as the butter melts, baste pan drippings over top of chicken pieces. The flesh of the chicken is flavored deliciously by this method.

Chicken Teriyaki

Marinate chicken pieces in Teriyaki Sauce. Broil under broiler unit or over charcoal, 6 inches from heat, turning frequently until well browned on all sides—about 25 to 45 minutes. (The pieces should be cut fairly small: separate drumsticks from thighs, cut breast into 4 pieces.) Serve with rice and braised celery.

Barbecued Chicken

Marinate chicken in any favorite barbecue sauce for 1 hour before cooking. Orange Barbecue Sauce, Tomato Barbecue Sauce, Red Wine Marinade, and Tomato Glaze are all delicious with chicken. Turn pieces frequently and watch carefully to avoid burning.

Barbecued Chicken Wings

8 chicken wings
1 cup prepared barbecue sauce
  (commercial or homemade)

½ cup orange juice
1 teaspoon Worcestershire
  or soy sauce

Marinate chicken wings in mixture of remaining ingredients for 1 hour. Remove from marinade, arrange in foil-lined broiler pan or over grid of charcoal fire. Broil 6 inches from heat, turning several times, until crisply browned, about 25 minutes. Watch carefully to make sure the pieces do not char. *Makes 4 servings.*

Chicken Paprika

2 small broilers, cut up
1 cup chicken stock
4 tablespoons flour
2 teaspoons salt

1 tablespoon paprika
8 tablespoons butter, clarified
1½ cups chopped onion
1 cup sour cream

Separate the breasts, wings, liver, and legs from the other parts of the chicken. Make stock of remaining pieces, cooking 30 minutes. Strain the stock; measure, set aside.

Dredge reserved chicken pieces in mixture of flour, salt, and paprika, shaking in a paper bag until pieces are well covered. Clarify the butter; strain into large heavy skillet or electric skillet set at 360° F. Fry the chicken pieces until crisply browned in the butter (only part of chicken at a time—do not crowd the pan). Keep warm in casserole.

After chicken is fried, add the onions to the pan drippings, cook over lowered heat (300° on electric skillet) until golden and soft. Stir in remaining flour mixture; blend well. Add the strained chicken stock; simmer until sauce is thickened. Turn off heat. Gradually blend in sour cream. Pour sauce over chicken in casserole. Bake, covered, in 350° oven until sauce bubbles—about 30 minutes. *Makes 14 chicken pieces (including livers)—enough for a dinner party of 6.*

SUGGESTED GO-WITHS. Rice or noodles, broccoli, salad of avocado, orange, and onion rings.

CHICKEN GULYÁS. Prepare as for Chicken Paprika, but cook 1 green pepper, seeded and chopped, with the onion, and add ½ cup tomato sauce to chicken stock.

ANOTHER WAY. Instead of 2 broilers, sauté 4 whole chicken breasts, each divided in half. Cook green pepper with the onion; add 1 carrot, finely diced. Instead of chicken stock, make the sauce with 1 can condensed cream of chicken soup and 1 can tomato sauce. Stir in 1 cup sour cream; pour over chicken breasts in casserole; proceed as for Chicken Paprika.

Chicken in Wine (Basic Recipe)

1 broiler-fryer, cut up	3 tablespoons clarified butter,
1 cup chicken broth	or 1 tablespoon olive oil and
¼ cup flour	2 tablespoons butter, or
1 teaspoon salt	3 tablespoons oil
¼ teaspoon freshly ground	1 cup wine*
black pepper or other spice	

Separate neck, giblets, wing tips, and less attractive trimmings from back; make broth by simmering these in 2 cups water and ½ teaspoon salt for 30 minutes. Strain; measure.

Dust remaining chicken pieces with mixture of flour, salt, and

*Use all white wine, or rosé wine; or use ½ cup sherry and ½ cup water; or ¼ cup Madeira and ½ cup water (in this case, do not boil down as much).

pepper. (Or, use paprika instead of pepper for deeper color.) Use clarified butter as described in preceding paragraph, or a mixture of olive oil and butter. (An electric skillet is excellent for sautéing chicken; set at 360° F.) When butter sizzles, add pieces of chicken, but do not crowd pan. Cook until crisply brown on each side; remove. Repeat until all chicken is browned. Pour off all but 1 tablespoon fat. Add wine and broth; cook over high heat until reduced to 1 cup, stirring to loosen browned bits from pan. Return chicken to sauce; simmer, uncovered, for 10 to 15 minutes or until fork-tender. Or, reheat chicken in sauce when time to serve. *Makes 4 or 5 servings, depending on size of chicken and the way it is cut up.*

FOR THICKENED SAUCE. When chicken is browned, do not pour off fat, but stir in 2 tablespoons flour. Use only ½ cup wine with 1 cup broth; simmer until slightly thickened, but not as thick as gravy.

CHICKEN TARRAGON. Prepare as for Chicken in Wine, but use only 2 tablespoons flour and reduce chicken broth (by boiling) to ½ cup. Soak 1 tablespoon dried tarragon in 1½ cups white wine for ½ hour; strain wine when adding to pan.

For the crispest, brownest pieces of chicken, dust the pieces with a flour mixture, then sauté in *clarified* butter. By clarifying the butter, you get rid of the bits of casein that cause burning. Simply melt the butter and pour it through a very fine sieve into the skillet in which the chicken is to be browned. Next best is to use a mixture of butter and olive oil. Do *not* use margarine for browning chicken in a skillet.

CHICKEN WITH PORT AND CREAM. Prepare as for Chicken in Wine, seasoning with a little nutmeg instead of pepper. After all chicken pieces are cooked, pour off fat, return chicken to pan, and add ¾ cup port wine. Cover tightly; simmer over lowest heat for about 40 minutes. Remove chicken to casserole; keep warm. Add ½ cup concentrated chicken broth to pan, boil up, cook until reduced and slightly thickened, stirring up to loosen browned bits on bottom of pan. Beat 2 egg yolks, blend with ½ cup heavy cream. Add some of hot sauce to egg-cream mixture, then with whisk stir this into remaining sauce in pan. Cook over lowest heat, stirring constantly, until thickened and very smooth. Pour over chicken in casserole; sprinkle minced parsley or cilantro over top.

COQ AU VIN. Prepare as for Chicken in Wine, but when chicken pieces are browned add 2 tablespoons brandy to pan drippings, set aflame (see How to Flame with Brandy). When flame has died out, remove chicken pieces to casserole. Add 1 cup red wine to pan, plus 1 teaspoon tomato paste, ¼ teaspoon thyme, and 1½ cups chicken broth. Simmer until reduced by about one-third. Thicken with ¾-ounce package gravy mix. To chicken in casserole, add Glazed Onions and Glazed Button Mushrooms. Cover with sauce. (This part can be done ahead.) Complete by baking in 350° F. oven for 40 minutes.

CHICKEN AMANDINE. Prepare as for Chicken in Wine, but after chicken pieces have been browned, add ¼ cup blanched slivered almonds to pan drippings; sauté until browned; remove and set aside. Cook ¼ cup thinly sliced onion and ¼ cup diced pimiento in pan drippings for 2 minutes. Pour off excess fat; add 1 cup chicken broth, 1 tablespoon catsup, and ¼ cup medium sherry; simmer 10 minutes. Replace chicken. Simmer until tender. Serve garnished with reserved almonds.

CHICKEN À L'ORANGE. Prepare as for Chicken in Wine, but add 1 teaspoon grated orange peel (or fine slivers of orange peel); instead of wine, use ½ cup orange juice plus 2 tablespoons medium-sweet sherry, Madeira, or brandy.

CHICKEN VÉRONIQUE. Prepare as for Chicken in Wine, but use only 2 tablespoons flour, and when chicken is browned, flame with 2 tablespoons brandy. When flame has died, add 2 cups seedless white grapes and 2 tablespoons minced onion. Cook until lightly browned. Add ¾ cup white wine and ½ cup reduced chicken broth; cook, stirring up browned bits, for 3 or 4 minutes. Return chicken to pan (or place chicken in casserole, cover with sauce). This may be done ahead; reheat chicken in sauce, adding 1 tablespoon brandy.

CHICKEN ORIENTALE. Prepare like Chicken Véronique, but use only ½ cup grapes plus 4 to 6 peach halves and add ¼ teaspoon powdered cumin and ¼ teaspoon curry powder. (Either canned or fresh peaches may be used; if fresh, sweeten lightly with sugar before adding to pan. Instead of seedless white grapes, seeded Tokay grapes may be used.)

INCREASING THE YIELD. To serve any of preceding or following chicken dishes for a dinner party of 8, buy 2 good-sized (2½- to 3-pound) chickens or 6 large chicken breasts, each cut in half (to allow for seconds). Increase other ingredients by half (6 tablespoons flour, 4 or 5 tablespoons butter, 1½ cups broth, 1½ cups wine).

SUGGESTED GO-WITHS. Rice is the best accompaniment for any chicken dish with an interesting sauce. Add a green vegetable and salad, and a light pastry or liqueur-laced ice cream for dessert.

Poulet aux Pêches

2 large chicken breasts, cut in halves
4 tablespoons clarified butter
4 tablespoons (¼ cup) cognac or brandy
4 scallions, chopped, or 2 small white onions, minced
1 tablespoon minced parsley
½ teaspoon salt
Dash of freshly ground pepper
2 tablespoons peach syrup
1 1-pound can cling peach halves, drained
Hot cooked rice
1½ cups chicken stock
1 teaspoon cornstarch
2 tablespoons heavy cream

Sauté chicken breasts in butter over high heat until crisply brown. Lower heat; add cognac a spoonful at a time, setting ablaze. When flame has burned out, add minced scallions or onion, parsley, salt, pepper, and the 2 tablespoons peach syrup. Cover; simmer 20 minutes at reduced heat. Add peach halves during last 5 minutes, uncover pan. When chicken is browned and tender, remove chicken and peaches to platter, arranging chicken over mounds of rice. Skim off excess fat from pan, add 1½ cups rich clear chicken stock and boil 3 minutes over high heat until reduced. Thin cornstarch with a little broth, add to pan, cook until slightly thickened and smooth. Add cream, blend well. Spoon a little of sauce over chicken breasts, pass remaining sauce. *Makes 4 servings.*

Poularde Portugaise

1 2½- to 3-pound fryer, cut up*
3 tablespoons flour
1½ teaspoons salt
¼ teaspoon freshly ground
  black pepper
2 tablespoons olive oil
3 tablespoons butter
1 large onion, chopped
1 clove garlic, minced
1 large or 2 medium green peppers, seeded, cut in squares

1 cup button mushrooms, or
  ¼ cup soaked dried mushrooms
  chopped
2 tomatoes, cut in thick slices
¼ cup minced cilantro or parsley
¾ cup dry white wine, or half
  wine, half chicken broth, or a
  mixture of wine and mushroom
  liquid
½ cup pitted sliced green or black
  olives
½ cup heavy cream

Dust chicken pieces with mixture of flour, salt, and pepper. Heat oil and butter in skillet (electric skillet at 350° F.); brown chicken pieces until outside is crisp but pieces are not cooked through. Remove. Add onion and garlic; cook until soft; add green pepper and mushrooms, cook about 2 minutes. Replace chicken over vegetables in skillet, or pour vegetable mixture in casserole and place chicken pieces over vegetables. Arrange tomato slices and cilantro or parsley over top. (This part can be done ahead.) Add wine, cover tightly and cook over very low heat for 30 to 40 minutes; or bake, uncovered, in oven set at 350° F. for 45 minutes. Add olives and cream during last 10 minutes. Serve from casserole or skillet with mashed potatoes, crusty rolls, and salad. *Serves 4.*

*To serve this superb casserole to a dinner party of 8, buy 2 chickens, cut each in 12 pieces (each breast in 4 pieces). Separate necks, giblets, wing tips and bonier parts of back. The other ingredients will be the same, except that you may need a little more seasoned flour and more liquid (1½ cups combined wine and chicken broth).

Poulet Cintra

1 2½- to 3-pound fryer, cut up
½ cup chicken broth
Salt
3 tablespoons butter
2 tablespoons olive oil
1 shallot, minced,
  or 3 scallions, minced
1 clove garlic, peeled

½ cup white port
¼ cup brandy
¼ cup cherry liqueur (optional)
2 egg yolks
1 cup heavy cream
Fried parsley or minced chives
  for garnish

Make broth with neck, wing tips, and giblets; strain; reduce to ½ cup by boiling. Discard cooked chicken pieces. Sprinkle remaining chicken pieces with salt. Heat butter and oil together until butter is melted (or use 5 tablespoons clarified butter). Add chicken a few pieces at a time without crowding skillet; cook over moderately high heat (360° F. on electric skillet) until well browned. While browning last pieces of chicken, add shallot and whole garlic to pan; when garlic is golden and soft, crush with tines of fork into fat in pan (discard shreds). Return all chicken pieces to pan, add port, chicken broth, brandy, and cherry liqueur. Bring to a boil; set liquid aflame. When flame dies, cover pan; simmer until chicken is very tender. (This can be done ahead of time: keep chicken pieces in the liquid, then reheat in the liquid, uncovered, until pieces are heated through.)

Remove hot chicken pieces to a platter or shallow serving dish; keep warm in oven set at 300° F. Reduce liquid by boiling to ½ cup. Beat egg yolks until thick and light; beat in cream. Slowly beat hot liquid into egg yolk mixture, then return to pan and simmer over very low heat, stirring constantly with whisk until sauce is smooth. Keep sauce warm until serving time (over hot but not boiling water), then pour over chicken pieces to serve. Garnish with fried parsley or minced chives. *Makes 4 servings.*

SUGGESTED GO-WITHS. Hot fluffy rice, glazed carrots, mixed green salad; for dessert, Peach Custard Tarts.

Chicken à la Señorita

A quick, easy, wonderful sauce that will have everyone guessing.

1 2½-pound chicken, cut up
2 tablespoons flour
1 teaspoon salt
2 or 3 tablespoons olive oil
1 medium onion, sliced

1 8-ounce can minced clams
1 can condensed cream of
  mushroom soup
½ soup can water

Shake chicken pieces in bag with flour and salt; brown in olive oil until crisp on all sides. Add onion; cook until golden and soft. Add remaining ingredients; cover. Simmer gently until chicken is very tender—about 20 minutes. *Makes 4 or 5 servings.*

SUGGESTED GO-WITHS. Rice, spinach, green salad with Roquefort dressing; for dessert, fruit compote.

Pepitoria of Chicken

1 broiler-fryer, cut up
1 cup chicken broth
2 tablespoons flour
1 teaspoon salt
¼ teaspoon freshly ground
  black pepper
3 or 4 tablespoons olive oil

¼ cup blanched almonds
2 cloves garlic
1 tablespoon minced parsley
1 large onion, chopped (about ¾ cup)
¼ teaspoon saffron
Yolks of 2 hard-cooked eggs
Minced parsley

Use neck, giblets, wing tips, and back of chicken to make broth. Shake remaining chicken pieces in bag with flour, salt, and pepper. Sauté in hot oil until browned, with a slice or two of onion in oil to prevent spattering. Crush blanched almonds into paste with garlic and parsley.

When chicken is browned, remove to casserole. Cook onion in oil until very soft; add almond mixture. Add saffron to strained chicken broth; heat to boiling. Strain broth into pan, stirring to remove all browned bits from bottom. Mash egg yolks, add a little of broth to blend, then stir into sauce and cook until fairly smooth. Pour over chicken. Serve at once, or reheat chicken in sauce in oven preheated to 350° F. for 30 to 40 minutes. Serve garnished with minced parsley. *Makes 4 or 5 servings.*

SUGGESTED GO-WITHS. Rice, artichoke hearts or asparagus, tomato-orange salad.

Mexican Chicken with Fruit

1 3-pound chicken, cut up
¼ cup flour
1 teaspoon salt
4 tablespoons shortening
½ green pepper, seeded, diced
2 cloves garlic, minced
1 cup minced onion
1 small can pineapple chunks,

  drained
1 cup dry white wine
1/3 cup seedless raisins
¼ teaspoon dried hot chili pepper
1 cup water
Hot cooked rice
¼ cup blanched toasted almonds
1 avocado, peeled, sliced

Dust chicken with flour mixed with salt; brown in hot shortening until crisp on all sides. Remove to casserole. Add green pepper, garlic, and onion to pan; cook until soft, then push to one side; add pineapple, brown in pan drippings. Sprinkle 2 tablespoons of the flour-salt mixture over the onion; stir until blended, then stir in wine; add raisins, chili pepper, and water. Pour mixture over chicken in casserole, cover. Simmer gently or bake at moderate heat until chicken is very tender—about 2 hours. Serve with hot cooked rice, with almonds and avocado for garnish. (This makes a one-dish meal; nothing else is needed but rice.) *Makes 6 servings.*

Chicken Marengo

1 3-pound chicken, cut up
¾ cup concentrated chicken broth
2 tablespoons flour
½ teaspoon salt
¼ cup olive oil
2 medium onions, sliced
1 clove garlic, minced

½ pound mushrooms, sliced
3 tomatoes, peeled, seeded,
   or 1-pound can peeled tomatoes
1 tablespoon tomato paste
1/3 cup Marsala wine or
   cream sherry
Salt

Make broth of neck, giblets, and wing tips. Shake remaining chicken pieces in bag with flour and salt. Brown in hot oil until crisp on all sides; remove as pieces are cooked. Cook onion, garlic, and mushrooms in oil until lightly browned. Add tomatoes, tomato paste, and Marsala or sherry; simmer until well blended—about 10 minutes. Add chicken stock and salt, if needed; replace chicken. Simmer 20 minutes and serve from pan in which it cooked; or, transfer to casserole, reheat in oven 40 to 45 minutes before serving. Serve with rice and a simple green salad. *Makes 4 to 6 servings.*

To serve a dinner party of 8, use 2 chickens, cut up, or 4 whole chicken breasts and 4 chicken legs cut into a total of 16 pieces.

Chicken Cacciatore

2 broiler-fryers, cut up
Salt, pepper
About ¼ cup flour
½ cup olive oil
8 small white onions, peeled
2 green peppers or pimientos,
   seeded, chopped
1 large clove garlic, minced
2 cups canned peeled tomatoes,

chopped
1 bay leaf, crumbled
1 tablespoon minced parsley
¼ teaspoon thyme
1 teaspoon beef stock
   concentrate
Hot cooked fettucini,
   spaghetti, or rice

Shake chicken pieces with salt, pepper, and flour. Sauté in hot oil until crisply browned on all sides, removing as pieces brown. Pour off all but about 3 tablespoons oil. Add onions, green pepper or pimiento, and garlic to oil; cook until very soft. Add tomatoes, herbs, and stock concentrate. Simmer until well blended—10 to 15 minutes; adjust seasonings if necessary. Replace chicken in sauce; cover; simmer 1½ hours over very low heat (or bake in covered casserole in moderate oven, 350° F.).

Serve with fettucini, spaghetti, or rice, tossed with butter and
Parmesan cheese, plus a simple green salad. *Makes 8 to 10 serv-*
ings.

Caril do Frango (Chicken Curry Portuguese Style)

1 broiler-fryer, about	1 bay leaf
2½ pounds	¼ teaspoon grated nutmeg
2 tablespoons flour	½ teaspoon powdered ginger
3 or 4 tablespoons butter,	⅛ teaspoon cayenne or Tabasco
clarified	¼ teaspoon cinnamon
1 large onion, minced	¼ teaspoon saffron
2 cloves garlic	1½ cups white wine
½ green pepper, seeded, chopped	2 anchovies, boned, minced
1 tablespoon minced ham	2 tablespoons minced cilantro
1 tablespoon curry powder	or parsley
¼ teaspoon thyme	

Cut chicken into small pieces, using poultry shears. Dust with
flour (do not add salt). Brown in clarified butter, in heavy
top-of-stove casserole, a few pieces at a time. Remove. Add onion, whole garlic cloves, and green pepper to casserole; cook
over reduced heat until garlic is soft enough to crush into fat
with tines of fork. Add ham and all the spices and herbs except
saffron; stir to blend. Add saffron to wine; let stand 10 minutes.
Add to remaining ingredients in casserole. Replace chicken.
Cover; cook over very low heat 1 to 1½ hours. Add anchovy at
the last. (Ham and anchovy together should provide all the salt
needed, but taste to make sure.) Garnish with cilantro or
parsley and serve over rice with assorted condiments, such as
grated coconut, chutney, chopped toasted almonds, and fried
bananas. *Makes 4 to 6 servings.*

Chicken with Sauce Suprême

1 large stewing hen, 4 to 5 pounds,	3 tablespoons flour
cut up	Salt, pepper
1 cup concentrated chicken broth	½ cup heavy cream
3 tablespoons butter	2 egg yolks (optional)

The deliciousness of this dish depends on the chicken broth.
Separate neck, giblets, back, and wing tips from remaining
parts; cook these in 2½ cups water with ½ teaspoon salt, for 30
minutes. Strain. Cut remaining chicken into serving portions;
add to the strained stock; simmer over low heat until very
tender—about 1 hour. Remove from broth; skin chicken pieces
and discard skin. Strain broth and measure. If more than 1 cup,
cook down; if less than 1 cup, add water as needed.

Melt butter; stir in flour. Slowly stir in chicken broth and cook 20 minutes. Add salt and pepper as needed. Add cream a little at a time, beating with whisk. If the egg yolks are to be added (as I prefer it), save out ½ the cream, beat egg yolk and remaining cream together, add part of hot sauce to egg yolk mixture, then add to remaining sauce, beating with whisk until smooth. Taste for seasoning; add salt and pepper as needed. Place skinned cooked chicken pieces in casserole; cover with sauce. If made ahead, reheat in 350° F. oven, covered, for 30 minutes. Serve over rice, with Petits Pois à la Française and a tossed salad of watercress and Boston lettuce, with fruit compote for dessert. *Makes 6 to 8 servings.*

Chicken with Dumplings

1 large 4- to 5-pound stewing hen, cut up	1 cup biscuit mix
	1/3 cup milk
Water	1 egg
1 teaspoon salt	Minced parsley

Place chicken parts in Dutch oven, pressure cooker, or heavy kettle with cover. Add water so that it almost but not quite covers the chicken pieces; in a pressure cooker, less water is needed. Add salt and cover tightly; cook until chicken is tender—about 45 minutes over low heat; or, in a pressure cooker at 15 pounds pressure, for 15 minutes. When chicken is cooked, uncover. Combine biscuit mix, milk, and egg to form a sticky dough; spoon the dough over the chicken pieces. Cover again; bring back to a boil (do not place petcock on pressure cooker); cook 12 minutes. Serve from a casserole, garnish with minced parsley, spooning the chicken broth over the dumplings at table. *Makes 6 to 8 servings.*

For 3 to 4 servings, use only half the chicken pieces, or use a smaller chicken.

Indiana Church Supper Chicken Pie

2 stewing chickens, 3 to 4 pounds each, cut up	sliced (optional)
	3 tablespoons flour
4 cups water	1 teaspoon gravy coloring
1 teaspoon salt	(optional)
3 or 4 tablespoons butter	Rich Biscuit Dough or piecrust
½ pound mushrooms,	(for 2-crust pie)

Simmer the chicken in water with salt until very tender—about 1½ hours. Remove chicken; skin and bone and cut meat into small pieces. Strain stock. Melt butter; cook mushrooms (if used) until lightly browned. Stir in flour. Slowly add 3 cups chicken stock; simmer until sauce is smooth and thickened. Taste for seasoning; add salt if needed. If desired, add a teaspoon of gravy coloring. Combine cut-up chicken and gravy. Place in long shallow oval casserole or baking dish (or use two 9 x 9-inch Pyrex baking dishes). Cover with Rich Biscuit Dough, rolled ¼ inch thick, or piecrust made with mix or your favorite recipe; dough should overlap edges of dish, but with a slash or cut-out portion in center. Bake in oven preheated to 375° F. until crust is golden and gravy can be seen bubbling up through slashes in center—about 40 minutes. *Makes 10 to 12 servings.*

CHURCH SUPPER TURKEY PIE. Instead of a stewing hen, cook a 10-pound turkey, cut up, in 8 cups water with 1 tablespoon salt until tender—about 4 hours. Make gravy with the broth; place diced turkey meat and gravy in roasting pan, use half again the recipe for Rich Biscuit Dough; or, cover pan with pastry, using piecrust mix or your favorite recipe. *Makes 12 to 14 servings.*

Individual Chicken (or Turkey) Pies

2 cups cooked chicken or turkey, diced or cubed
8 small white onions (cooked or canned)
2 carrots, scraped, cubed, cooked
1 cup frozen peas
3 cups Velouté Sauce (1½ recipes), or 2 cans condensed cream of chicken soup and 2/3 cup light cream
Seasonings to taste
Pastry for 2-crust pie

Combine chicken or turkey with vegetables; divide among 4 individual casseroles. Divide the sauce or soup with cream; pour over top. Season to taste.

Divide pastry dough in 4 parts; roll out each to fit over top of individual casseroles, make slashes in the center. Bake in oven preheated to 400° F. until crust is golden and flaky—about 40 minutes. *Makes 4 pies.*

Chicken Pot Pie

1 4- to 5-pound stewing chicken, cut up
3 to 4 cups water
½ cup minced onion
½ cup minced celery
2 teaspoons salt
¼ teaspoon white pepper
2 tablespoons chopped parsley

Place chicken in kettle with remaining ingredients except parsley; simmer, covered, 1½ to 2 hours. (Add more water if necessary.) When tender, add Pot-pie Dumplings a few at a time;

keep broth boiling and avoid sticking. Stir with a large fork occasionally. Cook, loosely covered, 10 minutes altogether; sprinkle with parsley; cook 3 or 4 minutes longer.

POT-PIE DUMPLINGS

1½ cups sifted flour	2 eggs, well beaten
1 teaspoon salt	2 tablespoons milk

Combine flour and salt, form a well in center, place eggs and milk here. Stir with fork, gradually blending flour into liquid, until a stiff dough is formed, then knead with fingers until smooth. Roll out ¼ inch thick. Cut into 2-inch squares with pastry wheel or sharp knife. Let stand on board 15 minutes to dry.

Chicken or Turkey à la King

2 cups diced cooked chicken or turkey	¼ cup chopped pimiento
1 tablespoon minced onion	1 tablespoon butter
½ green pepper, seeded, chopped	2 cups Velouté Sauce
	1 tablespoon sherry

A good use for leftover chicken or turkey; if you don't have as much as 2 cups, extend it with canned button mushrooms or minced celery. Cook onion, green pepper, and pimiento in butter until soft (add mushrooms and celery now, if to be used). Add chicken (or turkey) plus Velouté Sauce and sherry. Simmer until well blended. Serve over rice or in patty shells, accompanied by green peas or beans. *Makes 4 to 6 servings.*

Peking Chicken with Almonds

¼ cup oil	1 5-ounce can water chestnuts, halved, drained
½ cup blanched almonds	
1 small onion, thinly sliced	1 teaspoon salt
1 whole chicken breast, boned, cubed	½ cup chicken broth
	1 tablespoon soy sauce
1 green pepper, seeded, cut in squares	1 tablespoon dry sherry
	2 teaspoons cornstarch
1 white turnip, peeled, cubed, or	½ teaspoon sugar

Heat half the oil; add almonds; sauté until lightly browned; remove. Add remaining oil and onion; cook onion until soft. Add chicken; cook until lightly browned on edges. Add green pepper and turnips; cook 6 to 7 minutes. Sprinkle with salt. Blend together broth, soy sauce, sherry, cornstarch, and sugar; add to pan with almonds. Simmer until sauce thickens. Serve over rice. *Makes 4 to 6 servings.*

Deep-fried Peking Chicken

1 broiler-fryer, about
  2½ pounds
1 teaspoon sugar
¼ teaspoon white pepper
1 scallion, minced
2 slices green ginger root,

or ¼ teaspoon ground ginger
3 tablespoons soy sauce
2 tablespoons sherry
1/3 cup cornstarch
Oil for deep frying
Soy-Vinegar Sauce

Cut chicken into pieces about 2 inches long, using poultry shears. Place in bowl; combine sugar, pepper, scallion, ginger, soy sauce, and sherry; pour over chicken. Let stand 2 to 3 hours at room temperature, turning occasionally. Drain well; discard marinade. Dredge chicken pieces with cornstarch. Heat oil to 375° F. and fry a few pieces at a time until crisply browned. Remove from oil. Cool. Drain thoroughly. (This can be done ahead.) Reheat oil to 375° and return chicken, a few pieces at a time, to fry until crisp and well browned. Drain again on absorbent paper. Serve with Soy-Vinegar Sauce as part of a Chinese dinner. *Makes 4 to 6 servings.*

Chicken Kiev

¼ pound butter
4 whole chicken breasts, boned
¼ cup flour
½ teaspoon salt

1 egg, well beaten, blended
  with 2 tablespoons water
¼ cup fine dry crumbs
1 cup oil

Cut butter into 4 pieces; place in freezer until very hard. Meanwhile, pound boned chicken breasts until flat and very thin. Insert frozen butter in center of each breast, fold over, pound edges together with mallet or heavy end of hammer to seal. Roll chicken breasts in flour blended with salt, then in egg, finally in the crumbs. Fry in hot oil in electric deep fryer or electric skillet set at 350° F. until chicken is crisp and brown all over. Serve at once. When chicken is cut, butter will ooze out. *Serves 4.*

SUGGESTED GO-WITHS. French-fried parsley, buttered peas, and creamed potatoes.

Poulet du Cloître

2 whole chicken breasts, cut in
  halves
Salt, pepper
6 tablespoons clarified butter
2 tablespoons cream sherry
8 small white onions, peeled

4 serving portions ham, ¼ inch
  thick
1 6-ounce can mushroom crowns,
  drained
1 cup light cream
2 egg yolks

Sprinkle chicken breasts with salt and pepper; sauté in 4 table-spoons of the butter over high heat until well browned. Add sherry; lower heat; spoon mixture of sherry and pan drippings over chicken. Add onions and liquid of canned mushrooms; cover; simmer over lowest heat until onions are tender—about 30 minutes. Separately brown ham slices in remaining 2 table-spoons butter; remove to serving platter. Brown mushrooms in same butter; add to platter. Place a chicken breast over each slice of ham. Add onions to platter. To pan drippings, add cream, stir to blend. Add some of this to beaten egg yolks, then combine the two over low heat, beating with whisk until thick-ened to consistency of heavy cream. Taste; add salt if needed. Pour sauce over chicken breasts. *Makes 4 elegant servings.*

Chicken Lau-laus with Coconut-Curry Sauce

4 whole chicken breasts, boned
1½ tablespoons flour
1 teaspoon salt
4 to 6 tablespoons butter

2 teaspoons soy sauce
2 small onions or 6 scallions, minced
2 pounds spinach

Cut chicken into ¼-inch cubes; roll in flour mixed with salt. Sauté chicken in butter until browned—about 2 minutes; add soy sauce and onions; cook 1 minute. Use about 6 large spinach leaves for each lau-lau: spread out 3 or 4 leaves on a square of aluminum foil; place chicken mixture over spinach; cover with more leaves; roll up. Place in squares of foil and crimp edges together to seal. Place foil-wrapped lau-laus in glowing coals of charcoal fire, bake 30 to 40 minutes, turning once; or, bake in 350° F. oven for 30 to 40 minutes. Serve lau-laus topped with Coconut-Curry Sauce. *Makes 12 to 16 lau-laus; allow 2 for each portion.*

COCONUT-CURRY SAUCE

¾ cup packaged coconut
2 cups milk, scalded
2 tablespoons butter
1 small onion, minced
1 large clove garlic, minced or crushed

½ teaspoon salt
¼ teaspoon powdered ginger
½ tablespoon curry powder, or to taste
1½ tablespoons flour
2 tablespoons Jamaican rum

Add grated coconut to milk. Let stand 1 hour; strain, squeezing with back of spoon until coconut is dry. Discard coconut; save milk. Melt butter; add onion and garlic; cook until soft; add salt, ginger and curry powder, then flour, stirring until smooth.

Slowly add coconut milk; simmer over low heat until smooth and thickened. Add rum; cook 1 minute longer. *Makes 2 cups sauce.*

BAKED CHICKEN LUAU. Sauté floured chicken pieces in butter as in recipe for Chicken Lau-laus; remove. Cook onion until soft. Arrange spinach, chicken, and onion in layers in casserole; cover with coconut milk or Coconut-Curry Sauce. Bake, uncovered, in oven set at 325° F. for 45 minutes. *Makes 8 servings.*

Roast Chicken, Capon, Turkey, or Cornish Hens (Basic Recipe)

The same rules apply to all these birds; the only difference is size, and length of cooking time. For approximate cooking times, see Poultry Roasting Timetable.

First wash the bird (or birds), pat dry with paper towel inside and out, then sprinkle with salt inside and out. Rub olive oil or other fat all over outside, especially the legs. Olive oil is the best; it helps to keep the skin supple, induces more even browning, and because the consistency is heavier it sticks better to the surface. Softened butter lends delicious flavor, but makes the skin more brittle (unless cheesecloth is used, dipped in melted butter); margarine is less desirable because the additives in margarine separate in melting and tend to cause spotty browning.

If stuffing is to be used, allow approximately 1 cup stuffing per pound weight. Stuff loosely—do not pack tight. Some birds come dressed so that trussing is not necessary: the legs fit into a pocket. (Remove legs from pocket while poking stuffing inside breast cavity, then fit legs back into the pocket.) Place a small piece of aluminum foil over exposed stuffing. Stuffing in the neck cavity can be closed over simply by fastening overlapping skin with poultry skewers.

If breast opening must be trussed, fasten skin together with 3 or more skewers placed horizontally; lace up with butcher's cord just as for tightening the laces on skates.

Instead of bread stuffing, herbs, onion, fruit, or a combination of two or more of these may be placed in the cavity, to flavor the flesh delicately from the inside. This is much easier; and in these days of weight watching, why is a bread (or rice) stuffing necessary?

For capons or turkeys, insert a meat thermometer in thick part of drumstick or breast, without touching bone. Cook until internal temperature of 180° to 185° F. is reached. Small birds (small chickens, Cornish hens, game birds) can be tested easily by touching one of the legs: if it moves easily, bird is done.

A tent of aluminum foil should always be placed over turkey to prevent bird from browning too rapidly. This is not necessary for smaller birds.

Spit-roasting Poultry

Any bird (including a turkey) can be spit-roasted if it will fit on a rotisserie spit without touching the drip pan beneath as it revolves. This rules out most turkeys: only those of about 9 pounds or less will fit on the spit. Prepare as for oven-roasted birds: dust with salt inside and out, rub skin with oil or fat, stuff or not as you please. If rotisserie is thermostatically controlled, set heat at 375° F.; over charcoal, keep briquets widely spaced to reduce heat; throw water on fire occasionally if bird (or birds) seem to be browning too rapidly. Otherwise bird may char before it is cooked through.

Only smaller birds (Cornish hens or small broilers) should be marinated in a sweetened barbecue sauce in advance. Brush barbecue sauce over larger birds during last half hour.

For larger bird, insert meat thermometer in leg or breast, almost horizontally so that it will not touch drip pan as bird revolves. Internal temperature should reach 185° before bird is done. Smaller birds can be tested by moving leg.

It may be possible to get 3 Cornish hens on one spit, but usually no more than 2 small chickens or 1 capon or roasting chicken.

Chicken or Turkey Gravy

Make broth with necks, giblets, and any trimmings while bird is roasting or spit-roasting. When bird is cooked, remove to platter; pour off excess fat from pan drippings, saving only the fat streaked with brown, not the clear liquid. Measure this; add same amount of flour and 1 cup strained liquid (chicken broth plus water) for each 2 tablespoons fat. Simmer until well blended and smooth; taste for salt, add as needed.

Quick Seasoning Variations

All the following can be used either for oven-roasted or spit-roasted birds. Quantities given are sufficient for 2 small chickens, 4 Cornish hens, or 1 capon. Use half again as much for a turkey over 10 pounds.

ORANGE-STUFFED. Cut an orange in half; place half the orange in cavity of chicken, capon, or small turkey. If 2 chickens are being roasted, place ½ orange in each. For 4 Cornish hens, place ¼ orange in each. For a large turkey, place both halves of orange in cavity. Parsley sprigs and a small peeled onion may also be added, if desired. Orange flavors the flesh deliciously.

SOY-ORANGE GLAZE. Place an orange half in cavity as described above; while bird (or birds) turn on spit, brush with mixture of ¼ cup soy sauce, ½ cup orange juice, 1 tablespoon sherry.

ORANGE-CINNAMON GLAZE. Baste birds with mixture of 1 cup orange juice, ½ teaspoon cinnamon, dash of freshly ground black pepper, and ¼ cup olive oil.

HERB-FLAVORED. Lift up skin in several places; insert dabs of Herb Butter under the skin; replace skin. Or, use a blend of ¼ teaspoon ginger, ¼ teaspoon garlic salt, ¼ teaspoon orégano, and 8 tablespoons softened butter (enough for 2 broilers or 1 capon).

VERMOUTH-ORANGE GLAZE. Baste bird with mixture of ¼ cup sweet vermouth, ½ cup orange juice, ¼ teaspoon cinnamon, ½ teaspoon salt. (This is also delicious with duckling.)

TOMATO GLAZE. Brush bird with Tomato Glaze (see index) after skin has begun to turn golden.

HERB-STUFFED. In cavity, place sprigs of fresh herbs (fresh cilantro is especially delicious) or bouquet garni, plus an onion stuck with cloves.

Beer-basted Cornish Hens

4 Cornish hens, ¾ to 1 pound each	1 6-ounce can beer
Salt	1 teaspoon dry mustard
1 package herb-flavored bread stuffing	1 teaspoon brown sugar
	2 tablespoons chili sauce
	1 teaspoon salt

Wash birds inside and out; sprinkle with salt inside and out. Prepare bread stuffing according to package directions; use to stuff the hens. Combine remaining ingredients; marinate hens in beer mixture for several hours, turning several times. Spit-roast on rotisserie if spit is long enough to hold them all; or bake in oven preheated to 400° F. for 1 hour, until leg of largest bird moves easily. Baste frequently with beer marinade. When birds are done, remove to individual plates. Make gravy with pan drippings. *Serves 4.*

SUGGESTED GO-WITHS. Corn on the cob, green tomato salad, fresh pineapple au kirsch.

Baby Chickens Baked in Sherry

2 broilers, 1¾ to 2 pounds each	butter
Salt, paprika	1 cup medium sherry
8 tablespoons (½ stick) softened	1 cup chicken broth

Wash broilers inside and out; dust with salt and paprika. Rub all over with softened butter. Arrange birds in large roasting pan. Add sherry to pan. Bake in oven preheated to 375° F. (moderate) until leg of largest chicken moves easily—about 45 minutes. Baste occasionally with pan drippings.

As chickens roast, make broth with necks and giblets; strain. When chickens are done, remove to platter. Make sauce of pan drippings and chicken broth, with salt to taste. Cook, stirring, until well blended. Serve unthickened over chicken. *Serves 6.*

CORNISH HENS BAKED IN SHERRY. Prepare the same way, but use 4 small (¾-pound) Cornish hens instead of chickens.

Rice-stuffed Baby Chickens or Cornish Hens

Prepare 2 small (1¾-pound) broilers or 4 Cornish hens (¾ pound each) as for Baby Chickens Baked in Sherry, but fill with following stuffing, and baste with sherry as they cook. Allow longer cooking time—about 1¼ hours.

RICE-HAM STUFFING

3 cups cooked rice (1 cup uncooked)

2 tablespoons minced ham

2 chicken livers, sautéed in butter, chopped

6 blanched almonds, toasted, chopped

1 tablespoon minced parsley

2 tablespoons melted butter

Combine ingredients; use as stuffing for 2 small chickens or 4 Cornish hens, or 1 6- to 7-pound capon.

Roast Turkey with Corn Bread Stuffing

2 quarts crumbled corn bread (1 12-ounce package corn muffin mix)

1 pound chestnuts, boiled, chopped

½ pound pork sausage meat, cooked

2 cups stale bread crumbs

2 medium onions, chopped

3 stalks celery, minced

Salt, pepper

¼ teaspoon thyme, crushed

½ teaspoon basil, crushed

¼ cup butter

2 eggs, beaten

1 12-pound turkey, dressed

Make corn bread with mix according to package directions, baking in 8-inch-square pan. To prepare chestnuts, make a slit in each shell, cover with water, bring to a boil, and cook until shells crack; cool; cut off shells with sharp knife; chop coarsely. Cook sausage meat; drain off all excess fat. Combine crumbled corn bread, chestnuts, sausage, and bread crumbs in large mixing bowl (3-quart size or larger). Cook vegetables and herbs in the butter until soft; add to corn bread mixture. Stir in beaten eggs; taste for seasoning. Pack stuffing loosely into neck and tail cavities of turkey. Truss by closing the two cavities with poultry skewers; lace and pull tight with heavy cord. Rub outside of turkey with softened butter, or dip cheesecloth in melted butter and wrap over top of turkey. Place in large shallow roasting pan, cover loosely with aluminum foil. Roast at 325° F. until leg moves easily up and down—about 3½ hours. If using meat thermometer, insert on inside of thigh; it should register 185° F. when bird is cooked. Remove turkey from pan with pancake turner and/or spatula; let stand on platter while making gravy—bird is easier to carve after 15 minutes.

To make turkey gravy: While turkey is roasting, make broth with neck and giblets, using 4 cups water and 1 teaspoon salt. After turkey has been removed from roasting pan, pour off all fat (reserving brown essence); measure 6 tablespoons fat; return to pan; blend with 6 tablespoons flour. Measure broth; add water to make 3 cups. Stir, scraping pan to loosen all browned bits. Finally add 1 cup (½ pint) light cream, if desired. Taste for seasoning, add salt and pepper as needed. *Makes 4 cups gravy.*

Boned Stuffed Turkey

1 12-pound turkey	Pinch of ginger
1 pound lean raw pork, minced	2 cups stale crumbs,
1 pound sweet Italian sausage,	crumbled fine
diced	1 package frozen peas
4 tablespoons butter	1 teaspoon minced anchovy
1 calf's brain	2 tablespoons sherry
2 cups minced celery	Olive oil
1 cup minced onion	Salt, pepper
½ teaspoon orégano	

To bone turkey, place breast down on board, with small sharp knife slit along backbone from neck to tail. Insert knife between meat and bone, carefully work meat loose, first on one side, then the other. Sever breast bones from joints at drumsticks and wings, remove breast and back bones. Leave wings and drumsticks intact. Sew up with thread along back to close opening. Turn breast side up; force stuffing through regular opening until plump and natural-looking.

To make stuffing: Sauté minced pork and sausage in butter until lightly browned. At same time, cook calf's brain in acidulated water (see recipe for Calf's Brain). Add celery and onion to pork; cook until soft. Add orégano, ginger and diced cooked brain. Transfer to large bowl, add bread crumbs and remaining ingredients. Blend very well. Season to taste. Truss turkey.

Place turkey in large double thickness of foil; rub olive oil over outside, sprinkle with salt. Seal edges of foil. Place in large roasting pan; bake in oven preheated to 400° F. until meat thermometer registers 185°. (Insert thermometer in breast so that it goes deep into stuffing; stuffing must be thoroughly cooked.) Open foil and continue cooking until turkey browns. Remove to platter.

To make gravy: Scrape out pan drippings from foil into saucepan; remove clear fat, saving only brown-streaked drippings. Stir in 4 tablespoons flour; cook until mixture bubbles. Slowly add 2 cups water or broth (made with giblets) and salt to taste. Simmer until smooth and thickened. If desired, add 2 tablespoons cream.

This is perfect for a buffet, for the turkey slices easily and serves 16 to 18 persons.

Stuffed Chicken Breasts

Shape these so that they look like little birds; serve 1 breast to each person.

¼ cup cooked ham, chopped, and
  ¼ cup minced chorizo sausage, or
  ½ cup minced ham
1 tablespoon minced white onion
1 cup slightly stale bread crumbs
1¼ teaspoons salt

4 whole chicken breasts
¼ cup oil
1 teaspoon paprika
1 cup seedless white grapes
½ cup cream sherry or
  orange juice

Combine ham, and chorizo, onion, bread crumbs, and ¼ teaspoon salt; use as stuffing for the chicken breasts. Tie with string to hold together during baking. Brush outside of breasts with oil blended with paprika and 1 teaspoon salt. Lay in shallow casserole. Place stemmed whole grapes around chicken. Bake in oven preheated to 350° F. until delicately browned—about 35 minutes. Baste with sherry or orange juice once or twice. *Serves 4.*

Roast Pheasant Viennoise

2 pheasants, dressed
Buttermilk
1 large onion, sliced
1 carrot, minced
1 cup minced celery root
  (celeriac) or Pascal celery

1 parsnip, diced fine
4 tablespoons butter
Salt, pepper
2 strips bacon
¾ cup red wine
½ cup sour cream

Marinate the pheasants overnight in buttermilk to cover. In saucepan, cook vegetables in butter until soft; transfer to roasting pan. Remove birds from marinade; place over cooked vegetables and season; cover with bacon strips. Roast in oven preheated to 325° F. until birds are crisply brown—1½ to 1¾ hours. Baste occasionally with pan drippings. Remove to platter. Keep warm.

Strain pan drippings or purée in blender. Add red wine; simmer 5 minutes; taste for seasoning and add salt as needed. Turn heat very low; blend some of sauce with sour cream, then combine the two, beating with a whisk. Serve sauce with pheasants. *Makes 4 servings.*

CORNISH HENS VIENNOISE. Use 4 Cornish hens instead of the 2 pheasants.

SUGGESTED GO-WITHS. Tiny parsley potatoes, red cabbage, Lemon Relish.

Partridges on Toast

4 partridges*
1 tablespoon minced onion
4 tablespoons olive oil
Salt, pepper
2 tablespoons softened butter

¼ cup cream sherry
4 slices bread, trimmed
½ cup canned beef or chicken gravy
1 tablespoon minced parsley

Sauté the livers of the partridges with onion in 1 tablespoon of the olive oil. Mash to a paste with mortar and pestle or purée in blender. Season with salt and pepper; add butter; beat until creamy. Set aside. Brush the partridges with the remaining oil; place in oven preheated to 450° F. for 20 to 25 minutes; after 15 minutes, baste with the sherry. Meanwhile, lightly toast bread, spread with liver. When partridge is done, remove from oven, add beef gravy to drippings in pan and simmer, stirring, until well blended. Place partridges on liver-spread toast and garnish with parsley. Serve gravy on the side. *Serves 4.*

*Cornish game hens, pheasants, or squab chickens may be prepared the same way.

Roast Chicken Karachi

1 5-pound roasting chicken, or 1 6- to 7-pound capon
Rice-Almond Stuffing
½ pint (1 cup) yogurt

2 tablespoons minced green ginger, or 1 teaspoon powdered ginger
1 small onion, chopped

Prepare chicken as in basic recipe; stuff with Rice-Almond Stuffing. Truss. Prick skin all over with fork so that yogurt will penetrate. Combine yogurt with ginger and onion; rub into skin of chicken with back of spoon. Marinate 1 to 3 hours.

Preheat oven to 325° F.; place chicken in oven in open roasting pan; roast for 2½ hours. Make a clear unthickened gravy with pan drippings. *Serves 6.*

RICE-ALMOND STUFFING

3 cups partially cooked rice
2 hard-cooked eggs, chopped
1 cup cooked peas
2 tablespoons blanched toasted

almonds
¼ cup seedless raisins
2 slices lemon, seeded, minced (with peel)

Combine all ingredients; season to taste with salt and pepper. *Makes 5 cups,* but rice will swell somewhat during cooking.

Squabs with Cumberland Sauce

4 to 6 squabs*
Rice-Almond Stuffing
Melted butter, about 6 tablespoons

Broth made of giblets and necks
Cumberland Sauce

Ask the game merchant to give you the giblets and necks of the birds to make the broth. Wash and dry birds; sprinkle inside and out with salt; fill with Rice-Almond Stuffing (divided among the birds). Stuff loosely. (If any stuffing is left over, cook it separately in a casserole.) Place in open roasting pan, baste with melted butter.

Preheat oven to 400° F. (hot); bake birds at this heat for 10 minutes, then reduce heat to 300° and bake until legs move easily—1 to 1¼ hours longer. Baste occasionally with pan drippings. As birds are cooking, make broth of giblets and necks with a sprig of celery leaves. Strain; reduce to 1 cup. During last half-hour, baste birds with the broth.

Serve hot with Cumberland Sauce, adding the broth to the sauce. *Makes 4 to 6 servings.*

*Any small birds may be prepared this way—quail, partridge, grouse, or Cornish hens.

SUGGESTED GO-WITHS. Oriental Soup with Vegetables as a first course; with the birds, braised celery and Salade Valenciana.

STUFFINGS

Celery-Onion Stuffing

1 large onion, chopped
1 cup minced celery
6 to 8 tablespoons butter or margarine
½ teaspoon thyme
¼ teaspoon orégano

⅛ teaspoon sage
2 tablespoons minced parsley
8 cups (2 quarts) slightly stale bread cubes
Salt

Cook onion and celery in butter until softened; add herbs. Pour all of mixture over bread cubes in bowl; stir to blend thoroughly. Add salt to taste. Makes enough stuffing for a 10-pound turkey.

For a 6- to 7-pound capon, use 1 medium onion, ¾ cup celery, 4 to 6 tablespoons butter or margarine, herbs to taste, and 5 to 6 cups crumbs.

For 4 Cornish hens, divide all ingredients in half.

Apple-Prune Stuffing

1 package herb-seasoned
  bread stuffing
½ cup chopped dried prunes
1 cup chopped apples
½ cup chopped walnuts

¼ cup minced celery
2 slices bacon, cooked, crumbled
2 tablespoons rum, brandy, or
  Madeira wine
2 tablespoons melted butter

Moisten bread stuffing according to package directions; add remaining ingredients, blend well. Makes enough stuffing for a 6-pound capon, a 4- to 5-pound duckling, or 2 broiler chickens.

For a 10-pound turkey, or a goose, double all ingredients.

Bacon-Clam Stuffing

3 to 4 tablespoons olive oil
1 large Spanish onion, chopped,
  or 2 medium onions
1 or 2 cloves garlic, crushed
6 strips bacon, diced
10 cups seasoned poultry dress-

ing, or 10 cups stale bread
  cubes, 1½ teaspoons salt and
  mixed herbs
½ cup minced parsley
2 7- or 8-ounce cans minced
  clams, drained

Place olive oil, onion, garlic, and bacon in heavy skillet; cook until bacon is crisp and onion soft (do not allow onion to brown). Add about 1 cup of the bread cubes to pan; stir to mix. Add this to remaining bread cubes or seasoned poultry dressing along with parsley and drained minced clams. Makes 10 cups, enough for 10- to 12-pound turkey.

For 6 Cornish hens, divide all ingredients in half.

Chestnut-Sausage Stuffing

1½ pounds chestnuts in shell
1 pound sausage meat
1 large onion, minced
4 tablespoons butter or
  margarine
¼ cup hot water

1 tablespoon poultry seasoning
1 tablespoon salt
6 cups slightly stale coarse
  bread crumbs
6 tablespoons bourbon

Slit shells of chestnuts; bake in oven preheated to 450 F. (very hot) for 15 minutes. Remove from oven; when cool enough to handle, remove shells. (Or, chestnuts may be boiled in shells for 30 minutes.) Chop coarsely.

Cook sausage meat and onion in butter or margarine until sausage is browned—about 15 minutes. Add chestnuts; cook 5 minutes, stirring occasionally. Add remaining ingredients. Toss to mix thoroughly. Enough stuffing for 10- to 12-pound turkey.

Spanish Stuffing

½ pound lean pork, diced
3 tablespoons olive oil
1 medium onion, chopped
½ cup (2¼-ounce package)
   slivered almonds or pine nuts
¼ pound mushrooms, chopped
6 cups stale bread crumbs

½ cup seedless raisins
1 teaspoon thyme
½ teaspoon marjoram
½ cup minced parsley
½ teaspoon salt, or to taste
¼ teaspoon powdered ginger

Sauté pork in olive oil until lightly browned; add onion, nuts, and mushrooms. Cook until lightly browned. Add to bread crumbs with raisins, herbs, and seasonings. Toss to blend well. *Makes enough for breast cavity of a 12-pound turkey, or breast and neck cavities of a 10-pound turkey.*

Wild Rice and Mushroom Stuffing

2 cups wild rice
2 large onions, chopped
1 cup chopped celery, with
   leaves
8 tablespoons butter
4 cups chicken broth

1 cup chopped nuts
1 6-ounce can chopped mushrooms, drained
½ teaspoon poultry seasoning
Salt, pepper

Cook wild rice, onions, and celery in butter 5 minutes; add broth; bring to a boil; cover; simmer 30 minutes. Add remaining ingredients; mix thoroughly. *Makes about 6 cups—enough for 6 Cornish hens or 1 6-pound capon.*

Oyster Stuffing

1 cup minced onion
1 cup (½ pound) butter
1 pint small oysters, drained.
   chopped (with liquor)
1½ teaspoons salt

½ cup chopped parsley
½ cup chopped celery leaves
10 cups (2½ quarts) stale bread
   crumbs

Cook onion in butter until soft and golden; add all remaining ingredients except bread; cook 5 minutes. Add mixture to bread crumbs, stir to blend. *Makes about 10 cups stuffing—enough for breast and neck cavities of a 12-pound turkey, or the breast cavity of a 15-pound turkey.*

Quick Tricks with Turkey Roll

A boned 2-pound turkey roll is versatile and makes a comparatively inexpensive family dish. The following are some of the ways it can be varied; in each case, the roll is to be cooked in the aluminum foil package in which it comes.

WITH SHERRY-ORANGE SAUCE. Add ½ cup orange juice and 2 tablespoons medium or sweet sherry to foil pan before baking; serve as a clear sauce.

TURKEY-VEGETABLE CASSEROLE. Add 1 package frozen mixed vegetables (thawed enough to separate) to foil package before cooking, along with 1 tablespoon instant minced onion, ½ teaspoon salt for vegetables, and a pinch of thyme. Bake, covered, as directed. When cooked, slice the turkey, add vegetables and sauce. Serve from a casserole. Serve with baked potatoes (baked in same oven).

BRANDIED IN CREAM. Add 2 tablespoons brandy and ½ cup light cream to foil package before baking. Thicken sauce or not as preferred.

CURRIED TURKEY ROLL. Add to package before baking, ½ to 1 tablespoon curry powder, ¼ cup raisins, 1 teaspoon instant minced onion, ¼ teaspoon garlic powder or garlic salt, and 1 tart apple, peeled, seeded, and chopped. When turkey is cooked, slice or dice and serve in the sauce. Add salt to sauce if needed.

Using Leftover Chicken and Turkey

Turkey or Chicken Hash (Basic Recipe)

2 cups diced turkey or chicken*	2 tablespoons heavy cream or sour cream
1 cup gravy†	

Combine turkey and gravy; heat, stirring, until sauce bubbles. Turn off heat; stir in cream. Serve over toast or rice or with mashed potatoes. *Makes 4 servings.*

For 6 servings, use 3 cups meat, 1½ cups gravy, 3 tablespoons cream.

*When there is not this much meat, add mushrooms, chopped olives, grapes, or leftover cooked vegetables (such as peas or green beans) to make 2 cups. Do the same when you wish to make 6 servings and have only 2 cups meat; add other ingredients to make a total of 3 cups; use 1½ cups gravy.

†If you have no gravy, use ¾ cup canned gravy or gravy made with mix, add ¼ cup white wine or sherry, and ¼ cup cream (rather than 2 tablespoons).

CURRIED TURKEY HASH. Heat leftover diced turkey in Curry-Cream Sauce, or add 1 teaspoon curry powder to basic recipe.

TURKEY HASH AMANDINE. Prepare Turkey Hash as in basic recipe; separately toast ¼ cup blanched slivered almonds, or sauté almonds in butter. Serve almonds over hash. Or, combine almonds and hash, layer with cooked noodles in casserole, bake until sauce bubbles.

TURKEY PIE. Combine 3 cups meat (or a mixture of meat, mushrooms, chopped olives, and/or frozen or cooked vegetables), with 1½ cups gravy. Place in 1½-quart casserole; top with pie crust made with ½ package piecrust mix or your favorite recipe for 1-crust pie. Bake in oven preheated to 375° F. until crust is crisply golden and sauce can be seen bubbling through the slits.

Creamed Chicken on Waffles

1½ cups diced cooked chicken (or turkey)
1 4-ounce can button mushrooms with liquid
1 can condensed cream of
mushroom soup
¼ cup heavy cream
Dash of nutmeg
Waffles, homemade or frozen

Combine chicken and *drained* mushrooms. Add mushroom liquid to soup, blend well, then stir in cream. Add to chicken; stir over moderate heat until steaming. Season with nutmeg. Serve over hot crisp waffles.

Turkey Crêpes

Combine diced leftover cooked turkey (or chicken) with gravy, as for Turkey Hash. Use as a filling for thin pancakes, rolled up. Place rolled pancakes in a shallow casserole; cover with Béchamel or Mornay Sauce, sprinkle grated Parmesan cheese over top. (This can be done ahead.) Place casserole 5 inches from heat in broiler oven, or in oven preheated to 450° F. until cheese is melted and sauce lightly browned. A nice luncheon dish for ladies.

OTHER WAYS TO USE TURKEY OR CHICKEN LEFTOVERS

• Add to Basic Curry Sauce as an entree.
• Use with a package of Noodles Almondine.
• Use in salad with oranges and grapes.

- Turn into a sandwich filling (sliced or in salad).
- Combine with leftover cooked pork or ham, all minced, in Sauce Soubise or Mornay Sauce.
- Use to make Turkey Cocido.
- Use to make Turkey or Chicken Divan.
- Add to Spanish Rice or almost any pasta casserole.

Chicken Livers

These can be purchased by the pound in almost every market, and they may be used alone or in combination with mushrooms or other ingredients to make an inexpensive and delicious entree.

Chicken Livers in Sauce Robert

1 pound chicken livers
2 tablespoons butter or margarine
1 ¾-ounce envelope brown gravy mix

1 ½ cups boiling water
1 envelope (3 tablespoons) onion soup mix
¼ cup white wine

Cut each liver in half. Sauté livers in butter until well browned on both sides. Blend gravy mix with boiling water; add to livers with soup mix and wine. Simmer, stirring, 10 minutes. Serve over hot cooked rice or with noodles. *Makes 4 servings.*

Chicken Livers and Mushrooms in Sherry Sauce

1 pound chicken livers
4 tablespoons butter
½ pound button mushrooms, trimmed
½ teaspoon salt, or to taste

2 tablespoons flour
Pinch of nutmeg
½ cup medium sherry
1 cup chicken broth
2 tablespoons heavy cream

Cut each liver in half. Sauté chicken livers in butter until well browned. Add mushrooms; cook until lightly browned. Sprinkle with salt. Stir in flour and nutmeg. Slowly add sherry and chicken broth; simmer 5 minutes. Turn off heat, stir in cream. Serve with rice or noodles.

CHICKEN LIVERS AND GRAPES. Prepare as above, but use 1 cup seedless white grapes instead of mushrooms; omit flour and cream. Serve over rice.

DUCKS AND GEESE

The most important thing to keep in mind in preparing either of these birds is that they contain a great deal of fat, and efforts must be made to drain off all excess fat before preparing any sauce or gravy. First, remove all visible fat. Next, prick holes all over the skin of the bird and place it breast side down on a rack, over an open roasting pan, during the first half-hour of roasting. Another way is to precook the bird for 15 to 20 minutes in boiling water to draw out excess fat, then cool and prepare for roasting.

Duck is excellent spit-roasted, over reduced heat. (If using an electric rotisserie, set it at 350° F.) Be sure to have a deep pan to collect the dripping fat.

In the Orient, duck is often skinned (a good way to get at all the fat beneath the skin), then braised in butter with seasonings.

Goose is always best oven-roasted. One way is to bag it, in a large brown paper bag, with holes in the bottom through which the fat can drip, placing on a rack in a roasting pan. The bag keeps the meat moist, and the bird will brown very well inside the bag. The only tricky part is removing the bag, for there will still be considerable grease inside. Remove cooked goose *in the bag* to a large clean roasting pan, then cut away the paper. Remove goose to a platter, then pour off all the grease from the pan but the part streaked with brown.

For approximate cooking time, see Poultry Roasting Timetable.

To make any sauce for duck or goose, pour off all pan drippings, place in freezer or coldest part of refrigerator until fat has congealed, then discard *all fat* but brown essence on bottom. Use only this in the sauce.

Most ducks and geese are frozen when purchased. Allow 24 to 36 hours at room temperature to thaw completely.

Roast Duckling (Basic Recipe)

1 4- to 5-pound duckling	or 1 parsley or celery sprig,
1 cup giblet broth	1 onion, or 1 apple
½ lemon	1 tablespoon cornstarch
Salt, pepper	1 teaspoon gravy coloring
4 cups seasoned bread stuffing,	(optional)

Thaw duckling completely at room temperature the preceding day. Remove neck and giblets; use to make broth. Strain broth; chill. Remove all visible fat from duck, including as much as possible from under the skin. Prick skin of duckling all over.

Rub duck with cut side of lemon; sprinkle with salt and pepper. If desired, fill with 4 cups herb-seasoned bread stuffing (or 1 8-ounce package prepared according to package directions), or with Apple-Prune Stuffing. Or, instead of bread stuffing, place in cavity a parsley or celery sprig and/or a peeled whole onion stuck with cloves, or a quartered apple.

Place on rack in roasting pan, breast side down. Preheat oven to 450° F.; bake ½ hour. Pour off all accumulated fat in pan; turn duck breast side up; reduce oven heat to 325°. Return to oven; bake until skin is crisp and brown and leg moves easily—1 to 1½ hours longer.

Remove duck to platter. Pour off all drippings from pan except brown-streaked essence. Add cornstarch thinned with water. Remove all fat from chilled giblet broth. Add broth to pan; cook, stirring, until gravy is smooth and thickened. If desired, add 1 teaspoon gravy coloring. Serve duck with gravy, accompanied by applesauce. *Makes 3 servings.*

For 6 servings, roast 2 ducklings, double stuffing.

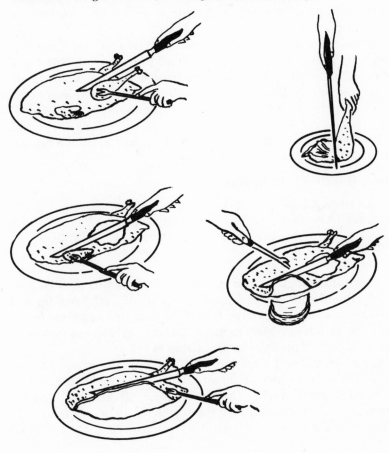

Duck Montmorency

1 4- to 5-pound duckling	½ cup port
1 cup giblet broth	2 tablespoons brandy
1 whole onion	1 cup pitted sweet cherries
½ lemon	Watercress
Salt, pepper	

Prepare duckling as in basic recipe for Roast Duckling; make broth with giblets. Insert whole onion in cavity; rub cut side of lemon over skin and season with salt and pepper. Bake on rack, breast side down, in oven preheated to 450° F. for first half-hour. Pour off pan drippings; turn duck so breast side is up; return to oven with lowered heat as in basic recipe.

Start basting with mixture of port and brandy every 15 minutes until duck is browned and leg moves easily—about 1 hour longer. Again pour off pan drippings; place in bowl; chill. Add cherries to pan; increase heat again to 400° When duckling is very crisp and brown, remove to platter.

Add to cherries in pan the giblet broth (with all fat removed) and the chilled pan drippings with all fat removed. Bring to a boil; scrape up browned bits from bottom. Garnish with watercress and serve the duckling with the unthickened sauce, accompanied by Rissole Potatoes and a green salad. *Makes 3 servings.*

For 6 servings, roast 2 ducklings and use half again the quantity of broth, port, brandy, and cherries.

Roast Duckling with Apples

2 4-pound ducklings	2 teaspoons horseradish
2 cups giblet broth	1 teaspoon raisins
6 apples	1 teaspoon sugar
Salt, pepper	3 tablespoons flour
Whole cloves	

Prepare ducklings as in basic recipe for Roast Duckling. Prepare giblet broth. Place 1 apple in cavity of each; sew up and season. Instead of roasting in hot oven at first, parboil for 30 minutes in salted water. Remove; pat dry; arrange in rack over roasting pan. Place in oven preheated to 350° F.

Core remaining 4 apples; insert whole cloves around top of each; fill with mixture of horseradish, raisins, and sugar.

Several times during first hour, pour off accumulated fat from pan; chill. When ducklings have been in oven 1 hour, add apples, placing around pan. Continue baking until skin of duckling is crisp and leg moves easily. Remove ducks and apples to platter.

Pour off all pan drippings but brown essence. Make gravy by stirring in 3 tablespoons flour, slowly adding giblet broth and any brown essence from pan drippings (but no fat at all). Cook until gravy is smooth and thickened. *Makes 4 to 6 servings.*

Roast Duck à l'Orange

1 large duckling (about 5½ pounds)
1 cup giblet broth
½ lemon
2 navel oranges
Sprig of celery
Salt

1 cup orange juice
½ cup dry white or red wine
1 tablespoon cognac, Grand Marnier, or Curaçao
1 teaspoon gravy coloring (optional)

Prepare duckling as in basic recipe for Roast Duckling. Prepare broth from giblets. Before rubbing with cut side of lemon, carefully remove thinnest outer part of lemon peel; cut in fine slivers. Remove peel from one of the oranges; cut in slivers. Blanche lemon and orange slivers in 1 cup boiling water; drain; set aside.

Place celery sprig and ½ orange inside duckling and sprinkle with salt; place breast side down on rack in roasting pan, roast in oven preheated to 450° F. for 30 minutes. Pour off all drippings, turn over duck, reduce heat to 325°, bake until leg moves easily and duck is crisply browned, about 1½ hours longer. Baste frequently with mixture of 1 cup orange juice and ½ cup wine (saving ½ cup of mixture for sauce).

Remove skin from remaining orange, and cut in slices or break into segments. When duck is done, remove to platter. Pour off all but brown essence from pan. Add slivers of lemon and orange peel and skinned orange segments to pan; simmer in pan drippings 5 minutes. Add remaining basting sauce, the fat-free giblet broth, cognac, or orange liqueur, and (if sauce is not dark enough) gravy coloring. Simmer 10 minutes, reducing to 1 cup sauce. Serve duck with the sauce. *Makes 4 servings.*

Braised Duckling (Basic Recipe)

1 duckling, cut in pieces	1 ½ cups giblet broth
½ cut lemon	1 tablespoon cornstarch
1 teaspoon salt	

When duckling is completely thawed, cut in serving portions with poultry shears. Rub with lemon and season with salt. Place skin side down, tightly packed together, in large heavy skillet or electric skillet *without water or fat*. Cook over moderate heat (350° F. in electric skillet), pouring off accumulated fat about every 20 minutes. Make broth with neck and giblets in separate pan while duck cooks.

When duck is fairly tender, remove. Pour off pan drippings, saving only brown essence. Stir in cornstarch; slowly add broth. Cook until smooth and thickened (consistency of heavy cream). Taste for seasoning; add salt if needed. Replace duck; simmer until very tender—about ½ hour. Serve the duckling with the gravy. *Makes 4 servings.*

CHINESE DUCK WITH MUSHROOMS. Prepare as for Braised Duckling, but rub skin of duckling with mixture of 2 tablespoons sherry and 1 teaspoon powdered ginger before placing in pan. When duckling is fairly tender, remove and pour off all fat. Replace in pan; add mixture of ½ cup soy sauce, 1 tablespoon canned peach or pineapple syrup, 1 teaspoon vinegar, 1½ cups giblet broth, and ½ cup sliced mushrooms (fresh or reconstituted dried). Simmer over very low heat until duck is very tender—about ½ hour longer. Serve with rice.

DUCK WITH OLIVES. Prepare as for Braised Duckling, but when duck is fairly tender, remove, pour off pan drippings, then add ¼ cup sherry or white wine, 1 cup giblet broth, and 1 cup canned chicken gravy. Simmer until smooth. Replace duck pieces; add 1 cup pitted or stuffed green olives. Simmer, uncovered, until duck is very tender. Sprinkle a few drops lemon juice over duck before serving.

Barbecued Duck Orientale

1 4- to 5-pound duckling	½ cup sweet vermouth
Salt, pepper	1 teaspoon powdered cumin
1 small onion, peeled	1 tablespoon honey
Parsley sprigs	1 teaspoon salt

Thaw duck completely. Remove and discard neck and giblets and all visible fat. Prick skin all over. Dust inside and out with salt and pepper. Place onion, parsley, and a spoonful of vermouth-cumin-honey mixture inside duck. Truss, closing cavity and tying legs close to body. Fasten neck skin to back. Place on rotisserie spit, spit-roast over reduced heat until skin is crisp and legs move easily—1½ to 2 hours. Have deep pan directly beneath duck to catch drippings (if roasting over charcoal, place briquets on either side of narrow drip pan or boat made of heavy-duty foil).

After 45 minutes, start basting with sauce composed of vermouth, cumin, honey, and 1 teaspoon salt. Continue basting until duck is done. Remove from spit to platter. Pour off all fat from pan drippings; make sauce with brown essence and any remaining basting sauce. Pour sauce over carved duck. Serve with braised yellow squash and tomato salad. *Makes 3 servings.*

Pressed Almond Duck

1 duckling, about 4 pounds	black pepper
1 teaspoon cinnamon	1 teaspoon grated orange peel
½ teaspoon cloves	½ cup cornstarch
1 teaspoon ground anise or fennel	½ cup blanched almonds, ground
1 teaspoon freshly ground	Oil for deep-frying

Split duck lengthwise through backbone. Place flat in kettle; cover with salted water (2 tablespoons salt to 4 cups water). Add spices and grated orange peel; bring to a boil; cook 40 minutes. Cool in broth. Remove from broth; bone duck, trying to keep meat in one piece. Combine cornstarch and almonds; pat thickly over outside of duck. Press duck flat with rolling pin to ¾ inch thick. Place on rack in steamer (or on rack over water in roasting pan, covered with tent of foil). Steam, covered, on top of stove or in oven until cornstarch appears cooked—about 10 minutes. Remove duck from rack, cut in squares. Deep-fry in oil preheated to 375° F. until crisp—about 8 minutes. Serve over shredded lettuce with rice and Frenched green beans. *Makes 4 servings.*

Roast Goose

These are not available in all markets, and usually when available are frozen. Defrost completely before preparing for the oven. Remove all visible fat, including that under skin. Prick all over. European cooks do not add bread stuffing, using only apples and prunes in the cavity. If bread stuffing is preferred, double the recipe for Apple-Prune Stuffing for an 8- or 10-pound goose. Just as for duck, roast breastside down during first half-hour; pour off pan drippings frequently.

It is impossible to judge the age or tenderness of a frozen goose, and since this is a costly bird in our markets, to be on the safe side it is advisable to sprinkle the goose with meat tenderizer inside and out before roasting (omit salt). Roast in a bag for greater moistness (see page 27).

Sauerkraut is the traditional accompaniment to goose, along with mashed potatoes and, sometimes, applesauce. Sauerkraut may also be used for stuffing, instead of bread stuffing.

5 SEAFOOD

For most Americans, seafood means principally three things: shrimp, canned tuna, and fillet of sole. Lobster or crabmeat now and then as a special treat, perhaps; clams and oysters if you live in coastal areas. But the enormous range and variety of fish and other less familiar shellfish is all but unknown to the average family, and since Friday is no longer a day of abstinence, interest in fish cookery is slipping more rapidly than ever.

A pity, because really fresh fish, properly prepared, can be utterly delicious, and seafood happens to be the best of all weight-reducing protein foods, low in cholesterol, high in essential minerals and vitamins. Some seafood is also inexpensive, though this can't be said any longer for shrimp, lobster, or even for fresh fillet of sole. Cod, haddock, and canned tuna, however, are still bargains.

When cooking either fish or shellfish, two things are important. First, *low heat* is necessary for tenderness and to retain natural juices. Second, most forms of seafood are more succulent if cooked in liquid, braised, or baked, rather than fried or broiled. If broiled, use reduced temperatures.

Frozen fish has less flavor and coarser texture than fresh fish—a further reason for cooking it in flavored liquid. Fortunately, shrimp and lobster lose less in the freezing process; in fact, if cooked with care, they can be almost as good as when freshly caught.

SHRIMP

Virtually all shrimp sold in American markets is frozen when caught. Some of the catch is thawed before it is offered for sale, and therefore seems fresh. Most of the frozen already shelled and deveined shrimp was frozen when caught, thawed at the factory in order to remove shells and veins, then frozen again. There is enormous difference in quality and flavor in the shrimp offered for sale, whether frozen or apparently fresh. In many cases, this is because of carelessness at the packing plant. A certain amount of trial and error is necessary on the part of the consumer in order to determine which brands of frozen shrimp are best, or what markets can be relied on for best quality.

That bitter iodine flavor often encountered in shrimp is not a mark of poor quality; it is characteristic of the shrimp from certain waters, or of certain varieties. To make sure cooked shrimp will not have this bitter taste, always add a little acid (vinegar, lemon juice, or tomato) to the liquid in which it is cooked.

"Boiled" Shrimp

Boiled shrimp should never be boiled; the liquid should reach no more than a gentle simmer, and cooking time should be brief—just long enough for the shrimp to turn pink and the flesh opaque. Bring salted, acidulated water (1 tablespoon vinegar and ½ teaspoon salt for each 2 cups water) to a rapid boil; add shrimp (still frozen, partially defrosted, or completely defrosted), and bring liquid again almost, but not quite, to a boil. Turn heat as low as possible; cook, tightly covered, 3 minutes for fresh or thawed, 5 to 6 minutes for the frozen shrimp, no longer. Turn off heat; let shrimp remain in liquid another 5 to 10 minutes. If not to be used immediately, store in liquid, covered.

Shrimp Poached in Beer

Instead of cooking shrimp in water, cook in a mixture of beer (any stale or leftover beer, even that left in glasses—it will be sterilized with boiling), water, mixed herbs, and a tablespoon of vinegar.

Shrimp Poached in Herb Bouillon

Instead of cooking shrimp in acidulated water, cook in the following Herb Bouillon, but do not allow to boil; cook at a gentle simmer just until shrimp have turned pink.

1 cup water	Pinch of thyme
1 cup white wine, or ½ cup dry	Pinch of fennel or tarragon
sherry and 1 teaspoon vinegar	¼ teaspoon marjoram
1 teaspoon salt	

Bring mixture to a rapid boil; cook 10 minutes; add shrimp. Cook 3 to 6 minutes longer. Enough liquid for 1 pound shrimp in shell or 12-ounce package already shelled frozen shrimp.

SHRIMP IN CURRY MOUSSELINE SAUCE. Cook shrimp by either of previous methods; add to Curry Mousseline Sauce; serve over rice.

SHRIMP IN CURRY-CREAM SAUCE. Cook shrimp, add to Curry-Cream Sauce. Serve with buttered noodles; or add to noodles in a casserole, topped with slivered almonds.

SHRIMP AVGHOLEMONO. Cook shrimp; serve topped with Avgholemono Sauce, over rice, on artichoke bottoms, or on toast.

SHRIMP HOLLANDAISE. Serve "boiled" shrimp (or herb-poached shrimp) over artichoke bottoms, topped with Hollandaise Sauce.

SHRIMP WITH HOT SALSA VERDE. Prepare Hot Salsa Verde, pour over cooked shrimp. Serve with boiled new potatoes and peas.

SHRIMP RÉMOULADE. Serve cooked shrimp with Rémoulade Sauce.

Shrimp Newburg

1½ pounds shelled medium to	1 cup heavy cream
large shrimp	Salt, pepper
2 tablespoons butter	2 egg yolks, beaten
2 tablespoons flour	2 tablespoons cream sherry
1 cup shrimp broth	

Cook shrimp as in basic recipe for "Boiled" Shrimp, using 1 tablespoon lemon juice with 2 cups water, ½ teaspoon salt. Pour off 1 cup broth; set aside. Keep shrimp stored in remaining liquid *until ready to add to sauce.* Melt butter; stir in flour; cook until mixture bubbles. Stir in the reserved 1 cup broth; cook, stirring, until slightly thickened; add heavy cream, and salt and pepper as needed. *Shortly before time to serve,* reheat shrimp in broth without boiling; separately reheat cream sauce. Beat egg yolks until very thick; slowly add *warm* cream sauce, beating with whisk, then add sherry. Drain shrimp; add to sauce. Pour mixture into top of double boiler, over warm water, or into casserole, to keep warm in oven set at 325° F. Serve from a shallow casserole with rice and artichoke salad. *Makes 4 servings.*

For 6 servings, cook 2 pounds shrimp; increase sauce ingredients by one-half.

For 2 servings, halve all ingredients in basic recipe.

SEAFOOD NEWBURG. Instead of shrimp, use a combination of mixed seafood, such as shrimp, lobster, and white-meat tuna; or shrimp, lobster, and shucked fresh or frozen oysters; or lobster and chunks of halibut.

For 6 servings, allow total of 2½ cups meat; increase sauce ingredients by one-half.

LOBSTER NEWBURG. Use 2 cups diced cooked lobster meat in basic recipe, instead of 1½ pounds shrimp (for 4 servings).

Shrimp Braised in Wine (Basic Recipe)

1½ pounds shelled small shrimp	1 teaspoon salt
1 medium tomato, peeled,	½ teaspoon paprika
seeded, chopped	¼ cup dry white wine
4 tablespoons butter	2 tablespoons chopped parsley

Sauté shrimp (completely thawed) and chopped tomato in butter over low to moderate heat until shrimp start to turn pink—about 3 minutes. Sprinkle with salt and paprika as they cook. Add wine; cook 3 or 4 minutes longer over low heat. Sprinkle with parsley just before serving. Serve with rice and Frenched green beans. *Makes 4 servings.*

SHRIMP CREOLE. Cook shelled shrimp in butter as in basic recipe, but add 1 peeled clove garlic and a few slices of onion with tomato; when garlic is soft, crush into the butter with tines of fork. Add ¼ cup chopped green pepper; cook 1 minute. If desired, add a pinch of cayenne. Instead of ¼ cup white wine, add 1 cup tomato sauce and 1 tablespoon sherry.

PRAWNS AL JEREZ. Use large shrimp, shelled, instead of small shrimp, sauté in olive oil instead of butter; instead of tomato, add 2 tablespoons minced parsley, 1 small (4-ounce) can pimientos, drained and chopped, and 1 clove garlic (optional). Season with ¼ teaspoon cumin. Instead of ¼ cup dry white wine, add ¼ cup dry sherry, ½ cup water, and 1 teaspoon lemon juice. Serve with rice and braised zucchini.

MIXED SEAFOOD MARINARA. Use 1 pound shelled shrimp and 2 or 3 lobster tails in above recipe, plus 1 7-ounce can drained minced clams. Use clam liquid plus water to make ½ cup broth; reduce salt to ¼ teaspoon.

Shrimp in Coconut Milk

1 can shredded or flaked coconut
1 cup milk
2 tablespoons butter
½ cup minced onion
1 small tomato, peeled,
　seeded, chopped
½ green pepper, diced
2 tablespoons flour
Salt, pepper
2 pounds shelled shrimp
Fried Bananas, or sautéed pine-
　apple slices

Prepare coconut milk by soaking coconut in milk ½ hour; drain, saving milk. Melt butter; add onion, tomato, and green pepper; cook until tender. Stir in flour and salt and pepper to taste. Add coconut milk; cook until slightly thickened. Add defrosted but uncooked shrimp; transfer to casserole, bake, covered, in preheated 350° F. oven for 30 minutes. Serve with rice, accompanied by Fried Bananas or pineapple. *Makes 6 servings.*

Phoenix-tail Shrimp

1 pound shrimp, in shell
4 tablespoons vegetable oil
2 small onions or scallions,
　chopped
1 tablespoon chopped green
　ginger root, or ¼ teaspoon
　powdered ginger
1 clove garlic, crushed
½ green pepper, seeded, diced
2 tablespoons very dry sherry
3 tablespoons soy sauce
2 teaspoons cornstarch
½ teaspoon sugar
½ cup shrimp broth

Shell shrimp, leaving tails on. Simmer shells for 20 minutes in salted water to make broth. Heat oil in pan, add onion, ginger, garlic, and green pepper. Cook until onion is tender, then add shrimp and cook 2 or 3 minutes longer. Add the sherry; cook 1 minute longer. Remove shrimp. Mix soy sauce, cornstarch, sugar, and broth to a thin paste; add to onion mixture. Cook until sauce is thickened and smooth. Return shrimp to pan; cook about 30 seconds longer. *Makes 4 servings*, to be served as part of a Chinese dinner.

Broiled Shrimp (Basic Recipe)

1½ pounds shelled medium to
  large shrimp, or 2¼ pounds
  shrimp, in shell
½ cup olive or corn oil
3 tablespoons lemon juice

¾ teaspoon salt
¼ teaspoon freshly ground
  black pepper
2 tablespoons minced parsley

If shrimp are in shell, remove all but tails; devein. Marinate the shrimp in mixture of oil, lemon juice, salt, pepper, and parsley for 15 to 30 minutes before cooking. Remove from marinade; place on foil-lined broiler pan; cook 4 inches from reduced heat in broiler, or over charcoal, just until shrimp turn bright orange. Serve warm with lemon wedges, Tomato Sauce with Capers, or Tartar Sauce. *Makes 4 servings.*

SHRIMP TERIYAKI. Marinate shrimp ½ hour in mixture of ¼ cup peanut oil, ¼ cup orange or pineapple juice, a pinch of ginger, ¼ cup soy sauce, 2 tablespoons sherry, and ¼ teaspoon salt. Place shrimp on bamboo skewers alternately with green pepper squares or pineapple chunks; broil, turning once or twice, as in basic recipe. Serve with rice, accompanied by cucumber salad.

Batter-fried Shrimp

1½ pounds shelled shrimp or
  about 30 shrimp shelled (but
  with tails left on)
½ cup flour

2 eggs, beaten
¾ teaspoon salt
Oil for deep-frying

Wash and dry shrimp; dredge in flour in deep bowl. Add eggs and salt; mix well with wooden spoon to form a batter. Let shrimp stand in batter about 15 minutes. Heat oil to 370°; add shrimp a few at a time (do not crowd pan) until golden on each side. Remove; drain on absorbent paper. *Makes 4 to 6 servings.*

Shrimp a Rebozados

This renowned dish is a specialty at the Granados Restaurant in New York's Greenwich Village.

1 recipe Batter-fried Shrimp
2 cups chicken broth
1 cup chopped onion
½ cup minced parsley
½ cup chopped pimiento

1 teaspoon orégano
2 cloves garlic
4 tablespoons olive oil
4 tablespoons flour
½ cup white wine or dry sherry

Prepare Batter-fried Shrimp as in previous recipe. Keep warm while making sauce. Combine broth, onion, parsley, pimiento, and orégano; simmer 10 minutes. Place garlic cloves in olive oil; sauté until soft and golden; crush into oil with tines of fork. Stir in flour; cook until it bubbles; slowly add the broth, then wine or sherry. Cook until smooth and thickened. Pour sauce over fried shrimp. *Makes 4 to 6 servings.*

Shrimp alla Romana

1 recipe Batter-fried Shrimp	3 or 4 slices onion
6 large or 12 small mushrooms, cut in slivers	3 tablespoons butter
	1 teaspoon Worcestershire sauce
1 cup prosciutto, cut in slivers	Lemon wedges

Prepare Batter-fried Shrimp as in basic recipe. Separately sauté mushrooms, prosciutto, and onion in butter until lightly browned; sprinkle with Worcestershire and season to taste. Serve fried shrimp with mushroom mixture as a sauce; sprinkle lemon over shrimp at table. *Makes 4 to 6 servings.*

Butterfly Shrimp

These differ from the basic recipe for Batter-fried Shrimp only in the way the shrimp is cut. Buy shrimp in the shell; leave the tail on, but cut deep down the back when removing the black vein. Dip in batter, holding by the tail, then fry until crisp and golden in deep hot oil. The two sides will spread out like wings. Serve with Tartar Sauce or any soy-flavored dip.

Shrimp Tempura

1 recipe Beer Batter or Tempura Batter	Oil for deep frying
	Soy-Horseradish Dip
2 to 2½ pounds shrimp in shell	

Shell shrimp, leaving tail on. Holding by the tail, dip in batter, then into oil preheated to 370° F. (cube of bread browns in 30 seconds). Fry until golden on each side; do not crowd pan. Serve the shrimp alone, or with an assortment of other foods, also dipped in batter and fried in the hot oil, such as sliced mushroom crowns, tender stringless beans, carrot slices, squares of flounder fillet, or even bite-size pieces of pork or ham. Serve very hot, right out cf the kettle, with Soy-Horseradish Dip. *Makes 4 to 6 servings.*

Shrimp Curry

1 recipe Basic Curry Sauce   Shredded coconut
1 cup pineapple chunks   Fried Bananas
1½ pounds shelled shrimp

Prepare Basic Curry Sauce, adding half the pineapple cut in small pieces. Add shrimp during last 5 minutes. Serve topped with coconut and remaining pineapple as garnish, with Fried Bananas on the side. *Makes 4 to 6 servings.*

LOBSTER AND CRABMEAT

Review Buying and Storage Guide relating to Shellfish, Book 1. Lobster meat may be substituted for crabmeat, and vice versa, in all recipes calling for diced or bulk lobster or crab.

Boiled Maine Lobster

It's best to buy lobsters while they are alive. Cook within a few hours after purchase. You need a large (10-quart) kettle and tongs for holding live lobsters. Add 6 tablespoons salt to 6 quarts water; bring to a rapid boil. Plunge the lobsters into the water one at a time; promptly place the lid back. It takes no more than 30 seconds for merciful death. Reduce heat after water has again returned to a boil. For 1-pound lobsters, 10 to 12 minutes' boiling is enough. Let water cool about 5 minutes, then remove lobsters with tongs and lay on back. With small sharp knife slit thin undershell from head to tail. Remove and discard dark vein and small sac 2 inches below head. Do not remove green liver (tomalley) or red roe (the caviar); these are choice bits. Crack large claws with hammer or nutcracker and drain off moisture. Serve while lobster is still warm, with individual bowls of Drawn Butter Sauce and lemon wedges. Each diner should be given a paper bib, nutcrackers or lobster hammers, and lobster forks. For the best way to remove meat, see sketches. This is gourmet food, but the manner of eating it is strictly informal.

Broiled Live Lobster

While lobsters are still alive, lay on back, insert a small sharp knife at the point where body and tail of lobster come together. This instantly kills lobster. Slit through thin undershell down the center from tail to head. (It may be possible to have your fish man do this for you, but be sure to cook lobster within a short time afterward.) Discard dark vein and small sac 2 inches below head. Cut away thin undershell. Lay lobsters on back on broiler pan. Brush generously with melted butter; sprinkle with salt, paprika, and pepper, if desired. Broil 4 inches from heat until meat is opaque—12 to 15 minutes. Brush occasionally with melted butter. Allow a 1-pound lobster for each serving.

"Boiled" Lobster Tails (Basic Recipe)

Before cooking the lobster tails, defrost in advance, or hold under warm running water a few minutes to thaw enough to handle easily. Cut away thin undershell with kitchen shears. With fingers, pull the meat partially away from the shell (but not entirely—the meat should still cling to the shell). Otherwise, much of the meat clings to the shell when cooked. If you prefer the cooked meat in the shell to lie flat, either crack the shell by putting your thumbs in the center and bending both ends backward, or with a small sharp knife, cut a slit vertically down the back of the shell.

Bring salted water to a boil in a large saucepan or kettle (depending on the number of lobster tails). When boiling rapidly, add lobster, bring water again to boil, reduce heat, cover pan, and cook just until white meat is opaque, allowing 1 minute per ounce weight of largest tail (3 minutes for 3-ounce tails, 7 minutes for 7-ounce tails). Turn off heat, let lobster remain in water a few minutes longer. Serve this way with Drawn Butter Sauce, Lemon Butter, Herb Butter, Vinaigrette Sauce, Hollandaise, Avgholemono Sauce, homemade Mayonnaise, or Green or Caper Mayonnaise.

Broiled Lobster Tails

Allow 1 5- or 6-ounce lobster tail per serving. Completely defrost tails, cut away undershell, and partially separate meat from shell, as in preceding recipe. Crack so that shell will lie flat. Arrange on broiler pan with shell side up; broil shell side 3 inches from heat for 5 minutes; turn, baste with melted butter, margarine, or oil; continue broiling until meat is opaque and very lightly browned. Serve hot, with lemon wedges or any of the sauces suggested for "Boiled" Lobster.

WITH SHERRY BUTTER. For 6 rock lobster tails, melt 1 stick (8 tablespoons) butter; add 1 tablespoon each minced onion, minced parsley, lemon juice, and sherry. Simmer 2 minutes; use as basting sauce brushed over lobster tails as they cook.

BARBECUED LOBSTER TAILS. Combine ¼ cup oil, ½ cup vinegar, 1 teaspoon each salt, paprika, and Angostura bitters, and ¼ cup each celery and onion. Simmer until onion is soft. Use as a basting sauce for broiled lobster tails as they cook.

Lobster Thermidor

4 live 1½-pound Maine lobsters	2 teaspoons dried mustard
4 tablespoons butter	½ teaspoon salt
¼ teaspoon tarragon (optional)	⅛ teaspoon freshly ground
¼ pound mushrooms, sliced	black pepper
1 teaspoon lemon juice or sherry	1 egg yolk
3 tablespoons flour	Fine dry crumbs tossed with
2 cups homogenized milk or	2 tablespoons melted butter
light cream	

Place lobsters in 3 quarts rapidly boiling salted water in large kettle; cover; boil 20 to 25 minutes. Remove lobsters immediately, let them cool, then remove meat; cut and dice. Clean shells for restuffing.

Melt butter in heavy pan; add tarragon and sliced mushrooms; sauté gently until mushrooms are lightly browned. Remove mushrooms; sprinkle with lemon juice or sherry. Stir flour into butter in pan; allow to cook until it bubbles without turning brown. Add a little of the milk or cream at a time; stir and cook after each addition until smooth and creamy. Add mustard, salt, and pepper; beat in egg yolk. Cool sauce slightly, then stir in lobster meat and reserved mushrooms; mix well. Stuff the lobster shells with this mixture. Top with butter-moistened crumbs. (This can be done ahead.) Before serving, place lobsters under broiler until crumbs are browned. *Serves 4.*

Lobster Tails Thermidor

Prepare as for Lobster Thermidor, but cook 6 5- to 6-ounce rock lobster tails as in basic recipe for "Boiled Lobster Tails." Remove meat; dice. Clean shells. Cook mushrooms and prepare sauce as in preceding recipe; add lobster meat; mix well. Stuff tails with mixture. Top with butter-moistened crumbs. (This can be done ahead.) Before serving, place under broiler until crumbs are browned. *Makes 6 servings.*

BAKED LOBSTER TAILS AMANDINE. To crumb mixture, add ¼ cup blanched chopped almonds; spread this over lobster before placing under broiler.

BAKED LOBSTER TAILS MOUSSELINE. Stuff lobster tails with mushroom-lobster mixture as for Lobster Tails Thermidor, but prepare 1 cup Mousseline Sauce and spread over the top; place under broiler until sauce is delicately browned.

STUFFED LOBSTER DIABLO. Prepare as for Lobster Tails Thermidor, but add ½ cup pitted sliced black olives and ¼ cup diced pimiento to mushroom mixture. Top with crumbs blended with grated Parmesan cheese.

Stuffed Lobster Orientale

4 1-pound lobsters, cooked	1 tablespoon brandy
3 tablespoons butter	1 cup Béchamel or Velouté
½ cup diced apple	Sauce
2 shallots, chopped	1 egg yolk, beaten
2 tablespoons chopped mushrooms	Salt (optional)
½ teaspoon curry powder	½ cup shredded coconut
1 teaspoon chopped raisins	

Remove all edible meat from cooked lobsters, saving shell for stuffing. Melt butter; add apple, shallots, mushrooms, and curry powder; sauté in butter for 5 minutes over low heat. Add raisins and brandy. Blend warm Béchamel or Velouté Sauce with beaten egg yolk; stir in other ingredients plus the diced lobster meat. Add salt to taste if needed. Fill shells with mixture. Spread shredded coconut over top. (This can be done ahead.) Bake in oven preheated to 350° F. until coconut is lightly browned—about 20 minutes. Serve with chutney and Pine Nut Pilaf. *Serves 4.*

Lobster in Butter-Cream Sauce

3 cups diced cooked lobster meat	¼ cup heavy cream
5 tablespoons butter	Pinch of cayenne pepper
1 tablespoon lemon juice	Salt

Heat lobster meat in butter with lemon juice in top of double boiler until butter has melted; stir in cream, cayenne, and salt to taste; heat just until cream is warmed through. Serve in patty shells or over rice. *Makes 4 to 6 servings.*

Lobster in Vermouth Velouté

3 cups diced cooked lobster meat; or 5 5- or 6-ounce lobster tails, cooked	1 tablespoon cornstarch
	1 can condensed clear chicken broth
3 egg yolks	¼ cup dry vermouth
½ teaspoon salt	1 tablespoon lemon juice

If lobster tails are used, remove meat from shells and dice. Blend beaten egg yolks with salt and cornstarch; stir in chicken broth and vermouth. Cook, stirring constantly with whisk, over very low heat or in top of double boiler until smooth and thickened. Remove from heat; stir in lemon juice. Add lobster meat; heat thoroughly. Serve in the shells or over rice. *Makes 6 servings.*

LOBSTER IN SALSA VERDE. Prepare as for Lobster in Vermouth Velouté, but serve the lobster with Hot Salsa Verde.

Cape Town Chafing Dish

6 5- to 6-ounce South African rock lobster tails	1 tablespoon flour
	1½ cups milk
1 8-ounce package cream cheese, softened	1 teaspoon salt
	Pinch of cayenne
1 cup cream	3 egg yolks
3 tablespoons butter	

Cook lobster tails as in basic recipe, but for only 1 minute after water comes again to boil. When cool, remove meat in one piece, carefully so that pink side is kept intact. Slice thickly. Blend cream cheese with 2 tablespoons of the cream; set aside. Melt butter; stir in flour; slowly add milk. Cook until smooth and thickened, stirring constantly. Remove from heat. Add seasonings, cream cheese, and lobster. Beat egg yolks with remaining cream; slowly add to lobster mixture over low heat, stirring until heated thoroughly (but do not allow to boil). Keep warm in casserole in oven set at 300° F. or in chafing dish. Serve with parsley rice. *Makes 8 servings.*

Scalloped Crabs

4 tablespoons butter
1 tablespoon minced onion
¼ pound mushrooms chopped, or 1 3-ounce can mushroom bits and pieces. drained
3 tablespoons flour
½ teaspoon salt

1¾ cups milk
1 egg yolk
1½ cups flaked crabmeat, gristle removed
½ cup fine crumbs
2 tablespoons grated Swiss cheese
Lemon wedges

Cook onion and mushrooms in 3 tablespoons of the butter until lightly browned. Stir in flour and salt, then slowly add milk. Simmer 10 minutes, stirring occasionally. Turn off heat; beat in egg yolk. Add crabmeat (fresh, frozen, or canned); blend. Pour into a buttered 6 x 10-inch baking dish. or into individual rame-kins. Over top, spread mixture of crumbs, cheese, and remaining 1 tablespoon melted butter. Bake in oven preheated to 375° F. until crumbs are golden—about 25 minutes; or, under broiler, 6 inches from heat, until lightly browned. Serve with lemon wedges. *Makes 4 to 6 servings.*

LOBSTER AU GRATIN. Use 1½ cups diced lobster meat instead of crab in above recipe.

ESCALLOPED CRABMEAT AMANDINE. Prepare as above, but add ½ cup blanched, toasted almonds, chopped, to crabmeat mixture. Omit cheese; reduce milk to 1½ cups; add 2 tablespoons cream and 2 tablespoons sherry, or ¼ cup white wine.

Coquilles St. Jacques

1 pint sea scallops
2 tablespoons chopped onion or shallot
1 teaspoon chopped parsley
2 tablespoons butter

¼ cup white wine
1 cup Béchamel Sauce, or 1 can condensed cream of celery soup and 2 tablespoons heavy cream
Buttered crumbs for topping

Chop sea scallops: sauté with onion and parsley in butter for 2 to 3 minutes. (Avoid overcooking—it toughens scallops.) Add wine; cook 1 minute longer. Add sauce (or soup and cream). Divide into 4 large or 6 small ramekins; sprinkle buttered crumbs over top. Place in oven preheated to 450° F. for 10 minutes, or 6 inches from heat in broiler just until crumbs are lightly browned. *Makes 4 to 6 servings.*

434

Easy Seafood Scallop

2 cans frozen cream of shrimp
  soup
¼ cup milk or light cream
Freshly ground black pepper
2 teaspoons Worcestershire sauce
1 pound shelled shrimp, or 2 6½-
  ounce cans crabmeat, drained

½ pound mushrooms, chopped
2 tablespoons butter
1 7-ounce can tuna,
  well drained
4 tablespoons sherry
Buttered crumbs

Defrost soup; heat with milk, pepper and Worcestershire, stirring until smooth. Cook shelled shrimp or crab and chopped mushrooms in butter about 5 minutes over low heat. Add tuna; combine with soup. Blend in the sherry. Divide into 6 greased ramekins or bake in 1½-quart casserole. Top with buttered crumbs. May be left in refrigerator until ready to bake. Bake 20 minutes for ramekins, 30 minutes for large casserole, in oven preheated to 400° F. *Makes 6 servings.*

Crab Cakes Maryland

1 pound (2 cups) crabmeat
1 cup soft bread crumbs,
  soaked in ¾ cup milk
  or light cream
3 eggs, separated
½ teaspoon dry mustard

1 teaspoon salt
2 teaspoons Worcestershire sauce
1 tablespoon chopped parsley
¼ teaspoon cayenne
About 1/3 cup fat for frying

Fresh bulk crabmeat should be used, if available; canned or frozen crabmeat is second best. Flake to remove all gristle. Combine milk-soaked crumbs with the yolks of the 3 eggs, mustard, salt, Worcestershire, parsley, cayenne, and crabmeat. Blend thoroughly but lightly. Beat egg whites until stiff; fold in. Chill mixture, then form into 8 crab cakes. Melt fat (vegetable shortening, or a mixture of 2 parts shortening and 1 part butter, or fresh country lard); add cakes; fry until crisply browned on each side. Serve hot with Tartar Sauce, cole slaw and sliced sun-ripened tomatoes, with iced or hot tea as the beverage. *Makes 8 servings.*

ANOTHER WAY. Combine crabmeat, 2 eggs beaten, seasonings as in preceding recipe, and 2 tablespoons mayonnaise; beat in blender until well blended. Chill. When cold enough to handle, form into cakes and roll each in fine dry crumbs, using 1 cup fine crumbs. Fry as above.

CRAB BALLS. Use either of the above recipes, but form into 1-inch balls (for appetizers) or 1½-inch balls for entree servings. Fry in deep hot fat until a deep crusty brown on all sides.

CLAMS, MUSSELS, AND OYSTERS

Review Buying and Storage Guides regarding these three mollusks, Book 1. Those living in coastal areas are fortunate in being able to buy all three in the shell, though mussels are rarely available except close to areas where gathered. Always scrub clams and mussels mercilessly before opening, to make sure all sand and grit has been removed. The "beard" on mussels should be cut and discarded.

To open oysters in the shell, lay the oyster on a countertop and try to force a knife between the shells at the thin end. If this doesn't work, break that end by pounding with a hammer. (See sketches.) Cut the muscle loose from the shell. Save shells for serving raw, or for cooking (as Oysters Rockefeller).

To open clams or mussels in shell, watch when shells open (as the creatures breathe), slip a knife in quickly before the shell closes, and force open. This is necessary only when they are to be served raw, for the shells open by themselves in cooking.

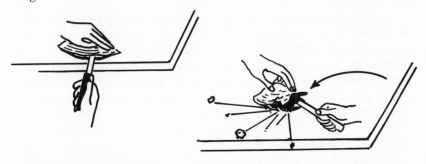

Mussels Bordelaise

1 quart mussels, scrubbed, beards removed	Juice of 1 lemon
1 cup mussel broth	2 egg yolks
1 tablespoon sweet butter	Salt, pepper
	Finely chopped parsley

Cook scrubbed mussels in salted water to cover until shells open. Remove from pan with slotted spoon, and remove mussels from shells. Let broth stand ½ hour so any remaining sand can settle. Strain through paper towel. Measure 1 cup.

Melt butter; add lemon juice. Beat warm strained butter into egg yolks until thickened. Heat broth; stir broth into egg mixture, beating with whisk until smooth. Add mussels. Adjust seasoning, adding salt and black pepper if needed; add parsley. Serve as a delicious first course, or over rice as an entree. *Makes 3 or 4 servings.*

CLAMS BORDELAISE. Shucked clams or canned whole clams can be prepared like Mussels Bordelaise. Prepare the sauce with butter, lemon, and egg yolks, as in preceding recipe. Heat clams in liquid; remove; set aside. Slowly add warm liquid to egg sauce, beat with whisk. Add clams to sauce.

Mussels Provençale

1 quart mussels, scrubbed
1 cup water
½ cup white wine
1 teaspoon salt
1 medium onion, chopped
1 clove garlic, minced

3 tablespoons olive oil
2 tomatoes, peeled, chopped, or
 1 tablespoon tomato paste
2 tablespoons chopped parsley
1 teaspoon grated lemon rind
Freshly ground black pepper

Scrub mussels with stiff brush; rinse through several waters until water is clear. Trim away beards. Place water, wine, and salt in saucepan, bring to a boil; when boiling rapidly, add mussels, cover, and lower heat. Cook until shells are open—about 5 minutes. Remove mussels; set aside. Let liquid stand so any remaining sand will sink to bottom.

Cook onion and garlic in olive oil until soft and yellow; add tomatoes or tomato paste and parsley; simmer until well blended and thick. Add 1 cup strained mussel broth, lemon rind, and pepper to taste; simmer 10 minutes longer. Just before serving, add mussels to sauce; reheat just until thoroughly hot; serve in soup plates with crusty bread for scooping up sauce. *Makes 4 servings.*

Oriental Seafood Pilaf

1 onion, thinly sliced
 or chopped
4 tablespoons butter
½ teaspoon salt
½ teaspoon ground allspice
 or cinnamon
¼ teaspoon freshly ground
 black pepper

¼ cup currants or raisins
¼ cup pine nuts
1 cup long-grain rice
1 tablespoon tomato paste
2 cups chicken broth
1 quart mussels or clams,
 in shells

Cook onion in butter until soft and golden; add salt, spices, currants or raisins, and pine nuts; stir to blend. Add rice; stir until glazed. Add tomato paste and chicken broth; bring to a boil; cover; turn heat low. Cook 15 minutes. Insert mussels or clams still in shell (previously very well scrubbed and beards of mussels removed) in rice. Continue cooking until shells open and all liquid is absorbed. *Makes 6 servings.*

WITH CANNED CLAMS. Instead of clams or mussels in shell, use 2 7-ounce cans clams. Drain, measuring liquid. Use only 1 cup chicken broth plus clam juice to make a total of 2 cups liquid. Omit salt.

Scalloped Oysters

1 pint shucked small oysters
4 tablespoons oyster liquor
½ cup stale bread crumbs
1 cup fine cracker crumbs

½ cup butter, melted
2 tablespoons milk or cream
½ teaspoon salt

Drain oysters; measure liquor; set aside. Bread crumbs should be fairly small but not crushed. Mix bread and cracker crumbs; stir in melted butter. Place a thin layer of crumbs (about one-third) in bottom of baking dish about 10 x 6 inches in size. Add a layer of oysters, then half the mixture of milk or cream, oyster liquor, and salt. Add another third of the crumbs, remaining oysters, and remaining milk-oyster liquor mixture, and top with crumbs. Bake in oven preheated to 350° F. until crumbs are lightly browned—about 30 minutes. *Makes 6 servings.*

Pan-fried Oysters

1 quart large shucked oysters
2 eggs, beaten
2 tablespoons milk or water
1 teaspoon salt

Freshly ground black pepper
1 cup fine bread or cracker
  crumbs; or corn meal
About ½ cup fat for frying

Drain oysters thoroughly; pat dry with absorbent paper. Combine beaten eggs, milk, and seasonings; dip each oyster in mixture, then roll in crumbs. Chill 15 to 30 minutes. Heat fat in heavy skillet to depth of ½ inch. Fry oysters until browned on each side. Drain on absorbent paper. Serve hot with Tartar Sauce, catsup, lemon wedges, or Mustard-Cream Sauce. *Makes 6 servings.*

For 2 to 3 servings, cook 1 pint large oysters; divide remaining ingredients by half.

Batter-fried Oysters

1 quart shucked oysters,
  well drained
½ cup flour

1 egg, beaten
½ teaspoon salt
Oil for deep-frying

Preheat oil to 375° F. Combine flour, egg, and salt (this makes a thick batter); dip oysters in batter; drop into sizzling-hot fat; fry until crisply browned on each side. **Makes 6 servings.**

FRIED CLAMS. Use shucked clams, quahogs, razor clams, or cherrystones, or canned whole clams; prepare by either of methods for Fried Oysters.

FRIED MUSSELS. Scrub, debeard, and shuck mussels. Dip in batter and fry until crisply browned, as for Fried Oysters.

See also Beer Batter; All-purpose Fritter Batter.

Deviled Oysters or Clams

1 pint oysters, drained, chopped, or 2 7-ounce cans chopped sea clams, drained	Pinch of nutmeg Salt Pinch of cayenne
2 tablespoons chopped onion	1 teaspoon prepared mustard
3 tablespoons butter	1 tablespoon Worcestershire sauce
3 tablespoons flour	1 egg, beaten
1½ cups milk	1 tablespoon chopped parsley
½ cup oyster liquor or clam juice	Buttered crumbs

Drain oysters or clams; measure liquid, adding water if needed to make ½ cup. Sauté onion in butter until soft; stir in flour; cook until it bubbles, then slowly stir in milk, then oyster or clam liquid. Add seasonings. Simmer, stirring, for 10 minutes. Remove from heat; stir in beaten egg and chopped oysters or clams and parsley. Pour into shallow casserole, top with crumbs. (This can be done ahead.) Bake in oven preheated to 400° F. until crumbs are browned—about 15 minutes. (May be frozen to be reheated when needed; in this case allow more baking time.) *Makes 6 entree servings.*

Oysters Rockefeller

2 dozen oysters, in shells	1 tablespoon parsley
Rock salt	½ teaspoon salt
6 slices bacon	6 drops Tabasco
1 package frozen chopped spinach	½ cup buttered bread crumbs
4 tablespoons onion	

Open oysters and shuck (see page 435). Line bottom of broiler pan with coarse rock salt. Place in oven to preheat. Cook bacon; crumble and divide among 24 oyster shells. Place oysters over bacon. Place partially thawed spinach, onion, parsley, salt, and Tabasco in blender; beat until puréed. Spoon spinach mixture over oysters. Top with buttered crumbs (which should be in small pieces but not crushed). Bake in oven preheated to 400° F. until oysters curl up—about 5 minutes. *Makes 4 entree servings, or 8 first-course servings.*

SUGGESTED GO-WITHS IF SERVED AS A SUPPER EN-TREE. Caesar Salad and garlic bread; for dessert, Caramel Custard or a pastry.

ANOTHER WAY. Instead of broiled oysters, fill with creamed oysters, using the same ingredients as for Deviled Oysters; hollow a loaf of Italian·bread; make fine crumbs of bread scooped from loaf; toss with butter; spread over top. Place under broiler until crumbs are lightly browned.

Mariscada

6 lobster tails, about 4 ounces
    each
1 pound large shrimp, shelled
    but with tails intact
½ pound scallops, fresh
    or frozen
1 pound clams in shell, or 1 10-
    ounce can whole clams, drained
½ cup olive oil
2 or 3 cloves garlic

½ cup minced parsley
4 to 6 scallions, chopped
2 tablespoons cornstarch
1 cup milk or light cream
1 cup white wine
½ teaspoon powdered ginger
Salt
2 hard-cooked eggs,
    quartered (optional)

First prepare lobster tails, as described in basic recipe for "Boiled" Lobster Tails, loosening meat partially from shells; (the bright red of shells makes the finished dish more attractive.) Prepare shrimp, leaving tails on. Place olive oil in large skillet; cook peeled slit garlic cloves in oil until soft; remove; set aside. Add all shellfish to oil; cover pan; cook over moderate heat 7 to 10 minutes. Mash garlic in mortar and pestle with parsley and chopped scallions. Blend together cornstarch, milk or cream, wine, ginger, and salt to taste; beat until smooth. Stir in garlic-parsley mixture. Stir sauce into pan with shellfish; add quartered eggs, if desired. Cook over *low* heat until sauce is thickened, shaking pan to prevent sticking. Serve at once or keep warm in casserole in 275° F. oven. A beautiful party dish. *Serves 8.*

SUGGESTED GO-WITHS. Rice, Avocado and Grapefruit Salad, rolls; chilled dry wine; for dessert, Peach Custard.

Peacemaker

1 round or long thick loaf   Dash of cayenne
   Italian bread   ½ pound butter, melted
1 quart or 2 dozen large oysters,   ½ cup minced parsley
   well drained   1 lemon, thinly sliced

Cut slice from top of bread; remove crumbs from center to form
a shell. Preheat broiler oven. Add cayenne to butter; dip each
oyster in butter; place on foil-lined broiler pan; broil 4 inches
from heat just until oysters curl and are lightly browned on
each side (turn once)—about 3 minutes. Remove; place oysters
in hollowed bread, which has been warmed in oven. Pour butter mixed with parsley over oysters, and lay lemon slices over
top. Cut loaf in quarters and serve hot. *Makes 4 servings.*

"FINNY FISH"

The following recipes have been grouped according to method, since the same method may be applied to many different
varieties of fish, and it is important first to learn the principles
of fish cookery.

Broiled fish will be more succulent and tender if first dipped
in oil or marinated in an oil mixture. Another way is to marinate fish in milk or buttermilk. It should be broiled on only one
side, unless it is a thick steak.

Baked fish will be improved in flavor if laid on a bed of
minced vegetables, or covered with a blanket of vegetables,
with wine or tomato (or both) added for liquid.

Poached Fish (Basic Recipe)

This is one of the most delicious methods of cooking fish
fish, and for weight watchers it is particularly worth knowing
about as it may be served plain, with only a sprinkling of lemon
juice, brushed very lightly with oil or melted butter—no rich
sauces. Simply prepare a flavored broth, using herbs and onion
and perhaps some wine, and lower the fish into broth that is
simmering gently but not boiling. Cook until the skin is firm to
the touch and flesh is clear white or translucent—about 15 minutes for a 2- to 3-pound fish or piece of fish.

If a large piece of fish (such as the tail end of halibut) or a
whole fish (such as salmon, carp, or mackerel) is to be poached,
you must have a pan large enough to hold the fish without
crowding. It is also wise to wrap a large piece of fish in cheese-

cloth, to make it easier to remove without breaking in pieces.

Drain the fish well; serve garnished with sprigs of parsley or watercress, with lemon wedges or a sauce. (Weight watchers can stick to lower-caloried sauces; those not concerned with weight may enjoy Drawn Butter, Hollandaise, or almost any of the egg-enriched sauces over the fish.)

This method is particularly suitable for bass, carp, red snapper, and whiting.

Pike with Dill Sauce

1 2- to 3-pound walleyed or yellow
  pike, dressed, cut in pieces
4 cups water
1 teaspoon salt
6 whole allspice berries, or ½
  teaspoon ground allspice

3 tablespoons butter
3 tablespoons flour
1 hard-cooked egg, minced
1 tablespoon minced fresh dill
2 tablespoons heavy cream

Heat water with salt and allspice in deep frying pan; gently lower in the fish; simmer at low heat, covered, 15 to 20 minutes. Pour off 1½ cups fish stock, leaving fish in remaining stock to keep warm. Melt butter in second pan, stir in flour, then slowly add measured fish stock. Cook, stirring, until sauce thickens, then reduce heat to very low and cook 10 minutes longer. Add chopped egg and minced dill; stir in cream. Remove fish to serving platter, cover with sauce. *Serves 3 or 4.*

HALIBUT WITH DILL SAUCE. Instead of pike, use halibut steak (fresh or frozen, thawed); prepare as in preceding recipe.

Poached Cod, Norwegian Style

2 pounds fresh or frozen cod
4 cups water
1 teaspoon salt

Minced parsley
Boiled potatoes
Drawn Butter Sauce

If fish is frozen, thaw. Bring salted water to boiling; gently lower cod into water; simmer, uncovered, below the boiling point, until fish is firm to touch and flesh clear white—about 15 minutes. (A thicker piece may require 20 to 25 minutes.) Serve sprinkled with parsley, with boiled potatoes and Drawn Butter Sauce. *Makes 6 to 8 servings.*

For 3 to 4 servings, use 1 pound cod, 3 cups water, and ¾ teaspoon salt.

Poached Sole Mornay

1 1¼- to 1½-pound sole, or 2 smaller   ½ teaspoon salt
  sole, dressed   1 cup Mornay Sauce with
1 small onion, thinly sliced   egg yolk
½ cup white wine

Place a layer of sliced onion over bottom of wide pan. Place dressed whole fish, white skin side down, on onion. Add wine and salt. Bring just to a boil; lower heat; cook, covered, until skin can be easily removed—about 7 minutes. Pull off skin; detach fish from bones. (Sole is easy to fillet because there is only the center bone and small bones at the edges on either side.) Lay the poached fillets in a shallow casserole. Cover with the Mornay Sauce; cook in broiler oven 5 inches from heat until sauce is lightly glazed. *Makes 3 servings.*

Salmon Poached in Court-bouillon

The court-bouillon is best when made with fish broth, made by cooking the fish head or tails, or smaller inexpensive fish, in seasoned liquid. However, it can be made of herbs and vegetables only, as in the following recipe.

COURT-BOUILLON

2 quarts water   piece
1 tablespoon salt   ½ teaspoon thyme
2 small white onions   1 teaspoon orégano
1 bay leaf   2 whole cloves
½ cup parsley   5 whole peppercorns
3 to 4 pounds fresh salmon, in one   1 cup white wine

Combine ingredients for court-bouillon; bring to a boil, simmer 20 minutes; strain. Reheat. Wrap salmon in cheesecloth, gently lower into simmering broth (do not allow broth to boil). Cook until fish is firm to touch—about 30 minutes. Pour off part of broth to facilitate removal of fish; gently raise from liquid; place on platter; remove cheesecloth.

Serve like this, warm, with Drawn Butter Sauce, Hollandaise, or homemade Mayonnaise; or, chill, mask with Mayonnaise Chaud-Froid, garnish with vegetable slivers to resemble flowers, and cover with Clear Aspic.

Trout au Bleu

Prepare a court-bouillon as in the preceding recipe, but add 1 cup vinegar. When court-bouillon is boiling rapidly, add *fresh* trout; cook until flesh is firm to touch—about 10 minutes. (The skin turns blue, which explains the name.) Serve with Drawn Butter Sauce and lemon wedges.

CARP AU BLEU. Prepare as for Trout au Bleu, except that carp is a larger fish and a larger kettle will be needed to hold it without crowding.

Sole Meunière

1 pound fillet of sole or flounder	4 tablespoons butter
½ teaspoon salt	Lemon juice
1 tablespoon flour	Minced parsley

Dust the fish with mixture of salt and flour. Melt butter in large skillet (electric skillet set at 275° F.); place fish in butter; cook gently until lightly browned on each side. Turn with spatula, taking care not to break fish. Baste with butter in pan. Sprinkle lemon juice over fish before removing from skillet, and garnish with minced parsley. *Makes 3 servings.*

For 6 servings, double all ingredients except butter (6 tablespoons butter should be enough).

SUGGESTED GO-WITHS. Boiled new potatoes, tiny peas and onions, citrus salad.

Sole Véronique

1 pound fillet of sole or flounder	or seeded Tokay grapes
1 tablespoon flour	½ cup dry vermouth or
½ teaspoon salt	white wine
4 tablespoons butter	⅛ teaspoon curry powder
1 cup seedless white grapes,	(optional)

Dust fillets with flour and salt and cook gently in melted butter, as for Sole Meuniere, but saute grapes in butter at same time. When fish is lightly browned on bottom, turn, add vermouth or wine to pan, and sprinkle with curry powder. *Makes 3 servings.*

SUGGESTED GO-WITHS. Frenched green beans, glazed carrots, chilled white wine as a beverage; peach and pear compote for dessert.

SOLE WITH ORANGE SAUCE. Prepare as for Sole Véronique, but omit grapes and curry powder; instead of wine, simmer in orange juice, add 1 teaspoon grated orange rind.

Flounder à la Normande

2 bay leaves
¼ teaspoon thyme
1 tablespoon minced parsley
1 clove garlic
¼ teaspoon salt
½ teaspoon freshly ground
  black pepper
Dash of cayenne

2 pounds fillet of flounder
8 scallions or shallots
2 tablespoons butter
2 tablespoons flour
1 cup bouillon made with
  vegetable bouillon cube
1 4-ounce can button mushrooms
2 egg yolks, beaten

Crush bay leaves, thyme, parsley, garlic, salt, and black and cayenne pepper into paste with mortar and pestle. Rub paste into fish. Mince the scallions or shallots; cook in 1 tablespoon of the butter in large skillet until soft. Place fish over the scallions; cook, covered, over lowest heat for 10 minutes; turn; cook, uncovered, 10 minutes longer.

Meanwhile, in a second saucepan, melt the other tablespoon butter with the flour; slowly stir in bouillon and the canned mushrooms and liquid. Cook, stirring occasionally, until reduced and thickened—about 10 minutes. Stir a little of this sauce into beaten egg yolks; combine the two. Cook another 10 minutes, beating with whisk to prevent curdling, keeping heat very, very low (or place over hot water). Remove flounder to platter. Add sauce in skillet to mushroom sauce; cook another 5 minutes, beating to blend. Pour this sauce over the fish. Garnish with croutons. *Serves 6 generously.*

Cod Braised in Spanish Sauce

1 pound fresh or frozen cod
1 large or 2 medium onions,
  chopped
2 pimientos, diced
¼ cup olive oil

1 large (15-ounce) can tomato
  sauce, or 2 8-ounce cans
Salt
½ cup white wine
½ cup minced parsley

If codfish is frozen, thaw. Slowly cook onion and pimiento in olive oil until soft but not browned; add tomato sauce, salt, wine, and parsley; simmer 30 minutes. Add codfish; spoon sauce over fish so that it is completely covered; simmer, uncovered, until fish flakes easily—about 20 minutes longer. *Serves 3.*

BACALAO IN SALSA TOMATE. Soak 1 pound dried codfish overnight, changing water several times. Prepare sauce as above; simmer codfish in sauce until soft—about 1 hour.

COD À LA RIOJANA. Cook onions and pimiento in olive oil as for Cod in Spanish Sauce, but instead of tomatoes, add 3 potatoes, very thinly sliced; cook these in oil, covered, with onions until soft, turning occasionally. Add codfish and wine or ½ cup tomato juice; simmer, covered, until codfish flakes easily—about 20 minutes longer.

Red Snapper Creole

3 pounds red snapper steaks	1 clove garlic, minced
Salt, pepper, cayenne	¼ teaspoon thyme
½ cup Madeira or cream sherry wine	⅛ teaspoon basil
3 tablespoons butter	1 medium (1-pound) can peeled tomatoes
1 large onion, chopped	1 teaspoon sugar
2 tablespoons minced parsley	1½ cups water or fish stock

Sprinkle fish with salt, pepper, and cayenne and a little of the wine. Melt butter in large skillet or top-of-stove casserole. Add onion, parsley, garlic and herbs, simmer 5 minutes. Strain canned tomatoes, placing whole tomatoes with onions, chopping with knife; after 5 minutes, add tomato juice and sugar; simmer 5 minutes longer. Add wine and water or stock and additional salt to taste. Cook 30 minutes. (This can be done ahead.) Add fish. Sauce should completely cover fish. Cook, uncovered, at low heat (liquid should just "smile")—10 minutes for steaks, 15 minutes for whole fish. (Or, place casserole in oven set at 325° F. and bake, uncovered, for 30 minutes.) *Makes 5 or 6 servings.*

SEA BASS CREOLE. Instead of red snapper, use a 3- or 4-pound sea bass in above recipe.

MACKEREL CREOLE. Instead of red snapper, use a 3-pound mackerel.

Fried Fish (Basic Recipe)

Whether you are frying fillets or small whole fish, the flesh will be more tender and moist if first soaked in milk for 15 minutes. Remove from milk; dredge with seasoned flour, fine crumbs, or corn meal (or a combination of flour and corn meal). Fry in sizzling-hot ½-inch-deep fat in skillet; if using electric skillet, it should be set at 350°. When crisply browned on each side, serve at once, with Tartar Sauce, catsup, Mustard-Cream Sauce, or Celery-Horseradish Sauce.

The best fish for frying this way are fillets of flounder, sole, haddock, and perch; scrod, porgy, trout, bass, pike; and sliced eel.

Fried Puffs of Sole

1 to 1¼ pounds fillet of sole or
   flounder
2 eggs, separated
2 tablespoons flour

1 teaspoon salt
½ cup oil
Lemon wedges

Cut fish into pieces about 4 x 3 inches each. Beat the egg whites until stiff; set aside. Beat the egg yolks until thick, stir in flour and salt, then fold in the stiffly beaten whites until well blended. Meanwhile, heat the oil in a heavy 10- or 12-inch skillet until tiny bubbles form around the edge. Dip each piece of fish in the foamy batter, covering completely with batter, and place in the hot oil. Carefully turn with spatula. cooking until golden on both sides. Serve at once with lemon wedges. *Serves 4.*

Trout or Bass Fried in Butter

6 fillets of trout or lake bass
2 large or 3 small eggs
¼ cup light cream
¾ teaspoon salt

¼ cup flour
4 to 6 tablespoons butter
Lemon wedges

Beat together eggs, cream. salt, and flour. Coat each fillet in the batter. Melt 4 tablespoons butter in large heavy skillet: add dipped fillets; fry quickly until golden and crisp on each side. Add more butter if needed. Remove; drain on absorbent paper. Serve with lemon wedges, accompanied by parsley potatoes and a green salad. *Makes 6 servings.*

Trout Baked in Corn Husks

Any small, fresh-caught fish can be cooked this way in a charcoal brazier or over a campfire, but brook trout is especially delicious. Clean and scale the fish. In each cavity place a generous lump of butter, some freshly ground black pepper, and a strip of bacon—preferably thick-sliced country bacon, green-hickory smoked. Remove fresh corn from the husks, leaving husks intact. Place each fish in emptied corn husks; tie at ends. Place over glowing embers of fire; rake a few live embers over the top; bake until husks are well browned.

Tender Broiled Fish Fillets (Basic Recipe)

1½ pounds fillets of fish,* cut in
   serving portions
½ cup olive oil or salad oil

¾ teaspoon salt
½ teaspoon paprika
Lemon wedges

Marinate fillets in oil seasoned with salt and paprika for 15 minutes. Remove from oil, holding up with a fork so oil will

*Sole, flounder, red snapper, Boston scrod, haddock, pompano, or whiting. Any frozen fillets can also be prepared this way, but defrost completely before cooking.

drain off; transfer to foil-lined broiler pan. Broil in preheated oven 4 inches from heat until fish is golden and flakes easily—about 15 minutes. *Do not turn; cook on one side only.* Remove to platter or serving plates; sprinkle with lemon juice. *Makes 4 servings.*

For 6 servings, use 2 pounds fillets and ¾ cup oil.

For 2 servings, use ¾-pound fillets and same amount of oil.

HERB-FLAVORED. Add ¼ teaspoon thyme, tarragon, or basil to oil mixture.

WITH LEMON BUTTER. Instead of sprinkling with lemon juice, put "nuts" of lemon butter on each serving portion just before removing from broiler.

GARLIC-FLAVORED. Add to the seasoned oil mixture ½ teaspoon homemade Garlic Salt instead of regular salt. Or, top the cooked fish with "nuts" of Cold Garlic Butter just before removing from broiler.

SOLE WITH CURRY-CREAM SAUCE. Marinate fillets as in basic recipe; transfer to foil-lined pan; sprinkle with ½ to 1 teaspoon curry powder. After 10 minutes, spoon ½ cup sour cream over fish; continue cooking until fish is lightly browned.

SUGGESTED GO-WITHS. Asparagus, small beets, hot Parker House rolls; Ambrosia for dessert.

Flounder Marquis

2 scallions or shallots, chopped	Pinch of ground coriander
1 teaspoon minced parsley	or cumin
2 tablespoons butter	Freshly ground black pepper
2 tablespoons olive oil	2 tablespoons sour cream or
2 tablespoons brandy	heavy sweet cream
½ teaspoon salt	1 pound fillet of flounder

Cook scallions or shallot and parsley in combined butter and oil until soft—about 1 minute; add brandy and seasonings; cook 1 minute longer. Remove from heat; blend in cream. Arrange fillets in shallow casserole; spoon cream mixture over top. Cook 3 to 4 inches from heat in preheated broiler until top is golden and fish flakes easily—about 15 minutes. *Makes 6 servings.*

HALIBUT MARQUIS. Prepare the same way, but use halibut steaks or fillets, cut thin.

FRESH COD BROILED IN CREAM. Use cod steaks or fillets (cut thin) instead of flounder in above recipe.

SUGGESTED GO-WITHS. Creamed potatoes, tiny peas, lettuce salad.

Broiled Swordfish

1½ pounds swordfish steak	3 tablespoons olive oil
1 small white onion, sliced	1 tablespoon lemon juice
1 clove garlic, split (optional)	½ teaspoon salt
1 tablespoon minced parsley	Sherry, or brandy (optional)

Marinate the swordfish in remaining ingredients for ½ hour, turning several times. Remove from marinade; place on foil-lined broiling pan; broil 3 inches from heat until lightly browned on both sides, turning once. If desired, sprinkle with sherry or brandy just before serving; or serve brushed with some of the marinade as a sauce. *Makes 4 servings.*

SUGGESTED GO-WITHS. Sautéed eggplant (or Eggplant Creole) and garlic bread.

Herb-flavored Salmon Steaks

These are especially delicious when broiled over charcoal, and because it is marinated in advance the fish remains moist and succulent.

MARINADE

½ cup dry vermouth	Few shreds anise or fennel
½ cup olive or salad oil	⅛ teaspoon thyme
1 tablespoon lemon juice	¼ teaspoon marjoram
½ teaspoon salt	⅛ teaspoon sage
Dash of freshly ground black pepper	2 teaspoons minced parsley

Combine all ingredients for marinade; pour over steaks. Allow to stand 3 to 4 hours or longer.

To broil in oven: Remove from marinade; broil 3 inches from heat until lightly browned *on one side only.*

To cook over charcoal: Grease rack or charcoal brazier; remove steaks from marinade; cook 6 inches from heat until brown; turn; brown on the other side until fork-tender—about 15 minutes altogether. Brush frequently with marinade. *Serves 6.*

SUGGESTED GO-WITHS. Braised zucchini, carrot sticks, and stuffed green olives; coffee ice cream laced with Tia Maria liqueur for dessert.

Cod al Jerez

1 to 1½ pounds cod, fresh or frozen
2 tablespoons olive or salad oil
¾ teaspoon salt
¼ teaspoon orégano

2 tablespoons minced parsley
2 tablespoons blanched slivered almonds
½ cup dry sherry

Defrost frozen cod before cooking. Brush shallow baking dish with 1 tablespoon of the oil, place codfish in dish, sprinkle with salt and remaining oil. Sprinkle orégano and parsley over top of codfish, lay almonds over the herbs, then pour sherry over all. Bake in oven preheated to 350° F. until fish flakes easily—25 to 30 minutes. *Makes 3 to 4 servings.*

HALIBUT AL JEREZ. Instead of cod use fresh or frozen halibut fillets in above recipe.

SUGGESTED GO-WITHS. Mashed turnips (homemade or frozen), Brussels sprouts; for dessert, Apple Crisp.

Baked Sole au Gratin

1 pound fillets of flounder
   or sole*
½ cup milk
½ cup fine dry crumbs
½ cup grated Parmesan cheese

½ teaspoon salt
¼ cup oil
1 small onion, minced
Lemon wedges

Cut fish in serving portions (defrost completely if frozen); soak in milk at least 15 minutes. Remove from milk; roll in mixture of crumbs, cheese, and salt. Brush half the oil over bottom of shallow casserole, spread chopped onion over oil, then lay crumbed fillets over onion. Sprinkle remaining oil over fish. Bake in oven preheated to 375° F. for 20 minutes. Serve with lemon wedges. *Makes 3 or 4 servings.*

*Cod, haddock, halibut, and whiting can be prepared the same way.

SOLE BAKED IN CREAM. Instead of marinating fish in milk, lay fish on a bed of the onion sautéed separately in 3 tablespoons butter; sprinkle fish with salt, then cover with ½ cup light cream and sprinkle ¼ cup each fine crumbs and cheese and 2 tablespoons chopped parsley over top. Bake in oven preheated to 350° F. for 25 minutes.

BAKED SOLE WITH MUSHROOMS. Soak sole in milk as in basic recipe; lay fish over minced onion in oiled or greased casserole; drain 4-ounce can sliced mushrooms; place mushrooms in casserole beside fish. Combine mushroom liquid with dry vermouth to make ½ cup; add mixture of salt, pinch of mace, and ¼ teaspoon each thyme and tarragon. Pour over fish. Dot with butter; bake as in basic recipe.

Red Snapper Ambassadeur

1 3- or 4-pound red snapper*	1 teaspoon curry powder
Salt	½ teaspoon salt
2 tablespoons butter	¼ cup dry vermouth
1 small white onion, minced	2 to 3 tablespoons heavy cream

Remove backbone from fish (or ask fish man to do it for you). Sprinkle fish with salt inside and out. Melt butter; sauté onion until soft, adding curry powder and salt. Brush mixture over fish inside and out. Lay in buttered baking dish; add vermouth. Bake in oven preheated to 375° F. until outside of fish is firm to touch—35 to 45 minutes. Serve with parsley rice. *Makes 4 to 6 servings.*

   *Salmon, mackerel, bluefish, and pompano may be prepared the same way

Psari Plaki (Greek Baked Fish)

1 3- or 4-pound fish (sea bass, etc.)	3 medium tomatoes, sliced, or 1
2 teaspoons salt	1-pound can peeled tomatoes
Freshly ground black pepper	2 tablespoons minced parsley
Few drops lemon juice	12 black Greek olives, pitted
½ cup olive oil	½ cup white wine
2 large onions, chopped	1 tablespoon soft bread crumbs
	1 lemon, sliced

Sprinkle fish with half the salt, the pepper, and lemon juice. Brush olive oil over bottom of long baking dish, place layer of onion and tomato in dish, sprinkle with a little salt, place fish over vegetables, then cover with remaining vegetables, parsley, and olives, and sprinkle with remaining salt. Pour remaining olive oil and the wine over all. Sprinkle bread crumbs over top. Bake, uncovered, in oven preheated to 350° F. for 45 minutes to 1 hour, basting occasionally with sauce. Serve with lemon slices over top. *Makes 6 servings.*

FRESH COD PORTUGUESA. Sprinkle a 3-pound cod steak with lemon juice and salt; let stand 15 minutes. Place over layer of onion as in preceding recipe, but lay sliced tomatoes over top of fish; sprinkle tomatoes with salt and minced fresh cilantro or parsely. Omit bread crumbs.

MEXICAN FISH IN GREEN SAUCE. Use fish steaks instead of whole fish; sprinkle with lime juice instead of lemon juice. In addition to chopped onion, add minced parsley, minced seeded green peppers, and chopped green tomatoes instead of ripe tomatoes; place half the mixture under the fish, the remainder spread over the top. Use only ¼ cup oil; sprinkle top of fish with vinegar and oil before placing in oven. Bake until fish flakes easily—about 30 minutes.

SWEDISH-STYLE BAKED PIKE. Use a 2- to 3-pound yellow pike or similar fish; brush casserole with melted butter instead of oil. Add a little sugar to the tomato; 10 minutes before removing from oven, pour 6 tablespoons heavy cream over fish. Omit olives and wine. (Halibut steak is also excellent prepared this way.)

SUGGESTED GO-WITHS. Baked potatoes (started before the fish), green salad, Lemon-Cream Pudding for dessert.

Haddock Tropical Style

1½ pounds haddock	¼ cup seeded raisins
Lemon juice	1 teaspoon minced parsley
¾ teaspoon salt	1 small can pineapple chunks,
3 tablespoons butter or oil	drained
2 small bananas	¼ cup water
16 blanched almonds, chopped	¼ cup very dry sherry
1 teaspoon grated onion	

Sprinkle fish with lemon juice and salt. Sauté gently in butter or oil until delicately colored; transfer to casserole. Slice bananas lengthwise; sauté in same pan as fish; lay around fish in casserole. Add nuts and onion to butter or oil; sauté until colored; add remaining ingredients; stir, scraping all bits from bottom of pan. Pour over fish. Bake in oven preheated to 350° F. for 20 minutes or until fish flakes easily. *Makes 4 servings.*

SUGGESTED GO-WITHS. Saffron rice, watercress and green olive salad, garlic bread; melon for dessert.

Salmon Steaks with Olives

4 salmon steaks
4 tablespoons olive oil
1 medium onion, chopped
1 tablespoon minced parsley
12 pimiento-stuffed olives,

sliced
½ teaspoon salt
1 tablespoon vinegar
½ cup clam juice or white wine

If salmon is frozen, defrost completely. Brush 2 tablespoons oil over bottom of shallow casserole; add onion, parsley, and olives. Lay salmon over mixture; sprinkle salmon with salt. Combine remaining oil with vinegar and clam juice or wine; pour over steaks. Bake in oven preheated to 325°F. until fish flakes easily—about 30 minutes. To serve, turn steaks upside down on platter so minced vegetables are on top. Add more sliced olives for garnish. Serve with Hollandaise, or Avgholemono Sauce. *Makes 4 servings.*

SUGGESTED GO-WITHS. Creamed corn and Brussels sprouts; baked apples for dessert.

Sole Delicias

1 pound spinach, cooked,
  chopped, or 1 package frozen
  chopped spinach
Pinch of nutmeg
¼ teaspoon salt

1 tablespoon cream
4 bananas
¼ cup melted butter
1½ pounds fillet of sole
1 cup Béchamel Sauce

Combine spinach, nutmeg, ¼ teaspoon salt, and cream in blender; beat to purée. Place a layer in bottom of shallow casserole. Slice bananas lengthwise; sauté in half the butter until lightly browned. Transfer to casserole, on either side of the spinach. Sauté sole in same butter until lightly browned on one side only; place over spinach. Prepare Béchamel Sauce; pour over fish. (This part can be done ahead.) Shortly before serving, place under broiler until top is lightly browned and sauce bubbling. *Makes 4 to 6 servings.*

Norwegian Fish Pudding

2 pounds raw boned pike, whitefish, halibut, or whiting (fresh
  or frozen), or 2 cups cooked fish
1 tablespoon minced parsley
1 teaspoon salt
¼ teaspoon ground white pepper

¼ cup butter
¼ cup flour
2 cups milk
3 eggs, separated
Drawn Butter Sauce

Cut the fish in pieces; add to blender to puree, or put through food grinder. Add parsley, salt, and pepper; blend thoroughly.

Melt butter; stir in flour; slowly add milk. Simmer sauce 5 minutes. Add some of hot sauce to beaten egg yolks, then combine egg yolks with remaining sauce. Add to fish. Beat egg whites until stiff; fold into fish mixture. Lightly but evenly butter a 1½-quart casserole or mold; add the fish mixture; fill to top. Place casserole or mold in larger pan, with water up to half the depth of the casserole or mold. Bake in oven set at 325° F. until firm to touch and knife inserted in center comes out clean—about 45 minutes. Let cool 10 minutes, then turn out on platter. Serve while warm with Drawn Butter Sauce. *Makes 8 servings.*

SUGGESTED GO-WITHS. Buttered carrots, cole slaw, and hot corn muffins.

Hot Sole and Crab Mousse

¾ pound fillet of sole
1 cup crabmeat
2 egg yolks
2 whole eggs, separated
¾ cup milk or half-and-half
3 tablespoons flour
1 teaspoon salt
Pinch of nutmeg

1 tablespoon lemon juice
1 tablespoon brandy
1 pint heavy cream, whipped
1 can frozen cream of shrimp soup
¼ cup white wine or dry vermouth

Cut raw sole in pieces, feed to blender with crabmeat (from which all gristle has been carefully removed) until puréed. Turn into bowl. Add the 4 egg yolks, beating in one at a time. (Set aside the 2 egg whites.) In blender beat together the milk, flour, salt, nutmeg, lemon juice, and brandy; add to sole-egg mixture. Whip cream until stiff (but save out 2 tablespoons for the sauce); fold into fish mixture. Beat the 2 egg whites until stiff, fold in. Lightly but evenly butter a 1-quart ring mold. Turn fish mixture into the mold. Place mold in pan with hot water (halfway up sides of mold), bake in oven preheated to 350° F. until puffed and firm and knife inserted in center comes out clean—about 35 minutes. Remove from oven; cool 10 minutes, then invert on round platter that is larger in diameter than the mold. Serve with a shrimp sauce made by beating frozen cream of shrimp soup with ¼ cup white wine or dry vermouth and the 2 tablespoons cream saved out from the pint of heavy cream. Heat, stirring, until smooth. *Makes 6 very elegant servings.*

SUGGESTED GO-WITHS. Asparagus and butterfly rolls; individual cherry tarts for dessert.

Gefilte Fish

3 pounds fresh white-fleshed fish (pike, whitefish, whiting, carp, etc.)
1 medium onion
1 medium carrot, scraped
1 slice bread soaked in water, or ¼ cup matzo meal
Salt, pepper
1 egg
1 cup cold water

Remove skin from fish, set skin aside. Bone fish, put into blender with quartered onion and cubed carrot; beat until puréed. (Or feed into food grinder.) Squeeze out all water from bread, add to fish mixture (or add meal). Season mixture with salt and pepper to taste; add egg and 1 cup water, mix until very smooth. Shape into small balls, or place in the reserved skin and fasten skin to keep mixture in shape. Make a stock with the bones of the fish, another peeled onion, and a stalk of celery. Strain. Pour over fish balls (or stuffed skin); simmer very gently until fish is firm and set—about 1 hour. If necessary, add water to stock to keep fish covered. Remove fish carefully to platter; reduce broth by boiling until thickened. Strain; pour over fish. Serve fish hot with noodles and assorted pickles, or chill and serve as an appetizer on lettuce leaves. *Makes about 14 servings.*

Bacalão Vizcaina

Salt codfish is a staple in all the Mediterranean countries, where the ways of cooking it are infinite (in Portugal, it is said to be prepared in more than a thousand different ways).

In the United States, only in New England and in Greek, Italian, and Spanish neighborhoods can one find the dried fish for sale, and its popularity is never likely to reach that in southern Europe. But for those who have grown up with *bacalão*, the very word evokes nostalgia. The following recipe is one from the Basque country of northern Spain, and it is one even those not otherwise excited by salt cod can enjoy, for the fish when cooked slowly in the sauce becomes tender and delicious.

1 pound salt codfish
4 or 5 medium onions, chopped
2 or 3 cloves garlic, minced
¼ cup minced ham or chorizo
½ cup olive oil
¼ cup chopped pimiento, or 1
teaspoon paprika (optional)
¼ cup minced parsley
4 to 6 tomatoes, peeled, chopped, or 2 1-pound cans tomatoes
3 slices white bread

Soak codfish for 24 hours, changing water several times. Place cod in fresh cold water; bring to a boil; turn off heat; let fish cool in water. Remove; discard bones and skin. Meanwhile, cook onions, garlic, and ham slowly in about two-thirds of the

olive oil until tender. Add pimiento or paprika and parsley;
cook 2 minutes. Add tomatoes: cook until well blended. Separately fry the bread in remaining olive oil until browned on
both sides; break up, add to tomato sauce. Add the boned fish
cut in serving pieces; cook over very low heat or bake in oven
(305° F.) until fish is very tender—about 1 hour. Serve sprinkled with additional minced parsley for garnish. *Makes 6 servings.*

Bouillabaisse

This is company food, for it is impossible to make a proper
Bouillabaisse for fewer than 6 people, and just as easy to make
one to serve 10. The fish must be fresh: shop for it or, still better, catch it yourself.

1 pound shrimp, in shells
3 pounds assorted fish (sea bass, cod, red snapper, sunny, mullet, etc.)

5 small (3- or 4-ounce) lobster tails
1 pound clams or mussels, in shells, or 1 7-ounce can chopped sea clams

COURT-BOUILLON

Fish heads, tails, shells of shrimp
6 cups water
1 teaspoon salt
1 medium onion

2 tablespoons butter
1 teaspoon orégano
1 bay leaf
½ teaspoon thyme
1 cup white wine

SAUCE

1 cup chopped onion, or 3 leeks, chopped (white part only)
2 cloves garlic, minced
½ cup olive oil
1 1-pound can tomatoes

1 bay leaf
¼ teaspoon thyme
2 tablespoons minced parsley
½ teaspoon salt
1 teaspoon saffron, crushed

First, shell the shrimp; put the shrimp shells in the kettle in
which the court-bouillon is to be made. Cut large fish into
serving-size pieces. The assortment of fish should include both
delicate and strong-flavored types, small whole fish, and at
least 1 large fish to cut into steaks. Rinse and vigorously brush
clam or mussel shells to clean thoroughly. Cut lobster tails in
half; loosen lobster meat by pulling partially from shells (see
page 248).

Second, combine all ingredients for the court-bouillon; bring
to a boil; simmer 20 minutes, uncovered. Strain; add water if
necessary to make 6 cups liquid.

Third, simmer onion and garlic in olive oil until golden and
tender. Add tomato forced through sieve or food mill, bay leaf,

thyme, parsley, and salt. Mash the saffron in a mortar or with the back of a wooden spoon; dissolve in a little hot water; add to the sauce. Simmer sauce 40 to 60 minutes. Combine with the strained court-bouillon.

Fourth, when guests have arrived, place all the fish in the combined sauce and court-bouillon; bring to a boil; simmer for exactly 20 minutes. During last 8 minutes, add shrimp, lobster, and clams or mussels. Taste for seasoning; add salt if needed. Serve in soup dishes, placing a slice of French bread in each. *Serves 8 to 10 persons.*

Calderete Asturiana

This delicious Spanish fish stew is good even when made with frozen or canned cod and lobster tails, though fresh ingredients, if available, are to be preferred, of course. An excellent low-calorie entree, also recommended for those on low cholesterol diets.

3 cups water	1 pimiento, chopped (optional)
¼ cup dry sherry or white wine	1 tablespoon minced parsley
2 teaspoons salt	½ cup olive oil
1 pound fresh or frozen codfish	1 1-pound can peeled tomatoes
3 4- or 5-ounce lobster tails	⅛ teaspoon saffron
1 7-ounce can minced clams	3 tablespoons chopped
and liquid	blanched almonds (optional)
1 medium onion, minced	Toasted or fried croutons

Heat water, wine, and salt to boiling in kettle. Add cod (previously thawed if frozen) and lobster tails (prepared as for "Boiled" Lobster Tails, each cut in half). Reduce heat; simmer gently until cod flakes easily—about 15 minutes. Remove cod and lobster; save stock.

Cook onion, pimiento and parsley in olive oil until onion is soft and golden. Drain tomatoes, add whole tomatoes to onion, chop in small pieces. Add saffron to tomato juice, combine with reserved fish stock, bring to a boil; strain into onion mixture. Add canned clams. Chop or crush the almonds in blender or mortar and pestle; add to stew. (All this can be done ahead.) Shortly before serving, replace cod and lobster in stew, bring just to a boil, simmer until thoroughly hot. Serve in soup plates topped with croutons. *Makes 6 to 8 servings.*

Cioppino (San Francisco's Famous Fish Stew)

1½ cups chopped onion
2 green peppers, seeded,
  chopped
¼ cup sliced or chopped mushrooms, or ½ cup chopped celery
2 garlic cloves, minced
¼ cup olive oil
2 cups (8-ounce bottle) clam
  juice
1 1-pound can peeled tomatoes
1 cup dry red wine

1 cup water
1 teaspoon salt, or to taste
Freshly ground black pepper
Pinch of cayenne
½ teaspoon orégano
2 6-ounce lobster tails, each cut
  in thirds
1 pound sea bass, boned, cut in
  pieces
1 pound shelled shrimp
1 tablespoon brandy (optional)

Cook onion, peppers, mushrooms or celery, and garlic slowly in olive oil until lightly browned—about 10 minutes. Add clam juice, tomatoes forced through sieve, wine, water, and seasonings. Cook 15 to 20 minutes. Cut lobster tails in thirds; pull meat partially away from shells. Add lobster and sea bass to tomato sauce; cook 10 to 15 minutes. Add shrimp and brandy; cook 5 minutes longer. Taste for seasoning; add salt if needed. Serve in soup plates with toasted French or Italian bread. *Makes 6 to 8 servings.*

Zarzuela de Mariscos

A famous seafood mélange of Barcelona. A *zarzuela* is a type of musical comedy; the seafood is usually served in individual earthenware casseroles, piping hot, with crusty bread for scooping up the luscious sauce.

1 pound large shrimp, in shells
1 pound halibut
3 tablespoons olive oil
2 tablespoons brandy
1 medium onion, chopped
1 large clove garlic
1 pimiento, diced

2 tomatoes, peeled, chopped
¼ cup blanched almonds, ground
1 teaspoon salt
½ cup white wine
1 quart mussels or clams in shells,
  well scrubbed
1 tablespoon minced parsley

Shell shrimp, keeping tails intact. Cut halibut in chunks. Sauté halibut in olive oil until lightly browned on one side; when golden, add shrimp; cook about 2 minutes, stirring once. Add brandy; set aflame. When flame has died, add onion, garlic (split in half), pimiento, and tomatoes. Cook until garlic is soft; then remove and set aside. Add almonds and salt; cook briefly. Add wine and mussels, cook uncovered until mussels open. Meanwhile, mash garlic with parsley to a paste, return to sauce. *Makes 6 servings.*

THE EVERYTHING COOKBOOK

SEAFOOD QUICKIES

Tuna à la King

2 tablespoons butter
3 or 4 thin slices onion,
  chopped
2 pimientos, chopped
1 green pepper, seeded, chopped
2 tablespoons flour
Salt, pepper

1 cup milk
½ cup cooked green peas or
  canned, drained mushrooms
2 hard-cooked eggs, quartered
1 7-ounce can chunk tuna,
  drained

Melt butter, add onion, pimiento and green pepper; sauté until lightly colored. Stir in flour, salt, and pepper, then slowly add milk. Cook 5 minutes until thickened and smooth; stir once or twice. Add peas or mushrooms, quartered eggs, and tuna broken into pieces. Heat thoroughly. Serve over rice or toast. *Makes 4 servings.*

QUICK SHRIMP À LA KING. Use 1 6½-ounce can shrimp instead of tuna in above recipe; add 1 tablespoon sherry or brandy; serve in patty shells.

Crisp Tuna Cakes

1 large (15-ounce) can tuna, or
  2 7-ounce cans
2 cups mashed potatoes
¼ cup grated Parmesan or Swiss
  cheese
3 eggs, well beaten
½ teaspoon salt

¼ teaspoon pepper
1 clove garlic, crushed
4 tablespoons minced parsley
½ cup fine dry crumbs
3 or 4 tablespoons oil
  for frying

Drain excess oil from tuna; mash with fork. Add mashed potatoes (which may be made with mix), cheese, beaten eggs, salt, and pepper. Mash garlic and parsley into paste; add to tuna mixture; blend thoroughly. Chill about 15 minutes for easier handling, then shape into 12 patties. Roll each patty in crumbs. Heat oil until sizzling; fry patties, about 4 at a time, until crisp on each side. Serve with catsup, accompanied by green beans and carrot cole slaw. *Makes 6 servings.*

CRAB-TUNA CAKES. Use 1 can crabmeat and 1 can tuna in above recipe.

NUTTY FISH CAKES. Use 1½ cups any cooked leftover fish in above recipe; instead of cheese, add ¼ cup finely chopped nuts.

Basque Sardine Casserole

2 large cans sardines
2 medium onions, chopped fine
4 canned pimientos or roasted

sweet peppers, diced
¼ cup olive oil

Rinse sardines under warm water. Pour part of olive oil over bottom of shallow casserole; arrange sardines, onions, and pimiento in casserole; cover with remaining olive oil. Bake at 350° F. for 30 minutes. Wonderful hot or cold. *Makes 4 servings.*

Finnan Haddie in Cream

1 can imported smoked haddock
2 or 3 medium potatoes
4 medium onions

1 tablespoon butter
1 teaspoon flour
1 cup light cream

Drain haddock, reserving liquid. Place fillets in 10 x 10-inch shallow baking dish. Peel potatoes, cut into ¼-inch slices; peel and slice onions same thickness. Cover onions and potatoes with cold water, bring to a boil, cook 10 minutes. Meanwhile, melt butter, stir in flour, add fish liquid from can; when smooth, add cream, stir until sauce reaches boiling point, then remove from fire. Drain potatoes and onions, place beside haddock in pan, cover with sauce. Place in 350° F. oven for 30 minutes until potatoes are tender and sauce bubbly-smooth. *Makes 4 servings.*

Fish Sticks Creole

1 package frozen fish sticks
2 tablespoons minced onion
4 tablespoons minced celery
½ green pepper, minced, or ¼ cup
  sliced or chopped pimiento-
  stuffed olives

1 tablespoon butter or margarine
1 15-ounce jar spaghetti sauce,
  or 2 cups spaghetti sauce made
  with mix
½ cup grated Parmesan cheese

Place fish sticks in shallow baking pan or dish, 9 x 9 x 2 inches. Bake in oven preheated to 400° F. until fish sticks are crisply browned. Meantime, sauté the onion, celery and green pepper (or olives) in butter; when onion is soft, add the spaghetti sauce and continue cooking over low heat about 10 minutes. Pour over fish sticks. Sprinkle cheese over sauce. Return to oven, bake 10 to 15 minutes longer. This is very good with baked potatoes (which can be placed in a 400° oven to bake 1 hour before dinner is to be served, then, the oven will already be hot when it is time to bake the fish sticks). *Makes 4 servings.*

Crabmeat à la Russe

1 can condensed cream of celery
  soup
½ cup sour cream
1 tablespoon catsup
1 tablespoon horseradish
1 cup cooked peas, or 4-ounce

can button mushrooms, drained
1 tablespoon chopped pimiento
1 6½-ounce can crabmeat, flaked,
  or 6-ounce package frozen
  crabmeat
1 hard-cooked egg, chopped

Combine soup, sour cream, catsup, and horseradish; heat, stirring, until well blended (do not allow to boil). Add peas or mushrooms, pimiento, and the crabmeat (make sure all gristle is removed). Cook over low heat until thoroughly hot. Serve over toast, garnished with chopped egg, accompanied by broccoli spears and a salad. *Makes 4 servings.*

6 RICE, PASTA, BEANS, AND SUCH

The various kinds of starch foods—rice, noodles, macaroni, dried beans, dried peas, and the grains, such as corn, millet, and buckwheat—have been serving mankind as staples since prehistoric times.

For the poor they often provide the biggest part of the diet, for they are cheap and filling. Only in our modern affluent society have we come to avoid them as being too high in calories. Yet as the rising cost of living makes us search for ways to keep food costs within an established budget, these grain foods and legumes once again come into their own. They can be used to extend a small amount of meat, or even to replace meat in the menu (the legumes are rich in protein), and bits and scraps of leftovers combined with any one of these starch foods may be rebuilt into wonderfully enticing casseroles.

The role of grain foods and legumes in making one-dish meals will be covered more completely in Chapter 7, "Casseroles, Plain and Fancy." Here we are concerned primarily with the best ways of cooking these high-starch foods, and with recipes for serving them as "go-withs," to accompany meat, poultry, fish, or eggs, or for the entree in quick, inexpensive family meals.

461

RICE

The best type of rice for everything but puddings is *long-grain*; it is less glutinous and holds its shape better, and is therefore more attractive and tasty.

For a summary of the different kinds of rice, see page 44. Make sure you understand the difference between regular and precooked rice. If a recipe in this book calls merely for rice, without specifying a particular type, assume that *uncooked* regular or converted long-grain rice is meant. If cooked rice is required, the recipe will say so. As a general rule, expect to get 3 cups cooked rice from 1 cup uncooked long-grain rice, 4 cups from converted rice.

Steamed Rice (Basic Recipe)

For each cup long-grain rice (regular or converted), use 1 teaspoon salt and 2 to 2½ cups water, depending on the texture desired. (The more water, the softer and stickier the rice.) Place salt and water in saucepan; bring to a boil. Add rice; cover pan. When water is again boiling, turn heat as low as possible, cook 20 minutes or until all water is absorbed: many vertical tunnels can be seen through the rice.

YIELDS. Allow ½ cup *uncooked* rice for each 2 to 3 servings, but do not try to cook less than 1 cup at a time. (Cooked rice can be easily reheated, or use it in other recipes.) *To serve 4 persons,* cook 1 cup; to serve *6 persons,* cook 1½ cups; for *8 persons,* 2 cups, and so on. In case of doubt, always cook more, not less; it can always be reheated or used in other dishes later.

Mediterranean Rice (Basic Recipe)

For each cup rice, place in a wide shallow saucepan (3 to 4 inches deep) 1 tablespoon butter or olive oil. Heat to sizzling; add rice, stir until every grain is glazed. Add ½ teaspoon salt for each cup rice. Then slowly (1 cup at a time, or less) add boiling hot chicken or beef broth, 2 to 2½ cups altogether. After each addition of broth, bring again to a boil. After all liquid has been added, reduce heat, cover, cook over lowest heat for 15 minutes. Remove lid, stir once, place linen cloth or paper towel over rice to absorb steam, cook 5 minutes longer over very, very low heat (use an asbestos pad under pan). This will produce rice that is fluffy and puffed, with every grain separate.

GREEK METHOD (PILAF). Use butter (rather than oil) and chicken broth in above recipe. Serve rice with tomato sauce. Peas, fresh or frozen, are sometimes cooked with the rice (1 cup peas for each cup uncooked rice).

ITALIAN METHOD (RISOTTO). First sauté a little chopped onion in olive oil, then add the rice and stir to glaze. To the glazed rice, add 2 cups beef or chicken broth. For Risotto Milanese, season the broth with ¼ teaspoon saffron, add the boiling-hot broth to the rice 1 cup at a time, pouring through a strainer (to strain out saffron leaves). When rice is cooked, add ½ cup grated Parmesan cheese and 2 tablespoons butter. Stir quickly so butter and cheese will melt and coat the rice grains. Place in oven covered with napkin or paper towel for a few minutes before serving. (Bits of chopped cooked meat or sausage, or chopped chicken, or cooked fish or shrimp may be sautéed with the onion, to turn the risotto into an entree.)

SPANISH METHOD (SAFFRON RICE). Use olive oil; glaze the rice just as in the basic Mediterranean Rice, but add ½ teaspoon paprika with 1 teaspoon salt. Instead of chicken or beef broth, add plain water, flavored with saffron (¼ to ½ teaspoon for 2 cups water), to the rice boiling hot, all of it at once. Bring the water to a boil again, cook 3 to 5 minutes over high heat, then place the pan over very low heat (or in an oven, uncovered) to continue cooking until all liquid is absorbed. A linen cloth or paper towel may be placed over the pan during the last 5 minutes. Some Spanish cooks add other herbs besides saffron to the water and may also season the rice with a little cumin. (In Latin America, Yellow Rice gets its color from a vegetable extract called ajiote; saffron is rarely used.)

Oriental Rice

First wash the rice through several waters, stirring to get rid of excess starch, until the water is clear. Place rice in saucepan, add water so that it is ½ inch above top of rice (or up to the first knuckle of your forefinger)—whatever the quantity of rice. This can be done ½ hour before time to cook the rice. Add salt; bring to a boil, covered (but watch carefully to make sure you know when water is boiling). Reduce heat, cook 15 to 18 minutes over lowest possible heat until all liquid is absorbed. Do not remove lid from pan during first 20 minutes of cooking. Turn off heat; remove lid, stir rice to fluff it up, place napkin or paper towel over pan. Let stand 10 to 15 minutes. (Another way, but one I do not recommend, is to use twice the quantity of water, bring it to a rapid boil, then add the rice; cook, uncovered, for 15 to 18 minutes. Not all liquid will be absorbed; drain the rice and rinse under *hot* water. However, rice so cooked tends to have less flavor and certainly much of the nutrients are washed away.)

This oriental method is recommended for those anxious to reduce the starch content of their meals, though rice processors point out that the pre-washing and pre-soaking also rids the rice of vitamins and minerals.

For whiter rice, add 1 teaspoon lemon juice to the cooking liquid. (The lemon flavors rice deliciously. In Spain, lemon wedges are always served with cooked rice dishes, a little of the juice sprinkled over the rice at table.)

To reheat leftover rice, place in a covered baking dish or casserole in a preheated 350° to 375° oven for 15 or 20 minutes. Or, place in top of double boiler, heat covered over hot water for 15 minutes. Or, melt butter in a heavy saucepan or small skillet, add the rice, heat covered over lowest heat.

Baked Rice (Oven Method)

Place rice in a casserole with cover. *For each cup rice*, add 1 teaspoon salt, 1 tablespoon butter or margarine, and 2 to 2½ cups *boiling* water (or, ½ teaspoon salt and the same quantity boiling chicken or beef broth). Cover. Stir once after first ½ hour; replace cover. Bake with an oven dinner for a total of 50 to 55 minutes, or until all liquid is absorbed.

PARSLEY RICE. Prepare white steamed rice by any preferred method. When rice is cooked, add 1 tablespoon minced parsley and 1 or 2 tablespoons butter; stir to blend quickly.

ALMOND RICE. Prepare according to recipe for Mediterranean Rice (or Saffron Rice), but before adding rice to melted butter, sauté ¼ cup blanched slivered almonds in the butter; proceed as in basic recipe. Or, cook white rice by any preferred method; after rice is cooked, stir in ¼ cup almonds, which have been sautéed separately in 1 or 2 tablespoons butter.

PINE NUT PILAF. Prepare rice according to Greek Method, sautéing ¼ cup pine nuts in butter before adding rice to the butter. If desired, ¼ cup chopped seedless raisins or ¼ cup currants may also be added.

MEXICAN GREEN RICE. Cook rice by any preferred method. Separately cook 1 package frozen chopped spinach (or 2 pounds fresh spinach). While warm, add spinach to rice, with 1 tablespoon chopped fresh cilantro (or Italian parsley), ¼ teaspoon cumin or chili powder, a generous amount of freshly ground black pepper, a pinch of cayenne (if desired), and 2 tablespoons butter or margarine. Stir quickly to blend through rice. Serve with steak, hamburgers, or fried fish.

MUSHROOM RICE. Sauté ¼ pound mushrooms in 3 tablespoons butter; add rice and salt, stir to glaze rice. Add water or chicken broth, cook as in Mediterranean Rice.

RISI E BISI. Cook rice according to Italian Method, but add 1 cup frozen tiny peas with 1 cup rice; omit saffron. Toss with butter, parsley, and Parmesan cheese when rice and peas are cooked.

FRUIT-NUT PILAF. Prepare rice according to Greek Method. Separately sauté in butter ½ cup blanched slivered almonds, ¼ cup raisins, and ½ cup chopped pitted dates. Add to cooked rice. Excellent with cold roast pork or turkey.

MATAI PULÃO. Melt butter in saucepan as in Mediterranean Rice; add ¼ cup chopped onion, ¼ teaspoon cinnamon, ¼ teaspoon curry powder, ⅛ teaspoon cumin or powdered coriander, and a few caraway seeds. Simmer until onion is soft; add 1 cup rice and 1 cup frozen peas. When rice is glazed, add 1 teaspoon salt and 2 cups chicken or beef broth; bring to a rapid boil. Reduce heat; cook, covered, until all liquid is absorbed. Add 1 tablespoon minced parsley, stir to blend. Place in preheated oven until rice is fluffy and grains separate. Serve with broiled meats, with Beef or Pork Satay, or with cold cuts.

Brown Rice

This is far more nutritious than plain rice, though it has such a decided flavor of its own that it cannot be served as a substitute for white rice. Best for a vegetable dinner, or to be served with pork, ham, or sausages. Soak ½ hour in salted water before cooking; do not drain—cook in the same water, bringing slowly to a boil. Cook according to package directions until all water is absorbed. Place in uncovered baking dish in oven 15 to 20 minutes before serving so that rice will puff up and be fluffy-dry.

Kidney Beans and Rice (Basic Recipe)

2 tablespoons butter, margarine,
  or oil
1 or 2 cloves garlic (optional)
¼ cup chopped onion
1 cup rice

1 teaspoon salt
1 can (1 pound) red kidney
  beans, drained
2½ cups water
1 tablespoon minced parsley

Melt butter, add peeled garlic, cook until garlic is soft, then press into fat and discard shreds. Add onion, cook until soft. Add rice, salt, and kidney beans, stir to glaze; add water 1 cup at a time, bringing back to a boil after each addition. Cover; reduce heat; cook until all liquid is absorbed. Remove cover, stir in parsley. Steam rice over low heat with a linen napkin or paper towel over pan; or, place uncovered in oven for 15 minutes. Serve with roast or grilled meat. Especially good with hamburgers. *Makes 6 to 8 servings.*

KOREAN RICE WITH BEANS. Prepare as in basic recipe, but season with ⅛ to ¼ teaspoon cayenne, omit parsley.

JAPANESE RICE WITH BEANS. Prepare as in basic recipe but season with ¼ teaspoon powdered ginger, omit parsley, and serve sprinkled with soy sauce and lemon juice, or with Soy-Horseradish Sauce.

Celery Rice

2 tablespoons butter
½ cup chopped celery
1 cup rice
1 teaspoon salt

1 onion bouillon cube (or 1
  teaspoon instant minced onion)
2 cups boiling water
2 tablespoons parsley

Melt butter, cook celery 2 minutes. Add rice and salt, stir until rice is glazed. Dissolve bouillon cube in the boiling water, add to rice, bring again to a boil. Cover, cook over lowest heat until all water is absorbed. When rice is cooked, stir in parsley. *Makes 4 to 6 servings. (For 6 to 8 servings,* increase all ingredients by half.)

Rice and Limas

2 tablespoons olive oil or butter
10 blanched almonds, coarsely
  chopped
1 tablespoon minced onion
1 cup rice

1 teaspoon salt
1 package frozen Fordhook
  limas
2 to 2½ cups water

Heat oil or butter, add almonds, sauté until lightly browned. (Can be cooked in electric skillet set at 250° F.) Add onion, cook 1 minute; add rice, salt, and limas, and the water heated to boiling. Cover pan, cook over reduced heat (200° on electric skillet) for 20 minutes, or until all liquid is absorbed. Stir to distribute beans through rice. Serve this way, or garnish with minced parsley. *Makes 6 to 8 servings.*

Tomato Rice

Cook rice by any preferred method, but use 1 can (1 pound) peeled tomatoes in place of 1 cup water. Chop whole tomatoes in fine pieces. Or, peel, seed, and chop 2 or 3 fresh tomatoes, sauté with onion in butter or oil, proceed as in Mediterranean Rice, using 2 cups water, 1 teaspoon salt.

Rice and Peppers

Sauté seeded chopped sweet green (or red) peppers in olive oil until lightly browned. Add a clove of garlic to the oil (if desired), crush in oil when soft. Add rice as in Mediterranean Rice; use chicken broth as the liquid. Serve as a vegetable or, topped with a poached egg, as a luncheon or supper entree.

RICE AND PIMIENTO. The same, except use canned pimiento or roasted sweet red peppers, well drained. Excellent with spit-roasted chicken.

Caribbean Rice and Peas

1 can (1 pound) *gandule*, or pigeon peas (available in Spanish markets)
3 tablespoons golden shortening, lard, or bacon fat
1 pinch saffron
¼ pound salt pork, minced
1 onion, chopped
1 or 2 cloves garlic, minced
1 green pepper, seeded and minced
1 pimiento or sweet chili pepper, minced
½ teaspoon orégano
½ tablespoon salt
1½ cups rice
3 cups liquid

Drain peas, saving liquid; set peas aside. Heat shortening, lard, or bacon fat, add saffron and salt pork, cook until lightly browned. Add onion, garlic, pepper, and pimiento (these can all be minced in electric blender to save time). Cook until vegetables are tender. Add drained peas, orégano, salt, uncooked rice, and the reserved liquid plus water to make 3 cups. Cover, bring to a boil, reduce heat, and cook over lowest heat until liquid is absorbed—about 20 minutes. *Makes 6 servings.*

Arroz con Garbanzos (Rice with Chick-peas)

1 clove garlic
2 tablespoons olive oil
1 large onion, chopped
½ cup minced parsley
1 pimiento, diced

1 package saffron rice mix*
1 can (1 pound) garbanzos (chick-peas), drained
½ teaspoon salt
2 cups boiling water

Sauté garlic in olive oil until soft; crush into oil with tines of fork. Add onion and parsley, cook until onion is soft. Add pimiento and entire contents of package of mix. Stir to glaze rice with oil. Add well-drained garbanzos, salt, and boiling water. Bring again to a boil, cover, reduce heat, cook 20 minutes or until all liquid is absorbed. *Makes 6 servings.*

GARBANZO CASSEROLE. To above recipe, add 1 cup diced cooked meat (pork, ham, beef, chicken, or turkey) for an inexpensive and delicious one-dish meal.

*If saffron rice mix is not locally available, use 1 cup regular or converted rice, add ½ teaspoon paprika, ¼ teaspoon saffron, and 1 teaspoon salt.

Rice and Corn Casserole

4 to 6 tablespoons bacon
  drippings or butter
2 medium onions, sliced
1 can (12 ounces) Mexican-style
  kernel corn, drained
2 teaspoons chili powder (or to
  taste)

1½ teaspoons salt (or to taste)
2 cups packaged precooked rice
1 can (7½ ounces) pitted
  black olives, drained
2¾ cups water
2 beef or chicken bouillon cubes

Melt fat in heatproof 3-quart pot or casserole (cast-iron enameled casseroles can be used over high heat). Add onion, brown slightly; add corn, chili powder, salt, and rice. Stir to coat rice. Add olives, water, and bouillon cubes. Cover tightly, bring to a boil, turn heat low, simmer 10 minutes. Served with baked ham, this makes (almost) a 1-dish meal. *Makes 10 to 12 servings.*

Spanish Rice American Style

1 large onion, sliced
½ green pepper, seeded,
  minced
2 to 3 tablespoons oil or fat
1 cup rice
1 can (1 pound) tomatoes, or 2

cans (8 ounces each) tomato
sauce
1 teaspoon salt
1 cup water
1 tablespoon minced parsley

Sauté onion and green pepper in oil until lightly browned; add rice, stir to glaze. Add tomatoes with liquid, chop whole tomatoes into small pieces (or add tomato sauce). Add salt, water, and parsley; bring to a boil. Cover, cook over lowest heat 20 minutes, or until all liquid is absorbed. *Makes 4 to 6 servings.*

SPANISH RICE PRONTO. Prepare as in above recipe, but use 1 1/3 cups packaged rice instead of 1 cup regular rice, and add an extra ½ cup water; cook, uncovered, for only 5 minutes after water comes to a boil. *Makes 3 or 4 servings.*

SPANISH RICE WITH MEAT. Sauté with the onion and green pepper any bits of leftover cooked meat or poultry, or ½ cup ground beef, or 2 or 3 frankfurters, sliced. If desired, sprinkle rice with grated Parmesan cheese just before serving.

Instant Risotto

1 1/3 cups water
1 beef, chicken, or onion
  bouillon cube
¼ teaspoon saffron (optional)
1 tablespoon butter

½ teaspoon paprika
1 1/3 cups packaged precooked
  rice
½ cup grated Parmesan
  cheese

Heat water, bouillon cube, and saffron together; when boiling, add butter and paprika. Stir in rice; cover and remove from heat. Let stand 5 minutes. Add cheese, blend thoroughly. Serve plain or with tomato sauce. *Makes 3 or 4 servings.*

PASTA

We use the Italian word *pasta* to include all the products made with a rolled-out flour-egg-water dough, even though some are of quite different national origin. Most American cooks today buy these products ready to cook, since there is such enormous variety of types, shapes, and sizes available. The only products not available are doughs for wonton, kreplach, or ravioli, and the *spätzle* of Germany. For the benefit of those who would like to try producing homemade noodles and pastas, a basic recipe follows. It is more difficult to roll out these pastas than to roll out piecrust, yet there is a freshness and flavor to the homemade pastas that the factory-made products lack. (Spaghetti and macaroni, however, are best purchased in packages.)

Homemade Noodles (Basic Recipe)

2 cups unsifted all-purpose flour   2 eggs
½ teaspoon salt   1 to 4 tablespoons water

Combine flour and salt in mixing bowl, blend well. Form a well in the center, add the eggs (unbeaten) and 1 tablespoon water. With mixing spoon, beat the eggs and water, gradually beating in flour to form a stiff dough, then work with fingers until smooth and dough comes away easily from the sides of the bowl. If necessary, add more water, but not more than 4 tablespoons altogether. Continue to knead for about 10 minutes, then place a moistened cloth over the bowl and let stand 20 to 30 minutes. Roll out on floured board as described in following variations. Cut in any desired widths or shapes. Let dry as specified in variation. Cook all noodles and pastas in a *large quantity of boiling salted water or broth* (a 10-quart kettle is good), making sure they do not stick together. The entire recipe as given need not be cooked immediately. After drying completely, all or part of the shaped pasta can be stored in a tightly covered jar.

EGG NOODLES. Roll out until so thin the dough is almost transparent. Cut into desired widths. (For very narrow noodles, roll up dough, cut all the way through with very sharp knife first dipped in flour.) Spread out or hang up to dry. When completely dry, cook 7 to 8 minutes in rapidly boiling salted water or broth; remove with slotted spoon or pour into colander.

SPÄTZLE. Roll out to ⅛ inch thick. Snip with scissors or small sharp knife into thin pieces about ¾ inch long. *Do not dry;* push immediately into rapidly-boiling salted water or broth. Cook 5 minutes; remove with slotted spoon.

RAVIOLI. Roll out like piecrust, just a little thinner. Cut into strips 2 inches wide. Place spoonfuls of filling* on one strip of dough, at regular intervals 2 inches apart. Cover with a second strip of dough. With tines of fork, press edges together and press down between fillings. Cut apart with pastry cutter or knife. Let dry for 2 hours before cooking. Cook until ravioli rise to top.

Suggested fillings. Use cooked seasoned spinach, grated cheese moistened with beaten egg, chopped meat or chicken, or a mixture of minced ingredients, seasoned to taste.

KREPLACH. Prepare dough as in basic recipe, but do not allow to dry. Cut into 3-inch squares. In center of each square place a teaspoonful of filling (seasoned chopped beef and onions; or chopped sautéed chicken livers and onions; or mashed potatoes and cottage cheese moistened with sour cream and seasoned to taste). Fold over, seal edges. Cook in rapidly boiling salted water or broth until they rise to top. Serve in soup; or, fry boiled kreplach in chicken fat and serve as appetizers.

WONTON. Prepare dough as in basic recipe. Roll out on board sprinkled with cornstarch rather than flour until paper-thin, almost transparent. Cut into 3-inch squares. Fill each with a teaspoonful of minced or diced cooked meat, seafood, or vegetables (such as celery, onion, or Chinese cabbage). Cover each with a second square of dough; press edges together to seal. Cook without crowding in rapidly boiling salted water or broth until they rise to top—about 10 minutes. After boiling, they may be fried in oil or butter, to be served as appetizers or snacks; or they may be served in soup (see Wonton Soup).

LASAGNE NOODLES. Prepare noodle dough as in basic recipe; roll out to thickness of piecrust. Cut in strips 1½ inches wide. Let dry ½ hour. Cook in rapidly boiling salted water for 20 minutes. Drain in colander. Use as directed in casserole recipe.

Easy Ways to Dress Noodles, Spaghetti, or Macaroni

Cook either commercial or homemade pastas in large quantity of rapidly boiling salted water until as tender as desired; stir once or twice to make sure strands do not stick together. (A tablespoon of olive oil or butter in the water will help to keep them separate.) Thin spaghetti will be cooked *al dente* in about 10 minutes; egg noodles may require no more than 7 or 8 minutes; heavier strands of macaroni may require 15 minutes. Taste by breaking off a small piece. When tender enough, pour into colander, let drain thoroughly.

While still warm, dress in one of the following ways:

BUTTER SAUCE. Add 2 to 3 tablespoons butter for each ½ pound pasta, stir so that melted butter coats the strands.

PARSLEY BUTTER. Add 2 to 3 tablespoons minced Italian parsley and a similar amount of butter to pasta; blend well.

GARLIC SAUCE. Sauté 1 or 2 peeled garlic cloves in olive oil or butter until soft and golden; press with tines of fork to crush. Add this to hot pasta, toss to blend. (If desired, a little orégano may also be added with garlic.)

PESTO GENOVESE. Prepare Pesto Genovese while pasta is cooking; add to hot pasta, toss to blend.

FETTUCINE ALFREDO. The thin-cut Italian noodles called fettucine are traditionally dressed this way, but any noodles or thin macaroni can be treated the same: add 1 stick (¼ pound) sweet (unsalted) butter and 1 cup freshly grated Parmesan cheese for ½ pound cooked noodles. Toss to blend thoroughly. (This is rich enough to serve as an entree, accompanied only by a green salad and red wine.)

WITH TUNA SAUCE. To ½ pound cooked hot pasta (noodles or thin spaghetti), add 1 can tuna, well drained, 2 tablespoons minced parsley, 1 tablespoon olive oil or butter, and ¼ cup grated Parmesan cheese. Toss to blend, serve immediately (tuna will be warmed by hot pasta). Serve as supper entree with a big mixed-vegetable salad.

HAM-ONION SAUCE. Sauté ¼ cup chopped onion, ½ cup chopped ham, and 1 tablespoon parsley in 2 tablespoons oil or butter until onion is soft. Add to ½ pound cooked hot pasta. (This "sauce" is also very good with Spätzle.) Serve with an omelet for supper.

EGG-CHEESE SAUCE. Add to 1 pound cooked hot spaghetti (or Spätzle), 1 raw egg (lightly beaten), 1 or 2 tablespoons butter, and ½ cup grated Parmesan or Romano cheese; toss very quickly to blend. Pass the pepper grinder at table.

SWISS CHEESE AND SAGE. To hot noodles, spaghetti, or Spätzle, add 1 cup shredded Swiss cheese, ½ teaspoon crumbled dried sage, and 2 tablespoons butter; toss quickly to blend, until cheese melts.

MUSHROOMS AND PEPPERS. For ½ pound pasta, sauté ¼ pound mushrooms (sliced) and ½ green pepper (seeded and chopped) in 3 tablespoons oil or butter until lightly browned. Add to hot cooked pasta with ¼ cup grated or shredded cheese. Serve with or without a topping of tomato sauce.

WITH TOMATO SAUCE. Toss pasta with any homemade tomato sauce, or with Quick Spaghetti Sauce, or a commercial spaghetti sauce. Serve topped with grated Parmesan.

BOLOGNESE SAUCE. Toss spaghetti or macaroni with Bolognese Sauce.

Macaroni and Cheese I

1 8-ounce package elbow
  macaroni, cooked
1 cup shredded Cheddar or
  American cheese

2 cups Béchamel Sauce
½ cup buttered fine
  dry crumbs

Arrange cooked macaroni in layers with cheese in greased 1½-quart casserole. Cover with sauce. Top with crumbs. Bake in oven preheated to 400° F. until crumbs are browned and sauce bubbling—about 40 minutes. *Makes 6 servings.*

Another way: Instead of grating cheese, place cubes of cheese in sauce as it cooks, stir until cheese is melted.

BAKED MACARONI AND HAM. Add 6 slices (serving portions) of ham, use only ½ cup cheese in above recipe.

Macaroni and Cheese II

1 cup shredded cheese (Cheddar,
  American, or Swiss)
¼ cup flour
½ teaspoon salt
Freshly ground black pepper

1 8-ounce package elbow
  macaroni, cooked
2 cups milk
Buttered crumbs

Combine cheese, flour, salt, and pepper; blend well. Arrange in layers with macaroni (macaroni first, then cheese mixture, etc., with macaroni on top). Add milk. Spread crumbs over top. Bake in oven preheated to 350° F., for 1 hour. *Makes 4 to 6 servings.*

BAKED MACARONI AND PEAS. Prepare as for Macaroni and Cheese II, but add 1 package frozen peas, thawed enough to break up, adding a layer of peas over each layer of cheese-flour mixture.

Baked Macaroni and Tomatoes

1 8-ounce package macaroni
  (any size), cooked
2 cups Homemade Tomato Sauce
1 cup soft white bread crumbs

1 tablespoon butter, melted
½ cup shredded American
  cheese

Arrange macaroni in greased 1½-quart casserole in layers with tomato sauce. Toss finely shredded bread crumbs with melted butter and cheese; spread over top. Bake, covered, in oven pre-heated to 375° F. for 45 minutes; uncover, bake 15 minutes longer to brown crumbs. *Makes 4 to 6 servings.*

Macaroni with Celery Sauce

½ cup chopped celery
2 tablespoons butter
1 teaspoon instant minced
  onion
2 10½-ounce cans condensed
  cream of celery soup

2 tablespoons tomato paste
¾ cup milk
1 8-ounce package macaroni,
  cooked
½ cup grated cheese

Sauté celery in butter until soft; add onion, cook 1 minute. Add condensed soup, tomato paste, milk; stir until heated and smooth. Season to taste. Add macaroni and cheese, stir to blend. Serve this way with baked ham (hot or cold), or layer in a casserole with ham slices, top with buttered crumbs, and bake as for Macaroni and Cheese. *Makes 4 to 6 servings.* ·

MACARONI AND TUNA CASSEROLE. Prepare as for Macaroni with Celery Sauce, but omit tomato paste; instead, season with 1 teaspoon prepared mustard, add 2 cans (7 ounces each) tuna, drained, or 1 can tuna and 3 hard-cooked eggs, quartered. Bake in oven preheated to 375° F. until cheese-crumb topping is browned—about 45 minutes.

NOODLES ROMANOFF. Add to hot cooked noodles ½ cup grated Parmesan cheese and ½ cup sour cream. Toss to blend. Grate pepper over the top; or serve topped with toasted slivered almonds.

Noodle Casserole (Basic Recipe)

4 cups cooked noodles (2 cups
  before cooking)
1½ cups cooked or canned meat,
  poultry, fish, or vegetables

2 cups sauce
½ cup buttered crumbs
¼ cup grated or shredded
  cheese

Grease a 1½-quart casserole. Layer the noodles with other ingredients as suggested in following variations. Cover with sauce (Béchamel, Velouté, Soubise, Cream of Mushroom, Curry-Cream, Sauce Allemande, or Cheese-Celery Sauce made with Swiss cheese). Top with mixture of crumbs and cheese. **Bake in oven preheated to 375° F. for 30 to 40 minutes until** crumbs are browned and sauce bubbling. If vegetables are added to the casserole, this may serve as a "1-dish meal." Otherwise, serve with it a green vegetable and a tossed salad for a simple, quick dinner. *Makes 4 to 6 servings.*

CHICKEN NOODLE CASSEROLE. Use 1½ cups cooked or canned chicken with the noodles, add Sour Cream-Mushroom Sauce.

TUNA-NOODLE CASSEROLE. With noodles, use 2 cans (7 ounces each) tuna, drained and flaked, and Cheese-Celery Sauce or Double-quick Mushroom Sauce. Or, use 1 can tuna, and 3 hard-cooked eggs with Curry Cream Sauce. Or, combine 1 can tuna with 1 cup frozen peas (defrosted) and Sauce Soubise.

HAM AND VEGETABLE CASSEROLE. Use ¾ cup minced ham, a 12-ounce can kernel corn, and ½ cup cooked or frozen (thawed) lima beans; layer with cooked noodles. Cover with Curry-Cream Sauce or Sauce Soubise.

Spaghetti Casserole (Basic Recipe)

½ pound spaghetti, cooked
2 cups sauce*
1 to 1½ cups ground beef or
  cooked meat, poultry, or fish
or a combination of meat and vegetables
¼ cup grated or shredded cheese
Buttered crumbs

Basically the same as the Noodle Casserole, except that a tomato sauce is nearly always used. If uncooked ground meat is used, it should be sautéed first in a tablespoon of oil or fat with a little chopped onion (and garlic, if wanted), then the sauce added to the meat. If cooked leftover meat, poultry, or fish is used, it is simply layered with the spaghetti. Almost any combination of meat and vegetables may be used. This makes a heavier casserole than the noodle casserole, and stronger-flavored ingredients are therefore appropriate (sausage, frankfurters, ham, diced pork, and such vegetables as limas, Italian broad beans, corn, kidney beans, and tiny whole onions). An excellent way to extend leftovers. For the topping, use any desired cheese blended with crumbs. Bake in preheated 375° F. oven until crumbs are browned and sauce bubbling. *Makes 4 to 6 servings.*

*Any variation of the Homemade Tomato Sauce; or Quick Spaghetti Sauce, or a commercial sauce such as marinara, mushroom, or pizza sauce.

Spaghetti and Meatballs

1 recipe Meatballs I or II
Homemade Tomato Sauce, or
　Quick Spaghetti Sauce

1 pound thin spaghetti
1 cup Parmesan or Romano
　cheese, freshly grated

Cook meatballs in heavy skillet; when well browned, add Tomato or Spaghetti Sauce, simmer 15 to 20 minutes. Cook spaghetti separately in large quantity rapidly boiling water; drain thoroughly. Serve spaghetti topped with sauce; pass the cheese. *Makes 4 servings.*

Quick Macaroni Lunch

1 small onion, sliced
2 tablespoons olive or
　corn oil
1 1-pound can peeled tomatoes
1 cup uncooked elbow macaroni

or shells
1 cup water
1 teaspoon salt
Grated Parmesan cheese

Sauté onion in oil until soft; add chopped canned tomatoes with liquid, macaroni, water, and salt. Cover, bring just to a boil, lower heat, simmer gently 12 to 15 minutes (watch carefully to avoid sticking), stirring once or twice. Serve topped with cheese. *Makes 2 or 3 servings.*

CORN MEAL, BULGUR, OTHER GRAINS

Corn-meal mush, that good old-fashioned Yankee food on which our forebears thrived (they called it "Hasty Pudding"), has its counterpart in the Polenta of Italy and the dish called Mamaliga in Rumania.

Corn-meal Mush

Bring 4 cups salted water (1 teaspoon salt) to a rapid boil; slowly stir in 1 cup yellow or white corn meal. Cook over hot water in double boiler, or in a saucepan over very low heat (use an asbestos pad if heat cannot be thermostatically controlled) for 30 minutes, stirring occasionally until thick, smooth, and free from lumps. Or cook over direct heat, stirring constantly, for 10 to 15 minutes. Serve hot with butter and milk as a breakfast cereal, or for supper as a "vegetable" with fried bacon or ham and eggs. *Makes 6 servings.*

FRIED CORN-MEAL MUSH. Cook Corn-meal Mush as above; pour into buttered shallow pan (9 x 15 x 2 inches). Let cool.

When cold and firm, cut into squares or rectangles, dust with **flour, fry in hot bacon fat, lard, or shortening. Serve with maple** syrup for breakfast, or with ham and turnip greens for supper.

HOMINY GRITS. Prepare like Corn-meal Mush, but use hominy grits instead of corn meal. Make Fried Hominy Grits exactly like Fried Corn-meal Mush.

POLENTA. Prepare exactly like Corn-meal Mush. Turn into wide shallow casserole, top with a generous amount of unsalted butter and shredded mild cheese (Fontina, mozzarella, domestic Swiss, etc.). Blend with cheese and butter. Serve with a green salad for lunch or supper.

POLENTA WITH CHICKEN LIVERS. Sauté chicken livers and diced bacon in butter with a little chopped onion; season with a pinch of dried sage or orégano, salt, and freshly ground pepper. Serve the chicken livers over hot Polenta; pass grated Romano or Parmesan cheese.

POLENTA GNOCCHI. Prepare Polenta as in basic recipe; pour out into greased pan (9 x 15 x 2 inches). Let cool. When cool and firm, cut into rounds with a 2-inch biscuit cutter. Lightly dust each with flour; place in overlapping layers in a buttered shallow casserole. Top with a generous amount of butter (3 or 4 tablespoons) and 1 cup freshly grated Parmesan or Romano cheese. Place under broiler, 5 inches from heat, or in preheated 450° F. oven, until lightly browned. (Sometimes a cup of tomato or spaghetti sauce is also poured over the polenta gnocchi with the butter and cheese before baking; or, hot tomato sauce may be served over the baked gnocchi.) *Makes 4 to 6 servings.*

MAMALIGA. Prepare exactly as for Corn-meal Mush; when cooked, pour into a shallow pan, let cool. When cold and firm, cut into squares or rectangles; brush on either side with melted butter or dip in melted margarine, and lay in a wide, shallow baking dish. Cover with Brindza cheese (if available), creamed cottage cheese, or sautéed mushrooms. Bake in preheated 450° F. oven until a crust has formed that is lightly browned and butter-crisp Serve with sausages or bacon.

Virginia Spoonbread

¾ cup white or yellow corn meal   1 tablespoon sugar
1 1/3 cups boiling water   1¼ teaspoons baking powder
2 tablespoons butter or   4 eggs
  margarine   2 cups milk
1 teaspoon salt

Preheat oven to 375° F. Place corn meal in large mixing bowl.
(Virginia cooks prefer white water-ground corn meal, but it is
also good made with yellow meal.) Add the boiling water, stir
until meal is thoroughly moistened. Add butter, salt, sugar, and
baking powder; beat to blend. Add eggs and milk, beat with rotary beater until smooth (mixture will be thin). Pour into
2-quart casserole. Bake 1 hour or until firm and delicately
browned. Serve from casserole, topping each serving with a
piece of butter. This is the consistency of soufflé, not really
bread at all. *Makes 5 or 6 servings. See also* Corn-meal Pancakes, Corn Muffins, Tamale Pie, Corn Bread, Corn-meal
Dumplings.

Gnocchi Genovese

½ cup cream of wheat or farina   About 1 cup flour
2 cups milk, heated to steaming   1 cup grated Parmesan cheese
3 tablespoons butter   1 cup Tomato Sauce (optional)
1 egg, beaten

Stir cream of wheat into hot milk over low heat; continue to
cook and stir until thick and smooth. Remove from heat, briskly
beat in 1 tablespoon of the butter and the beaten egg, until mixture is well blended. Let cool enough to handle; add flour to
make a stiff dough, then knead with fingers until pliable, and
turn out onto floured board. Cut into pieces about 1 inch long.
Drop into kettle of rapidly boiling salted water until dumplings
rise to top. Remove with slotted spoon. Place in shallow baking
dish, top with remaining butter and the cheese (as for Polenta)
or with Tomato Sauce, butter, and cheese. Place under broiler,
4 inches from flame, until cheese melts and top is lightly
browned. *Makes 4 to 6 servings.*

Kasha

A favorite with those of Russian background, buckwheat
groats (called *kasha* in Russian) may be served as a "vegetable," or as a casserole ingredient in the Jewish dish Cholent, a
slow-cooking bean casserole to which the buckwheat groats are

added during the last 15 minutes. Another way is to blend the uncooked groats with a beaten egg, stir in a saucepan over low heat until the cereal grains are coated and separate, then add 2 cups boiling water and 1 teaspoon salt for 1 cup groats; cook, covered, over very low heat 15 minutes or until water is absorbed. Or, cook buckwheat groats according to package directions and serve topped with onions fried in chicken or goose fat. Still another way is to serve cooked Kasha topped with cottage cheese and sour cream.

Bulgur

Cracked wheat (or "wheat pilaf," as this is sometimes called) is available in Greek and Syrian groceries and in some specialty shops. It may be cooked according to package directions and blended with pine nuts, dried fruit, and butter (as for Pine Nut Pilaf or Fruit-Nut Pilaf). Or, added to a casserole of chick-peas, sautéed lamb and onions, and broth during the last 20 minutes of cooking, it becomes a Syrian dish known as Burul bi Tfeen. Somewhat similar is the North African dish couscous, also a blend of bulgur, chick-peas, and lamb. A favorite Greek way of serving bulgur is the following:

1 medium onion, chopped   broth
3 tablespoons olive oil   1 cup bulgur
2½ cups chicken or beef

Sauté onion in olive oil until lightly browned. Add broth, bring to a boil. Stir in bulgur. Bring again to a boil, reduce heat, and cook, covered, until all liquid is absorbed—20 to 30 minutes. Remove lid, let stand 5 minutes. Serve hot. *Makes 6 servings.*

BEANS, PEAS, AND OTHER LEGUMES

There are now many quick-cooking beans and peas on the market, so before presoaking any of these dried legumes, check package directions—it may not be necessary. Lentils never need presoaking; only check the water level periodically to make sure they are covered with liquid as they cook. Chick-peas may also be cooked without presoaking, by adding an extra 2 hours' cooking time and replenishing the pot with water now and then. Canned chick-peas and kidney beans are also delicious, and cut preparation time to almost zero.

Chick-peas Sicilian Style

2 1-pound cans chick-peas
2 tablespoons olive oil
¼ cup wine vinegar

2 tablespoons minced parsley
A few very thin slices onion
Freshly ground black pepper

Drain the canned peas, saving half the liquid; add peas with reserved liquid to serving dish (to serve cold), dress with olive oil, vinegar, parsley, onion, and pepper. Or, heat peas with these ingredients and serve as a hot vegetable with meat (beef, pork, or ham) or fried fish or chicken. *Makes 6 servings.* (A 1-pound can serves 3.) *See also* Garbanzo Salad and Cocido.

Garbanzos à la Sevillana (Chick-peas Seville Style)

2 small or 1 large onion,
    sliced
2 or 3 cloves garlic, minced
4 tablespoons olive oil
2 cups canned tomatoes
2 cans (1 pound each) chick-

peas, drained
½ cup rice
2 sweet potatoes (or 1 large)
2 cups water
1 teaspoon salt
1 tablespoon minced parsley

Sauté onion and garlic in olive oil until soft; add tomatoes, chick-peas, rice, and sweet potatoes (peeled and cut into 1-inch cubes). Add water and salt, cover, cook 20 minutes or until potatoes are tender. Add parsley a minute before removing from stove. *Makes 6 servings.*

Plaki (Dried Beans in Tomato Sauce)

1 pound dried marrow beans
½ cup olive oil
3 or 4 cloves garlic, crushed
    or minced
4 or 5 medium onions, thickly
    sliced
¼ teaspoon marjoram or
    orégano

¼ teaspoon thyme
1 bay leaf, crumbled
2 tablespoons minced fresh
    parsley
6 tomatoes, peeled and diced,
    or 1 large can tomatoes (1 pound
    12 ounces), chopped
2 teaspoons salt, or to taste

Soak beans overnight in water to cover. Drain thoroughly and wash with cold water. Heat olive oil—the best quality—in a heavy iron pot. Add garlic, onions, and herbs. Cook in olive oil until onions are soft but not brown. Add tomatoes; simmer until well blended. Add drained beans and water enough to cover. Bring to a boil; turn heat as low as possible and simmer, covered, for 1 hour. Add salt, remove cover, and simmer 1 hour longer. *Makes 6 servings.*

Red Kidney Bean Casserole

6 small white onions, sliced
1 green pepper, chopped
1 garlic clove, minced
1/3 cup butter
2 cans (1 pound each) red

kidney beans, drained
Salt and pepper
1/8 teaspoon ground cloves
2 tablespoons tomato paste
1 cup cider

Sauté onions, pepper, and garlic in the butter. Add to the beans along with seasoning, tomato paste, and cider. Bake 40 to 45 minutes in oven preheated to 375° F. Serve with baked potatoes and salad for a meatless meal. *Makes 6 servings.*

Lentils with Rice

3 large onions, chopped
½ cup olive oil
1 cup lentils
6 to 7 cups water*

1 cup long-grain rice
1 tablespoon salt
Minced parsley

Cook onions slowly in olive oil until very soft and golden. Meanwhile, cook the lentils (without previous soaking) in the water for 35 minutes; add rice, salt, and onions. Cook another 20 minutes, or until most of the liquid is absorbed. Equally good hot or cold. Serve garnished with minced parsley. *Makes 6 servings.*

*The amount of water needed will vary according to the lentils themselves and the utensil they are cooked in. With some pans there is more evaporation than with others.

Lentils Monastery Style

1 cup lentils (about ½ pound)
5 cups water
1 tablespoon salt, or to taste
1/8 teaspoon thyme
1/8 teaspoon marjoram or orégano
3 large onions, chopped
1 carrot, diced fine or grated
¼ cup minced parsley

¼ cup olive oil
1 or 2 tomatoes, chopped
  (optional)
¼ cup dry sherry or 2 tablespoons
  brandy (optional)
¾ cup shredded Swiss cheese or
  Gruyère

Place lentils in water with salt and herbs, bring to a boil, simmer gently 15 minutes. Meanwhile, slowly cook onions, carrot, and parsley in olive oil. Add this to the lentils with tomato and wine. Simmer until lentils are tender—45 minutes to 1 hour longer.

When lentils are ready, place some cheese in each serving dish, then spoon the lentils over the cheese. *Makes 6 hearty servings.*

Beans à la Castillana

½ pound white, navy,
  or marrow beans,
  cooked, drained
4 to 6 cups water
Salt
1 onion, chopped
3 cloves garlic, crushed

4 tablespoons Spanish olive oil
2 pimientos, drained, chopped
3 whole cloves
1 celery stalk, chopped
1 bay leaf
1 tablespoon minced parsley
Grated cheese (optional)

Cover beans with water, add salt, slowly bring to a boil. Separately cook the onion and garlic in the olive oil slowly until yellow and soft, then crush the garlic with a fork or back of wooden spoon. Add the pimientos, cook 1 or 2 minutes longer. Add this mixture with the cloves, celery, and bay leaf to the beans, continue cooking until beans are tender. Just before serving, add parsley. Serve topped with grated cheese, if desired. *Makes 6 servings.*

Boston Baked Beans

1 pound pea beans, soaked,
  drained
½ teaspoon dry ginger, or
  1 teaspoon dry mustard
¼ cup molasses

2 teaspoons salt
1 pound salt pork
1 small onion, peeled
About 4 cups warm water

An earthenware bean pot adds greatly to the deliciousness of this New England specialty. If beans are the quick-cooking kind, they may be placed in bean pot without previous soaking. Add mixture of ginger or mustard, molasses, and salt; stir through beans. Cut slashes in pork, bury in center of beans with onion. Add enough *warm* water to cover beans completely. Cover pot, place in 250° F. oven, and bake 10 to 12 hours. Check halfway through to see if more water is needed. *Makes 8 to 10 servings.*

SUGGESTED GO-WITHS. Steamed Boston brown bread or corn muffins and cole slaw.

Quick Bean Bake

Use canned New England style baked beans, but to give them fresher flavor, add 1 tablespoon molasses, 1 tablespoon catsup, and a little instant minced onion. Bake in a bean pot or casserole, covered, in 350° F. oven, for about 40 minutes.

VARIATIONS. Add 2 or 3 frankfurters, cut in cubes; or a tablespoon of sherry; or partially cooked bacon and a small can of pineapple chunks (drained); or diced ham and dry ginger.

7 CASSEROLES, PLAIN AND FANCY

What is a casserole? The word in French means an earthenware pot which may be used, with cover, on the top of the stove (over very low heat), but more often goes into the oven. In American usage, the word has become synonymous with "one-dish meal," meaning a dish containing meat (or a meat substitute) and vegetables, so that nothing else is needed to complete the meal but a beverage, bread, salad or relishes, and dessert.

Most stews so qualify, and therefore could just as well be called casseroles. Many rice, pasta, or bean combinations make enticing "one-dish meals." And there are the entrees in which chicken (or meat) and seafood are combined with vegetables. Most Chinese dishes fall within the casserole category; so do curries. Inevitably there is overlapping between the recipes collected here and those to be found in other recipe chapters. The criterion used in the selection of the following recipes is that each makes a fine party dish—since nothing is more in demand by American hostesses than glamour-touched "one-dish meals," the easiest kind to serve to company. A few homely casseroles, such as Shepherd's Pie and Hash Pie, are thrown in for good measure because these are good emergency dishes to serve unexpected or drop-in guests.

Paella

The darling of the adventurous host is this renowned Spanish rice creation which is often a banquet in one dish. Actually, paella can be a very simple dish. In Valencia, the city of its origin (the full name is Paella à la Valenciana), I once watched a chef make four different rice dishes, one after another, and none required more than 25 minutes' cooking time. He insisted that the *auténtico* Paella à la Valenciana contained only chicken, snails, and green beans—no seafood of any kind, no pork, no pimientos. His recipe for this *auténtico* Paella follows, and if one uses the imported canned escargots, it is very easy indeed to prepare, and quite delicious.

A proper paella should be made in a paella pan, that shallow metal pan with two side handles in which the dish is always served in Spain. A few gourmet bazaars now sell these pans, and so directions are also given for cooking the dish in such a utensil. But for the benefit of the many thousands of other Americans who do not have a paella pan, basic directions are given for cooking it in a 3-quart casserole.

Original Paella

1 large chicken breast, cut in
  4 to 6 pieces, or 1 very small
  (1½-pound) chicken, cut up
¼ teaspoon saffron, dissolved in
  2 to 2¼ cups boiling
  chicken broth
¼ cup olive oil
1 clove garlic
1 small onion, chopped
2 teaspoons paprika
¼ teaspoon white pepper
1 teaspoon salt
1 cup tender young green beans,
  or ½ package frozen beans,
  thawed
1 cup rice
24 snails (escargots) with shells
Lemon juice
Sherry (optional)

If cut-up chicken is used, cut tender parts into 8 to 10 pieces, and use remainder for making broth. Add saffron to broth; bring to a boil. Heat oil in 10-inch skillet (an electric skillet may be used). Brown chicken in olive oil over high heat; push to one side of pan. Lower heat, add garlic, onion, paprika, pepper, and salt. When garlic is lightly browned, crush into the oil. Add green beans, broken into 1-inch pieces (or thawed, if frozen), and the rice; stir to glaze rice. Strain boiling hot broth into the skillet. Bring liquid again to a boil; cook 10 minutes over high heat.

Open can of imported escargots; drain; place snails in the shells which come with the package. Place snails down into the rice so that liquid will enter the snail shells. Complete cooking of paella over very low heat, or transfer to a casserole and complete cooking in oven preheated to 350° F. During last 5 minutes, place a moistened cloth over top. Remove cloth to serve; sprinkle top of paella with lemon juice, or a mixture of lemon juice and sherry. Total cooking time from start to finish is only 25 minutes (not including time required to make broth). *Serves 4.*

To serve 6, use 2 chicken breasts (or, use 1 chicken breast and add a 6-ounce package frozen shelled shrimp with the snails). Instead of 1 cup beans, use 1 package frozen peas or lima beans. Increase rice to 1½ cups, broth to 3 or 3½ cups.

Family Paella

Start out with the same ingredients as for the original version, but bone chicken breast and add ½ pound lean pork, diced, and 2 tablespoons diced pimiento. Instead of green beans, frozen peas or limas may be used. Omit snails; instead add a 6-ounce package frozen shelled shrimp. Cook in the same manner as for the Original Paella, using a large skillet. Bring skillet to table. Or, if using an electric skillet, start the dish in the kitchen; finish cooking at table.

Paella à la Valenciana

1 2- to 2½-pound chicken, cut up	1 pimiento, drained, chopped
1 pound large shrimp, in shell, or	2 cups rice
4 7-ounce lobster tails	1 cup frozen peas, thawed
6 cups water	1 teaspoon salt
½ teaspoon saffron	1 quart mussels or clams,
½ to ¾ cup olive oil	scrubbed thoroughly
Paprika	1 tablespoon olive oil
1 pound lean pork, diced	1 tablespoon sherry (optional)
2 whole cloves garlic	Lemon wedges
2 to 3 tablespoons minced parsley	Minced parsley
1 medium onion, minced	

Separate tender parts of chicken: cut these into 12 pieces with poultry shears: breast into 4 pieces, legs each in 2 or 3 pieces, wings with tips removed, the back so that only meaty portions are preserved (and bones removed from these). Put aside with chicken livers. All remaining pieces (including tips of the wings) are used to make the broth, along with shells of shrimp (or undershell of lobster); cook in 6 cups salted water *with the saffron* for 30 minutes; strain, reserve stock, measure 4 cups. (Broth will probably have cooked down to this.)

Devein shrimp, saving tails; or, if lobster tails are used, pull meat partially from upper shell (see page 428); cut each in 1-inch pieces right through the shell.

Heat ½ cup olive oil (add a few slices of onion to prevent spattering); brown chicken quickly without crowding pan. Sprinkle chicken with paprika as it cooks. Remove chicken to plate. Brown pork and garlic in the same oil (add more oil if needed). Remove pork; crush garlic into oil. Lower heat; add parsley, onion, and pimiento; cook until onion is soft. Add rice, peas, and salt; stir to glaze rice with oil. Transfer mixture to large (3-quart) casserole, preferably a wide, fairly shallow casserole that can be used both on top of the stove and in the oven. Replace the chicken (including browned chicken liver) and pork; add shrimp or lobster to rice, distributing in pattern. (This part can be done ahead; cover tightly; keep at room temperature.) During last ½ hour before dish is to be served, bring broth to a boil, pour boiling hot over rice, bring again to a boil *uncovered*. Cook over moderately high heat for 10 minutes, stirring once. Turn heat as low as possible (or place in oven set at 325° F.); **continue cooking another 15 minutes. Arrange the** mussels or clams over the rice. Sprinkle with a little olive oil, or a mixture of olive oil and sherry (1 tablespoon each). Place over the casserole a moistened linen cloth or paper towel; continue cooking until mussels or clams are open—another 5 minutes. By now all liquid should be absorbed and rice should be fluffy. Bring to the table in the casserole, garnished with lemon wedges and a little minced parsley. Serve 1 lemon wedge to each person, to sprinkle lemon over each serving portion at table. *Serves 8.*

To cook in a paella pan. The true Spanish way is to cook the paella out of doors. Stick three iron pipes in the ground in such a way that the broad shallow paella pan may be rested evenly on them. Build a twig fire within the area described by the pipes; when it has settled down to a red glow, place the pan over the fire. First brown the chicken in olive oil, then add the remaining ingredients (the broth will have been made in advance in the kitchen) in the order given. Feed the fire with more twigs from time to time to keep it brisk, until the liquid can be seen to disappear. *The pan is never covered;* when all liquid has been absorbed and the rice is fluffy, the paella is ready to serve. *For indoor cooking,* place the pan over high heat during the first 15 minutes of cooking, then transfer to an oven (or on the back of a big iron range) to complete cooking.

VARIATIONS

- Instead of cut-up chicken, use 2 whole chicken breasts, cut in 2-inch pieces, and use clear soup or stock concentrate for broth.
- Instead of pork, use ½ pound chicken livers; or use ½ pound each pork and veal, diced; or use chorizo sausage or ham; or use part pork, part diced salami.
- If fresh mussels or clams are not available, use canned minced clams; drain and use clam juice for part of broth. Add minced clams with rice.
- Instead of frozen peas, add frozen artichoke hearts, Fordhook limas, or Frenched green beans.
- Instead of, or in addition to pimientos, add 1 or 2 tomatoes, peeled and chopped. (In this case, use slightly less liquid.)
- In addition to pimiento, ¼ cup chopped seeded green pepper may be added.
- Sliced or chopped stuffed green olives may be added for garnish, if desired (but do not add to rice itself during cooking).
- Use less rice (1½ cups), add 1 1-pound can chick-peas, well drained, with the rice.
- Packaged saffron rice may be used, if preferred, in which case omit saffron and salt from basic recipe.

Rosetxat

¼ cup olive oil
1 clove garlic
2 medium tomatoes, chopped
1 medium onion, chopped
1 tablespoon minced parsley
¼ cup lean ham, minced
1 teaspoon paprika
1 pound butifarra sausage, or Italian sweet sausage, cut in 1-inch lengths
1½ cups rice
½ to 1 teaspoon salt
¼ teaspoon saffron, dissolved in 3 cups boiling beef broth
1 1-pound can garbanzos (chick-peas), drained

Place olive oil in casserole or heavy skillet; add the whole garlic and the tomato; when garlic is golden, mash into the oil with fork. Add onion, parsley, ham, and paprika. Cook until onion is soft; add the sausage; brown lightly. Add rice, salt, and the boiling-hot saffron-flavored broth. Finally add drained chick-peas. If skillet will not hold all ingredients, transfer to a deeper oven casserole. Complete cooking in oven at 350° F. until all liquid is absorbed, about 20 minutes. *Makes 6 servings.*

SUGGESTED GO-WITHS. Simple green salad, herb-toasted bread; for dessert, fruit compote.

Arroz Alicantara

1½ pounds large shrimp
1 pound flounder or halibut, cut in pieces
2 cups water
1 teaspoon salt
¼ teaspoon saffron
1 8-ounce can minced clams
¼ cup olive oil
1 large onion, sliced

2 or 3 cloves garlic, crushed
1 bay leaf
1 small can pimientos, drained, diced
1 cup rice
1 package frozen artichoke hearts, thawed, or 1 can artichoke hearts in brine, drained

Remove shells from shrimp. If fresh fish is used, have it filleted but save bones and head for fish stock. (Frozen fillets may be used if fresh is unavailable.) Cook shrimp shells and fish bones in the salted water for 15 to 20 minutes, adding saffron during last 5 minutes. Drain; combine clear fish stock with minced clams. Meantime, sauté cut-up fillets in the olive oil until lightly browned; add onion, garlic, bay leaf, and pimiento. Cook until onion is soft. Add rice; stir until coated with olive oil. Add artichoke hearts, fish stock, and shrimp; bring to a boil; lower heat and cook gently, uncovered, until liquid is absorbed and rice fluffy—20 to 25 minutes. Shake pan several times to prevent sticking. *Makes 6 servings.*

SUGGESTED GO-WITHS. Thin-sliced tomatoes, green pepper and raw onion salad; for dessert, Orange-Coconut Pudding.

Arroz con Pollo

1 chicken, cut up
3 to 4 tablespoons olive oil
½ cup minced ham
1 medium onion, chopped
¼ cup diced pimientos
1 cup canned tomato
¼ teaspoon saffron or *ajiote*

(available in Spanish markets)
½ bay leaf
1 teaspoon salt
1 cup rice
2 cups water
8 to 10 pimiento-stuffed olives

Brown chicken pieces in olive oil in large skillet; push to one side of pan. Add ham, onion, and pimiento; cook until soft. Add tomato mixed with saffron (or *ajiote*), bay leaf, and salt; simmer until well blended. Add rice; stir to glaze. Add water. Cook uncovered over low heat until most of water is absorbed; cover with moistened linen cloth and cook until all rice is dry and fluffy (or complete cooking in moderate oven). Add olives during last 5 minutes. *Makes 4 to 6 servings.*

WITH GARBANZOS. Add 1 1-pound can chick-peas, drained, with rice. This increases the yield to 6 heartier servings.

SUGGESTED GO-WITHS. Avocado halves filled with Vinaigrette Sauce for first course; tossed salad with the rice; fruit salad for dessert.

Rice Limeno

A delicious Latin American cousin of paella.

1 tablespoon blanched, slivered almonds	1 teaspoon salt
4 tablespoons olive oil	1 cup shelled or frozen peas
1 small onion, chopped	2 tablespoons raisins
1 small clove garlic, minced	12 veal scallopini
1 green pepper, seeded, diced	1 tablespoon flour
1 canned pimiento, chopped, or 1 3-ounce jar diced pimientos, drained	½ teaspoon salt
	¼ pound lean pork, cut in slivers
	4 tablespoons butter
1¼ cups converted rice	½ cup sherry
2½ cups water	½ cup beef bouillon or water
1 teaspoon salt	1 teaspoon minced parsley

Sauté slivered almonds in oil until lightly browned; remove; set aside. Add onion, garlic, green pepper, and pimiento; cook until soft but not brown. Add rice; stir to coat with oil. Add water, salt, peas, and raisins. Cover; bring to a boil; reduce heat; cook until water is absorbed—about 20 minutes. Spoon into large shallow casserole, keep in warming oven (250° F.). Meanwhile pound veal slices with flour and salt; dust pork with flour mixture. Sauté meat in butter quickly until golden on each side, taking care not to overcook. Add sherry; simmer a minute or two. Remove veal; continue to cook over high heat until liquid is reduced to half. Add broth; simmer until well blended, stirring to deglaze. Place overlapping slices of veal around edge of rice in shallow casserole, pork in center; cover meat with sauce; sprinkle minced parsley and the reserved browned almonds over top. Keep warm in oven until time to serve. *Makes 6 servings.*

SUGGESTED GO-WITHS. Avocado salad, butterfly rolls; for dessert, pineapple sherbet over melon wedges.

Chicken, Lima, and Rice Dinner

1 3-pound chicken, cut in 10 pieces	½ teaspoon curry powder
5 cups water	1 large or 2 small tomatoes, peeled, chopped
1 teaspoon mixed herbs	1½ cups rice
1 onion	1 package frozen Fordhook limas, thawed
3 tablespoons butter or margarine	
1 teaspoon salt	

Separate tender parts of chicken. Make stock of remaining pieces with water, herbs, and onion, cooking 30 minutes; strain broth and set aside 3½ cups. Brown tender pieces of chicken in butter over high heat (an electric skillet is excellent; set at 350° F.). Dust with salt and curry powder. Add tomatoes; reduce heat (electric skillet to 210°). Add rice; stir to coat with fat. Add broth and limas; cover; cook until all liquid is absorbed—20 to 25 minutes. Turn off heat and remove cover; let stand covered with paper towel or linen napkin for 10 to 15 minutes. *Makes 6 servings.*

SUGGESTED GO-WITHS. Watercress salad, corn muffins; peaches and cream for dessert.

Jambalaya

This Creole casserole is a direct descendant of the Spanish paella, introduced to the luxury-loving people of Old New Orleans when Louisiana belonged to Spain.

1 pound shrimp, in shells	½ green pepper, seeded, chopped
2 cups water	¼ teaspoon cayenne
Salt	1 teaspoon salt
6 smoked sausage links, or 1 pound chorizo	1 cup rice
2 tablespoons butter	¼ teaspoon thyme
1 cup diced ham	1 bay leaf, crumbled
2/3 cup chopped onion	1 cup canned tomatoes
2 cloves garlic, minced	

Shell shrimp; set aside. Simmer shells in salted water 30 minutes to make shrimp stock. Brown sausage links in large heavy skillet (or electric skillet set at 360° F.). Remove sausages; pour off fat. Add butter to pan with ham, onion, and garlic; cook until lightly browned. Lower heat (to 300° on electric skillet), add green pepper, cayenne, and salt. Stir in rice until glazed. Add 1½ cups shrimp stock and remaining ingredients; bring to a boil, uncovered; cover; lower heat (to 210° on electric skillet);

simmer covered until all liquid is absorbed—about 20 minutes. During last 5 minutes, add cooked sausage and the uncooked shrimp. Let stand 10 minutes before serving, or place in pre-heated oven (transferred to casserole) about 10 minutes. *Makes 4 to 6 servings.*

SUGGESTED GO-WITHS. Oriental Consommé as a first course; lettuce salad with garlic dressing with the Jambalaya; strawberries in orange juice for dessert.

Turkish Pilaf

2 pounds boned lamb	3 cups water
4 tablespoons butter	1½ cups rice
2 large or 3 medium onions, sliced	¾ cup chopped pitted prunes
(2 cups)	½ cup raisins
¼ teaspoon cinnamon	1½ tablespoons melted butter
¼ teaspoon freshly ground black	3 tablespoons lemon juice
pepper	1 tablespoon minced fresh pars-
Salt	ley

Cut lamb into small pieces with sharp knife or kitchen shears; place in heavy skillet with cover (or porcelain-lined cast-iron casserole) with 4 tablespoons butter. Sauté slightly. Add onions, cinnamon, and pepper; turn heat very low; cook, tightly covered, 2½ to 3 hours. (Considerable liquid will be drawn from the meat.) Add 1 teaspoon salt; stir to blend; set aside to cool.

Meanwhile, heat 3 cups water to boiling in saucepan, add rice and 1½ teaspoons salt. Bring to a boil; cover; turn heat very low and cook 15 minutes. Remove cover; place clean cloth towel over saucepan. Leave saucepan over very low heat 5 minutes; turn off heat; leave 15 to 20 minutes.

During this time, cover prunes and raisins with boiling water; let stand about 5 minutes; drain. When meat has cooled, spoon out as much of the sauce as possible, reserving in small bowl. Skim off and discard excess fat. Add fruit to meat mixture. If meat was cooked in a skillet, transfer mixture now to large casserole. Cover meat with rice. (This part may be done hours in advance.) To reserved sauce from meat, add 2 tablespoons water; spoon this over rice. Cover casserole; place in oven set at 300° F.; bake 40 to 45 minutes. Uncover, spoon over rice the 1½ tablespoons melted butter blended with 3 tablespoons lemon juice, then top with minced parsley. To serve, lightly mix rice with other ingredients. An unusual and superb party dish. *Makes 6 to 8 servings.*

SUGGESTED GO-WITHS. Lettuce and tomato salad: for dessert, yogurt topped with blackberry jam.

Persian Pilaf

1 2½-pound chicken
5 cups water
6 tablespoons butter, clarified
1½ teaspoons salt
¼ teaspoon cinnamon
¼ teaspoon freshly ground black pepper

½ cup dried apricots, snipped
½ cup seedless raisins or currants
1 large onion, chopped
1½ cups rice
½ cup chopped fresh or frozen dill, or 2 tablespoons dill weed

Cut the tender portions of chicken in 12 pieces, including the liver; use remaining parts to make chicken broth with the water. Melt the butter; pour through a strainer to clarify. Add 4 tablespoons of the butter to heavy casserole or large heavy skillet; brown the chicken pieces in the butter over high heat until crisp. Sprinkle chicken with mixture of ½ teaspoon salt, cinnamon, and black pepper as it cooks. Meanwhile soak apricots and raisins in boiling water to cover for 15 minutes.

Remove chicken from casserole or skillet. Add remaining 2 tablespoons butter, the onion, and the soaked, drained fruit to skillet; cook until onion is soft. Add rice and remaining 1 teaspoon salt; stir to glaze. Slowly add 3½ to 4 cups *boiling hot* chicken broth; bring again to a boil. Replace chicken, add dill. Cover pot or skillet with paper towel, then place fitted cover over paper and turn heat as low as possible. Cook until all liquid is absorbed—about 20 minutes. Stir rice once to fluff; if still moist, place in preheated oven a few moments to dry out. *Makes 6 to 8 servings.*

SUGGESTED GO-WITHS. Green bean salad with black olives; ice cream laced with curaçao for dessert.

Pellão of Pork Indienne

1 tablespoon slivered green ginger, or ½ teaspoon powdered ginger
2 cloves garlic
4 peppercorns
¼ teaspoon ground cloves
2 cardamom seeds, or ¼ teaspoon crushed cardamom
½ teaspoon cumin
2 teaspoons salt

2 pounds lean pork
1 cup yogurt or buttermilk
4 tablespoons butter, clarified
2 onions, chopped (1 cup)
2 cups long-grain or converted rice, cooked (6 to 8 cups after cooking)
¼ cup Lemon Butter
Toasted almonds
Shredded coconut

In mortar or electric blender, crush all spices and seasonings to a paste. Rub into meat on both sides; let stand 15 minutes, then cover meat with yogurt or buttermilk. Marinate 1 hour, or in refrigerator until needed, turning once or twice. (This and cooking of rice can be done a day ahead.)

Remove meat from marinade; drain thoroughly; cut into cubes. Brown on all sides in the clarified butter. Add onions; cook until soft. Add marinade; cook over low heat until almost dry. Add rice; stir quickly to blend and to heat through. Transfer to casserole; pour hot melted Lemon Butter over top. Cover tightly; bake in oven set at 275° F. for about ½ hour. (If dinner cannot yet be served, turn off oven and keep casserole tightly covered.) Serve topped with toasted almonds and shredded coconut, with a minted cucumber and watercress salad, and tea as the beverage. *Serves 8.*

Greek Pilaf with Shrimp Sauce

2 cups rice, cooked according to Greek Method	1 tablespoon minced fresh or frozen dill
1 medium onion, minced	¼ teaspoon cinnamon
1 or 2 cloves garlic, minced	1 teaspoon sugar
¼ cup olive oil	¾ teaspoon salt
1 1-pound can peeled tomatoes	1 pound shelled shrimp
1 6-ounce can tomato paste	

Cook rice according to Greek Method at same time as sauce is prepared.

To make sauce, sauté onion and garlic in olive oil; add tomatoes and tomato paste, chopping tomatoes into small pieces. Add dill, cinnamon, sugar, and salt; simmer 15 minutes. (Rice should be nearly cooked by now.) Thaw frozen shrimp sufficiently to chop into small pieces. Add shrimp to tomato sauce; cook 2 minutes longer. Arrange the rice in a ring, with the shrimp sauce inside. (To do this in advance, when dish is prepared for company, arrange in shallow casserole; cover casserole with its own cover or with foil; keep warm in 250° F. oven until needed, up to 1 hour.) Serve with Greek Salad and garlic bread, with cantaloupe or Persian melon for dessert. *Makes 6 to 8 servings.*

SHRIMP PILAF WITH TOMATOES. Prepare the rice according to Greek Method; when cooked, add 1 pound chopped cooked shrimp and 1 cup cooked peas. Place in casserole; cover top *completely* with sliced tomatoes; sprinkle tomato slices with mixture of ¼ cup grated cheese, 1 teaspoon sugar, ¾ teaspoon salt, and ¼ teaspoon thyme, and dot generously with butter. Shortly before serving, place in preheated broiler oven 5 inches from heat until tomato is shriveled and lightly browned.

Nasi Goreng

Peculiar to Indonesian cuisine is the frequent use of peanuts or peanut butter; that is what makes this Indonesian version of a pilaf different from all others.

1 2½-pound chicken, cut in small pieces	1 teaspoon cumin
5 cups water	1 teaspoon paprika
4 medium onions, chopped	¼ teaspoon mace
2 cloves garlic, minced	⅛ teaspoon cayenne
6 tablespoons peanut oil	1 6-ounce package frozen shelled shrimp
2 cups rice	1 cup crabmeat (fresh, frozen, or canned)
4 tablespoons peanut butter or crushed peanuts	1 cup diced ham
2 teaspoons crushed coriander	Assorted garnishes

The first part of this should be done a day ahead. First separate the tender portions of chicken (breast, legs, wings, meaty parts of back, and liver) and cut into 2-inch pieces. With remaining parts and water, make seasoned broth. (Keep cut-up chicken in refrigerator until needed.) Strain broth; measure; add water if necessary to make 4 cups. Sauté onion and garlic in 3 tablespoons of the peanut oil until soft; add rice, brown lightly. Add the strained broth and the peanut butter (if crushed peanuts are used, add later with the crabmeat). Bring to a boil; cover; turn heat very low; cook until all liquid is absorbed. Remove cover; place paper towel over pan and cook 5 minutes longer. Stir rice and transfer to a bowl.

About an hour before dish is to be served, heat remaining 3 tablespoons oil; brown tender chicken pieces a few at a time over high heat until crisp on all sides; blend the spices; sprinkle over the chicken as it cooks (if necessary, add more oil). When all chicken is cooked, add cooked rice, shrimp, crabmeat, and ham (and crushed peanuts are added now). Stir to blend thoroughly. Transfer to casserole, cover, and place in oven set at 325° F. for another 20 to 30 minutes of cooking. (Turn off oven if not to be served immediately.) *Serves 8.*

SUGGESTED GO-WITHS. Any of the same garnishes as for a curry, especially chutney, thinly sliced cucumber salad, coarsely chopped nuts, fried bananas, chopped hard-cooked egg. Sometimes the egg is sprinkled over the casserole when it is served. Tea is usually served with the meal. For dessert, a compote of tropical fruits in orange juice.

Chinese Fried Rice (Basic Recipe)

3 cups cooked rice

3 tablespoons vegetable or peanut oil

4 green onions (scallions). chopped, or ¼ cup chopped onions

1 or 2 garlic cloves, minced (optional)

½ green pepper, seeded, chopped

½ cup other minced crisp vegetables*

½ teaspoon salt

1 cup cooked meat, poultry, or seafood

2 eggs, beaten

2 tablespoons soy sauce

Minced scallions, parsley or cilantro, for garnish

The rice must be cooked ahead so that it will be dry and fluffy. Prepare according to basic recipe for Steamed Rice or Oriental Rice. Heat oil in a heavy skillet or wok; add scallions and garlic; stir-fry until lightly browned—about 2 minutes. Add green pepper and other vegetables. Stir-fry until lightly browned, sprinkling with salt. Add rice and meat or poultry or seafood. Stir to blend thoroughly; turn heat as low as possible; cook 5 minutes longer. (If using a skillet, cover pan; if cooked in a wok, it need not be covered.) Combine beaten eggs and soy sauce; stir quickly and deftly through rice so that egg is completely absorbed and rice seems dry (it must not be all slimy). Serve in a casserole topped with minced scallion, parsley, or cilantro. *Makes 4 servings by itself; if served as one dish in a Chinese dinner, it may be served to 6 persons.*

*Raw slivered carrots, minced celery, chopped water chestnuts, slivers of white turnips, or tender raw green beans cut fine.

BACON AND PEPPER FRIED RICE. Cut ½ pound bacon into squares. Use only 1 tablespoon oil; cook bacon in this until crisp. Remove bacon, set aside. Proceed as in basic recipe, using 1 whole green pepper and ¼ cup celery. Other meat may be omitted.

SHRIMP FRIED RICE. Uncooked frozen shrimp may be used, minced before being added to the rice mixture. Or, use 4 slices bacon, diced, and 1 6½-ounce can shrimp, minced.

PORK FRIED RICE. Leftover cooked pork may be used as the meat, by itself or in combination with shrimp, chicken, or ham.

TO EXTEND FRIED RICE. Any mild-flavored cooked or canned vegetables may be added, such as peas, green beans, mushrooms, kernel corn (yes!), or baby limas. (But *not* broccoli, spinach, or any strong-flavored vegetable.)

ALMOND FRIED RICE. Serve topped with ¼ cup chopped toasted almonds.

TUNA FRIED RICE. Sauté 1 cup sliced mushrooms with the green pepper; use 1 can chunk tuna, well drained, instead of meat.

To serve 2 persons, use 1½ cups cooked rice; halve all other ingredients. An excellent quick entree for a 2-person household.

If you have just 1 cup leftover cooked rice, divide all other ingredients by half, except the vegetables, which are increased to 1 cup, including cooked (or canned) vegetables.

When frozen chopped onions are used in any recipe, make sure the onions are completely thawed and drained before adding to fat—or the fat will spatter badly and onions will not brown at all.

Baked Lasagne (Basic Recipe)

1 pound lasagne, cooked
2 cloves garlic
3 or 4 tablespoons olive oil
1 cup chopped onion
½ cup chopped parsley
1 pound chopped beef
  (hamburger)
4 cups tomato or spaghetti sauce

(homemade or commercial)
¼ to ½ teaspoon orégano
½ teaspoon basil
1 cup ricotta or cottage cheese
¾ pound mozzarella cheese, thinly sliced
4 tablespoons grated Parmesan or Romano cheese

Cook the lasagne in a large quantity of rapidly boiling salted water until tender; drain thoroughly; rinse with *hot* water. Separate and cut lengths to fit large (3-quart) baking dish or casserole. Heat whole or split garlic cloves in olive oil until soft and yellow; press into oil with tines of fork (remove and discard shreds, if preferred). Add onion and parsley; cook until onion is soft. Add meat; cook, stirring, until meat has lost its pink color.

Add sauce, orégano, and basil. Cook until thoroughly hot.

Layer the lasagne with the sauce and the ricotta and mozzarella cheeses, with sauce and part of the mozzarella on top. Sprinkle Parmesan cheese over the mozzarella. (All this can be done ahead.) Bake in oven preheated to 400° F. until top is lightly browned and sauce is bubbly—about 45 minutes. *Makes 10 servings.*

WITH PORK. Instead of ground meat, use 2 cups diced cooked pork, or 1 pound lean raw pork, sautéed until browned.

WITH CHICKEN LIVERS. Instead of ground meat, use 1 pound chicken livers, sautéed separately in butter; or, use a combination of ½ pound chicken livers and ½ pound sliced mushrooms; or a combination of ½ pound chicken livers and ½ pound ground veal or pork.

MUSHROOM LASAGNE. Omit meat; instead use 1 pound fresh mushrooms, sautéed in butter, for a vegetarian entree.

SPINACH LASAGNE. Omit meat; use 1 package frozen chopped spinach; add to onion; break up in fat until thoroughly thawed.

For 5 to 6 servings, divide all ingredients in basic recipe in half.

SUGGESTED GO-WITHS. Roquefort Salad, garlic bread, spumoni or Biscuit Tortoni for dessert.

Baked Manicotti

Use same ingredients as for Baked Lasagne (or any of the same variations), but substitute 1 pound manicotti shells (cooked in rapidly boiling salted water) for lasagne, and fill the shells with ricotta cheese. Place filled manicotti in casserole layered with the sauce.

ANOTHER WAY. Make thin crepes with basic pancake batter; spoon ricotta cheese in each, and roll up. Cover these with meat sauce and slices of mozzarella; bake until sauce is bubbling.

Fettucine with Chicken Livers

½ pound fettucine or egg noodles
1 pound chicken livers
6 or 7 tablespoons butter
¼ pound fresh mushrooms, sliced
½ teaspoon salt
Dash of freshly ground black

pepper
¼ cup red table wine
½ cup grated Parmesan cheese
¼ cup light cream
2 eggs, lightly beaten

Cook noodles in salted water until tender; drain, keep warm Meanwhile, sauté chicken livers in 3 to 4 tablespoons butter until well browned. Add mushrooms; cook a minute or two. Sprinkle with salt and pepper, add wine; lower heat; simmer 3 or 4 minutes. To hot drained noodles, add remaining 3 tablespoons butter, cheese, and cream; toss until well blended. Add eggs; toss again. If necessary, place pan over very low heat to cook eggs (but if noodles are hot, this will not be necessary). Arrange fettucine around edge of shallow casserole, chicken livers in center. Serve this way immediately or if to be served later, sprinkle top with buttered crumbs, when ready to serve, place under broiler 6 inches from heat until crumbs are lightly browned. *Serves 6.*

SUGGESTED GO-WITHS. Artichoke and black olive salad, red wine as the beverage; strawberry cheesecake for dessert.

Crab Fettucine

1½ cups crabmeat (fresh, frozen, or canned)
4 tablespoons butter
½ cup cream
1 cup (4 ounces) grated Parmesan cheese

1 package frozen peas and onions, cooked
Salt
1 pound wide egg noodles, cooked
Freshly ground black pepper

Place crabmeat in top of double boiler with butter, cream, and cheese. Heat over hot water until butter and cheese are melted; stir to blend. Add peas and onions. Taste; add salt if needed. At same time, cook egg noodles. Drain thoroughly. Place in casserole with crab-pea mixture; stir to blend. Grind pepper over top. Serve at once with a mixed salad and hot crisp rolls or muffins (corn muffins would be excellent). *Makes 4 servings.*

WITH ARTICHOKES. Instead of peas and onions, use 1 package frozen artichoke hearts, cooked.

WITH GREEN BEANS AND MUSHROOMS. Use 1 package frozen green beans and mushrooms, cooked, instead of frozen peas and onions.

Chicken Tetrazzini

1 stewing chicken, about 4 pounds, cut up	½ cup heavy cream
6 cups water	2 tablespoons medium sweet sherry
1 teaspoon salt	Salt, pepper
1 celery sprig	Nutmeg
1 small onion stuck with cloves	1 pound thin spaghetti, cooked
3 tablespoons butter or margarine	½ cup grated Parmesan cheese
3 tablespoons flour	

Cook the chicken in water with salt, celery sprig, and onion until very tender with water barely "smiling"—about 1 hour. Remove chicken. When broth is cool, strain and measure. *Reduce by boiling to 1 cup.* Set aside.

When chicken is cool enough to handle, skin, bone, and cut meat in small pieces. Use 2 to 2½ cups chicken meat, but not the liver or giblets. Make Velouté Sauce by melting butter, stir in flour, then slowly add strained broth, cream and sherry. Simmer over very low heat 10 minutes, stirring with whisk until smooth. Add salt, pepper, and nutmeg to taste. Arrange cooked spaghetti in greased 2-quart casserole in layers with chicken; cover with the sauce. Spread Parmesan cheese over top. (All this can be done ahead.) Bake in oven preheated to 350° F. until cheese is lightly browned and sauce bubbling—30 to 40 minutes. *Serves 6.*

SUGGESTED GO-WITHS. Caesar Salad, Parker House rolls; Peach Tarts for dessert.

QUICK CHICKEN TETRAZZINI. To serve 3 or 4, use 1½ to 2 cups diced cooked or canned chicken, and for the sauce, 1 can condensed cream of chicken soup, 1/3 cup light cream, and 1 egg, beaten. Season sauce with a dash of nutmeg and a tablespoon of sherry, if desired. Layer with ½ pound spaghetti, cooked, in 1-quart casserole; top with mixture of ½ cup each fine dry crumbs and Parmesan cheese; dot with butter. Bake as directed in basic recipe.

TURKEY TETRAZZINI. Use 2 to 2½ cups diced turkey meat (from leftover roast turkey), and make sauce as in basic recipe, using 1 cup chicken broth or broth made by cooking turkey carcass; or, make sauce with 2 cans condensed cream of chicken soup, 2/3 cup cream, and 1 egg, beaten. Layer with spaghetti; top with cheese as in basic recipe.

PORK AND MUSHROOM TETRAZZINI. To serve 6, use 1½ pounds lean pork, diced, instead of chicken; add ¼ pound mushrooms, sliced. Sauté pork in 4 tablespoons butter until lightly browned; add mushrooms; brown lightly. Stir in 3 tablespoons flour and, for broth, make chicken broth with stock concentrate (or use canned clear chicken soup). Proceed as in basic recipe, alternating layers of pork and mushrooms and spaghetti.

CHICKEN AND HAM TETRAZZINI. Use 1 cup cooked or canned chicken and 1 cup diced ham; for chicken broth, use canned condensed clear chicken soup (reduce to 1 cup by boiling). Or, to serve 3 or 4, use ½ cup each chicken and ham, and proceed as for Quick Chicken Tetrazzini.

See also Macaroni-Ham Casserole, and Noodle Casserole (basic recipe with variations) in preceding chapter.

Spaghetti-Ham Casserole

1 1-pound can Danish ham	¼ cup sherry
1 8-ounce can tomato sauce	1 package frozen lima beans
½ teaspoon orégano	½ pound spaghetti, cooked
½ teaspoon salt, or to taste	½ cup shredded sharp cheese
1 teaspoon instant minced onion	

Remove ham from can, saving gelatin. Cut ham into thin crosswise slices; set aside. Add water to gelatin to make 1½ cups; combine with tomato sauce, orégano, salt, instant onion, and sherry. Simmer until well blended; add limas; cover; cook 10 minutes longer. Meanwhile, cook spaghetti until just tender; drain; place in greased 2-quart casserole in layers with ham and sauce. Top with cheese. Bake in oven preheated to 400° F. for 30 to 40 minutes until cheese is melted and sauce bubbly. *Makes 4 to 6 servings.*

For 8 to 10 servings, use a 2-pound can of ham, double remaining ingredients.

WITH LEFTOVER BAKED HAM. Use large slices, about ¼ inch thick, allow 1 slice per serving.

Quick Chicken Divan

3 whole chicken breasts	2 packages frozen broccoli
1½ cups Mornay Sauce	spears, thawed
1 egg, beaten	½ cup grated Parmesan cheese

Cook chicken breasts, covered, in salted water until tender—about 20 minutes; remove chicken; save broth. Skin and bone chicken; slice the breast meat. Use broth in making Mornay Sauce. When sauce is somewhat cooled, beat in egg. Cook broccoli about 3 minutes; drain thoroughly. Butter a shallow 2-quart casserole; arrange broccoli in a layer over the bottom; cover with one-third of the sauce; add the chicken; cover with remaining sauce. Spread cheese over top. Cover casserole. (This can be done ahead.) Bake in oven preheated to 350° F. until sauce is bubbling and cheese melted—30 to 40 minutes. Remove cover; glaze sauce under broiler a few moments before serving. *Makes 6 to 8 servings.*

SAUCE SHORT CUT. Use 1 can condensed cream of chicken soup, ½ cup chicken broth, ¼ cup heavy cream, and ½ cup shredded Swiss or natural Gruyère cheese. Stir until well blended and cheese is melted. Add to beaten egg, blend well.

QUICK TURKEY DIVAN. Use 6 large slices of cooked turkey breast instead of chicken.

WITH ASPARAGUS. Instead of broccoli, use asparagus spears—either fresh asparagus spears, briefly cooked (still crisp), or frozen asparagus spears placed in casserole (thawed but not cooked).

HAM AND MUSHROOM DIVAN. Instead of chicken, use sliced ham (1 large slice for each serving portion) and add sliced mushrooms (sautéed in butter) to basic recipe; use either broccoli or asparagus. Top with Mornay Sauce and grated cheese as in basic recipe.

SUGGESTED GO-WITHS. Toasted Herb Bread or rolls, sliced tomato and watercress salad; for dessert, honeydew with juice of lime.

Ham and Artichokes Madeira

6 slices canned or cooked ham
1 package frozen artichoke
  hearts, or 2 cans imported Spanish artichoke hearts, packed in
  brine
2 tablespoons butter
2 tablespoons flour

1½ cups broth*
½ cup light cream
2 tablespoons Madeira wine,
  cream sherry, or brandy
Salt, pepper to taste
½ cup grated Parmesan cheese

Arrange half the ham slices in bottom of greased shallow casserole. Cook frozen artichoke hearts according to package
directions; save cooking liquid. Or, drain canned artichoke
hearts, save liquid. Melt butter, stir in flour, cooking until mixture bubbles. Add broth; stir and cook until smooth and thickened. Add cream and Madeira; season to taste. Place artichoke
hearts in layer over ham; add remaining ham; cover with sauce.
Sprinkle cheese over top. Place under broiler in preheated
broiler oven, 5 inches from heat, until top is glazed and lightly
browned. *Serves 6.*

    *Artichoke liquid plus water, or gelatin from can of ham, if canned
ham is used.

HAM AND ARTICHOKES IN MUSHROOM SAUCE. Omit butter, flour, and broth in above recipe; use instead 1 can condensed cream of mushroom soup, a 2-ounce can of mushrooms
with liquid plus 1/3 cup cream and 2 tablespoons Madeira.*

    *Cream sherry or brandy may be used instead of Madeira.

SHRIMP AND ARTICHOKES MADEIRA. Instead of ham, use
12 ounces frozen shelled shrimp, cooked briefly; add ¼ pound
mushrooms sautéed in butter (1 4-ounce can mushrooms). In
casserole, place first a layer of artichoke hearts, then mushrooms, then cooked shrimp. Cover with sauce, as in basic recipe
(or above variation), and top with cheese.

SUGGESTED GO-WITHS. Crusty rolls, Green Beans Vinaigrette; for dessert, mixed fruit compote.

Curried Creamed Shrimp in Patty Shells

¼ cup minced shallots or white onions

¼ pound sliced mushrooms, or 1 4-ounce can sliced mushrooms

¼ cup minced celery

2 tablespoons butter or margarine

1 can frozen condensed cream of shrimp soup, thawed

1 cup sour cream

½ to 1 teaspoon curry powder, according to taste

1 6-ounce package frozen shelled shrimp, cooked

4 patty shells

Sauté shallots, mushrooms, and celery in butter until tender. Add soup; stir until well blended. Combine sour cream and curry powder; add some of hot sauce, then combine the two. Remove from heat; add shrimp. (This can be done ahead.) Reheat in top of double boiler over hot water; serve in patty shells purchased from bakery. *Makes 4 luncheon servings.*

SUGGESTED GO-WITHS. Avocado Vinaigrette as a first course; with the shrimp, grilled tomatoes. For dessert, mélange of fruit with pineapple sherbet.

CURRIED CRAB IN PATTY SHELLS. Use 1 cup or 6 ounces of crabmeat (fresh, frozen, or canned) in place of shrimp in above recipe.

Chicken and Lobster Costa Brava

4 to 6 small (3- or 4-ounce) frozen rock lobster tails

1 3-pound chicken, cut up

2 cups water

1 teaspoon salt

4 tablespoons olive oil

2 tablespoons butter

2 carrots, peeled, grated

2 leeks or 6 scallions, minced

½ cup very dry sherry

¼ cup brandy

½ cup beef gravy

1 tablespoon tomato paste or catsup

Defrost lobster tails; cut away undershell; pull meat partially away from heavy upper shell. Cut each tail in half. Separate wing tips, neck, giblets, and ugly pieces of back from other chicken pieces; use to make chicken broth with water. Cut up remaining chicken pieces in small portions; dust with salt.

Heat olive oil and butter together until butter is melted and sizzling. Add chicken pieces; cook until well browned; remove (do not crowd pan). Add lobster; cook just until shell turns red; turn once. Remove. Add carrots and leeks; sprinkle with salt; cook until very soft over low heat. Add sherry; simmer 2 minutes. Replace chicken and lobster; add brandy; set aflame. When flame has died out, remove chicken and lobster to casserole; blend beef gravy with catsup and ½ cup strained chicken broth; add to vegetables; cook, stirring, about 2 minutes. Pour over chicken and lobster in casserole. (All this can be done ahead.)

About 1 hour before dinner, place casserole in oven; turn on oven to 325° F.; bake, covered, 30 minutes. Reduce oven heat to 250° F.; leave casserole in oven until time to serve. *Serves 6; double ingredients to serve 12.*

SUGGESTED GO-WITHS. Rice, salad of artichoke hearts, pimiento, and black olives. For dessert, Black-bottom Pie. Either red or white wine may be served with the entree.

Cazuela Americana

This is my own adaptation of Chicken and Lobster Costa Brava, created especially for a holiday buffet supper when I expected about 20 guests. All the pieces of meat, chicken, and the shrimp can be speared on cocktail picks to be removed from a shallow casserole, or the dish may be served as an entree, accompanied by rice or saffron rice.

6 chicken breasts, boned
2 cups water
2 teaspoons chicken stock concentrate
¼ cup olive oil
4 to 6 tablespoons butter
2 pounds lean pork, diced
1 pound lean ham, diced
1 pound sweet Italian sausage, or butifarra, cut in 1-inch pieces
3 carrots, peeled, grated
2 leeks, minced
1 medium onion, minced
2 cloves garlic, minced
2 pounds shelled shrimp
1 cup very dry sherry
½ cup brandy
1 can (1¼ cups) beef gravy
Salt
2 tablespoons minced parsley

Use the bones taken from the chicken breasts to make chicken broth with water and stock concentrate. Cut remaining chicken meat into 1-inch pieces. Sauté the chicken in 2 tablespoons each oil and butter until well browned; remove to large casserole.

Sauté the pork until well browned in same fat, adding more if needed; remove to casserole with chicken. Continue with ham and sausage. When all meat has been browned, add the minced vegetables and remaining oil and butter; cook until very soft. Return chicken and some of meat to pan with the shelled shrimp; add sherry; simmer until thoroughly hot—about 2 minutes. Add brandy; set aflame. When flame has died out, remove chicken, the meat, and shrimp again to casserole. Add beef gravy blended with 1 to 1½ cups chicken broth; simmer 5 minutes. Taste for seasoning; add salt if needed (or, if too salty, add water). Pour over chicken and meat in casserole; liquid should almost cover other ingredients. Cover casserole. (This can be done ahead; in fact, it can be frozen to be reheated.)

Reheat in oven set at 325° F. for 40 minutes before serving; add 20 minutes more if frozen. *Makes about 30 servings.*

Chinese Pork and Peppers

½ pound lean pork, cut in slivers
2 tablespoons peanut or other bland vegetable oil
1 small onion, chopped
1 clove garlic, minced
1 cup sliced celery
1 green pepper, seeded, cut in 1-inch squares
1 small (5-ounce) can water chestnuts, drained, sliced, or 2 white turnips, cut in matchstick slivers
1 tablespoon cornstarch
3 tablespoons soy sauce
2 tablespoons dry sherry
1 cup water
1 teaspoon chicken stock concentrate, or 1 bouillon cube

Sauté the pork in oil until well browned on all sides; remove, or push to one side of pan. Add onion, garlic and celery, sauté over moderate heat until tender. Add green pepper and water chestnuts (or turnip); replace the pork; cook 1 minute. Blend together cornstarch, soy sauce, sherry, and water; add to the pork mixture. Add stock concentrate or bouillon cube; stir until dissolved. Cook until sauce is thickened—about 3 minutes. Serve as part of a Chinese family dinner. *Makes 3 or 4 servings.*

Indonesian Pork and Chicken

1 pound lean pork
2 tablespoons peanut oil
3 whole chicken breasts, cut in 2-inch pieces
1 cup chopped onion
1½ cups celery, sliced diagonally
1 tablespoon curry powder
⅛ teaspoon ground ginger
⅛ teaspoon cayenne
1 1-pound can mixed Chinese vegetables, thoroughly drained
1 tablespoon cornstarch
1 tablespoon brown sugar
2 tablespoons soy sauce
½ cup chicken broth
1 cup Coconut Milk
1 cup chopped peanuts
Hot cooked rice

Cut pork into slivers; sauté in oil over high heat until well browned—about 5 minutes; remove. Add chicken; brown until crisp on all sides; remove. Add onion and celery; reduce heat; cook until tender—about 3 minutes. Add seasoning; stir to blend. Add Chinese vegetables; replace pork and chicken. Blend cornstarch and sugar together; thin with soy sauce and broth. Add to casserole; bring to boil; cook until almost dry. Add Coconut Milk; simmer, stirring, until sauce is smooth and thickened. Serve garnished with peanuts, accompanied by hot cooked rice. Nothing else is needed but a pot of tea, with a compote of fruit for dessert. *Makes 6 to 8 servings.*

Chop Suey (Basic Recipe)

4 tablespoons peanut or vegetable
oil
2 medium onions, minced
1 or 2 cloves garlic, minced
1 cup celery, sliced diagonally
½ green pepper, seeded, cut in
squares
½ teaspoon salt
1½ cups meat, poultry, or sea-

food, chopped*
½ cup canned or frozen vegeta-
bles†
3 tablespoons soy sauce
2 teaspoons cornstarch
¾ cup chicken broth
1 tablespoon very dry sherry
Hot cooked rice

Prepare all ingredients, place in bowls ready to use, but do not cook until shortly before meal is to be served (a total of approximately 10 minutes' final cooking time is all that's needed). Separately cook rice in advance; reheat rice when needed over steam (place in colander or sieve above hot water, without permitting water to touch rice; cover with linen cloth or paper towel).

Heat half the oil in a heavy skillet or wok; add onion and garlic first; cook 2 minutes. Add celery; cook 2 minutes longer. Add green pepper; cook 1 minute. Sprinkle vegetables with salt as they cook. Add meat, chicken or duck, or seafood; stir-fry until lightly browned. (If raw, a little longer cooking is required; if already cooked, no more than 1 minute is necessary—just enough to heat thoroughly and brown very lightly.) Add frozen or canned vegetable; combine soy sauce and cornstarch; stir to dissolve cornstarch. Combine with chicken broth and sherry; add to pan; cook, stirring, until sauce is thickened and glazed. Serve with rice, by itself, or as part of a Chinese family dinner. *Makes 4 to 6 servings.*

*Slivers of pork, chicken breast (uncooked), cut in 1-inch pieces, diced cooked duck, chopped shelled shrimp, cubes of raw or frozen fish fillets, or a combination of any two of these may be used. To supplement a smaller amount of meat, add blanched almonds (sauté in oil before the onion is cooked), or increase the amount of canned or frozen vegetable.

†Frozen peas, Frenched green beans, sliced mushrooms, sliced water chestnuts, bamboo shoots, bean sprouts, or artichoke hearts may be used. *Fresh* snow peas and slivers of *raw* turnip are other possibilities.

Chicago Chop Suey

¾ to 1 cup minced ham
½ cup chopped onion
1 or 2 cloves garlic, minced
3 tablespoons oil
½ green pepper, seeded, chopped
1 12-ounce can kernel corn, well drained
1 5-ounce can water chestnuts, sliced
½ teaspoon salt
1 recipe Oriental Brown Sauce
Slivered toasted almonds (optional)
Hot cooked rice

Sauté the ham, onion, and garlic in 2 tablespoons oil until lightly browned—about 2 minutes. Add the green pepper; cook 1 minute. Add the corn and water chestnuts; sprinkle with salt. Cook 1 minute longer. Add Oriental Brown Sauce; simmer until sauce is thickened, smooth, and shiny. Serve topped with almonds and accompanied by fluffy rice as part of a Chinese family dinner. *Makes 4 to 6 servings.*

Moo Goo Gai Pan

2 whole chicken breasts
Salt, pepper
3 tablespoons peanut or vegetable oil
½ cup blanched almonds
3 scallions, minced
1 cup thinly sliced mushrooms
1 cup diced seeded green pepper
3 or 4 thin slices green ginger, or ⅛ teaspoon ground ginger
1 cup frozen tiny peas, thawed
2 teaspoons cornstarch
¾ cup chicken broth
2 tablespoons very dry sherry
2 tablespoons soy sauce

Skin and bone chicken breasts; cut into 1-inch pieces. Sprinkle chicken with salt and pepper. Heat oil in skillet or wok; quickly sauté chicken until meat turns solidly white (this requires only 3 or 4 minutes). Push to one side of pan; add almonds, stir-fry until browned. Add scallions, mushrooms, green pepper, and ginger; stir-fry 2 minutes. Add peas; stir until broken up and coated with oil; cook 2 minutes. Dissolve cornstarch in some of the chicken broth; add remaining chicken broth, sherry, and soy sauce; add to chicken and vegetable mixture. Cook, stirring once or twice, until sauce is smooth, thickened, and shiny—about 4 minutes longer. Serve with rice, by itself or as part of a Chinese dinner. *Makes 4 to 6 servings.*

Chicken Hekka

A Hawaiian dish very similar to what we call chop suey, except for the addition of yams or sweet potatoes—a very delicious touch.

1 medium onion, thinly sliced	1 tablespoon brown sugar
½ pound mushrooms, sliced	3 cups diced cooked chicken or
3 tablespoons oil	turkey
3 sweet potatoes or yams	1 tablespoon cornstarch
(uncooked), peeled, diced	1 tablespoon dry sherry
1½ cups chicken broth	Hot cooked rice
1/3 cup soy sauce	

Sauté onion and mushrooms in oil until tender but not browned. Add diced raw sweet potatoes; sauté 1 minute. Add chicken broth mixed with soy sauce and sugar; stir to dissolve sugar. Simmer, *covered,* until potatoes are nearly done—about 15 minutes. Add chicken; remove cover; cook just until heated through—about 5 minutes. Blend cornstarch with enough water to dissolve; add sherry. Stir this into vegetable-chicken mixture. Cook until sauce is thickened and shiny and potatoes are tender. Serve with rice. *Makes 6 servings.*

Chicken and Pork Adobo

1 broiler, about 2 pounds, cut in	1 bay leaf
10 to 12 pieces	2 tablespoons soy sauce
2 cups water	1 teaspoon salt
2 pounds lean pork, cut in 1-inch	¼ teaspoon pepper
cubes	3 to 4 tablespoons oil or fresh lard
½ cup vinegar	1 cup Coconut Milk
4 cloves garlic	

The chicken should be cut with poultry shears right through the bone, into 2-inch pieces. Reserve liver; use giblets, neck, and water to make stock. Marinate remaining chicken pieces and pork for 2 hours or more in mixture of vinegar, garlic, bay leaf, soy sauce, salt, and pepper. Remove from marinade; pat dry. Heat oil or lard. Brown the chicken liver; remove, crush, and set aside. Brown chicken pieces and pork, without crowding pan. When all pieces are browned, return to pan; add strained marinade, 1 cup chicken stock and the crushed liver; cook until almost dry. Add Coconut Milk (made by soaking shredded coconut in hot milk) ½ cup at a time; cook until reduced. Serve with rice, accompanied by a salad of avocado and sliced onion. *Serves 8.*

Malayan Chicken and Shrimp Curry

1 small (2-pound) chicken,
cut in 10 to 12 pieces
2 cups water
4 tablespoons oil or shortening
2 large or 4 small onions, cut in
matchstick slivers
1 clove garlic, minced
2 teaspoons curry powder
1 teaspoon coriander

½ teaspoon cumin
Dash of Tabasco or cayenne
4 large potatoes, peeled, diced, or
1 cup rice
1 6-ounce package frozen shelled
shrimp
1 cup Coconut Milk
½ cup chopped peanuts

Make broth of the chicken neck, giblets, bonier parts of back, and the water. Brown the chicken pieces in 2 tablespoons of the oil, without crowding pan. Remove as pieces are browned. Add remaining oil; cook onion and garlic with spices until soft. Replace chicken; add potatoes or rice and shrimp with 1 cup chicken broth. Cover tightly, simmer over low heat 15 minutes, shaking pan occasionally. Add Coconut Milk (made by soaking shredded coconut in hot milk) ½ cup at a time; cook, uncovered, until most of liquid is absorbed. Serve from casserole topped with chopped peanuts, accompanied by assorted garnishes as for an Indian curry. *Makes 6 servings.*

Sweet and Pungent Pork

2 pounds lean pork, cut in 1-inch
cubes
2 tablespoons oil

1 recipe Chinese Sweet and Pungent Sauce

Fry pork in oil over high heat until browned on all sides. Add ingredients for sauce. Serve as part of a Chinese dinner.

SWEET AND PUNGENT SPARERIBS. Have butcher cut lean spareribs into 2-inch lengths. Blanch with boiling water to remove excess fat. Prepare Chinese Sweet and Pungent Sauce; add spareribs; simmer 20 minutes.

See also Phoenix-tail Shrimp; Korma Curry; Caril do Frango.

Moussaka

1 small or ½ large eggplant	½ cup wine
½ to ¾ cup olive oil or shortening	½ cup canned tomatoes or tomato
2 tablespoons butter	sauce
1 pound very lean ground meat*	8 tablespoons fine dry crumbs
4 medium onions, sliced	2 eggs, separated
2 or 3 cloves garlic, minced	1½ cups Béchamel Sauce
½ teaspoon thyme	Dash of nutmeg
½ teaspoon orégano	

Slice the eggplant lengthwise *without peeling* (discard outer slices, which are mostly peel). Add about 4 tablespoons of the oil to skillet at a time; sauté the eggplant slices until lightly browned on each side, adding more oil as needed. Set aside. When all eggplant has been cooked, add butter and 2 more tablespoons oil to pan; to this add the ground meat; cook, stirring, until all pink color is gone and meat is lightly browned. Add onion, garlic, thyme, and orégano; cook until onion is soft. Add wine and tomato. Simmer 10 minutes. Stir in 4 tablespoons of the crumbs and the whites of the 2 eggs (unbeaten).

Place 2 tablespoons of the remaining crumbs in bottom of well-greased casserole. Add a layer of eggplant slices, then part of the meat mixture, then more eggplant, until all have been used. Eggplant slices should be on top. (This part can be done ahead.)

Prepare Béchamel Sauce; beat the 2 egg yolks; stir into the sauce; season with nutmeg. Pour the sauce over the casserole. (It should completely cover other ingredients.) Top with remaining 2 tablespoons crumbs. Bake in oven preheated to 350° F. for a total of 1 hour. When moussaka is served, it should come from the casserole in wedges with the sauce forming a soft crust. *Makes 8 to 10 servings.*

*Lean lamb is used in Greece, but ground lean beef, or a mixture of beef, veal, and pork, is also very good.

SUGGESTED GO-WITHS. Green salad and crusty rolls with the main course; Fruit Punch Cup for dessert.

Escalloped Corn and Lobster

1½ cups lobster meat, or 2	½ teaspoon salt
6½-ounce cans lobster	½ teaspoon dry mustard
1½ tablespoons butter	1 egg, beaten
1 12-ounce can cream-style corn	½ cup sherry
2 tablespoons flour	Buttered crumbs
1 cup light cream	

Drain lobster and cut larger pieces into chunks. Melt butter, add corn blended with flour, then stir in cream, seasonings, and egg; stir over medium heat about 2 minutes. Add lobster and sherry. Divide into 4 ramekins. Top each with buttered crumbs. Shortly before serving, place in preheated broiler, 6 inches from heat; cook until crumbs are browned. Serve with salad and hot rolls, with cheesecake for dessert. *Serves 4.*

Golubtsi (Russian Stuffed Cabbage)

12 large cabbage leaves	½ pound ground beef
Salt	1 egg, beaten
1 medium onion, chopped	1½ cups puréed tomatoes, or 1
4 tablespoons butter	cup tomato sauce
2 tablespoons minced parsley	½ cup water
1 cup cooked rice	1 tablespoon cornstarch
½ pound ground lean pork	½ cup sour cream

Separate outer cabbage leaves carefully, trimming away hard core. Place in deep pot; cover completely with boiling water; sprinkle with salt; cover pot; simmer 2 minutes, then let stand 10 minutes. Meantime, simmer the chopped onion in 2 tablespoons of the butter until yellowed; add parsley, rice, the two kinds of meat, and 1½ teaspoons salt; cook until meat has lost its pink color. Cool. Stir in beaten egg and 1 tablespoon of the tomato purée or sauce. Remove cabbage leaves from water, draining well. Place 1 to 1½ tablespoons of the meat mixture in each cabbage leaf, fold over sides, then roll up tightly. Melt remaining 2 tablespoons butter in large (12-inch) skillet or large shallow baking dish. Place rolled cabbage leaves in butter, overlapped side down. Simmer in butter 2 minutes. Add the remaining tomato purée and water, cover skillet (use foil if it has no cover), and simmer over low heat 40 minutes, or bake in preheated 350° F. oven 1 hour. When cabbage is tender, make a thin paste of corn starch and some of sauce from skillet or baking dish; add to rest of sauce; simmer 5 minutes. Pour sour cream over top, stirring into tomato sauce. Serve with baked or boiled potatoes. *Serves 6.*

ANOTHER WAY. Instead of rice, use 1 cup stale bread crumbs in filling; soak crumbs in water, then squeeze out water. Proceed as in above recipe, but for sauce, use 1 cup beef stock instead of tomato.

Pastel de Choclo

Choclo is the name of a white variety of corn popular in Latin America. This *pastel*, or pie, is often baked in pastry. Or, it may be served in a casserole, over rice, with the corn spread over the top; use sliced olives for garnish. The following is very easy, however, and quite delicious, especially for a spur-of-the-moment luncheon. Canned chicken and leftover roast pork may be used.

½ cup diced cooked chicken
2 cups (1 pound) lean boneless pork, cooked, diced
1 12-ounce can white corn, drained
2 hard-cooked eggs, minced
4 green olives, pitted, minced
8 chopped black olives
½ tablespoon chili powder
½ teaspoon cumin or curry powder
¼ teaspoon cayenne
1 teaspoon sugar
¼ cup raisins
1 tablespoon instant minced onion
2 tablespoons olive or vegetable oil
1 can beef gravy
½ cup medium dry sherry
Stuffed olives, sliced

Combine all ingredients except stuffed olives; place in oiled casserole. Bake or cook over very low heat until heated through and bubbly—about 20 minutes. Serve in a rice ring or over rice, with sliced stuffed olives for garnish. *Serves 4.*

Calabacines Rellenos (Stuffed Zucchini)

4 zucchini (each 6 to 8 inches long)
1 pound ground meat
¼ cup fine dry crumbs
1 to 2 cloves garlic, crushed
3 tablespoons minced parsley
1 teaspoon salt
½ cup olive oil
3 slices very stale bread
1 cup water
1 teaspoon paprika
5 or 6 toasted almonds, crushed
1 hard-cooked egg
2 tablespoons tomato catsup (optional)

Scrape the squash, cut lengthwise slices from top of each, then scoop out the centers. Blend the zucchini pulp with meat, crumbs, garlic, 1 tablespoon parsley, and salt; stuff into the squash "boats." Form meatballs of remaining meat mixture. In a skillet, brown both the meatballs and the outside of the stuffed squash in olive oil, quickly, without cooking through; transfer to top-of-stove casserole or large sauce pan. In same skillet, fry the stale bread in the olive oil until crisp on both sides; remove from oil; place in bowl containing 1 cup water. Pour off all but 2 tablespoons olive oil from skillet; add the paprika, almonds, egg yolk forced through a sieve, and the catsup, then the bread with the water in which it soaked. Simmer this mixture for 5 minutes to form a sauce, then pour sauce over the squash and the meatballs in casserole; cover; simmer over low heat or complete baking in oven preheated to 350° F. for 20 to 25 minutes longer. Just before serving, sprinkle with remaining minced parsley and minced egg white. Serve with mashed or baked potatoes and a salad. *Serves 4.*

Baked Stuffed Eggplant

1 large eggplant (about 2 pounds)	minced
½ cup olive oil	1 or 2 cloves garlic, minced
½ pound chopped meat (beef or lamb)	2 large tomatoes, peeled, chopped
	¼ teaspoon orégano
½ chopped onion	½ cup minced parsley
½ cup minced celery	1 teaspoon salt
2 pimientos or sweet red peppers,	1 cup soft bread crumbs

Cut a long slice lengthwise from the top of the eggplant; scoop out center, leaving a shell ½ inch wide. Brush the eggplant shell inside and out with olive oil. Discard seedier sections of eggplant pulp. Sauté the remainder of eggplant pulp in ¼ cup of the olive oil along with meat, onions, celery, pimiento, and garlic. When onions are soft, add tomatoes, herbs, and salt. Simmer 30 minutes. Fill eggplant shell with mixture; top with crumbs, pushing crumbs down into stuffing. Brush additional oil over top. Bake in oven preheated to 350° F. for 1 hour. *Makes 4 to 6 servings.*

Oyster-Mushroom Casserole

20 large mushroom caps	1 cup fine dry bread or cracker crumbs, blended with 1 tablespoon melted butter
3 tablespoons butter	
Salt, pepper	
1 quart oysters	2 tablespoons grated Swiss cheese
½ cup cream of mushroom soup	
1/3 cup cream sherry	

Trim mushrooms, saving trimmings. Finely mince the trimmings. Sauté the caps in butter until lightly browned. Place mushrooms in buttered 1-quart shallow casserole; sprinkle with salt and pepper. Cover with oysters and their liquid. Blend soup with sherry and the minced mushroom trimmings; pour over oysters. Spread crumb mixture and cheese over top. (This may be done ahead.) Cook in preheated broiler, 6 inches from heat, until crumbs are lightly browned. Serve on Christmas Eve with eggnog, rolls, and a bowl of assorted fruit. *Makes 4 to 6 servings.*

Turkish Stuffed Tomatoes

8 medium or 6 large tomatoes
Salt
6 tablespoons olive oil
2 large onions, chopped
1 cup uncooked rice
1 tablespoon pine nuts
2 tablespoons raisins
1 teaspoon chopped fresh or frozen dill
1 teaspoon chopped mint, or ¼
teaspoon dried mint
¼ teaspoon freshly ground black
pepper
1 cup water
1 teaspoon sugar

Cut tops from tomatoes; scoop out insides carefully, leaving ¼-inch shell. Reserve 1 cup chopped seeded tomato pulp. Sprinkle inside of shells with salt and 1 tablespoon olive oil. Simmer onion in 3 tablespoons olive oil until soft; add rice and pine nuts; stir to glaze. Add raisins, dill, mint, pepper, and 1 teaspoon salt, plus reserved tomato pulp and 1 cup water. Bring to a boil; cook 10 minutes, covered (rice will still be hard). Add sugar. Fill tomatoes *loosely* with mixture (the rice will swell with cooking). Place tomatoes in shallow baking pan; brush outside with remaining 2 tablespoons oil. (This can be done ahead.) Prepare oven to 350° F.; bake tomatoes for 45 minutes. Delicious hot or cold. Can be served with sliced turkey or ham and macaroni salad for a buffet. *Makes 6 to 8 servings.*

PILAF-STUFFED TOMATOES. Add 1 cup cooked minced lamb, pork, or beef to onions; reduce amount of rice to ½ cup. Omit mint. Season with pinch of saffron, if desired.

See also Baked Stuffed Cucumbers.

Veal-stuffed Peppers

6 large green peppers
4 tablespoons olive oil
1 medium onion, chopped
2 cloves garlic, minced
1 pound ground veal (or meatloaf
mixture)
½ cup minced celery
1 cup stale bread crumbs, broken
in small pieces
½ teaspoon thyme
Salt, pepper
2 tablespoons pine nuts (optional)
¼ cup grated Parmesan or Romano cheese
Butter
1 cup chicken broth or tomato
juice

Select peppers that have a fairly solid bottom so that they will stand upright in dish. Cut a very thin slice from bottom of each if necessary to prevent toppling over. Cut off slice from top and carefully remove all seeds and white membrane from inside.

Place on a rack or in a colander over boiling water; steam, covered, 5 minutes. Drain thoroughly, turned upside down.

Heat olive oil; sauté onion and garlic in oil until soft. Add meat; stir until it loses its pink color. Add celery and crumbs; stir until crumbs are well moistened. Add seasonings, nuts, and cheese. Fill peppers with the mixture. Place a small lump of butter on top of each. Place peppers upright in shallow casserole; pour chicken broth or tomato juice around peppers. *This can be done ahead.*

Bake in oven preheated to 350° F. until peppers are tender and top lightly browned—45 minutes to 1 hour. Serve with potatoes, noodles, or rice. *Serves 6.*

PORK-STUFFED PEPPERS. The same, but use 1 pound ground lean pork instead of veal, and use 2 tart apples, chopped, instead of celery, plus 2 tablespoons chopped seedless raisins, if desired.

RICE-STUFFED PEPPERS. Prepare peppers as in recipe for Veal-Stuffed Peppers, but omit meat; add to the onion 3 cups cooked rice, ¼ cup pine nuts, 2 tablespoons raisins, ¼ cup grated cheese. Reserve some of cheese to sprinkle over tops of stuffed peppers. Bake in tomato juice, as in preceding recipe.

BAKED STUFFED TOMATOES. Any of the stuffings suggested above for peppers may be used for tomatoes. Select large, well-shaped tomatoes; scoop out center, leaving a shell ¼ inch wide. Brush inside and out with olive oil and sprinkle with salt before filling tomatoes.

Cassoulet

1 hind shank of beef (about 2 pounds)
3 quarts water
1 duckling, cut up
1 pound dried white beans
¼ pound salt pork, diced
1 pound lean pork or lamb, diced
1 cup chopped onion
2 or 3 cloves garlic, minced

Pinch of powdered clove
¼ teaspoon thyme
3 tablespoons tomato paste, or ½ cup tomato sauce
2 tablespoons brandy or cognac
1 pound smoked pork sausage links
1 cup seasoned bread crumbs

The dish should be started *at least* 1 day ahead for easiest preparation. Make stock with the hind shank of beef and water; defrost duckling (if frozen); cut up into serving-size pieces; cook in the beef stock. When cooked, dice duck meat and beef (lean only); place in refrigerator until needed. Strain, cool, and chill stock.

Next day, remove fat from chilled stock. Cover beans with fresh *boiling* water; bring again to a boil; cook 10 minutes. Turn off heat, let beans soak 1 hour, then drain.

Place diced salt pork in skillet; draw out fat; set aside crisp brown cubes of salt pork for garnish. Brown lean pork or lamb in the pork fat; remove; add to duck-beef mixture. Sauté onion and garlic in the same fat; remove; add to meat mixture. Combine drained beans with meat mixture, cloves, thyme, tomato paste (or sauce), and brandy. Place in Dutch oven or heavy pot; add 2 quarts strained beef stock; cook, covered, over *very low heat* until beans are soft—2 to 3 hours. (This should be done at least 6 hours before dish is to be served.) Turn off heat. As beans cool, fat will rise to top. Skim and discard fat. Taste beans; adjust seasonings as needed. Transfer beans to earthenware casserole. (Freeze at this stage, if desired.)

Parboil sausage links in water to remove excess fat. Arrange bread crumbs over top of beans, with sausage links and salt pork cubes over crumbs. About an hour before dinner is to be served, turn on oven to 350° F.; bake until crumbs and sausages are well browned—about 40 minutes. Turn off oven; cassoulet will keep warm another ½ hour. *Makes 10 to 12 servings.*

Family Cassoulet

2 to 3 cups any leftover cooked meat and poultry
1 pound quick-cooking dried beans
1 cup chopped onion
1 or 2 cloves garlic
1 tablespoon minced parsley

2 tablespoons fat
3 tablespoons tomato sauce
1 quart beef stock (made with concentrate)
6 to 8 small pork sausage links
1 cup seasoned bread crumbs

Use any combination of meat and poultry, but only the lean of the meat. Add boiling water to beans, according to package directions. Sauté onion, garlic, and parsley in fat until soft. Combine meat, beans, onions, tomato sauce, and beef stock; place in 2-quart casserole. Parboil sausage links to remove excess fat; place bread crumbs over top of beans and sausage links over crumbs. Bake, covered, in oven set at 350° F. for 1 hour; remove cover; bake until beans and sausage are browned—about ½ hour longer. *Makes 8 to 10 servings.*

Székely Gulyás

2 pounds lean pork, cubed
1 tablespoon vegetable shortening
2 cloves garlic, crushed or minced
1 small onion, chopped (about ¼
  cup)
1 tablespoon paprika

1 teaspoon salt
2 pounds sauerkraut
1 cup canned tomatoes
½ cup sour cream
½ teaspoon caraway seeds
  (optional)

Sauté the pork in melted shortening until browned lightly on all sides. Add garlic, onion, paprika, and salt; cook 2 minutes. Add sauerkraut and tomatoes; stir to mix ingredients. Cover tightly; cook over very low heat at least 2 hours. Turn off heat. Blend sour cream with some of hot liquid from pan; stir cream and caraway seeds into sauerkraut. Serve from a casserole with boiled or baked potatoes and Green Beans Vinaigrette. *Makes 6 servings.*

Cocido con Pavo

Leftover roast turkey
1½ quarts water
Salt
Soup vegetables
1 pound chick-peas (garbanzos)
1 or 2 large onions, chopped
3 cloves garlic, minced
¼ cup olive oil
1 1-pound can peeled whole to-

  matoes
2 cups chopped ham
¼ cup chopped Italian parsley
Ham bone
1 pound sweet potatoes, peeled,
  cubed
Minced parsley and hard-cooked
  eggs for garnish

Trim leftover turkey carcass, removing all meat carefully; set meat aside. Place carcass in kettle; cover with water; add 2 teaspoons salt and the usual soup vegetables (celery leaves, parsley sprigs, onion). Cover; simmer 1 to 2 hours. Strain and measure 4 cups.

While turkey carcass is simmering, soak the dried chick-peas in boiling water to cover for the same length of time, then drain.

Simmer onions and garlic in olive oil until soft; add tomatoes, ham, parsley, and ½ teaspoon salt; cook 5 to 10 minutes. Transfer tomato mixture to deep heavy pot. Add strained turkey broth to pot with chick-peas and the ham bone. Bring to a boil; lower heat; simmer 2½ to 3 hours. Taste for seasoning; add more salt if needed. Add sweet potatoes and reserved turkey meat, simmer until garbanzos are tender—about ½ hour longer. Garnish with parsley and chopped hard-cooked eggs. *Makes 6 servings.*

Choucroute Garnie

2 pounds sauerkraut	chops*
½ teaspoon caraway seeds	½ pound smoked pork sausage
12 whole peppercorns	links
1 medium carrot, scraped, cubed	½ pound picnic ham butt, cooked,
1 cup dry white wine	sliced
4 to 6 smoked or cured pork	2 pigs' feet (optional)

A large kettle or Dutch oven is needed for cooking this. Combine in bottom of kettle, sauerkraut, caraway, peppercorns, carrot, and wine. Arrange meat over top. Cover tightly; simmer over very low heat 2 to 3 hours. Or, cook the day before, refrigerate, and reheat before serving (the flavor will be improved upon reheating). Nothing else is needed but boiled potatoes and perhaps vegetable relishes. Either beer or white wine may be served as the beverage. *Makes 8 servings.*

*These are sold in packages, 4 to a package, in many supermarkets. If not locally available, fresh pork loin chops may be used.

Fabada al Asturiana (Asturian Bean Stew)

1 pound dried white marrow	or ½ pound salami, cut in
beans	chunks
6 to 8 cups cold water	½ cup chopped lean ham, or 4
1 large onion, quartered	slices lean bacon, diced
¼ cup Spanish olive oil	½ teaspoon saffron
¼ pound chorizo sausage, sliced,	1½ to 2 teaspoons salt

Place beans (without previous soaking) in large earthenware casserole or heavy Dutch oven; add 4 cups cold water; bring just to a boil; turn heat as low as possible; cover; simmer gently 1 hour. Twice during the hour, add 1 to 2 cups cold water (this slows down cooking and allows beans to swell gradually). Keep beans well covered throughout cooking period. When liquid has come again to a boil, add onion and olive oil; simmer 10 minutes; add chorizo or salami and ham or bacon. (If you happen to have a ham bone and the final remains of a baked ham, be sure to add it.) Crush saffron, blend with salt, add a little warm water, then add this to beans. Continue to simmer beans until very tender—another 2 to 2½ hours. Add additional water if necessary. *Makes 8 to 12 servings.*

Beef and Vegetable Pie

1 pound stewing beef, in 1-inch cubes
1 tablespoon shortening
1 package frozen peas and carrots
1 cup (8-ounce can) kernel corn or white corn, drained

1 1-pound can whole onions, including liquid
1 10-ounce can beef gravy
2 tablespoons sherry
Piecrust mix or pastry for 1- or 2-crust pie

This can be made as one big pie, in a 10 x 10-inch Pyrex baking dish, with 1 crust, or as individual pies, in individual casseroles (which requires additional pastry). For individual pies, cut the meat in smaller pieces. Sauté the meat in shortening until well browned. Combine with remaining ingredients except pastry.

Prepare piecrust dough; roll out to ⅛ inch. Place beef-vegetable mixture in baking dish or ramekins; cover completely with pastry, overlapping edges. Cut slits in the center of each. (Pie can be made days ahead, if desired, and kept frozen until time to bake.) Bake in oven preheated to 400° F. until crust is golden and crisp and sauce can be seen bubbling through the slits—about 45 minutes. Nothing else is needed but salad and bread. *Makes 4 to 6 individual pies (depending on size of casseroles), or 4 to 6 servings.*

Shepherd's Pie

¼ to ½ cup minced onion
2 to 3 tablespoons shortening
2 to 3 cups minced cooked meat (lamb, beef, pork, or veal)
1 cup cooked leftover vegetables

(optional)
1 cup gravy
2 tablespoons water or sherry
2 cups seasoned mashed potatoes
Melted butter

Sauté the onion in shortening until lightly browned; add meat; stir until thoroughly moistened. Add cooked or canned vegetables, if desired, to extend meat (if you have 2 cups of meat or less). Best vegetables to use are peas, green beans, corn, carrots, turnips, sweet potatoes (but *not* broccoli, Brussels sprouts, spinach, or cabbage). Stir in gravy and water or sherry. Transfer to 1½-quart casserole. Cover with mashed potatoes (freshly made or made with instant mashed potatoes). Brush melted butter over top or dot with butter. Bake in oven preheated to 425° F. until potatoes are lightly browned—about 20 minutes. Nothing else is needed but salad or relishes. *Makes 4 servings.*

For 2 servings, halve all ingredients and bake in 1-quart casserole.

Hash Pie

2 tablespoons bacon drippings	2 bouillon cubes
1½ pounds ground meat, or 2	1½ cups water
cups diced cooked meat*	2 tablespoons sherry
2 medium raw potatoes	Pastry for 1-crust pie, or topping
2 medium onions, chopped	made with corn muffin mix or
¾ teaspoon salt	biscuit mix

Heat bacon drippings in skillet: add meat; stir until it loses its pink color. Peel potatoes and chop in small pieces. Add potatoes and onions to skillet, stir-fry until lightly browned. Add salt, bouillon cubes, water, and sherry; simmer until bouillon cubes are dissolved. Transfer to casserole; top with pastry crust (purchased ready to bake, if you approve of that type) or make topping with corn muffin mix, quick and easy corn bread mix, or biscuit mix. Bake in oven preheated to 400° F. until topping is golden and filling can be seen bubbling around the edges. Add a salad, garlic bread, and assorted relishes and pickles. *Makes 4 to 6 servings.*

*Any kind of leftover meat may be used, alone or in combination. A good way to clean out the refrigerator of bits and pieces of leftovers.

The quickest way to thaw frozen ground meat is to place it in a hot skillet which has been just moistened with fat (only enough to prevent meat from sticking). As the meat becomes soft, scrape it off and return to skillet to soften another layer. When only a small inner layer of frozen meat is left, break that up with a sharp knife. This is not satisfactory for making hamburgers, but it's fine when the meat is to be used in a casserole or sauce, as in the preceding recipes.

Sausage and Sweet Potato Casserole

1 pound pork sausage links, or	2 large or 4 small sweet potatoes
bulk sausage meat	4 tart greening apples
Pinch of sage or poultry seasoning	1 tablespoon brown sugar
(optional)	¼ cup orange juice

Cook the sausage first. If sausage links are used, precook in water according to package directions (which gets rid of excess fat), then drain off this liquid and cook sausages until *lightly* browned. If bulk sausage is used, form into patties (add just a pinch of sage or poultry seasoning to these, if you like, but no salt); pan-broil until browned on each side.

The sweet potatoes must also be precooked, or they will turn black. Peel; slice thickly; cook in salted water about 5 minutes (they should not be cooked through). Drain; arrange in bottom of lightly greased 1½-quart casserole. Arrange sausage links or patties over sweet potatoes; top with peeled, cored, sliced apples. Sprinkle apples with brown sugar. Add orange juice. Bake, covered, in oven set at 350° F. for about 40 minutes. Serve with Brussels sprouts and relishes. *Makes 4 to 6 servings.*

Tamale Pie

2 1-pound cans chili con carne with beans	Instant minced onion (optional)
½ pound ground beef	½ package (1 cup) corn muffin mix
Salt	1 egg
Pinch of chili powder	½ cup milk

This is a great emergency dish. Simply empty the canned chili into a 1½-quart casserole, add ground beef (you should keep some in the freezer). Add pinch each of salt and chili powder and a sprinkling of instant onion. Mix together well. Blend corn muffin mix with egg and milk, spread over the top. Bake in oven preheated to 400° F. until the topping is golden brown—about 25 minutes. While waiting for the pie to bake, serve assorted relishes, such as cherry tomatoes, celery, olives (black and green), and radishes. Cottage cheese is a good relish to serve with the pie. Nothing else is needed to round out the meal but an ice cream dessert from the freezer. *Makes 4 to 6 servings.*

To serve 8, increase amount of hamburger meat, add canned mushrooms (drained), pitted black olives, a can of kernel corn (drained), and perhaps some chopped pimiento. Place mixture in long shallow casserole and use an entire package of corn muffin mix (with 1 egg and 1 cup milk). Or, divide filling in half, make 2 casseroles, top each with the quick and easy type of corn bread mix that comes in a packet (requiring 2 packages of this mix).

8 VEGETABLES

Cooking vegetables properly is such a simple thing, yet how few cooks have mastered it!

The secret is simply this: cook them as brief a time as possible, in as little water as possible, and while hot (well drained), bathe them with butter or margarine. Not much butter is needed (and margarine in this case is often just as good). A teaspoonful may serve for 3 cups cooked vegetables. Yet that single teaspoon of butter or margarine makes a world of difference.

Certain vegetables become special with the fragrance of herbs: dill or parsley for carrots, thyme or basil with tomatoes, mint with limas. Peas are always better with a thin slice or two of onion added to the cooking water, or with a pinch of mint or fennel added to the butter. Nutmeg does wonders for spinach. Caraway perks up green cabbage.

A satisfying meal can be made with nothing but vegetables, if all the vegetables are lovingly cooked, and those concerned with weight control should remember that most vegetables are much lower in calories than meats, and the fibrous vegetables are low in starch.

Artichokes

These are available in five forms: fresh, frozen hearts, canned imported hearts in brine, canned artichoke bottoms (very expensive and useful chiefly for salads and hors d'-oeuvres), and artichoke hearts in an oil-vinegar sauce. I have yet to open a jar of the latter whose oil was not rancid—and once the oil has gone rancid, nothing can be done to save the artichokes. This means that the best year-round product is the frozen, and except in those areas where artichokes are locally grown, it's also the most economical. The canned hearts in brine cost even less on a per-portion basis, but are not attractive served by themselves; as a vegetable they are useful chiefly in salads, hors d'oeuvres, and casseroles.

FROZEN ARTICHOKE HEARTS (BASIC RECIPE). Place frozen block in saucepan with ¼ cup olive oil, a garlic clove, and ¼ teaspoon salt. Bring to a boil; lower heat; cook, tightly covered, until tender; after 3 minutes, uncover; break up frozen block. When tender, remove and discard garlic; sprinkle with lemon juice and parsley. Delicious either hot or cold. *Makes 3 servings.*

ARTICHOKES WITH HAM. Prepare frozen artichoke hearts as in basic recipe, but add ¼ cup minced ham and 2 slices onion. Serve sprinkled with lemon juice, with strips of pimiento over top.

ARTICHOKES COOKED IN WINE. Simmer 2 tomatoes, peeled, chopped (or canned, peeled tomatoes, drained) in ¼ cup olive oil with ½ teaspoon salt, a pinch of thyme, and a pinch of powdered coriander or celery seed. Add package of artichoke hearts and ½ cup dry white wine; cover; bring to a boil. Break up frozen block; continue cooking, covered, until tender. Serve sprinkled with lemon juice or grated lemon rind.

ARTICHOKES GRANADA. Cook 1 sliced onion and 1 diced carrot in ¼ cup olive oil until onion is yellow. Add block of frozen artichoke hearts and ½ teaspoon salt. Cover; cook over low heat 3 minutes; break up frozen block; add 1 cup chicken broth and 1 teaspoon rosemary. Bring broth to a boil; simmer, uncovered, until artichokes are tender—about 4 minutes longer. Serve hot, sprinkled with lemon juice. *Makes 4 or 5 servings.*

Artichokes à la Grecque

2 small carrots, scraped, cubed
6 small onions, peeled
2 cups water
½ teaspoon salt, or to taste
2 packages frozen artichoke
  hearts

1 teaspoon minced fresh or frozen
  dill
½ cup olive oil
1 teaspoon cornstarch or arrowroot
Juice of ½ lemon (2 tablespoons)

Cook carrots and onions in salted water until onions are tender—about 15 minutes. Add artichoke hearts and dill; cook, covered, until artichokes are tender—about 7 minutes. Remove vegetables, saving water. Blend olive oil with cornstarch; add lemon juice; add to 1 cup vegetable water. Cook and stir until a thickened smooth sauce is formed. Replace the vegetables. *Chill. Serve cold for a buffet. Makes 8 servings.*

FRESH ARTICHOKE HEARTS (BASIC RECIPE). Wash artichokes and cut stems 1 inch from leaves. Also cut off with sharp knife the sharp points of leaves. Stand upright in saucepan; add boiling water to depth of 1 inch, 1 tablespoon olive oil, 1 tablespoon vinegar, and 1 teaspoon salt. Bring to a boil; cook, covered, until base of artichoke can be easily pierced with fork—about 40 minutes, depending on size. Remove from pan; drain upside down on rack. Serve warm or cold, one to each person, with Vinaigrette Sauce, hot Garlic Butter, Hollandaise Sauce, or Homemade Mayonnaise. The leaves are pulled off one at a time, dipped in sauce, and sucked. Remove and discard the fuzzy center (the choke); the bottom of the artichoke is the tenderest and most delicious part.

Asparagus

Fresh green asparagus is one of the delights of spring. The frozen are a poor substitute, unless cooked very briefly. Canned white asparagus is better than the canned green, useful as an ingredient in casseroles, or served cold in Vinaigrette Sauce, as a "cooked salad" for winter menus.

FRESH ASPARAGUS (BASIC RECIPE). Scrub spears with a vegetable brush to rid them of sand. Break off tough ends. Place spears horizontally in a skillet with water barely to cover; add salt. Do not completely cover pan; place lid so that most of pan is covered, leaving space from which steam can escape (otherwise the asparagus quickly loses its beautiful green color). Cook just until spears can be pierced with a fork, about 6 minutes. *Avoid overcooking.* Drain most but not all the liquid; add a lump of butter or margarine. Serve immediately.

ASPARAGUS ON TOAST. Prepare asparagus as in basic recipe but do not drain. Place 3 or 4 spears on each piece of buttered toast; sprinkle with asparagus liquid blended with melted butter (1 tablespoon butter for 3 tablespoons asparagus stock).

ASPARAGUS MILANESE. Prepare as in basic recipe; place a poached egg on each serving of 3 or 4 asparagus spears, if to be served as a luncheon entree; or, sprinkle each serving with grated Parmesan cheese and bathe with melted butter or margarine.

ASPARAGUS WITH ROQUEFORT BUTTER. Prepare asparagus as in basic recipe; over the asparagus spoon a sauce made of 4 tablespoons butter or margarine and 2 tablespoons Roquefort cheese, stirred over low heat until cheese is melted. Sprinkle with lemon juice. (This is enough sauce for 6 servings, or 1½ pounds asparagus.)

ASPARAGUS HOLLANDAISE. Top cooked asparagus with Hollandaise Sauce—one of the most delicious of all ways to serve this wonderful vegetable.

ASPARAGUS OMELET. Frozen asparagus spears may be used successfully in this recipe; melt butter in an omelet pan; arrange the spears (thawed but not cooked) like wagon spokes. Sprinkle with salt. Beat 3 eggs until light; add 3 tablespoons cream, ¼ teaspoon salt, freshly ground black pepper. Pour egg mixture over asparagus. Place strips of pimiento between asparagus. Cook over low heat, lifting up egg as it firms, until lower half of egg is cooked. Place under broiler with reduced heat, 4 to 5 inches from heat, until top is firm and lightly browned. Slip out of pan. Serve immediately with a green salad and hot coffee for brunch or lunch. *Makes 3 or 4 servings.*

ASPARAGUS IN BACON. Wrap frozen jumbo asparagus spears (thawed but not cooked) each with ½ slice bacon; place under broiler, turning as bacon cooks. When bacon is crisp, asparagus is ready to serve. Makes an unusual first-course appetizer.

Asparagus au Gratin

2 packages frozen asparagus
  spears. partially cooked. or 1
  large can white asparagus.
  drained
1 cup Mornay Sauce or Quick

Sauce Soubise
½ cup grated Cheddar cheese
½ cup herb-seasoned bread
  crumbs

Arrange asparagus spears in shallow baking dish. Cover with the sauce. Top with mixture of cheese and crumbs. (This can be done ahead.) Place under preheated broiler, 4 to 5 inches from heat, until sauce is bubbling and crumbs lightly browned. Serve with lamb chops (broiled in same oven) and sliced tomatoes. *Makes 4 to 6 servings.*

BEANS. See Green Beans; Italian Beans; Lima Beans.

Beets

Fresh beets are in the markets throughout the year, but they are most tender and flavorful in the spring. When buying beets, select those with fresh-looking tops, and you buy two vegetables in one. Canned beets are available as whole or sliced beets, as pickled beets, and in Harvard Sauce. None of these has as much flavor as the fresh beets, but they can be made to taste quite good if skillfully seasoned.

FRESH BEETS (BASIC RECIPE). Trim leaves, wash, and store in refrigerator for another meal. Parboil the whole beets *without peeling*; if large and not young, they may require as long as 40 to 50 minutes' cooking time. Small spring beets are sometimes cooked tender in 15 minutes. Test for doneness by piercing with a fork. Allow to cool until they can be handled easily then peel off skins (obviously it is necessary to cook them ahead of time). Reheat with butter or margarine, or in one of the following sauces.

HARVARD BEETS. Cook 2 bunches of fresh beets as in basic recipe; slice. Or use a 1-pound can of sliced beets, drained. Blend together 2 tablespoons sugar, 1 teaspoon cornstarch, ½ teaspoon salt, a pinch of powdered ginger or dry mustard, and a tablespoon of cider vinegar. Stir in 2 tablespoons water or beet liquid (from can). Add 3 tablespoons butter or margarine; stir over heat until smooth and bubbling. Add to sliced beets. *Makes enough for 6 servings.*

BEETS IN ORANGE SAUCE. Combine 2 tablespoons butter, 1 tablespoon honey, ½ teaspoon grated orange rind, ⅛ teaspoon crushed cardamom, and ¼ cup orange juice. Stir over heat until well blended. Add whole or sliced beets; heat beets in the sauce. *Makes enough sauce for 6 to 8 beets.*

BEETS IN MUSTARD SAUCE. Add to beets in saucepan 2 tablespoons olive oil, butter or margarine, 1 tablespoon prepared mustard, and 1 tablespoon vinegar. Stir until beets are coated with sauce. Sprinkle with salt and pepper to taste. *Makes enough sauce for 6 to 8 beets* (or for a 1-pound can).

CARAWAY BEETS. Prepare as for Beets in Mustard Sauce, but omit mustard and add ½ teaspoon crushed caraway seeds. If desired, add 1 teaspoon sugar.

BEETS IN SOUR CREAM SAUCE. Combine ¼ cup sour cream, 1 tablespoon vinegar, 1 teaspoon sugar, dash of cayenne, a little crushed mint; pour over hot cooked beets, serve immediately.

BEETS VINAIGRETTE. Dress beets (cold or hot) with Vinaigrette Sauce.

BEET GREENS. Wash leaves thoroughly as for spinach. Cut away pink stems; chop them very fine. Place greens and chopped stems in heavy saucepan with ¼ teaspoon water and a sprinkling of salt; bring to a boil; cook, tightly covered, for 5 minutes. Taste for tenderness; a little longer cooking may be necessary. Drain thoroughly. Dress with vinegar and sugar, or vinegar and butter (or margarine). Especially good with pork or ham.

Broccoli

FRESH BROCCOLI (BASIC RECIPE). Separate flowers; cut stems in thin slivers, discard tougher portions of stalk. Place in saucepan; cover with *boiling* water; add ½ teaspoon salt for 2 cups water; bring again to a boil. Place the lid on the pan so that it is only partially covered, allowing escape of steam. Cook only until stems can be pierced with fork—no more than 10 minutes, and while vegetable is still bright green. Drain, add butter or margarine and, if desired, sprinkle with lemon juice.

FROZEN BROCCOLI (BASIC RECIPE). Lay spears in saucepan, add ½ cup boiling water and ½ teaspoon salt, bring water again to boil, cook only partially covered for 4 to 5 minutes. Drain, add butter or margarine.

BROCCOLI HOLLANDAISE. Serve cooked broccoli (fresh or frozen) with Hollandaise Sauce.

BROCCOLI AMANDINE. Serve cooked broccoli sprinkled with slivered blanched almonds which have been sautéed in butter. Serve with lemon wedges; sprinkle broccoli with lemon at table.

BROCCOLI MAYONNAISE. Cover hot cooked broccoli with a sauce of cold commercial mayonnaise to which a few drops lemon juice, a sprinkling of salt, and a dash of cayenne have been added.

TOPPED WITH BACON. Cook 2 or 3 slices of bacon until crisp; drain; crumble. Serve crumbled bacon over cooked broccoli as garnish.

Brussels Sprouts

BRUSSELS SPROUTS (BASIC RECIPE). The same basic rule applies to both the fresh and the frozen vegetable: add boiling water (and salt), bring again to a boil, cover only partially so steam can escape, and cook *only 4 to 5 minutes*, just until fork-tender. Drain immediately; add butter or margarine (the stems of the fresh sprouts should be trimmed before cooking, and any discolored leaves removed, but otherwise they are ready for the pot as they come from the market). The sprouts should still be bright green when cooked; avoid overcooking. Never leave the lid on the pan after they are cooked—that will cause the leaves to turn a sickly color and give the vegetables a strong, unpleasant taste.

WITH CARAWAY. Add a few caraway seeds to the sprouts with the butter. Serve with lemon wedges, the lemon to be squeezed over the sprouts *at the table* (not before).

CREAMED BRUSSELS SPROUTS. Cook sprouts as in basic recipe, saving the cooking liquid. With this make a Medium White

Sauce, using the broth as part of the liquid; add cream for the remainder. Serve topped with slivered toasted almonds.

BRUSSELS SPROUTS SALAD. When sprouts are left over, cover before storing with 3 parts oil and 1 part vinegar. They can then be added to a mixed vegetable salad, or served cold tossed with crumbled cooked bacon as a "cooked salad."

BRUSSELS SPROUTS AND MUSHROOMS. Cook sprouts as in basic recipe. Separately, sauté an equal quantity of mushroom caps in butter. Combine the two; sprinkle with minced parsley. Very nice for a gala dinner, such as Thanksgiving.

Cabbage

Fresh cabbage of one variety or another is available in abundance throughout the year. For cole slaw, the crisp smooth heads are best. For a cooked vegetable, the curly-leafed Savoy cabbage is delicious. Red cabbage goes naturally with roast pork. All cabbage should be cooked briefly, served still a little crisp. If cooked as a separate vegetable (rather than in soup or stew), use a very small amount of liquid—cabbage contains considerable water which will be drawn out with cooking.

BRAISED CABBAGE. Cut a small head of cabbage (or ½ a large head) in wedges. Wash thoroughly; drain. Chop 2 onions; sauté in 2 tablespoons butter, margarine, or olive oil until soft and golden. Add cabbage, a 1-pound can of peeled tomatoes, salt, pepper, and parsley. Cook, covered, until cabbage is fork-tender—about 10 minutes.

COOKED CABBAGE SALAD. Shred 3 or 4 cups cabbage (Savoy or green). Cook, uncovered, in 1 cup boiling salted water until limp and fork-tender—about 10 minutes. Drain. Toss immediately with 3 tablespoons olive oil and 1 tablespoon vinegar (or ½ teaspoon lemon juice). Good hot or cold.

CABBAGE WITH GINGER-CREAM SAUCE. Thinly slice 1 small onion; sauté in 2 tablespoons butter until yellow and soft. Add 3 cups shredded cabbage, salt, pepper, and ½ cup water. Cover tightly; simmer until cabbage is fork-tender but still a little crisp—about 10 minutes. Remove cover; cook until liquid has evaporated. Turn off heat; add ½ cup sour cream blended with ¼ teaspoon powdered ginger; stir to blend.

CURRIED CABBAGE. Prepare as in preceding recipe, but use ½ teaspoon curry powder instead of ginger with the sour cream; or use curry powder and yogurt.

CARAWAY CABBAGE. Shred cabbage, cook in salted water just until fork-tender; drain. Add butter and about ½ teaspoon caraway seeds; toss. Sprinkle with vinegar or lemon juice.

CABBAGE BAKED IN CREAM. Shred a medium head of green cabbage; cook in boiling salted water just 5 minutes. Drain; chill. Melt 1 tablespoon butter in saucepan; stir in 1 tablespoon flour; then add ½ cup cream and salt and pepper to taste; simmer until smooth and thickened. Chop *cold* cabbage; toss with the cream sauce; place in buttered baking dish. Bake, uncovered, as part of an oven dinner, for 30 to 40 minutes. (The cabbage will exude juice with cooking, so that when done it will have at least 1 cup sauce.) If desired, top with buttered crumbs. *Makes 6 servings.*

CABBAGE WITH PEANUTS. Shred and partially cook cabbage as in preceding recipe. Add 2 tablespoons butter, ¼ cup chopped peanuts, salt, and pepper. Place in casserole, cover tightly, and bake as part of an oven dinner, as in preceding recipe.

RED CABBAGE WITH APPLES. Melt butter in large saucepan or heavy pot; add an onion (sliced) and an apple (peeled, diced); cook until lightly browned. Add 4 cups shredded red cabbage, 3 to 4 tablespoons vinegar, 2 to 4 tablespoons brown sugar, and a pinch of powdered clove. Stir until coated with butter. Add ½ cup red wine. Cover; simmer until cabbage is tender—about 12 minutes. Serve this way, or thicken the sauce, if preferred, with 1 tablespoon flour or ½ tablespoon cornstarch.

See also New England Boiled Dinner: Cole Slaw; Cabbage Salad: Baked Stuffed Cabbage; Golubtsi; Sauerkraut.

Carrots

PARSLEYED CARROTS (BASIC RECIPE). Scrape carrots with a vegetable parer; cut lengthwise into quarters or eighths (depending on thickness of carrot), or slice thinly. Cook, covered, in salted water (1 cup water for 4 large carrots) for 3 minutes; drain; add 2 or 3 tablespoons butter and a tablespoon of minced parsley. Cover tightly and cook over lowest heat until fork-tender—2 to 3 minutes longer. Baste butter from pan over carrots to serve. (Brief cooking makes a world of difference in the flavor of carrots; when cooked this way, it's possible to get even children to eat them.)

DILLED CARROTS. Prepare as for parsleyed carrots, but use minced fresh or frozen dill (dried dill weed is not the same). Or add a little of the juice from dill pickles to the butter for the last part of the cooking.

GLAZED CARROTS. Scrape and quarter carrots, as in basic recipe, but cook in 1 cup chicken broth (made with chicken stock concentrate) instead of water; do not add salt. Pour off half the chicken broth, retaining ½ cup. Add 3 tablespoons butter and 2 tablespoons sugar; simmer, uncovered, until sauce is reduced and shiny.

CARROTS AND CAULIFLOWER. This makes a pretty combination, and a tasty one, too. Scrape and quarter carrots, as in basic recipe; break cauliflower into individual buds. Place the two vegetables together in the same saucepan, about equal quantities of each. Add boiling salted water enough almost to cover; bring again to a boil; cover; cook 5 minutes. Drain; add butter or margarine, toss while warm so melted butter will coat vegetables.

CARROTS PIEDMONTESE. Partially cook carrots as in basic recipe; drain. Add to pan with butter ¼ cup very thinly sliced onion and, if desired, a peeled garlic clove. Continue cooking over low heat until carrots are tender. Remove and discard garlic. Sprinkle carrots with vinegar and minced chives or parsley.

CARROTS IN VINAIGRETTE SAUCE. Cold cooked carrots (leftovers) can be marinated in vinaigrette sauce and served as a "cooked salad." Or dice, marinate in the sauce with a few thin slices of onion, add to a mixed vegetable salad.

Cauliflower

BASIC RECIPE. Divide cauliflower into buds: discard stem and leaves except for a few crisp small green leaves near the stem, add these to the buds. Cook in 1 cup water, with ½ teaspoon salt, tightly covered, until barely fork-tender—4 to 5 minutes. Drain: add butter or margarine and a few drops lemon juice and, if liked, a few caraway seeds. Or, sprinkle with minced parsley or minced fresh cilantro. *One medium cauliflower makes 6 to 8 servings.*

CAULIFLOWER WITH CHEESE SAUCE. Cook cauliflower, as in basic recipe. Serve topped with Quick Cheese Sauce (condensed Cheddar cheese soup plus 1/3 cup beer, white wine or cream).

CAULIFLOWER WITH CORIANDER-CELERY SAUCE. Serve cooked cauliflower topped with a sauce made of 1 can condensed cream of celery soup, 1/3 cup light cream, ½ teaspoon crushed coriander, and ¼ teaspoon paprika.

Celery

Celery makes a delicious hot vegetable, one very low in calories and starch and high in vitamins.

BRAISED CELERY (BASIC RECIPE). Slice 4 or 5 stalks Pascal celery diagonally in 1-inch pieces. Place in heavy saucepan with 2 tablespoons butter, a few thin slices of onion, ¼ cup water or tomato juice, salt, and pepper. Cook over low heat until tender, but still a little crisp—about 10 minutes. Or, instead of water or tomato juice, peel and chop 2 tomatoes; cook with the celery. *Makes 4 or 5 servings.*

TENDER CREAMED CELERY. Slice 6 or 7 stalks celery at an angle, as in basic recipe, but cook, covered, in 1 cup boiling salted water until quite tender—10 to 12 minutes. Drain, saving liquid. Make a medium White Sauce of 2 tablespoons each butter and flour, and the cooking liquid, plus milk or cream to make 1 cup. Season with salt, pepper, and a dash of nutmeg or mace. Beat sauce into 1 egg, beaten, using a whisk. Add cooked celery to the sauce; keep warm over hot water until time to serve. *Makes 6 servings.*

CELERY AVGHOLEMONO. Braise celery in water as in basic recipe; drain; add to Avgholemono Sauce (or Quick Avgholemono Sauce).

Celery Cabbage

This elongated crisp green is also called Chinese cabbage and Chinese celery. It is frequently used as an ingredient in Chinese entrees, but it may also be cooked as a separate vegetable (besides being a delicious raw salad ingredient). Cut in thin diagonal slices; cook like green cabbage in a small amount of salted water, until barely crisp. Add butter or margarine and plenty of freshly ground black pepper. Or, braise in oil without any water at all, with a few thin slices of onion, season with soy sauce.

Celery Knob, or Celeriac

Also called celery root, this big ugly-looking vegetable is nearly all root with a few sorry-looking leaves. Not widely available, and then only seasonally, but when you do see it, try it.

BASIC RECIPE. Peel root, cut into matchstick slivers, or dice. Cook in boiling salted water until fork-tender—10 to 12 minutes. Drain, add butter or margarine, and minced parsley. Or season with crushed coriander, a pinch of cayenne, and black pepper.

CELERY KNOB CILANTRO. Cook celery knob as in basic recipe; add butter, season with minced fresh cilantro. This is a particularly delicious flavor combination.

CREAMED CELERY ROOT (OR KNOB). Cook as in basic recipe. Make a medium White Sauce, using the stock for part of the liquid; beat into beaten egg (as for Tender Creamed Celery). Or, make a Quick Velouté Sauce with condensed cream of chicken soup, heavy cream, and a few tablespoons of the liquid from cooking.

CELERY KNOB SALAD. Cook as in basic recipe. When cold, dress with Vinaigrette Sauce or equal parts oil and vinegar, salt, and pepper. Serve as a "cooked salad" with Pork or Veal Schnitzel or Roast Pork.

Corn

CORN ON THE COB. The great American favorite is now available fresh in markets throughout the year, though it is still at its best and sweetest during late summer, from local farms. Do not remove husk and silk until shortly before time to cook the corn, and do not cook until last minute. Have a kettle of salted water boiling briskly; drop the stripped ears into the water; bring again to a boil; cook 5 minutes tightly covered. Drain thoroughly. *If it's only the family,* pass a butter plate and let each person rub his ear of corn over the butter (much easier than trying to get cold butter to stay on the kernels when spread with a knife). Pass the salt shaker. *When guests are present,* the nice way is to brush the corn with melted butter in the kitchen, using a pastry brush, before bringing it to the table.

ROASTING EARS. The original way of cooking corn on the cob: soak the ears in salted water, without removing husks, for 1 hour, turning once or twice. Remove from water; place on grid of barbecue grill, or right in the ashes; cook, turning occasionally, until husks are lightly browned. When the husks are removed, the corn silk comes off with them. Rub each ear over a stick of butter; dust with salt. Wonderful eating.

CORN ROASTED IN FOIL. Strip corn of husks and silk, place each ear in a piece of foil large enough to enclose completely, and place a "nut" of butter inside the foil. Seal by twisting ends. Bake in the coals of a barbecue fire or in a moderate oven for 15 to 20 minutes.

SUCCOTASH. A very good use to make of leftover corn on the cob; can also be made with fresh corn, the kernels scraped from the ear, or with canned kernel corn. Fresh uncooked corn requires longer cooking (about 5 minutes), but otherwise the recipe is the same. Combine cooked or canned corn with cooked lima or green beans; simmer in butter and cream, tightly covered, over very low heat. Season with salt and plenty of freshly ground black pepper.

Corn Fritters

½ cup flour	2 cups corn cut from cob, or
½ teaspoon baking powder	canned kernel corn, drained
½ teaspoon salt	Fat for deep-frying
2 eggs	

Combine flour, baking powder, and salt; stir to blend well.

Make a hole in center; break eggs into hole. Stir eggs with spoon, gradually beating in the flour to form a batter. Stir in the corn. Heat fat in a skillet to a depth of ½ inch, or 2 inches in a deep-frying kettle or deep heavy pot. Drop mixture into sizzling-hot fat by the tablespoon; cook until browned on both sides. Do not crowd skillet or pot. Remove with slotted spoon; drain on absorbent paper. Serve with crisp cooked bacon (the fritters may be fried in hot bacon fat, if preferred) and maple syrup, for brunch or supper. *Makes 4 to 6 servings.*

Corn Pudding

2 cups raw corn cut from cob, or 1 1-pound can cream-style corn
¼ cup flour
2 eggs, beaten
½ teaspoon salt
¼ teaspoon freshly ground black pepper
2 cups milk
2 tablespoons butter

If raw corn is used, first cut with a small sharp knife down the ear through the center of the kernels, then scrape down the ear in such a way as to remove all the milk and the pulp. Add flour, eggs, salt, and pepper to corn (use less salt with canned corn). Stir in milk. Pour into buttered 1½-quart casserole. Dot butter over top. Bake in oven set at 325° F. until pudding is firm and top is golden—about 1 hour. Superb with baked ham or fried chicken. *Makes 6 servings.*

CARAWAY CREAMED CORN. Melt 1 tablespoon butter in saucepan; add a 1-pound can of cream-style corn, ½ teaspoon salt, ¼ teaspoon pepper, ½ teaspoon caraway seeds. Cook, covered, over high heat just to bring to a boil; lower heat; cook 5 minutes, stirring once or twice. *Makes 4 servings.*

CORN AND PEPPERS. Sauté 1 green pepper, seeded and chopped (or ½ green pepper and ½ sweet red pepper), and a few slices of onion in butter until lightly browned. Add 2 cups corn cut from cob (leftover cooked, or raw) or 1 12-ounce can kernel corn, drained. Cook 3 or 4 minutes longer. Especially good as part of a vegetable dinner.

Cucumbers

These are most in demand for salad, served raw, but they can be braised as in the following recipe, or stuffed, like zucchini, or used to make soup (as for green cabbage soup, using sliced peeled cucumber instead of cabbage).

CUCUMBERS WITH BACON. Peel and slice cucumbers to make 3 cups. Sauté 6 scallions (green onions), sliced, in 2 tablespoons butter or margarine; add the cucumbers and 2 peeled, chopped tomatoes. Sprinkle with salt, sugar, and cumin to taste. Simmer, uncovered, for 3 or 4 minutes. Serve sprinkled with crumbled cooked bacon. *Makes 6 servings.*

BAKED STUFFED CUCUMBERS. Blanch 6 cucumbers, each about 6 inches long, by soaking in boiling salted water 10 minutes. Remove; cut a lengthwise slice from top of each; scoop out pulp. Discard seedy portion; save remainder. Use the filling given for Baked Stuffed Eggplant or the rice filling for Turkish Stuffed Tomatoes, or Pilaf-stuffed Tomatoes. Top with buttered crumbs; bake in moderate oven about 40 minutes until crumbs are browned and rind of cucumber can be pierced with fork. Halfway through, spoon ½ cup yogurt over cucumbers. *Serves 6.*

Eggplant

The deliciousness of eggplant depends to a very large extent on how fresh the vegetable is. When locally in season, the eggplant can be eaten peel and all (except for the cap at the end), and the peel imparts distinctive flavor. But when shipped from far away, or gathered at the very end of the season, the vegetable is often bitter, especially the peel. When in doubt, it's best to peel the eggplant before cooking. Many cookbooks recommend that sliced eggplant be soaked in salted water before cooking. I have tried this, and found it made very little difference. Smaller elongated eggplant seem to have more flavor than the big overgrown ones.

BRAISED EGGPLANT. Cut in dice, retaining the peel if vegetable is garden-fresh. Cook over low heat, covered, in a generous amount (1/3 to ½ cup) of best-quality olive oil, until limp and soft—about 8 minutes. No water is needed because the vegetable itself is high in water content, though it is wise to turn the pieces once or twice with a spatula, to prevent sticking. Sprinkle with salt and minced parsley to serve.

BRAISED EGGPLANT À LA GRECQUE. Cut unpeeled eggplant in ½-inch cubes; simmer in 1/3 cup olive oil with 2 large onions, sliced, 1 or 2 garlic cloves, minced, 2 tablespoons minced parsley, and 2 tomatoes, peeled, chopped (or 1/3 cup tomato sauce). Add thyme, salt, and pepper to taste. Cook, covered, over low heat about 30 minutes. *Makes 6 to 8 servings.*

MEDITERRANEAN FRIED EGGPLANT. Cut unpeeled eggplant in very thin slices, either horizontally or vertically, depending on size of eggplant. Fry in a generous amount of olive oil until lightly browned on each side, adding more oil as needed. Sprinkle with salt. Serve at once, passing vinegar cruet.

BATTER-FRIED EGGPLANT. Peel eggplant, cut in rectangles about ½ inch by 2½ inches. Dip in All-purpose Fritter Batter (or the same batter as for Corn Fritters). Fry in deep fat, or in a skillet in hot fat ½ inch deep, until crisp and browned on all sides. Serve hot.

Imam-Baildi (Turkish Eggplant Casserole)

1 large or 2 small eggplants	Salt, pepper
¾ to 1 cup olive oil	4 medium tomatoes, peeled,
5 or 6 onions, sliced	sliced
2 or 3 cloves garlic, crushed	½ cup fine crumbs moistened
1 tablespoon minced parsley	with oil

Slice unpeeled eggplant very thin. Sauté 4 or 5 pieces at a time in olive oil (starting with ¼ cup oil) until lightly browned on each side; add remaining oil as needed. Remove and set aside. Cook onions and garlic in same oil, simmering over low heat until yellow and tender. Add parsley, salt, and pepper. Arrange layers of eggplant and layers of onion alternately in shallow baking dish. Place sliced tomatoes over top. Sprinkle tomatoes with salt; cover with the moistened bread crumbs. Bake in oven set at 350° F. for 1 hour. Remove from oven. Cool to room temperature. Do not chill. Serve at room temperature, neither warm nor cold. Excellent with barbecued lamb. *Makes 6 to 8 very rich servings.*

BARBECUED EGGPLANT. In large sheet of heavy-duty foil (or double thickness of foil) place 2 cups diced eggplant, 1 teaspoon onion powder (or instant minced onion or grated onion), 1 teaspoon minced parsley, 3 tablespoons oil or butter, ¼ teaspoon salt, and 3 tablespoons tomato sauce. Seal foil completely; bake in glowing coals of charcoal fire for about 1 hour; test for doneness by opening packet and piercing eggplant with fork. *Makes 4 to 6 servings.*

See also Ratatouille; Pisto Manchego; Caponatina; Baked Stuffed Eggplant; Eggplant Caviar.

Endive

The word is applied to two completely different vegetables: the salad green, which is also called chicory, and the elongated, cigar-shaped vegetable known as Belgian endive. Both are used primarily for salads—at least with American cooks. Both have a slightly bitter taste.

BRAISED BELGIAN ENDIVE. Soak endive in ice water for 15 minutes; drain. Allow 1 per serving; cut each in half. Braise in butter, covered, for 2 minutes, then add a cup of chicken broth (for 4 to 6 endives). Cook, covered, over low heat until tender but still slightly crisp. Vegetable should have semi-transparent look. Serve sprinkled with lemon juice and white pepper.

STUFFED BELGIAN ENDIVE. Cut each endive in half lengthwise; remove small outer leaves. Fill these with seasoned bread stuffing to which minced parsley has been added; dot butter over top. (If desired, chopped ham may be added to the crumbs.) Place stuffed endive halves in shallow casserole; pour 1 cup chicken broth around them. Bake in preheated 350° F. oven until leaves are tender and crumbs are lightly browned—about 20 minutes. Serve sprinkled with lemon juice.

Fennel

A celerylike vegetable with a licorice flavor. The feathery top is the herb we know by the same name; cut it off and keep it in a plastic bag in the freezer to use like frozen dill weed. Slice or chop the curious-looking bulb; braise like celery (see Braised Celery). Or, cook in boiling salted water until tender, drain, toss with Vinaigrette Sauce and serve as "cooked salad," at room temperature. Delicious with roast lamb, ham, or pork.

BAKED FENNEL. Cut 1 or 2 heads of fennel lengthwise; cook in boiling salted water just until tender—8 to 10 minutes. Drain. Arrange in shallow baking dish; dot with 2 tablespoons butter. Sprinkle with mixture of 2 tablespoons fine dry crumbs, 1 tablespoon grated Parmesan cheese, and 1 tablespoon of the chopped fennel leaves; dot with 2 more tablespoons butter. Sprinkle with paprika. Bake in oven preheated to 400° F. or cook 4 inches from heat in broiler just until crumbs brown. *Makes 6 servings.*

Green Beans

These were known as "string beans" until horticulturists developed varieties without strings; some people still call them "snap beans." Of all vegetables, these are probably the most widely popular, with youngsters as well as grownups. They are available fresh, frozen, and canned, in various styles, throughout the year.

FRESH GREEN BEANS (BASIC RECIPE). Break into 1-inch pieces, removing tip. Cook, tightly covered, in boiling salted water (not quite enough water to cover beans) just until fork-tender—about 8 to 10 minutes. Drain; add butter or margarine.

FRENCHED GREEN BEANS. Slice lengthwise. Cook as in basic recipe, but may be tender in less time (about 6 minutes).

BEANS WITH SOUR CREAM SAUCE. Dress hot cooked beans (fresh or frozen, cut or Frenched) with a mixture of 3 tablespoons sour cream, 1 tablespoon grated Parmesan or Romano cheese, and ¼ teaspoon crushed caraway seeds; stir to blend. Delicious hot or cold.

CURRIED GREEN BEANS. Toss hot cooked beans with sour cream blended with ¼ teaspoon curry powder.

GREEN BEANS IN ORANGE SAUCE. Cook fresh or frozen beans in salted water until almost tender; drain. Add 2 tablespoons butter, a few thin slices of onion, 1 teaspoon grated orange peel, and 2 tablespoons orange juice. Cover tightly; continue to cook over low heat until tender.

GREEN BEANS AND MUSHROOMS. Separately sauté mushrooms in butter; add to hot cooked beans.

GREEN BEANS WITH CHEESE TOPPING. To hot cooked green beans (fresh or frozen) add 2 tablespoons cheese instead of butter (Roquefort, shredded Swiss mozzarella, or mild Cheddar).

Fassoli Fresca

1½ pounds (1 quart) green beans
2 or 3 large tomatoes, peeled,
   chopped, or 1 1-pound can
   peeled tomatoes
1 medium onion, sliced

⅛ teaspoon orégano
¼ cup olive oil
½ teaspoon salt
Dash of freshly ground black
   pepper

Beans that are past their prime and becoming just a little tough are fine for this dish. Break in 1-inch lengths; place in heavy pot with remaining ingredients; simmer tightly covered until beans are very tender—about 1 hour. Even better cold (room temperature) than hot. *Makes 6 servings.*

Green Peas

There is nothing to compare with new green peas fresh from the garden, but alas, most of the fresh peas available at supermarket counters have traveled far before reaching their destination. Frozen peas sometimes have better flavor—if cooked with care.

FRESH PEAS (BASIC RECIPE). Shell peas shortly before cooking, keeping 3 or 4 of the brightest-colored pods for the cooking water. Place peas and pods in saucepan with a few thin slices of onion and 1 to 1½ cups salted water (barely enough to cover peas). Bring to a boil; lower heat; cook just until the peas are wrinkled—about 8 minutes. Drain; discard pods; add butter or margarine. *One pound peas in shells makes 3 servings; buy 2 pounds to serve 6.*

FROZEN PEAS (BASIC RECIPE). Place in saucepan 2 tablespoons butter and 2 tablespoons water. Over butter place block of frozen peas (1 10-ounce package). Add 2 or 3 very thin slices of onion and ¼ teaspoon salt. Cover; bring to a boil; reduce heat; stir to break up frozen block, if possible. Continue cooking, tightly covered, over lowest heat; remove cover only to stir peas once or twice more. As soon as peas are wrinkled, turn off heat. Leave covered in pan until time to serve. Do not drain. *Makes 4 servings.*

To serve 6 or 8, use 2 packages and double remaining ingredients.

MINTED PEAS. Cook fresh or frozen peas just until wrinkled. Drain; add butter or margarine and ¼ teaspoon crushed dried mint, or a dash or two of mint extract.

PEAS WITH FENNEL. Cook fresh or frozen peas: season with a pinch of powdered fennel or minced fresh fennel leaf (the feathery part).

PEAS WITH DILL. The same, but use minced fresh or frozen dill for seasoning.

Petits Pois à la Française

1 small head Boston lettuce, shredded	½ teaspoon salt
2 pounds fresh peas in pod	4 to 6 tablespoons butter
2 tablespoons minced shallot, or 2 or 3 thin slices onion	Pinch of nutmeg
1 teaspoon sugar	¼ cup water
	1 tablespoon minced parsley

Place layer of shredded lettuce in saucepan with tight-fitting lid. Add shelled peas with 3 or 4 of the freshest pods. Add shallot or onion, sugar, salt, butter, and nutmeg. Cover with more shredded lettuce. Add water: place lid on pan: bring to a boil. Reduce heat, shaking pan once or twice. Cook over very low heat until peas are wrinkled—about 15 minutes. Remove and discard lettuce. Serve sprinkled with parsley. *Makes 6 servings.*

Made with canned peas. Buy the best-quality early June peas: drain thoroughly, saving liquid. Add to liquid the butter, onion, sugar, and salt: cook to reduce to half. Place layer of shredded lettuce in saucepan, then the peas, and ½ dozen very tiny white onions, cooked separately. Cover with seasoned liquid. Add another layer of lettuce. Simmer 10 minutes over very low heat.

Using frozen peas. Over the layer of shredded lettuce, place defrosted frozen tiny peas with onions. Add butter, sugar, salt, and nutmeg. Cover with more shredded lettuce. *Add no water.* Cover tightly; cook over very low heat about 15 minutes. Remove and discard lettuce.

PETITS POIS CREOLE. Cook 2 pounds fresh peas or 2 packages frozen peas according to preceding recipe, but omit lettuce and add 2 tablespoons water (for frozen), ¼ cup water (for fresh peas). Cook over very low heat until peas are wrinkled. Remove cover: turn off heat when all liquid is evaporated. Beat 1/3 cup cream with 1 egg yolk and 1 teaspoon sugar. Add to cooked peas, stir until sauce is thickened. *Makes 6 servings.*

Greens (Kale, Mustard Greens, Turnip Greens, Collards, Swiss Chard, Dandelion Greens)

All these are bursting with vitamins and minerals, and all are cooked according to the same basic rules: wash thoroughly, to get rid of all sand and grit, then cook in a small amount of water until tender. Some water must be added—about ¼ cup. The length of cooking time depends on the vegetable and its youth or age. Taste to test doneness. Drain thoroughly, chop with small sharp knife. Sprinkle with salt, add butter, margarine, oil, or meat drippings. Pass the vinegar.

Swiss chard differs somewhat from the others: the coarser white stems should be removed from the leaves and cooked first, for they require longer cooking. This tastes best dressed with oil or vinegar. The type of fat or oil used for the others is pretty much a matter of personal taste. In the Deep South, greens are often cooked in a large amount of liquid, flavored with sow belly.

KALE WITH BACON SAUCE. Cook 6 strips bacon until crisp; remove; drain on absorbent paper. To bacon fat, add ¼ cup sugar, ¼ cup vinegar, ¼ cup water, and ¼ teaspoon celery seed. Bring to a boil. Add as a sauce to cooked fresh or frozen chopped kale. Sprinkle kale with crumbled bacon. (The same sauce is good with other greens.)

Italian Beans

The name has been applied to a variety of flat bean called *haricot* in Europe (and generally thought of as French, though it was Alexander the Great who first brought the haricot to Europe from India). Available only in frozen form in most markets; cook according to package directions, as briefly as possible. Dress in any of the ways suggested for Green Beans.

Kohlrabi

Prepare the same way as Celery Knob or Fennel. Especially good in cream sauce or German Hollandaise.

Leeks

The flavor of leeks is sweet and delicious, much more delicate than onions, and if they weren't so costly they could be served frequently as a vegetable. Only the white part should be used, the beards carefully trimmed, and the stalks separated enough to wash out all sand. Cut in 1½- to 3-inch pieces. Simmer in salted water until tender. Drain; add butter and lemon juice. Or for creamed leeks, add to Béchamel Sauce.

Lima Beans

The frozen limas are less expensive than the fresh and generally better in flavor.

FRESH LIMA BEANS (BASIC RECIPE). Shell pods. Discard any beans that are tinged with brown or shrunken and yellowed. Cook in boiling salted water until beans are slightly shriveled—15 to 20 minutes. Add butter or margarine.

FROZEN FORDHOOK LIMAS. The large beans cook as quickly as the baby limas and have more flavor. Cook according to package directions; season with butter only, or in one of the following ways.

SPANISH-STYLE LIMAS. No water needed to cook frozen limas this way. Heat 2 tablespoons olive oil in heavy saucepan, add 1 small onion sliced, cook about 1 minute. Add 1 package frozen Fordhook limas, 2 tablespoons chili sauce, ½ teaspoon salt, and a dash of fresh pepper. Cover tightly; cook over very low heat until limas are tender, stirring once or twice with fork to break up block.

LIMAS IN TOMATO SAUCE. Similar to the above, but with more sauce. Cook 1 package frozen Fordhook limas in 1 cup tomato sauce with 2 tablespoons olive oil and 1 teaspoon instant minced onion. Season with orégano, salt, and minced parsley.

Barbecued Limas

1 package frozen Fordhook limas	¼ cup olive oil
2 slices bacon, diced	2 tablespoons minced onion
3 tomatoes, peeled, diced	1 tablespoon minced parsley
¼ teaspoon salt	

Combine ingredients; place in center of large sheet of heavy-duty foil; secure edges; bake among hot coals of fire or on grid for about 30 minutes. *Makes 4 servings.*

Mushrooms

Cultivated mushrooms are available fresh, frozen, and canned. The canned come in three styles: crowns (also called caps or buttons, depending on size), sliced, and bits and pieces. Should you buy more fresh mushrooms than you need immediately, simply place the remainder in a plastic bag, seal, and stick in the freezer for later use. Always thaw frozen mushrooms completely before adding to butter.

Do not peel mushrooms unless they are very badly discolored. Trim only the root end of the stems (and save these trimmings for use in stocks or broth). If not to be used immediately, sprinkle mushrooms with lemon juice, keep tightly covered, but do not add water.

Mushrooms shrink greatly while cooking, and the longer they cook, the more they shrink. This is why a 4-ounce can of mushrooms represents an original ½ pound. They also shrink after cooking, if allowed to stand for some time—so serve immediately if possible.

If mushrooms are cooked with onion, the amount of onion should be less than half that of the mushrooms; otherwise the delicate mushroom flavor is lost.

Canned mushrooms should be added to a stew or sauce during last part of cooking. Cook as briefly as possible.

MUSHROOMS SAUTÉED IN BUTTER (BASIC RECIPE): Cut mushrooms as specified: slice, dice, or leave caps on (remove stems, or cut stems parallel with bottom of caps). Rinse just before cooking, pat dry. (Use trimmings for stock or broth.) Use 3 to 4 tablespoons butter for ½ pound mushrooms. Melt butter (do not allow it to sizzle); keep heat low. Add mushrooms; cook, turning once or twice, until delicately tinged with brown on each side—about 10 minutes. Sprinkle with salt and paprika. If to be served this way, add minced parsley and sprinkle with a few drops of lemon juice. Allow 6 to 8 servings to a pound, 3 to 4 servings for ½ pound, when served as a vegetable.

MUSHROOMS COOKED IN CREAM. Simmer sliced or button mushrooms in butter, as in basic recipe, for 10 minutes. Sprinkle with salt. Add 1 cup light cream for ½ pound mushrooms; continue to cook over lowest heat, uncovered, until sauce is reduced by half. Thicken sauce with flour or arrowroot, if desired.

MUSHROOMS LYONNAISE. Simmer ¼ cup minced or thinly sliced onion in 4 tablespoons butter until delicately colored; remove with slotted spoon. Add 1 pound sliced large or whole button mushrooms to same butter; cook 10 minutes, sprinkling with salt, and 1 teaspoon paprika. Replace onions, add 1 cup light or sour cream. Continue to cook, uncovered, 5 minutes longer over very low heat. Sprinkle with minced parsley or chives.

GRILLED MUSHROOM CAPS. Trim caps; sprinkle with lemon juice. Sauté in melted butter over moderate heat until lightly browned; or, brush with melted butter or oil and, while broiling meat or fish, place on broiler rack, broil until lightly browned—5 to 8 minutes.

DUXELLES. Chop 1 pound fresh mushrooms into very small pieces. Cook in ¼ cup (4 tablespoons) butter in a heavy skillet with a few slices of onion or a minced shallot and, if desired, 1 clove garlic, minced. Cook over low heat, turning now and then, until the mushrooms are almost black in color and the butter absorbed—about 45 minutes. Sprinkle with salt to taste. Use as a topping for broiled meats or fish or to garnish vegetables (such as grilled tomatoes, cooked green beans, limas, or artichoke hearts). Can be made ahead and stored in a jar in refrigerator. *Makes about 1 cup.*

Peppers

There are many types of peppers (the botanical name is *capsicum*), but the availability of chili, Tabasco, and cayenne peppers (the spicier varieties) is limited chiefly to the west and southwest and to specialty markets. *Green peppers* are the most widely used, the sweet variety. When fully ripe, these turn red, though they are not the same variety as those canned as *pimientos* (which are also sweet and red).

Green peppers are available throughout the year, but only during autumn, the period of seasonal abundance, are they cheap enough to prepare and serve as a vegetable. The rest of the time, their use is limited (because of cost) primarily to that of seasoner or garnish. *Frozen chopped green pepper* is available in many frozen food counters, but in freezing it has lost most of its flavor and color. *Canned pimiento* and canned *roasted sweet red peppers* are a better buy and can be used as a substitute for chopped green peppers in many recipes.

SAUTÉED GREEN PEPPERS. First remove the thin outer peel, either by piercing the raw pepper with a fork and holding directly over a gas flame until the outside is blackened (when it can be easily peeled off) or roasting in a very hot oven (preheated to 550° F., or at broil) until blackened; cool before handling. (Omit this step, if preferred.) Trim and seed peppers; remove all white membrane; cut in large flat pieces. Sauté over moderate heat in olive oil, with a peeled garlic clove in the oil, until fork-tender. Remove and discard garlic. Serve peppers sprinkled with vinegar and salt.

Green peppers are better when the outer skin is removed, but I have often done this without removing the skin, and being a lover of green peppers, I like them this way, too. Trim and seed the peppers, remove all white membrane, and cut in large flat pieces. Sauté over moderate heat in olive oil (¼ inch deep) with a peeled garlic clove in the pan, until fork-tender. Remove and discard garlic when browned. Serve the peppers sprinkled with vinegar and salt.

See also Stuffed Green Peppers; Mixed Pepper Relish; Sausage Grinders.

Okra

This curious vegetable, called "lady's-finger" by the English, came to our shores from Africa, where it is still called *gombo*. The African slaves that came to Louisiana introduced its use in stews, and thus the name came to be associated with gumbo, the most famous of Creole stews. Okra is widely used as a vegetable in the southern United States and is available in frozen form in nearly all supermarkets. Aside from its use in Creole stews, it is delicious cooked with tomatoes or combined with eggplant and tomatoes in a casserole. The Greeks use it in lamb stew. If overcooked, okra becomes slimy, though this same gelatinous substance in the vegetable is what serves as a thickening in gumbos. Frozen *okra* is available both in whole pods and sliced.

Okra with Tomatoes, Greek Style

1 package frozen okra pods	¼ teaspoon thyme
1 medium onion, sliced	½ teaspoon salt, or to taste
¼ cup olive oil	Dash of freshly ground black pepper
2 cups tomato juice, or 1 cup canned tomatoes and 1 cup water	1 teaspoon lemon juice

Allow okra to defrost at room temperature as onions simmer in the olive oil. When onions are soft, add tomato juice or canned tomatoes and water, thyme, salt, and pepper. Cook about 20 minutes. Add okra and lemon juice; cook 15 minutes longer. *Makes 3 to 4 servings.* Double all ingredients to serve 6.

OKRA AND EGGPLANT CASSEROLE. Combine in a large heavy saucepan or an earthenware casserole 1 package frozen sliced okra (thawed enough to break up), 1 medium onion, sliced, 2 cups diced eggplant, a 1-pound can peeled tomatoes (or 3 ripe tomatoes, peeled, quartered), and ¼ cup oil. Add salt and pepper to taste. Simmer, covered, until all vegetables are tender—about 30 minutes. Serve sprinkled with minced parsley. *Makes 4 to 6 servings.*

Onions

Review Buying and Storage Guides for summary of kinds of onions and their use. Frozen chopped onions are available in most markets and are appreciated by those whose eyes water when they chop fresh onions, but must always be defrosted completely, then drained well and patted dry before being added to fat.

To chop fresh onions without tears, use a covered vegetable chopper, available in houseware departments, or chop in electric blender.

Canned whole onions are useful for stews or shish kabob. They don't have the flavor or texture of the fresh but are nevertheless very handy as a short cut, and in recipes calling for small whole onions the liquid in the can is useful as a broth.

To slice onions, first cut off a slice at one side so onion can be held firmly in place, then slice *horizontally* with a sharp French knife. If your eyes water, place a slice of bread in your mouth (it will absorb the gaseous onion moisture that causes eyes to smart). Or stop once or twice to rinse the onions under running water and to rinse off the knife blade.

BOILED ONIONS (BASIC RECIPE). Peel whole onions (small white, medium or large, depending on use). Cook in broth or salted water to cover until tender enough to be pierced easily by fork—20 to 40 minutes, depending on size. Drain, saving the broth. Serve as a vegetable bathed with butter or margarine. (When they are to be served as a vegetable, small white onions are usually preferred; they are more delicate in flavor.)

ONIONS COOKED IN CREAM. Parboil small peeled white onions in salted water 15 minutes (they will still be crisp). Drain (save broth for stock or sauces). Place in top of double boiler with light cream or dairy half-and-half (1 cup cream for 12 to 16 small onions). Add salt, pepper, and nutmeg to taste and 1 tablespoon butter. Cover; cook over hot water until onions are tender—15 to 20 minutes longer. *Allow 3 or 4 onions per serving, depending on size.*

CREAMED ONIONS. Parboil small white onions until tender, as in basic recipe. Prepare a Medium White Sauce, using the reserved onion broth with light cream or half-and-half for the liquid. Serve sprinkled with minced parsley.

ESCALLOPED ONIONS. Prepare Creamed Onions; place in casserole or baking dish; cover with buttered crumbs. Bake with oven dinner.

GLAZED ONIONS. Boil small white onions as in basic recipe, just until barely tender. Place in a heavy skillet with 2 tablespoons sugar and 4 tablespoons melted butter. Cook over low heat, turning occasionally, until shiny golden brown on the outside. Or, cook onions in 1 cup chicken broth, tightly covered, for 15 minutes; uncover; reduce broth to half by boiling; add sugar and butter; continue cooking, uncovered, turning onions occasionally until they are glazed and tender. Serve with the remainder of the broth as a sauce.

FRIED ONIONS. Slice onions fairly thin. Simmer in olive oil, butter or meat drippings until lightly browned and very tender. Sprinkle with salt and paprika as they cook, turn occasionally with spatula to prevent sticking. Cook uncovered if you prefer them well browned. For softer texture, cover the pan, uncovering only to turn onions now and then. For very soft texture, cook over lowest heat about 1 hour (the latter are not really fried but braised, as the natural juices of the onion are drawn out with slower cooking).

FRENCH-FRIED ONIONS. Slice raw onions ¼ inch thick; separate into rings; dip each ring in All-purpose Fritter Batter. Fry in deep hot fat until crisp on both sides. Drain on absorbent paper. Frozen French-fried onions will be improved if refried in hot fat before serving. Drop while still solidly frozen into fat

½ inch deep, but stand well back from stove, because fat will spatter the moment the frozen food touches it.

Parsnips

This old-fashioned vegetable deserves more attention. It's easy to prepare, requires little cooking time, and if browned in butter is sweet and nutty. Scrape the parsnips with a vegetable parer, cut off the tops, and cut into cubes or lengthwise slices. (If very large, remove pithy inner core.) Precook 5 minutes in salted water, then sauté in butter; or place raw in heavy skillet with 3 tablespoons water and 3 tablespoons butter, cook over low heat, turning once until fork-tender—about 12 minutes altogether. Sprinkle with salt, pepper, and a pinch of allspice or ground clove.

Potatoes

BOILED POTATOES (BASIC RECIPE). Peel potatoes; cut large ones in halves or quarters. Cook in boiling salted water until fork-tender—about 20 minutes. Drain; immediately add butter or margarine and shake pan so potatoes will be coated with the golden fat.

SALZKARTOFFELN (GERMAN-STYLE SALTED POTA-TOES). Boil potatoes as in basic recipe. Drain; sprinkle with salt; add 1 or 2 tablespoons butter for 4 to 6 potatoes. Cover pan; place over very low heat for 5 minutes. Shake pan several times without lifting it from unit. This causes starch to expand, making potatoes more mealy and tender, with much the same texture as baked potatoes.

PARSLEY POTATOES. Cook potatoes as in basic recipe, or as for Salzkartoffeln; add a generous amount of minced parsley with butter.

BOILED NEW POTATOES. Instead of peeling potatoes, scrape the thin outer skin. Many people prefer them with their skins. Cook small potatoes whole, as in basic recipe.

POTATOES COOKED IN THEIR JACKETS. Boil potatoes in salted water *without peeling* until fork-tender; drain as soon as cool enough to handle; slip off skins. Especially recommended for small new potatoes, or for potato salad. (The potatoes tend to be darker in color, especially old or fully mature potatoes, when cooked this way. If snow-white potatoes are wanted, it's best to peel or scrape them first.)

MASHED POTATOES. Boil potatoes as in basic recipe, making sure they are completely soft. Drain thoroughly; immediately add a generous amount of butter or margarine, about ¼ teaspoon salt (for 4 to 6 potatoes), and a generous amount of freshly ground black pepper. Mash with fork until all lumps are gone. Add milk—about ¼ cup for 4 potatoes, 1/3 cup for 6 potatoes. Mash furiously, beating until fluffy. (For fluffier, more moist potatoes, add slightly more milk.) Spoon into serving dish; place a big lump of butter in the center.

DUCHESS POTATOES. Prepare extra-fluffy mashed potatoes: for 2 cups potatoes, add 1 beaten egg, beat until thoroughly blended. Transfer to buttered baking dish. Bake until top is lightly tinged with gold.

POTATO CAKES. Before storing leftover mashed potatoes in the refrigerator, shape into flat cakes, like thin hamburger patties. Store in covered dish. Reheat by browning the potato cakes in hot fat (bacon drippings or vegetable shortening), until crisp on both sides. These are so good you may want to make mashed potatoes ahead to have potato cakes next day. Especially recommended with hamburgers or baked fish.

POTATOES STEAMED IN BUTTER. The success of this depends largely on having a good heavy skillet with tight-fitting cover. Peel potatoes and slice thickly. Melt a generous amount of butter in a skillet—about 4 tablespoons for 6 large potatoes. Add potatoes, a few thin slices of onion, a generous amount of minced parsley, and a sprinkling of salt and pepper, but only 2 tablespoons water. Cover lid, cook over high heat until steam comes from lid, then turn heat as low as possible. Cook, shaking pan occasionally, until potatoes are tender. Turn over with spatula once or twice to prevent sticking. They should be tender and yellowed, but not browned.

COTTAGE-FRIED POTATOES. Much the same as Potatoes Steamed in Butter, except that potatoes are cooked in bacon drippings or vegetable shortening rather than butter, the raw potatoes are sliced quite thin, and while they are cooked covered, they are supposed to become brown and crisp—at least some of the slices. Onion is optional. Paprika may be sprinkled over them for color.

POTATOES LYONNAISE. Like Cottage-fried Potatoes,except that equal amounts of onion and sliced potatoes are cooked together in fat, covered, and minced parsley is added just before serving.

HASHED BROWN POTATOES. Either raw or leftover cooked potatoes may be used. Cut in small dice. Heat butter, bacon fat, or other shortening in heavy skillet; add the potatoes, cook over high heat until they start to brown, then lower heat and cook slowly until tender and a crisp brown crust has formed over the bottom; chop potatoes with small sharp knife as they cook. If potatoes stick, add more fat, lifting up crust to force fat under. When solid crust has formed over bottom, fold over like an omelet and serve.

GERMAN-FRIED POTATOES. Slice either raw or cooked potatoes quite thin. If raw, soak potatoes in cold water (to which a drop or two of lemon juice has been added) for 15 minutes; drain; pat dry with absorbent paper. Heat fat ½ inch deep in heavy skillet; add potatoes; sprinkle with salt. Cook, uncovered, over moderately high heat, turning occasionally, until potato slices are crisp—about 15 minutes. If precooked, potatoes should now be ready to serve. If raw when added to fat, cover pan, turn heat very low, and continue cooking until fork-tender.

FRENCH-FRIED POTATOES. Cut raw potatoes into sticks about ¼ inch thick by 2 inches long. Soak in iced salted water while fat is heating. For frying, a thermostatically controlled frying kettle is best, set at 370° F.; if you have a thermostatically controlled top burner, set it at high and place over it a deep heavy pan with fat or oil 2 to 2½ inches deep. Fat is right temperature when a small cube of fresh bread browns in 30 seconds (remove and discard cube). Before adding potatoes to hot fat, drain potatoes and pat with towel; add only part at a time to hot fat (do not crowd pan). If fat is the right temperature they will be crisply brown in 10 to 12 minutes. Remove with slotted spoon; drain on absorbent paper. Sprinkle with salt while hot.

POTATO-TOMATO SKILLET. Cook 6 to 8 sliced raw potatoes and 3 or 4 sliced onions in 6 tablespoons olive oil (or butter) over moderately low heat, uncovered, until they become yellow but not browned. Pour off excess oil; add 4 tomatoes, sliced, and 2 tablespoons minced parsley; turn so tomato is on bottom. Sprinkle with ¾ to 1 teaspoon salt. Cover pan; turn heat as low as possible; continue cooking until potatoes are very tender. *Makes 8 servings.*

POTATOES WITH ALMONDS CASTELLANO. Cook 4 or 5 potatoes (sliced), 1 large onion (sliced), and a pimiento (diced) in 3 or 4 tablespoons olive oil. As in the previous recipe, the vegetables are cooked slowly, over low heat, covered, until tender. During the last part of the cooking, add ¼ cup chopped or slivered almonds and a teaspoon of minced parsley. Sprinkle with salt and white pepper. *Makes 6 servings.*

RISSOLE POTATOES. Select fairly small potatoes, of uniform size. Peel; boil in salted water for 10 minutes. Drain thoroughly. Sauté in fat ¼ inch deep in heavy skillet, browning on all sides; or drop into deep hot fat and fry until browned on all sides. Or, if other foods are being cooked in the oven, brush potatoes with oil, place in baking dish, and bake until crisply golden on the outside, turning once.

OVEN-BROWNED POTATOES. Parboil potatoes 5 minutes; drain; place around meat in the roasting pan; cook in the meat drippings, turning once, until crisply browned on the outside but fork-tender.

BAKED POTATOES. Idaho potatoes are much the best; other large potatoes tend to have a more watery texture. Scrub the outside; cut away the peel in one spot or pierce with a fork (otherwise the expanding starch could make the potato explode). Bake in a hot oven (400° to 450°) until largest potato can be easily pierced with a fork—about 1 hour. Cut a cross in top of each. Squeeze to open. Place a lump of butter in the opening.

BAKED POTATOES WITH SOUR CREAM. Instead of butter, top baked potatoes with sour cream blended with minced chives, or sour cream blended with crumbled cooked bacon.

STUFFED BAKED POTATOES. Bake extra-large potatoes; when done, carefully cut off lengthwise slice of peel. Scoop out the potato, preserving the shell. Mash the potatoes with butter and milk, stir in grated cheese, salt, pepper, and a dash of cayenne (optional). Replace potatoes in skins. Brush exposed part with melted butter. (This can be done an hour or two before dinner is scheduled.) Reheat in oven to serve.

CREAMED POTATOES. Select small, fairly uniform potatoes; or cut large potatoes into quarters or halves. Boil in salted water until tender; drain. Add Béchamel Sauce, using 1 cup sauce for 6 medium potatoes.

Potatoes Anna

4 large potatoes, peeled (4 cups sliced)   6 tablespoons melted butter   Salt, pepper

The potatoes should be of fairly uniform size, so that slices will be uniform. Cut very thin, crosswise. Soak in ice-cold water 5 minutes; drain, pat dry with towel. Have ready a buttered 9 x 9-inch baking dish. Dip potato slices in melted butter; lay in overlapping slices in skillet or dish, to form 3 layers. Sprinkle each layer with salt and pepper. Pour any remaining butter over top. Preheat oven to 450° F. (very hot); bake potatoes, uncovered, for 10 minutes. Reduce heat to 350°; bake about 30 minutes longer. A brown crust should have formed over both top and bottom. Remove from oven; invert onto serving dish. *Makes 6 servings.*

For 8 servings use 6 cups sliced potatoes and ½ cup (8 tablespoons) butter.

POTATOES ANNA WITH CHEESE. Sprinkle 1 tablespoon grated Parmesan cheese over each layer of potatoes.

ESCALLOPED POTATOES I. Slice raw potatoes. Place in a buttered 9 x 9-inch baking dish, sprinkling each layer with salt, pepper, and a little flour (1 tablespoon flour for each layer). Add milk enough to cover potatoes completely. Bake until potatoes are tender and a brown crust has formed on top.

ESCALLOPED POTATOES II. Cook potatoes and cut into cubes or dice. Add to Béchamel Sauce, as for Creamed Potatoes. Place in shallow baking dish; top with mixture of buttered crumbs and grated cheese. Bake in moderate to hot oven until top is browned and sauce is bubbling. (This can be prepared in the morning, and need not be put into the oven until about 20 minutes before dinner is to be served. Especially good with baked ham.)

ESCALLOPED POTATOES AND HAM. Prepare according to either of the preceding recipes for Escalloped Potatoes, adding a layer of thin slices of ham between layers of potatoes.

Rutabagas. *See* Turnips.

Sauerkraut

Sauerkraut is cabbage that has been fermented in brine. The fermentation serves as a preservative, but if the kraut is not well rinsed before cooking, and cooked thoroughly, it can cause stomach distress. The flavor is better, too, if kraut is cooked slowly for a long time with additional ingredients. *Canned sauerkraut,* having been processed at high heat, need only be heated through, but its flavor is also improved by long, slow cooking, an exception to all other vegetable cookery.

SAUERKRAUT SIMMERED IN BUTTER (BASIC RECIPE). Rinse kraut in warm water; drain well. Place in heavy saucepan or pot with 1 tablespoon butter and 1 cup liquid for each pound of kraut. Simmer, covered, over low heat ½ to 1 hour. Season to taste with pepper or caraway. (Salt is not needed.)

SAUERKRAUT WITH APPLES. Prepare sauerkraut as in basic recipe, but add, for each pound of kraut, 1 tart apple, peeled and sliced, and 1 small onion, sliced (or 1 large onion for 2 pounds kraut). If desired, grated potato may also be added (1 small potato for 2 pounds kraut). This produces a thicker sauce. Season to taste: a small amount of salt may be needed.

CHAMPAGNE KRAUT. Prepare as in basic recipe, but add a little grated or sliced onion, and instead of water add dry white wine.

ANANASKRAUT. With 1 pound kraut, cook ¼ cup crushed pineapple and 1 tablespoon minced parsley; instead of water, add pineapple juice.

Sauerkraut and Potato Casserole

½ cup chopped or sliced onion
2 tablespoons butter or shortening
1 pound sauerkraut, drained

½ cup sour cream
4 cups seasoned mashed potatoes
½ cup grated cheese

Cook onion in butter until soft. Add sauerkraut; simmer 10 minutes. Stir in sour cream. Place half the mashed potatoes in bottom of buttered casserole; add sauerkraut, then remaining potatoes. Spread cheese over potatoes. (This can be prepared ahead). Bake in moderate (350° F.) oven until cheese is melted and potato topping is lightly browned. Very good with roast pork, pork chops, or baked spareribs. *Makes 6 servings.*

See also Székely Gulyás; Choucroute Garni.

Spinach

FRESH SPINACH (BASIC RECIPE). The best way to cook spinach is the simplest. Trim stems, wash thoroughly in cold water (even the packaged, ready-to-cook fresh spinach should be washed). Drain, place drained leaves in a large pot with ¼ teaspoon salt per pound (no water). Cover tightly, bring to a boil. As soon as steam appears from lid, lower heat and cook just until leaves are wilted—about 3 minutes. Drain thoroughly; chop with sharp knife to cut leaves and any bits of stem. Add a lump of butter and a dash of nutmeg. Lemon wedges may be served with the spinach, if desired.

FROZEN SPINACH. This takes longer to cook than the fresh; its only advantage is that no washing is necessary. Because of the tendency to burn, it must be cooked in the amount of water suggested in packaging instructions—and this robs it of flavor, for when the cooking water is drained off, so is much of the flavor. *Frozen chopped spinach,* however, is quite good prepared by any of the three following recipes.

Spinach in Red Wine

1 package frozen chopped spin-   Dash of freshly ground black
  ach   pepper
1½ tablespoons butter   2 tablespoons red wine
½ teaspoon salt

Allow spinach to thaw enough so that it can be cut into 1-inch cubes. Melt butter in heavy skillet; place spinach over it; sprinkle with salt and pepper. Add wine. Cover tightly; cook over high heat 2 minutes; turn heat low; cook 4 to 5 minutes longer, breaking up with a fork to hasten thawing. Serve this way, or sprinkle with lemon juice, or garnish with sieved hard-cooked egg. *Makes 4 servings.*

Quick Creamed Spinach

1 package frozen chopped spin-   ½ teaspoon salt
  ach   ½ teaspoon instant minced onion
1½ tablespoons butter   ½ cup sour cream

Place partially thawed spinach in pan with butter; sprinkle with salt. Add onion. Cook, covered, over high heat 1 minute; stir to mix with onion. Lower heat; cook 5 minutes longer or until completely thawed and soft. Stir in sour cream; blend well; turn off heat. *Makes 4 servings.*

Spinach Catalán

2 pounds fresh spinach, thorough-   2 tablespoons olive oil
  ly washed   2 tablespoons seedless raisins or
½ teaspoon salt   currants, chopped
1 tablespoon minced onion   Vinegar and olive oil in cruets
1 tablespoon pine nuts (pignoli)

Prepare spinach as in basic recipe. Sprinkle with salt. Cover; bring to a boil; cook just until leaves are limp, then drain and chop. In a skillet, sauté the minced onion and pine nuts in olive oil until lightly browned. Add the chopped raisins or currants, then the well-drained spinach. Serve this way, passing cruets of vinegar and olive oil, for a little of each to be sprinkled over the servings. *Makes 6 to 8 servings.*

Squash and Pumpkin

With all the different varieties of squash available in the markets it is necessary only to distinguish between the hard- and soft-shelled varieties, for otherwise pretty much the same cookery methods may be followed. The soft-shelled varieties include zucchini, yellow summer squash (now available throughout the year), and pattypan. (Cucumber can also be described as a variety of summer squash.) These need only brief cooking, and the rind is edible when cooked.

The hard-shelled varieties are available mostly in winter: they include acorn, hubbard, butternut, and pumpkin. These are best either baked or cooked until tender enough to scoop out and mashed (like potatoes).

Frozen whipped squash is produced from a winter variety, cooked and mashed before freezing.

SUMMER SQUASH SIMMERED IN BUTTER. This is an especially good way to prepare yellow squash. Cut squash in ¼-inch slices; use 2 tablespoons butter and 2 tablespoons water for each pound of squash. Sprinkle with salt and pepper. Simmer, covered, until tender—about 10 minutes. Sprinkle with parsley before serving.

PATTYPAN IN CREAM. Dice or cube pattypan squash. Simmer in butter, covered, as in preceding recipe, for 5 minutes. Add ¼ cup cream, continue cooking until tender. Add 1 teaspoon cornstarch thinned in a little water; cook until sauce is thickened.

ZUCCHINI ITALIENNE. Scrape off outer part of rind with small sharp knife, but rind should still be green. Cut in ¼-inch slices, sauté in olive oil until browned on both sides. Brown a peeled garlic clove in the olive oil (optional) at the same time. Remove and discard garlic. Sprinkle zucchini with salt. Serve sprinkled with parsley.

Braised Squash (Basic Recipe)

2 pounds yellow summer squash or pattypan
1 medium onion, chopped or sliced
½ green pepper, seeded, chopped
1 tablespoon minced parsley
4 tablespoons butter or olive oil
½ teaspoon salt, or to taste

Wash squash, slice or dice without peeling. Sauté in heavy sauce pan, skillet or casserole, with remaining ingredients, simmering gently, covered, until tender, about 10 minutes. *Makes 6 to 8 servings.*

For 3 or 4 servings, divide ingredients in half; or cook full recipe, serve leftovers cold next day as a cooked salad.

BRAISED ZUCCHINI. Prepare as in basic recipe, or Spanish style, but cook *uncovered*, turning as squash browns.

SPANISH STYLE. Add 1 small to medium tomato, peeled and chopped, to basic recipe.

SQUASH IN SOUR CREAM. Prepare yellow or pattypan squash as in basic recipe, but instead of parsley add chopped fresh or frozen dill or dill weed. When tender, stir in ½ cup sour cream.

BARBECUED SQUASH. Slice or dice zucchini or yellow squash; place in large sheet of heavy-duty foil with onion, green pepper, parsley, olive oil, and salt, as in basic recipe. Seal packet; place in coals of charcoal fire; cook for about 40 minutes. Turn packet so that heat reaches all sides.

SQUASH CASSEROLE. Prepare basic recipe, place in casserole, and cover with sliced tomatoes. Sprinkle tomatoes with salt, pepper, and orégano, then spread a mixture of fine crumbs and cheese over top. Dot with butter. Bake in oven preheated to 350° F. until crumbs are browned and tomatoes shriveled and soft—about 30 minutes. *Makes 6 to 8 servings.*

SQUASH KABOBS. Use a combination of yellow and zucchini squash, or squash with eggplant. Cut in thick slices or cubes. Marinate in seasoned olive oil for ½ hour: remove from marinade, arrange alternately on barbecue skewers. Cook, turning frequently, over charcoal until lightly browned. Serve sprinkled with salt, pepper, and lemon juice squeezed from lemon wedges.

See also Stuffed Baked Zucchini.

Honey-glazed Acorn Squash

3 small acorn squashes	½ teaspoon salt
5 tablespoons melted butter or margarine	½ teaspoon ground allspice
	¼ cup honey

Wash squash; cut each in half through the heavy outer rind; remove and discard seeds and stringy fibers. Cut a thin slice off bottom of each half if necessary to stand upright. Place squash in baking pan. Add water up to ¼ inch deep. Combine butter.

salt, allspice, and honey. Spoon 1½ tablespoons mixture in each squash cavity. Brush mixture over all exposed parts of cut side. Bake in oven preheated to 350° F. until inside of squash is very tender and top is glazed—about 45 minutes. Baste butter-honey mixture around the edges once during baking. *Serves 6.*

MAPLE-GLAZED HUBBARD OR BUTTERNUT SQUASH. Prepare the same way, except that these are larger in size and one will make 6 to 8 servings. Serve from the two halves of the cut shell.

Squash Soufflé

3 cups cooked winter squash, or 2 packages frozen whipped squash, thawed
¼ cup milk
3 tablespoons flour
1 tablespoon brown sugar
3 eggs, beaten

½ teaspoon salt
½ teaspoon ground nutmeg
Pinch of freshly ground black pepper
2 tablespoons sherry or 1 tablespoon honey or maple syrup

Preheat oven to 350° F. Combine all ingredients, beat to blend well. Spoon into buttered 1-quart casserole. Place immediately in hot oven; bake until top is lightly browned—about 35 minutes. Especially good with roast turkey. *Makes 6 to 8 servings.*

Squash or Pumpkin Fritters

1 cup cooked squash, frozen whipped squash (thawed), or canned pumpkin
1 cup sifted flour
1 egg, beaten

½ cup milk or light cream
½ teaspoon salt
1 teaspoon baking powder
Oil or fat for deep-frying

Combine all ingredients except fat; beat until very smooth. Place oil in deep heavy skillet (or electric skillet) to depth of 1 inch. Heat to 370° F. (until a cube of bread browns in 30 seconds). Drop a rounded tablespoonful of the mixture at a time into the hot fat; do not crowd pan. Fry until golden on each side. *Makes 18 to 20 fritters—enough for 6 to 8 servings.*

It isn't necessary to throw away all that golden pulp from the inside of a Halloween jack-o'-lantern. Cook it to make fritters, as in the above recipe, or pumpkin soup, or mashed pumpkin—a favorite dish of our Colonial forebears. In Colonial days, in fact, Bostonians were known popularly as pumpkins because they ate so many.

Mashed Pumpkin

3 to 4 cups diced pumpkin
¼ cup sugar (white or brown)
Dash of freshly ground black pepper
Dash of ground ginger
Dash of ground allspice
3 tablespoons butter
¼ teaspoon salt

Simmer diced pumpkin in boiling salted water until fork-tender. Drain; mash with fork or force through food mill. Add remaining ingredients; beat to a fluff. Serve hot with a lump of butter on top. *Makes 4 to 6 servings.*

See also Cream of Pumpkin Soup; Beef Stew in a Pumpkin.

Sweet Potatoes and Yams

Today's sweet potatoes and yams are more perishable than those of former times; they should be stored in the refrigerator until needed. Buy only as much as you need for immediate meals. When peeled, the vegetable quickly turns black, so it's best to cook them in their jackets, then peel afterward. Or, drop potatoes in hot salted water as they are peeled; cook immediately. Serve them this way, bathed with butter or margarine, as the perfect accompaniment for ham or pork chops. Yams are more moist and a deeper orange color than sweet potatoes, but either may be used in the recipes that follow. Frozen and canned candied sweet potatoes are available in nearly all markets.

BAKED SWEET POTATOES. Scrub, cut away any black spots or withered areas, place in a hot (400° F.) oven, and bake until fork-tender—45 minutes to 1 hour, depending on size. Cut open as for baked white potatoes; fill with a lump of butter or chive-flavored sour cream. Mash potatoes at table; sprinkle with salt.

WHIPPED SPICED YAMS. Boil yams in their jackets in salted water until fork-tender—about 15 minutes for medium size. Or, peel, drop into boiling salted water, and cook covered until tender. Remove skins, add a big lump of butter, a pinch each of ground cinnamon, cloves (or allspice), and crushed cardamom (or nutmeg), and 1 or 2 tablespoons cream or orange juice (enough for 6 to 8 yams). Beat to a fluff. Excellent with pork chops; or, for a meatless meal, serve with broiled tomatoes and buttered green beans.

Candied Sweet Potatoes

6 large sweet potatoes or yams (about 5 cups peeled, sliced)
6 to 8 tablespoons melted butter or margarine
½ cup light brown sugar
⅛ teaspoon cinnamon
½ teaspoon salt
Grated rind and juice of 1 orange
1 cup unsweetened pineapple juice

Peel and slice potatoes; arrange in buttered casserole promptly, basting each layer with melted butter to prevent darkening. Sprinkle each layer with mixture of sugar, cinnamon, salt, and grated orange rind. Combine orange juice and pineapple juice; pour over potatoes. Bake, covered, in moderate (350° F.) oven for 1 hour; uncovered during last ½ hour. A thick syrup should form over the potatoes. Excellent with roast chicken or turkey, accompanied by Brussels sprouts. *Makes 6 to 8 servings.*

QUICK CANDIED SWEETS. Boil sweet potatoes or yams in their jackets. Slip off skins; cut in quarters or slice thickly. For 4 large potatoes, melt 4 tablespoons butter in a heavy skillet; add 5 or 6 tablespoons brown sugar; stir until sugar is dissolved. Place sliced or quartered potatoes in mixture, basting so they are completely covered. Cook, covered, over lowest heat until potatoes are warmed through. Serve sprinkled with grated orange or lemon peel.

SWISS CHARD. See Greens.

Tomatoes

When tomatoes are in season locally they should be enjoyed to the full, for out-of-season tomatoes do not have the same flavor or succulence. Canned peeled tomatoes are preferable to the fresh the rest of the year.

BROILED TOMATOES. Cut large tomatoes in thick slices, smaller tomatoes in halves. Sprinkle with salt and pepper; dot with butter. If desired, sprinkle with grated or shredded cheese. Place tomatoes on broiler pan 2 to 3 inches from heat until lightly browned and somewhat shriveled, but firm enough to hold their shape.

FRIED GREEN TOMATOES. Select large firm tomatoes which have just started to turn red and are still mostly green. Cut in thick slices; dredge with mixture of flour, salt, and freshly ground black pepper. Heat bacon drippings in skillet to depth of ¼ inch; fry the tomatoes until browned on each side. Serve hot.

FRIED TOMATOES WITH GRAVY. Select firm but fully ripe tomatoes; slice thickly; dredge with seasoned flour, as above. Fry in bacon fat, butter, or shortening until browned on both sides. Some of the slices will break up; push these to one side of the pan until all tomatoes are fried; add a little flour (only enough to absorb the liquid), then stir in half-and-half, top milk, or light cream, adding about 1 cup milk or cream for 2 table-spoons flour. Simmer as for meat gravy; season with salt and pepper to taste. Serve with mashed potatoes for a meatless meal, the gravy spooned over both tomatoes and potatoes. With tender garden beans and a salad, this makes a fine supper for a summer evening.

FRIED TOMATOES ITALIENNE. Slice firm ripe tomatoes; sauté in melted butter over very low heat. Sprinkle with salt, pepper, a little oregano, and a little thyme. When browned on the bottom, turn and sprinkle the top with seasonings. Handle gently to avoid breaking. When done they should be very soft but still intact. Excellent with scrambled eggs or omelet for brunch.

Baked Stuffed Tomatoes

6 large firm tomatoes	crumbs
2 tablespoons chopped onion	½ teaspoon marjoram
1 or 2 cloves garlic, crushed	½ teaspoon salt
4 tablespoons olive oil	1 tablespoon minced parsley
2 slices bread, broken into	

Scoop centers from tomatoes, saving pulp. Sauté onion and garlic in half the olive oil until soft but not brown. Add bread crumbs, toss until lightly toasted. Combine with marjoram, salt, parsley, and scooped-out tomato pulp. Stuff tomatoes with mixture, mounding high over top. Sprinkle remaining olive oil over top of tomatoes. Arrange in shallow baking dish; bake 40 to 50 minutes to 350°F. Good either hot or cold. *Makes 6 servings.*

STUFFED WITH RICE. Instead of bread, use 1 cup cooked rice in preceding recipe. Add 2 to 3 tablespoons each pine nuts and currants or raisins, if desired.

Escalloped Tomatoes

1 large (1-pound 12-ounce) can peeled tomatoes	Freshly ground black pepper
	1 to 2 teaspoons sugar (optional)
1 cup stale bread crumbs	2 to 3 tablespoons butter
Salt	

Pour tomatoes into baking dish. Push crumbs into the juice so as to cover them completely. Sprinkle salt, pepper, and sugar (if desired) over top; dot with butter. Bake, uncovered, as part of an oven dinner, or in an oven preheated to 400° F. until tomatoes are reduced by one-third and crumbs are lightly browned—about 1 hour. Excellent with baked potatoes either for a meatless meal or with roast meat or chops. *Makes 4 to 6 servings.*

For 2 servings use a 1-pound can of tomatoes, ½ cup crumbs, ¼ teaspoon salt, and 1 to 1½ tablespoons butter.

STEWED TOMATOES. The same as Escalloped Tomatoes, except that mixture is simmered in a covered saucepan. A few slices of onion, or instant minced onion, may be added, if desired.

Turnips

The big yellow turnips called rutabagas (also known as Swedish turnips) have much the same flavor as the small white purple-tinged ones. Mashed yellow turnips mixed with an equal amount of mashed potatoes are often received with more enthusiasm than when plain; frozen mashed yellow turnip is one of the more successful of the frozen vegetables. White turnips, cut into matchsticks and briefly cooked, make an excellent ingredients in Chinese entrees in place of canned Chinese vegetables—more flavorful and crisp.

Curried Turnips

6 to 8 small white turnips, thinly sliced	1 teaspoon curry powder
2 medium onions, sliced	½ teaspoon cumin
4 to 5 tablespoons butter	½ teaspoon salt, or to taste
½ teaspoon powdered coriander	½ cup water
	1 cup yogurt

Cook turnips and onions gently in butter until onions are golden. Add spices and water. Simmer, uncovered, 5 minutes over lowest heat. Add yogurt, ½ cup at a time, until well blended and creamy. *Makes 4 to 6 servings.*

Wax Beans

Prepare in any of the ways suggested for Green Beans, but allow more cooking time. The following makes a fine entree for a budget supper, accompanied by baked potatoes and corn on the cob.

Wax Beans Estofada

2 cloves garlic
¼ pound chorizo or similar sausage, sliced, or ½ cup minced
  ham
1 pimiento or sweet pepper, diced
1 medium onion, chopped
½ cup olive oil

2 carrots, scraped, quartered
2 pounds wax beans, ends
  trimmed
½ cup water
½ teaspoon salt
1 tablespoon minced parsley

Cook garlic, chorizo, pimiento or sweet pepper, and onion in olive oil over low heat until onion is soft; add carrots, beans, water, and salt; cover; cook over low heat until vegetables are soft. Serve topped with parsley. Good hot or cold. Excellent with lamb or pork chops. *Makes about 8 servings.*

ZUCCHINI. See Squash.

Vegetable Casseroles

When there is an abundance of fresh vegetables in the market, they can be combined in a stew or casserole tasty enough to serve as the main course. As most of the following are also delicious served cold (rather, at room temperature—not chilled), they also make fine dishes to serve with barbecued meats or poultry on the patio.

Ratatouille

1 eggplant, 7 to 8 inches long (1
  pound)
Salt
2 or 3 zucchini or yellow squash, 4
  to 6 inches long (1½ pounds)
1 large onion, sliced or chopped
2 or three cloves garlic, minced
½ cup olive oil

3 large ripe tomatoes, peeled,
  chopped, or 1 1-pound can
  peeled tomatoes
¼ teaspoon orégano
2 tablespoons minced parsley
¼ teaspoon thyme
1 green pepper, seeded, chopped
  (optional)

Peel and chop eggplant and sprinkle with salt; let stand ½ hour, then drain off excess salt. Partially scrape squash; cube. Cook onions and garlic in olive oil at moderate heat unil onion is soft and golden; add eggplant and squash; cook, uncovered, until eggplant is delicately browned. Add tomatoes, herbs, green pepper, and salt to taste. Simmer, uncovered, 1 hour. Usually served warm but also good cold. *Makes 6 to 8 servings.*

AS AN ENTREE. Add ¼ to ½ pound ground beef (top round or chuck) with onions.

Pisto Manchego

¼ cup olive oil
1 large or 2 small potatoes.
  peeled. diced
1 medium onion, sliced
1 4-ounce can pimientos, drained,
  diced
1 or 2 cloves garlic, minced

1 small eggplant, diced, or 2 cups
  sliced zucchini or yellow squash
¼ cup diced bacon or ham
1 cup canned tomatoes
½ teaspoon salt, or to taste
1 tablespoon minced parsley

Heat oil in large heavy skillet (or an electric skillet set at 300° F.). Add potatoes, onion, pimientos, garlic, eggplant, and diced bacon or ham. Cook, turning occasionally with spatula, until lightly browned. Add tomatoes, salt, and parsley; cook until all vegetables are tender. Serve as an entree topped with poached egg or wedges of hard-cooked egg, or serve as the vegetable with grilled meats. *Makes 4 to 6 servings.*

Ceylon Vegetable Curry

6 tablespoons shortening
1 medium onion, sliced
1 clove garlic, crushed
1 tablespoon curry powder, or
  mixture of cumin, ginger, fennel, dry mustard, cinnamon,
  and nutmeg to taste. with a dash
  of Tabasco
½ pound (2 cups) tender green
  beans
1 large carrot. scraped. quartered

  lengthwise
1 cup corn cut from cob
1 green pepper, seeded, cut in
  squares
1 package frozen peas
1 cup water
2 chicken or onion bouillon cubes
3 cups cooked rice
½ cup shredded coconut
2 hard-cooked eggs

Melt shortening; add onion, garlic, and curry powder or spices. Cook 2 minutes over high heat; add remaining vegetables; low- er heat; cover; cook 5 minutes. Add water and bouillon cubes; bring water to a boil; cook until vegetables are tender. Serve with rice, garnished with coconut and chopped egg, for a vege- tarian entree or a meatless meal. *Makes 6 servings.*

Tian

2 pounds spinach or Swiss chard
½ cup olive oil
Salt, pepper
2 medium onions, chopped
1 or 2 cloves garlic, minced
6 to 8 small (4-inch) zucchini,
  sliced

½ cup chopped fresh basil or
  fresh parsley
4 eggs
1 cup grated Parmesan cheese
1 cup fine dry crumbs, moistened
  with butter or oil

Thoroughly wash spinach or chard; discard stems; chop leaves coarsely. Heat oil in large skillet; add chopped spinach or chard; cook, covered, until wilted—about 2 minutes. Remove with slotted spoon; press out all liquid; season with salt and pepper. Add to same pan the onions, garlic, zucchini, and basil or parsley. Cook, uncovered, until onion and zucchini are lightly browned. Sprinkle with salt and pepper. Remove from oil. Place in wide shallow earthenware casserole. Arrange cooked spinach or chard over the other vegetables. Break each egg first into a saucer (to make sure yolk doesn't break) then slip into casserole over spinach. Sprinkle mixture of cheese and moistened seasoned crumbs over top. (This can be done ahead.) Bake in oven preheated to 375° F. until eggs are just set, the yolks still soft. *Makes 4 entree servings.*

Sweet Potato, Carrot, and Prune Tzimmes

1½ pounds pitted prunes
3 cups boiling water
2 or 3 tablespoons shortening
2 onions, chopped
1 to 1½ teaspoons salt
3 or 4 carrots, scraped, cubed

(2½ cups)
3 medium sweet potatoes
½ cup honey or maple-blended
  syrup
½ teaspoon cinnamon
¼ teaspoon cloves

Soak prunes in boiling water ½ hour. Melt shortening in heavy pot; add onions; cook until golden and soft. Add salt, carrots, soaked prunes, and the water in which they soaked. Cover; cook over low heat 1 hour. Peel sweet potatoes, quarter if large, and add to the pot with honey and spices. Continue to cook, covered, until potatoes are very tender and liquid has cooked down to a sauce—40 minutes to 1 hour longer. *Makes 6 servings.*

Hot Vegetable Salad

½ pound (2 cups) string beans, sliced diagonally
2 or 3 carrots, scraped and thickly sliced or diced
1 cup cauliflower broken in small pieces, or 1 package frozen artichoke hearts
3 or 4 potatoes, peeled, diced
¼ cup olive or salad oil
2 tablespoons vinegar, or to taste
Salt, pepper

Cook the beans, carrots and cauliflower (or artichoke hearts) in boiling salted water, in one saucepan, the potatoes in another saucepan. Vegetables should be just fork-tender but not soft—avoid overcooking. Drain well; combine in serving dish; immediately dress with olive oil, vinegar, salt, and pepper. Serve hot, to accompany omelet, hamburgers, or cold cuts. *Makes 4 to 6 servings.*

Vegetable Plate Combinations

- Asparagus Milanese, broiled tomatoes, buttered carrots
- Broccoli Amandine, baked potatoes, Beets in Orange Sauce
- Corn on the Cob, Braised Squash, buttered limas
- Escalloped Tomatoes, Brussels sprouts, Hashed Brown Potatoes
- Cabbage Baked in Cream, buttered green beans, Baked Rice-stuffed Tomatoes
- Baked Honey-glazed Acorn Squash, Braised Celery, limas
- Green Peas with Onions, parsnips, whipped sweet potatoes
- Carrots and Cauliflower, spinach, Steamed Skillet Eggs with Cheese
- Cabbage with Ginger-Cream Sauce, limas, Broiled Tomato Halves Topped with Grated Cheese
- Fassouli Fresca, Corn on the Cob, Cole Slaw

9 SALADS

"It takes four men to make a salad," according to an old Andalusian saying: "a spendthrift for oil, a miser for vinegar, a counselor for salt, and a madman to mix them all up."

This describes the most basic of all salads, the one that is served in most countries if you ask for simply "a salad," and probably closely resembles the original salad of the ancients: lettuce, or a mixture of greens, tossed with oil, vinegar, and salt—nothing more. Such a salad goes with any meal and supplies the healthful green leafy vegetables that belong in every daily menu; and if the greens are crisp and fresh, and the oil of the very best quality, it will please the most critical gourmet.

But "salad" has come to mean anything from hors d'oeuvre mixtures to luncheon entrees to desserts. Sometimes the word signifies simply that the dish is composed of a mixture of ingredients, chopped or minced, as in chicken salad or Salade Russe. A fruit salad may closely resemble a fruit compote, except that the ingredients are cut in small pieces. Most salads are cold, but then how to explain hot potato salad and hot vegetable salad?

568

Some salads are composed mainly of raw vegetables and/or fruits; but again there are cooked salads, meaning cooked vegetables dressed with oil and vinegar or an oil-based sauce.

Gelatin salads are peculiarly American. They are related to the aspics of Continental cuisines, but only distantly. The dressing (or sauce) for a gelatin salad must be a thickened one—mayonnaise, a sour cream mixture, boiled dressing, or a combination of one or more of these with other ingredients added for special flavor.

You will find many recipes for salad dressings in Chapter 2, "Sauces and Soups." All of these are listed in the index under *Salad Dressings*. In addition there are hundreds of commercial salad dressings and seasoned dressing mixes in supermarkets, so that the choice of dressing for the salad is without limit.

One important thing to remember is that *no dressing is any better than the oil that goes into it*. No amount of herbs or spices can cover up the taste of rancid oil. This is just as true of commercial dressings as of those made at home, with or without mixes. Refrigerating oils does not prevent rancidity; most oils—olive oil especially—are better if not refrigerated. The oil should be fresh to begin with (which can be determined by simply holding the oil to one's nose), stored in clean containers in a dry, not too warm place, and not mixed with other ingredients until a reasonable time before serving. A combination of olive and vegetable oil will go rancid more quickly than pure olive oil; a prepared dressing, if not used within 24 hours, may turn rancid, which is also true of an opened bottle of mixed dressing, even if it was fresh when purchased. It is the addition of other ingredients, or impurities from exposure to air, that cause oil to go bad. For this reason, *mixed* dressings should always be kept tightly covered and refrigerated.

Mayonnaise and mayonnaise mixtures also need to be refrigerated after opening. This is true, of course, of sour cream dressings as well, and any dressings containing eggs, cream, butter, or other perishable ingredients.

Tossed Green Salad (Basic Recipe)

Allow ¾ to 1 cup greens for each serving. A mixture of greens is more interesting than simple lettuce—unless the lettuce is very fresh and very crisp. Mixed greens should include some bland greens, some peppery or bitter, some very crisp, others softer in texture. For example: Boston or bibb lettuce with curly endive; iceberg lettuce with raw spinach or watercress; romaine with Boston lettuce; mustard greens (shredded) with bibb or garden lettuce (also shredded) and green new cabbage (shredded).

The greens should be soaked in ice water when first brought home, shaken vigorously to get rid of excess water, then stored in a vegetable crisper or large plastic bag (see page 22). Leave them there until shortly before time to serve, then tear into pieces or shred, according to the type of green or the recipe. *Do not add dressing until the last minute*—just before bringing to the table, or at the table.

The choice of oil is important. If it's olive oil, buy only top quality. (In the end, this is better economy, because top-quality oil remains fresh longer.) Some like a strong-flavored, very green oil; others prefer the blander golden oil. A top-quality refined olive oil is more bland in flavor than most virgin oils. If olive oil is not to your taste, use equal care in selecting another salad oil that has no trace of rancidity.

The choice of vinegar may range from a simple cider vinegar to red or white wine vinegar, to herb vinegars (including tarragon vinegar with a feathery wisp of tarragon leaves in the bottle). Since normally only a tablespoon of vinegar is required for a bowl of tossed salad, the cost of a more esoteric vinegar is minimal. (If a pint of vinegar costs as much as 75¢ for example, the cost of each tablespoonful will be less than 2½¢.)

Here you have the necessary ingredients. The bowl of salad greens may be brought to the table, along with cruets of oil and vinegar, a salt shaker, and a pepper grinder: douse the greens with oil "like a spendthrift," toss to coat the greens, then shake salt over the greens and toss again. Sprinkle vinegar over them "like a miser," and grind pepper madly. One more toss and the salad is ready. No headaches, no trauma—no worrying about measurements. It's the easiest, the simplest, and in the estimation of many, the best way of dressing a salad.

WITH PREPARED DRESSING. If an herb-flavored dressing is more to your liking, prepare it in advance (see recipes for Vinaigrette Dressing and variations). Bring the bowl of greens to the table, with the dressing in a separate container. Sprinkle the dressing over the greens; toss. Remember that ¼ cup of salad dressing is ample for a quart of greens (4 to 6 servings).

DRESSING TRICKS

To add garlic flavor, either (1) rub the salad bowl with a clove of garlic (split), crushing with the back of a spoon, before greens are placed in the bowl, or (2) rub a piece of slightly stale bread with garlic, cut bread in cubes, and add to salad greens, or (3) add a garlic clove (split) to *prepared* dressing several hours in advance (remove garlic before adding dressing to salad), or (4) use homemade garlic salt instead of plain salt in making a prepared dressing.

Sweeten prepared dressings with onion slices. A few slices of raw onion added to a prepared dressing an hour or so before the dressing is to be used makes a miraculous difference in flavor. If raw onion disagrees with you (as it does with me), simply do not eat the onion rings (push them to the side of the plate) or remove them from the dressing before adding it to the greens. The sweet onion flavor will already have been imparted to the sauce.

Herbs add interest to a simple oil and vinegar dressing, but use them cautiously. The best are chives, tarragon, fennel, and thyme. If orégano is added, make it only a pinch. Chopped *fresh* basil is pleasant; so is fresh dill or fresh chervil (though in my estimation parsley is too strong in flavor for lettuce salad).

Of the **spices**, mustard is the most frequently used, but for variety try a pinch of curry powder, ginger, cumin, or chili powder. Freshly grated lemon or orange peel also adds delightful fragrance.

ROQUEFORT SALAD. This can be made in one of three ways: (1) crumble Roquefort or other blue cheese right into the bowl of greens and add oil, vinegar, salt, and pepper at the table; or (2) add the cheese to Vinaigrette Sauce in advance (¼ cup cheese to ½ cup sauce) and beat until creamy; (3) add prepared Blue Cheese-Cream Dressing to the greens. Use ½ cup dressing for 6 to 8 cups greens.

TOSSED SALAD WITH CREAM DRESSING. Instead of Vinaigrette Sauce, add Sour Cream-Mayonnaise to greens, using ¼ cup dressing for each quart (4 to 6 servings) of greens.

MIXED TOSSED SALAD. Add to greens either raw or cooked vegetables cut into small pieces, such as:

Diced avocado	Cooked lima beans
Slivers of green pepper	Cooked or canned artichoke
Diced celery	hearts
Sliced Chinese cabbage	Cooked peas
Raw white turnips, cut in slivers	Cooked or canned sliced beets
Tiny radishes	Sliced heart of palm (canned)
Green or black olives	Sliced water chestnuts (canned)
Cooked or canned green beans	Slivers of canned pimiento

Do not add sliced or chopped tomatoes until the last moment. Most cooked (or canned) vegetables taste better in mixed salads if first marinated in prepared dressing, before they are added to the greens.

Tomato-Roquefort Salad

6 ripe tomatoes, cut in wedges	½ cup crumbled Roquefort
1 cup thinly sliced celery	cheese
½ cup sliced scallions	½ cup oil
(green onions)	¼ cup vinegar
1 tablespoon minced parsley or	¼ teaspoon salt
chives	½ cup black olives
1 tablespoon slivered orange peel	1 bunch watercress, trimmed

Place tomatoes in bowl with celery, scallions, parsley, and orange peel. Combine half the cheese with the oil, vinegar, and salt; shake or beat in blender until creamy. Pour over tomatoes. Let stand at room temperature until time to serve (no more than 1 hour). The watercress should be trimmed of stems and freshened in ice water, then thoroughly shaken and chilled in a covered container. Just before serving, place in a salad bowl the tomatoes, dressing, olives, watercress, and the remaining cheese. Toss at the table. *Makes 6 to 8 servings.*

Salade Valenciana

1 seedless orange	6 to 8 cups mixed greens, in small
1 small white onion, thinly sliced	pieces
1/3 cup olive oil	¼ cup slivered pimientos or
3 tablespoons red wine vinegar	sliced pimiento-stuffed olives
Salt	

Cut off very fine slivers of orange peel containing no white; place in salad bowl. Peel the orange so that no white remains on orange segments, then slice or dice the orange; add to salad bowl. Add onion, olive oil, vinegar, and about ¼ teaspoon salt. Marinate at least 30 minutes (up to 2 hours). Prepare greens—a mixture of romaine, watercress, and Boston lettuce is very good. Tear into bite-size pieces but keep covered in refrigerator. At last moment, add pimientos or olives and the greens to the salad bowl, over the oranges. Toss at table. *Makes 8 servings.*

Mushroom and Green Pepper Salad

½ pound raw fresh mushrooms
1 green pepper, cut in thin slivers
A few thin slices onion
1 teaspoon capers

¼ cup Vinaigrette or Sherry-
  Vinaigrette Sauce
1 teaspoon grated orange rind
4 to 6 cups mixed greens

Combine mushrooms, green pepper, onion, and capers. Add sauce and orange rind. Marinate at least 2 hours. At table, toss with mixed greens. *Makes 8 servings.*

Cucumber Salad

Remove most, but not all, of peel from cucumber (leave lengthwise strips). Cut into paper-thin slices. Sprinkle generously with salt and sparingly with sugar. Let stand ½ hour or longer, then drain off any liquid. Sprinkle with vinegar, or, if desired, vinegar and oil. Add a little minced parsley for garnish.

Cucumber and Tomato Salad

Use more or less equal quantities of cucumbers and fresh ripe tomatoes. Partially peel cucumber; cut in thin slices. Cut tomatoes in thin slices. Arrange in layers with a few thin slices of onion (if desired). Sprinkle each layer with salt. Cover with Vinaigrette Sauce. If desired, add a little minced parsley or minced chives. Serve within ½ hour.

TOMATO AND PEPPER SALAD. Instead of (or in addition to) cucumber, layer tomatoes with slivered green or red sweet peppers (or pimiento).

Bermuda Salad

Thinly slice 1 or 2 large Bermuda (red) onions. Layer with 4 or 5 ripe tomatoes, thinly sliced. Cover with ½ cup Roquefort-Vinaigrette Dressing. Marinate ½ to 1 hour. Serve this way or over iceberg lettuce. *Makes 6 to 8 servings.*

Egg and Green Bean Salad

About 2 cups cooked or canned
  green beans
Few slices onion
1 or 2 anchovy fillets, minced
½ cup Vinaigrette, Herb

Vinaigrette, Italian, or
  Sherry-Vinaigrette Dressing
4 to 6 cups salad greens
3 hard-cooked eggs, cut in wedges

Marinate the beans, onion, and minced anchovy in the dressing for 1 or more hours at room temperature. Just before serving, add salad greens and eggs. Toss. *Makes 8 servings.*

Orange and Avocado Salad

2 seedless oranges
1 small onion, thinly sliced
1 ripe avocado, sliced
2 tablespoons lemon juice
2 tablespoons vinegar

½ cup olive oil
Pinch of curry (optional)
Salt, pepper
4 to 6 cups mixed greens

Peel oranges so that no white remains on segments. Slice or dice oranges. Place in salad bowl with onion and sliced avocado. Sprinkle with lemon juice, so that avocado is well covered with juice. Add vinegar, oil, curry, salt, and pepper. Cover bowl tightly with plastic wrap or foil; marinate at room temperature ½ to 1 hour. Add greens just before serving; toss. *Makes 8 to 10 servings.*

Marinated Avocado Halves

This is one of the easiest and most elegant dishes to serve as a first course. Select avocados that are fully ripe, buttery-soft, yet without any tinges of brown in the flesh. (If not ripe when purchased, leave them at room temperature until properly soft to the touch.) Cut in halves, *without peeling.* Remove only the pits. Cut slits in the flesh with a small sharp knife so that dressing can penetrate. Fill with a mixture of 2 parts olive oil and 1 part vinegar. Let stand at room temperature, covered with plastic wrap, for several hours before serving. Serve in the shell, 1 avocado half to each person, to be eaten with spoons.

AVOCADO HALVES WITH SHRIMP OR CRABMEAT SALAD. Prepare avocado halves as in above recipe, but merely brush with dressing. Fill with Shrimp or Crabmeat Salad.

Hearts of Palm Vinaigrette

Easy and delicious. Marinate hearts of palm (available in cans at gourmet counters) in Vinaigrette Sauce or Italian dressing with pimiento strips and minced parsley. Serve with pimiento strips laid across the palm hearts, as a first course or a side salad.

Artichoke Hearts and Pimiento

Instead of hearts of palm, marinate canned Spanish artichoke hearts and pimiento in Vinaigrette Sauce. Also suitable as either first-course appetizer or salad.

Green Beans Vinaigrette

Tender whole green beans should be used—either canned Blue Lake beans or fresh young beans cooked *au point*. If freshly cooked beans are used, add Vinaigrette Sauce while they are still warm. Sprinkle with minced parsley. Use enough sauce to cover beans completely. Chill about 1 hour only. Serve cold. (Instead of simple Vinaigrette, Ravigote Vinaigrette or Italian Dressing may be used.)

GREEN BEANS AND BLACK OLIVE SALAD. Marinate canned or cooked green beans as for Green Beans Vinaigrette, with thinly sliced onion and black olives (preferably Italian or Greek olives). Add to mixed greens just before serving.

Canned-tomato Salad

When locally grown tomatoes are not in season, canned peeled tomatoes may be served as a salad—but be sure you buy the best quality. Carefully remove the whole tomatoes from the juice (save the juice for other uses). Marinate ½ to 1 hour in Vinaigrette Sauce. Or add to Vinaigrette Sauce a dried-up lemon half, cut in quarters; heat in a small skillet with several parsley sprigs and about 1/3 cup olive oil until the lemon peel is browned. Strain while hot over the tomatoes. Grind black pepper over the tomatoes. Garnish tomatoes with wedges of hard-cooked egg,

Double Bean Salad

Marinate cooked lima beans and cooked whole or cut-up green beans in Vinaigrette or Italian dressing to which a pinch of curry has been added, for ½ to 1 hour. Add to mixed salad greens just before serving, along with green or black olives, pimiento strips, or chopped hard-cooked egg.

Greek Salad

1 small head bibb or iceberg lettuce
1 cup (approximately) chopped
curly endive
2 tomatoes, quartered
1 small white onion, thinly sliced
1 green pepper, seeded, chopped

1 cucumber, unpeeled, thinly
sliced
8 to 10 pitted black Greek olives
½ cup olive oil
Salt, pepper
2 tablespoons red wine vinegar

Tear lettuce and endive into small pieces. Arrange in salad
bowl with tomatoes, onion, green pepper, cucumber, and olives. Add olive oil. Toss to blend. Sprinkle with salt and pepper.
Toss again. Add vinegar, toss again. Serve immediately. *Makes
4 to 6 servings.*

Swiss Onion Salad

½ cup Vinaigrette or Lorenzo
Sauce or Italian dressing
1 teaspoon prepared mustard
1 medium yellow onion, thinly
sliced
½ pound imported Swiss cheese.

finely diced
About 2 cups lettuce
½ cup diced celery (optional)
1 tomato, cut in wedges
1 hard-cooked egg, sliced

Combine sauce or dressing with mustard; blend well. Marinate
onion and cheese in sauce 1 hour or longer. Arrange remaining
ingredients in salad bowl; keep chilled. Add sauce with onion
and cheese just before serving. Toss lightly. *Makes 4 entree
servings, or 6 to 8 side servings.*

Caesar Salad

4 slices stale white bread
2 cloves garlic, split
6 tablespoons olive oil
2 quarts lettuce or mixed greens,
torn in pieces
6 anchovy fillets, chopped

2 coddled or raw eggs
½ teaspoon salt, or to taste
½ teaspoon prepared mustard
½ cup grated Parmesan cheese
2 tablespoons vinegar

Cut bread into ½-inch cubes to form croutons. Heat garlic in 2
tablespoons of the olive oil until lightly browned; add bread;
sauté until golden on all sides. Remove bread and save. Discard
garlic. Place lettuce in large salad bowl, add anchovies, croutons, and the 2 tablespoons olive oil in which croutons were
sautéed. Break eggs into small bowl. Add to eggs remaining 4
tablespoons olive oil, salt, mustard, cheese, and vinegar. Beat
lightly to blend; add at once to lettuce; toss quickly and lightly
until no trace of egg can be seen. *Makes 8 servings.*

Winter Salad

2 large tart apples, peeled, seeded, chopped
1 stalk celery, minced
6 hazelnuts or walnuts, chopped
2 raw white turnips, peeled,
  chopped

½ green pepper, chopped
8 pitted dates, chopped
Pinch of curry powder
½ cup Vinaigrette or French
  Dressing
Iceberg lettuce

Combine apples, celery, nuts, turnips, green pepper, and dates. Stir curry powder into dressing; toss mixture with half the dressing. Marinate until needed. Arrange mounds of the salad mixture on crisp lettuce; pass remaining dressing. *Makes 6 to 8 servings.*

Waldorf Salad

2 cups diced red apples
  (unpeeled)
Lemon juice
½ cup diced celery

¼ cup coarsely chopped walnuts
5 tablespoons mayonnaise
1 tablespoon sour cream
Lettuce

Sprinkle diced apples with lemon juice to prevent discoloring. Add remaining ingredients (except lettuce); toss to blend. Serve on lettuce cups. *Makes 6 servings.*

ROQUEFORT-WALDORF. Prepare as for Waldorf Salad, but instead of mayonnaise use ¼ cup sour cream beaten until smooth with ¼ cup Roquefort cheese and a teaspoon of lemon juice.

Salade Niçoise

About 2 cups cooked or canned
  whole green beans, drained
2 small potatoes, cooked, peeled,
  diced
2 tomatoes, quartered
¼ cup sliced pimiento-stuffed

  olives
4 to 6 black olives, sliced
1 tablespoon capers
2 anchovy fillets, chopped
½ cup Vinaigrette Sauce
Lettuce

Combine first 6 ingredients in a bowl; add chopped anchovies to Vinaigrette Sauce; pour over vegetables. Marinate at room temperature 1 to 2 hours; toss to blend lightly. Arrange vegetables in mounds on lettuce, with olives, capers, and chopped anchovies over the top; sprinkle any sauce left in bottom of bowl over the vegetables. *Makes 4 to 6 servings.*

WITH TUNA OR SARDINES. For a first-course or entree salad, add 1 7-ounce can white-meat tuna (well drained) or 1 can Portuguese sardines (well drained) to salad on plates.

Macédoine Salad

1 package frozen peas, cooked 3 minutes
1 small onion, thinly sliced
3 small carrots, scraped, diced, cooked 3 minutes
½ cup Vinaigrette or French Dressing
1 cucumber partially peeled,
sliced
Salt, pepper
1 ripe avocado, sliced
Lettuce
1 1-pound can whole pickled beets, drained
1 hard-cooked egg, sliced

Place peas and half the onions in one bowl, the carrots and the rest of the onions in another. Marinate each mixture in ⅛ cup of the dressing for at least ½ hour (preferably longer). Sprinkle cucumber slices with salt. Let stand. Marinate the avocado in remaining dressing. During last hour before serving, arrange crisp lettuce cups on large platter. Place peas and onions in some of the cups, carrots and onion slices in others, beets in still others. Arrange cucumber, avocado, and egg slices in between the lettuce. Sprinkle with salt and pepper. Sprinkle dressing (left in bowls in which vegetables marinated) over all. Keep chilled and covered with plastic wrap until time to serve. An attractive buffet salad. *Makes 6 to 8 servings.*

Ribboned Vegetable Salad

3 cups shredded Savoy cabbage
2 cups shredded carrot, or finely sliced carrot sticks
½ cup sliced pimiento-stuffed green olives
1 lemon, thinly sliced, each slice cut in half

DRESSING
1 clove garlic
½ teaspoon salt
2 tablespoons fresh basil leaves or minced dill
½ cup minced fresh parsley
2 tablespoons lemon juice
½ cup olive oil

Arrange the shredded cabbage and carrots in alternate rows across a platter. Place the pimiento-stuffed sliced olives between the rows. Arrange the lemon slices round the edge or across the top. Cover the platter tightly with plastic wrap. Refrigerate until time to serve.

To make the dressing, crush the garlic clove with salt, add the basil or dill, then the parsley, mashing each to a paste. Add the lemon juice, then the olive oil. Beat to blend well. Pour half the dressing over the salad just before serving; pour the rest in a cruet, serve separately. *Makes about 8 servings.*

Cole Slaw with Cream Dressing

2 cups shredded cabbage
1 teaspoon salt
¼ teaspoon dry mustard
½ tablespoon sugar
1 to 1½ tablespoons vinegar, or to

taste
1½ tablespoons sour cream
1 tablespoon mayonnaise
Pimiento or green pepper strips
(optional)

To cut cabbage, either rub across the largest holes of a four-sided grater, or cut cabbage in half, place flat side down on a chopping board, and cut as thinly as possible with large French knife, then cut again across the grain so cabbage will be in very fine pieces. Sprinkle with salt; toss. Combine mustard, sugar, and vinegar (with 1 tablespoon vinegar to start). Add to cabbage. Finally add sour cream and mayonnaise and more vinegar, if desired. Chill. Serve cold, garnished (if desired) with pimiento or green pepper strips. *Makes 4 to 6 side servings.*

Cole Slaw with Poppy-seed Dressing

Shred 4 cups cabbage as instructed in previous recipe. Toss with ½ cup boiled dressing and 1 teaspoon poppy seeds. *Makes 8 generous servings.*

CARROT COLE SLAW. Combine 2 cups shredded cabbage with 1 carrot, coarsely grated, and 1 tablespoon chopped parsley. Add ¼ cup Boiled Dressing or mayonnaise. Sprinkle with celery salt and a dash of cayenne, if desired.

PINEAPPLE COLE SLAW. Shred 2 cups cabbage, add 1 cup well-drained crushed pineapple, ¼ cup minced green pepper, and 1 tablespoon minced fresh or frozen dill (or 1 teaspoon dill weed). Toss with ¼ cup Sour Cream-Mayonnaise or Boiled Dressing.

ROQUEFORT COLE SLAW. Shred 3 cups cabbage, add 1 tart apple, peeled and diced, and ¼ to 1/3 cup Blue Cheese-Cream Dressing. Garnish with pitted black olives.

MISSOURI COLE SLAW. Dress shredded cabbage with Missouri Cream Dressing, using ¼ cup dressing for 2 cups cabbage. Garnish with sliced pimiento-stuffed olives.

Wilted Lettuce

2 small heads garden or bibb lettuce
4 strips bacon
2 tablespoons vinegar

2 tablespoons water
1 tablespoon sugar (brown or
white)
Salt, pepper

Wash lettuce thoroughly; shake dry. Tear into pieces; place in porcelain or glass (not wooden) salad bowl. Cook bacon in skillet until crisp; remove; drain on absorbent paper. Add vinegar, water, sugar, salt, and pepper to bacon drippings; boil to reduce by about one-third. Add hot sauce to lettuce; toss until lettuce is wilted. Serve at once. Especially good with new potatoes and peas, to accompany cold roast beef. *Makes 4 to 6 servings.*

PORK CHOP SALAD. Omit bacon in above recipe. After pork chops have been pan-fried, remove and use the pan drippings from the chops for the fat. Or, instead of garden lettuce, spinach may be prepared with this same Pork Chop Dressing.

Mimosa Salad

1 pound fresh raw spinach
1 tablespoon grated onion
(optional)
½ cup Italian Dressing

6 slices bacon, cooked, crumbled
3 hard-cooked eggs
1 small cucumber, thinly sliced

Select very fresh spinach. Soak through several changes of water, to make sure all grit is removed. Shake to remove excess water. Break off stems. Crisp leaves by placing in vegetable crisper in refrigerator.

Add grated onion to dressing. Cook bacon; crumble; set aside in small bowl. Separate the hard-cooked eggs; sieve the yolks; place in a second small bowl. Mince the egg whites; add them to the dressing. When ready to serve, place spinach in salad bowl. Arrange bacon, sieved egg, and thinly sliced cucumber over spinach. Toss with dressing at table. *Makes 4 to 6 servings.*

Hot Potato Salad

2 pounds small new potatoes
1 pound lean bacon
3 onions, chopped

½ cup vinegar
Salt, pepper
10 hard-cooked eggs, quartered

Cook potatoes in their jackets until just tender. Drain; immediately cover with cold water. Peel as soon as cold enough to handle. Dice while warm.

While potatoes cook, fry bacon in a skillet. When crisp, remove and drain bacon on absorbent paper. Add onions to bacon fat; cook until soft and yellow. Add vinegar, salt, and pepper. Add this mixture to potatoes, toss quickly but lightly to blend. Serve warm, garnished with the cooked bacon slices and quartered hard-cooked eggs. Great for an outdoor fall barbecue with hamburgers and corn on the cob. *Makes about 10 servings.*

Sweet and Sour Potato Salad

8 medium potatoes, boiled
1 stalk celery, diced
2 hard-cooked eggs, chopped
2 or 3 scallions, minced
3 bread-and-butter pickles, diced
1 tablespoon minced parsley
4 slices bacon
2 eggs, well beaten

1 cup sugar
¼ teaspoon dry mustard
½ teaspoon salt
¼ teaspoon freshly ground black pepper
½ cup vinegar, diluted in ½ cup cold water

Boil potatoes in their jackets. When cooked but still warm, peel and dice. Add celery, hard-cooked eggs, minced scallions, chopped pickles, and parsley. Cook bacon until crisp. Drain, crumble. Add bacon to potato mixture. Beat eggs; add sugar, seasonings, and the vinegar diluted in water. Add egg mixture to hot bacon fat in skillet; stir constantly until thickened like mayonnaise. Pour over potato mixture and toss to mix lightly. *Makes 6 servings.*

Swedish Potato Salad

2 tart apples
4 potatoes, cooked, peeled
4 sweet gherkins, sliced
1 3½-ounce jar herring fillets, drained
1 tablespoon minced onion
1 tablespoon minced parsley

1/3 cup olive oil
Yolk of 1 hard-boiled egg
½ teaspoon salt
Freshly ground black pepper
2 tablespoons vinegar
1 medium can small whole beets

Core and thinly slice apples; slice potatoes. Add pickles, herring, onion and parsley, toss with 1 tablespoon of the olive oil. Mash egg yolk, add salt and pepper, beat in remaining olive oil until smooth and thick, then add vinegar. Add this sauce to potato-apple mixture. Serve shaped into a mound. Garnish with small whole beets and additional minced parsley. *Makes 4 to 6 servings.*

Midwestern Potato Salad

8 potatoes, cooked, peeled, diced   per
1 small onion, grated or minced   Freshly ground black pepper
1 teaspoon salt   ½ cup minced celery
¼ cup salad oil   ¼ cup vinegar
2 tablespoons minced green pep-   ¼ cup mayonnaise

Do not overcook potatoes. Combine all ingredients in the order given. Chill thoroughly. Serve with cold cuts and sliced tomatoes. *Makes 8 servings.*

FRENCH POTATO SALAD. Peel potatoes; cook whole (cut only very large ones in halves or quarters) until fork-tender. Drain. While still warm, cut in slices, then sprinkle with olive oil, salt, pepper, and a very little vinegar. Serve at room temperature (not chilled). If desired, sprinkle with minced parsley, chives, or dill.

Florida Shrimp and Potato Salad

1 envelope garlic salad dressing   lengthwise into 8 strips
   mix   1 avocado, peeled, cut into 8
¼ cup wine vinegar   wedges, sprinkled with lemon
2 tablespoons water   juice
2/3 cup olive oil   1 pound shelled shrimp, cooked
3 cups hot diced cooked potatoes   1 tablespoon capers
2 medium onions, minced   Cherry tomatoes, green or ripe
¼ cup chopped parsley   olives, green pepper rings, and
Boston or iceberg lettuce   watercress sprigs for garnish
1 medium cucumber, peeled, cut

Prepare salad dressing with vinegar, water, and oil as directed on envelope. Combine potatoes, onions, and parsley in bowl; toss with 1/3 cup of the dressing. Line a large oval platter with the lettuce; mound the potato salad in the center. Stand cucumber and avocado strips on end alternately around sides of mound. Arrange cooked shrimp over top; sprinkle capers over shrimp. Arrange garnishes around base of mound. Serve with remaining dressing. *Makes 4 to 6 entree servings.*

Danish Macaroni Salad

½ pound (8-ounce package) el-   1 cup mayonnaise
   bow macaroni, cooked   Few drops of lemon juice
1 1-pound 1-ounce can peas,   ½ teaspoon salt
   drained   Dash of white pepper
2 carrots, cooked and finely   ¾ to 1 teaspoon curry powder
   diced   1 teaspoon grated onion

To well-drained cooked macaroni, add drained peas and diced carrots. Blend mayonnaise with remaining ingredients; toss vegetables with this mixture. *Makes 8 cups salad—enough for 10 to 12 servings.*

See also Garbanzo Salad; other appetizer salads in Chapter 1, "Appetizers."

Mediterranean Bean Salad

1 1-pound can cannellini beans, or 2 cups cooked pea beans	¼ cup olive oil
¼ cup thinly sliced or minced onion	1 tablespoon lemon juice, or 2 tablespoons wine vinegar
1 or 2 cloves garlic, crushed	¾ cup minced parsley
	Salt to taste

Heat canned or cooked beans in their juice, then drain well. Add onion, garlic, and olive oil to warm beans. When cool, add lemon juice or vinegar and the parsley. Serve at room temperature. *Makes 4 servings.*

Viennese Rice Salad

3 cups cooked rice	½ cup minced parsley
1 clove garlic, crushed	4 tomatoes, cut in wedges
2 teaspoons paprika	Artichoke hearts
1 cup Vinaigrette Sauce	6 small radishes
2 teaspoons grated onion	Black olives
1 pimiento, chopped	

The rice should be fluffy, with every grain separate, but thoroughly chilled before sauce is added. Crush garlic in mixing bowl; add paprika, the sauce, and grated onion. Reserve ¼ cup sauce; pour remainder over rice. Add chopped pimiento and parsley to rice. Toss to blend. Marinate tomato wedges and artichoke hearts in remaining sauce. Serve rice in a mound, surrounded by tomato wedges, radishes, artichoke hearts, and olives. *Makes 4 to 6 servings.*

Curried Rice Salad

3 cups cooked rice	2 tablespoons minced green pepper
½ cup mayonnaise	1 tablespoon minced pimiento
1 teaspoon curry powder	¼ cup minced celery
1 teaspoon Dijon mustard	Orange sections
1 teaspoon grated onion	

Toss rice with all the ingredients except the orange sections, blending well. Serve on lettuce, shaped into a mound, with orange sections as garnish. *Makes 4 to 6 servings.*

Buffet Vegetable Platter

3 medium potatoes, peeled, cooked
3 carrots, cooked, cubed
1 or 2 zucchini, cooked
1 cup string beans, cooked
1 package frozen artichoke hearts, cooked
½ cup olive oil

¼ cup vinegar
1 teaspoon salt, or to taste
¼ teaspoon black pepper
1 tablespoon grated onion
¼ cup chopped stuffed olives
2 tablespoons minced parsley
1 tablespoon capers

All vegetables should be cooked until tender but still crisp. Drain; cool. Combine olive oil, vinegar, salt, pepper, and grated onion. Divide dressing among vegetables, marinating each vegetable separately. Shortly before dinner is to be served, arrange vegetables attractively on platter. Combine chopped olives, parsley, and capers and sprinkle over top. *Serves 8 to 10.*

Salad-stuffed Tomatoes

To prepare tomatoes for stuffing, cut off green stem end and scoop out insides, discarding seeds and more watery portions. Save firm solid pulp to use in filling.

Or, cut each tomato into 5 or 6 sections, cutting down far enough to spread out tomato in flower shape. Sprinkle with salt. Pile stuffing over the tomato "flowers." *Each of the following recipes makes enough stuffing for 8 large tomatoes.*

CURRIED CHICKEN STUFFING

2 cups chopped cooked chicken
1 cup minced celery
1 cup cooked rice
¼ cup pine nuts (pignoli) or chopped pecans
1 cup firm tomato pulp

1 teaspoon minced parsley
1 teaspoon curry powder
1 teaspoon salt
¼ cup olive or salad oil
2 tablespoons vinegar
1 tablespoon mayonnaise

Combine all ingredients, tossing lightly. Fill tomatoes; chill well before serving.

CRAB AND ASPARAGUS STUFFING

1 6½-ounce can crabmeat, gristle removed
1 small (10½-ounce) can white asparagus tips, drained, chopped
2 hard-cooked eggs, chopped
½ cup cooked tiny green peas

1 tablespoon oil
½ teaspoon salt, or to taste
Freshly ground black pepper
¼ teaspoon ground cumin
¼ cup mayonnaise
Few drops lemon juice

Chop larger pieces of crabmeat; combine all crabmeat with remaining ingredients in order given. Handle lightly to avoid breaking up crabmeat. Pile in or on tomatoes. Serve cold surrounded by pimiento-stuffed and black olives and crisp radishes.

AVOCADO AND CELERY STUFFING

2 large ripe avocados, peeled, diced	½ teaspoon salt, or to taste
1 cup diced celery	⅛ teaspoon cayenne
1 tablespoon minced onion	1 tablespoon mayonnaise
3 tablespoons olive oil	1 tablespoon minced parsley
1 tablespoon lemon juice	Tomato pulp

Combine avocados, celery, onion, and olive oil; toss so that avocado is well covered. Add lemon juice; toss again. Add remaining ingredients. Pile lightly in tomato cups or over tomato "flowers." Chill well before serving.

Fruit-filled Avocado

3 avocados	½ teaspoon salt
1 teaspoon lime juice	⅛ teaspoon freshly ground pepper
1 cup diced fresh pineapple	¼ teaspoon cumin
2 oranges, peeled, seeded, diced	1 teaspoon sugar
¼ cup olive oil	Dash of rum
1 tablespoon vinegar	

Cut fully ripe avocado in half; do not peel. Remove and discard pits; sprinkle exposed flesh with lime juice. Place pineapple and orange cubes in bowl. Make dressing of remaining ingredients; pour half of dressing over mixed fruit to marinate. Fill avocado halves with diced fruit; pass remaining dressing. *Makes 6 servings.*

Orange Baskets

4 large navel oranges	¾ cup sour cream
1½ cups large halved red grapes, seeded	¼ cup mayonnaise
	Orange juice
½ cup (2 ounces) crumbled Roquefort cheese	1/3 cup chopped pecans

Cut oranges into halves. Scoop out meat with sharp knife. Reserve shells. Slice a thin piece from the bottom of each shell so that it will stand flat on the plate. Cube orange meat and mix with seeded grape halves. Spoon mixture into orange cups, heaping high. Chill. Mix Roquefort with sour cream, mayonnaise, and enough orange juice to make mixture the consistency of heavy cream. Chill. When ready to serve, spoon Roquefort mixture over orange cups. Sprinkle tops with chopped nuts. Serve at once. *Makes 8 servings.*

FRUIT AND COTTAGE CHEESE SALAD. For each serving, place on an individual salad plate a canned peach or pear half, or a slice of canned pineapple. Place a spoonful of cottage cheese in the cavity. Spoon over each French Dressing, or Blue Cheese-Cream Dressing, or Curry Mayonnaise.

FRUIT SALAD WITH CHUTNEY-CHEESE BALLS. Soften an 8-ounce package of cream cheese at room temperature until it can be easily molded with the fingers. Add 1 tablespoon minced commercial chutney; blend well; roll into balls ¾ to 1 inch in diameter. Chill. Toast 1 cup grated or flaked coconut on a baking sheet until golden; roll the cream cheese balls in the coconut. Serve 1 cheese ball in the center of a canned peach or pear half or a slice of pineapple. Or, make smaller balls and use 2 for each serving; use as garnish for a salad of orange and grapefruit segments dressed with French Dressing, Spanish Dressing, or Curried French Dressing. *Makes enough for 6 to 8 servings.*

First-course Fruit Salads (Basic Recipe)

2 cups diced mixed fruit	Russian Dressing, or Curried
½ to ¾ cup Fruit Dressing, Chutney Mayonnaise, Sour Cream-	French Dressing
	Iceberg lettuce

Marinate the fruit in the dressing for 1 hour before serving. Serve fruit piled on lettuce cups. Recommended as a first course or a luncheon salad. *Makes 4 servings.*

CITRUS SALAD. Combine orange and grapefruit segments in equal proportions with a little minced green pepper; or lay pimiento strips over the top.

AVOCADO AND PAPAYA SALAD Combine 1 cup diced fully ripe papaya with 1 cup diced ripe avocado. Dress with Spanish Dressing, or a dressing of ¼ cup lime juice, ½ cup salad oil, salt, and pepper. (If papaya is not available, use diced cantaloupe.)

AVOCADO AND GRAPEFRUIT SALAD. Dice or slice avocado. Cover with Fruit Dressing or Curried French Dressing. Marinate until needed, then add grapefruit segments and, if desired, a few thin slices of onion.

CANTALOUPE SALAD. Combine diced cantaloupe with diced peaches or oranges and seeded Tokay or emperor grapes. Dress with Chutney Mayonnaise. Top each serving with a strawberry.

ORANGE, BANANA, AND NUT SALAD. Dice peeled oranges: combine with diced bananas, using a proportion of 2 parts oranges to 1 part bananas. Marinate in Curried French Dressing or Fruit Dressing. Sprinkle chopped peanuts, walnuts, or pecans over top of each serving.

Entree Salads

Green Goddess Salad

4 to 6 anchovy fillets, chopped
1 scallion (green onion), minced
1 clove garlic, crushed
¼ cup minced parsley
½ cup mayonnaise
¼ cup sour cream
½ teaspoon dried tarragon

2 tablespoons vinegar
2 cups diced cooked crabmeat, shrimp, lobster, chicken or a combination
1 large head romaine lettuce
Yolks of 2 hard-cooked eggs sieved

Mash together anchovies, scallion, and garlic with mortar and pestle or electric blender to form a paste. Add half the parsley; mash it into a paste. Transfer to mixing bowl; add remaining parsley, mayonnaise, sour cream, and the tarragon soaked in the vinegar. Beat until thoroughly blended. Marinate the seafood (or a mixture of seafood and chicken) in half the sauce. Remove coarse outer leaves of romaine; thoroughly wash remaining romaine, shake dry, then tear into bits. Toss the romaine with the remaining sauce. Serve seafood and sauce over the top. Garnish with sieved egg yolk. *Makes 6 entree servings.*

Crab Louis

2 large Dungeness crabs,
  cracked, shelled, or 1½ pounds
  crabmeat
1 cup mayonnaise
¼ cup heavy cream, whipped
¼ cup chili sauce
1 tablespoon grated onion

1 teaspoon minced parsley
Few drops lemon juice
1 head iceberg lettuce
¼ cup minced green pepper
4 tomatoes, cut in wedges
4 hard-cooked eggs, in wedges

If Dungeness crabs are used, chop the body meat and clean the legs (reserve the legs for garnish). Make sauce by combining mayonnaise with the whipped cream, chili sauce, onion, parsley, and lemon juice. Add half of this to diced crabmeat. Separate lettuce leaves; arrange on a platter or on individual plates. Place the crabmeat mixture over the lettuce. Arrange green pepper, tomato and egg wedges, and the reserved crab legs over the top. Spoon the remaining sauce over the salad. *Makes 6 entree servings.*

Mexican Chicken Salad

3½ cups diced cooked chicken or
  turkey
3 medium tomatoes, cut in
  wedges
1 large onion, thinly sliced
½ cup olive oil
¼ cup red wine vinegar
1 teaspoon salt

½ teaspoon freshly ground black
  pepper
1 small crisp head lettuce
2 oranges, peeled, sliced
2 avocados, peeled, sliced and
  sprinkled with lemon juice
1 bunch small radishes, trimmed

Toss together diced chicken or turkey, tomatoes, and onion with a dressing of olive oil, vinegar, salt, and pepper. Shred half the lettuce; add shredded lettuce to chicken mixture. Arrange remaining lettuce leaves on platter, fill with salad mixture, and garnish with the orange and avocado slices and the small whole radishes. *Makes 8 entree servings.*

Meat and Potato Salad

Iceberg lettuce
4 or 5 large slices rare roast beef,
  cut in thin slivers
2 cups tender whole green beans,
  cooked
3 medium potatoes, cooked,
  peeled, diced
½ cup garlic-flavored French

Dressing
¼ cup mayonnaise
4 slices crisp cooked bacon,
  crumbled
4 anchovy fillets, drained,
  minced
2 hard-cooked eggs, sliced

Separate lettuce leaves, use the best-shaped leaves as a base for the salad. Shred remaining lettuce, place in center. Over the lettuce arrange in bundles the roast beef, green beans, and the diced potatoes (previously marinate the potatoes in a little of the dressing to prevent discoloring). Beat together remaining French dressing and the mayonnaise. Combine bacon and anchovies; sprinkle over the top. Arrange egg slices around the edges. Keep salad chilled until time to serve, then bring to table with the dressing; toss at table. *Makes 4 entree servings.*

Chef's Salad

1 head iceberg lettuce	1 cup Swiss cheese, cut in slivers
2 cups romaine or Chinese cabbage, shredded	8 to 10 small radishes
	1 or 2 tomatoes, cut in wedges
1 cup cooked chicken or turkey, cut in slivers	2 hard-cooked eggs, cut in wedges
1 cup tenderized cooked ham, cut in slivers	1 cup Vinaigrette, Ravigote Vinaigrette, or Italian Dressing

Separate lettuce into cups, shred the inner part of the lettuce, and combine with the shredded romaine. Make a bed of this in a very large salad bowl. Over the greens, arrange the chicken, ham, and cheese in separate bundles. Arrange the radishes, tomato, and egg wedges between these bundles. Toss with the prepared dressing at table.

Other possible ingredients: Use slivers of salami instead of ham, add a sliced avocado (marinated in part of the dressing to avoid discoloring), or add slivers of green pepper, or artichoke hearts. *Makes 6 to 8 entree servings.*

Ensalada Mixta

1 7-ounce can white-meat tuna, drained	¼ cup mayonnaise
	2 tablespoons olive oil
1 cup cooked green peas	1 teaspoon lemon juice
1 cup very thinly sliced celery	Salt
3 or 4 slices onion	Salad greens
¼ cup cooked ham cut in thin slivers	Tomato or egg wedges
	Black or green olives

In a bowl combine tuna, peas, celery, onion, and ham. Blend mayonnaise with olive oil, lemon juice, and salt; add to salad ingredients; toss lightly. Serve on salad greens with tomato wedges and olives as garnish. *Makes 6 to 8 servings.*

Viennese Lobster Salad

An impressive party salad, easier to prepare than an aspic.

1½ cups Italian or Spanish
  Dressing
6 7-ounce lobster tails
1 cup tiny peas or lima beans,
  cooked
½ cup diced cooked carrots
2 cups diced cooked potatoes

½ cup mayonnaise
1 tablespoon capers
1 pimiento, cut in strips
Sliced stuffed olives
Lettuce leaves, radishes, and
  carrot curls for garnish

First mix dressing to marry flavors. Partially defrost lobster tails. Cut away undershell; pull flesh partially away from outer shell. Cook in simmering (not boiling) water until shells are bright red and flesh snowy white—about 10 minutes. When cool, carefully remove meat from shell to preserve red-veined steaks. Cut into slices, saving the most attractive pieces for garnish, and finely dice the remainder. Marinate diced lobster, peas, and carrots in ½ to 1 cup of the dressing. Toss potatoes with remaining dressing while hot; marinate in dressing ½ hour; drain off excess. Combine potatoes and minced vegetable-lobster mixture; toss lightly with mayonnaise and capers. Pile 1 tablespoon mixture at a time on round platter, mounting high. Arrange reserved lobster slices, pimiento strips, and olive slices around top. Cover with plastic wrap. When ready to serve, place lettuce leaves, radishes, and carrot curls around sides for garnish. *Makes 12 servings.*

MOLDED CRAB SALAD. Use 1½ pounds crabmeat instead of lobster in above recipe.

Galician Seafood Salad

2 7-ounce rock lobster tails,
  cooked
3 hard-cooked eggs, chopped
2 gherkins, chopped
1 medium onion, thinly sliced
½ pound shelled shrimp,
  cooked, chopped
12 capers
4 tablespoons olive oil

2 tablespoons wine vinegar
1 tablespoon dry sherry
½ teaspoon sharp mustard
2 tablespoons mayonnaise
Salt, pepper, cayenne
Salad greens
2 canned pimientos, cut in strips
2 lemons, quartered

Carefully remove the lobster meat from the shell, so as to preserve the bright red color of the back. Dice lobster; add remaining ingredients except the last three, toss lightly to blend. Serve over salad greens, garnish with strips of pimiento, and a lemon wedge for each serving. *Makes 8 servings.*

Gelatin Salads and Aspics

Molded salads and gelatin aspics have the advantage of remaining fresh and pretty-looking for hours—at least for as long as they remain in the refrigerator and (except in very warm weather) for several hours at room temperature after removing from the refrigerator. For buffets, when a large number of people are expected and the work of preparation must be spaced over one or more days, this can make a great difference.

Still another advantage of gelatin salads is that often they are more acceptable to children than tossed salads, especially those salads that combine fruits and vegetables and are served with sweetened mayonnaise or cream dressings.

Some fruit salad molds may be served either as salads or as desserts. Most of the following are more suitable as salads.

For hints on using gelatin (how to speed jellying, how to unmold, which molds to use, and so on), see index.

Tomato Aspic

4 cups tomato juice (2 1-pint cans)
½ teaspoon instant minced onion
2 bay leaves
4 whole peppercorns
3 cardamom seeds, or ⅛ teaspoon ground nutmeg or mace
½ teaspoon salt
Pinch of cayenne
2 3-ounce packages or 1 6-ounce package lemon-flavored gelatin

Heat 2 cups of the tomato juice to boiling with the onion and seasonings. Simmer covered 5 minutes; strain. Add strained juice to gelatin, stir until dissolved. Add remaining 2 cups tomato juice. Pour into 1-quart mold or 8 x 8-inch pan. Chill until firm; unmold. If chilled in square pan, cut into cubes to serve; serve on watercress or lettuce. If chilled in 1-quart ring mold, fill center with cottage cheese, chicken or shrimp salad, or Blue Cheese-Cream Dressing. *Makes 8 servings.*

Perfection Salad

1 envelope unflavored gelatin
2 to 4 tablespoons sugar
½ teaspoon salt
1 ¼ cups water
¼ cup mild vinegar

1 teaspoon lemon juice
¾ cup finely shredded cabbage
1 cup chopped celery
1 pimiento, chopped, or 2 table-
    spoons chopped green pepper

Place gelatin, sugar and salt in a saucepan. Add water; stir over low heat until gelatin and sugar are dissolved. Remove from heat; add vinegar and lemon juice. Chill until thickened to consistency of unbeaten egg white. Fold in cabbage, celery, and pimiento or green pepper. Pour into a 1-quart mold or 6 individual ¾-cup molds. Chill until firm; unmold. Serve on lettuce with mayonnaise, Sour Cream Mayonnaise, or Russian Dressing. *Makes 6 servings.*

QUICK BLENDER METHOD. Place in blender 1 package lemon-flavored gelatin and 1 cup hot water (omit sugar); beat 20 seconds. Add ¾ cup cold water, vinegar, and coarsely chopped vegetables. Beat until vegetables are finely chopped. Proceed as above.

Golden Glow Salad

1 3-ounce package lemon-
    flavored gelatin
½ teaspoon salt
1½ cups hot water
¾ cup well-drained crushed

    pineapple
1/3 cup pineapple juice
1 tablespoon lemon juice
1 cup grated raw carrot

Dissolve gelatin and salt in hot water; add pineapple with juice and the lemon juice. Chill until syrupy. Fold in carrots. Pour into 8 x 8-inch pan. Chill until very firm—about 3 hours. Unmold. Cut into squares. Serve on lettuce or watercress with mayonnaise or Sour Cream Mayonnaise. *Makes 6 servings.*

Spiced Peaches in Jelly

1 1-pound can cling peach halves
¼ cup vinegar
6 whole cloves
1 stick cinnamon

¾ cup water
1 3-ounce package lemon- or
    raspberry-flavored gelatin

Drain peaches; set aside. Combine ¾ cup of the peach syrup with vinegar, cloves, cinnamon, and ¾ cup water. Bring to a boil; cover; simmer 5 minutes. Add mixture through a strainer to gelatin in bowl. Stir until dissolved; pour into 8 x 8-inch pan. Chill until syrupy. Place peach halves in gelatin, rounded side up. Chill until very firm. When firm, unmold; cut around the peach halves in squares. Serve as an accompaniment to roast pork or ham with Creamed Cottage Cheese or Sour Cream-Horseradish Sauce. *Makes 6 servings.*

Ginger Ale-Fruit Mold

2 envelopes unflavored gelatin
½ cup lemon juice
½ cup sugar
½ teaspoon salt
1½ cups hot fruit juice (orange

or canned pineapple)
1 14-ounce bottle ginger ale
2 cups chopped fruit*
¼ cup chopped pecans or walnuts

Place gelatin, lemon juice, sugar, and salt in saucepan; add hot juice; stir constantly until gelatin dissolves (or place in blender and beat 20 seconds). Add ginger ale; chill until syrupy. Stir in chopped fruit and nuts. Pour into 1-quart ring mold. Chill until very firm. Unmold. Fill center with Creamed Cottage Cheese or a dressing made of equal parts whipped cream and mayonnaise. *Makes 6 to 8 servings.*

*Fruit may be all chopped canned peaches; or a mixture of peaches, diced pineapple, and seeded grape halves; or diced oranges, banana, and pineapple; or strawberry and oranges. This may serve as either salad or dessert.

Pickled Beet Ring

1 package lemon-flavored gelatin
1 cup boiling water
¾ cup beet juice
2 tablespoons vinegar
1 tablespoon horseradish
½ teaspoon salt

2 tablespoons grated onion
1 1-pound can pickled beets,
 drained
¾ cup diced celery
¼ cup finely chopped apple
Lettuce

Dissolve gelatin in boiling water; add beet juice, vinegar, horseradish, salt, and onion. Cool until consistency of egg white. Chop drained beets and add them with the celery and apple to the gelatin mixture. Stir to distribute evenly. Pour into 1-quart ring mold. Chill in refrigerator until very firm. Unmold on lettuce. Serve plain or fill center with cottage cheese, Sour Cream-Horseradish Sauce, or Chicken Salad. If Chicken Salad is used, serve with the following Chicken Salad Dressing. *Makes 6 to 8 servings.*

Chicken Salad Dressing

1 cup hot chicken broth
½ cup vinegar
5 egg yolks, well beaten
2 tablespoons prepared mustard
1 tablespoon salt

¼ teaspoon freshly ground
   black pepper
Pinch of cayenne
½ cup heavy cream
6 tablespoons butter

Add hot chicken broth to vinegar, then stir broth slowly into beaten egg yolks, beating constantly with whisk until thoroughly blended. Add seasonings; cook mixture on top of double boiler, stirring constantly until mixture thickens. Add the cream and butter; stir briskly until butter has melted. Cool. *Makes 2 cups.*

Chicken and Pineapple Mold

1 envelope unflavored gelatin
½ cup cold water
1 cup chicken broth, heated to
   boiling
½ teaspoon salt
1 tablespoon lemon juice
¼ cup syrup drained from

   pineapple
1½ cups diced cooked chicken
½ cup drained crushed pineapple
¼ cup diced celery
¼ cup minced green pepper or
   pimiento

Soften gelatin in cold water. Stir in boiling hot chicken broth; stir until dissolved. Add salt, lemon juice, and pineapple syrup. Chill until syrupy. Combine chicken, pineapple, celery, and green pepper; stir into gelatin. Turn into 4-quart mold. Chill until firm. Unmold; serve with Curry Mayonnaise or Chutney Mayonnaise. *Makes 6 servings.*

Weight Watcher's Chicken-stuffed Tomatoes in Aspic

1 envelope unflavored gelatin
¼ cup cold water
1½ cups hot chicken broth
8 large tomatoes
Salt
1½ cups diced cooked chicken or

   turkey
½ cup minced celery
16 pimiento-stuffed olives
Cumin, pepper
2 hard-cooked eggs, sliced

Soften the gelatin in the cold water; dissolve in hot broth. Scoop centers from tomatoes, discarding seeds. Chop more solid portions of tomato pulp, sprinkle with salt. Add to diced chicken, celery, and half the olives, chopped. Season mixture to taste with salt, pepper, and cumin or other desired seasonings. Spoon a little of the gelatin into each tomato. Add enough chicken mixture to fill almost to top; spoon more gelatin over the chicken, then add enough more chicken to fill completely. Place tomatoes on rack over baking sheet; spoon gelatin over outside of tomatoes as well as over the stuffing. Chill until partially set. Place a slice of egg on each stuffed tomato; glaze with gelatin; chill until partially set. Add sliced olives around the egg; glaze with gelatin and chill until completely set. When firm, unmold and serve on lettuce, with Low-calorie Dressing (or no dressing at all), for a dieter's luncheon entree. *Makes 8 servings.*

Soufflé Salad (Basic Recipe)

1 package lemon-flavored gelatin
1 cup hot water
½ cup cold water
2 tablespoons vinegar
½ cup mayonnaise, or ½ cup sour cream

Salt, pepper
2 cups diced or sliced vegetables, or chopped chicken or fish, or a mixture of vegetables, meat, and nuts

Dissolve gelatin in hot water; add cold water, vinegar, mayonnaise or sour cream, and salt and pepper to taste. Beat with rotary beater until smooth. Pour into refrigerator freezing tray; chill in freezer until firm 1 inch from edge—15 to 20 minutes. Turn into bowl; beat until fluffy. Fold in remaining ingredients; turn into 1-quart mold. Chill in refrigerator (not freezer) until very firm. Unmold. Garnish with fresh fruit or crisp vegetable relishes. Serve as a luncheon or buffet entree. *Makes 6 to 8 servings.*

SHERRIED CHICKEN SOUFFLÉ SALAD. Prepare as in basic recipe, but use ½ cup medium sweet sherry instead of cold water, and sour cream rather than mayonnaise; fold into the fluffy gelatin mixture 1½ cups finely minced chicken, ¼ cup chopped nut meats or shredded coconut, and ¼ cup minced celery or green pepper.

SALMON MOUSSE. Prepare as in basic recipe, using a mixture of Homemade Mayonnaise and sour cream. Add to the souffléed gelatin 1½ cups flaked cooked or canned salmon, 1 tablespoon capers, ¼ cup minced celery, and ¼ cup minced pimiento. Season with a pinch of fennel, if desired.

10 EGGS AND CHEESE

These two high-protein foods have much in common. Both can be kept on hand for snacks whenever needed; both can be used (separately or together) to make quick inexpensive luncheon or supper dishes; both are near-perfect food nutritionally.

Review Buying and Storage Guides relating to eggs and cheese, Book 1; also, review the role of eggs and cheese in nutrition in Book 2. For those on special diets, remember that egg whites are lower in calories than egg yolks and are fat-free, and the least fat of the cheeses are cottage and pot cheese and firm cheeses made partially of skimmed milk. (See Glossary of the World's Cheeses.)

EGGS

Eggs for breakfast, eggs for lunch, hard-boiled and deviled eggs for snacks, soufflés for dinner, and a flaming rum omelet for a fancy dessert—the egg belongs to everybody.

Tips on Egg Cookery

•Always cook eggs at low heat or over water. Only exceptions: shirred eggs (the French call them *oeufs sur le plat*), which are baked in hot oven just until the whites are firm, the yolks still soft.

•When you think of it in time, remove eggs from the refrigerator ½ hour before using. The shells of hard-cooked eggs are less likely to break; uncooked eggs will separate more easily; egg whites will beat to greater volume.

•If the white of the egg is cloudy and the yolk promptly breaks into shreds, the egg isn't fresh. Better throw it out.

•Whenever a hot mixture is to be combined with beaten eggs or egg yolks, *always* beat a little of the hot mixture first into the egg, then add the egg to the rest of the hot mixture, beating constantly until smooth and thickened.

•When you have an excess of egg whites (after preparing a recipe calling for yolks only) here are possible solutions:

1. Use whites instead of whole eggs in batters, meat loaf, meatballs, or for breading.
2. Make them into meringue, to top chocolate or butterscotch pie made with mix, or meringue shells to hold fruit or ice cream.
3. Brush egg white over bottom of pastry shell before adding a custard-type filling, to prevent the filling from soaking into the pastry.
4. Brush over outside of sweet yeast breads for a glossier, more golden crust.

•Leftover egg whites may be kept in a clean, tightly covered jar or refrigerator dish for 1 week.

"Boiled" Eggs

Boiled eggs should never be actually boiled. Observe these cardinal rules:

•Examine each egg shell before placing in water (hot or cold). If there is the slightest crack, use the egg for other purposes.

•If possible, remove from refrigerator ½ hour before cooking. When this is not possible, hold each egg under warm running water to warm the shells gradually (otherwise hot water on cold shells may cause cracking).

•Never let the water boil, only simmer very gently. Boiling water may cause the shell to crack and also toughens the egg white.

•If, despite all precautions, you remove the lid to find one or more eggs cracked and the insides spilled out, don't be upset. **Some eggs are too utterly fragile, or there may have been a** crack you didn't notice. It's tough luck, but there's nothing much to do but throw the ruptured egg away.

•Large eggs require longer cooking time than small eggs: those eggs previously warmed to room temperature require less cooking time than those that are refrigerator-cold. That's why the following cooking times are variable.

•To remove the shells of *hard-cooked* eggs, leaving a neat, unbroken surface, first cool the cooked eggs in cold water until the shell is completely cold, then crack the shell lightly, roll the egg between your hands, and start peeling at the large end.

COLD-WATER METHOD. Place eggs in pan with cold water to cover; bring water to a rapid boil; cover pan; turn off heat. *Coddled eggs* should be left in hot water 1 minute; *soft-cooked eggs,* 2 to 4 minutes, depending on how soft you like them. *Hard-cooked eggs* should be left covered in hot water 15 to 20 minutes, depending on size of egg (the larger the longer).

BOILING-WATER METHOD. Fill saucepan half full of water; bring water to a rapid boil. Lower eggs into water one at a time, in a slotted spoon. Turn heat as low as possible; cover pan. For *soft-boiled eggs,* simmer 2 minutes; turn off heat; let stand 1 to 2 minutes longer. For *hard-boiled eggs,* simmer gently 10 minutes; turn off heat; let stand 5 to 10 minutes longer, depending on size of egg. For *coddled eggs,* turn off heat as soon as eggs are added to water; turn off heat; cover; let stand 2 minutes only.

Creamed Eggs (Basic Recipe)

Hard-cook eggs, allowing 1 or 2 per serving. Shell; cut in quarters. Separately prepare Béchamel Sauce or Quick Velouté Sauce, using 1 cup sauce for 4 eggs. Add eggs to sauce; serve on toast or in a rice ring as the entree for a meatless meal, accompanied by Frenched Green Beans and Broiled Tomatoes, or Glazed Carrots.

CREAMED HAM AND EGGS. For 2 servings use 2 hard-cooked eggs, quartered, and ½ to ¾ cup diced ham in 1 cup Quick Velouté or Cheese Sauce. Add a tablespoon of chopped pimiento, or chopped chives or dill, if desired.

CREAMED EGGS À LA KING. Sauté a few slices of onion, about 2 tablespoons each chopped green pepper and pimiento, and 1 tablespoon minced parsley in 1 tablespoon butter or margarine. Add a can of condensed cream of chicken or celery soup, ¼ cup light cream or homogenized milk, 4 hard-cooked eggs, quartered, and a small (2-ounce) can button mushrooms with liquid. Simmer about 5 minutes; serve with rice. *Makes 2 to 3 servings.*

CREAMED CHICKEN AND EGGS. Prepare like creamed Ham and Eggs, but use ½ to ¾ cups diced chicken or turkey instead of ham. Add a pinch of curry powder, cumin, or ginger, if desired.

CREAMED TUNA AND EGGS. Sauté 2 tablespoons minced onion, ¼ cup celery, and 2 tablespoons chopped green pepper or pimiento in 1 tablespoon butter until soft. Add 2 cups any desired sauce (Quick Velouté, Cheese-Celery, Quick Soubise, or Celery-Horseradish Sauce), a 7-ounce can tuna, well drained, and 4 to 6 hard-cooked eggs, quartered. Heat thoroughly. Serve with rice or noodles for a quick, easy family supper. *Makes 4 to 6 servings.*

EGGS IN CURRY-CREAM SAUCE. Prepare as in basic recipe, but add ¼ to ½ teaspoon curry powder to sauce. (The curried sauce is also good with all the other variations.)

See also Stuffed Eggs and variations.

Poached Eggs (Basic Recipe)

   These are simply soft-cooked eggs which are shelled before cooking. A shallow wide saucepan is best for cooking them: combine water to a depth of 2 inches with ½ teaspoon salt and a teaspoon vinegar. Heat water until small bubbles appear on surface, but do not allow to boil. Break each egg first into a cup or small bowl (to make sure the yolk does not break), then slip gently into the simmering water. Simmer at lowest heat from 3 to 5 minutes until the egg white is snowy; push straggly ends toward the solid egg. Remove one at a time with a slotted spoon. Serve on buttered toast.

OTHER USES FOR POACHED EGGS. To top Corned Beef Hash, or for Beefsteak à la Mayer (instead of Fried Eggs), or with Eggs a la Cubana.

Eggs Benedict

1 recipe Hollandaise Sauce   4 slices toast, or 2 toasted English
4 slices ham   muffins, split
1 to 2 tablespoons butter or mar-   4 poached eggs
garine

First prepare the Hollandaise; keep warm in top of double boiler over warm (not hot) water. Sauté the ham in butter until lightly browned on one side. Place a slice of ham on each piece of toast or muffin. Poach the eggs as in basic recipe. Place a Poached Egg on each slice of ham. Cover with Hollandaise Sauce. Serve immediately for brunch or lunch. *Makes 4 servings.*

"Fried" Eggs

Fried eggs should never be actually fried; they should be either sautéed gently or steamed over low heat.

SUNNY SIDE UP. Melt butter or margarine in a skillet (a 10-inch skillet for 4 eggs, a 6- or 7-inch skillet for 1 egg), enough to moisten the surface generously. For 4 eggs, use 1 to 2 tablespoons,fat; for a single fried egg, use 2 to 3 teaspoons. As soon as butter is melted, gently slip 1 egg at a time into the skillet. Sprinkle salt over top. Cook over *low heat* until white is firm but still tender, and yolk is glazed over but still soft. Baste occasionally with butter in pan (tilt pan slightly so butter will run to one side). Remove with pancake turner or spatula.

ONCE OVER LIGHTLY. Prepare eggs as for Sunny Side Up, but use more butter or margarine (about 1 tablespoon per egg) and cook the eggs more firm—the edges may curl slightly. When lightly browned on the bottom, lift up with a spatula and turn over. (If necessary, add more butter to pan before turning over, to prevent sticking.) Cook about 10 seconds, then slip out of the skillet onto a warm plate.

SKILLET-STEAMED EGGS. Melt butter in skillet as for eggs Sunny Side Up, gently add eggs to skillet, sprinkle salt over top, then *cover the skillet tightly.* Cook over lowest heat just until white is translucent. Slip out of the pan with a spatula. Baste eggs with any butter left in pan. These are much more tender and delicate than eggs Sunny Side Up, almost like Poached Eggs..

BACON AND EGGS. Allow 2 slices of bacon for each serving. Cook bacon in a skillet until crisp on both sides, or broil in broiler oven until crisp, without turning. If cooked in skillet, drain off *all* the bacon fat, add a tablespoon or two of butter, and break eggs into the pan. Cook Sunny Side Up, Once Over Lightly, or skillet-steam the eggs, as preferred. Serve eggs with bacon on the side.

HAM AND EGGS. Allow 1 small slice of ham for each serving. Sauté the ham in butter or margarine until lightly browned on one side; turn; lower heat. Break eggs into skillet on top of ham. Sprinkle eggs very lightly with salt (and, if desired, a pinch of curry). Cover skillet. Cook until white of eggs is translucent. Use pancake turner or spatula to remove, slipping out so that each piece of ham is topped with an egg.

Skillet Eggs and Cheese

2 tablespoons butter or olive oil	4 eggs
4 very thin slices Swiss or Provo-lone cheese	Salt, pepper
	Toast

Melt butter in 10-inch skillet. Place slices of cheese in the butter; lower heat. Break eggs over the cheese. Sprinkle with salt and pepper. Cover skillet; cook just until whites of eggs are set. Carefully cut the eggs and cheese to separate, then remove from pan one by one with pancake turner. Serve on or with toast. *Makes 2 to 4 servings, depending on appetites.*

Rice a la Cubana

4 cups hot cooked rice	2 tablespoons butter
8 slices bacon	4 eggs
2 large bananas, peeled, quartered	¼ teaspoon salt

Prepare rice. Cook bacon until crisp; drain on paper towel. In separate pan, sauté the bananas in butter until golden; remove carefully. Break eggs gently into same pan in which bananas were sautéed. Sprinkle with salt; cover pan; turn off heat; cook eggs in retained heat of pan until whites are set, yolks still soft. Pile rice on each of four serving plates; arrange bananas and bacon around rice on each plate, place an egg on top of each serving of rice. The soft egg yolk is like a sauce when mixed with the rice. An excellent brunch or luncheon dish needing only salad or fresh fruit and a beverage to complete the menu. *Serves 4.*

WITH CURRIED BANANAS. If desired, sprinkle bananas with a mixture of ½ teaspoon each sugar and curry powder as they are sautéed.

Scrambled Eggs

There are three ways of scrambling eggs:

FRENCH METHOD

4 eggs, beaten	2 tablespoons milk
¼ teaspoon salt	1 to 2 tablespoons butter

Beat eggs with a fork just until whites and yolks are blended. Add salt and milk. Melt butter in an omelet pan or small skillet with sloping sides; tilt pan so butter covers entire surface. Pour in egg mixture; as soon as egg starts to firm, lift up and over and continue to turn until all liquid is firm (this is much like a French omelet, except that the egg is turned over continuously, so it is fluffier than an omelet). *Serves 2 or 3.*

AMERICAN METHOD

5 eggs	Freshly ground black pepper
½ cup milk	1 to 2 tablespoons butter
½ teaspoon salt	

Beat eggs just until whites are blended with yolks. Add milk, salt, and pepper. Heat butter in omelet pan or skillet until melted. Pour in egg mixture. Cook, turning up constantly with a spatula, until consistency is creamy. *Serves 3 or 4.*

IN-THE-PAN METHOD

Melt 1 or 2 tablespoons of butter in a skillet (not an omelet pan); break eggs right into the skillet, sprinkle with salt and pepper, then stir with fork before eggs can set, until all liquid is firm. (My principal objection to this method is that the pan is such a mess to wash afterward, whereas when eggs are scrambled the French way is a well-seasoned omelet pan, the pan usually need not be washed at all, only rubbed dry with paper towel.)

Scrambled Eggs and Tomatoes

2 tablespoons butter	Salt, pepper
1 medium tomato, peeled, chopped	2 to 3 eggs, beaten

Melt the butter in a 7- or 8-inch skillet; add the tomatoes; cook until soft and lightly browned; sprinkle with salt and pepper.

Add the beaten eggs; lift up and over continuously with spatula until egg is firm and well blended with tomato. Serve immediately. *Makes 2 servings.*

ITALIAN-STYLE SCRAMBLED EGGS. Sprinkle chopped tomato, as eggs cook, with a pinch of orégano.

SCRAMBLED EGGS WITH CHEESE AND TOMATOES. Prepare as for Scrambled Eggs and Tomatoes, but add 2 tablespoons grated or shredded cheese to the beaten eggs.

SCRAMBLED EGGS WITH FRIED TOMATOES. Instead of chopping the tomato, use 2 tomatoes; slice thickly; sprinkle both sides of each slice with salt, pepper, and a pinch each of orégano and thyme. Sauté the tomato slices over low heat until lightly browned on each side. Remove; keep warm. Scramble eggs in the same pan according to any of the three methods suggested in the basic recipe, using 4 eggs for 2 or 3 servings.

Scrambled Eggs and Avocado

1 ripe avocado, peeled, finely diced	1 tablespoon milk
2 tablespoons butter	¼ teaspoon salt
4 eggs, beaten	Freshly ground black pepper
	Pinch of curry (optional)

Sauté the diced avocado in butter until lightly browned. Combine eggs, milk, salt, pepper, and curry; blend well. Pour egg mixture over avocado; lift up and over with spatula until egg is firm. *Serves 2 or 3.*

Omelets

There are many types of omelet, from the simple individual French omelet, which is rolled over and out of the pan, to larger stuffed French omelets, to puffy or soufflé omelets, and finally the Spanish-type omelet, which is a mixture of vegetables and sometimes meat held together with egg. Chinese Foo Yong is also an omelet, similar to the Spanish type, but made in pancake size and served with a sauce. Pipérade, which is sometimes described as Basque-style scrambled eggs, is very much like a Spanish omelet, that is, filled with peppers, onion, ham, and sometimes tomato.

A certain dexterity must be utilized in getting any type of omelet to slip out of the pan easily and all in one piece, but there is nothing really mysterious or difficult about it. The type of pan used is important: for a delicate French omelet, it is wise to have a well-seasoned omelet pan, and to use this *only* for French omelets, skillet-steamed eggs, and plain scrambled eggs.

Do *not* use such an omelet pan for a Spanish-type omelet, for sautéing foods in the pan will later cause the French omelets to stick. For the Spanish-type omelet, any skillet will do, though one with sloping sides is easier to manage.

Classic French Omelet

3 eggs
¼ teaspoon salt
1 tablespoon butter

1 tablespoon heavy cream (optional)

For an omelet of this size, a 7-inch omelet pan should be used. Use only the freshest eggs. First break each egg into a small bowl, to be sure of freshness. Add salt to the eggs; beat with fork just until whites are blended through yolks. Melt butter in the pan but do not permit it to sizzle. Tilt pan so that butter covers entire bottom and part of the sides. Lower heat; add the beaten eggs; tilt pan so egg mixture covers entire bottom of pan (liquid egg should be no more than ¼ inch deep). As egg firms, lift up sides gently with spatula and tilt pan again so that liquid egg runs under. Lift up gently with spatula to loosen. When bottom seems firm throughout but omelet is still creamy-soft on top, place a spoonful of heavy cream in center if desired, and fold over omelet. Slip out onto warm porcelain plate or small platter. Serve immediately. *Makes 2 servings.*

OMELETTE AUX FINES HERBES. Prepare exactly like the Classic French Omelet, but add to beaten eggs 1 tablespoon minced fresh parsley, or a mixture of minced parsley and other fresh (never dried) herbs.

OMELETTE AU FROMAGE. Prepare as for individual French Omelet, but after egg has begun to firm sprinkle about 2 tablespoons shredded Cheddar or Swiss cheese over top. Cheese will melt by the time omelet is folded over.

Stuffed French Omelet (Basic Recipe)

This must be a larger omelet, and so a larger pan must be used, but it should be one with sloping sides for greater dexterity in slipping the omelet out of the pan. If it is not possible or desirable to keep special omelet pans in two sizes in the kitchen, this larger omelet may be made in a Teflon-coated 10-inch skillet, preferably one with sloping sides.

6 eggs	2 to 3 tablespoons butter
½ teaspoon salt	Filling as desired (see varia-
1 tablespoon cream	tions)

Beat eggs with rotary beater until thoroughly mixed. Add salt and cream; stir to blend thoroughly. Melt butter in skillet, tilting so that surface is well covered. Add egg mixture, cook over lowered heat until egg begins to firm, then gently lift up sides with spatula and tilt to allow moist egg to run under. Loosen with spatula so that it does not stick at any point. When omelet is firm and starting to turn golden underneath, spread the filling over one half of the omelet. With spatula, fold over the other half, with the filling inside the "pocketbook" shape. Slide out onto warm platter. *Makes 4 servings.*

TOMATO OR "SPANISH" OMELET. Before starting to cook the omelet, make a tomato sauce as follows: Sauté in 1 tablespoon butter 2 to 3 tablespoons chopped onion and about 2 tablespoons minced celery or green pepper. Peel and chop 3 large ripe tomatoes; add to pan. (Or, use 1 cup canned tomato sauce; cook until reduced to ¾ cup.) Sprinkle with salt, pepper, and a pinch of thyme or orégano. Simmer until mixture is well blended and fairly smooth. Keep mixture warm until ready to add to omelet as filling.

SHRIMP-STUFFED OMELET. Sauté 12 shelled shrimp (or a 6½-ounce can shrimp, drained) in 2 tablespoons butter with 1 large tomato, peeled, chopped. 1 teaspoon minced parsley, 2 tablespoons minced onion, and, if desired, 2 tablespoons chopped green pepper or pimiento. Simmer 4 minutes. Use as filling for omelet in basic recipe.

CRAB- OR LOBSTER-STUFFED OMELET. Defrost 1 10½-ounce can frozen cream of shrimp soup; heat with ¼ cup cream; stir to blend. Add 1 6½-ounce can crabmeat or lobster and a 2-ounce can sliced mushrooms, drained. Simmer until thoroughly hot. Use as filling for omelet.

SPINACH OMELET. Use cooked leftover spinach as the omelet filling, or use frozen creamed spinach, heated according to package directions.

Soufflé or Puffy Omelet

6 eggs, separated   2 tablespoons cream
½ teaspoon salt   2 tablespoons butter

For this, a skillet with a heatproof or removable handle should be used, for it must go into the oven for the second part of the cooking. First, turn the oven to 400° F. Next, beat the egg whites until stiff. Separately, beat the egg yolks until thickened: stir in salt and cream. Gently fold the egg yolk mixture into the egg whites until thoroughly blended but still fluffy. Melt butter in skillet without allowing it to sizzle; add egg mixture. Cook over moderate heat until omelet is lightly browned on the bottom. (Lift up with spatula to check browning.) Now, transfer to oven, or if the broiling oven is deep enough, place it 6 inches below the broiling unit at reduced heat. Continue cooking until top is golden and springs back when touched. Slip out onto warm platter; serve immediately. *Makes 4 to 6 servings.*

CHEESE SOUFFLÉ OMELET. Prepare as for Soufflé Omelet, but add ½ cup grated Swiss or natural Gruyére cheese to the beaten yolks.

SHRIMP SOUFFLÉ OMELET. Prepare as for Soufflé Omelet, but add ½ to ¾ cup coarsely chopped cooked or canned shrimp and 1 tablespoon minced parsley to the yolk mixture.

Spanish Omelet or Tortilla

What is called "Spanish omelet" in most American cookbooks bears little relation to the type of omelet cooked in Spain, which there is called a "tortilla" (with no similarity to the corn-meal pancake of that name in Mexico). A Spanish omelet is a hearty entree, thick, chock full of minced vegetables and sometimes meat or seafood. It is cooked in an entirely different way from the French omelet. The first step is always to sauté vegetables (including onion) in olive oil. The egg is added to the vegetable mixture, in the same pan (whereas, for a French omelet, any vegetables or other ingredients for the filling are always cooked separately). I have often watched cooks preparing these omelets in Spain and Portugal and it is fascinating to observe their dexterity. This is not a low-calorie dish, but it is an inexpensive one, and can be put together at any time, on the spur of the moment. It is even delicious cold, served as an appetizer with drinks. In Spain, peasants carry wedges of it with them for their lunch in the fields. Almost any ingredients that happen to be on hand may be added to the omelet: bits of leftover vegetables, meat, seafood, chicken. It always contains some onion, and should always be cooked in olive oil—this is the secret of its superb flavor.

Three different techniques may be used in the cooking of the Spanish omelet.

1. Cook the omelet over moderately low heat until it is browned and firm on the bottom; then, by holding a plate over the top of the skillet, flip it over upside down on the plate. Now return the omelet to the skillet, moist side down, to brown on the other side.

2. Brown the omelet on the bottom in the same way, but instead of flipping it over, place the pan under the broiler unit, 4 to 5 inches from the heat, with reduced flame, until lightly browned on top. (This is the easiest way, but does not have as delicious a flavor as when cooked by the first technique. Also, one must have a skillet with heatproof or removable handle.)

3. Use a larger quantity of olive oil and get the oil quite hot before the vegetables and egg are added, so that the egg immediately begins to brown. Turn heat low as soon as egg has been added. Lift up the mixture and gradually roll it over so that the liquid egg runs into the bottom, and finally it is a large thick roll golden brown on the outside.

Tortilla con Patatas (Basic Recipe)

¼ to ½ cup olive oil	minced
1 large onion, minced	½ teaspoon salt, or to taste
1 large raw potato, peeled,	5 large or 6 small eggs, beaten

If a Teflon-coated skillet is used, ¼ cup oil will be sufficient, but in an iron skillet, and when a golden-brown exterior is wanted, the larger amount of oil should be used. Heat the oil to sizzling, then immediately turn the heat to low, add onions and potatoes (these must both be cut very fine—some Spanish cooks instead slice the raw potato paper-thin). Cook until vegetables are quite soft; sprinkle with half the salt. Beat the eggs until well mixed; add remaining salt. Add one-third of the eggs at a time to the pan, lifting up around the edges with the spatula to let the liquid egg run under. When all the egg has been added, and the mixture is golden on the bottom, proceed with one of the three techniques described above (flip it out and slide back into the pan with the moist side down, or brown the top under the broiler, or gradually roll the thick omelet until all liquid egg has begun to firm and outside is golden brown).

Serve at once, accompanied by a simple tossed salad (or lettuce and tomato salad), crusty bread, and red wine. *Makes 4 hearty servings.*

TORTILLA CON JAMÓN. Prepare as for Tortilla con Patatas, but add to minced onion and potato about ½ cup minced cooked ham or Canadian bacon.

OMELETA CON LEGUMBRES. Prepare as for Tortilla con Patatas but omit potatoes; instead add about 1 cup other cooked or canned chopped vegetables with minced onion.

PORK CHOP OMELET. Cut the lean meat from 2 pork chops; trim into slivers. Sauté the pork and about ½ cup chopped onion in oil until pork is browned. Add beaten egg; proceed as in basic recipe.

Pipérade

1 small onion, minced	½ teaspoon salt
1 clove garlic, minced	1 large ripe tomato, peeled, chopped
½ green pepper, cut in thin strips	2 tablespoons minced ham
3 to 4 tablespoons olive oil	4 eggs, beaten

Sauté the onion, garlic, and green pepper in olive oil until lightly browned. Sprinkle with salt. Add chopped tomato and ham; cook until tomato is very soft. The eggs may now be added, as for a tortilla, or may be cooked separately, as for a French omelet, with the vegetable mixture spread over the top to serve. (The omelet is not folded over, simply served with a vegetable topping.) Serve with lettuce salad, crusty bread, and red wine. *Makes 2 servings.*

Western Omelet

This was probably introduced to Montana and Oregon by Basque shepherds, of whom there are many in that mountain region. Its similarity to Pipérade is striking. Sauté onion, green pepper, and garlic in bacon drippings or shortening (rather than olive oil) until lightly browned. Add beaten eggs; sprinkle with salt. Turn over continuously as egg firms (as for Scrambled Eggs, French method). Tomato catsup is usually served on the side.

Cheese Western

The same as a Western Omelet, but with ½ cup shredded Cheddar or American cheese sprinkled over the top as the egg begins to firm.

Egg Foo Yong

4 eggs, beaten
2 scallions, minced
¼ cup minced celery
½ cup mushrooms, thinly sliced
¼ cup cooked vegetables*

½ cup minced seafood, chicken, pork, or ham†
1 tablespoon soy sauce
4 tablespoons peanut or soy oil
Chinese Brown Sauce

Add to the beaten eggs all remaining ingredients except the oil and Chinese Brown Sauce. Use a small (7-inch) skillet. Heat the oil to sizzling; drop 2 tablespoons of the egg mixture into skillet at a time, forming a small pancake. Tilt the pan so that egg will spread out thin. As soon as lightly browned on one side, slip a pancake turner or spatula under the pancake or omelet; flip over to brown on other side. Remove. Keep the individual omelets warm until all are cooked. Serve topped with Chinese Brown Sauce, as part of a Chinese family dinner or for luncheon or supper dish preceded by an oriental soup, followed by a fruit dessert. *Serves 4 to 6.*

*Vegetables to be used could be peas, chopped green beans, pimiento, green pepper, diced cooked eggplant, diced cooked zucchini, chopped cooked spinach, sliced water chestnuts, or canned bean sprouts or bamboo shoots.

†Shrimp is especially good in Foo Yong, or a mixture of shrimp and pork, or of shrimp and cooked bacon. Other good mixed combinations: minced ham and chicken, minced clams and cooked diced bacon, or minced pork and chicken livers.

Chinese Pork Omelet

3 pork chops
1 tablespoon soy sauce
4 tablespoons peanut oil
½ cup chopped onion

¼ cup minced celery or drained bean sprouts
4 eggs, beaten
¼ teaspoon salt

Remove all meat from bones. Discard fat. Cut lean pork into slivers. Toss the pork with soy sauce. Heat oil in skillet; brown the pork slivers over high heat. Add the onion and celery; cook about 2 minutes. Beat the eggs; add salt. Pour the egg mixture over the pork; lower heat. Lift the egg and turn it over with a spatula as it firms, much as in the French method of scrambling eggs, until all the moist egg is firm. Remove the omelet from the skillet. To be part of a Chinese dinner. *Serves 6.*

French Toast

1 egg	2 to 3 slices white bread
¼ cup milk	1 to 2 tablespoons bacon fat, but-
2 teaspoons sugar	ter, or margarine

Beat together in a wide shallow bowl the egg, milk, and sugar. Briefly soak bread in mixture, 1 slice at a time. Sauté soaked bread in sizzling hot fat until golden on each side. Serve with maple or maple-blended syrup. *Serves 2.*

FRENCH TOAST AND BACON. First fry bacon, allowing 2 slices per person. Pour off excess bacon fat, leaving no more than 2 to 3 tablespoons fat in skillet. Cook the French toast in the hot bacon fat.

CHEESE FRENCH TOAST. Add ¼ cup grated Parmesan or ½ cup shredded Cheddar, Swiss or American cheese to the egg mixture; beat with rotary beater to blend thoroughly. Soak bread in mixture; cook as in basic recipe.

See also Croque Monsieur.

Shirred Eggs, or Oeufs sur le Plat (Basic Recipe)

These must be cooked in wide shallow ramekins, available in gourmet shops. The best kind are the porcelain or earthenware ramekins, with small handles on either side. They are also available in copper. They come in two sizes. To cook 1 egg, the smaller size should be used; for 2 eggs, use the larger size. The flavor of eggs prepared this way is completely different from that of poached or fried eggs. It is essential that the eggs be absolutely fresh; if the flavor is the slightest bit off, it will be more apparent than with any other method of cookery.

This is the simplest of all egg dishes, yet its variations offer infinite variety.

Place a small piece of butter (about ½ teaspoon) in each ramekin. Place ramekins in a preheated 400° F. oven until the butter is melted; use potholders to remove hot ramekins from oven; tilt each ramekin so that butter spreads over the bottom. Break each egg first into a small bowl (to make sure yolk does not break), then slip into ramekin. Sprinkle each egg with salt; drop a teaspoon of cream or milk into each ramekin. Return ramekins to oven; bake until whites are set, yolks still soft, only slightly glazed over. For a small ramekin containing 1 egg, this may require only 5 minutes; for 2 eggs in a larger ramekin, 10 minutes. Eggs cooked in a sauce require longer. Serve immediately, with rolls or toast to scoop out the luscious egg yolk.

HAM AND EGGS SUR LE PLAT. Prepare as for Oeufs sur le Plat, but place a slice of tenderized ham in each large ramekin after butter has melted, add a dot of butter over ham, then slip 2 eggs into each ramekin. Bake until whites have set.

BAKED EGGS AND CHEESE. Prepare like Oeufs au Plat, but before adding eggs to ramekins (after butter has melted) add to each ramekin ¼ cup sour cream blended with 2 tablespoons shredded Swiss or Cheddar cheese. Slip eggs into dish over the sour cream-cheese mixture. Bake as for Oeufs sur le Plat.

Eggs a la Riojana

1 8-ounce can tomato sauce	1 teaspoon instant minced onion
2 tablespoons olive oil	8 eggs
1 tablespoon minced parsley	2 tablespoons grated Parmesan
¼ teaspoon orégano (optional)	cheese

Preheat oven to 400° F. Heat together tomato sauce, olive oil, parsley, orégano, and instant onion until sauce bubbles. Divide sauce among 8 large ramekins. Break eggs carefully; place 2 eggs in each ramekin. Sprinkle cheese over eggs and sauce. Place ramekins in preheated oven and bake until whites are set, yolks still soft—about 15 minutes. Serve with crusty rolls and a tossed green salad for lunch or supper. Serves 4.

Eggs a la Flamenca

1 large onion, chopped	3 large tomatoes, peeled and
2 cloves garlic, minced	chopped, or 1 1-pound can
2 tablespoons olive oil	peeled tomatoes
½ cup chopped ham or chorizo	½ teaspoon salt
sausage	8 eggs
1 teaspoon minced parsley	1 cup cooked or frozen peas
1 pimiento, drained, sliced	8 cooked asparagus spears

Sauté onion and garlic in olive oil until soft. Add ham or chorizo; cook until lightly browned. Add parsley, pimiento, and tomatoes; cook until tomato is reduced and thickened. Add salt. Divide sauce into 4 large ramekins. Place 2 eggs in each. Arrange cooked or frozen peas and asparagus on either side of the eggs. Bake in oven preheated to 350° F. until eggs are set, yolks still soft—about 20 minutes. Serve at once. Serves 4.

Huevos en Arroz (Eggs Baked in Rice)

1 large onion, chopped	½ teaspoon salt
2 tablespoons olive oil	Dash of cayenne
1 cup uncooked rice	6 eggs
2 cups chicken broth	½ cup grated Swiss cheese

Cook onion in olive oil until soft, add rice, then add broth, salt, and cayenne. bringing to a boil. Lower heat: cook, covered, until liquid is absorbed, then spoon into casserole. Make 6 indentations in rice; break an egg into each. Sprinkle salt and cheese over top of eggs. Bake in oven preheated to 400° F. until eggs are set—about 15 minutes. *Serves 6.*

EGGS ON SAFFRON RICE NESTS. If preferred in preparing above recipe, use packaged saffron rice mix, omitting salt and cayenne; cook the rice in water instead of chicken broth, according to package directions.

Soufflés

One of the most marvelous of inexpensive supper dishes is a cheese soufflé, whose fragrance alone is enough to provoke the appetite before the lovely delicate thing is removed from the oven. Its only disadvantage is its fragility; it must be served the moment it comes from the oven, or the soufflé may collapse and lose all its charm.

There are steps to take in advance, so that the soufflé need not be placed in the oven until family or guests are present, and the rest of the meal may be all prepared, ready to place on the table. One way is to combine all ingredients but the egg white ahead of time, then beat the egg whites until stiff just before the soufflé is to be added to its prepared casserole or soufflé dish. Another way is to freeze it—but longer baking time is necessary in this case, which means everyone must wait that much longer for the soufflé to appear.

Cheese Soufflé (Basic Recipe)

3 tablespoons butter	pepper
3 tablespoons flour	4 large or 5 small eggs, separated
1 cup milk	¼ pound Cheddar or American
1 teaspoon salt	cheese, grated (1½ cups)
½ teaspoon freshly ground black	

Melt butter in skillet; stir in flour; cook until mixture bubbles. Slowly stir in milk; cook until smooth and thickened. Blend in salt and pepper. Beat egg yolks with whisk until thick and smooth; add the sauce a little at a time. Stir grated cheese into this mixture. (This part can be done ahead.) In a separate bowl, beat egg whites until stiff. Fold beaten whites gently into cheese-yolk mixture. Butter the bottom and sides of 1½-quart casserole. Dust flour over butter, then shake out excess flour. Pour egg mixture into casserole. Make a groove with spoon 1 inch from edge. Bake in oven preheated to 325° until puffed high and golden — about 45 minutes. Serve immediately. *Serves 4.*

SWISS SOUFFLÉ. Use ¼ pound grated Swiss or Gruyère cheese (1½ cups) instead of American or Cheddar in basic recipe.

VEGETABLE SOUFFLÉ. Add 1 cup cooked chopped vegetables to above recipe; use only ¾ cup cheese. Asparagus, green beans, limas, kernel corn, and artichoke hearts are all delicious possibilities.

NUT SOUFFLÉ. Add ½ cup chopped nuts (dry-roasted cashews, or peanuts, or chopped walnuts) to basic recipe, reducing cheese to ½ cup. Or use 3-ounce package cream cheese cut into small pieces instead of grated processed cheese with nuts.

Spinach-Noodle Soufflé

4 eggs, separated
2 shallots, minced
1 10-ounce package frozen
  chopped spinach, defrosted

½ pound egg noodles, cooked,
  drained
Salt

Combine egg yolks, minced shallots, defrosted spinach, cooked noodles, and salt. Beat egg whites stiffly and fold in. Spoon into greased 1½-quart baking dish. Bake in oven preheated to 350° F. for 30 minutes. Serve immediately. *Serves 4.*

Easy Cheese Soufflé

1 10½-ounce can condensed
  Cheddar cheese soup, undiluted

4 eggs, separated
¼ teaspoon cream of tartar

Heat soup; do not allow to boil. Remove from heat and cool slightly. Beat egg yolks until thickened; add some of warm soup, then combine the two. Beat egg whites with cream of tartar until stiff. Fold yolk-soup mixture into whites gently. Turn into ungreased straight-sided 1½-quart casserole or soufflé dish. With a spoon, make a groove 1 inch from edge. Place casserole in pan containing 1 inch of hot water. Bake in oven preheated to 325° F. until puffed high and golden—about 45 minutes. *Makes 4 servings.*

Shrimp Soufflé

1 can frozen cream of shrimp
  soup, defrosted
1 6½-ounce can shrimp, drained,

coarsely chopped
4 eggs, separated
¼ teaspoon cream of tartar

Heat defrosted soup (undiluted) until hot, but do not allow to boil. Stir shrimp into soup. Beat egg yolks until thickened; add some of the warm soup, then combine the two. Beat egg whites with cream of tartar until stiff; fold egg yolk mixture into white. (Or, omit cream of tartar and use 5 egg whites.) Pour into ungreased 1½-quart casserole with straight sides. Make a groove around the edge with a spoon. Bake in oven preheated to 325° F. until puffed high and golden—about 45 minutes. Serve with artichoke hearts, radishes, and grilled cherry tomatoes for a ladies luncheon. *Serves 4.*

Frozen Swiss Soufflé

3 tablespoons butter
¼ cup flour
½ teaspoon salt
⅛ teaspoon freshly ground pepper
½ cup cream

½ cup dry vermouth
1½ cups coarsely grated natural
  Gruyère cheese
4 eggs, separated
¼ teaspoon cream of tartar

Melt butter in heavy pan; add flour, salt, and pepper; stir over medium heat until well blended. Slowly stir in cream, vermouth, and cheese and cook, stirring, over low heat until cheese melts; remove from heat. Beat egg yolks until thick; combine with cheese mixture. Beat egg whites slightly, add cream of tartar, beat until stiff. Carefully fold cheese mixture into egg whites. Pour into ungreased 1½-quart freezer-to-oven casserole. Cover. Place in freezer. When ready to bake, remove from freezer and place frozen in 300° F. oven, removing cover. Bake until puffed high and golden—65 to 75 minutes. Serve immediately. *Serves 4 to 6.*

CHEESE

Cheese offers everything: glamour, utility, nourishment, infinite variety. There's a cheese for every taste and every use. Almost every American city now has at least one cheese store, offering a hundred or more types of cheese for sale, along with accessories for serving cheese.

The best types for *cooking* include American, Cheddar (and its many offspring), Swiss or Emmentaler, Gruyère (especially natural Gruyère), Parmesan (or its cousin Romano), mozzarella, and the various types of fresh cheese (cottage, pot, ricotta, farmer). Add to the list the blue cheeses for use in salads and certain sauces.

Grating cheeses include Parmesan, Romano, Asiago, Sbrinz (a Swiss import) and very firm aged Cheddars. For best flavor, such cheese should be grated only as needed. The already grated cheese, even when purchased in tightly sealed containers, hasn't half the flavor.

The best cheeses for *sandwiches* are the easy-to-slice firm or semifirm types, or the easy-to-spread types. The former include American, Swiss, Muenster, brick, provolone, Jack, Edam, Gouda, and the semifirm Cheddars, including those spiced with caraway. The spreadable cheeses range from the fresh soft category (cream cheese, cottage cheese, Neufchâtel) to the pasteurized process cheese spreads, to the blue cheeses and blue cheese spreads.

Appetizer cheeses include both firm and semifirm types, cheese spreads (especially those blended with wine or other spirits), and soft cheeses, but it is the sharper, more pungent and odorous cheeses and the exotic cheeses that are more at home on the cocktail table than in the kitchen. These include genuine Roquefort, Gorgonzola, little goat cheeses, spiced cheeses, Limburger, Liederkranz, sharp aged Cheddars, pungent Port-Salut, salty feta.

Dessert cheeses are the soft or semisoft types: Brie, Camembert, Crema Danica, Bel Paese, a young semifirm Gorgonzola, crème de Gruyère (a French import) and the many small

double-cream French cheeses now available, though some of
the semifirm cheeses are also suitable to serve following the
main course of dinner. These include Stilton (served with port
wine), Roquefort, with a red table wine, Edam or Gouda, Swiss
(with a white wine such as Sauternes), or pungent crumbly fontinella (an especially delicious firm cheese now made in Wisconsin).

Definition of Terms

With all the *natural* cheese available, most of the cheeses offered for sale in American supermarkets have been *pasteurized.*

Natural cheese is produced by the time-honored method of
extracting the curd of the milk from the whey, pressing the curd
into desired shapes. *Fresh* cheeses are those natural cheeses
made from the curd, but not ripened. These are perishable and
must be kept under refrigeration at all times. *Ripened* cheeses
are the natural cheeses that are permitted to go through a process of fermentation, during which the cheese is stored in an
atmosphere where it will absorb certain desired bacteria and
molds to give it distinctive flavor. The more of the whey extracted from the curd, the more firm the cheese will be, and the
longer its keeping qualities.

Pasteurized process cheese is a mixture of natural ripened
cheese and milk solids, heated to a melting temperature to kill
all bacteria, then poured into molds. Such cheeses have longer
keeping qualities (if tightly sealed, they will keep under refrigeration almost indefinitely) but blander flavor and more rubbery texture.

Pasteurized process cheese spreads have a larger proportion
of milk solids and more liquid, with vegetable gum added for
thickening. *Pasteurized process cheese foods* may contain less
than 20 percent actual cheese content, the rest being milk solids, water, artificial flavorings and vegetable gum. Most of
these are quite bland and therefore popular with the young.

Glossary of Cheeses

The following list includes only the most available and popular of cheeses, domestic and imported. There are many dozens
of others to be found in cheese shops, with new varieties being
offered all the time.

AMERICAN. A pasteurized cheese resembling Cheddar in
appearance and flavor, sold chiefly in packages already sliced.

BEL LAGO. A semisoft cheese from Switzerland, suitable either as an appetizer or as a dessert cheese.

BEL PAESE. A distinctive-flavored Italian cheese, creamy-soft and mild; may be served as an appetizer or dessert cheese. An American cheese by the same name is produced in Wisconsin.

BLUE OR BLEU CHEESE. Any semisoft cheese veined with blue or green mold. It varies in pungency from mild to very sharp; generally, the younger the cheese, the more delicate the flavor.

BONBEL. A soft yellow French cheese, widely available in American markets, bland in flavor, very good for snacks or appetizers.

BRICK. An American cheese; pale, firm, brick-shaped, more odorous than Cheddar, but not as strong as Limburger. Slices easily.

BRIE. One of the world's great cheeses, a French import; should be runny-soft when purchased, and always removed from refrigerator 1 to 2 hours before serving. Primarily a dessert cheese, but may also be served with cocktails. Distinctive flavor, unlike any other.

BRINDZA. A Rumanian sheep or goat cheese; white, salty, used in making the Rumanian corn-meal dish called Mamaliga. An American imitation is now produced in the West.

CACIOCAVALLO. A firm Italian cheese with smoky flavor (though it is not smoked—the flavor is the result of the way it is aged, rubbed with olive oil, hung from rafters); something like provolone.

CAMEMBERT. The original Camembert has been produced in France since the Middle Ages; a distinctive, soft dessert cheese, and the French Camembert is still the best, though cheeses of this name are now being produced in many other countries. American Camembert is much more bland than the original. Any Camembert should be creamy-soft but without the slightest tinge of ammonial odor when purchased. Warm to room temperature for at least 1 hour before serving.

CANTAL. A semifirm French cheese that may be found in many gourmet shops and cheese stores; has been produced in France for more than 2000 years. Mild but with distinctive flavor; deep gold in color. Suitable for snacks, as appetizer, or after the salad, with red wine.

CARAWAY-SEEDED CHEESE. There are now many of these available, some domestic, others imported. Semifirm or firm, pungent, similar to Cheddar in flavor; good for sandwiches.

CHEDDAR. The name given to a wide variety of cheeses, ranging in texture from semisoft to semifirm, firm, and very firm. Named after a village in England where cheese is no longer made. A good natural Cheddar is pungent, well aged, just a little crumbly. Of the domestic cheddars, the finest are produced in Vermont, Wisconsin (Longhorn), New York State (Herkimer County and Coon are two outstanding New York Cheddars), and Colorado (Colorado Blackie). A natural Cheddar frequently has a black rind, the remnant of the black cloth used to wrap the curd as it ripens. Jack, or Monterey Jack, as it is frequently called, is a type of Cheddar, and so is Tillamook, a salt-free cheese produced in Oregon. An excellent English Cheddar type is called Dunlop. Many pasteurized cheeses are also called "Cheddars," and many of the pasteurized process cheese foods try to imitate Cheddar in flavor.

CHESHIRE. An English cheese, from the region of Chester; produced in "red" (orange), white, and blue (blue-veined) varieties.

COON. A New York State Cheddar; superb for cocktails.

COTTAGE CHEESE. Fresh cheese; the simple, pressed curd of naturally soured whole or skimmed milk, or of pasteurized milk treated with a culture. It is lightly salted and blended with a little cream to give it a softer texture. (Pot cheese is the same but without cream.)

CREAM CHEESE. A fresh cheese made from the curd of pure cream and whole milk, lightly salted. Very perishable. Keep under refrigeration; use within 1 week. Useful in cooking, for sauces, in sandwiches, in making such desserts as Coeur à la Crème.

CREMA DANICA. A soft white dessert cheese imported from Denmark, very high in butterfat.

CRÈME DE GRUYÈRE. A soft ripened French cheese with the flavor of Gruyère but the consistency of Camembert. A fine dessert cheese.

DANISH BLUE. A very sharp blue-veined cheese imported from Denmark.

DOUBLE CRÈME. Any soft ripened French dessert cheese containing 60 percent butterfat.

EDAM. A cheese of Dutch origin in characteristic cannonball shape with a bright red rind. Several American Edams are now being produced, but a well-aged Dutch Edam is a thing very difficult to surpass. Primarily for appetizers or snacks.

EMMENTALER. See Swiss.

ESROM. A very fine semisoft Danish cheese. For sandwiches, smorgasbord, appetizers.

FARMER CHEESE. A fresh natural cheese made from whole or skimmed milk, forced through a fine sieve so that it is firmer and closer-textured than cottage cheese. Mild; some is firm enough to slice.

FETA. A Greek cheese made of sheep's milk; white and flaky, kept moist by storing in brine. An excellent appetizer cheese, especially when served with black olives.

FONTINA. A semisoft cheese that melts easily, may be used to top polenta, pizzas, or casseroles. Cheeses of this name are produced in Italy, Switzerland, and the United States. When aged, fontina becomes semifirm with nutty flavor.

FONTINELLA. A firmer cheese than fontina, with zestier, sharper flavor. An excellent fontinella is made in Wisconsin.

GORGONZOLA. An Italian blue-veined cheese; semisoft and delicate when young, becomes very sharp when aged. Many domestic Gorgonzolas are now being produced.

GOUDA. A Dutch cheese, larger and richer in butterfat than Edam. Some are round, others in loaf shape. When aged, the cheese becomes piquant and flaky. There are now a number of American imitations.

GRUYÈRE. One of the world's finest cheeses, produced in Switzerland for many centuries. It has smaller holes and higher butterfat than the cheese Americans know as "Switzerland Swiss." *Natural Gruyère* is one of the finest cheeses for use in cooking. The *pasteurized Gruyère* sold in supermarkets in foil-wrapped wedges is not nearly as useful for cooking (these are better served for snacks and appetizers) because the flavor is more bland and the texture more rubbery.

JACK. Also known as Monterey Jack. A type of Cheddar produced in California, available in soft, semisoft, and semifirm varieties. Mild, buttery, excellent for use in cooking and also for sandwiches or on the cocktail buffet.

LIEDERKRANZ. An American cheese created in the Gay Nineties by a German delicatessen owner. Named after his favorite singing society. Soft, creamy, pungent. Serve with beer or as a dessert cheese.

LIMBURGER. Of Belgian origin but now made in many countries, including Germany and the United States. Odorous, creamy, the king of "smelly" cheeses. Best with beer.

MANCHEGO. A firm Spanish cheese somewhat like Swiss, excellent at its best but varies greatly in quality.

MONTEREY JACK. See Jack.

MOZZARELLA. The original Italian cheese of this name was made entirely of the milk of water buffalo, but now is made more often of partially skimmed cow's milk. American mozzarella is produced entirely from cow's milk. Melts easily; commonly known as the "pizza cheese."

MUENSTER, MÜNSTER, or MUNSTER. The original cheese of this name comes from the Vosges Mountains of Alsace-Lorraine. A soft, pancake-shaped cheese, usually served with white wine. The American Muenster is entirely different, a semifirm cheese with small holes, made in wheels or loaves. The latter is fine sandwich cheese, good for cooking and for appetizers. But be sure to warm it to room temperature before serving.

MÜTSCHLI. A semisoft cheese from Switzerland, mild, creamy.

NATURAL GRUYÈRE. See Gruyère.

NEUFCHÂTEL. The domestic cheese of this name is similar to cream cheese but with lower butterfat, and may be used in the same ways as cream cheese. The French Neufchâtel is a soft cream-colored cheese with a velvety white crust, a dessert cheese.

PARMESAN. Of Italian origin, a firm pungent grating cheese. American Parmesan is milder. Sold both in wedges and already grated in jars or packages.

PONT L'ÉVÊQUE. A French dessert cheese from the province of Normandy.

PORT DU SALUT, or PORT-SALUT. A semisoft cheese made originally by Trappist monks in France, now made by Trappists in many parts of the world. Some of the American cheeses of this name, however, have never known a monastery. Particularly fine with cocktails; also as dessert.

POT CHEESE. See Cottage Cheese.

PROVOLONE. A firm smoked Italian cheese made with characteristic brown shiny rind. Cured by hanging from rafters. American provolone is a rather poor imitation. For sandwiches, snacks, also for cooking.

RICOTTA. The cheese of this name sold in supermarkets is always a fresh unripened cheese, similar to cottage cheese but finer in texture. An essential ingredient in making lasagne and other Italian dishes. However, in Italy ricotta is sold in several forms, including a ripened aged type hard enough to grate. Italian delicatessens in the United States sometimes offer both the hard ricotta for grating and one called ricotta salata, which is something like feta cheese.

ROMANO. A hard aged grating cheese similar to Parmesan. The Italian Romano, imported from Italy, is made from the whey of sheep's milk. American Romano is made from whole cow's milk and is so similar to American Parmesan that it's difficult to distinguish the difference.

ROQUEFORT. A blue-veined sheep's milk cheese produced in southern France since Roman times. Genuine Roquefort always bears the red imprint of a sheep on its foil wrapper. A superb cheese, frequently used in the kitchen, but at its prime so delicious that it's a shame to serve it in any way but enthroned on crusty French bread.

SAINT-PAULIN. A variation of Port du Salut, also produced by Trappist monks.

SAMSØ. A very fine Danish cheese, golden, semifirm, buttery.

SAPSAGO or SCHABZIEGER. A hard greenish cheese of Swiss origin, flavored with clover.

SBRINZ. A grating cheese from Switzerland, made since ancient times.

STILTON. The English blue cheese of world renown. No English gourmet would think of serving it without a glass of fine port to wash it down.

SWISS. The American name for the type of cheese known in Europe as Emmentaler. Natural Swiss is produced in huge wheels weighing as much as 200 pounds. A firm buff-yellow cheese with big holes—though the size of the holes is no criterion of the quality of the cheese. Some very fine Swiss cheeses are produced in Wisconsin, others in Ohio. An all-purpose cheese, for snacks, cocktails, cooking, even for dessert when the cheese is a particularly fine one. Pasteurized versions of what is called Swiss cheese are also available, in foil-wrapped wedges and ready sliced for sandwiches in sealed packets.

SWITZERLAND SWISS. The rather ridiculous name by which Emmentaler cheese, imported from Switzerland, is known in the United States. Some is even available already sliced for sandwiches, but like all ready-sliced cheese, this has lost much of its zest in the prepackaging process.

TILSITER. A semifirm pungent cheese with small, irregular holes. Excellent for cocktails or snacks. Produced in all Scandinavian countries, in Germany, Switzerland, and also the United States.

Tips on Serving Cheese

•All cheese has richer, fuller flavor if served at room temperature. If possible, remove from refrigerator 1 hour before serving.

•A cheese tray offering at least three different varieties is one of the easiest and most fun things to serve with cocktails. Select the cheeses for variety in texture (one firm, one soft, the third in between), flavor (one mild, one very pungent or smelly, the third with interestingly different flavor), and appearance (shape and size).

If you feel unsure of your own tastes, ask the man behind the counter for suggestions: he will give you tiny samples of cheese to taste.

•A cheese board is nice to have if you plan to serve cheese frequently. Put only the cheese and a cheese knife or butter knives on the board. Set out a variety of breads and crackers separately.

•Good go-withs: radishes, black and green olives, dill pickles with certain cheeses (such as Muenster or brick), fruit (especially grapes and apples), nuts, pretzels, or bread sticks.

•Most cheese tastes best if accompanied by red wine. Some seem made for beer. There's no better food to put into a picnic hamper than cheese (two kinds are better than one), along with wine or beer, crusty bread, and fruit.

11 BATTERS AND BREADS

The story of mixes is the story of basic recipes. Take biscuit mix: it was first introduced in the 1930's, when hot biscuits fresh from the oven were still considered by many an indispensable part of the American breakfast. Company home economists, asked to find ways for promoting the product, began dreaming up a myriad of other uses, treating the mix as a basic recipe, going on from there. Today biscuit mix is as much a staple as baking powder was to our great-grandmothers.

The same principle lies behind all packaged mixes and many other convenience products as well. There's no reason for apologizing about using a mix as a short cut, if the end result is a proud one. Contrariwise, if a particular mix isn't available, the cook, knowing what ingredients the mix contains (what the basic recipe is, in other words), can always reconstruct the recipe from scratch.

All *batters* are a mixture of flour, salt, a leavener, liquid, and shortening. The leavener may be baking powder or baking soda (for *quick breads*), yeast (for *yeast breads*), eggs, or a combination of one of the first two with eggs. Biscuit mix contains flour, salt, baking powder, and shortening. By altering the amount of liquid, making the batter thinner or thicker, the mix may be used to make everything from pancakes to nut bread.

Pancake mix contains several cereal grains crushed into flour, plus salt and baking powder. Most pancake mixes do not contain shortening.

Fritter batters (used to coat foods to be fried) may have no leavener but eggs. However, when the liquid used to make a fritter batter is beer, a fermentation occurs which, upon standing, causes the batter to rise slightly and thicken. In fact, the first commercial yeast cakes were made from beer dregs, sold by a Connecticut brewer named Fleischmann who developed the yeast as a by-product.

Yeast is an organism, a spore. Commercial dried yeast comes to life when warm water is added, just as seeds come to life when placed in moist soil. Before compressed yeast cakes (the forerunner of today's dried yeast) were developed, each family had to keep a "starter" lump of dough for making bread; the starter would be passed on from mother to daughter. Dried yeast is a marvelous convenience food but its shelf life is limited. Therefore it is important always to note the date on the package. This is also true of hot roll mix, or any mix containing a yeast packet.

Yeast is the most dramatic of all the leaveners. When the yeast has been coaxed into life by warm water, then blended with a mixture containing flour and placed in a protected warm spot, the yeast "feeds" on the sugar in the wheat starch; this causes the formation of a gas that makes the dough swell like a balloon. According to legend, the first yeast bread was an accident, when a baker in ancient Egypt left a batch of dough in a warm dark spot and forgot about it until next day. The warmth had caused the fermentation. "Salt-rising bread" is made with such a leavener: a mixture of salt, water and grated raw potato is left overnight in a warm moist place until the mixture ferments, when it is added to the flour just as yeast would be added. "Sourdough," the bread of frontiersmen in the early West, was also made according to the same principle.

The most primitive form of bread contains no leavener, only wheat flour or some other crushed cereal grain, salt, and water. This was true of the "hearth cake" or "ash cake" of our forebears. Such unleavened breads are still made in many parts of the world and some of them, such as the *chapati* of India, are very good indeed. Pancakes are a refinement of hearth cakes.

From pancakes made only of crushed grain and water, more delicate cakes were developed using more liquid, adding eggs or some other leavener, or both. Crepes, the French pancakes, contain almost as much egg as flour. Chinese pancakes are made almost entirely of egg, with only a few tablespoons of flour.

Some breads, such as dumplings and Boston brown bread, are steamed, some are fried rather than baked. Doughnuts and crullers come into the latter category. We don't think of these as breads because they are sweetened, but many of our favorite hot breads are sweet, and some yeast breads could pass for cakes. In fact, the words "cake" and "bread" were used synonymously in earlier times.

The difference between a dough and a batter lies primarily in the amount of liquid used. A dough must be stiff enough to handle with the hands; a batter is of pouring consistency. Doughs are *kneaded* to form a smooth protective outer crust that keeps the inside moist and tender. ⸙

In preparing all the recipes in this section, *level measurements* are important. Read the recipes through once to make sure you understand. Get out all the utensils you need before you start mixing, and pay particular attention to *pan sizes* for all those breads that are to be baked in the oven.

In multiplying or dividing recipes for breads or batters, it is a good idea to write out the revision in full and follow the revised ingredient list.

PANCAKES, CREPES, BLINTZES, AND WAFFLES

Pancakes (Basic Recipe)

1 cup all-purpose flour	2 tablespoons shortening
1½ teaspoons baking powder	¾ to 1 cup milk*
½ teaspoon salt	1 egg

Sift together flour, baking powder, and salt (the flour need not be presifted). Melt the shortening (butter, margarine, vegetable shortening, or bacon drippings). Combine milk and egg in a 1-quart mixing bowl; beat with rotary beater until frothy. Add flour mixture; stir just enough to moisten all the flour. Stir in melted shortening.

*Use smaller amount of liquid if puffy, spongy cakes are preferred; use larger amount for thinner cakes.

If using an electric skillet, preheat the skillet to 400° F. If using a griddle or frying pan, heat until a few drops of water sprinkled on the surface bounce and disappear immediately. Before baking the first batch it usually helps to moisten the surface of skillet or griddle with a very small amount of fat (rub a piece of brown paper with fat; rub the paper over the surface of the skillet). Additional greasing is not necessary for later batches. Drop the batter into the hot skillet from a pitcher or a large spoon to form cakes 4 inches in diameter. Cook until batter puffs up and small bubbles appear and the cakes are lightly browned on bottom; flip over with pancake turner; bake until lightly browned on the other side. Turn only once. Serve immediately with butter and syrup, or as recipe specifies. *Makes 8 to 10 cakes, enough for 2 or 3 servings.*

For 4 to 6 servings, double all ingredients.

Using Pancake or Biscuit Mix. Substitute 1 cup mix for the flour, baking powder, and salt in basic recipe. Omit shortening.

BLUEBERRY PANCAKES. Add to basic recipe or mix ½ cup fresh blueberries sweetened with 2 tablespoons sugar, or ½ cup canned blueberries, well drained. Bake in skillet or on griddle. Serve topped with maple or maple-blended syrup.

APPLE PANCAKES. Add ½ cup pared and thinly sliced apples and 2 tablespoons sugar to basic recipe or mix. If desired, ¼ teaspoon cinnamon may also be added. Sprinkle confectioners' sugar over hot cakes; serve with crisp bacon.

HAM PANCAKES WITH SPICY ORANGE SYRUP. Add ½ cup chopped ham to basic recipe. Serve cakes topped with a syrup made by heating together 1 cup maple-blended syrup, 1 teaspoon frozen orange juice concentrate, 1 teaspoon prepared mustard, ⅛ teaspoon powdered cloves, and 2 tablespoons butter.

BUTTERMILK PANCAKES. Instead of 2 teaspoons baking powder, use 1 teaspoon baking powder and ½ teaspoon baking soda. Instead of milk, use buttermilk. Allow batter to stand a few minutes before baking pancakes.

Corn-meal Griddlecakes

¾ cup all-purpose flour
¾ cup corn meal
2 teaspoons baking powder
½ teaspoon salt
1 to 2 teaspoons sugar or maple

syrup
1 egg
1 cup milk
2 tablespoons shortening or oil

Blend together flour, corn meal, baking powder, salt, and sugar in mixing bowl. Make a well in the center; add egg and milk; stir until all flour is moistened. Melt shortening (bacon fat is recommended); stir into batter. Let batter stand 5 minutes while heating griddle or skillet to 400° F. Moisten surface with a very small amount of fat. Bake as for regular pancakes. *Makes about 16 cakes, enough for 4 servings.*

CORN-MEAL-BUTTERMILK CAKES. Instead of 2 teaspoons baking powder, use 1 teaspoon baking powder and ½ teaspoon baking soda. Instead of milk, use buttermilk.

USING CORN MUFFIN MIX. To 1 cup mix (½ package), add 1 egg, ½ cup milk, and 1 tablespoon melted shortening. *This makes enough for 2 servings. For 4 servings,* use entire package of mix with 1 egg and 1 cup milk.

OATCAKES or BANNOCKS. Prepare as for Corn-meal Griddlecakes but use ¾ cup old-fashioned rolled oats in place of corn meal, and 2 eggs instead of 1. Serve topped with butter and cottage cheese.

Soufflé Pancakes

3 eggs, separated
1½ cups flour
2 teaspoons baking powder
1 tablespoon sugar (optional)

¾ teaspoon salt
1½ cups milk
3 tablespoons butter, melted

Beat egg whites until stiff. Sift together flour, baking powder, sugar, and salt. Beat egg yolks with milk until frothy; add flour mixture; stir just until flour is moistened. Stir in melted butter. Fold in egg whites. Bake 4-inch cakes in preheated skillet or griddle until lightly browned on bottom; flip and lightly brown on the other side. Serve with blueberry syrup, jam, or Orange Syrup, accompanied by crisp bacon. *Makes about 12 cakes, enough for 4 servings.*

Orange Syrup. Heat together 1 teaspoon frozen orange juice concentrate, 1 cup maple-blended syrup, and 2 tablespoons butter.

Made with Mix. Instead of flour, baking powder, and salt, use 1 ½ cups pancake mix.

Crepes (French Pancakes) (Basic Recipe)

¾ cup sifted flour	3 eggs
½ teaspoon salt	1½ cups milk
1 tablespoon sugar (optional)	2 tablespoons butter, clarified

Combine flour, salt, and sugar. Beat eggs with fork just until whites and yolks are blended; add flour mixture; beat with whisk until smooth. Add milk; beat again just until smooth. Cover bowl with cloth; let stand 1 hour at room temperature, or place in refrigerator and chill 3 hours. Batter will thicken as it stands.

Crepes are easiest to prepare in a 5-inch crepe pan—a copper skillet with very low sides. A 7-inch skillet may be used but crepes are not likely to be so uniform in shape. Add about 1 teaspoon butter to pan for first crepes; add more as needed. Add 2 tablespoons batter to pan; tilt so that batter spreads out very thinly to edge of 5-inch pan. Cook over moderate heat until golden on bottom—about 1 minute; flip; cook the other side. If not to be served at once, place cooked crepes on plate; cover each with waxed paper; place linen cloth over top. *Makes 12 crepes, enough for 4 servings.*

SHRIMP-STUFFED CREPES. Heat 1 can frozen cream of shrimp soup with ¼ cup heavy cream; add 8 to 10 shelled shrimp, cut in pieces, and 2 tablespoons sherry or brandy. Simmer until shrimp turn pink. Prepare Crepes. Spoon shrimp mixture onto each crepe; roll crepes around filling; place in shallow casserole. Top with 1 cup grated Swiss cheese. Crepes may be prepared ahead to this point. Reheat under broiler, 4 inches from unit, until cheese is melted and sauce is bubbling.

CREPES MORNAY. Fill Crepes with creamed spinach (frozen creamed spinach may be used), or a mixture of minced lobster and mushrooms, or diced chicken and mushrooms blended with ½ cup Mornay Sauce. Place in shallow casserole; cover with 1 cup Mornay Sauce. Glaze under broiler, 4 inches from heating unit.

MANICOTTI ALLA ROMANA. Prepare Crepes as in basic recipe. Fill each with cottage cheese or ricotta cheese; roll up. Place rolled crepes in shallow casserole. Cover with 2 cups well-seasoned tomato sauce. Place thin slices of mozzarella cheese over top. Glaze under broiler, 4 inches from heating unit, or bake in preheated 425° F. oven until top is glazed and sauce bubbling.

CHEESE BLINTZES. Prepare Crepes as in basic recipe. While warm, fill with mixture of cottage cheese and sour cream (¼ cup sour cream to 1 cup cottage cheese), about 1½ tablespoons cheese per crepe. Roll up. Shortly before serving, sauté crepes in butter until lightly browned all over. Serve as a supper entree topped with dollops of sour cream.

BLUEBERRY BLINTZES. Fill prepared Crepes with a mixture of fresh or canned blueberries: 1½ cups fresh berries mixed with 3 tablespoons sugar and 1 tablespoon cornstarch; or a 1-pound can blueberries in syrup mixed with ¼ cup of the syrup blended with 1 tablespoon cornstarch; or 1 can ready-to-use blueberry pie filling. Place rolled blintzes in shallow casserole. Brush melted butter over top. Bake in oven preheated to 425° F. until delicately browned—about 20 minutes. Serve warm for dessert topped with sweetened sour cream.

STRAWBERRY CREPES. Fill Crepes with crushed sweetened strawberries. Dust confectioners' sugar over top. Serve as dessert topped with whipped cream.

SWEDISH DESSERT PANCAKES. Prepare Crepes as in basic recipe but add 2 tablespoons sugar to batter. While warm, place a teaspoonful of currant jelly, cherry preserves, or Cranberry-Orange Relish in each crepe; roll up. (In Sweden, lingonberry preserves would be used.) Dust confectioners' sugar over top. Cover lightly; keep warm in 250° F. oven. Serve topped with sweetened whipped cream flavored with a little brandy.

Crepes Suzette

1 recipe Crepes	¼ cup sugar
4 lumps of sugar, or 1 tablespoon sugar	4 tablespoons sweet butter
1 orange	¼ cup Grand Marnier or Curaçao
½ lemon	¼ cup brandy or cognac

This is a show-off dish that requires practice to master, but since it can be prepared ahead (except for the final reheating and flaming), it makes a fine company dessert.

Prepare the batter for the crepes; let stand 1 hour, then cook the crepes; stack with waxed paper between each.

Rub the lumps of sugar over the rinds of the orange and lemon so that the flavorful oil or zest of the fruit rind will be absorbed by the sugar. (Or grate half of the orange rind and one-fourth of the lemon rind; blend with 1 tablespoon sugar). Carefully peel off the remaining orange and lemon rind without cutting into the white part. Cut into fine slivers. Squeeze juice from orange and lemon; dissolve the lump sugar in the juice.

Beat sugar and butter together by hand or with an electric blender or mixer until fluffy and creamy. Add fruit juice, the slivers of orange and lemon peel, and 2 tablespoons of the Grand Marnier. Marinate to blend flavors for several hours.

To prepare the dessert at the table, a chafing dish is almost essential. Place the flavored butter in the blazer of the chafing dish; heat until bubbling; add the crepes one at a time. As each crepe is warmed, fold it in half, then in quarters, and push to one side of pan. When all have been so heated and wrapped, add the remaining Grand Marnier, then the cognac which has been warmed separately. Tip the pan so that the flame of the alcohol burner touches the vapor rising from the bubbling cognac mixture (this is the professional way—if you are too timid to try it, touch the cognac mixture with a lighted match instead). The mixture should burst into flames. Spoon it up to keep the flame alive until all the alcohol in the cognac has burned out. Serve 2 to 3 crepes to each person, spooning the sauce over the crepes. *Makes 12 crepes, or 4 to 6 servings.*

Chinese Pancakes

4 eggs
4 tablespoons flour
¼ cup milk or water

1 teaspoon soy sauce
Oil

Beat eggs lightly; sprinkle flour over eggs; beat with whisk until smooth. Add the milk or water and soy sauce; let stand about 10 minutes to thicken. A 5-inch crepe pan is best for cooking these, but a 7-inch skillet may be used. Brush pan lightly with oil to moisten, then add 2 tablespoons batter; tilt so that mixture spreads to edges. As soon as it is lightly browned, turn gently; cook the other side. Fill each with one of following fillings; roll up as for crepes. Serve with Chinese Brown Sauce. *Makes about 6 servings.*

Shrimp Filling. Drain and mince a 6½-ounce can shrimp; combine with 2 chopped scallions, some chopped water chestnut or bamboo shoots, and soy sauce to taste.

Pork Filling. Cut the lean meat of 1 pork chop into fine slivers; sauté in oil with a little chopped onion or scallion, chopped bamboo shoots or green pepper, and minced celery. Add soy sauce to taste.

Waffles (Basic Recipe)

2 cups sifted all-purpose or cake
  flour
3 teaspoons baking powder
1 teaspoon salt

2 eggs, separated
1¼ cups milk
1/3 cup butter, melted

Preheat the waffle iron while mixing the batter. Combine flour, baking powder, and salt; blend well. Make a well in the center; add the egg yolks and milk; beat lightly until well blended (do not overbeat). Stir in melted butter. Separately beat egg whites until stiff; fold into batter. If waffle iron is well seasoned, it should not be greased. Spoon about 2 tablespoons batter into each grid or section; avoid filling more than two-thirds full. When waffle has stopped puffing up and no steam comes from the iron, open to see if waffle is sufficiently brown. If so, remove; divide into sections and serve the first go-round while baking additional waffles. Close lid of iron briefly to reheat before adding more batter. *Makes 6 4-section waffles, or 6 to 8 servings.*

Using Biscuit or Pancake Mix. Substitute 2 cups mix for the flour, baking powder, and salt. If using biscuit mix, only ¼ cup melted butter is needed. Eggs may be used whole rather than separated, though the waffles will not be quite as crisp and light.

HAM WAFFLES. After batter has been added to the iron, sprinkle ¼ cup minced ham over the top; ham will bake into the waffles.

CHEESE WAFFLES Add ½ cup grated cheese to basic recipe or mix.

CHOCOLATE DESSERT WAFFLES. Prepare waffles as in basic recipe, but use cake flour and add 3 tablespoons sugar. Melt 2 squares unsweetened chocolate in top of double boiler over hot water· stir into batter. Bake waffles in preheated iron until steam stops coming from the iron. Serve warm topped with whipped cream, ice cream, or vanilla pudding flavored with brandy.

GINGERBREAD WAFFLES. Prepare gingerbread batter with mix according to package directions. Bake in waffle iron as for regular waffles; serve warm topped with a mixture of whipped cream cheese and crushed pineapple, or cream cheese and chopped canned peaches.

WAFFLE SECRETS

Using plenty of butter in the batter is the secret of crispness.

Do not add sugar to the batter if you want waffles to be crisp—the sugar causes them to "wilt" if they stand longer than 10 minutes.

Never wash a waffle iron; simply clean the grids with steel wool. Washing will cause it to stick next time.

Fritter Batters

"Fritter" is an all-inclusive term applied to any food that is dipped in a protective batter (or egged and crumbed), then fried. In most cases, solid pieces of food are so dipped, but some fritters are made by adding minced food to a thick batter (this is true of corn fritters, clam fritters, and apple fritters or beignets). Most fritters are fried in deep fat, a few in shallow fat, but all are fried.

A fritter batter is thicker than a pancake batter, but not as thick as the dough for dropped biscuits. Some batters contain no liquid at all, only eggs and flour. Make sure foods are dry before dipping them in batter. A little olive oil added to fritter batter makes the coating more crisp. (Olive oil is more effective than butter, and the flavor will not be discernible.) Most important of all, the fat or oil for deep frying must be preheated to the correct temperature and kept at that temperature throughout the frying process. Drain all fried foods on absorbent paper before serving.

All-purpose Fritter Batter (Basic Recipe)

1 cup flour	1 or 2 eggs
1 teaspoon baking powder	1/3 to ½ cup milk or other liq-
¼ teaspoon salt	uid*
1 tablespoon olive oil	

Combine flour, baking powder, and salt (flour need not be pre-sifted); stir to blend; make a well in center. Place olive oil and unbeaten egg in center; stir in flour from sides until well blended. Gradually add liquid until mixture is the consistency of melted Cheddar. Let stand 30 minutes to 1 hour, if possible. Prepare foods for frying; drain well or pat dry with paper towels. Preheat fat to 370° F. Dip foods in batter; drop into hot fat; cook until outside is golden and crisp. Turn if necessary. Drain well on fresh paper towels. Also may be used for clam fritters, corn fritters, oyster fritters, or sweetbread fritters. *Makes 1½ cups batter.*

*If water is used instead of milk, less will be needed. Fruit juice or wine may be used as the liquid when appropriate.

Using Mix. Substitute 1 cup pancake mix for flour, baking powder, and salt in basic recipe. Or substitute 1 cup biscuit mix, omitting olive oil.

HAM FRITTERS. Add 1 cup minced ham and 1 tablespoon minced parsley to above batter. Drop batter by spoonfuls into deep, hot fat.

FISH FRITTERS. Add 1 cup cooked, flaked leftover fish, 1 tablespoon minced parsley, and 1 tablespoon minced onion to above batter. Drop by spoonfuls into hot fat.

BEER BATTER. Use beer as the liquid; use 2 eggs. *Makes 1½ cups batter.*

TEMPURA BATTER. Use 2 eggs, with water as the liquid; ½ teaspoon baking soda instead of 1 teaspoon baking powder. Let batter stand ½ hour before using. *Makes about 2½ cups batter.*

BANANA BEIGNETS. Peel and quarter 6 bananas. Prepare All-purpose Batter, using fruit juice as the liquid. Dip bananas in batter and sauté in hot butter using 6 to 8 tablespoons clarified butter in all until golden on all sides. Fry only part at a time; do not crowd pan. As they are cooked, sprinkle bananas lightly with rum. Superb as an accompaniment to ham or fish, or as a dessert.

APPLE BEIGNETS. Prepare All-purpose Batter, using fruit juice as the liquid. Peel, core, and dice tart apples to make 2 cups. Add the apples to the batter before the stiffly beaten whites are folded in. Drop by tablespoons into hot fat. When golden on all sides, remove with slotted spoon; drain on absorbent paper; dust while warm with confectioners' sugar.

PEACH OR APRICOT BEIGNETS. Prepare All-purpose Batter. Use canned peaches or apricots, and use the canned fruit syrup for the liquid in the batter. Add well-drained diced fruit to the batter before the stiffly beaten egg whites are folded in. Fry until golden; dust while warm with confectioners' sugar.

Puffy Egg Batter

2 eggs, separated
2 tablespoons flour
¼ teaspoon salt
2 tablespoons water

Blend the egg yolks with the flour, salt, and water. Beat the egg whites until stiff; fold into yolk mixture. Use immediately; dip fillets of fish in batter; sauté on both sides in blend of 3 tablespoons each olive oil and butter, heated to sizzling. Enough for 1½ pounds fish fillets, or 4 *servings.* (Also good for coating slices of sweetbread or brains, or for apple slices to be served topped with syrup.)

Doughnuts

Originally doughnuts actually contained nuts; they were sometimes called "nut cakes." Today's tubular "fried cakes" owe their shape to Hanson Gregory of Camden, Massachusetts. His mother's doughnuts were soggy in the center so often that he suggested she cut out the center—and she did.

4 tablespoons butter, softened
1 cup sugar
2 eggs
4 cups sifted flour
1 tablespoon baking powder
½ teaspoon salt
½ teaspoon nutmeg
¾ cup milk
Oil for deep frying

Cream butter and sugar together in large bowl of electric mixer until light and fluffy. Add eggs, one at a time. Combine presifted flour with baking powder, salt, and nutmeg. Set mixer at medium speed; add flour to butter mixture alternately with milk. When well blended, cover bowl; place in refrigerator; leave for 2 hours.

Remove a quarter of the dough at a time from bowl; roll out on lightly floured board to ¼ inch thick. Cut with doughnut cutter. Heat fat to 370° F. in an electric fryer or in a wide, deep pan on a thermostatically controlled range burner, or use electric skillet set at 370°, with fat 1 inch deep. Drop doughnuts in hot fat, frying only 2 or 3 at a time; turn once to brown on both sides. Remove with tongs; drain on absorbent paper. While warm, shake in a paper bag with confectioners' sugar or with a mixture of granulated sugar and cinnamon. When all are cooked, fry the holes. *Makes about 3 dozen.*

ORANGE-GLAZED DOUGHNUTS. Add 1 tablespoon grated orange peel to doughnut batter; instead of milk, use ¾ cup orange juice. When doughnuts are cooked, spread an orange glaze made by adding ¼ cup orange juice to 1½ cups sifted confectioners' sugar over the top of each.

See also Dutch Apple Doughnuts.

Biscuits and Muffins

These are the quick breads particularly beloved by Americans. Although a bride is no longer judged by the lightness of her breakfast biscuits as was the case 50 years ago, these quick breads, steaming-moist from the oven, make any simple supper seem special.

Besides the many mixes available, there are also oven-ready refrigerated biscuits and rolls. Many of these have very interesting recipe variations suggested on the package.

Baking Powder Biscuits (Basic Recipe)

2 cups sifted all-purpose flour	¼ cup vegetable shortening
3 teaspoons baking powder	¾ cup milk
½ teaspoon salt	

Sift flour before measuring; sift again with baking powder and salt. Cut in the shortening until mixture resembles coarse meal, or work the shortening into small particles with your fingers. Add the milk a little at a time, stirring to blend after each addition. Handle lightly. Dough will be soft; you will probably have to dust flour over your hands in order to pick it up. Turn out on lightly floured pastry board; knead just to make it smooth;

avoid too much kneading. Roll out to ½ inch thick. Cut into rounds with a 2-inch biscuit cutter, or into squares or diamonds. Place biscuits on ungreased baking sheet; place close together if you want them to rise high and be quite soft, apart if you prefer crusty biscuits. Bake in oven preheated to 450° F. (Let the biscuits stand in a warm place while the oven is heating.) Bake until tops are golden—12 to 15 minutes. Split while hot; spread with butter. *Makes about 14 biscuits, enough for 4 to 5 servings.*

For 2 or 3 servings, divide all ingredients in half, using 6 tablespoons milk.

DROP BISCUITS. Increase milk in basic recipe to 1 cup, or use 1 cup biscuit mix with 1 cup milk. Do not roll out. Drop by spoonfuls on greased baking sheet. Bake in preheated oven until golden.

BUTTERMILK BISCUITS. Use only 2 teaspoons baking powder; add ½ teaspoon baking soda to basic recipe; use buttermilk instead of whole milk.

CHEESE BISCUITS. Add ½ cup grated Cheddar cheese to basic recipe or to 2 cups biscuit mix.

DUMPLINGS. Use 1 cup biscuit mix, ½ cup milk, and 1 egg; or divide basic recipe in half but use a scant ½ cup milk and add 1 beaten egg. Do not roll out. Drop by spoonfuls over the top of beef stew, stewed chicken, or other recipe as specified. Cover pot; cook 12 minutes. Serve from the pot with "pot liquor" spooned over the dumplings. *Makes enough for 4 servings.*

PARSLEY DUMPLINGS. Prepare as for plain Dumplings but add 2 tablespoons minced parsley.

In any recipe calling for biscuit mix, the basic recipe for baking powder biscuits (without the milk) may be used. Conversely, in any recipe calling for flour, baking powder, salt, and shortening in approximately the same proportions, biscuit mix may be substituted.

Honey Buns

2 cups biscuit mix	2 tablespoons melted butter
1 egg	1/3 cup brown sugar
1/3 cup milk	1/3 cup chopped walnuts
2 tablespoons firm butter	or almonds
¼ cup plus 2 tablespoons honey	1/3 cup raisins

Combine biscuit mix, egg, and milk; beat with fork until sticky. Flour fingers, then knead biscuit dough until it can be handled easily. Roll out on floured board to a rectangle about 14 x 10 inches. Dot dough with bits of butter. Combine ¼ cup honey with melted butter and brown sugar; spread over dough; add chopped nuts and raisins. Roll up. Cut with knife into 8 slices. Place close together on greased baking sheet or baking pan. Spread remaining honey over top. Bake in oven preheated to 400° F. until golden—about 20 minutes. *Makes 8 buns.*

Golden Muffins (Basic Recipe)

2 cups sifted flour	1 egg, beaten
3 teaspoons baking powder	1 cup milk
½ teaspoon salt	¼ cup shortening, melted
1 tablespoon sugar	

Grease 12 muffin cups.* Preheat oven to 425° F. Sift together presifted flour, baking powder, salt, and sugar. Place in bowl; form a well in center. In well place egg and milk; stir in flour just until all flour is moistened (do not beat). Stir in melted shortening. Spoon into muffin cups. Bake until puffed and golden—20 to 25 minutes. Serve immediately with butter, jam, or jelly. *Makes 12.*

To make 6 muffins, divide all ingredients but egg in half.

*Greasing may not be necessary if Teflon-coated muffin tins are used.

Made with Biscuit Mix. Use 2 cups biscuit mix instead of flour, baking powder, and salt in basic recipe. Add only 2 tablespoons melted shortening.

For 6 muffins, use 1 cup biscuit mix and 1 tablespoon shortening, but use 1 whole egg or 1 egg yolk or 1 egg white.

BLUEBERRY MUFFINS. Add 1 cup fresh blueberries to basic recipe or to 2 cups biscuit mix.

DATE MUFFINS. Add ½ cup chopped pitted dates to basic recipe or to biscuit mix.

ORANGE MUFFINS. Add 1 tablespoon grated orange rind to basic recipe or to 2 cups biscuit mix; use orange juice instead of milk.

SPICED RAISIN MUFFINS. To basic recipe (or to 2 cups biscuit mix), add ½ teaspoon cinnamon, ½ teaspoon cloves or allspice, ¼ teaspoon nutmeg, and ½ cup raisins.

Beaten Biscuits

Throughout the states below the Mason-Dixon Line, beaten biscuits are a subject of nostalgia. To make them, even with the help of an electric mixer, requires great patience for they must be kneaded vigorously until the dough blisters. They are crackerlike in consistency, with a flavor all their own.

4 cups sifted all-purpose flour	shortening
1 teaspoon salt	1 cup milk
¾ cup fresh lard or vegetable	2 to 3 tablespoons water

Sift together flour and salt; set aside. Add lard and milk to bowl of electric mixer; beat at low speed until thoroughly blended; gradually add flour mixture. Increase speed of mixer to medium. Stop every now and then to remove dough that gets clogged in beater; add water a tablespoon at a time as dough thickens. Beat in mixer for five minutes. Remove; knead by hand until **dough blisters. Roll out on lightly floured board to ¼ inch thick;** cut with biscuit cutter. Prick each biscuit with fork. Bake in oven preheated to 375° F. until golden—for about 30 minutes. *Makes 20 biscuits.*

Bran Muffins

1½ cups sifted flour	real, or 1 cup wheat kernels
4 teaspoons baking powder	1 egg, beaten
1½ teaspoons salt	1½ cups milk
2 to 3 tablespoons sugar	3 tablespoons melted shortening
1 cup whole bran breakfast ce-	

Grease 12 muffin cups. Preheat oven to 400°F. Sift together presifted flour, baking powder, salt, and sugar. Add bran or wheat kernel; stir to blend. Make a well in center of flour; add egg and milk. Beat in flour from the sides just until all flour is moistened (avoid overbeating). Add melted shortening. Spoon into greased muffin cups. Bake until well browned—25 to 30 minutes. Serve immediately with butter and jam. *Makes 12.*

Corn Muffins

1 cup sifted flour	1 cup corn meal
3 teaspoons baking powder	1 egg, beaten
1 teaspoon salt	1 cup milk
2 to 3 tablespoons sugar	2 tablespoons melted shortening

Grease 12 muffin cups. Preheat oven to 400° F. Sift together presifted flour, baking powder, salt, and sugar. Stir in corn meal. Form a well in center; place egg and milk in well; beat in flour just until all flour is moistened. Stir in melted shortening. Pour into muffin cups; bake until top is golden-brown and firm—20 to 25 minutes. *Makes 12.*

For 6 muffins, divide all ingredients in half but use 1 whole egg.

Made with Mix. Substitute a packaged corn muffin mix for the flour, baking powder, salt, sugar, corn meal, and shortening in the above recipe. Only egg and milk need be added to the mix.

PINEAPPLE-CORN MUFFINS. Instead of milk, add ½ cup crushed pineapple (including juice) to package of corn muffin mix; use 2 eggs instead of 1. Or substitute crushed pineapple for milk in basic recipe, adding 1 more egg.

Popovers

1 cup sifted flour	ening
½ teaspoon salt	1 cup milk
1 tablespoon oil or melted short-	2 eggs

In contrast to muffin batter, which should be beaten no more than 12 strokes or until the flour is moistened, popover batter needs vigorous beating with a rotary beater or an electric mixer. Preheat oven to 425° F. Grease 12 muffin cups. Place all ingredients in mixing bowl; beat until very smooth. Fill muffin cups two-thirds full (batter may not be enough for 12 cups; place a little water in any empty cups.) Bake until crust is very brown—30 to 35 minutes. Prick tops with fork; leave in oven 10 minutes longer to allow steam to escape so popovers will not be soggy inside. Serve hot with plenty of butter. *Makes 10 to 12.*

Quick Loaf or Supper Breads

Orange-Cinnamon Bread

¾ cup sugar
1 egg
1¼ cups orange juice
3 cups biscuit mix
¼ teaspoon cinnamon

1 cup finely chopped nuts
½ cup chopped pitted dates, prunes, or seedless raisins
1 teaspoon grated orange rind

Preheat oven to 350° F. Grease 9 x 5 x 3-inch loaf pan. Combine sugar, egg, orange juice, biscuit mix, and cinnamon; beat vigorously for 30 strokes. Stir in nuts, fruit, and orange rind. Pour into pan. Bake until toothpick inserted in center comes out clean—55 to 60 minutes. Cool before slicing. *Makes 1 loaf.*

Lemon-Prune Bread

1 cup sugar
1 egg
1¼ cups milk
3 cups biscuit mix

¾ cup chopped walnuts
¾ cup chopped pitted prunes
1 tablespoon lemon juice
1 tablespoon grated lemon rind

Preheat oven to 350° F. Grease 9 x 5 x 3-inch loaf pan. Combine sugar, egg, milk, and biscuit mix; beat vigorously for 30 strokes. Stir in remaining ingredients, blending well. Pour into pan. Bake until toothpick inserted in center comes out clean—50 to 55 minutes. Cool before slicing. *Makes 1 loaf.*

LEMON-ALMOND BREAD. Make as above, but use crushed almonds instead of walnuts, omit prunes and lemon juice. Bake 45 to 50 minutes.

Cranberry-Nut Bread

¾ cup sugar
1 egg
1¼ cups orange juice
1 tablespoon grated orange rind
3 cups biscuit mix

¾ cup chopped nuts
1 cup chopped cranberries (fresh or frozen: if frozen, do not thaw)

Preheat oven to 350° F. Mix together sugar, egg, orange juice, orange rind, and biscuit mix. Beat vigorously for 30 seconds (batter may still be lumpy). Stir in nuts and cranberries. Pour into well-greased 9 x 5 x 3-inch loaf pan. Bake until toothpick stuck into center comes out clean—55 to 60 minutes. Remove from loaf pan. Cool before slicing.

Corn Bread (Basic Recipe)

1 cup sifted all-purpose flour
3 teaspoons baking powder
1 teaspoon salt
2 tablespoons sugar
1 cup yellow or white corn meal

2 eggs
1 cup milk
¼ cup oil or melted vegetable
  shortening

Grease an 8 x 8-inch baking pan. Preheat oven to 400° F. Sift together presifted flour, baking powder, salt, and sugar; place in mixing bowl; stir in corn meal. Make a well in center of flour mixture; add eggs and milk; stir in flour from sides and beat just until dry ingredients are moistened. Add shortening. Pour into baking pan; bake until top is lightly browned—about 30 minutes. Cut into squares and serve immediately with butter. *Makes about 12 squares.*

Using Mix. The basic recipe is equivalent to 1 package corn muffin mix. The quick-and-easy corn bread mix that comes complete with a foil pan makes less than half this quantity. Use corn muffin mix, adding 2 eggs and 1 cup milk, for the same number of servings, or buy 2 packages quick-and-easy corn bread mix and follow package directions.

NEW ENGLAND CORN BREAD. Follow basic recipe but use ¼ cup molasses and ¾ cup milk instead of 1 cup milk. Omit sugar.

Southern Corn Bread

2 cups white corn meal
1 teaspoon baking soda
1 teaspoon salt

1 egg
2 cups buttermilk or sour milk
¼ cup melted bacon fat

Preheat oven to 500° F. Grease a 12 x 8-inch or 13 x 9-inch pan. Combine corn meal, soda, and salt in mixing bowl; make a well in center; add egg and buttermilk. Stir in corn meal from the sides; beat just until all dry ingredients are moistened. Stir in melted fat. Pour into baking pan. Bake until crisp and brown—about 20 minutes. Cut into squares. Serve with butter or maple syrup and crisp bacon. *Makes about 16 squares, or 8 servings.*

CRACKLIN' BREAD. Make Southern Corn Bread but instead of bacon fat, use the fat saved from pork sausages, or use crackling (the crisp skin of pork fat) broken into small pieces. Bake either in muffin pans or corn-stick molds.

Quick Coffee Cakes

These are not "quick" in today's sense because they require 25 to 30 minutes' baking time, but, because the leavener is baking powder rather than yeast, they can be whipped together in time for late breakfast, kaffeeklatsch, or brunch.

Streusel Coffee Cake

1½ cups sifted flour
3 teaspoons baking powder
¼ teaspoon salt
¼ cup butter

1 cup sugar
1 egg
½ cup milk

STREUSEL TOPPING

½ cup brown sugar
2 tablespoons flour
2 teaspoons cinnamon

¼ cup butter, melted
¼ cup finely chopped or crushed
nuts (optional)

Preheat oven to 375° F. Combine flour, baking powder, and salt; place in mixing bowl. Cream butter and sugar together until light and fluffy (this may be done in blender); add egg, then milk. Add mixture to flour, stirring in flour from sides; beat just until all flour is moistened. Pour into greased 9 x 9-inch pan.

Prepare Streusel Topping by blending together with fingers the sugar, flour, cinnamon, and butter, until mixture is in fine pieces. Add nuts. Spread mixture over top of coffee cake batter before baking. Bake until top is golden and a toothpick in center comes out clean—25 to 35 minutes. *Makes about 9 squares.*

Made with Mix. Substitute 1½ cups biscuit mix for the flour, baking powder, and salt; add only 2 tablespoons butter. Or use quick and easy coffee cake mix according to package directions and add ½ the Streusel Topping before baking.

FRUIT-TOPPED COFFEE CAKE. Make Streusel Coffee Cake but for topping use only ¼ cup brown sugar, and instead of ¼ cup nuts, use ½ cup mixed candied fruit.

BLUEBERRY COFFEE CAKE. Stir 1½ cups fresh blueberries into coffee cake batter. Use the same streusel mixture but omit nuts.

PINEAPPLE COFFEE CAKE. Add ½ cup well-drained crushed pineapple to coffee cake batter; decrease sugar to ¼ cup. Omit nuts from Streusel Topping.

NUT COFFEE CAKE. Add ½ cup chopped walnuts or pecans or ¼ cup each nuts and raisins to coffee cake batter. Use orange juice for half the liquid in the batter. Add grated orange rind to topping; omit nuts from topping.

Baking with Yeast

There are few satisfactions greater than that of producing a home-baked loaf of bread, or a stollen redolent of fruit and spices, or golden-soft yeast rolls whose very aroma is enough to awaken hunger long before they are brought, still warm, to the table.

Successful baking with yeast demands that certain tricks be mastered and many precautions be observed, but anyone can learn to do it for it does not require great skill. And when one is in the right mood for it, baking with yeast is fun. The husband of one of my friends who started baking bread as a lark found punching down the dough to be a marvelous release from tension after a hard day at the office.

While measurements must be exact, and oven temperatures reliable, the yeast itself must be treated with patience. So sensitive is this "living plant" to temperatures that a few degrees one way or the other may completely alter the rising time. Also, kneading the dough requires dexterity: A smooth, pliable dough must be formed but it must not be kneaded so that the elasticity is worked out of it. It's a "feel" one learns.

A few pointers:

- Check the expiration date printed on the package before buying or using yeast. If the time is up, you may still be able to use it *if* it has been stored in a cool place, but be warned that the finished bread may be a little on the heavy side. It is usually better not to chance it.
- A cold bowl could chill the yeast. Rinse out both the bowl in which the yeast is to be dissolved and the big mixing bowl with hot water just before using; dry thoroughly before adding ingredients.
- Use only water for dissolving the yeast even if the recipe specifies milk or some other liquid. Water dissolves the yeast more quickly and thoroughly.
- The temperature of the water should be blood temperature—more than lukewarm but not hot. Test by letting a few

drops fall on the inside of your wrist—if you can't feel it, the temperature is just right. If it feels either cold or hot, try again.

•The perfect temperature for the spot on which the dough is to rise is 85° F. In summer, you may only have to place the bowl, covered with a clean cloth, in a corner free from drafts. In winter (when home-baked breads are most in demand), it may be necessary to place the bowl in a spot where warmth from stove or radiator will help (but not on the range or radiator). Or, place it in an unlighted oven; beneath the mixing bowl place a large pan of hot water. Close the oven door.

•Even the temperature of the flour can make a difference, if the flour is stored in a cold pantry. This won't be a problem for most American cooks, but it just gives you an idea of how temperamental yeast can be.

•How do you know when the yeast is properly risen—"doubled in bulk"? Press two fingers deep into the dough; pull them out. If a deep indentation fills up immediately, let the dough have a little more time.

There are three basic methods of preparing a yeast dough. The newest and quickest is called the "batter method." This requires no kneading. For the beginner, it will probably seem the easiest method even though the product is not quite so desirable: The texture of the bread is not so fine and the crust is rougher, more uneven.

The method most used is called the "straight-dough method"; it requires two risings. The third method, called the "sponge method," is the oldest. It requires three stages: first the yeast is fermented with water and a small amount of flour into what is called a "sponge," then the remaining flour is added to form a dough that must rise to double in bulk, and finally the dough is shaped for a third rising.

A variation of the straight-dough method is the "refrigerator method"; this makes it possible to start the dough one day and bake bread or rolls shortly before dinner on the following day or even a week later.

The first step in all yeast baking is to get out all necessary utensils and ingredients. Read the recipe through to see what you need. Warm the bowls with hot water, especially in midwinter. Be sure to have plenty of wax paper, a rubber spatula for removing the dough from the bowl and from the mixer blades, a linen cloth to place over the dough, and cooling racks.

White Bread

¼ cup warm water	2 tablespoons sugar
1 package active dry yeast	2 teaspoons salt
1 cup milk	6 cups unsifted all-purpose flour
1 tablespoon butter or margarine	1 cup lukewarm water

Test water temperature on inside of wrist; place ¼ cup warm water in small bowl (previously warmed). Sprinkle yeast over water; stir to dissolve. Heat milk, butter, sugar, and salt until butter is melted; stir to dissolve. Cool milk to lukewarm, then place in large mixing bowl (previously warmed). Add 2 cups of the flour to milk mixture; stir to blend. Add yeast and 1 cup lukewarm water. Beat to blend well. Add remaining 4 cups flour all at once and beat with spoon or electric mixer until smooth.

Grease the palms of your hands; turn over dough until you can handle it easily, then turn out onto lightly floured board. Knead and punch dough with fingers, over and over, until it is a smooth ball.

Clean out the mixing bowl; wash with warm water; dry, then rub with shortening. Place ball of dough in mixing bowl; brush oil or melted butter over top. Cover bowl; place in warm place free from drafts until doubled (dents remain in dough when poked).

Punch down the dough (see sketch), then pull edges of dough to center and turn so a round ball again is formed. Turn out on board; cut dough in half; shape each half into a ball. Cover with linen towel; allow to rest 5 to 10 minutes, then shape. You may want to bake two loaves exactly alike or vary one of the loaves (making Cheese Bread or Caraway Bread) or make one loaf of bread and a dozen rolls.

Place each ball of dough in a greased 9 x 5 x 3-inch loaf pan. Cover with linen towel; place again in warm spot until dough has risen to the tops of the pans.

Preheat oven to 400° F. Bake until tops are golden and crusty—about 40 minutes. Remove from oven; tip the bread out of the pans and tap the bottoms to see if the bread has a hollow sound. If not, return it to the oven for another 5 minutes of baking; test again. When bread is baked, place on wire racks to cool. The aroma will have everyone mad with hunger, but do not slice bread until it has cooled on a rack for at least an hour. *Makes 2 loaves.*

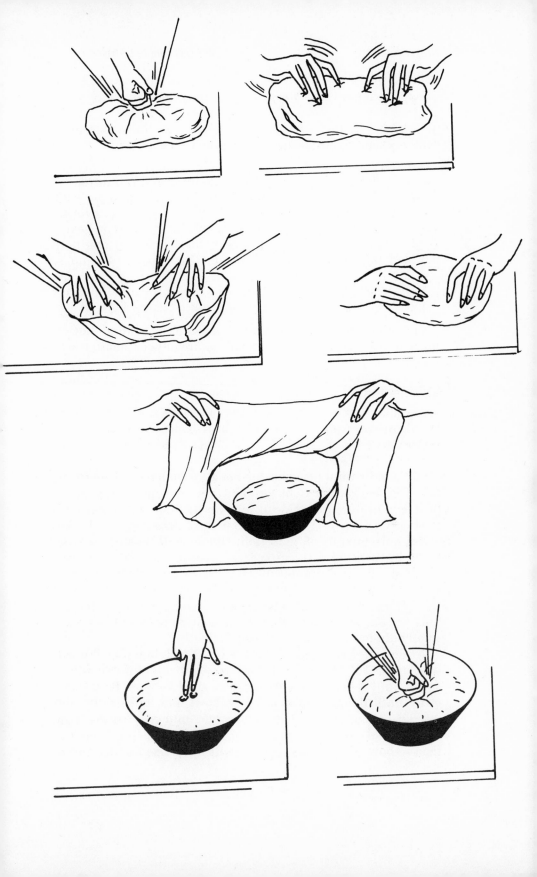

CHEESE BREAD. To half the dough, work in 1 cup grated sharp Cheddar cheese when kneading after the first rising.

CARAWAY BREAD. To half the dough, work in 1 tablespoon caraway seeds when kneading after the first rising.

CRUSTY ROLLS. Form half the dough into rolls as follows: cut dough into 12 pieces with knife dipped in flour. Roll out each piece into an oblong; fold ends of oblong to center; overlap slightly, then pinch edges together. Place 1 inch apart on baking sheet. Brush melted shortening over top; cover; let rise until doubled. Bake until crust is golden and firm—about 15 minutes.

WHOLE-WHEAT BREAD. Instead of using all white flour, use equal parts whole wheat and white flour in basic recipe.

Baked bread or rolls should be frozen *after* baking; they require only defrosting at room temperature or brief heating to be ready to serve when wanted.

Batter Bread

½ cup milk	½ cup warm water
1½ tablespoons sugar	1 package active dry yeast
1½ teaspoons salt	2¼ cups unsifted flour
1 tablespoon margarine	

Heat the milk until it steams (do not allow to boil). Stir in sugar, salt, and margarine. Cool to lukewarm. Measure warm water (test temperature on inside of your wrist). Pour water into large mixing bowl; sprinkle in yeast; stir until dissolved. Add lukewarm milk mixture. Stir in flour; batter will be stiff. Beat by hand or with electric mixer at medium speed until well blended—about 2 minutes. If using mixer, remove dough from blades with rubber spatula. Cover bowl; place in warm spot free from draft until dough has more than doubled in bulk—about 40 minutes. Batter will look rough and moist with small bubbles just beneath the surface.

While batter is rising, grease a 9 x 5 x 3-inch loaf pan. Preheat oven to 375° F. When batter has doubled, stir it down with a spoon until it is reduced almost to original volume. Beat vigorously until dough leaves sides of bowl and looks shiny and smooth—about 30 seconds. Turn batter into greased loaf pan. Immediately place in oven; bake until crust is golden and firm—about 50 minutes. (Bread will have risen above top of pan.) Remove from oven; immediately turn out of pan. Tap bottom; it should sound hollow—if not, put back into the oven for another 5 minutes. Cool on wire rack. Allow to cool completely before slicing. *Makes 1 loaf. Double all ingredients to make 2 loaves.*

Apple-Crumb Coffee Cake (Batter Method)

¼ cup warm water	½ teaspoon salt
1 package active dry yeast	3 eggs
8 tablespoons (1 stick; ¼ pound) butter or margarine, softened	¼ cup lukewarm milk
	2 1/3 cups unsifted flour
½ cup sugar	Apple-Crumb Topping

Test water temperature with drops on inside of wrist; measure into small, warm bowl. Sprinkle in yeast; stir until dissolved. Cream together butter and sugar with electric mixer until light and fluffy. Add yeast mixture, salt, eggs, and milk (which has been heated to steaming, then cooled to lukewarm). Set mixer at medium speed, and gradually add flour; blend well. Spread the batter into a well-greased 9 x 9 x 2-inch baking pan. Arrange Apple-Crumb Topping over the dough. Cover. Let rise in warm spot free from drafts until doubled—about 1 hour.

Preheat oven to 375° F. Bake coffee cake until golden and firm—about 35 minutes. Turn out of pan immediately and cool 10 minutes on wire rack. Serve warm. *Makes about 9 squares.*

APPLE-CRUMB TOPPING. Peel, core, and slice 3 large apples; arrange slices over top of dough. Mix together 2/3 cup sugar, ½ cup flour, 2 teaspoons cinnamon, and 6 tablespoons softened butter or margarine until mixture resembles coarse crumbs. Sprinkle mixture over apples.

PANNETONE. Prepare as for Apple-Crumb Coffee Cake but instead of topping, add to the batter itself 2 tablespoons chopped citron and ¼ cup golden raisins. Instead of a 9 x 9 x 2-inch pan, 2 greased small loaf pans (7½ x 4 x 2¼-inches) may be used. Brush ¼ cup melted butter over dough before placing pans in oven.

Sweet Egg Rolls

1/3 cup milk	¼ cup warm water
2 tablespoons sugar	1 package active dry yeast
½ teaspoon salt	1 egg
2 tablespoons butter or margarine	2¾ cups unsifted flour

Heat milk until it steams: do not allow to boil. Add sugar, salt, and butter: cool to lukewarm. Measure warm water (test temperature with drops on inside of wrist): place in large mixing bowl. Stir in yeast until dissolved. Add the lukewarm milk mixture, egg, and about half the flour. Beat until smooth. Stir in enough remaining flour to make a soft dough.

Turn out on lightly floured board: knead until smooth and elastic—about 10 minutes. Place dough in greased bowl: cover with linen cloth. Let rise until doubled—about 30 minutes. Punch dough down: divide into 12 even pieces: form each piece into a small round. Place rolls on greased baking sheet. Let rise again for about 30 minutes. Brush tops with melted butter or margarine. Bake in oven preheated to 375° F. until rolls are golden—about 15 to 20 minutes. Serve warm. *Makes 1 dozen.*

For 2 dozen, double all ingredients.

PAN ROLLS. Form dough into a roll about 12 inches long. Cut into 12 equal pieces: form each into a smooth ball. Place in greased shallow pan about ¼ inch apart. Allow to rise again, then bake as in basic recipe.

PARKER HOUSE ROLLS. Roll out dough into 9-inch circle: cut into rounds with 2½-inch cutter. With dull edge of table knife, make an indentation in center of each: fold over so edges just meet: brush tops with melted butter or margarine. Let rise again: bake as in basic recipe.

CRESCENTS. Divide dough into two parts. Roll out each into a 9-inch circle. Brush with melted shortening. Cut each circle into 8 pie-shaped wedges. Roll up, beginning at wide end. Seal ends by pressing dough firmly together. Place about 2 inches apart on greased baking sheet: place with points underneath. Curve to form crescents. Let rise again: bake as in basic recipe.

CLOVER LEAF. Cut off pieces of dough about 1 inch in diameter. Grease palms of hands: roll each piece of dough into a ball.

Place 3 balls in each of 12 greased muffin cups. Brush more melted shortening over tops. Let rise again; bake.

Refrigerator Rolls

¾ cup hot water or warm milk	1 cup warm water
½ cup sugar	2 packages active dry yeast
1 tablespoon salt	1 egg
3 tablespoons shortening	5½ to 6 cups flour

Combine hot water or milk, sugar, salt, and shortening; stir until shortening is melted and sugar dissolved. Cool to lukewarm. Measure warm water (first tested for temperature on inside of wrist) into large mixing bowl. Sprinkle in yeast; stir until dissolved. Stir in water or milk mixture. Add egg; beat until yolk and white are blended. Add half the flour; beat until dough falls from spoon. Stir in remaining flour a little at a time until soft dough is formed. Cover tightly with plastic wrap or waxed paper held in place with rubber band. Store in refrigerator until doubled in bulk, then punch down and remove only as much dough as wanted at a time. Shape rolls; place in pans; let rise until doubled, then bake in preheated 400° F. oven until golden—15 to 20 minutes. *Makes 24 rolls*; dough will keep in refrigerator for 1 week. When wanted, dough may be formed into any of previously described shapes, or into sweet buns.

PECAN BUNS. Melt 1 stick (¼ pound or 8 tablespoons) butter or margarine; add 1 cup brown sugar and ¾ cup chopped pecans. Make dough for Refrigerator Rolls. Use approximately half the dough for plain rolls; roll out remainder on floured board into a 12-inch square. Sprinkle pecan mixture over dough, leaving a ½-inch-wide border around edges. Roll up; cut into 1-inch slices. Place in 12 greased muffin cups. Cover; let rise until doubled—about 1 hour. Bake in oven preheated to 350° F. about 25 minutes. *Makes 12.*

CINNAMON BUNS. Make dough for Refrigerator Rolls. Use approximately half the dough for plain rolls; roll out remainder into a 12-inch square. Melt 6 tablespoons butter; spread over dough with pastry brush. Sprinkle mixture of cinnamon and sugar over butter. (Also sprinkle ¼ cup raisins over dough, if desired.) Roll up. Cut into 1-inch slices. Place 1 inch apart on greased baking sheet. Cover; let rise until doubled. Bake in oven preheated to 400° F. about 20 minutes. Cool on rack. Frost with Vanilla Glaze. *Makes 12.*

Sweet Potato Buns

4 tablespoons butter, melted	2 eggs, well beaten
1 cup mashed cooked or canned sweet potatoes	1 teaspoon salt
	3 tablespoons sugar
1 envelope active dry yeast	3½ to 4 cups sifted all-purpose
½ cup warm water	flour
½ cup milk	

Add butter to sweet potatoes; beat to blend. Dissolve the yeast in warm water. Heat milk just until it steams; cool to lukewarm, then add to dissolved yeast. Add potatoes, eggs, salt, sugar, and 2 cups of the flour; blend well; spoon into large bowl. Cover and let rise in warm place until doubled. Sift in remaining flour; knead until smooth, then form into rolls about 1½ inches in diameter. Place rolls close together on buttered baking sheet. Let rise until doubled again. Preheat oven to 375°. Bake until tops are golden—20 to 30 minutes. Eat while hot with plenty of butter. *Makes approximately 30.*

Sally Lunn

6 tablespoons butter	2 tablespoons sugar
½ cup milk, heated	1 teaspoon salt
1 envelope yeast	4 cups sifted flour, or enough for
¼ cup warm water	stiff batter
4 eggs, well beaten	

Place the butter in the milk; heat milk until butter is melted. Cool to lukewarm. Meantime, thoroughly dissolve yeast in warm water (test temperature on wrist). Combine beaten eggs, milk, yeast, sugar and salt, in large bowl. Sift in flour, stirring until batter is stiff. Let rise in warm place until doubled in bulk. Turn out on floured board; knead well with lightly greased fingers. Butter 2 8 x 8 x 2-inch cake pans; divide the dough into two parts; place in the two pans. Let rise again until doubled. Bake in oven preheated to 400° until tops are a beautiful golden brown—15 to 20 minutes. Serve hot, cut in wedges, with plenty of butter. Leftover Sally Lunn may be split and toasted. *Makes 2 cake-size loaves.*

Dutch Apple Doughnuts

These yeast-raised doughnuts are made with hot roll mix. To make them from scratch, substitute 1 package active dry yeast, 2-1/3 cups sifted flour, and ½ teaspoon salt for the package of mix in the following recipe.

1 package hot roll mix
½ cup sugar
½ teaspoon nutmeg
¼ cup warm water
¼ cup orange juice

2 eggs, well beaten
1 cup peeled, diced tart apples
¼ cup raisins
Oil for deep-frying

Blend the flour in the package of hot roll mix with sugar and nutmeg. Test temperature of warm water by letting a few drops fall on the inside of the wrist; place water in small bowl; add yeast from package of mix; stir until dissolved. Add to this the orange juice (which should be at room temperature), eggs, apples, and raisins. Stir in the flour mixture to form a dough. Sprinkle pastry board with flour; turn out dough on board; knead until smooth. Return to clean bowl; cover; place in a warm spot free from drafts until dough has doubled in bulk. Punch down; knead lightly. Roll out a third of the dough at a time to ½-inch thick. Cut with doughnut cutter. Let rise again until doubled—about 30 minutes. Preheat oil to 375° F. in electric fryer, electric skillet, or in wide, deep pan on a thermostatically controlled burner. Fry a few doughnuts at a time until golden—about 2 to 3 minutes on each side; turn once. While warm, dust with confectioners or granulated sugar. *Makes about 2 dozen.*

OLIEBOLLEN. Prepare as for Dutch Apple Doughnuts, but instead of diced apple, add 2 tablespoons chopped candied orange peel. Instead of rolling out the dough when it has doubled in bulk, drop by tablespoons into hot oil or fat.

French Bread

1 cup warm water   ½ tablespoon sugar
1 package active dry yeast   2½ cups unsifted flour
1½ teaspoons salt   Corn meal

Test temperature of water; measure into large mixing bowl which has been warmed. Sprinkle in yeast; stir to dissolve. Add salt and sugar; stir to dissolve. Add the flour about a cup at a time; beat in with a wooden spoon, or beat with electric mixer at low speed. Add enough flour to make a smooth dough. Cover the bowl; let dough stand in warm place until doubled. Turn out the dough onto a floured board; let rest 10 minutes, then divide in half. Roll out each half into an oblong ¼ inch thick; fold the ends of the oblong to the center; overlap slightly, then seal the dough by pinching the center seam and ends together (see sketches). Twist seam slightly, if desired. The loaves should be long and slender; the more slender, the crustier the bread will be. Dust a baking sheet with corn meal; place the shaped dough on the sheet. Cut diagonal gashes (see sketch) over top. Brush with water. Cover; let rise again until almost doubled. Preheat oven to 400° F. Place a pan of water in the lower part of the oven. Bake loaves until golden and crusty—about 40 minutes. Remove; cool on racks. Do not slice until completely cold. *Makes 2 slender loaves.*

WHOLE-WHEAT FRENCH BREAD. Instead of using all white flour, use half whole wheat, half all-purpose flour.

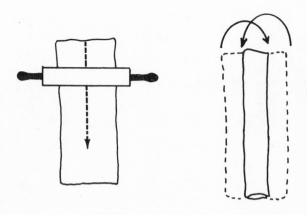

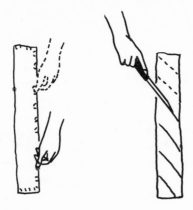

Whole-wheat Bread (Sponge Method)

1½ cups warm water
3 tablespoons sugar
2 packages active dry yeast
4 cups unsifted all-purpose white flour
1 cup milk

1/3 cup molasses
1 tablespoon salt
5 tablespoons margarine
3 cups unsifted whole-wheat flour

Measure and test temperature of warm water; place in large, warm bowl. Sprinkle in sugar and yeast; stir until dissolved. Add 1½ cups all-purpose flour. Beat until smooth. Cover; let rise in warm place until light and spongy—about 30 minutes.

Heat milk; stir in molasses, salt, and margarine; cool to lukewarm. Stir sponge down, then stir in lukewarm milk mixture, remaining white flour, and enough wheat flour to form a soft dough. Turn out on lightly floured board and knead until smooth and elastic—about 8 to 10 minutes. Place in greased bowl; turn to grease all over. Cover; let rise in warm place until doubled—about 30 minutes.

Punch down. Divide in half; shape into loaves. Place in 2 greased 9 x 3-inch bread pans. Cover; let rise again until doubled—about 30 minutes.

Preheat oven to 400° F. Bake bread until crisp brown crust has formed. Remove; turn out on rack; tap bottom. If loaves sound hollow, cool on racks at least 1 hour before slicing. *Makes 2 loaves.*

Swedish Rye Bread (Limpa)

½ teaspoon baking soda
2 cups buttermilk
½ cup water
½ cup molasses
1 tablespoon anise or fennel seed
1½ tablespoons salt

3 tablespoons shortening
1 envelope active dry yeast
3 cups sifted all-purpose flour
3 cups rye flour
2 tablespoons butter, melted

Add baking soda to buttermilk. In saucepan combine water, molasses, anise or fennel seed, salt, and shortening. Bring to a boil; boil 3 minutes. Remove from heat; cool to warm (test temperature on wrist). Add yeast to molasses mixture; stir until dissolved. Add buttermilk to yeast mixture in large mixing bowl; add all-purpose flour; beat hard to make a smooth dough. Add rye flour; mix well; turn out on lightly floured board; knead until smooth and elastic. Place in heated, greased bowl; cover; set in warm spot free from drafts; let rise until doubled—1½ to 2 hours. Punch down; knead again; divide in half and make two round balls. Place balls on greased baking sheet; brush tops with melted butter; let rise again until doubled—about 1 hour. Bake in oven preheated to 375° F. for 10 minutes; reduce heat to 350° F.; bake 35 to 45 minutes longer. Remove from oven and brush again with butter. *Makes 2 loaves.*

Onion Bread Ring

1 envelope active dry yeast
¼ cup warm water
2 tablespoons sugar
2 teaspoons salt
1 egg, beaten

3 tablespoons instant minced onion
¾ cup milk
3 to 3¼ cups flour
1/3 cup melted shortening

Soften the yeast in warm water (test temperature on wrist). Stir in sugar, salt, then the egg. Add instant onion to milk; heat milk; do not allow to boil. Cool to lukewarm; add to yeast mixture. Stir in 2 cups of the flour; beat vigorously until batter is smooth. Add melted shortening; mix well; add remaining flour; beat until dough is smooth and satiny. Grease a 1-quart ring mold; turn dough into mold. Cover; let rise in warm place free from drafts until dough is doubled or has risen ⅛ inch from top of mold—about 1 hour. Preheat oven to 400° F. Bake ring until top is nicely browned and bottom sounds hollow when tapped—about 20 minutes. Turn out onto a wire rack; cool. Serve still slightly warm; cut into thick slices. *Makes 8 to 10 servings.*

Hot Cross Buns

1 package active dry yeast
¼ cup warm water
3 tablespoons sugar
¾ cup milk
1½ teaspoons salt
1·teaspoon vanilla
1 egg
3 cups unsifted flour
5 tablespoons shortening, melted

¼ cup seedless raisins
¼ cup dried currants
2 tablespoons sliced citron
2 tablespoons candied orange peel
1 egg yolk
1 tablespoon milk
Vanilla Glaze

Add yeast to warm water (test temperature on wrist); stir to dissolve. Add sugar to milk; heat milk to steaming, then cool to lukewarm. Add lukewarm milk to yeast with salt, vanilla, and egg; beat until white and yolk of egg are blended. Stir in approximately half the flour and beat until batter falls from spoon. Cool melted shortening to lukewarm; stir in 3 tablespoons. Blend in fruit and peel. Gradually add remaining flour until soft dough is formed. Turn out onto floured pastry board; let rest 10 minutes, then knead until smooth and elastic. Shape into a ball; place in greased bowl. Brush remaining melted shortening over top of dough. Cover; let rise in warm place until doubled. Punch down dough; shape into a ball; cover; let rest 10 minutes. Cut dough into about 30 pieces; shape into small biscuit-shaped rolls. Place in lightly greased baking pan. Cut a cross in top of each with sharp knife. Brush tops with egg yolk mixed with milk. Let rise again until doubled. Bake in oven preheated to 400° F. until top is golden and shiny—about 15 minutes. While warm, make a cross over each bun with Vanilla Glaze. *Makes about 30.*

VANILLA GLAZE. Blend 1 tablespoon water and ¼ teaspoon vanilla with ¾ cup sifted confectioners' sugar.

Prune Baba

Prepare yeast dough as for Hot Cross Buns but add only 1 cup chopped, pitted dried prunes instead of other fruit. Place dough in greased and floured ½-quart ring mold; let rise until doubled in bulk, then bake in oven preheated to 400° F. until golden and firm to touch—about 25 minutes. Turn out on round platter and immediately spoon over it one half the following boiling-hot Rum Syrup. *Makes about 10 rich servings.*

RUM SYRUP. Combine 1 cup each sugar and water and ½ cup dark sweet rum. Bring to a boil and boil hard until syrup begins to thread. Spoon half the syrup over the hot Baba. When cake is cold, spoon remaining syrup over the Baba; if necessary, heat syrup a little to make it more fluid. Serve garnished with whipped cream.

Dresden Stollen

½ cup seedless raisins
¼ cup chopped citron
¼ cup chopped candied orange peel
¼ cup dark rum
1 package active dry yeast
¼ cup warm water
¾ cup milk
¼ cup sugar
½ teaspoon salt

4 tablespoons (½ stick) butter
2¾ to 3 cups unsifted flour
⅛ teaspoon ground cardamom
2 eggs, beaten
1 teaspoon grated lemon rind
½ cup (about 6 ounces) almonds, blanched, shredded
2 to 3 tablespoons melted butter
Confectioners' sugar

Soak fruit and peel in rum while preparing dough. Dissolve yeast in warm water (test temperature on wrist). Combine milk, sugar, salt, and butter; heat until sugar is dissolved and butter melted. Cool to lukewarm. Place 2 cups flour blended with cardamom in large bowl; form a well in center. In well, place yeast, milk mixture, and eggs. Stir to blend in flour, then beat until smooth and dough comes away easily from sides of bowl. Drain fruit; add with lemon rind and ¼ cup almonds to the ¾ cup reserved flour; toss until fruit and nuts are well coated. Add coated fruit and nuts to dough; work dough with fingers until fruit and nuts are well distributed. Knead on lightly floured board until smooth and elastic. If sticky, add a little more flour. Place in greased bowl, turning to grease the top. Cover; let rise in warm place until doubled—about 1 hour.

Turn out on board; roll dough into oblong shape ½-inch thick. Brush melted butter over top. Fold in half lengthwise in pocketbook shape so that upper half does not quite cover the lower edge. Form into crescent. Place on greased baking sheet. Brush top with more melted butter. Let rise again until doubled—35 to 45 minutes. Press remaining almonds into dough. Preheat oven to 350° F.; bake the stollen until golden and firm—about 40 minutes. Remove. Brush with a generous amount of melted butter. Dust with confectioners' sugar while warm. *Makes 1 loaf.*

Greek Easter Bread

¾ cup warm water
1 package active dry yeast
¼ cup milk
2 tablespoons sugar
2 teaspoons salt

Coarsely grated rind of 1 orange
2 tablespoons butter
3¾ to 4 cups sifted flour
1 large or 2 small eggs, beaten

GLAZE

2 to 3 tablespoons sesame seed
1 small egg, beaten

2 tablespoons cold water

Test water on wrist; add yeast to water; let stand a few minutes. Combine milk, sugar, salt, orange rind, and butter; heat together just to boiling; cool to lukewarm. Add half the flour and the milk mixture to yeast; stir to blend. Add remaining flour alternately with the beaten eggs, stirring until dough comes away from bowl; it should be very stiff. Turn out on floured board; knead until smooth—3 to 5 minutes. Place in large greased bowl; cover and place in warm spot free from drafts until doubled—about 45 minutes. Punch down the dough; turn over; let stand 20 minutes longer. Turn out on lightly floured board; shape two-thirds of the dough into a large ball; place in center of greased baking sheet; flatten slightly. Divide remaining dough into thirds; roll each into a long, thin ribbon, then weave into a braid long enough to encircle the center loaf. Place braid around the loaf; pinch ends of braid tightly together. Return to warm spot to rise again until doubled in bulk, then brush bread with mixture of sesame seeds, egg, and water for glaze. Finally, cut the shape of a cross in the center of the loaf with thin-bladed sharp knife. Place in oven preheated to 375° F.; bake until loaf is brightly golden and irresistibly fragrant—about 45 minutes. *Makes 1 loaf.*

WITH EGGS. Traditionally 5 eggs, colored red, are baked in the bread. Raw eggs should be used; dip them in red Easter-egg coloring. They are like hard-boiled eggs when cooked. Personally, I do not feel the eggs add anything but a colorful appearance to the bread, but Greeks may differ with this opinion.

Yulekake (Norwegian Christmas Bread)

2 envelopes active dry yeast	1 cup heated milk
½ cup warm water	½ cup seedless raisins
½ cup sugar	½ cup diced citron
¾ teaspoon ground cardamom	¼ cup butter or margarine, melted
2 teaspoons salt	
1 egg	6 cups all-purpose flour

Combine yeast, warm water, and 1 tablespoon of the sugar. Let stand at least 5 minutes to soften. Stir in remaining sugar, cardamom, salt, and egg. Cool milk to lukewarm and add along with raisins, citron, and butter or margarine. Stir in 3 cups of the flour and beat until batter falls from spoon. Add 2 more cups flour. Mix well. Turn out onto a pastry board and knead in remaining 1 cup flour. Turn into a large greased bowl. Cover and let rise in a warm place until doubled—about 1 hour. Divide dough in half; shape each half into a ball; place on pastry board; cover and let rest 10 minutes. Punch down one ball of dough at a time and divide it into 3 equal parts. Roll each part into a roll 16 inches long. Pinch one end of each roll together and braid into a loaf. Place in a greased 9 x 5 x 3-inch loaf pan. Repeat with the remaining ball of dough. Brush tops with melted butter or margarine. Cover and let rise in a warm place until doubled again—about 45 minutes. Bake in oven preheated to 350° F. until a deep, rich brown—about 45 minutes. Cool on rack; store in a closed bread box. *Makes 2 loaves.*

Brioche

This sweet eggy bread is a French specialty. It may be formed into almost any shape, but "top hats" are fairly easy to shape and are quite attractive. They freeze well after baking and can be reheated as needed.

½ cup milk	1 teaspoon salt
½ cup (1 stick) butter, softened	3 whole eggs
1/3 cup sugar	1 egg, separated
¼ cup warm water	3½ cups unsifted flour
1 package active dry yeast	1 tablespoon sugar

Heat milk until it steams; cool to lukewarm. Cream butter and sugar by hand or with electric mixer until light and fluffy. Measure warm water (test temperature on wrist) into small previously warmed bowl. Sprinkle in yeast; stir to dissolve. Add salt, lukewarm milk, yeast, 3 whole eggs, 1 egg yolk, and flour to the creamed mixture. Beat vigorously with wooden spoon for 2 minutes. Cover; let rise in warm place until *more* than doubled—about 2 hours.

Stir down; beat vigorously for 2 minutes; cover bowl with waxed paper held in place with rubber band, or with foil. Refrigerate overnight.

Next day punch down; turn soft dough onto lightly floured board. Shape as desired (see Top Hats). Let rise in warm place until doubled—about 50 minutes. Brush with mixture of unbeaten egg white and 1 tablespoon sugar. Bake in oven preheated to 375° F. about 15 to 20 minutes. *Makes 24 Top Hats.*

TOP HATS. Divide dough in 2 parts, one of which is about three-quarters of the whole, the other one-quarter. Cut larger part into 24 equal pieces; form into smooth balls. Place in greased muffin pans. Cut smaller piece into 24 equal pieces; form into smooth balls. Make a deep indentation in the center of each large ball; dampen slightly. Press small ball into each indentation. Let rise until doubled.

See also yeast-raised cakes (Gugelhupf; Baba au Rhum; Savarin Cake).

12 PASTRIES

Pies and cakes, tarts and tortes, cookies and cream puffs. This is the stuff that dreams are made of, dreams of home and Mom's cooking, of sugarplum trees and gingerbread houses. How could there be a birthday celebration without a birthday cake lavish with frosting, aglow with candles? How dare a patriotic family skip pumpkin pie for Thanksgiving dinner? What would spring be without a strawberry shortcake to usher in the season properly? And what is as American as apple pie?

The cookie jar does not have quite the nostalgic place in the home kitchen it once had, now that supermarkets offer packaged cookies in abundance to satisfy the hunger pangs of small fry, but brownies wrapped in foil and sent by army air post halfway around the world have helped many an American soldier to keep his sanity, knowing someone cared enough to whip up a batch of real American cookies for him and dispatch them to that alien land.

Packaged mixes have so changed the preparation of pies, cakes, and cookies that even the novice can now produce a glamorous-looking dessert. Whether the pastries made with mixes are as good as those made from scratch is moot, but there is no denying that the vast majority of American home cooks now use mixes, and the recipes that follow accept this premise.

Pies

A word of advice to users of piecrust mix: The hardest part of making piecrust is rolling out the dough. This you have to do even if you use mix in preparing the dough. Therefore, first-time makers of piecrust are advised to read the instructions for preparing Flaky Pastry Dough all the way through—even if they plan to use mix.

Flaky Pastry Dough I (For 1-crust 8- or 9-inch Pie)

1 1/3 cups sifted all-purpose flour
¼ teaspoon salt
1 tablespoon butter (*not* margarine)
½ cup vegetable shortening, less 1 tablespoon
3 tablespoons cold water

Put flour into a 1-quart mixing bowl. Add salt to the flour; blend well. Fill a glass measuring cup with water to the ½-cup line; add butter first, then enough vegetable shortening to force the water up to the 1-cup line. Pour out the water. Add the butter and shortening to the flour; chop with a knife or use a pastry blender until the butter and shortening are in fairly even pieces, each more or less the size of a pea. Add water 1 tablespoon at a time; toss with fork until all the flour is moistened, then use your fingers to work it into a smooth dough. Sometimes it is necessary to add a bit more water, but only a *teaspoon* of water at a time, for too much water is what makes piecrust tough. On the other hand, without enough water, the dough cannot be rolled out smoothly. Cover bowl; let dough stand about 3 minutes.

Dust the surface of the pastry board with flour; also rub flour over the rolling pin. (Or, if you are quite serious about making pies, buy a stockinette cover for the rolling pin and a cloth cover for the pastry board—these can be purchased at most housewares departments and using them is a guarantee that pastry will not stick to the board.) Place the dough on the board and with a quick, light motion roll out the dough into a circle until it is very thin, about ⅛ inch. Turn over the dough frequently as you roll, to be sure it is not sticking. If it does stick anywhere, scrape off the dough from the board with a knife and dust flour over the spot. Your circle will not be a perfect one—it almost never is—but make it as uniform as possible. If it goes way out in one direction, cut off the recalcitrant piece, moisten the edges of the shy side, and do some mending.

When the dough is about 1 inch larger in circumference than the edges of the pie pan, lift it up, place it in the pie pan, and fit it into the pan snugly, pushing it into place around the edges with fingers. If you have a nice generous edging, fold it over to make a standing rim, and pinch into fluted shape with thumb and forefinger. If there is not that much edging, press the dough down to the edge of the pan with tines of a fork.

If this is to be a baked pie shell (that is, if the filling will not be added until after baking), prick the bottom with the tines of a fork, place it in the freezer, and leave it there for 10 minutes, meanwhile preheating the oven to 450° F. Chilling the pastry helps avoid undue shrinking while it bakes—otherwise, you may look at your beautiful crust only to see the edges fallen down into the pan. (Another way to avoid this is to make a "lining" of foil to fit inside the pastry.)

Bake until crust is lightly browned—15 to 20 minutes. Remove; cool at room temperature. Do not add filling until pastry is completely cooled.

If making a custard-type pie, brush unbeaten egg white ovr the bottom of the pastry, chill in freezer 5 minutes, then add filling. The egg white forms a "lining" that helps prevent the filling from seeping into the crust. (Another way is to bake the crust for 5 minutes before adding the filling, but if you decide to do this, chill it in the freezer for 10 minutes before placing in the oven.)

Ingredients called for in this recipe are equivalent of 1 stick (½ package) piecrust mix.

An 8- or 9-inch pie (whether single- or double-crust) makes 6 servings.

Flaky Pastry Dough II (For 2-crust 8- or 9-inch Pie)

2 cups sifted all-purpose flour	(*not* margarine)
½ teaspoon salt	2/3 cup vegetable shortening
About 1½ tablespoons butter	¼ cup cold water

As in making the single-crust pie, sift the flour onto the pastry board, measure, and place the 2 sifted cups into mixing bowl; blend with salt. Place water in glass measuring cup to 1/3-cup line; add shortening and butter to bring water to the 1-cup line; pour off water. Add butter and shortening to flour; chop until size of small peas. Add water 1 tablespoon at a time, tossing after each addition; form into 1 large ball with fingers. Cut ball in half, but with slightly more in one half than the other. Roll out the larger half first, so the pieces left from trimming may be added to the second half

Follow the same instructions as for rolling out a single crust. After lower crust has been fitted into the pie pan, roll out the top crust, fold in half, cut slashes in the center (see sketch).

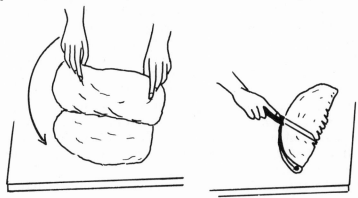

Place filling in pie; moisten.edges of bottom crust with water; cover with top crust. Press edges together with tines of fork, then flute, if desired (but this is not really necessary except for the decorative effect).

Preheat oven to 400° F. Bake pie until juices of filling can be seen bubbling up through slashes and crust is baked to a lovely golden color—35 to 40 minutes.

Ingredients in this recipe are the equivalent of 1 package pie-crust mix.

FLAKY PIE DOUGH FOR 10-INCH PIE. The most commonly used pie pan is 9 inches in diameter; 8-inch pans are used less frequently, and the difference in yield is almost negligible. The 10-inch size is useful chiefly for the large family, for it can be cut into 8 wedges rather than 6. For a 2-cruster, use 3 cups flour, 1 cup combined butter and shortening, and 6 to 8 tablespoons cold water. For a 1-crust 10-inch pie, use ½ these amounts.

CHEESE PASTRY. Add ¼ cup shredded Cheddar cheese to basic recipe for Flaky Pastry Dough for 1-crust pie or ½ package piecrust mix; ½ cup cheese to dough for 2-crust pie or 1 package mix. May be used to make cheese sticks, to enclose cocktail frankfurters for hot hors d'oeuvres, or may serve as the crust for an apple pie.

CINNAMON PASTRY. Work ¼ teaspoon cinnamon into pastry for 1-crust pie; roll out and cut into strips; twist; bake to be served with tea. Or, add ½ teaspoon to pastry for 2-crust pie (or 1 package piecrust mix); use as pastry for fruit pies, especially apple, cherry, or peach.

PIECRUST MADE WITH INSTANT-TYPE FLOUR. The chief difference in using these superfine flours is that the flour does not need to be presifted; proportions, however, are much the same, with just a little more shortening. Follow individual manufacturer's instructions for best results.

TART SHELLS. Prepare Flaky Pastry Dough for 2-crust pie, or use 1 package piecrust mix. Roll out; cut into 5-inch circles. Fit into individual tart pans; or, cut heavy-duty aluminum foil into 5-inch circles, shape the foil, and fit the pastry into it. Chill in freezer 10 minutes. Meanwhile, preheat oven to 450° F.; bake tart shells until golden—about 10 minutes. Cool before filling. *Makes 5 or 6, depending on size.*

Butter-Egg Pastry Dough I (For 1 9-inch Pie or Fruit Kuchen)

This German *Kuchen* dough is easier to prepare than piecrust, at least for a 1-crust pie, because it need not be rolled out.

1½ cups sifted all-purpose flour	½ cup (1 stick) butter
1 teaspoon baking powder	1 medium egg, beaten
Pinch of salt	Grated lemon rind (optional)
2 tablespoons sugar	

Combine flour, baking powder, salt, and sugar in mixing bowl. Chop in butter until very fine. Add beaten egg and lemon rind; work with fingers until smooth. Place ball of dough in 9-inch pie pan, press with fingers and heel of palm to fit pan, and come up the sides above the edges. Flute edges. Add filling and bake as directed in recipe until crust is golden and crisp.

Butter-Egg Pastry Dough II (For 2- or 3-layer Torte)

2 cups sifted all-purpose flour	1 large egg, or 2 small eggs, beaten
1 teaspoon baking powder	
¼ teaspoon salt	1 to 2 tablespoons cream or water
3 to 4 tablespoons sugar	Grated lemon rind (optional)
¾ cup butter	

Form dough as for 1-crust pastry shell. Press dough over bottom and up the sides of a 9-inch layer cake pan; proceed as recipe directs. Or, divide dough in half or thirds; roll out each to form a circle; transfer pastry circles to baking sheet; bake in hot oven until golden and crisp.

Crumb Crust (For 1-crust 8-inch Pie)

1 cup fine graham cracker or cookie crumbs*	¼ cup butter, softened 3 tablespoons sugar

Crumbs must be very fine. Crush in electric blender or with rolling pin. (Graham cracker crumbs may be purchased ready to use.) Blend crumbs, butter, and sugar together to form a paste; press into pie pan. Chill 1 hour before filling; use only a soft, clinging type of filling (gelatin, soft pudding, ice cream, etc.). For a firmer crust, bake in oven preheated to 375° F. for 8 minutes; cool before adding filling.

For a 9-inch pie, use 1 1/3 cups crumbs, 4 tablespoons sugar, and 4 to 5 tablespoons butter.

*Vanilla wafers, chocolate wafers, gingersnaps, or shortbread cookies may be used.

Coconut Crust (For 1-crust 8- or 9-inch Pie)

¼ cup (4 tablespoons) butter 2 cups shredded or angel flake	coconut

Melt butter; add coconut; stir constantly until golden brown—7 or 8 minutes. Turn mixture into 8- or 9-inch pie pan; press firmly to cover bottom and sides. Before adding filling, cool at room temperature about 30 minutes, or chill 10 or 15 minutes.

ICE CREAM PIE IN COCONUT CRUST. Fill prepared coconut crust with any desired flavor of ice cream, soften just enough to spread and swirl. Keep in freezer until time to serve. Chocolate, peach, black cherry, and butter pecan ice cream are especially good choices.

PEACH MELBA PIE. Prepare Ice Cream Pie, using vanilla ice cream. Top ice cream with sliced sugared peaches, cover peaches with frozen raspberries (drained of most but not all juice), and top with whipped cream. Keep in freezer up to 15 minutes before serving.

INSTANT CHEESE PIE. Prepare an 8-inch Crumb Crust (using vanilla or chocolate wafers). For the filling, use a package of instant vanilla pudding mix, but instead of milk, add 1 cup sour cream and 1 teaspoon grated lemon rind; pour filling into cooled crust. Chill in refrigerator until thickened.

NO-COOK PUMPKIN PIE. Prepare an 8-inch Crumb Crust, using gingersnaps. Bake 8 minutes; cool. For filling, add milk (according to directions) to a package of *instant* vanilla pudding mix; beat 1 minute. Combine a 1-pound can of pumpkin with 1½ teaspoons pumpkin pie spice; blend into pudding mixture. Spoon into cooled crumb crust; refrigerate at least 30 minutes before serving (or the preceding night). Just before serving, top with whipped cream or whipped topping mix. (Or, for a fluffier filling, prepare 1 package whipped topping mix according to package directions. Prepare instant pudding as directed, fold into whipped topping, then add *1 cup* (only) canned pumpkin, and ¾ teaspoon mixed pumpkin pie spice.)

SPANISH CHOCOLATE CHIFFON PIE. Prepare an 8-inch baked crust, or a graham cracker crust or coconut crust. Prepare a package of chocolate chiffon pie filling according to package directions, but just before pouring into crust, stir 2 or 3 tablespoons cream sherry into filling.

CHOCOLATE CHERRY CHIFFON PIE. Prepare chocolate chiffon pie filling as directed on package, but stir in ½ cup Cherry Kijafa wine, or ¼ cup kirsch or Cherry Heering before pouring filling into pie shell.

Cherry-Cream Tarts

6 baked tart shells	pie filling mix
1 package vanilla pudding and	1 jar cherry preserves

First bake the tart shells; cool. Cook the pudding mix according to package directions, but use part cream (instead of all milk) and, if desired, a tablespoon of brandy or sherry. Divide contents among tart shells. Heat cherry preserves until syrup is fluid; spoon over pudding. Cool. If desired, serve topped with whipped cream. *Makes 6.*

PEACH-CREAM TARTS. Instead of cherry preserves, place over pudding in each tart shell an inverted canned peach half. Melt ½ cup currant jelly; spoon a tablespoon of melted jelly over each peach half as a glaze.

PEACH-CHEESE TARTS. Instead of pudding, whip a 3-ounce package of cream cheese with 2 tablespoons cream or milk and ½ cup sugar; divide cheese among tart shells. Top each with a canned peach half; glaze each peach with melted currant jelly.

Rum Toffee Pie

Prepare a baked pie shell, coconut crust, or graham cracker crust. Cool. Cook butterscotch pudding and pie filling mix according to package directions; when pudding has thickened, stir in 2 tablespoons dark sweet rum; cook a few seconds longer. Pour into pie shell; arrange walnut halves or sprinkle slivered toasted almonds over top. Cool to room temperature. *Makes 1 pie or 6 servings.*

Butterscotch Meringue Pie

1 baked pie shell or coconut crust
1 package butterscotch pudding
  and pie filling mix
3 eggs, separated
2 tablespoons butter

1 tablespoon rum or brandy
  (optional)
3 tablespoons granulated sugar
¼ teaspoon cream of tartar

Prepare pie shell or crust; cool. Cook pudding according to package directions, but add the 3 egg yolks; cook and stir until mixture comes to a full boil. Stir in butter and rum. Cool 5 minutes; pour into pie shell or crust. Beat whites of eggs until foamy; gradually add sugar and cream of tartar. Spread over cooled filling. Bake in oven preheated to 425° F. until delicately browned, 5 to 10 minutes. Cool. *Makes 1 pie, or 6 servings.*

CHOCOLATE RUM PIE. Prepare as for Butterscotch Meringue Pie, but use chocolate pudding and pie filling mix instead of butterscotch mix; add 1 tablespoon rum. If desired, sprinkle shredded blanched almonds over meringue before placing in oven.

Banana Cream Pie

Fill a baked pie shell (or coconut or crumb crust) with prepared vanilla pudding and pie filling mix, adding one-half the pudding, then a layer of sliced bananas, then remainder of pudding. Chill. Serve garnished with additional banana slices and whipped cream, if desired. Or, use a package of vanilla-flavored whipped dessert mix (instead of pudding and pie filling mix); prepare according to package directions, with sliced bananas layered into the filling.

BANANA CREAM-COCONUT PIE. Instead of vanilla pudding and pie filling mix, use coconut cream pudding mix for the filling; or, prepare in either of the ways suggested for Banana Cream Pie and, instead of whipped cream, sprinkle shredded coconut thickly over the top.

Lemon-Walnut Chiffon Pie

1 baked 9-inch pie shell or Coconut Crust
1 envelope unflavored gelatin
¼ cup cold water
3 eggs, separated
2/3 cup sugar

½ cup lemon juice
½ teaspoon salt
1 teaspoon grated lemon rind
¼ cup chopped walnuts
½ cup heavy cream, whipped
(optional)

Prepare pie shell or crust. Soften gelatin in cold water in 1-quart mixing bowl. Place in top of double boiler the yolks of the 3 eggs, 1/3 cup of the sugar, the lemon juice, and the salt; stir over hot (not boiling) water until mixture thickens. Remove from heat; add to softened gelatin; stir until dissolved. Stir in grated lemon rind. Chill in refrigerator until mixture is the consistency of unbeaten egg whites; beat until fluffy with rotary beater. Separately beat egg whites until stiff, add to egg whites the remaining 1/3 cup sugar. Fold egg whites and walnuts into gelatin mixture. Beat cream until peaks form. Fold into gelatin mixture. (May be made without cream or nuts for less caloric but still delicious dessert.) Pile filling high in pie shell or crust. Chill. *Makes 6 very fluffy, creamy servings.*

Rum Chiffon Pie

This fabulous pie involves time and trouble—but it's worth it when you want to impress someone very special.

1 baked 9-inch pie shell
1½ envelopes (1½ tablespoons)
unflavored gelatin
½ cup cold water
3 eggs, separated

½ cup sugar
1 cup strong black coffee
3 tablespoons dark sweet rum
1 cup heavy cream, whipped

Prepare pie shell. Soften gelatin in cold water. Beat egg yolks until thick, add sugar, beat again, add ¼ cup of the coffee. Cook in top of double boiler over hot (not boiling) water, stirring almost constantly, until mixture thickens—about 5 minutes. Add softened gelatin and remaining coffee; chill until mixture starts to set. Beat with rotary beater until fluffy; add rum. Fold in whipped cream and the 3 egg whites beaten until very stiff. Everything must be stiff, for this filling is to be piled high in the crust; otherwise it may flow over the sides of the crust. Pour into baked pie shell; chill until firm. *Makes 6 rich servings.*

Apple Kuchen (Basic Recipe)

Not as American as apple pie, but actually easier to prepare because there is only 1 crust and it need not be rolled out.

Butter-Egg Pastry Dough I
3 to 4 cups sliced apples
1 teaspoon cornstarch, or 2 teaspoons flour
½ cup granulated sugar

½ cup cream
1 egg, beaten
2 tablespoons confectioners'
  sugar

Prepare pastry dough; press with fingers into bottom and up sides of 9-inch pie pan, raising above edges. Blend sliced apples with cornstarch or flour mixed with sugar; spread mixture over bottom of crust. Bake in oven preheated to 400° F. for 25 minutes. Blend cream with beaten egg and confectioners' sugar; pour mixture over apples in pie pan. Continue baking until crust is golden and crisp—about 40 minutes total baking time. Remove from oven; cool but do not chill. *Makes 6 servings.*

WITH CANNED APPLES. Use a 1-pound can of sliced apples; omit cornstarch and granulated sugar.

PEACH KUCHEN. Line pastry with sliced ripe peaches instead of apples.

PLUM KUCHEN. Pit red plums enough to cover bottom of pastry. Increase cornstarch to 1 tablespoon and sugar to ¾ cup. Omit cream and egg in filling.

KIRSCHKUCHEN (CHERRY KUCHEN). Fill pastry with either pitted Bing cherries or sour red cherries. With Bing cherries, use ½ cup sugar; with sour cherries, ¾ cup. Or, use canned tart pie cherries packed in heavy syrup, using ¼ cup syrup with ½ cup sugar. Add, besides sugar, 2 tablespoons kirsch (optional, but very good). Bake this way; or for a richer dessert, after 25 minutes add the cream, egg, and confectioners' sugar as in the basic recipe.

Classic Apple Pie

Flaky Pastry Dough for 2-crust
  pie, or 1 package piecrust mix
4 cups sliced apples
½ cup sugar

¼ teaspoon cinnamon or nutmeg
  (optional)
2 tablespoons butter

Roll out pastry; fit bottom crust into pie pan. Fill with sliced apples, sprinkle apples with mixture of sugar and cinnamon or nutmeg. Dot apples with butter. Cover with top crust; seal edges. Bake in oven preheated to 400° F. or until syrup can be seen bubbling through slits and crust is golden—about 40 minutes. Serve still slightly warm, with wedges of sharp Cheddar cheese. *Makes 6 servings.*

APPLE PIE À LA MODE. Serve each piece of pie topped with a scoop of vanilla ice cream.

APPLE PIE IN CHEESE CRUST. Add ½ cup grated Cheddar cheese to pastry; fill with apples. Sprinkle apples with a teaspoon of lemon juice, or add 1 teaspoon grated lemon rind to apples.

YANKEE BREAKFAST PIE. Use brown sugar or maple syrup instead of white sugar. Serve pie warm for breakfast (it can be reheated in oven).

BAKED APPLE DUMPLINGS. Prepare 3 cups flaky pastry dough, or use 1½ packages (3 sticks) piecrust mix. Roll out a third at a time. Peel and core 6 large or 8 small firm tart apples; leave whole. Cut squares of pastry large enough to cover apples, about 6 inches square (depending on size of apples). Place an apple on each square; place a teaspoon of sugar and a little grated lemon rind in each apple. Seal edges of pastry, pinching together to form a cross over top of each apple. Bake in oven preheated to 400° F. until crust is deep gold—about 50 minutes. Serve still warm, with cream (if desired). Or, serve cold with Hot Lemon Sauce. These are somehow more delicious and fruity than sliced apples in pie. *Makes 6 to 8 dumplings.*

Cherry Pie

Because sour red pie cherries are so seldom seen in American markets any more, only a recipe calling for canned pie cherries is given here. One disadvantage of the canned cherries is that the canning process robs them of color. For better appearance, a few drops of red food coloring should be added to the fruit before it is placed in the crust.

Pastry for 2-crust pie
½ to ¾ cup sugar
2½ tablespoons tapioca
⅛ teaspoon salt
½ cup cherry juice
Few drops red food coloring

2 cups canned sour red pie cherries, drained (1-pound can)
⅛ teaspoon cinnamon or nutmeg, or few drops lemon juice (optional)
1 teaspoon butter

Prepare pastry. Blend sugar with tapioca and salt; add cherry juice and food coloring. Let stand while rolling out pastry. Fit bottom crust into 9-inch pie pan; add cherries; sprinkle with spice, if desired, or lemon juice. Dot with butter. Cover with top crust; seal edges. Bake in oven preheated to 475° F. for 10 minutes; reduce temperature to 400° F., bake until crust is golden and crisp and fruit syrup is bubbling between the slits—about 35 minutes. Cool to room temperature before serving, but do not chill. *Makes 6 servings.*

CHERRY-WINE PIE. Instead of ½ cup cherry juice, add ¼ cup juice and ¼ cup Cherry Kijafa wine; or 6 tablespoons juice and 2 tablespoons kirsch or Cherry Heering. Gives the cherries very special flavor.

WITH READY-TO-USE CHERRY PIE FILLING. Line an 8-inch pie pan with pastry. Blend ¼ cup cherry wine or 2 tablespoons liqueur with prepared pie filling; cover with top crust.

LATTICED CHERRY PIE. Instead of a top crust, cut the second half of the pastry into long strips and arrange in lattice formation over the top, weaving in and out. (See sketch.)

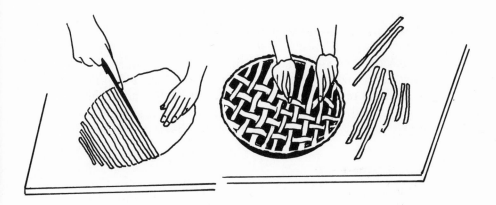

Blueberry Pie

Pastry for 2-crust pie	2 tablespoons cornstarch
1 quart fresh blueberries	1 teaspoon lemon juice
½ cup sugar	Grated rind of 1 lemon

Line 9-inch pie pan with pastry. Wash and pick over blueberries. Combine sugar and cornstarch, blending well; add to berries, then place berries in pastry. Sprinkle lemon juice and grated rind over berries. Cover with top crust; seal edges. Bake in oven preheated to 400° F. for 40 minutes or until syrup can be seen bubbling between slits and crust is golden and crisp. *Makes 6 servings.*

WITH CANNED BLUEBERRIES. Use an 8-inch rather than a 9-inch pie pan. Drain a 1-pound can of blueberries packed in heavy syrup; measure out and reserve ½ cup of the syrup; to this add 1/3 cup sugar blended with 2 tablespoons cornstarch, and the lemon juice and rind. Place drained blueberries in pastry, cover with syrup-sugar mixture. Cover with top crust; seal and bake. (Or, use canned ready-to-use blueberry pie filling, adding a few drops lemon juice.)

BLACKBERRY PIE. Use 1 quart ripe blackberries instead of blueberries; otherwise proceed as for Blueberry Pie.

PEACH PIE. Fill pastry-lined 9-inch pie pan with 3 to 4 cups sliced *fresh* peaches; add ¾ cup sugar blended with 1 tablespoon cornstarch (or 2 tablespoons flour) and a pinch of nutmeg or a dash of almond extract. Cover with top crust; seal edges. Bake as for Blueberry Pie.

PEACH PIE A LA MODE. Serve pie slightly warm topped with vanilla or butter pecan ice cream.

RHUBARB PIE. Select tender pink stems of rhubarb; dice. Fill pastry-lined pie pan with 4 to 5 cups fruit. Blend 1¼ to 1½ cups sugar with 3 tablespoons tapioca, ¼ cup water, and a pinch of salt. Let stand 5 minutes, then spoon over rhubarb. Dot with 1 tablespoon butter. Cover with top crust. Bake as for Blueberry Pie.

Rhubarb Cream Pie

Flaky Pastry Dough or Butter-Egg Pastry Dough I for 1-crust pie	4 cups diced fresh rhubarb
1¼ to 1½ cups sugar	1 tablespoon butter
6 tablespoons flour	1 teaspoon vanilla
	¾ cup heavy cream

Line 9-inch pie pan with pastry. Combine sugar and flour; spread half the mixture over bottom of pie pan. Add rhubarb; cover with remaining sugar-flour mixture. Dot with butter; sprinkle with vanilla. Preheat oven to 400° F.; bake pie in oven 20 minutes, then pour cream over the fruit. Lower oven temperature to 300° F.; bake until filling is bubbling and crust golden—35 to 40 minutes longer. Cool to room temperature but do not chill. *Makes 6 servings.*

WITH FROZEN RHUBARB. Instead of fresh, use 2 10-ounce packages frozen rhubarb in **preceding recipe; use** ¾ to 1 cup sugar.

RHUBARB-CUSTARD PIE. Use only 3 cups diced fresh rhubarb; blend with ¾ to 1 cup sugar and 2 tablespoons flour. Place in pastry-lined 9-inch pie pan. Preheat oven to 425° F.; bake 20 minutes. Beat together 3 egg yolks, 1 cup milk, and ½ teaspoon vanilla; pour over rhubarb. Lower oven temperature to 350° and continue baking until knife inserted in center comes out clean—about 30 minutes longer. *Makes 6 servings.*

Deep-dish Fruit Pies

Double the amount of fruit filling (including sugar and thickening) for apple, peach, berry, or cherry pie; place in 9 x 9-inch baking dish. Prepare pastry for 1-crust pie; roll out to fit top of baking dish. Cut slashes in center; lay on top of fruit. Bake in oven preheated to 425° F. until pastry is golden and syrup of fruit bubbling—about 50 minutes. Serve at room temperature (not chilled) with cream or ice cream. *Makes 8 to 10 servings.*

Concord Grape Pie

4 cups Concord grapes	Pinch of ground clove
1 cup sugar	1 tablespoon lemon juice
1 ½ tablespoons tapioca	1 tablespoon water
Pinch of salt	Pastry for 2-crust pie

Slip peels from grapes; set peels aside. Place the peeled grapes in a saucepan and cook until soft enough to force through a sieve or food mill to remove seeds. Add the grape peels, sugar, tapioca, salt, ground clove, lemon juice and water. Let stand 10 minutes while preparing pastry. Line 9-inch pie pan with half of the pastry; add grape mixture; cover with remaining pastry and seal edges. Bake in oven preheated to 425° F. until syrup can be seen bubbling through slits and pastry is golden—about 40 minutes. *Makes 6 servings.*

Mince Pie

2 tablespoons brandy or bourbon
2 tablespoons peach or apricot
  syrup
3 to 4 cups mincemeat (1

30-ounce jar, or 2 9-ounce packages)
Pastry for 2-crust pie

Blend brandy and fruit syrup (from canned fruit) with prepared mincemeat. (If desired, a cup of chopped canned fruit,
peaches or apricots, may be used with 3 cups mincemeat to
make a total of 4 cups.) If packaged mincemeat is used, the
brandy and fruit juice may replace part of water required to
reconstitute mix. Let stand several hours to "season" while
preparing pastry. Line pie pan with pastry and add filling. Cover with pastry and seal edges; bake in oven preheated to 400°
F. until filling can be seen bubbling through the slits and pastry
is golden brown. Remove from oven; add another tablespoon of
brandy or rum through the slits in the crust, using a syringe.
Cool to room temperature but do not chill. Reheat just before
serving. Serve with Hard Sauce or ice cream. *Makes 6 servings.*

Brandied Pumpkin Pie

Pastry for 1-crust 9-inch pie
1 egg white, unbeaten
2 cups cooked or canned pumpkin
2 whole eggs, slightly beaten
1 egg yolk
1 cup brown sugar
½ teaspoon ground ginger

½ teaspoon ground cinnamon
¼ teaspoon ground nutmeg
¼ teaspoon ground mace or
  crushed cardamom
½ cup milk
½ cup cream
¼ cup brandy

Line pie pan with pastry, fluting the edges. Brush unbeaten egg
white over bottom. Chill in freezer for 10 minutes; preheat oven
to 425° F. Combine all remaining ingredients, beat with rotary
beater until smooth. Pour into chilled pie shell; bake 10 minutes. Lower oven temperature to 350° and bake until knife inserted in center comes out clean—about 50 minutes longer.
Remove from oven; cool to room temperature, but do not chill.
This makes a luscious spicy pie with light texture. Serve topped
with whipped cream if desired, but it is marvelous without
cream. *Makes 6 servings.*

YANKEE PUMPKIN PIE. Instead of brown sugar, add ¾ cup
molasses to pumpkin mixture; use only ¼ teaspoon each cinna-

mon and ginger (or ½ teaspoon mixed pumpkin pie spice). Omit brandy. This makes a heavier pie with distinct molasses flavor. Serve topped with ice cream.

PUMPKIN PIE WITH PRALINE TOPPING. Bake pie in either of the preceding recipes. Shortly before serving, spread over top a mixture of 1 cup coarsely chopped pecans, ¾ cup brown sugar, ¼ teaspoon cinnamon, and 3 tablespoons melted butter. Place 4 inches below broiler unit until topping is glazed and bubbling, about 5 minutes.

SOUR CREAM-PUMPKIN PIE. Prepare as for Brandied Pumpkin Pie, but use 1 cup sour cream instead of cream and milk; omit brandy.

Black-bottom Pie

Crumb crust for 9-inch pie
2 squares unsweetened chocolate
¼ cup milk
3 tablespoons sugar
1 egg, separated

1 package vanilla-flavored
   whipped dessert mix
1 tablespoon dark sweet rum
½ cup heavy cream, whipped
2 tablespoons confectioners
   sugar

Prepare the crumb crust, using graham crackers or vanilla wafers; bake 8 minutes, cool. Cut 1 of the 2 chocolate squares in half; place 1½ chocolate squares in saucepan; set aside remaining ½ square. Add milk and 1 tablespoon of the sugar to chocolate; stir over very low heat until chocolate is melted. Add melted chocolate mixture to egg yolk; beat quickly to blend. Cool.

Prepare whipped dessert mix as directed on package. Measure 1 cup of the dessert mix; blend the melted chocolate mixture into this; pour into crumb crust, chill in refrigerator about 15 minutes.

Beat the white of the egg until foamy; gradually beat in the remaining 2 tablespoons sugar, until egg white forms soft peaks. Fold this and rum into remaining dessert mix; gently spoon this mixture over the chocolate layer. Chill 3 hours or longer.

Before serving, beat the heavy cream until thick; sweeten with confectioners' sugar. Spoon over pie. Shave the remaining ½ square chocolate with a vegetable parer and sprinkle chocolate curls over whipped cream. *Makes 6 very rich servings.*

BLACK-BOTTOM-ICE CREAM PIE. Fill a chilled graham cracker crust first with chocolate ice cream (1 pint), then a layer of chocolate syrup, then vanilla ice cream. Top with whipped cream or whipped topping mix. Dribble more chocolate syrup over the cream. Freeze until time to serve.

Torta di Ricotta

Sweet Egg Pastry
1½ pounds ricotta cheese
½ cup toasted almonds, ground
½ cup confectioners' sugar

Grated rind of 1 lemon
½ teaspoon vanilla
4 eggs

Line pie pan with pastry, fluting edges. Combine ricotta with ground almonds (easiest way to grind them is in an electric blender), sugar, lemon rind and vanilla. Beat in eggs, one at a time, until smooth. Pour mixture into pastry. Cut foil or waxed paper to fit over top of filling, to edge of pastry. Bake for 5 minutes in hot (425° F.) oven; reduce heat; bake at 350° until center is firm—about 30 minutes. Cool. *Cut into 8 thin wedges for 8 rich servings.*

Lemon-Meringue Pie

1 baked 9-inch pie shell
1 cup sugar
5 tablespoons cornstarch
Dash of salt
2 cups water
3 eggs, separated

1/3 cup lemon juice
2 teaspoons grated lemon rind
2 tablespoons butter
2 tablespoons confectioners
   sugar

Bake and cool pie shell before starting the filling. If you have a blender, place in the blender, all at once, the sugar, cornstarch, salt, water, the 3 egg yolks, lemon juice, and grated rind. Beat until smooth. Place over hot water in top of double boiler; cook, stirring constantly, until thickened and smooth. Add butter, stir to blend. Pour into cooled pie shell. Let stand until filling is cold. Beat egg whites until stiff; fold in confectioners' sugar. Spoon meringue over filling so that it comes to the very edge. Bake in oven preheated to 400° F. until meringue is delicately browned, about 10 minutes. Cool (do not chill) before serving.

If you do not have a blender, cook sugar, corn starch, salt, and water together until mixture comes to a boil; beat this thickened hot mixture into egg yolks a little at a time, then add lemon juice, rind, and butter and cook, stirring constantly, over hot water until mixture is very thick. *Makes 6 servings.*

Southern Pecan Pie

Pastry for 1-crust 9-inch pie
3 eggs
2/3 cup dark corn syrup
2 tablespoons butter or margarine, melted
¼ teaspoon salt
2/3 cup brown sugar
1 cup pecan halves

Line pie pan with pastry; chill in freezer 10 minutes. Preheat oven to 375° F. Combine remaining ingredients except pecans, beat with rotary beater until smooth. Add the pecans; pour into chilled pie shell. (Pecans will rise to top.) Bake until filling is set and pastry crisp and golden—about 50 minutes. Cool. Serve topped with whipped cream or ice cream, if desired. *Makes 6 servings.*

French Custard Flan

In Spain, the word *flan* means a caramel custard. In France it means a 1-crust pie shell, which is used as often to hold cheese or a meat mixture for an entree as to hold custard or fruit for a dessert. Quiche Lorraine is actually a kind of flan. The following is an impressive but easy dessert when made with convenience foods.

1 baked 9-inch pie shell
Custard cream
1 1-pound can ready-to-use cherry pie filling
¼ cup kirsch
½ cup currant jelly

Bake the pastry shell first (using ½ package piecrust mix, or prepare Flaky Pastry Dough for a 1-crust pie, or line the pan with Butter-Egg Pastry Dough, fluting the edges). Cool. Prepare custard cream, using pudding and pie filling mix; flavor with brandy or kirsch. Pour into baked cooled pie shells; chill. Place the canned cherry pie filling in a saucepan with the kirsch; heat, stirring, until kirsch is well blended with cherries. Spread over chilled custard. Heat the currant jelly until melted; spread over cherries as a glaze. Cool or chill. Cut in pie-shaped wedges to serve. *Makes 6 servings.*

RASPBERRY-CUSTARD FLAN. Defrost a package of frozen raspberries, pour off most but not all of syrup, spread over chilled custard cream instead of cherries. Top with currant jelly glaze.

Clafouti Limousin (French Cherry Pastry)

1 cup flour
½ teaspoon salt
2 tablespoons granulated sugar
2 eggs
1 cup milk

2 cups pitted Bing cherries
½ cup confectioners' sugar
½ teaspoon almond extract, or 1
   tablespoon kirsch

Place flour in a mixing bowl; blend with salt and granulated sugar. Make a well in the center; add eggs and milk; stir until blended with flour, making a smooth batter (but do not beat). Butter an 8-inch layer cake pan or 9-inch pie pan; pour ½ the batter in the pan. Blend cherries with confectioners' sugar and almond extract or kirsch; spoon over batter. Top with remaining batter. Bake in oven preheated to 400° F. until top is puffed and golden and cake tester or toothpick inserted in center comes out clean—about 35 minutes. Sprinkle while hot with additional confectioners' sugar. Cool to room temperature *before removing from pan. Serve still slightly warm. Makes 6 servings.*

Strawberry Shortcake

1 quart fresh strawberries
½ cup plus 2 tablespoons sugar
2 cups biscuit mix
5 tablespoons butter or marga-

rine
½ cup light cream or milk
1 egg, beaten
Heavy cream or whipped cream

First prepare the strawberries: set aside about one-third of the berries, the best ones, for garnish. Trim the caps, wash, but leave whole; sprinkle with a little sugar. Wash, trim, and chop the remaining berries. Add sugar to taste (about ½ cup, possibly more for those with a sweet tooth). Set aside.

Combine biscuit mix and 2 tablespoons sugar; chop in 4 tablespoons of the butter until in fine particles. Stir in cream or milk and egg; mix lightly to form a dough. Turn out on lightly floured board; divide dough in half. Dust palms of hands with flour, knead one half lightly, then pat out to fit bottom of 9-inch pie pan. Dot remaining 1 tablespoon butter over top. Knead second half of dough; pat to form circle of the same size; place over top of the first circle of pastry. Bake in oven preheated to 450° F. until shortcake is golden brown—about 15 minutes. Remove; cool; split the 2 halves. Place lower half on a platter; cover with chopped sweetened berries; add top half, browned side on top. Place reserved berries over top crust. Serve at room temperature (not chilled), passing a pitcher of heavy cream, or garnish with whipped cream. *Makes 6 to 8 servings.*

PEACH SHORTCAKE. Fill baked shortcake with sliced sweetened peaches instead of strawberries; arrange peach slices in a circle over the top.

BLACKBERRY OR RASPBERRY SHORTCAKE. Use 1 quart blackberries or raspberries instead of strawberries.

Rich Biscuit Dough

1 cup sifted flour	rine
1½ teaspoons baking powder	4 to 6 tablespoons milk
½ teaspoon salt	1 medium egg
3 tablespoons butter or marga-	

Combine flour, baking powder, and salt; sift. Place in mixing bowl; chop in butter or margarine until in fine particles. Add 4 tablespoons of the milk and the egg; stir to blend, forming a sticky dough. If the mixture is quite dry, add more milk, a tablespoon at a time. Flour palms of hands; pick up mixture; knead just enough to form a ball. Turn out on lightly floured board; pat or roll to ¼ inch thick. Use as topping for meat pies, fruit cobblers, deep-dish fruit pies, or sugar-free shortcake dough. *Makes 1 8- or 9-inch biscuit crust.*

With Biscuit Mix. Instead of flour, baking powder, and salt, use 1 cup biscuit mix: instead of 3 tablespoons butter or margarine, add 1 tablespoon. Use same quantity of milk and 1 egg.

Cherry Lagkaga

A favorite Danish dessert pastry.

Butter-Egg Pastry Dough II
1 cup sugar
4 tablespoons cornstarch
1 cup boiling water*
1 cup Cherry Kijafa wine

1 tablespoon lemon juice
2 tablespoons butter
1 cup heavy cream, or 1 package
  whipped topping mix

First prepare the pastry; divide it into 3 even portions, press each to fit a circle of waxed paper 8 inches in diameter. Keeping the pastry on the waxed paper, invert and place on baking sheet or bottom of upturned cake pans. Bake in oven preheated to 375° F. until evenly golden. Remove; cool.

Blend sugar and cornstarch; add boiling water; stir to dissolve. Add wine; bring to a rolling boil over medium heat, stirring frequently. Add lemon juice and butter; stir until butter is dissolved. Cool until thickened, stirring once or twice.

Beat the cream until very thick, or prepare topping mix according to package directions. (The topping mix is really preferable, because it retains its shape longer.) Spread the first pastry layer with half of the filling. Add the second pastry layer, cover this with half of the whipped cream or whipped topping mix. Add the third pastry layer, and the remaining filling. Spread remaining whipped cream around the edges. Chill. *Makes 8 rich servings.*

*Instead of 1 cup boiling water and 1 cup wine, the filling may be made with ½ cup boiling water and 1½ cups pitted black cherries in heavy syrup, puréed in electric blender.

RASPBERRY LAGKAGA. Purée 1 10-ounce package frozen raspberries (defrosted) by beating in blender. Prepare preceding recipe, using only ½ cup boiling water and puréed raspberries instead of cherry wine.

Puff Paste

The chief difference between puff paste and Flaky Pastry is that true puff paste is made with butter rather than vegetable shortening, and with a larger proportion of fat to flour. It is hard to produce a really good puff paste in the United States because American dairy butter is inferior to that available in France and most other Western European nations. All the water has not been forced out during the churning process—and that small amount of water in the butter causes our puff paste to be dry and brittle.

A fairly successful method is to start out with a standard recipe for Flaky Pastry Dough, or a package of piecrust mix. Roll out the dough (half at a time), and dot the rolled pastry with more butter; fold over, chill in freezer, then roll out again. Over each half of the dough, dot 3 tablespoons *sweet* (unsalted) butter (6 tablespoons altogether for a recipe for a 2-crust pie, or 1 full package of piecrust mix). Fold over to center, then bring up ends to form a packet (see sketches). Chill in freezer 1 hour (dough should be firm but not hard). Roll out on cloth-covered board, using a rolling pin covered with stockinette, or roll out on a lightly floured pastry board. Small pastries, such as tart shells or rectangular forms, as for French Apple Tarts, are easier than larger shapes.

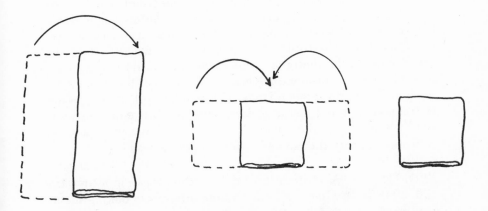

FRENCH APPLE TARTS. Cut rolled Puff Paste into rectangles 6 x 3 inches. Fold over edges and flute. In the center, place overlapping slices of apple. Cover apple slices with a glaze made by heating currant jelly to melting. Bake in oven preheated to 425° F. until pastry is golden. Remove; cool but do not chill.

JAM TARTS. Shape 3½-inch Puff Paste circles over outside of *inverted* muffin cups; pleat around edges to fit snugly. Bake in hot oven until golden. Cool. Place in bottom of each a tablespoon of whipped cream cheese; spoon red raspberry or blackberry jam over cheese. Just before serving, garnish each, if desired, with a dollop of whipped cream.

PORTUGUESE CUSTARD TARTS. Cut rolled Puff Paste into circles 3½ inches in diameter. Fit over the *inside* of muffin cups; brush unbeaten egg white over bottom of each. Chill in freezer 5 minutes. Combine 2 eggs (beaten) with ¾ cup sugar, a dash of almond extract, and 1½ cups milk (heated to steaming). Divide mixture among 8 of the chilled tart shells; bake in oven preheated to 400° F. until top of custard is glazed and browned and pastry is golden—about 20 minutes. Chill immediately, but when set, remove from refrigerator. Serve at room temperature.

Chou Paste

1 cup sifted all-purpose flour	1 teaspoon salt
1 cup water	1 teaspoon sugar (optional)
6 tablespoons best sweet butter	4 large eggs

Sift and measure flour first; set aside. Place water, butter, and salt in saucepan; bring to a boil; cook until butter has melted. (For cream puffs or éclairs, add sugar to hot water.) Remove from heat, add flour all at once, beat with a wooden spoon to blend thoroughly, then place again over moderately high heat; beat vigorously until mixture leaves the sides of the pan, forming a mass. Again remove from heat, make a well in the center of the paste. Add 1 egg at a time, beating after each addition until blended into the paste. After all eggs have been added, continue beating until smooth. *Makes about 2 cups.*

PROFITEROLES. Place a third of the Chou Paste at a time inside cloth pastry bag; force out into mounds onto baking sheet, making them 1 inch in diameter. Space 2 inches apart. Bake in oven preheated to 400° F. until puffs have doubled in size and are a deep brown, crusty to the touch—about 20 minutes. Remove from oven, puncture or slit top of each to allow steam to escape, then return to turned-off oven, with door slightly open, for another 10 minutes. Remove; let cool on a rack. When cold, cut away the soft portions from the inside, and add any desired filling.

QUICK CHEESE PROFITEROLES. Use a pressurized tube of soft cheese spread; insert nozzle of tube into opening in shells; force cheese inside. Or, prepare filling given in Chapter 1 ("Appetizers"); see Cheese Profiteroles.

CHOCOLATE PROFITEROLES. Make slightly larger puffs than for Cheese Profiteroles; when cool, cut off tops and remove soft insides. Fill with very firm vanilla ice cream; keep frozen until time to serve. Serve topped with warm Fudge Sauce.

CREAM PUFFS. Make puffs 3 inches in diameter. When baked, cut a slice from top of each, fill with sweetened whipped cream, Custard Cream, or Frangipani.

CHOCOLATE ÉCLAIRS. Press the Chou Paste into mounds about ½ inch high and 4 inches long. Bake until well browned. When cool, cut a slice from top of each; remove centers. Fill with Custard Cream to which 2 ounces of semisweet chocolate has been added (melted first over hot water). Or, fill with plain Custard Cream and cover the tops with Chocolate Glaze.

Whipped Cream Cones

2 eggs
½ cup sugar
½ cup sifted flour

Whipped cream
Jelly, jam, or candied orange peel

There is a trick to making these and it's a time-consuming process, but once made the cones last for weeks (in an air-tight tin) and make a conversation-piece dessert.

First grease 2 or 3 baking sheets, then sprinkle flour lightly over greased surface. Preheat oven to 400° F. Beat eggs until frothy; blend in sugar, then flour. Place a scant tablespoon (or heaping teaspoon) of the batter on the baking sheet; place in oven; bake until edges are golden—3 to 4 minutes. With spatula, lift cookies from sheet and promptly roll into cone shape. Place in narrow juice glass until cool. Proceed the same way with remaining batter, making only 1 or 2 cones at a time. Grease and flour baking sheet each time before adding batter. To serve, fill with whipped cream, placing generous dab of currant jelly, raspberry, or lingonberry jam, or candied orange peel in center. *Makes 12 to 16 cones.*

Almond Meringue

6 egg whites
½ teaspoon cream of tartar
¼ teaspoon salt
1½ cups sugar

¼ teaspoon cinnamon
1 teaspoon sweet sherry
¼ cup ground almonds

Preheat oven to 400° F. Beat egg whites until foamy, add cream of tartar and salt, continue beating until whites stand in soft peaks. Gradually add sugar and cinnamon, blended together, until very stiff. Add sherry; fold in almonds. Spoon into buttered spring-form pan or 9-inch cake pan with removable bottom. Place in oven; turn off heat immediately; leave 6 hours. Remove from oven; carefully release from pan. Serve topped with sliced peaches and whipped cream or ice cream. *Makes 8 servings.*

Mocha-Nut Torte

5 eggs, separated
1 cup sugar
1 tablespoon instant coffee powder
½ cup sifted all-purpose flour
½ cup hazelnut or walnut meats,

finely ground
2 pints heavy cream, whipped
and sweetened, or 1 quart coffee ice cream
Confectioners' sugar

Beat egg whites until soft peaks form. Add sugar gradually until mixture is stiff. Beat egg yolks separately until thick and light; fold in. Blend together coffee powder, flour, and nuts; gently but thoroughly fold into egg white mixture until no white streaks remain. Spoon into 9-inch tube pan (preferably one with a removable bottom) which has been greased, then floured. Stir once more to remove air bubbles. Bake in oven preheated to 325° F. for 50 to 55 minutes. Cool on rack. Split cake in 4 layers. Fill layers with whipped cream or coffee ice cream that has been softened until it can be spread easily. Put cake back together again; sprinkle confectioners' sugar over top. If ice cream is used, freeze; remove from freezer 10 minutes before serving. *Makes about 10 rich servings.*

Cheesecake

Cheesecake is not really a cake. It is a torte with a very rich custard filling. The richest type is made with cream cheese and heavy sweet cream—about as close to pure butterfat as one can get. Less caloric, but also less smooth in texture, is a cheesecake made with cottage cheese and sour cream. Both versions follow.

The crust may be made with zweiback mixed with sugar and melted butter, or with vanilla wafer crumbs and melted butter. (Do not use margarine.) For a deep cheesecake, it is essential to have a pan with a removable bottom, preferably a spring-form pan, though a 10-inch cake pan with removable bottom may be used. Otherwise, make it in a pie pan, using a smaller recipe (as the No-Bake Pie Pan Cheesecake).

Cream Cheesecake (Classic Recipe)

Zwieback or Vanilla Wafer Crust	¼ teaspoon salt
1½ pounds (3 8-ounce packages) cream cheese, softened	4 eggs, separated
	2 egg yolks
2 tablespoons cornstarch, or 4 tablespoons flour	1 cup heavy sweet cream
	Juice and grated rind of 1 lemon

Prepare crumb crust mixture. First rub a 9-inch spring-form pan (or 10-inch pan with removable bottom) with butter, over the bottom and up the sides. Sprinkle with enough leftover crumbs to form a film over the butter. Press ½ the crumb mixture over the bottom, the remainder up the sides (2 inches). Beat the softened cream cheese vigorously until light and fluffy; add, in the order given, flour, salt, and the 6 egg yolks, the heavy cream, and the lemon juice and rind, beating *after each addition* until smooth. Whip the 4 egg whites until stiff; fold into cheese mixture. Pour cheese mixture over crumbs. Sprinkle top with nutmeg, if desired. Bake in oven set at 325° F. for 1 hour; turn off oven, let cheesecake remain in warm oven for an additional 30 minutes. Remove. *When completely cool*, remove from pan, first removing the sides, then slip cheesecake off the bottom of the pan (after loosening with a spatula). *Makes 12 rich servings.*

ZWIEBACK CRUST. Crush contents of 1 6-ounce package of zwieback to make 2½ cups crumbs. Use about ½ cup crumbs to dust over buttered bottom and sides of pan. Combine remaining crumbs with ¼ cup sugar and 6 tablespoons butter, melted. (If desired, add ¼ to ½ teaspoon cinnamon to mixture.) Blend well to form paste.

VANILLA WAFER CRUST. Crush enough vanilla wafers to make 2 cups crumbs. Use about 1/3 cup to dust over buttered bottom and sides of pan. Blend remaining crumbs with 4 tablespoons butter, melted, to form a paste. (Add ¼ teaspoon cinnamon or nutmeg and 1 teaspoon lemon juice to mixture, if desired.)

COTTAGE CHEESECAKE. Instead of cream cheese and heavy sweet cream, use 1½ pounds cottage cheese (2 12-ounce packages) and 1 cup sour cream. Force cottage cheese through fine sieve before adding to other ingredients, or beat in blender with other filling ingredients until very smooth.

Blender Method. For either the Cream Cheesecake or the Cottage Cheesecake, use the same ingredients, but first place in blender the 6 egg yolks, sugar, flour, salt, and cream, and beat on high speed until smooth. With blender in motion, but turned down to medium speed, gradually add cheese until mixture is very smooth and well blended. (If preferred, a 12-ounce package of cottage cheese and an 8-ounce package of cream cheese may be used, instead of all cottage or all cream cheese.) Fold cheese mixture into egg whites beaten separately until stiff.

PINEAPPLE CHEESECAKE. Add ¾ cup thoroughly drained crushed pineapple to cream cheese in recipe for Cream Cheesecake.

CHEESECAKE WITH STRAWBERRY GLAZE. Prepare either the Cream Cheesecake or Cottage Cheesecake. *After cheesecake has been baked and cooled,* prepare following glaze.

1 quart fresh strawberries
1/3 cup sugar
1 tablespoon cornstarch
¼ cup water
1 teaspoon butter

Wash and hull berries; set aside best-shaped ones, enough to cover top of cake. Crush the remainder (enough to make ½ cup), combine with sugar, cornstarch, and water. Bring to a boil, cook 2 minutes. Turn off heat, stir in butter. Strain through sieve. Arrange berries, points up, over cake. Cover with cooled strained glaze. Chill until glaze is firm. Keep cake chilled until time to serve (and after serving, return to refrigerator—cheesecake is very perishable).

No-bake Piepan Cheesecake

Graham Cracker Crumb Crust for 9-inch pie
¼ teaspoon cinnamon (optional)
1 envelope unflavored gelatin
½ cup sugar
⅛ teaspoon salt
2 eggs, separated
½ cup milk
1 teaspoon grated lemon rind
2 cups (1 8-ounce package) cottage cheese, sieved, or 1 8-ounce package cream cheese, softened
½ teaspoon vanilla
½ cup sour cream

Prepare crust, adding cinnamon to mixture if desired, but press only two-thirds of the mixture over bottom and up sides of 9-inch Pyrex pie pan. Bake in 375° F. oven for 8 minutes; chill before adding filling. Combine gelatin with sugar and salt; blend well; place in top of double boiler with the 2 egg yolks and the milk. Cook, stirring, over hot (not boiling) water for 7 to 8 minutes. Remove from heat; stir in grated lemon rind. The cottage cheese must be forced through a fine sieve; the cream cheese, if used, must be beaten until fluffy. Beat egg-gelatin mixture into cheese; add vanilla. Chill until mixture is partially set (mounds when stirred with spoon). Beat egg whites until stiff; fold into chilled cheese mixture. Fold in sour cream. Spoon over crumb mixture. Sprinkle remaining crumb mixture over top. Chill until very firm—at least 3 hours. Serve from the pie pan. (Instead of a crumb topping, Strawberry Glaze may be added. In this case, divide crumb crust recipe in half; use only for bottom crust.) *Makes 6 servings.*

Cakes

With every supermarket carrying dozens of cake mixes and frosting mixes, to say nothing of the frozen ready-to-serve cakes and the fabulous array of ready-baked goods in pastry counters, few cooks any longer attempt to make family cakes from scratch. Yet cake recipes keep changing hands and sweet-toothed Americans drool over the very description of feather-light cakes and lavish frostings. Even the strong-willed are likely to succumb when brought face to face with a towering layer cake, a rich chocolaty devil's food or a nut-and-fruit-filled Christmas cake moistened with brandy or rum. "I really shouldn't, you know*"* is the sigh that marks surrender. And why not? Isn't life meant to be enjoyed?

There are two distinct advantages in making a home cake from scratch. A butter cake can be made with real butter—and you will be surprised what a difference that makes. And all cakes made with fresh, pure ingredients are more moist; they lack that chemical-plastic sort of dryness of the cake-mix cake.

When you mix your own batter, always use *cake* flour, not all-purpose flour—unless the recipe specifically says all-purpose flour will do. Level measurements are *very* important. So, too, is an oven with reliable controls, and be sure to use the pan size specified. An electric mixer simplifies cake making and so does a blender, but some recipes are easy enough by hand the original way. If the recipe specifies that egg yolk should be "thick and light," keep on beating until there is a noticeable difference in color (much lighter) and texture (much thicker). Egg whites need be only stiff enough to remain in peaks when the beater is removed—unless the recipe specifies "very stiff" (or "stiff and dry").

Not all cakes need to be frosted. Some are good simply sprinkled with confectioners' sugar; some may be drenched with sherry, brandy, or rum. Others are delicious served topped with a hot sauce. (*See* Pudding Sauces.)

Golden Butter Cake (Basic Recipe)*

2¾ cups sifted cake flour	2 cups granulated sugar
3 teaspoons baking powder	3 eggs
1 teaspoon salt	1 cup milk
½ pound (2 sticks) best quality sweet butter, softened	2 teaspoons vanilla

First prepare the cake pans. You may use 2 9-inch layer cake pans (each 1¼ inches deep), or 3 8-inch layer pans, or 1 8 x 12 x 2-inch pan, or a 9-cup (2¼-quart) Turk's head mold or tube pan. Layer cake pans or a long pan may be either greased or lined with paper; cut the paper to fit the *bottom* (not the sides) of the pans exactly. A tube pan must be greased, then dusted with flour (grease lightly but evenly, shake in flour so that all greased surface is filmed, then invert and shake out all flour but that clinging to the surface). Next, turn on oven to 350° F.

Now, sift and measure the flour onto a sheet of waxed paper. Measure the baking powder and salt; stir into flour. Place the butter in the large bowl of electric mixer (or any 1½-quart bowl, if using a portable mixer). Beat at low speed until the butter is creamed to a fluff. Start adding the sugar with mixer in motion, beat until fluffy. Add eggs 1 at a time (break right into the bowl). Now increase mixer to medium speed; start adding the flour mixture alternately with the milk; beat just until very smooth (no need to watch the second hand on the clock). Add vanilla at the last. Pour mixture into pans, dividing evenly; use a rubber spatula to get out every bit of batter. Shake down each pan on the countertop to level the batter. Place in oven, staggering position if 2 or more pans are used. Bake until toothpick or cake tester inserted in center comes out clean; also, cake should have started to draw away from sides of pan and spring back if lightly touched with fingers. (Requires about 30 minutes for

*This recipe is equivalent in yield to a package of yellow cake mix.

layers, 50 minutes for 1 large cake.) Remove from oven, cool in pans 10 minutes, then turn out on cake rack or racks. Allow cake to become completely cool before adding icing. *Makes 2 9-inch layers, 3 8-inch layers, or 1 large cake.*

ORANGE CAKE. Instead of milk, use ½ cup orange juice, 2 tablespoons lemon juice, and 1/3 cup water, plus 1 tablespoon grated orange rind. If made in layer pans, spread chocolate frosting between layers and over sides. If made in a long 1-layer pan, cut into squares, serve topped with Hot Lemon-Brandy Sauce or White Wine Sauce.

ORANGE CAKE MADE WITH CAKE MIX. Use similar mixture of orange and lemon juice and water instead of liquid called for in package directions. Add grated orange rind.

PINEAPPLE CAKE WITH COCONUT FROSTING. Thoroughly drain a small can of crushed pineapple; measure ½ cup fruit. Follow basic recipe, but use only 1½ cups sugar, add drained crushed pineapple after adding sugar, and use ½ cup of the pineapple syrup with ½ cup milk for the liquid. Bake in layers; when cake is completely cool, frost between layers and over top with White Mountain Frosting or white frosting mix. Sprinkle shredded coconut generously over top and sides. (Or, add ½ cup drained crushed pineapple to yellow cake mix and frost with white frosting and coconut.)

BROILED PRALINE TOPPING. Bake cake in 8 x 12-inch pan. Blend together 6 tablespoons softened butter, 2/3 cup firmly packed brown sugar, ¼ cup cream, and ½ cup coarsely chopped pecans. Spread over cake *in pan* while cake is still warm; place in broiler oven 4 to 6 inches from heat until mixture bubbles. Cool. No need to remove cake from pan—simply cut into squares and remove each square with a spatula.

Two-layer White Cake {Basic Recipe}*

2½ cups sifted cake flour	1½ cups sugar
3 teaspoons baking powder	1 cup milk
½ teaspoon salt	1 teaspoon vanilla
½ cup (¼ pound) best quality sweet butter	4 egg whites (½ cup)

First, prepare 2 8- or 9-inch layer cake pans (line pans with waxed paper; or grease, then flour). Preheat oven to 350° F. Sift, then measure *cake* flour; stir in baking powder and salt. Place butter in mixing bowl; beat with electric mixer at low speed until creamy; gradually add sugar; beat until fluffy. Increase speed to medium; add flour mixture alternately with milk until batter is smooth. Add vanilla last. Separately, beat egg whites until stiff with rotary beater (make sure blades of beater are completely free of grease). Fold egg whites into batter. Spoon into pans, dividing evenly. Bake until pick inserted in center comes out clean—30 to 35 minutes. Cool in pans 10 minutes; turn out on rack.

   *Recipe yield is equivalent to that of a package of white cake mix.

COCONUT CAKE. Prepare basic recipe or 1 package white cake mix, baking in 2 layers. Prepare 1 cup Lemon Filling; stir in ½ cup shredded coconut; spread between *cooled* layers. Frost top and sides with Fluffy White Frosting (or white frosting made with mix). Sprinkle 1 cup shredded coconut over frosting.

PEPPERMINT CANDY CAKE. Prepare basic recipe or 1 package white cake mix; stir into batter 1/3 cup crushed peppermint stick candy. Frost cake with mint-flavored white or pink frosting.

Four-tiered Birthday Party Cake*

3 cups sifted cake flour	sweet butter
4 teaspoons baking powder	2 cups sugar
½ teaspoon salt	1 cup milk
6 egg whites (¾ cup)	1 teaspoon vanilla
½ pound (2 sticks) best quality	

First, prepare pans (tiered cake pans in graduated sizes, available in every housewares department): line with waxed paper;

   *The yield is equivalent to 2 boxes cake mix.

or grease, then flour. Preheat oven to 350° F. Sift cake flour and measure; stir in baking powder and salt. Beat egg whites with electric mixer (make sure blades are clean of any grease). Set aside.

In a second mixing bowl, place butter, beat until creamy. Gradually add sugar with mixer in motion. Add flour mixture alternately with milk; when batter is very smooth, add vanilla. Fold in egg whites. Divide batter between cake pans, filling each half full. Bake until tester inserted in center of each cake comes out clean and cakes spring back when touched. (The smaller tier will be ready in about 25 minutes, the larger in about 30.)

Cool in pans for 10 minutes; invert on cake racks. When completely cool, use double recipe of White Mountain Frosting or white frosting mix, tinted as desired. Garnish with candies, commercial ("dine store") birthday party greetings or decorations, or animal crackers, or what you will. *Makes 15 to 20 servings.*

LANE CAKE. Prepare recipe for Four-tiered Birthday Party Cake, but use 8 egg whites, and divide among 3 9-inch layer cake pans. (Put aside yolks of the eggs for the filling.) Bake at 350° F. until cake springs back when pressed—25 to 30 minutes. Cool; turn out on racks. To the 8 reserved egg yolks, add 1 cup granulated sugar and ½ cup butter or margarine. Stir constantly over low heat until sugar is dissolved and mixture thickened to custardy consistency. Remove from heat; add 1/3 cup bourbon; blend well. Add 1½ cups mixed diced candied fruit and 1 cup coarsely chopped nuts (pecans or walnuts). Spread between the layers and over the top of cake layers. Chill cake overnight. Serve this way, or spread whipped cream around sides. A traditional Christmas cake in the South.

Prune Cake Ring with Rum Glaze

Prepare 1 package lemon cake mix according to package directions, but add to batter 1 cup chopped pitted prunes. Pour into greased and floured 1½-quart ring mold; bake in oven preheated to 350° F. until top springs back when touched—about 30 minutes. Remove from oven, cool in pan 5 minutes, then turn out on rack. When cool, spread with *Rum Glaze:* To 2 cups sifted confectioners' sugar, add 1 tablespoon boiling water and 1 tablespoon rum. Beat until smooth, drizzle over top of ring and down the sides.

Sour Cream Cupcakes

1½ cups sifted cake flour or all-purpose flour
1 teaspoon baking powder
½ teaspoon baking soda
½ teaspoon salt
1 cup sugar

2 large eggs
1 cup sour cream
1 teaspoon vanilla
½ cup coarsely chopped nuts or raisins (optional)

Grease 12 muffin cups; dust with flour (shake out flour). Preheat oven to 350° F. Sift flour, measure, add baking powder, soda, salt, and sugar. Place flour mixture in bowl; make a well in center; add eggs and sour cream; beat in flour mixture gradually. Add vanilla and nuts or raisins last. Beat until very smooth. Spoon into muffin cups; bake until top springs back when touched—18 to 20 minutes. Turn out on rack; cool. Serve plain, or, when cold, frost as desired. *Makes 12 cupcakes.*

Buttermilk Cake

½ cup butter (8 tablespoons or 1 stick)
1 cup sugar
2½ cups sifted cake flour
½ teaspoon baking soda

Pinch of salt
1 cup buttermilk
Grated rind of 1 lemon
5 eggs
Confectioners' sugar

Butter a Turk's head mold or tube pan; dust with flour; shake out excess flour. Turn on oven to 350° F. Beat butter and sugar together until creamy and fluffy. Sift together cake flour, baking soda, and salt; add this to butter mixture alternately with buttermilk, beating until smooth. Add lemon rind, then eggs, 1 at a time. When batter is smooth, pour into pan, bake until toothpick inserted in center comes out clean—about 50 minutes. Let stand in pan 10 minutes, then turn out on rack. Dust with confectioners' sugar. *Makes 1 large cake.*

German's Chocolate Cake

1 package (¼ pound) German's Sweet Chocolate
½ cup boiling water
1 cup vegetable shortening
2 cups sugar
4 eggs, separated

1 teaspoon vanilla
2½ cups sifted cake flour
1 teaspoon baking soda
½ teaspoon salt
1 cup buttermilk

Line 3 8- or 9-inch layer pans with waxed paper. Preheat oven to 350° F. Add chocolate to boiling water, stir until melted.

Cool. Place shortening and sugar in mixing bowl, beat until light and fluffy. Add the yolks of the eggs, one at a time, beating after each. Add vanilla and the melted chocolate, mix until blended. Sift flour with soda and salt; add alternately with buttermilk. Beat until batter is smooth. Fold in stiffly beaten egg whites.

Divide batter into the three pans; shake down to distribute evenly. Bake 35 to 40 minutes until top springs back when touched. Cool; turn out on rack. When cold, spread Coconut-Pecan Frosting between layers and over tops and sides. *Makes about 12 servings.*

COCONUT-PECAN FROSTING

1 cup evaporated milk	1 teaspoon vanilla
1 cup sugar	1 1/3 cups flaked coconut
3 egg yolks	1 cup chopped pecans
¼ pound margarine	

Combine milk, sugar, egg yolks, margarine, and vanilla in saucepan. Cook over low heat, stirring constantly, until mixture thickens. Remove from heat. Add coconut and pecans. Cool until of spreading consistency.

Chocolate-Rum Cake

1 ounce (1 square) unsweetened chocolate	½ cup (1 stick) butter, softened
1¾ cups sifted cake flour	1½ cups brown sugar
1½ teaspoons baking powder	3 eggs
½ teaspoon baking soda	½ cup water
1 teaspoon salt	5 tablespoons dark sweet rum

Melt chocolate over hot water. Combine sifted cake flour with baking powder, soda, and salt and sift again. Using an electric mixer at medium-low speed, cream butter, add sugar gradually until very fluffy, then add eggs 1 at a time, beating 15 seconds after each egg addition. Add flour mixture alternately with combined melted chocolate and water, adding flour last. When batter is smooth, add rum and beat 30 seconds longer. Divide batter equally in 3 8-inch layer pans which have been lined with waxed paper; bake in oven preheated to 350° F. until cake springs back when pressed—20 to 25 minutes (or use 2 9-inch layer pans and bake 35 minutes). Let cool in pans 5 minutes; turn out on racks. Frost with Chocolate Rum Frosting.

CHOCOLATE-RUM FROSTING. Melt 4 squares bitter chocolate and 3 tablespoons butter or margarine over hot water. Sift 4 cups confectioners' sugar (1-pound box); add a pinch of salt. Stir in 4 tablespoons milk, 3 tablespoons dark sweet rum, and the chocolate mixture. Blend well, let stand 1 minute, then spread lightly between layers and thickly over top and sides. Garnish with halved maraschino cherries. Season 2 to 3 days before serving; the cake becomes more mellow and richer in flavor with age, up to a week, if stored in a cake box.

NOTE. Do not judge this by the same standards as a cake-mix cake. It will not be as light or fluffy, but the flavor is so good that no one cares. The aging is what makes the difference. Excellent for the holidays, when guests are likely to drop in unexpectedly.

QUICK CHOCOLATE-RUM CAKE. Make a fudge or devil's food cake with mix, baking in 2 or 3 layers. Sprinkle cake with dark sweet rum. Frost with chocolate frosting mix, substituting rum for water called for on package of mix.

Chocolate Cupcakes

2 ounces unsweetened chocolate   1 cup self-rising flour
¾ cup sugar   ¾ cup minus 2 tablespoons milk
2 tablespoons softened butter   ½ teaspoon vanilla
1 or 2 eggs

Turn on oven to 375° F. Grease and flour 12 muffin cups (2 6-cup tins) or line cups with paper baking cups. Melt chocolate in top of double boiler over hot (not boiling) water. Beat sugar and butter together until fluffy; add eggs, 1 at a time, then the flour alternately with the milk. Add the chocolate and vanilla last, stirring to blend well. Spoon into muffin cups, filling only half full. Bake until toothpick inserted in center comes out clean—about 20 minutes. Frost with Orange or Coconut Frosting. *Makes 12 cupcakes.*

Red Devil's Food Cake

This is made with cocoa—unsweetened cocoa. Do *not* use cocoa mix. A good recipe to turn to when other forms of baking chocolate are not available. And it's so easy!

1 ¾ cups sifted cake flour
1 ½ cups sugar
1 ¼ teaspoons baking soda
1 teaspoon salt
1/3 cup unsweetened cocoa

½ cup vegetable shortening, or margarine
1 cup milk
1 teaspoon vanilla
3 eggs

Prepare 2 layer cake pans (8- or 9-inch). Preheat oven to 350° F. Sift flour, then measure it; place in mixing bowl; add sugar, soda, salt, and cocoa. Add, all at once, the shortening, milk, and vanilla. Beat with mixer at medium speed for 2 minutes (watch the clock). Add eggs (break right into bowl) beat exactly 2 minutes longer. Pour into the prepared pans, dividing batter evenly. Bake about 35 minutes, until cake springs back when touched and pulls away from sides. Cool in pans 10 minutes; turn out on rack. When completely cold, spread frosting between layers and over top. *Makes a 2-layer cake (equivalent in yield to 1 box chocolate cake mix).*

Good frostings for chocolate cake: Mint, orange, or strawberry-flavored whipped cream, or whipped topping mix, or whipped cream cheese (if cake is to be consumed the same day), or caramel—and, of course, fluffy white or deep dark fudge.

"Tell Your Neighbor" Cake

1 package yellow cake mix
1 package lemon-flavored *instant* pudding

1 cup water
4 eggs

Combine in the same bowl the cake mix, pudding mix, water, and eggs. Blend with mixer at low speed just to moisten, then beat 8 minutes at medium speed. Line 3 9-inch layer cake pans with brown paper (do not grease pans). Pour batter into pans. Bake in oven preheated to 350° F. until tester inserted in center comes out clean—25 to 30 minutes. Cool in pans 15 minutes, then turn out on rack. Cool thoroughly. Fill and frost with packaged frosting mix (white, chocolate, or strawberry). Store uncovered in refrigerator. *Makes 1 large cake.*

CHOCOLATE COCONUT "TELL YOUR NEIGHBOR" CAKE. Use a package of devil's food cake mix and coconut cream instant pudding mix; fill and frost with white frosting; sprinkle top and sides with coconut.

Chiffon Cake

Salad oil is the shortening—that's what makes this type of cake different from all others.

2¼ cups sifted cake flour or 2 cups all-purpose flour
1½ cups sugar
3 teaspoons baking powder
1 teaspoon salt
7 eggs, separated

½ teaspoon cream of tartar
½ cup salad oil
¾ cup cold water
2 teaspoons vanilla
2 teaspoons grated lemon rind

Use an *ungreased* 10-inch tube pan for best results. Preheat oven to 350° F. Sift and measure flour; add sugar, baking powder, and salt. Beat the whites of the eggs with cream of tartar until very stiff (make sure blades of beater are free of grease); set aside. To the flour mixture, add the 7 egg yolks and all remaining ingredients in the order given; beat with electric mixer at medium speed or with rotary beater until smooth (avoid overbeating). Add flour-yolk mixture to egg whites, folding in carefully. Pour into tube pan. Bake until top springs back when touched—about 1 hour. Remove from oven; invert cake in pan over top of a milk bottle; leave in pan until completely cold. To remove from pan, loosen edges with spatula, turn over on plate or platter, and tap sharply. Frost as desired. (This is more moist than Angel Food Cake.)

COCONUT CHIFFON. Add grated orange rind instead of lemon rind, and 1 1/3 cups angel flake coconut to flour-yolk mixture before adding to egg whites.

CHOCOLATE CHIP CHIFFON. Omit lemon rind; after folding flour-yolk mixture into whites, fold in ½ cup shaved sweet chocolate or semisweet chocolate bits.

Sponge Cake (Basic Recipe)

Sponge cake is so easy that anyone can make it. The flour needs to be sifted and measured carefully, but that's all. Baking powder is not necessary—except to cut down on the number of eggs. The pan need not be greased (though if very *lightly* greased, the cake may be easier to remove).

5 or 6 eggs, separated
1 cup sifted sugar
1 cup sifted cake or all-purpose flour

½ teaspoon baking powder (optional)*
Grated rind of 1 lemon

*If baking powder is used, 5 eggs will be sufficient.

Beat the egg yolks with sugar in blender or with rotary beater until very thick and light. Beat in the sifted flour (blended with baking powder, if used) about ¼ cup at a time, then the lemon rind. In a large mixing bowl, beat egg whites until stiff; gently fold in the yolk mixture. Pour into ungreased or very lightly greased pan or pans. Bake in oven preheated to 350° F. until cake springs back when touched and has started to draw away from edges of pan. Remove from oven; cool as directed in any of the following variations.

BIZCOCHO BORRACHO, OR TIPSY SPONGE CAKE. Bake sponge cake batter in ungreased or very lightly greased 10-inch tube pan for about 35 minutes. Cool upside down in pan (invert over milk bottle) 10 minutes, loosen around edges with spatula, then turn out on cake rack. While cake is still warm, drench with the following hot syrup: ½ cup sugar, ½ cup cream sherry, cooked together until thickened—about 4 minutes. Allow cake to cool, then place a lace doily over top and sprinkle with confectioners' sugar. When doily is removed, a lacy sugar pattern remains on cake.

ITALIAN RUM CAKE, OR ZUPPA INGLESE. Prepare sponge cake batter, but divide among 3 8-inch layer pans. Bake until cake springs back when touched—about 30 minutes. Cool in pan 5 minutes; turn out on racks. Sprinkle each cake layer generously with dark sweet rum, using ½ to 2/3 cup rum altogether. Prepare a Custard Cream filling; to one-third of the custard mixture add 1 ounce unsweetened chocolate, melted, or 1-ounce packet chocolate-flavored baking product. Spread plain custard over first layer, chocolate over second, plain custard over third. Chill in refrigerator overnight; spread Chocolate Frosting around sides of cake.

ANOTHER WAY. Instead of chocolate-flavored cream for the center layer, spread orange marmalade in center; spread remaining Custard Cream around sides.

Banana Meringue Cake

1 recipe Sponge Cake, baked in 2
  8-inch layers
3 large bananas, sliced
½ cup sugar

Custard Filling
3 egg whites, beaten stiff, sweetened with 3 tablespoons sugar

Split baked cooled sponge cake in half, lay half the banana slices over top of cake, sprinkle with sugar then cover with Custard Filling. Add second layer of cake; repeat with bananas, sugar, and custard. Sweeten stiffly beaten egg whites with sugar; spread over top and sides of cake. Place in preheated 325° F. oven until meringue is delicately browned. Serve hot or cold.

CUSTARD FILLING

2 cups milk
1 tablespoon cornstarch
¼ cup sugar

2 eggs
½ teaspoon vanilla

Bring milk just to a boil. Blend cornstarch with sugar. Beat eggs until light, stir in cornstarch mixture, place in top of double boiler, then slowly add the hot milk, stirring over hot water until custard coats spoon evenly. Add vanilla. Cool before spreading on cake.

Sponge Roll (Basic Recipe)

5 eggs, separated
¾ cup sugar
Grated rind of 1 lemon

½ cup sifted flour (all-purpose
  or cake flour)
Confectioners' sugar

Line a 15 x 10-inch pan with waxed paper; very lightly grease the paper. Preheat oven to 375° F. Beat the 5 egg whites until stiff. Separately beat yolks until very thick and light; gradually beat in sugar, then lemon rind and flour. Gently fold this into the whites, taking care to remove all air bubbles. Spread over pan as evenly as possible. Bake 15 minutes until cake springs back when touched. While cake is in oven, moisten a clean cloth dishtowel and sprinkle towel with sifted confectioners' sugar. Remove finished cake from oven, loosen around edges and immediately invert over towel. Carefully pull off waxed paper. Roll up the cake inside the towel; keep wrapped until filling is ready.

JELLY ROLL. Blend any desired jam or jelly (preferably a red or black one, such as strawberry, raspberry, currant, or blackberry), with just enough fruit juice or sweet wine to spread easily. Unroll Sponge Roll; spread thinly with jelly or jam; roll up again. Sprinkle top with confectioners' sugar. When cold, cut into 1-inch slices.

ICE CREAM CAKE ROLL. Fill Sponge Roll with ice cream (any flavor) softened enough to spread easily; roll up again, dust with confectioners' sugar. Freeze. Remove from freezer to cut into slices 10 minutes before serving.

LEMON CAKE ROLL WITH CHOCOLATE GLAZE. Fill Sponge Roll with Clear Lemon Filling; roll up again. Spread Chocolate Glaze over top.

GYPSY'S ARM (BRAZO DE GITANO). Prepare a Sponge Roll as in basic recipe, but in making the cake, use 6 egg whites and only 4 yolks. Put aside the yolks of the other 2 eggs to make a Custard Cream filling with vanilla-flavored pudding and pie filling mix or egg custard mix; follow package directions, but add to thickened pudding ¼ cup sherry. Beat hot pudding into the 2 reserved egg yolks; cool 2 to 3 minutes longer, stirring, over low heat. Spread half the custard cream over the sponge roll. If desired, sprinkle ½ cup chopped dates over the custard cream. Roll up. To remaining filling, stir in 1 cup whipped cream (½ cup heavy cream before whipping); spread over top and sides of cake roll.

LINCOLN LOG. Prepare Sponge Roll as in basic recipe, but use only ½ cup sugar, and add to the yolk mixture ¼ cup Dutch cocoa mix. For the filling, prepare Mocha Buttercream; use one-fourth of the recipe blended with 1 cup whipped cream (½ cup heavy cream before whipping). After sponge has been rolled-up cake. May be frozen; remove from freezer 10 to 15 outside, making elongated ridges in the cream with a knife blade. Chill or freeze until time to serve. (The same confection in France is called *Buche de Noël* when served on Christmas Eve as a sweet "yule log".)

STRAWBERRY ROLL. Prepare a Sponge Roll as in basic recipe. Wash, hull, and chop 1 quart strawberries, keeping out a few berries for garnish. Blend with 2 cups whipped cream (1 cup heavy cream, whipped); sweeten to taste. Use about 1/3 the mixture for filling; spread the remainder over outside of rolled-up cake. May be frozen; remove from freezer 10 to 15 minutes before cutting. (Or make the roll with 1 10-ounce package frozen strawberries, puréed in blender, blend berries with whipped topping mix.)

Dobos Torte

7 eggs, separated   ¼ teaspoon salt
¾ cup sugar   Chocolate Torte Filling
1 cup sifted cake flour   Caramel Glaze

This is a 6-layer cake. It may be baked in 3 layers, with each layer then split horizontally to make 6, or in 6 separate layers. The layers will be very thin. First prepare the pans: grease 3 8-inch layer pans, then line each with waxed paper cut carefully to fit, and grease the paper. (Otherwise the thin layers will be too hard to handle.) If you prefer to bake 6 separate layers, do 3 at a time, then repeat.

First beat the egg whites until stiff (soft peaks formed). Separately beat the yolks until fluffy, add sugar, beat until mixture is pale and thick, then add the flour and salt. Gently fold the egg whites into the yolks, taking care to remove air bubbles. Divide batter in pans as evenly as possible (if preparing 6 separate layers, 5 tablespoons per pan is about right; or, divide all the batter into the three pans). Preheat oven to 400° F., bake until lightly browned—8 to 10 minutes. Remove and immediately turn out on cake racks to cool, pulling off paper carefully. Use a long-bladed knife with serrated edge to cut layers horizontally in half. When cake layers are all baked and have cooled, spread Chocolate Torte Filling between layers and on the outside. Over the top spread Caramel Glaze. Mark serving portions in the glaze while it is still warm. Chill at least 4 to 6 hours, preferably 24 hours. *Makes about 12 servings.*

CHOCOLATE TORTE FILLING

4 squares (4 ounces) unsweet-   ½ cup sugar
  ened chocolate, melted   ¾ cup butter or margarine
4 eggs, beaten

Melt chocolate over hot water. Combine eggs and sugar; stir constantly over boiling water until mixture is thickened—about 10 minutes. Add thickened egg to chocolate, beat to blend, cook and stir over low heat 2 minutes, then add butter, beat until butter is thoroughly blended. Chill until mixture is thickened enough to spread easily.

CARAMEL GLAZE. Melt ¾ cup granulated sugar in a small skillet; add 1 tablespoon butter as soon as sugar is liquid; stir until golden. Spread *quickly* over top of cake (it will harden almost instantly).

QUICK DOBOS TORTE. Thoroughly chill a commercial pound cake, then slice horizontally (use a thin long-bladed knife) into 6 layers. Spread chocolate Buttercream Frosting thinly between layers and over top. Spread whipped cream around sides. Chill 24 hours, then cut in vertical slices. *Makes about 8 servings.*

POUND CAKE TORTE. Slice a chilled commercial loaf of pound cake horizontally into 4 layers. Prepare a package of whipped topping mix according to directions; fold in 1 cup *crushed* nuts (pecans, walnuts, or peanuts and, if desired, ½ cup coconut). Spread between cake layers and over top and sides. Chill 24 hours before cutting. Cut in vertical 1-inch slices. *Makes about 8 servings.*

Angel Food Cake

1 cup sifted cake flour	1 teaspoon cream of tartar
1½ cups sifted granulated sugar	¼ teaspoon salt
1¼ cups (10 to 12) egg whites, at room temperature	1 teaspoon vanilla
	¼ teaspoon almond extract

Preheat oven to 350° F. Have ready a 10-inch tube pan. Sift flour and sugar together 3 times. Place egg whites in large mixing bowl and beat at high speed until egg whites are foamy. Add cream of tartar, salt, and the two flavoring extracts. Continue beating egg whites at high speed until mixture forms soft peaks. Turn off mixer. Add ¼ cup of flour-sugar mixture at a time, folding in lightly after each addition. Carefully fold and blend until all air bubbles have been removed. Pour into tube pan. Bake until cake springs back when touched and is delicately golden—40 to 45 minutes. Remove from oven; invert pan over milk bottle; cool cake 1 hour before removing from pan. May be served plain or with frosting or filling; do not add frosting or filling until cake is completely cold.

Recipe is equivalent in yield to 1 package angel food cake mix.

DEVILISH ANGEL CAKE. Shave 3 ounces bitter (unsweetened) chocolate with vegetable parer. Stir into batter for angel food cake just before pouring into tube pan. Frost outside of cooled baked cake with chocolate frosting.

LEMON ANGEL CAKE. Prepare Angel Food Cake as in basic recipe or with mix; bake in tube pan. Slice cooled baked cake into 3 layers. Prepare lemon-flavored pudding and pie filling mix; spread half the cooled pudding between the cake layers; to remaining pudding add 2 cups whipped cream (1 cup heavy cream before whipping) or 1 package whipped topping mix. Frost outside of cake with this mixture. Chill 1 to 2 hours.

Pineapple Upside Down Cake

6 tablespoons butter or margarine
1½ cups firmly packed brown sugar
1 1-pound can sliced pineapple, drained
1 package yellow cake mix, or Golden Butter Cake made with 2 eggs only

MADE IN ELECTRIC SKILLET. Preheat electric skillet to 250° F. Melt butter in skillet; add sugar, stir to mix well over bottom of skillet. Arrange the drained pineapple slices over the sugar-butter mixture. Prepare cake batter as directed; pour batter over fruit carefully, spread evenly with rubber spatula. Place cover over skillet, open the vent. Bake 40 to 50 minutes or until toothpick inserted in center comes out clean. With spatula, loosen cake from sides of skillet. Invert over cake plate or platter. Serve warm or cold, topped with whipped cream or ice cream. *Makes 10 to 12 servings.*

BAKED IN OVEN. Pour melted butter into bottom of 10 x 10-inch pan or 12 x 9 x 2-inch pan. Add sugar, blend well and distribute over bottom. Arrange pineapple slices over sugar. Pour cake batter over fruit. Bake in oven preheated to 350° F. until tester comes out clean—35 to 40 minutes. Immediately invert over cake plate or rectangular serving tray, but do not try to remove from pan for 5 minutes.

APRICOT UPSIDE DOWN CAKE. Use canned unpeeled apricot halves (stoned) in place of pineapple slices.

PEACH UPSIDE DOWN GINGERBREAD. Thoroughly drain canned peach halves; arrange over brown sugar-butter mixture with rounded sides up. Instead of cake mix, cover with gingerbread made from 1 package gingerbread mix. Bake in electric skillet 50 minutes, in oven 35 to 40 minutes.

White Fruitcake

½ cup sifted all-purpose flour
2 cups mixed candied fruit and peel, chopped fine
2 cups chopped pitted dried prunes
2 cups walnuts, chopped fine

1 package white cake mix
1½ cups (13½-ounce can) crushed pineapple and juice
¼ cup water
3 eggs, well beaten
¾ cup rum

Prepare 2 loaf pans (9 x 3 x 5 inches), lining bottom of each with brown paper; grease paper on both sides. Sift flour over the candied fruit and prunes; toss to coat thoroughly. Add nuts and toss again. In another bowl, blend cake mix with pineapple, water, eggs, and ½ cup rum. Combine the two mixtures; stir to blend thoroughly. Spoon into pans. Bake at 300° F. until cake is firm and starts to pull away from sides of pan—about 1½ hours. Remove from oven, leave in pans five minutes, then turn out on cake racks. While still warm, sprinkle with some of remaining rum. When cake is cold, wrap in cheesecloth, sprinkle cheesecloth with rum on all sides, then wrap cake in double thickness of aluminum foil. Let age at least 30 days, preferably 2 months *Makes a total of 5 pounds fruitcake.*

Gugelhupf (or Kugelhopf)

1 package active dry yeast
¼ cup warm water
1 cup milk, heated
1/3 cup softened butter
½ cup sugar
3 eggs
1 teaspoon salt

2 teaspoons grated lemon rind
4 to 5 cups sifted flour
½ cup chopped candied cherries
½ cup chopped blanched almonds
Confectioners' sugar

Dissolve yeast in warm water (test temperature on wrist). Heat milk, cool to lukewarm. Beat butter and sugar together until creamy, add eggs one at a time. Add yeast mixture, salt, milk, and grated lemon peel to egg mixture. Set aside ¼ cup flour; toss with cherries and nuts. Add remaining flour a cup at a time to yeast mixture until soft dough is formed. Turn out onto lightly floured board: knead until smooth and elastic. Work in cherries and nuts. Grease a Turk's head mold; place the dough in the mold. Cover: let rise again. When dough is within 1 inch of top of mold, or when dents remain in the dough when poked, bake in oven preheated to 375° F. until golden. Remove from mold, cool on rack, but while still warm dust with confectioners' sugar. A favorite holiday cake in Austria. *Makes 1 cake.*

Rich Moist Fruitcake

This luscious fruitcake takes only 20 minutes to put together, and will keep moist and fresh all winter. A wonderful idea for holiday gifts; can be warmed to serve as pudding for holiday meals, or served sliced with eggnog at holiday parties. With the one recipe make 4 small (1¼-pound) cakes or 2 larger (2½-pound) cakes.

¼ cup all-purpose flour, sifted

2 1-pound jars (4 cups) mixed candied fruit

2 cups (8-ounce can) walnuts, coarsely chopped

1 package spice cake mix

1½ cups prepared mincemeat*

3 eggs, well beaten

1 cup rum

Prepare 2 loaf pans (9 x 3 x 5 inches) or 4 smaller (7½ x 3 x 5 inches) pans by lining bottom of each with brown paper; grease paper on both sides. Sift the flour over the candied fruit; toss to coat thoroughly; add the nuts and toss again. In another bowl, blend cake mix with mincemeat, eggs, and ¾ cup rum. Combine the two mixtures, stir to blend thoroughly. Spoon into cake pans. Bake at 300° F. until cake is firm and starts to pull away from sides of pan—about 2 hours. Leave on cake racks 10 minutes before removing from pans, then sprinkle warm cakes all over with some of remaining rum. Wrap with cheesecloth, sprinkle again with rum, wrap securely in double thickness of foil. Age 1 month or longer before using. *Makes 5 pounds fruit cake.*

*This is about half a jar of commercial mincemeat. Use the remaining mincemeat in the jar as a topping for ice cream, with a little rum or brandy.

Baba au Rhum

1 package active dry yeast

½ cup warm water

2 cups sifted flour

4 eggs

½ teaspoon salt

½ cup butter

1½ tablespoons sugar

¼ cup raisins, cut up

¼ cup candied citron, minced

¼ cup candied orange peel, minced

1 cup heavy cream, whipped and flavored with sugar and rum

RUM SYRUP

1 cup sugar

1 cup water

½ cup dark sweet rum

Add yeast to warm water (test temperature on inside of wrist); stir to dissolve. Add ½ cup sifted flour to yeast mixture, blend to make a sponge. Sift and measure 1½ cups flour into large mixing bowl; add yeast sponge, then eggs, one at a time, beating with wooden spoon to make smooth, sticky dough. Cover with towel. Put in warm place free of drafts for ¾ to 1 hour until doubled (dents remain when punched).

Work salt, butter, and sugar into risen dough with fingers, lifting repeatedly until dough is smooth and pliable. Work in lightly floured raisins and candied fruit, distribute evenly in batter. Pour into 10 well-buttered individual baba molds or into 1½-quart ring mold.

Bake in preheated 400° F. oven for 15 minutes; reduce to 350°, bake until toothpick inserted in cake comes out clean—about 10 minutes longer. Cool 10 minutes in molds; unmold; transfer to platter. While *cakes are warm*, drench with boiling hot Rum Syrup (heat sugar, water, and rum together until syrup spins a thread). Use only half the syrup now; add remainder 1 hour before serving. Serve topped with sweetened whipped cream flavored with rum.

Savarin Cake with Sherry-Apricot Glaze

1 recipe yeast-raised cake (as for Baba au Rhum)	½ cup sweet sherry
	¼ cup apricot jam
1 1-pound can apricot halves in heavy syrup	1 cup heavy cream, whipped, sweetened

Prepare the cake as for Baba au Rhum, baking in 1½-quart well-buttered ring mold. While cake is in the oven, drain the apricots, measure 1½ cups syrup; to this add the sherry; bring to a boil; boil 5 minutes. Turn baked cake out of pan onto rack. Immediately drench with ¾ cup of the boiling hot sherry syrup, adding a little at a time to the cake. Cool 10 minutes. Arrange apricots over top of cake. Combine remaining sherry-apricot syrup with apricot jam; beat until free from lumps. Spoon this over the apricots on the cake. Allow to cool completely. Whip the cream; chop any remaining apricots; blend into the cream. Pile the cream in the center of the cake ring. *Makes 12 rich servings.*

SAVARIN CAKE WITH SABAYON SAUCE. Bake the yeast-raised batter in a 1½-quart buttered ring mold, as for Baba au Rhum. Soak with hot Madeira. Serve with **Sabayon Sauce**.

Kentucky Bourbon Pecan Cake

3 cups all-purpose flour
1 pound white seedless raisins, chopped
1 pound pecans, shelled, chopped
2 teaspoons grated nutmeg
2 teaspoons baking powder

½ pound butter, softened
2 cups sugar
6 eggs, separated
1¼ cups bourbon
Pecan halves and sliced candied cherries for garnish

Preheat oven to 250° F. Line bottoms of 2 9 x 5 x 3-inch pans or a 10-inch tube pan with heavy brown paper, then grease the paper. Sift flour and toss fruits and nuts in 2 tablespoons of it. Sift remaining flour with nutmeg and baking powder. Cream butter and sugar until fluffy; add egg yolks one at a time, blending in after each addition.

Add flour and 1 cup of the bourbon alternately, beating until batter is very smooth. Stir in fruit and nuts, which have been tossed with flour. Beat egg whites until stiff; fold into batter so that no air holes remain. Spoon batter into tube pan or loaf pans. Place pecan halves and sliced red and green cherries over unbaked batter. Place cake on lower rack of oven, bake 4 hours; during the first 1½ hours, place shallow pan of water on top shelf of oven; remove during last 2½ hours of baking.

When cake has drawn away from sides of pan and cake tester comes out clean, remove cake from oven, let cool in pan 30 minutes, then remove carefully so that garnished side is upright.

When cake is completely cold, wrap with cheesecloth which has been soaked in remaining bourbon. Age 1 to 2 weeks before serving.

FROSTINGS AND FILLINGS

Quick Butter Frosting

½ cup softened butter or margarine
1 1-pound box confectioners' sugar
1 egg white, unbeaten (optional)*

2 to 3 tablespoons light cream, evaporated milk, or homogenized milk
1 teaspoon vanilla

Place butter and about one-fourth of the sugar in a bowl (sugar need not be sifted if electric beater is used, but should be sifted

*Can be made without egg white, but the egg white give it glossier, firmer texture. If egg white is omitted, use 5 tablespoons milk.

if beaten by hand). Beat until light and fluffy. Add egg white and continue beating in sugar alternately with cream or milk (1 tablespoon at a time) until mixture is very fluffy and smooth. Add vanilla last. Makes about 2½ cups frosting, enough for tops and sides of 2-layer cake (8- or 9-inch), or 30 cupcakes.

LEMON-OR ORANGE-BUTTER FROSTING. Add 1 teaspoon grated lemon or orange rind with vanilla.

MINT-BUTTER FROSTING. Instead of vanilla, add 1 teaspoon mint extract; color with a few drops green or red (for pink icing) food coloring.

MOCHA-BUTTER FROSTING. Add with the sugar ½ unsweetened cocoa and 2 tablespoons instant coffee powder; or, instead of milk, add 2 1-ounce packets unsweetened chocolate-flavored baking product and 2 tablespoons strong black coffee, or enough coffee for right spreading consistency.

Buttercream Frosting or Filling

½ pound (2 sticks) butter, softened	3 egg yolks
1 cup confectioners' sugar	1 teaspoon vanilla

Place butter in small bowl, beat with electric mixer until creamy; gradually add sugar, then egg yolks, until very creamy, soft, and fluffy. Add vanilla or other flavoring last. Place in refrigerator until firm enough to spread. Makes enough for filling and frosting a 2-layer cake.

ANOTHER WAY. Use granulated sugar; place in saucepan with ¼ teaspoon cream of tartar and ¼ cup water; bring to a boil; boil until syrup spins a thread. Beat syrup into egg yolks, then beat in butter until smooth.

MOCHA BUTTERCREAM. Blend with sugar 1½ tablespoons dark unsweetened cocoa, and 1 tablespoon instant coffee powder (not liquid).

CHOCOLATE BUTTERCREAM. Add 4 ounces chocolate-flavored baking product, or ½ cup dark unsweetened cocoa with the sugar.

RUM BUTTERCREAM. Use 1 tablespoon dark sweet rum instead of vanilla.

LIQUEUR BUTTERCREAM. Use 1 tablespoon any liqueur (such as Cointreau, Curaçao, Tia Maria, or Bénédictine) instead of vanilla.

ORANGE BUTTERCREAM. Add 1 tablespoon grated orange rind; for very special flavor, use Curaçao instead of vanilla.

Chocolate Cream Frosting

4 squares unsweetened chocolate

4 tablespoons butter or margarine

1 1-pound box confectioners'
sugar

⅛ teaspoon salt

½ cup milk

1 teaspoon vanilla, or 1 tablespoon rum

Melt chocolate and butter together over hot water. Place sugar in large bowl; add salt, milk, and vanilla; blend. Blend in chocolate. Let stand, stirring occasionally, until thick enough to spread. (Or, the bowl may be placed in a larger bowl containing ice to hasten thickening.) *Makes 2½ cups, enough for tops and sides of 2-layer cake (8- or 9-inch).*

Chocolate Fudge Frosting

3 cups granulated sugar

½ cup evaporated milk

Dash of salt

4 ounces unsweetened chocolate

4 tablespoons butter

1 teaspoon vanilla, or 1 tablespoon rum

Place sugar, milk, salt, and chocolate in saucepan; cook and stir over medium heat until sugar is dissolved; cook, stirring constantly, until mixture boils; cook until a little dropped in water forms a soft ball—about 5 minutes longer. Add butter and vanilla or rum; cool until bottom of pan feels lukewarm. Beat until frosting is creamy and of easy spreading consistency. Spread immediately. *Makes 2¾ cups, enough for filling and frosting of 2 9-inch layers or 3 8-inch cake layers, or 30 cupcakes.*

QUICK FUDGE FROSTING. Use confectioners' rather than granulated sugar; place only 1½ cups sugar in saucepan at start; use 3 1-ounce packets chocolate-flavored baking product instead of unsweetened chocolate. Stir over low heat until sugar is dissolved and mixture bubbles around edges. Remove from heat; cool 5 minutes. Add remaining 1½ cups confectioners' sugar, butter, and flavoring; beat until right consistency for spreading.

Gooey-soft Chocolate Frosting

1 12-ounce or 2 6-ounce packages   2 cups sifted confectioners' sugar
  semisweet chocolate bits   Dash of salt
1 cup sour cream

Place chocolate in top of double boiler over hot water; when about ¾ melted, remove from heat, stir until free from lumps. Add sour cream, sugar and salt, beat to blend well. Spread at once. *Makes enough for filling and frosting 2 9-inch cake layers or 24 cupcakes.*

Seven-minute Frosting

An electric mixer is almost essential for making this frosting—unless one has a very strong right arm.

2 egg whites   1/3 cup water
1½ cups granulated sugar   2 teaspoons light corn syrup
Dash of salt   1 teaspoon vanilla extract

Place all ingredients but vanilla in top of double boiler; beat 1 minute with electric beater until thoroughly mixed, then place over boiling water and beat constantly for 7 minutes (watch the clock) or until the frosting stands in stiff peaks. Remove from heat. Pour into a large bowl, add vanilla, and continue to beat until glossy. (It should be called "Nine-minute Frosting".) Tint, if desired, or cover with coconut, or fold in chopped candied fruit or nuts. *Makes 4½ cups, enough for very thick, high frosting and filling for a 2-layer cake, or not so high for a 3-layer cake.*

This is equivalent in yield to a package of white frosting mix, but has far better flavor—and no chemicals.

White Mountain Frosting

This, too, requires an electric mixer, or a very muscular arm.

1¼ cups light corn syrup   Pinch of salt
2 egg whites   1 teaspoon vanilla extract

Place the syrup in a small saucepan; bring to a boil. Beat the egg whites meantime with electric mixer at high speed until they form soft peaks. Blend in salt. Slowly add the boiling hot syrup with the beater in motion; beat until frosting is fluffy and forms stiff peaks. Fold in vanilla or other desired flavoring (mint, almond, rum, lemon, or liqueur). Tint if desired; sprinkle with coconut or other garnishes. *The yield is slightly less than that of Seven-minute Frosting, but quite enough for filling and frosting a 2-layer cake.*

Penuche Frosting

¼ pound (1 stick) butter   ¼ cup milk
1 cup brown sugar, firmly   2 cups sifted confectioners' sugar
  packed

Melt butter in saucepan; add brown sugar; cook over low heat for 2 minutes, stirring. Add milk; bring to a boil, stirring constantly. Cool to lukewarm; stir in confectioners' sugar, then beat until right consistency for spreading. (To hasten thickening, place bowl in larger bowl containing ice.) Especially good over spice or chocolate cake. *Makes enough for tops (not sides) of 2 8- or 9-inch layers, or 1 13 x 9-inch sheet cake.*

Confectioners' Glaze

Place 1 cup sifted confectioners' sugar in small bowl; beat in 1 tablespoon milk until mixture is thin enough to spread over top of sweet yeast bread, rolls, coffee cake, or cake. *Makes 1/3 cup glaze.*

Chocolate Glaze

Melt two-thirds of a 6-ounce package semisweet chocolate bits over hot water; stir in 1 tablespoon light corn syrup. Or, place a 4-ounce bar of German's sweet chocolate and 1 tablespoon vegetable shortening over hot water until melted. Drizzle melted chocolate over éclairs, or other cake frosting (to dribble down sides of white-frosted cake, for example). *Makes ¾ cup glaze.*

Clear Lemon Filling

¾ cup granulated sugar   1 tablespoon butter
3 tablespoons cornstarch   2 tablespoons grated lemon rind
¼ teaspoon salt   1/3 cup lemon juice
¾ cup water

Combine in saucepan the sugar, cornstarch, and salt, blending thoroughly. Add water; bring to a boil; boil hard 1 minute. Remove from heat, add butter, lemon rind, and lemon juice. Cool before spreading over cake for filling. *Makes 1 cup,* enough for covering 1 8- or 9-inch cake layer.

For filling both layers in a 3-layer cake, double ingredients.

CLEAR ORANGE FILLING. Instead of water, use strained orange juice; instead of lemon rind, add grated orange rind; add just 2 tablespoons lemon juice.

PINEAPPLE FILLING. Use only ½ cup sugar; thoroughly drain crushed pineapple, measure 1 cup crushed fruit and ¾ cup juice. Add pineapple juice to sugar mixture, bring to a boil; when thickened, add the crushed pineapple, butter, and 1 teaspoon lemon juice.

Quick Custard Cream Cake Filling

For a 3-layer cake, prepare 1 package vanilla-flavored pudding and pie filling but use only 1½ cups milk (or ½ cup less than required in package directions). When thickened, beat warm pudding into 2 egg yolks. For the filling of a 2-layer cake, use ½ package pudding, only ¾ cup milk and 1 egg yolk. Add brandy, rum, or sherry flavoring, if desired.

Choco-Mint Topping

For a quick, easy frosting, place chocolate-covered mints over the top of a baked cake (leaving a margin all around the edges); place in oven until candies have melted enough to swirl over the cake. (This can be done only on a single-layer cake or sheet cake. The cake will be easier to cut if first taken out of the pan, then placed on a baking sheet.)

Broiled Fruit Topping

6 tablespoons butter, melted	Dash of salt
½ cup brown sugar	1 cup chopped canned fruit*
2 tablespoons syrup from canned fruit*	½ cup chopped nuts †

Combine all ingredients, blend well. Spread evenly over top of sheet cake (13 x 9-inch) on baking sheet, place under broiler until mixture is bubbling—about 5 minutes. Let cool 10 minutes before cutting in squares. Serve this way or topped with whipped cream or whipped topping mix.

*Canned crushed pineapple, apricots, peaches, or fruit salad.
† Walnuts, pecans, dry-roasted peanuts, or blanched almonds.

Ways to Use Slightly Stale Cake

If cake is covered with frosting, scrape off and discard frosting first. Cut into squares or slices.

•Serve topped with a hot sauce, such as Lemon-Brandy Sauce. White Wine Sauce, or Hot Fudge Sauce. (This turns cake into a Cottage Pudding.)

- Layer thin cake slices with pudding (made from mix) or ice cream. Chill or freeze; cut into squares.
- Arrange layers of stale cake slices, vanilla pudding, and Pineapple Filling in a loaf pan; chill overnight. Serve topped with whipped cream or whipped topping mix.
- Use cake, cut into fingers, instead of ladyfingers to make a Charlotte Russe or similar dessert.

COOKIES AND BARS

No-bake Peanut Butter Balls

1¼ cups graham cracker crumbs
¼ cup sugar
½ teaspoon cinnamon
½ teaspoon nutmeg
½ cup peanut butter (creamy or chunk-style)
1/3 cup light corn syrup
Confectioners sugar

Combine crumbs, sugar, cinnamon, and nutmeg; blend well. Add peanut butter and syrup; form a dough. With moistened hands, roll into small balls. Chill on waxed paper. When firm, roll in sifted confectioners' sugar. *Makes about 2½ dozen.*

Walnut-Bourbon Balls

2½ cups crushed vanilla wafers
1 cup sifted confectioners' sugar
3 tablespoons light corn syrup
1 cup chopped walnuts
½ cup minced candied fruit (optional)
¼ cup bourbon

Combine all ingredients, knead into a dough; shape with fingers into small balls. Roll balls *in additional* confectioners sugar. Place on waxed paper. Chill overnight until firm. Store loosely covered. *Makes about 3 dozen.*

CHOCOLATE-BOURBON BALLS. Use crushed chocolate wafers instead of vanilla wafers.

PECAN SNOWBALLS. Prepare like Walnut-Bourbon Balls, but use 1 cup chopped pecans instead of walnuts, and instead of whiskey, use 1/3 cup carbonated cola drink or Dr. Pepper's drink. Roll in finely grated or flaked coconut instead of confectioners' sugar.

NUT-FRUIT BALLS. Use crushed vanilla wafers, nuts, and minced candied fruit, but instead of confectioners' sugar and corn syrup, use 2/3 cup sweetened condensed milk; omit whiskey. Add ½ teaspoon cinnamon, if desired. Store in refrigerator.

Easy Coconut Macaroons (Basic Recipe)

2 cups finely grated coconut	Dash of salt
¾ cup sweetened condensed milk	1 teaspoon vanilla
	¼ teaspoon almond extract

Combine ingredients: let stand 2 or 3 minutes. Preheat oven to 325° F. Spread brown paper on baking sheet; greast the paper. Drop mixture by teaspoons 1 inch apart on brown paper, flatten with back of spoon. Bake until golden—about 25 minutes. Remove immediately with spatula; cool on flat surface. Store in covered container. *Makes about 3 dozen.*

CHOCOLATE MACAROONS. Use only 1½ cups coconut; add 1 cup-semisweet chocolate bits to mixture.

CHERRY MACAROONS. Add ½ cup chopped candied (glacé) cherries to basic recipe.

Brownies (Basic Recipe)*

2/3 cup sifted all-purpose flour	2 eggs
½ teaspoon baking powder	1 cup sugar
¼ teaspoon salt	½ cup coarsely chopped nuts
1/3 cup margarine or vegetable shortening	1 teaspoon vanilla
2 squares unsweetened chocolate	

Preheat oven to 350° F. Grease an 8 x 8 x 2-inch pan. Measure and sift together the flour, baking powder, and salt. Melt shortening and chocolate together over hot water. Place eggs in mixing bowl; beat until light; beat in sugar, then chocolate mixture, then flour. Stir in nuts and vanilla. Spread chocolate mixture evenly over bottom of pan. Bake until no imprint remains when pressed—about 25 minutes. Remove from oven; cool in pan. When cold, cut into 1½-inch squares. Store in covered container. *Makes about 20.*

*This is equivalent in yield to 1 package brownie mix.

BROWNIE-ICE CREAM SANDWICHES. Prepare basic recipe, but separate eggs, beat egg whites until stiff, and fold into chocolate mixture before spreading into a greased 9 x 9-inch baking pan. Layer each 2 baked brownies with vanilla ice cream: serve topped with Chocolate Sauce.

CHOCOLATE-PEPPERMINT BROWNIES. After brownies are baked, place chocolate peppermint patties over top, return to oven until patties are soft. then swirl over top. Cool brownies in pan. then cut.

FROSTED BROWNIES. Spread cooled cut brownies with Orange-Butter Frosting; sprinkle frosting with shredded coconut, if desired.

FAMILY-SIZE BROWNIE BAKE. Double all ingredients in basic recipe; bake in 13 x 9-inch pan.

Fudge Brownies

These are more moist and richer, more cakelike, and the yield is slightly higher.

4 squares unsweetened chocolate
½ cup butter or margarine
2 cups sugar
4 eggs, beaten until light

1 cup sifted all-purpose flour
1 teaspoon vanilla
1 cup coarsely chopped nuts (walnuts, pecans, peanuts, or filberts)

Melt chocolate and butter over hot water; cool to lukewarm. Add sugar gradually to beaten eggs, beating after each addition (it's just as easy to do this by hand—no advantage in using a mixer). Blend in chocolate mixture, then the flour, until all flour is moistened. Add vanilla and nuts. Thoroughly grease a 9 x 9-inch pan.* Preheat oven to 350° F., spread brownie mixture evenly in pan and bake 25 minutes; or bake 40 minutes in oven preheated to 325°, or until no imprint remains when pressed. Cool in pan before cutting. *Makes about 30.*

*For chewier, more crisp brownies, bake above recipe in a 13 x 9-inch pan.

Lacy Oatmeal Cookies

¾ cup margarine or vegetable shortening
1 cup brown sugar, firmly packed
½ cup granulated sugar
1 egg
¼ cup water

1 teaspoon vanilla extract
1 cup sifted all-purpose flour
1 teaspoon salt
½ teaspoon soda
3 cups rolled oats, quick or old-fashioned
½ cup raisins or nuts, chopped

Beat together until fluffy the shortening, the two kinds of sugar, egg, water, and vanilla. Separately combine the flour, salt, and soda; add to first mixture. Stir in oatmeal and raisins or nuts; blend well. Grease 1 or 2 baking sheets. Preheat oven to 350° F. Drop mixture on baking sheet 2 inches apart; bake until delicately browned—12 to 13 minutes. Immediately remove from baking sheet; cool on flat surface. Repeat until all are baked. Store in covered container. *Makes 4 to 5 dozen.*

Hermits

½ cup margarine or vegetable shortening
1 cup brown sugar, firmly packed
1 egg
½ cup sour cream, or 1/3 cup strong black coffee

1 ¾ cups sifted all-purpose flour
1 teaspoon pumpkin pie spice or mixed cinnamon and nutmeg
½ teaspoon baking soda
½ cup raisins
¼ cup chopped nuts

Beat margarine or shortening in mixing bowl until fluffy; beat in sugar, egg, and sour cream or coffee, then the flour previously mixed with spices and soda. (Batter will be stiff, but it's as easy to mix by hand as with an electric mixer.) Stir in raisins and nuts. Grease 1 or 2 baking sheets. Preheat oven to 400° F. Drop batter on baking sheets by teaspoons 2 inches apart. Bake until just set (if touched with finger, no imprint remains)—8 to 10 minutes. Immediately remove from baking sheet with spatula; place on flat surface. Store leftovers in covered container. *Makes about 3 dozen cookies.*

CHOCOLATE JUMBLES. Increase flour to 2¾ cups; add 2 squares melted unsweetened chocolate; omit raisins.

Pineapple Drops

1½ cups sifted all-purpose flour
⅛ teaspoon salt
¼ teaspoon baking soda
½ cup vegetable shortening
½ cup sugar

1 egg
½ cup *undrained* crushed pineapple
1/3 cup crushed or finely chopped almonds

Preheat oven to 375° F. Grease 1 or 2 baking sheets. Measure flour, salt, and soda; combine. Place shortening in bowl; beat until creamy; beat in sugar and egg until light and fluffy. Add flour mixture, pineapple, and almonds; stir just until all flour is moistened. Drop by teaspoons on greased baking sheet, 2 inches apart. Bake until golden—10 to 12 minutes (do not overbake). Remove immediately from baking sheet with spatula; cool on flat surface. Store covered. *Makes about 3½ dozen.*

Almond Cookies

The perfect dessert for a Chinese dinner.

2 cups blanched almonds,   packed
  crushed   6 tablespoons butter
1 cup sifted all-purpose flour   1 to 2 teaspoons water
½ cup brown sugar, firmly   24 blanched almond halves

Grease baking sheet. Preheat oven to 350° F. Crush almonds in electric blender until very fine. Or, first toast blanched almonds, then crush with mortar and pestle or with a rolling pin. Combine flour and sugar; add almonds and then the butter; work butter into flour mixture with fingers to form a smooth dough; if necessary, add 1 or 2 teaspoons water—but no more. Form dough into balls about 1 inch in diameter; press flat on baking sheet, press a whole blanched almond in center of each. Bake in oven until golden—about 20 minutes (cookies will be crisp). Store loosely covered. *Makes about 24.*

Banbury Cakes

1 package piecrust mix   1 egg
Grated rind of 1 lemon   ½ teaspoon vanilla
½ cup chopped nuts   ¼ cup sifted confectioners' sugar
¾ cup granulated sugar

Preheat oven to 375° F. Empty piecrust mix into bowl; break up with fork. Add lemon rind, nuts, granulated sugar, egg, and vanilla; beat to form a sticky dough. Flour palms of hands, then take bits of dough and roll into 1-inch balls. Roll each ball in confectioners' sugar. Place 3 inches apart on ungreased baking sheet. Bake until golden (cookies will flatten out)—10 to 12 minutes. Remove from pan immediately. Store in covered container. *Makes about 36.*

Butterscotch Squares

1 package piecrust mix   ½ teaspoon vanilla
2 teaspoons baking powder   ½ cup chopped nuts
1 cup light brown sugar   ½ cup finely diced candied or-
2 eggs   ange peel

Grease a 13 x 9 x 2-inch pan. Preheat oven to 350° F. Break up piecrust mix with fork in mixing bowl. Combine baking powder and sugar; blend well; add to piecrust mix. Add eggs, beating after each. Blend in vanilla, nuts, and orange peel. Spread mixture with knife evenly over bottom of pan. Bake until top is golden and firm—35 to 40 minutes. Remove from oven; cool in pan 5 minutes, then cut into squares with sharp knife. Leave in pan until cold. Store in covered container. *Makes 24 to 30.*

Nut Sticks

1 package piecrust mix
½ cup granulated sugar
1 egg
1 teaspoon vanilla

2 cups crushed nuts (almonds,
   Brazil nuts, peanuts)
Confectioners' sugar

Break up piecrust mix; add sugar, egg, and vanilla, blend well. Mix in nuts. Shape dough into small balls then roll the balls between palms of hands to form thin sticks 2 inches long. Arrange on ungreased baking sheet. Bake in oven preheated to 350° F. until golden—about 20 minutes. Remove; while warm, roll in confectioners' sugar. Store loosely covered. *Makes about 50.*

Refrigerator Cookie Roll (Basic Recipe)

1½ cups sifted all-purpose flour
½ teaspoon baking soda
½ teaspoon salt
½ cup margarine

1 cup sugar*
1 egg
2 teaspoons vanilla

Measure flour; sift; sift again with soda and salt. Beat margarine until soft; beat in sugar and egg until light and fluffy. Add vanilla and flour mixture, blend well, then work with fingers into a stiff dough and shape into a smooth long roll about 1½ inches in diameter. Wrap securely in waxed paper, foil, or plastic wrap. Refrigerate at least overnight, or up to a week. Cut off thin (¼-inch) slices as needed; arrange on *ungreased* baking sheet. Bake in oven preheated to 375° F. until golden—about 10 minutes. Remove at once with spatula. Cool on rack; all those not eaten immediately should be stored in a covered container. *The entire recipe makes about 5 dozen.*

*Use all white granulated sugar, or half white, half brown sugar.

CHOCOLATE REFRIGERATOR ROLL. Add 2 1-ounce squares unsweetened chocolate, melted (or 1-ounce packets chocolate-flavored baking product), to the basic recipe.

ORANGE REFRIGERATOR ROLL. Add 1 tablespoon grated orange rind.

NUT ROLL. Work in ½ cup chopped nuts—pecans, almonds, walnuts, or Brazil nuts.

COCONUT ROLL. Work in ½ cup shredded or flaked coconut.

WHIRLIGIGS. Divide dough in half; add 1 square unsweetened chocolate (melted over hot water) to half the dough. Roll out the 2 halves of dough separately, between sheets of waxed paper. Remove paper; place the chocolate-flavored dough above the plain dough, then roll up like a jelly roll. Wrap; chill. When cold and firm, cut off very thin slices, bake on ungreased baking sheet as in basic recipe.
   Or, buy 2 rolls of commercial refrigerator cookie dough, one chocolate, one vanilla; soften enough at room temperature to roll out each, then place chocolate-flavored dough above vanilla-flavored, roll up together, wrap in waxed paper, and chill until firm. When cold and firm, slice and bake.
   Basic recipe is equivalent to 2 rolls commercial refrigerator ready-to-bake cookie dough.

PICTURE COOKIES. Make or buy 2 rolls refrigerator cookie dough, one chocolate, the other vanilla. Cut thin slices from each roll. With a tiny cookie cutter (or with a sharp knife), cut out silhouette pictures from center of each: place chocolate in center of vanilla, vanilla in center of chocolate. Place assembled silhouettes on baking sheet; bake.

CUT-OUT COOKIES. Both commercial and homemade refrigerator cookie dough can be rolled out and cut into any desired shapes with cookie cutters. The dough must have been chilled long enough to be very firm, then softened at room temperature just enough to manipulate with rolling pin on lightly floured board or countertop to ¼ inch thick (a little thicker than for sugar cookie dough, which follows). Cut into desired shapes; bake on ungreased baking sheet until lightly browned. Decorate either before or after baking. (See Ways to Decorate Cookies.)

Seed Cakes

An Early American favorite, fragrant with caraway.

¼ pound (1 stick) butter, softened
2 tablespoons light cream
½ cup granulated sugar

1 egg
1½ cups sifted all-purpose flour
1 teaspoon caraway seeds

Beat butter until fluffy; add cream, then sugar and egg. Beat until smooth. Add sifted flour and caraway seeds, beating again until smooth. Chill dough, then roll out between sheets of waxed paper as thin as possible. Cut with biscuit cutter or bottom of wineglass, or with decorative cookie cutters. Place on *ungreased* baking sheet. Bake in oven preheated to 375° F. until golden—about 15 minutes. Store in covered container. *Makes about 3 dozen.*

Rolled Sugar Cookies

12 tablespoons (¾ cup) butter or
  margarine, softened
Sugar
2 eggs

½ teaspoon vanilla
2½ cups sifted all-purpose flour
1 teaspoon baking powder
½ teaspoon salt

Beat butter until creamy; beat in sugar and eggs until fluffy. Add vanilla. Sift and measure flour; blend with baking powder and salt. Beat flour mixture into butter mixture to form a stiff dough. Knead just enough to make dough smooth. Chill at least 1 hour (the longer the better). Roll out about one-third at a time, keeping the rest chilled. Avoid working flour into dough; if possible, use a stockinette covering for the rolling pin and a cloth covering for the board. Or, break off just a small piece of dough at a time, flatten with the bottom of a glass tumbler, then cut with cookie cutters. If dough is rolled in 1 piece, cut shapes over the surface before trying to lift away from the board to the baking sheet, so as to handle as little as possible. Place on ungreased baking sheet.* Scraps of dough can be reshaped, pressed flat with bottom of tumbler, then cut into shape. Decorate with raisins or candies *before* baking, with Decorators' or Chocolate Glaze *after* baking. Bake in oven preheated to 400° F. until cookies are delicately golden (avoid overbaking) —about 6 minutes. Immediately lift from sheet with spatula to flat surface. Store baked decorated cookies in container with tight cover. *Makes about 40 cookies, depending on size.*

*When cookies are to be hung on Christmas tree, form a small hole near the top of each *before* baking.

Spritz Cookies

These are made with a cookie press—easy and fun. The same dough can be used for making rolled cookies, if well chilled before hand.

1 cup softened butter, margarine, or vegetable shortening
½ cup granulated sugar
½ cup brown sugar, firmly packed
1 tablespoon orange juice
1 teaspoon grated orange rind
1 egg
2½ cups sifted flour
¼ teaspoon salt
¼ teaspoon baking soda

Cream together shortening and both kinds of sugar until light and fluffy, beat in orange juice, grated rind, and egg, then the flour previously sifted with salt and baking soda. Place about one-fourth of the dough at a time in cookie press, using any desired decorative forms. Press out onto ungreased baking sheet, taking care to keep cookies small. Garnish with candies or colored sugar before baking. Bake in oven preheated to 375° F. for 10 to 12 minutes. Repeat until all are baked. Keep stored in airtight container. *Makes about 6 dozen.*

PEANUT BUTTER SPRITZ. Use only ½ cup shortening; add ½ cup peanut butter (smooth or chunky); use only 2 cups sifted flour.

CHOCOLATE SPRITZ. Use all granulated sugar (not brown); add 3 squares melted unsweetened chocolate.

PETITS FOURS. Make Spritz Cookies according to basic recipe; press into oblong, whirligig, or butterfly shapes. Place candies in centers, if desired. When baked and cooled, dip cookies into melted chocolate, or decorate with Confectioners' Glaze or Chocolate Glaze. Sprinkle minced pistachio nuts or toasted chopped almonds over glaze before it hardens.

SPITZBUBEN. Prepare as for Rolled Sugar Cookies, but omit eggs and use only 2 cups flour. (Or, use 2 rolls refrigerated ready-to-bake cookie dough, soften enough at room temperature to roll out.) Roll dough ¼ inch thick; cut 2-inch circles with biscuit cutter. Cut centers from half the circles. Bake until golden—about 10 minutes. Spread the full circles with a dab of jelly; top with "doughnut" circles. Sprinkle with confectioners' sugar.

CHRISTMAS WREATHS. Prepare dough for Rolled Sugar Cookies, or use refrigerated ready-to-bake cookie dough. Form 1-inch balls, dip each into finely chopped nuts, place on greased baking sheet 1 inch apart. Dip bottom of tumbler in sugar; press balls flat to form circles. Press indentation in center of each with thumb. Sprinkle with green sugar sprinkles. Bake in oven preheated to 375° F. for 5 minutes; again press center; bake until golden—about 10 minutes longer. Remove immediately from baking sheets. When cooled slightly, place a dab of red jam or jelly in center of each.

Tips on Decorating Cookies

Press the following into cookie dough before baking:

- Colored sugar sprinkles
- Seedless raisins (for eyes)
- Gumdrop slivers (red for mouth)
- Semisweet chocolate bits
- Chocolate sprinkles (brown hair)
- Shredded coconut (will turn straw color with baking)
- Glacé cherry halves
- Nut halves
- Slivers of candied fruit
- Cinnamon drops
- Candy hearts
- Animal crackers

Sprinkle over cookies during last 3 minutes of baking:

- Tinted coconut, or white coconut intended to remain white

Add these decorations to baked, cooled cookies:

- Confectioners' glaze (for fine lines, dip toothpick in glaze)
- Chocolate glaze
- Dip one end of cookie in melted chocolate
- Place small candies in glaze while soft
- Sprinkle minced nuts or colored sugar over glaze before it hardens

Lemon-Coconut Bars

½ cup softened margarine
¼ cup confectioners' sugar
1 cup flour
2 eggs
½ cup granulated sugar
1 package lemon-flavored pud-

ding and pie filling mix
½ teaspoon baking powder
1 cup chopped pitted dates
1 cup fine-grated or flaked coconut

Cream margarine and confectioners' sugar together until light and fluffy. Blend in flour. Press evenly into an 8 x 8 x 2-inch or 9 x 9 x 2-inch pan. Preheat oven to 350° F. Bake butter-sugar mixture until lightly browned—15 to 18 minutes. Meanwhile, beat eggs until thick and lemon-colored, gradually beat in granulated sugar, then add pudding mix (right from the box) and baking powder. Blend well. Stir in dates and coconut. Spread mixture over the hot crust, return to oven, bake 25 to 30 minutes longer until topping is puffed and browned. Cool in pan; cut into bars. Store in tightly covered container. *Makes about 18 bars.*

Butterscotch Crisps

½ cup softened butter or margarine
½ cup firmly packed brown sugar
1 package butterscotch pudding

and pie filling mix
1 egg
1½ cups sifted all-purpose flour
1 teaspoon baking soda
1 teaspoon cream of tartar

Grease baking sheet. Preheat oven to 350° F. Combine butter, sugar, and pudding mix (right from the package). Beat until creamy and smooth. Add egg; blend well. Sift flour; measure; add baking soda and cream of tartar; blend well. Add flour mixture to butter mixture; form a dough, kneading with fingers. Take small pieces of dough; roll into balls about 1 inch in diameter. Press on *greased* baking sheet; bake until golden—10 to 12 minutes. Store in covered container. *Makes about 4 dozen.*

PEANUT BUTTEB CRISPS. Add 1/3 cup chunk-style peanut butter to above.

CHOCOLATE CRISPS. Use chocolate pudding and pie filling mix instead of butterscotch.

Lemon-Prune Bars

1 6-ounce can frozen lemonade concentrate, thawed
1 cup chopped pitted prunes
½ cup granulated sugar
1 tablespoon cornstarch
Dash of salt
¼ cup chopped walnuts

½ cup softened margarine
1½ cups rolled oats, regular or old-fashioned
1 cup sifted all-purpose flour
½ cup brown sugar, firmly packed

Preheat oven to 350° F. Get out an 8 x 8 x 2-inch pan (do not grease). Add enough water to lemonade concentrate to make 1 cup. Add this to prunes; simmer until prunes are soft—about 5 minutes. Add granulated sugar, cornstarch, salt, and the nuts. Cook, stirring, until mixture is thick—about 8 minutes. Cool.

Combine margarine, oats, flour, and brown sugar; mix with fingers until crumbly. Pat half the oats mixture in bottom of pan; top with prune mixture, spreading evenly, then add remaining oats mixture. Bake until top is golden and firm—about 35 minutes. Cool in pan. Cut into bars. Keep leftovers in covered container. *Makes 16 bars.*

Lebkuchen

1 cup honey
1 cup sugar
4 eggs
2 tablespoons cocoa
1 cup milk (or 1 cup black coffee)
3 cups sifted all-purpose flour
½ teaspoon baking soda
¼ teaspoon ground clove
¼ teaspoon cardamom or nut-

meg
¼ teaspoon powdered ginger
½ teaspoon cinnamon
½ cup finely chopped citron or candied orange peel (optional)
Sugar Glaze
Whole blanched almonds
Citron pieces

Combine honey, sugar, and eggs; beat until thick. Add cocoa and milk or coffee. Sift together flour, baking soda, and spices. Combine with egg mixture; blend thoroughly. Fold in candied peel. Grease 2 baking sheets. Preheat oven to 400° F. Spoon batter over the sheets evenly to ½ inch thick. Bake until no imprint remains when touched—10 to 12 minutes. Prepare the glaze as lebkuchen bakes. Spread the glaze over the lebkuchen while warm; arrange almonds and cut pieces of citron over top. When cold, cut into squares. These should be soft and sweet, similar to gingerbread in flavor but more delicately spiced. If stored in an airtight container they will keep for weeks. *Makes about 35 squares.*

SUGAR GLAZE. Place in a small bowl ½ cup sifted confectioners' sugar. Add ½ teaspoon vanilla and 1 tablespoon water. Stir until smooth; add more water, 1 teaspoon at a time, until mixture is the consistency of cream. Spread at once over Lebkuchen. This glaze can also be used on cookies, coffee cake, and baked sweet yeast breads. *Makes about 1/3 cup.*

Pfeffernuss

2 eggs, beaten
1 cup sugar
¼ cup ground almonds
¼ cup candied orange peel and citron, finely chopped
1 teaspoon cinnamon
⅛ teaspoon ground clove

½ teaspoon freshly ground black pepper
¼ teaspoon ground ginger
Grated rind of 1 lemon
3 cups sifted all-purpose flour
About ¼ cup rum
Confectioners' sugar

Beat eggs and sugar together until frothy. Add almonds, orange peel, and citron. (An electric blender will quickly grind the almonds and mince the candied fruit.) Add spices and lemon rind to flour; combine with egg mixture; knead to form smooth dough. Shape into a long roll about 1½ inches in diameter. Chill, then cut into ½-inch slices. Place slices on greased baking sheets; let stand, uncovered, overnight. Next day, turn over the "nuts," then bake in 300° F. oven until lightly browned—about 20 minutes. While still warm, sprinkle with rum and confectioners' sugar. When they are completely cold, store in airtight container. *Makes 50 or more hard little "nuts" that become more chewy and flavorful with age.*

Gingerbread Men

3½ to 4 cups sifted all-purpose flour
1 teaspoon salt
2 teaspoons ground ginger
½ teaspoon ground nutmeg
¼ teaspoon ground allspice
1 teaspoon baking soda

1 cup molasses
¼ cup cold water
2 tablespoons rum
1 cup butter
¾ cup brown or white sugar
1 egg, beaten
Sugar Glaze

Sift 3½ cups of the flour with salt and spices. Add soda to molasses; combine with water, rum, butter, sugar, and egg. Bring slowly to a boil, then cool. Chill overnight. Add additional flour if necessary to make rolling easy. Roll to ¼ inch on a lightly floured board. Cut with gingerbread-man cutter. Insert raisins for eyes and make a small hole in head so that cookies may be hung on Christmas tree. Bake at 375° F. for 10 to 12 minutes. Let stand on baking sheet a minute or two before removing. Use Sugar Glaze to trace mouth, hair, and clothing (see sketch). Will keep fresh in covered container for weeks. *Makes about 2 dozen gingerbread men, 3 to 4 dozen smaller cookies.*

Pralines

8 tablespoons (1 stick) soft- ened butter	1 egg
1½ cups dark brown sugar, firm- ly packed	1½ cups sifted all-purpose flour 1 teaspoon vanilla 1 cup coarsely chopped pecans

Beat butter and sugar together until creamy; beat in egg, then flour, then vanilla and nuts. Chill 1 hour. Preheat oven to 375° F. Grease 1 or 2 baking sheets. Roll pieces of dough into 1-inch balls; place on baking sheets 3 inches apart. Moisten bottom of tumbler; press balls to flatten to ⅛-inch thickness. Bake until lightly browned. Remove immediately from baking sheet and cool. Store loosely covered. *Makes 3 dozen.*

Packing Gift Cookies

Certain cookies travel far better than others. The firmer, thicker ones are better travelers than the thin, crisp ones. Those flavored with a bit of whiskey or other spirit are also good choices for traveling. Here are some examples:

Brownies	Rolled Sugar Cookies (made
Walnut-Bourbon Balls	a little thicker than usual)
Hermits (made with coffee)	Gingerbread Men
Chocolate Jumbles	Lemon-Prune Bars
Lebkuchen	Pfeffernuss

TIPS ON PACKING COOKIES. Get sturdy cardboard cartons from a supermarket or local shop. Select boxes that are still in good shape. Line bottom with crumbled foil or newspapers, then with pieces of cardboard, to form a smooth base. Wrap cookies in foil, 2 or 3 to a package. Place packages in even layers. Put crumbled foil or newspapers between layers, with more cardboard on top. Leave room for a final layer of crumbled foil or newspaper. Seal flaps with gummed tape.

Wrap the box with heavy brown paper and tie securely with cord. Label front and back, using Magic Marker or paste-on labels. Write conspicuously.

13 FRUIT, PUDDINGS, AND FROZEN DESSERTS

Many people consider a bit of sweet at the end of the meal the climax of dinner, and having to give up desserts for a beautiful figure can be the cruelest of tortures.

A *fruit bowl* is the best dessert for the figure-conscious. In many countries, the fruit bowl is passed as a matter of course at every meal, and it's a very wise custom, because fresh fruit may be eaten without sugar, cream, butter, or flour; because fruit is nutritionally important; and because, from the viewpoint of the cook, raw fruit from the fruit bowl is the easiest dessert to serve.

Those fruits easiest to eat at the table include apples, pears, grapes, fresh apricots, purple plums (fresh prunes), bananas, sweet cherries, nectarines, and tangerines.

Almost as easy as fruit-bowl fruits are the melons and berries, whose seasonal arrival brings welcome variety. Melons need only be cut into wedges. Pass salt or lemon wedges if you like for cantaloupe and honeydew. Berries need only be washed and sprinkled lightly with sugar, though cream may be served to those not concerned with waistlines.

For those who prefer fruit cut up and served more daintily in sherbet dishes, suggested delicious and easy-to-prepare fruit salads and compotes follow along with other simple fruit desserts.

Ambrosia

In simplest terms, this means cut-up oranges and bananas topped with shredded coconut. Allow 1 orange and ½ banana for each serving. Peel the orange so that all white membrane is removed; cut through the sections in slices or dice; remove seeds. Peel and slice bananas. Add sugar to taste; toss to blend with fruit. Place fruit in a serving dish or in individual sherbets. Top with shredded coconut.

Baked Apples

The quickest and easiest way to prepare baked apples is to cut large, firm unpeeled apples in halves crosswise, remove the seeds, then place cut side up in a shallow casserole or baking dish and sprinkle with white or brown sugar. Add a little water to the bottom of the dish; bake in a 400° to 450° F. oven until tops are glazed and fruit has puffed up—about 20 minutes. (To bake apples with an oven dinner when oven is set at 325° or 350° F., allow 30 to 35 minutes.)

The best apples for baking are McIntosh, Winesap, Cortland, and Rome Beauty.

STUFFED BAKED APPLES. Leave unpeeled apples whole; cut out the cores from top to bottom. Place in shallow baking dish; fill hollowed cores with a mixture of sugar, grated lemon rind, and seedless raisins. One teaspoon sugar per apple is about right; put in as many raisins as will fit. Dot tops with butter. Bake until apples have puffed up, bursting the skin around the top, and skin is glazed—30 to 40 minutes. Serve with or without cream.

ORANGE-CRANBERRY APPLES. Instead of sugar and raisins, place a spoonful of Orange-Cranberry Relish in hollowed core of each apple and sprinkle tops with sugar. Baste with pan juices once or twice during baking.

Apricot Fluff

Cook 1 pound dried apricots until tender. Purée in electric blender or force through food mill or sieve. Blend with ¼ cup orange juice, and sugar to taste; fold in 1 cup sweetened whipped cream or whipped topping mix. If desired, add a spoonful of brandy. Serve topped with chopped pistachio nuts or toasted slivered almonds. *Makes 6 to 8 servings.*

SHORTCUT VERSION. Instead of dried apricots, use 2 junior-size jars strained applesauce and apricots (baby food); omit orange juice and sugar; flavor shipped cream with brandy or Curaçao. *Makes 6 servings.*

Bananas in Cream

Peel and slice bananas (allow ½ to 1 per serving, depending on size). Dust with sugar. Cover with heavy cream blended with 1 tablespoon brandy or cognac if desired, 15 minutes before serving.

ANOTHER WAY. Sprinkle shredded or toasted coconut over top of each serving.

Bananas Flambée

3 large or 6 small bananas	Dash of cinnamon (optional)
1 to 2 tablespoons confectioners' sugar	2 tablespoons butter
	¼ cup brandy or rum

Slice bananas lengthwise; cut larger ones in half again. Allow 2 pieces of banana per serving. Dust bananas with confectioners' sugar and cinnamon. At table, sauté bananas in butter in chafing dish or electric skillet until golden on each side. Warm brandy or rum; lower into pan and set aflame (or tilt blazer or chafing dish so that the brandy vapor is set afire by the alcohol burner). Spoon up to keep flame alive. Serve the bananas at once. Especially delicious over vanilla ice cream or topped with heavy cream. *Makes 6 servings.*

Spiced Bananas Baked in Port

3 large or 6 small bananas	¼ teaspoon nutmeg
2 tablespoons flour	4 tablespoons butter, melted
¼ cup white or brown sugar	1/3 cup port wine
½ teaspoon cinnamon	½ cup heavy cream
¼ teaspoon cloves	

Slice bananas lengthwise; cut large bananas in quarters. Combine flour, sugar, and spices. Dredge each piece of banana with the flour mixture. Pour 2 tablespoons melted butter in bottom of Pyrex pie pan or shallow baking dish; add the bananas; top with remaining butter. Add port. Bake in oven preheated to 375° F. until bananas are lightly browned—about 25 minutes. Serve warm, topped with cream. *Makes 6 servings.*

732   *THE EVERYTHING COOKBOOK*

BANANAS BAKED IN FRUIT SAUCE. Instead of port, use syrup from canned fruit, especially plums or peaches.

Cherries au Kirsch

Remove pits from fresh Bing cherries; add sugar to taste (about ¼ cup sugar for 1 quart cherries), and 1 to 2 tablespoons kirsch. Marinate at least 1 hour before serving. Serve in sherbet dishes.

Cherry-Peach Compote

Combine fresh Bing cherries, cut in half and pitted, with fresh peeled peaches (or use canned cherries and canned peach halves). If using fresh peaches, heat ¼ cup granulated sugar with 1 tablespoon brandy, kirsch, or cherry brandy until mixture comes to a boil; boil 1 minute, then pour hot over fruit. Allow to cool. If using canned peach halves blend ½ cup peach syrup with brandy or kirsch; pour over fruit. Marinate at least 1 hour before serving.

ANOTHER WAY. Omit brandy; add a dash of almond extract to syrup.

Cherries Jubilee

1 large (1-pound 12-ounce) can pitted Bing cherries, in syrup
¾ cup cherry syrup
2 tablespoons cornstarch
2 tablespoons brandy, rum, or kirsch
1 quart vanilla ice cream

Drain cherries, reserving ¾ cup syrup. Blend syrup with cornstarch and brandy or other liquor. Shortly before serving, add cherries to syrup; heat and stir until syrup is thickened and glossy. Serve warm over ice cream. *Makes 8 servings.*

ANOTHER WAY. Use only ¼ cup cherry syrup combined with ½ cup Cherry Kijafa wine and 1 tablespoon brandy or rum.

CHERRIES JUBILEE FLAMBÉE. Prepare as in basic recipe, but do not add brandy until time to serve the dessert. Separately warm the brandy; lower into hot sauce in a ladle; set aflame. Spoon up until flame dies out.

Frosted Grapes

Select very fresh, unblemished grapes (large red grapes are especially attractive). Cut into small clusters, allowing one cluster per serving. Roll in unbeaten egg white, then in granulated sugar. To make them even more special, the sugar may be moistened with brandy or sherry. Chill. Serve alone or with a dessert cheese such as Camembert.

Fruit Salads

Use imagination in combining seasonal fruits for salads, or combine fresh and canned fruits, using the syrup of the canned fruit, or marinate cut-up fruits in wine, rum, brandy, a favorite liqueur, or orange juice.

- **Florida Special**. Seeded black grapes, cut-up oranges, and sliced peaches in white wine.
- **Oranges au Château La Salle**. Diced seeded oranges and diced Tokay grapes in Château La Salle wine (a sweet dessert wine).
- **January Salad**. Diced apples, diced fresh pears, seeded muscatel grapes, and chopped walnuts, sweetened to taste.
- **Honeydew-Peach Salad**. Diced honeydew melon and cut-up fresh peaches, sugared to taste, marinated in orange juice.
- **Melon-Peach Combo**. Cantaloupe balls, honeydew balls, peaches, or oranges in rosé wine.
- **Tricolor Compote**. Blueberries, raspberries (fresh or frozen, drained), and peaches (fresh or canned) in Cointreau and fruit syrup.
- **Fruit au Kirsch**. Cut-up peaches, bananas, and Bing cherries marinated in kirsch (brandy is also good).
- **Melon-Berry Salad**. Diced watermelon, diced cantaloupe, and blueberries in red or rosé wine.
- **Tropical Special**. Wedges of pineapple (fresh or canned), sliced bananas, and diced oranges marinated in white rum.
- **Orange-Nut Salad**. Diced seeded oranges and chopped walnuts delicately laced with brandy or white wine.
- **Melon Balls in Port**. Cantaloupe and honeydew balls covered with port wine and marinated 1 hour before serving.
- **Pineapple-Orange Salad au Vermouth**. Two cups each fresh pineapple wedges and cut-up oranges marinated in a mixture of ½ cup sweet vermouth, ¼ cup sugar, and ½ teaspoon cinnamon for at least 1 hour before serving.

Fruit Compotes

American canned fruits are the finest to be found anywhere and may be served just as they come from the can, but to make them seem special, here are a few tricks.

•**Apricot Compote.** Drain a large can of apricots (either apricot halves or whole apricots, as preferred). Add about ½ cup white seedless grapes. Measure ½ cup of apricot syrup and add 1 to 2 tablespoons brandy, Curaçao, or Cointreau; pour over fruit; marinate 1 hour or until time to serve. *Makes about 4 servings.*

•**Apricot-Orange Compote.** Add to the above 1 or 2 oranges, peeled, seeded, and diced, and 1 banana, sliced. *Makes 6 to 8 servings.*

•**Brandied Peaches.** Drain peach syrup from canned peaches; heat ½ cup syrup with 2 tablespoons brandy (do not boil); pour over fruit. Marinate an hour or two. Serve as is or laced with cream.

•**Greengage Compote.** Serve greengage plums just as they come from the can topped with shredded coconut and a lacing of cream.

•**Queen Anne Compote.** Combine Queen Anne (white) cherries and canned peach halves. If desired, sprinkle with a few drops of brandy or bourbon.

•**Peach-Pear Compote.** Combine equal quantities canned Bartlett pear halves and canned home-style peaches. Spoon just enough syrup over top to keep fruit moist. Serve topped with shredded coconut.

•**Pear-Plum Compote au Rhum.** Combine pear halves and red plums; add a little rum (or a favorite liqueur) to the plum syrup and pour over the fruit.

•**Pineapple-Plum Compote.** Combine pineapple chunks and purple plums; blend some of fruit syrup with white wine, orange juice, or lemonade mix and toss with fruit.

•**Sherried Plums.** Drain purple plums; combine ¾ cup of the syrup with ¼ to ½ cup cream sherry; pour over the plums and marinate an hour. Serve sprinkled with grated orange peel.

•**Southern Comfort.** Combine canned figs, apricot halves, and sliced bananas; marinate in fig syrup and a little bourbon. Or combine chopped dried figs, chopped dried apricots, sliced bananas, and white raisins; cover with fruit syrup saved from a previous meal. Bring to a boil; cool; marinate several hours. A dash of brandy or bourbon may be added if desired.

Fruit Compote in Jelly

1 1-pound can pear halves, drained	1 13½-ounce can pineapple chunks, drained
1 1-pound can cling peach halves, drained	½ lemon, thinly sliced
	3 cups fruit syrup and water

5 whole cloves
1 stick cinnamon
1 3-ounce package strawberry-

flavored gelatin
2 teaspoons lemon juice

Arrange drained fruits in serving dish (not glass). Scatter lemon slices over top. Measure fruit juices; add water to make 3 cups. Add cloves and cinnamon; heat to boiling and simmer 5 minutes; strain.

Dissolve the gelatin in the hot liquid. Add lemon juice; cool to room temperature. Pour over fruits. Chill until gelatin is consistency of a thick syrup—1 to 1½ hours. Baste gelatin mixture over fruits once or twice during this period. *Makes 6 to 8 servings.*

FRUIT COMPOTE IN WINE JELLY. Instead of 3 cups fruit juices and water, use 2 cups fruit juices, and 1 cup Cherry Kijafa or port wine.

Peaches Flambée

Place canned peach halves in a shallow baking dish, pitted side up. Add enough syrup to cover bottom of dish. Bake in oven preheated to 400° F. for 15 minutes. Bring hot to table; ladle a tablespoon of brandy or rum into hot syrup and set aflame. Add a second spoonful of the spirit; keep flame alive by spooning up. Serve warm like this or over ice cream. *One large can of peaches makes 4 servings alone, 6 servings over ice cream.*

Grilled Curried Peaches

Arrange 12 peach halves, pitted side up, in a shallow baking dish. Combine ½ cup brown sugar and ¼ teaspoon curry powder; sprinkle over peaches. Place a dot of butter in each half and dribble peach syrup over all. Place under broiler unit until butter is melted and sugar bubbling. Serve warm this way or with cream. *Makes 4 servings.*

Cantaloupe Float

2 cups cantaloupe balls
2 cups watermelon balls, seeded
1 pint fresh blueberries
½ cup orange juice

½ cup pineapple juice or white wine
1 cup ginger ale
1 pint lemon or lime sherbet

Arrange melon and blueberries in serving dish—a glass bowl is especially attractive. Combine fruit juices (or juice and wine) and ginger ale; pour over fruit. Chill until time to serve. At serving time, place small scoops of sherbet over top, so that sherbet floats over fruit juice. *Makes 8 servings.*

FRUIT SALAD FLOAT. Instead of melon and blueberries, combine almost any seasonal fruits; marinate in wine; serve topped with scoops of sherbet.

Spiced Prunes

When stewing dried prunes, add a dash each of cinnamon and nutmeg, half a lemon cut in slivers, and any canned fruit syrup you happen to have on hand. You will never think of thém again as "stewed" prunes.

Prune-Pineapple Compote

1 pound pitted dried prunes	2 tablespoons dark sweet rum, or
1 1-pound can pineapple chunks	¼ cup sweet sherry
2 oranges	⅛ teaspoon cinnamon
1 tablespoon lemon juice	⅛ teaspoon allspice

A day in advance, cook prunes in water to cover until tender but not soft. Drain; reserve ½ cup liquid. Combine this with ½ cup of the pineapple syrup, grated peel of ½ an orange, lemon juice, rum, and spices. Heat just to boiling, then turn off heat. Add prunes, pineapple, and peeled diced oranges. Marinate 24 hours. Serve hot. *Makes 10 servings.*

APRICOT PRUNE COMPOTE. Instead of pineapple, use 1 can apricot halves or whole apricots, and apricot syrup instead of pineapple syrup.

PRUNES IN PORT. Soak dried prunes in port wine to cover for 24 hours, then add more wine (about 1 cup); simmer gently until prunes are soft. Cool, then chill. Marinate another 24 hours. Serve laced with cream.

PINEAPPLE GRAND MARNIER. Sprinkle slices of canned pineapple with Grand Marnier liqueur; soak maraschino cherries in cognac. Serve with a cherry in the center of each pineapple slice.

PINEAPPLE AU CRÈME DE MENTHE. Sprinkle canned pineapple slices with crème de menthe liqueur. Serve this way, or topped with coconut.

Baked Rhubarb Compote

In the old days rhubarb was considered one of the finest of spring tonics, but the stewed product is unattractive in appearance and has little appeal for today's younger generation. Bake it instead; it holds its shape better and the juice becomes more like a syrup.

BAKED RHUBARB (Basic Recipe). Cut stems in 1-inch pieces, using mostly the pinker part. Place in casserole with fitted cover; add 1 cup sugar for 2 cups rhubarb. Cover; bake at 350° F. for 1 hour. Cool, then chill before serving.

BAKED RHUBARB AND PEACHES. Combine 2 cups diced rhubarb with 1 cup canned sliced peaches or diced peach halves. Place in baking dish with ¾ cup sugar and ½ cup peach syrup. Add a dash of nutmeg. Bake, covered, for 1 hour. Cool before serving. Serve with or without cream.

Fruit Sundaes

Easy and fun: Mix and match different flavors of ice cream with toppings of fresh, frozen, or canned fruits.

RASPBERRY SUNDAE. Defrost a box of frozen raspberries. Serve both the berries and the syrup over vanilla ice cream.

BANANA SPLIT. In each sherbet glass or dessert dish place 1 or 2 scoops vanilla ice cream; garnish with lengthwise slices of banana. Top with crushed pineapple, and over the pineapple spoon chocolate syrup. A maraschino cherry usually crowns the top.

BRANDIED PEACH SUNDAE. Prepare as for Brandied Peaches, but chop canned peach halves in small pieces. Spoon over vanilla ice cream and top with whipped cream.

CANTALOUPE SUNDAE. Place a scoop of vanilla ice cream, or lemon or pineapple sherbet, in each cantaloupe half. Or, top a wedge of cantaloupe with sherbet or ice cream and a few strawberries or pitted sweet cherries or blueberries.

STRAWBERRY SUNDAE. Top vanilla ice cream with fresh sugared berries or frozen strawberries with their syrup. Top with whipped cream or whipped topping mix.

DOUBLE BLUEBERRY SPECIAL. Top blueberry or blueberry whirl ice cream with fresh sugared blueberries and chopped or sliced bananas.

BLACKBERRY-PEACH SUNDAE. Top peach ice cream with fresh sugared blackberries, or black raspberry ice cream or sherbet with fresh sugared peaches.

PEACH-RUM SUNDAE. Marinate fresh cut-up peaches in mixture of rum and sugar to taste. Serve over scoops of sherbet or ice cream (lemon, orange, or pineapple sherbet, or banana or peppermint-stick ice cream).

PEACH MELBA SUNDAE. In each dessert dish or parfait glass, place a few peach slices (fresh and sugared or canned "home-style"); over the peaches place a scoop of vanilla ice cream; over the ice cream place defrosted frozen raspberries with their syrup; top with more ice cream and finally with whipped cream. This can be stored in freezer for ½ hour but no longer or fruit will freeze to ice.

Coeur à la Crème

2 8-ounce packages cream
  cheese, softened
1 cup sour cream

1 quart strawberries
¼ cup sugar

Blend cream cheese with sour cream; beat to a smooth paste. Line a heart-shaped mold with cheesecloth (special molds are available in gourmet shops, or use a gelatin mold). Press the cheese mixture into the mold as firmly as possible. Chill. Trim berries; add sugar. Unmold cheese heart on serving platter; place berries around the heart. Makes 6 servings.

Gelatin Desserts

There are two quite different commercial types of gelatin: unflavored, which is 85 percent protein and contains no sugar or fruit flavor, and fruit-flavored gelatin, which is a blend of sugar, powdered gelatin, and artificial flavors.

In using gelatin, whether for molded salads, aspics, mousses, or fruited gelatin molds, the same basic rules apply.

•The gelatin must first be completely dissolved in liquid. Unflavored gelatin is usually softened in cold water, then dissolved in hot water. But if the gelatin is mixed first with sugar, hot water may be added immediately. Fruit-flavored gelatin (already mixed with sugar) is always dissolved first in hot water.

•It is important to use the exact size mold specified in the recipe, and the mold should be filled to the very top. This makes a difference in the appearance of the gelatin and also in the ease with which it can be removed from the mold.

•As a general rule, one envelope of unflavored gelatin or a 3-ounce package of fruit-flavored gelatin is the right amount necessary to jell 2 cups of liquid.

•The smaller the mold, the more quickly the gelatin becomes firm throughout. Conversely, the larger the mold, the longer the time required for setting. Metal molds (aluminum or copper) are speedier than those made of glass or ceramics.

•Tall molds are tricky, more likely to collapse when unmolded. To avoid this, use less liquid—if the recipe calls for 2 cups, use only 1¾ cups liquid.

•A ring mold is one of the easiest of all to use. The contents set more quickly because more surface is exposed. Because the shape is smooth, it is easier to unmold the contents. And the shape lends itself to attractive decoration.

•Gelatin should always be chilled in the refrigerator, not in the freezer. The only time the freezer is useful is for quick setting a thin layer. Gelatin should be in 0° cold no more than 5 or 10 minutes.

•For a layered mold, add and partially set one layer at a time. Do not let any one layer become completely firm, however, or the next layer may not adhere to it.

•Before adding any solid ingredients, the gelatin should be chilled until syrupy, the consistency of unbeaten egg white. When a decorative pattern of ingredients is to be placed on the outside, only a thin layer of gelatin should be added first. Let this become syrupy, then place the ingredients exactly where you wish them to be. Chill until firm enough so that they do not slip when the mold is picked up.

•Make sure the gelatin is firm throughout before unmolding (shake it to see). Have ready a plate or platter that is large enough to hold it. Dip the mold in warm (not hot) water almost, but not quite, to the top. Loosen around the edges with your fingers (see sketch). Invert the plate over the top of the mold; turn the whole thing over; tap the sides of the mold. The gelatin should come out immediately. If not, pat it with a warm towel and try again. Or dip it once more in warm water (but be careful—this could soften the contours too much).

Once it is unmolded, return the gelatin immediately to the

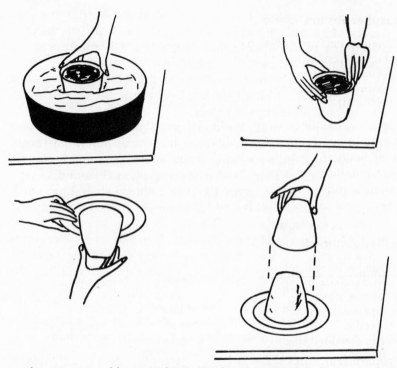

refrigerator and keep it there until time to serve.

•To speed up the setting of simple fruited gelatins, add ice cubes instead of cold water (10 to 12 large cubes for 1 cup cold water). Stir until the ice is nearly melted and the gelatin is syrupy; remove the bits of ice, then add the cut-up fruit. The dessert will be ready to serve after about half an hour of chilling in the refrigerator.

•Molded desserts look pretty but it is easier to prepare individual servings in sherbet or dessert dishes that needn't be unmolded. A fruited gelatin may also be served, topped with whipped cream, from a glass serving dish.

Jellied Peaches

1 cup canned peaches, diced and well drained	1¼ cups hot water
1 3-ounce package lemon- or orange-flavored gelatin	¾ cup canned peach syrup
	1 teaspoon lemon juice

Thoroughly drain the peaches. Dissolve gelatin in hot water; stir in peach syrup and lemon juice. Divide peaches among 4 sherbet dishes; cover each serving with gelatin. Chill until firm. Top each serving with heavy cream or whipped topping. *Makes 4 servings*.

Raspberries in Gelatin

1 3-ounce package raspberry- or black cherry-flavored gelatin
1¼ cups hot water
1 teaspoon lemon juice (optional)

1 package frozen raspberries
½ cup miniature marshmallows
¼ cup chopped walnuts (optional)
Whipped cream

Place gelatin in bowl and add hot water; stir to dissolve. Add lemon juice and the solidly frozen raspberries. Stir gently until fruit is completely separated and gelatin starts to set. Stir in marshmallows and nuts. Pour into a 1-quart mold, 6 individual ¾-cup molds or custard cups, or a glass serving dish. Chill until firm. Serve topped with whipped cream. *Makes 6 servings.*

Jellied Ambrosia

2 oranges, peeled and diced, or 1 can mandarin oranges, drained
1 banana, sliced
½ cup seedless white grapes, halved
½ cup shredded coconut

1 3-ounce package lemon- or orange flavored gelatin
1 cup hot water
12 large ice cubes
½ cup heavy cream, whipped and sweetened

Prepare fruit; mix with coconut. Dissolve gelatin in hot water; add ice cubes. Stir until most of ice has melted and gelatin has started to set, then remove remaining ice with slotted spoon and discard. Add fruit and coconut mixture to the gelatin; transfer to 1½-quart gelatin mold or 8- or 9-inch square baking pan, or to a serving dish. Chill until firm. Unmold and garnish with whipped cream, or serve directly from serving dish, passing whipped cream separately. *Makes 6 to 8 servings.*

Amethyst Parfait

1 package cherry- or raspberry-flavored gelatin
1 cup hot water
1 10-ounce package frozen raspberries

½ cup cold water
1 3-ounce package cream cheese, softened
¼ cup confectioners' sugar
1 to 2 tablespoons light cream

Dissolve gelatin in hot water; add frozen block of fruit. Stir gently until fruit thaws and separates and gelatin begins to thicken. Stir in cold water.

Combine cream cheese, confectioners' sugar, and cream; beat until fluffy. Spoon gelatin and cheese mixture in alternate layers into parfait glasses, ending with cheese mixture on top. *Makes about 6 servings.*

Amor Frio

3 eggs, separated
½ cup sugar
1 envelope unflavored gelatin
⅛ teaspoon cinnamon
1¼ cups heated milk

¼ cup cream sherry
2 cups cut-up fruit*
½ cup heavy cream, whipped, sweetened

Carefully separate eggs so that there is no trace of yolk in the whites. Beat the yolks until thick. Combine sugar, gelatin, and cinnamon. Add hot milk (heated only to steaming—do not allow it to boil); stir until gelatin is dissolved, then add to yolks. Place mixture in top of double boiler over hot but not boiling water; stir constantly until spoon is evenly coated. Add sherry; stir to blend. Do not overcook. Remove from heat. Beat egg whites until stiff. Fold egg whites into gelatin mixture. Pour into 1½-quart mold; chill until mixture is of soft-jelly consistency. Arrange cut-up fruit in gelatin (pieces should be of different sizes and shapes; reserve some for garnish). Return to refrigerator; chill until very firm. Unmold on platter. Return to refrigerator until time to serve, then garnish with sweetened whipped cream and slices of fruit or whole berries. *Makes 8 servings.*

Suitable fruit: Slices of fresh or canned peaches, sliced canned pears, fresh berries, seeded halved grapes, melon balls.

Molded Fruit in Sherry

3 cups mixed fruit*
2 envelopes unflavored gelatin
¼ cup cold water
1 cup hot water
¼ cup plus 2 tablespoons sugar
1¼ cups plus 1 tablespoon cream

sherry
2 tablespoons lemon juice
1¼ cups syrup from canned fruit
½ cup heavy cream, whipped and sweetened

A 1½ quart mold is needed; it should be chilled for quicker setting while the gelatin is being prepared. First prepare the fruit, choosing it for appearance and color. Sprinkle fresh fruit lightly with 2 tablespoons sugar. Drain thoroughly before adding to gelatin.

Soften gelatin in cold water; add hot water and remaining sugar; stir to dissolve. Add 1¼ cups sherry, lemon juice and fruit syrup. Place a third of gelatin mixture in chilled mold; chill in freezer until syrupy—about 5 minutes. Arrange first layer of fruit; chill until almost firm—about 10 minutes. Add a third more gelatin, chill until syrupy; add more fruit. Repeat with third and final layer, filling mold to the top. Now complete

*Sliced peaches, sliced pears, strawberries or other fresh berries, and halved and seeded black grapes make an attractive combination.

chilling in refrigerator (not freezer) until very firm—1 to 2 hours longer. Unmold by dipping quickly in a bowl of warm water; turn out on platter. Return to refrigerator to keep firm until time to serve. Garnish with whipped cream, sweetened and flavored with a tablespoon sherry, and with slices of the fruit or with berries. *Makes 10 to 12 servings.*

QUICK FRUIT IN WINE JELLY. Use 1 6-ounce or 2 3-ounce packages lemon-flavored gelatin; dissolve gelatin in 1 cup hot water. Add 1 cup sweet wine (sherry, Cherry Kijafa, Chateau La Salle, Madeira, or port) and 12 to 16 large ice cubes. (When using ice from an icemaker, at least twice this many cubes will be needed.) Stir until ice is nearly melted and gelatin syrupy; remove bits of ice. Stir in 3 cups cut-up fruit. Pour into glass serving dish. Chill until firm. Serve plain or with whipped cream or Custard Wine Sauce. *Makes 10 to 12 servings.*

For 6 servings, divide all ingredients by half.

Bavarian Cream (Basic Recipe)

1 envelope unflavored gelatin	1¼ cups milk
½ cup sugar	½ teaspoon vanilla
Pinch of salt	1 cup whipped heavy cream
2 eggs, separated	

Combine gelatin, sugar, and salt. Place in top of double boiler over hot water. Beat egg yolks until thick; stir in milk. Add this to the gelatin mixture and stir with whisk until gelatin is thoroughly dissolved. Remove from heat. Add vanilla; chill gelatin until it is the consistency of unbeaten egg whites. Beat egg whites until stiff. Beat cream until thickened but not stiff. Fold cream into gelatin, then fold in the beaten egg whites, blending well. Pour into a 4-cup mold or 4 individual 1-cup molds or a glass serving dish. Chill until firm. *Makes 4 to 6 servings.*

STRAWBERRY BAVARIAN. Wash and chop 1 cup strawberries; sweeten to taste with sugar. Prepare Bavarian Cream as in basic recipe; fold in fruit just before pouring into mold. Serve garnished with a few whole berries.

PEACH BAVARIAN. Prepare 1 cup peeled, stoned, and minced fresh peaches; sweeten to taste with sugar. Prepare Bavarian Cream as in basic recipe; fold in fruit just before pouring into mold. Serve garnished with peach slices sweetened and sprinkled with brandy.

COFFEE BAVARIAN. Prepare as in basic recipe but use 1 cup strong black coffee instead of 1¼ cups milk.

BAVARIAN PUNCH. Prepare as in basic recipe but use ½ cup sweet white wine or sherry, ½ cup peach syrup (from canned peaches), and 2 tablespoons brandy or rum instead of milk. Instead of vanilla extract, use 1 teaspoon grated lemon rind.

CHOCOLATE BAVARIAN. Prepare basic recipe; melt 2 ounces German's sweet chocolate over hot water; stir into mixture just before pouring into mold.

Lemon Cream

3 eggs, separated	1 cup hot water
2 tablespoons sugar	½ cup strained orange juice
Grated rind of 1 lemon	2 tablespoons fresh lemon juice
2 tablespoons brandy or Madeira	1 cup whipped heavy cream
1 package lemon-flavored gelatin	

Beat egg yolks with sugar and lemon rind until thick and light. Stir in brandy or Madeira. Dissolve gelatin in hot water. Add to gelatin the orange juice, lemon juice, and the egg-yolk mixture. Chill until it thickens to the consistency of unbeaten egg whites. Beat egg whites until stiff. Beat cream until thick but not stiff. Fold whipped cream into gelatin, then told in the egg whites. Pour into a 6-cup mold or a 1½-quart glass serving dish. Chill until firm. To unmold, dip quickly in hot water; invert over platter. Serve garnished with whole strawberries or black cherries. *Makes 6 to 8 servings.*

Nesselrode Pudding

A true Nesselrode pudding is made with puréed chestnuts and candied fruit. Two versions follow, one with and one without chestnuts.

½ pound chestnuts*	4 eggs, separated
2 cups steaming-hot milk	¼ cup sugar
½ cup white raisins	2 envelopes unflavored gelatin
½ cup mixed candied fruit	1 cup heavy cream, whipped
¼ cup glacé cherries, sliced	Marrons glacé for garnish
½ cup Madeira, brandy, or rum	

*Omit the chestnuts altogether and this is still a very delicious sweet—some may even prefer it this way.

Cut a slit in each chestnut; cover with water; bring to a boil. Cook until shell opens somewhat—about 30 minutes. Cool; remove shells. Chop chestnuts: place in electric blender with ½ cup hot milk; beat until puréed. Remove from blender; set aside. Place fruit in bowl; cover with wine or rum and soak while preparing the custard-gelatin mixture.

Beat the egg yolks in blender until very thick and light-colored. Combine sugar and gelatin; add remaining hot milk; stir until gelatin is dissolved. Add gelatin mixture to egg yolks in blender and beat until smooth. Add egg-yolk mixture to chestnut purée. Beat the egg whites until stiff; fold into chestnut mixture. Add the drained fruit and ¼ cup of the wine or rum. Beat the cream until stiff; fold in. Spoon mixture into 2-quart mold. Chill until very firm. Unmold. Serve garnished with marrons glacé. *Makes 12 servings.*

Quick Nesselrode Pudding

2 envelopes unflavored gelatin
¼ cup sugar
1 quart commercially prepared eggnog*
1 tablespoon dark sweet rum
1/3 cup thinly sliced glacé cher-ries
¼ cup minced candied citron
¼ cup minced candied orange peel
1 cup heavy cream

Combine gelatin and sugar; place in top of double boiler with 1 cup of the prepared eggnog; stir until gelatin and sugar are dissolved. Remove from heat; stir in rum and remaining eggnog. Chill mixture until syrupy, then beat with rotary beater until light and fluffy. Fold in fruit and the cream, whipped until stiff. Chill until very firm. Unmold. Garnish with shaved chocolate curls and additional whipped cream or with circles of maraschino cherries and citron "leaves" for a holiday dessert. *Makes 10 servings.*

*Or, use 4 eggs and 1 quart milk beaten together; increase sugar to ½ cup.

Molded Rice Pudding Royal Victoria

1½ cups mixed candied fruit

3½ tablespoons Jamaica rum

1½ cups packaged precooked rice

3 1/3 cups milk

½ teaspoon salt

¾ cup sugar

2 envelopes unflavored gelatin

½ cup cold water

3 eggs, separated

1 cup heavy cream, whipped

Fluffy Rum Sauce

Soak chopped candied fruit in 3 tablespoons of the rum; marinate 20 to 30 minutes. Chill a 2-quart mold. Meantime, combine rice and milk in a saucepan; stir to moisten rice thoroughly; bring to a full rolling boil, uncovered. Cover and remove from heat; let stand 8 minutes. Add salt, sugar, and the remaining ½ tablespoon rum. Soften gelatin in cold water; add to rice. Beat egg yolks until thick and lemon colored; add to rice, blending well. Fold in whipped cream, then fold in the stiffly beaten egg whites. Carefully drain all liquid from candied fruit; set aside ½ cup of fruit for decoration and stir remainder into rice. Pour rice mixture into mold; chill about 4 hours. Unmold; garnish with remaining candied fruit. Serve with Fluffy Rum Sauce (using the drained rum from the candied fruit in the sauce). *Makes 10 servings of a truly regal dessert.*

Princess Rice

¾ cup packaged precooked rice*

1 cup milk

¼ teaspoon salt

¼ cup sugar

1 envelope unflavored gelatin

¼ cup cold water

1 egg yolk

1 teaspoon grated lemon rind

2 tablespoons rum, or 1 teaspoon vanilla

½ cup slivered almonds

1 cup drained canned fruit (apricots, peaches, or pineapple)

½ cup heavy cream, whipped

Combine rice, milk, salt, and sugar in saucepan. Bring to a boil; cook over low heat 15 minutes, stirring occasionally. Soften gelatin in cold water. Add gelatin and egg yolk to hot rice; stir quickly to dissolve and blend. Add lemon rind, rum, almonds, and fruit (reserve a few pieces of fruit for garnish). Blend in the stiffly whipped cream. Pour into serving dish; chill; garnish with reserved fruit. Or, pour into 1-quart mold; chill until very firm; unmold and serve garnished with fruit. Red Fruit Sauce is delicious served with this. *Makes 6 servings.*

*Instead of precooked rice, 1/3 cup medium or long-grain rice may be used. Cook it in 1¼ cups milk in top of double boiler until very soft—about 35 minutes.

Danish Rum Pudding

2 envelopes unflavored gelatin	2 cups milk
½ cup cold water	6 tablespoons dark sweet rum
4 eggs, separated	½ cup heavy cream
½ cup sugar	Red Fruit Sauce

Soften gelatin in cold water. Combine egg yolks with sugar; beat until thick and light; add milk and beat until well blended. Stir mixture in top of double boiler over simmering water until custard evenly coats back of spoon. Remove from heat; stir into softened gelatin. Chill until mixture starts to set; blend in rum. Beat the whites of the eggs until stiff; fold into mixture. Whip heavy cream until stiff; fold in. Pour into 2-quart mold; chill until firm, preferably overnight. Serve with Red Fruit Sauce. *Makes 8 servings.*

Charlotte Russe

1 dozen ladyfingers	2/3 cup sugar
2 tablespoons Madeira, cream sherry, or cognac	2 envelopes unflavored gelatin
	½ cup cold water
2 cups milk	2 cups heavy cream
1 teaspoon vanilla	Whipped cream for garnish
4 egg yolks	Candied fruit for garnish

A spring-form mold or a deep cake pan with removable bottom and deep sides is needed for making this renowned dessert. Split the ladyfingers; sprinkle them with wine or cognac. Line bottom of pan with waxed paper; arrange ladyfingers in wagon spokes over bottom and upright around sides. Heat milk to steaming; add vanilla. Beat yolks and sugar (preferably in blender) until very frothy and light. Slowly add hot milk. Return to pan in which milk was heated; cook over very low heat, stirring constantly, until spoon is evenly coated with custard. Soften gelatin in cold water; add some of the hot custard and stir to dissolve. Add to remaining custard. Force custard through sieve into bowl; set bowl in larger bowl of ice and stir until custard begins to thicken. Whip cream until stiff; fold into thickened custard. Pour mixture into lined mold. Chill until very firm—at least 2 hours. Unmold on platter. Return to refrigerator until time to serve. Garnish with sweetened whipped cream and candied fruit. (The cream may be flavored with kirsch or cognac.) *Makes 8 to 10 servings.*

Custards and Puddings

By definition, a custard is a mixture of eggs and milk, and so many of the preceding puddings and Bavarians are really custards. Baked custards are the easiest to make: the eggs and milk need only be stirred together, then placed in the oven to bake. Soft custards and wine custards are much trickier for the heat must be low (the safest way to cook them is over hot water) and they must be stirred almost constantly to prevent curdling—yet if not cooked sufficiently, the resulting custard will be too thin.

In many recipes calling for soft custard or custard filling, vanilla pudding and pie filling mix—enriched with eggs and flavored with brandy, sherry, rum, or a liqueur—may be used as a short cut. A soft custard is more like a sauce than a pudding and is, in fact, used as a sauce in many recipes.

Baked Cup Custard (Basic Recipe)

¼ cup sugar
Pinch of salt
2 cups milk, heated to steaming
2 eggs, beaten

1 teaspoon vanilla extract or brandy
Nutmeg (optional)

Add the sugar and salt to the milk; stir until dissolved; do not allow milk to boil. Pour milk into beaten eggs; stir in vanilla or brandy. Divide among 4 or 5 Pyrex custard cups. Sprinkle nutmeg over top of each, if desired. Place in shallow roasting pan; add water to come 1 inch up sides of cups. Bake in 350° F. oven until knife inserted in center comes out clean—about 50 minutes. Remove from pan; chill immediately. Serve cold. *Makes 4 or 5 servings.*

FLAN. These are most successful if made in narrow metal flan cups, available in gourmet shops or stores carrying imported housewares. The custards cook more quickly and have a more interesting shape. The ingredients for the custard itself are the same as for Baked Cup Custard; the only difference is that the bottom of the molds are spread with a thin layer of caramel. To make this, melt ½ cup sugar in a small skillet until it turns a liquid brown. Divide melted sugar among the flan molds. Add the custard mixture. Place in pan; add water as for cup custard. Bake in a 400° F. oven until a knife inserted in center comes out clean—about 20 minutes. Chill immediately. When thoroughly cold, loosen around sides with knife blade; invert on individual dessert plates and tap the bottom or shake until the custard comes out. *Makes 6 to 8 servings,* depending on size of flan molds.

Flan can also be baked in standard pyrex cups, but longer, slower baking is required—about 50 minutes.

CRÈME CARAMEL. This French version of flan is usually baked in one pan. Melt ¾ cup sugar; pour over bottom of 9 x 9-inch pan. Add custard mixture, make with 3 eggs and 2 cups milk; place inside larger pan; add enough water to come partway up sides. Bake at 325° F. until knife inserted in center comes out clean. Chill. When cold and firm, invert over platter; tap or shake to unmold.

PEACH CUSTARD. Slice and sweeten fresh peaches, or use canned home-style sliced peaches. Place a few peach slices in bottom of each custard cup. Cover with custard mixture; bake as in basic recipe. Serve in custard cups or unmold, as preferred. A little whipped cream on top is delicious addition.

If a baked custard separates, it is probably because it cooked too long. If the custard looks very firm throughout when knife is inserted in center, plunge the cups or pan immediately into cold water to chill more quickly. If this is not done, the custard will continue to cook in the cups, even when placed in refrigerator.

Orange Custard

2 tablespoons honey	½ cup orange juice
2 tablespoons sugar	1 cup milk
4 eggs, well beaten	Grated rind ½ orange

Combine honey, sugar, and eggs; beat in orange juice, then milk and grated orange rind. Pour into custard cups. Place cups in pan containing water to depth of 1 inch. Bake at 300° F. until knife inserted in center comes out clean—about 50 minutes. *Makes 4 servings.*

Lemon Sponge Custard

¼ cup sifted all-purpose flour	2 eggs, separated
¾ cup sugar	¼ cup lemon juice
¼ teaspoon salt	1 cup milk
1 tablespoon grated lemon rind	

Combine flour, sugar, salt, and lemon rind; blend well. Stir in yolks of eggs and the lemon juice; when well blended, stir in milk. Beat egg whites until stiff; fold into lemon mixture. Pour into buttered deep 1-quart baking dish, or Pyrex custard cups, or flan cups. Place in pan containing water to depth of 1 inch. Bake in oven preheated to 350° F., 1 hour for large custard, 35 minutes for custard cups, 25 minutes for flan cups. The custard separates into two layers, the clear layer making a "crown." Chill; unmold before serving. *Makes 4 to 6 servings.*

Pots de Crème au Chocolat

1 6-ounce package semisweet   Pinch of salt
  chocolate pieces   ½ teaspoon vanilla
6 eggs   Whipped cream

Melt chocolate in top of double boiler over hot water. When
melted, remove from heat; stir until smooth. Beat eggs
(preferably in blender) until they have changed from foamy to
thick. Add salt, vanilla, and melted chocolate to eggs, using a
rubber spatula to get every bit of chocolate from pan. Spoon
into soufflé cups, sherbets, or dessert dishes. Chill 8 to 12 hours.
Serve topped with whipped cream. *Makes 6 to 8 servings.*

Chocolate Mousse

¼ cup sugar   chocolate pieces
1 tablespoon flour   1 tablespoon vanilla, or 1 table-
3 eggs, separated   spoon rum
½ cup milk   Grated rind ½ orange
4 tablespoons butter   1½ cups heavy cream
1 6-ounce package semisweet

Combine sugar, flour, and egg yolks; stir in milk; heat over low
heat, stirring with wire whisk, until mixture is consistency of
custard sauce. Add butter 1 tablespoon at a time, stirring after
each addition. Remove from heat; add chocolate; stir briskly
until melted. Stir in vanilla or rum and orange rind. Cool slightly, then fold in stiffly beaten egg whites and 1 cup of the cream,
whipped until stiff. Pour into sherbet dishes; chill until very
firm—about 5 hours. Whip remaining ½ cup cream; use as topping. *Makes 8 to 10 rich servings.*

ANOTHER WAY. Not quite so caloric in this version: Use 4 eggs
and 2 cups milk to make custard. Omit butter. Melt chocolate
separately over hot water; stir into custard. Flavor with 2 tablespoons rum and the grated orange rind. Whip only ¾ cup heavy
cream; stir into custard. *Makes 6 to 8 servings.*

Soft Custard (Basic Recipe)

  This is also frequently called boiled custard (though it must
never be allowed to boil) or English custard. The French call it
Crème à l'Anglaise.

¼ to ½ cup sugar   2 cups milk, heated to steaming
1 teaspoon cornstarch (optional) 1 teaspoon vanilla
4 eggs or 5 egg yolks, beaten

Combine sugar and cornstarch in top of double boiler; stir in eggs. Beat in hot milk and vanilla. Place mixture over hot (not boiling) water; cook, stirring, until mixture coats back of spoon evenly—about 7 minutes. *Do not overcook; do not allow to reach a boil.* Pour into chilled dish; chill until thickened. *Makes 4 to 5 dessert servings, or 2 cups custard sauce.*

CUSTARD CREAM. This is thicker than Soft Custard and may be used as a filling for éclairs and layer cakes such as Boston Cream Pie, as a filling for Gypsy's Arm, or in making Trifle. The classic recipe calls for flour but vanilla-flavored pudding and pie filling mix may be used as a shortcut with very satisfactory results. Prepare the mix according to package directions; when thickened, beat pudding mixture into 2 egg yolks or 1 beaten egg; stir over low heat about 3 minutes longer. Flavor, if desired, with brandy, rum, sherry, Madeira, or Curaçao, and grated rind of ½ lemon. *Makes 2¼ cups.*

ALMOND CREAM FILLING. Prepare Custard Cream, but flavor with ½ teaspoon almond extract; when cooled, stir in ¼ cup crushed toasted almonds.

FRANGIPANI. Prepare Custard Cream; add ½ cup crushed macaroons. Use as filling for cream puffs or baked tart shells.

NO-COOK CUSTARD CREAM. Prepare 1 package vanilla-flavored whipped dessert mix with 1½ cups *chilled* light cream: Beat mix in deep, narrow bowl with ½ cup of the cream for 1 minute at high speed; add remaining 1 cup chilled cream; beat 2 minutes longer. Blend 1 egg yolk with 2 tablespoons sugar and ½ teaspoon vanilla or other desired flavoring; fold into dessert mix. Chill 1½ hours before using as filling or topping. *Makes 3 cups.*

EASY CUSTARD SAUCE. Prepare vanilla-flavored pudding and pie filling mix according to package directions, adding ½ to 1 cup light cream (depending on consistency desired) in addition to milk called for. Flavor, if desired, with 1 to 2 tablespoons brandy, rum, sherry, or Curaçao. *Makes 2½ to 3 cups sauce.*

CUSTARD CROWNED WITH BERRIES. Prepare either Soft Custard or Easy Custard Sauce; flavor with 1 to 2 tablespoons Curaçao or brandy. Pour into serving dish; chill. Serve covered with sweetened strawberries, raspberries, blackberries, or blueberries. Top berries with whipped cream, if desired.

TIPSY PUDDING. Cut sponge cake or pound cake horizontally into slices 1 inch thick. Place in serving dish and sprinkle generously with sherry or rum. Cover with Easy Custard Sauce (flavored with sherry or rum) or Custard Cream. Sprinkle custard with crushed macaroons or slivered toasted almonds.

ENGLISH TRIFLE. It begins like Tipsy Pudding but becomes more elaborate: Spread the sherry- (or rum-) soaked cake with strawberry or raspberry jam thinned with enough sherry to spread easily. Cover with Easy Custard Sauce or Custard Cream, then cover the Custard with whipped cream. Nuts may be sprinkled over the top for garnish, if desired.

BOSTON CREAM PIE. Bake 2 8-inch cake layers or use commercial sponge-cake layers. Spread Custard Cream between layers. Spread Chocolate Glaze over top or, just before serving, pour Chocolate Sauce over top (a commercial sauce may be used).

See also Gypsy's Arm; Charlotte Russe; Danish Rum Pudding; Buttermilk Pie.

Zabaglione (Sabayon)

8 egg yolks
1 cup confectioners' sugar

½ cup Marsala, Madeira, or
   cream sherry

Combine egg yolks, sugar, and wine in top of double boiler over hot (not boiling) water, or in bowl placed over another bowl of hot water. Beat constantly with whisk until it doubles in volune and begins to thicken. Pour at once into sherbet glasses (unless it is to be served as a sauce) and chill. *Makes 6 to 8 servings.*

   For 10 fluffier servings, beat the egg whites until stiff; fold into the cooled mixture.

SABAYON SAUCE. Use only 4 egg yolks, ½ cup confectioners' sugar, and ¼ cup wine; prepare as above. This is the traditional sauce to serve with Savarin cake. *Makes 2 cups sauce.*

Peach Pudding

   Prepare vanilla pudding and pie filling mix according to package directions, but use ½ cup canned peach syrup for part of the milk. When pudding has thickened, stir in sliced canned peaches. Serve topped with cream or whipped cream.

PINEAPPLE-LEMON PUDDING. Prepare lemon pudding and pie filling mix according oo package directions, but use ½ cup syrup from canned pineapple in place of same amount of water. When pudding has thickened, stir in ½ cup slivered pineapple chunks. Chill. Serve topped with whipped cream or topping mix and slivered toasted almonds.

Bread Pudding

2 cups stale white bread crumbs
4 cups milk, heating to steaming
1/3 cup sugar
2 tablespoons butter, melted

2 eggs, slightly beaten
¼ teaspoon salt
¼ teaspoon mixed spices
(cinnamon, mace, nutmeg)

Place crumbs in bowl; cover with milk; soak until milk is cool. Add sugar, melted butter, eggs, salt, and spices; blend well. Pour into buttered 1-quart casserole. Bake, uncovered, in oven set at 325° F. until top is golden and custard is firm—about 1 hour. Serve warm, plain or with cream. *Makes 6 servings.*

PEACH-BREAD PUDDING. Add 1 cup cut-up fresh and sugared or canned peaches to basic recipe.

RUM-TOFFEE PUDDING. Prepare butterscotch pudding and pie filling mix according to package directions; when pudding has thickened, add 2 tablespoons dark sweet rum; continue cooking a few seconds longer. Serve topped with whipped cream flavored with a little rum. Garnish, if desired, with walnut halves or slivered toasted almonds.

Old-fashioned Rice Pudding

4 cups milk
½ cup long-grain rice
½ cup sugar

2 tablespoons raisins
Grated rind of ½ lemon
Pinch of salt

Combine all ingredients; place in buttered 1-quart casserole. Bake uncovered in oven set at 300° F. for 3 hours, stirring occasionally. Pudding will become browned and "nutty" as it bakes and will finally be quite thick. Serve warm with cold cream. *Makes 6 servings.*

Easy Rice Custard

4 eggs, slightly beaten
1 1/3 cups packaged precooked rice
2/3 cup sugar
½ teaspoon nutmeg
1 teaspoon salt
1 quart milk
2 teaspoons vanilla
¼ cup raisins (optional)

Combine all ingredients; pour into 2-quart casserole; place in pan and pour in hot water to reach halfway up side of casserole. Bake in oven set at 350° F. for 50 minutes; stir once. Remove from oven; let stand for 30 minutes without stirring. Serve warm or chilled. *Makes 8 servings.*

Rødgrød, or Röte Grutze (Red Fruit Pudding)

The Danes call this their national dessert, but across the border in Germany the same dish is claimed as a German original. Forget national differences and enjoy it—it is delicious.

1 1-pound can tart red pitted cherries packed in heavy syrup
1 10-ounce package frozen raspberries, defrosted
1½ tablespoons cornstarch
1 tablespoon lemon juice
1 tablespoon currant jelly
Few drops red food coloring
1 cup whipped and sweetened heavy cream

Drain the fruit, saving juice. In saucepan, blend cornstarch with a little of the juice; add the rest of the juice; bring to a boil, stirring until juice bubbles and is thickened. Add lemon juice, currant jelly, and food coloring. Fold in the fruit. Cool, then chill. Serve in a glass bowl or in individual sherbets, topping each serving with whipped cream. *Makes 5 or 6 servings.*

Note. If you have a blender, purée fruit and juices in it, then force through sieve to remove raspberry seeds. Thicken with cornstarch; add lemon juice, jelly and food coloring; cook until thickened.

Indian Pudding

6 cups milk
½ cup yellow corn meal
1 tablespoon butter
½ cup molasses
½ teaspoon salt
½ teaspoon ground ginger
½ cup raisins (optional)

Heat 2 cups milk to scalding; stir in corn meal and butter. Stir constantly over low heat until thickened. Add 2 cups cold milk, molasses, salt, and ginger. Pour into buttered 2½-quart baking dish; place in oven set at 275° F. Bake 1 hour, stirring two or three times, then add 1 more cup milk. Bake 1 hour longer; stir in remaining milk. Add raisins if desired; bake 2 hours longer. Don't worry if pudding has a curdled look in beginning; as it cooks down it will become creamy and smooth. Serve warm topped with heavy cream, vanilla ice cream, rum-flavored whipped cream, or Rum Hard Sauce. Leftover pudding is good cold, with cream. *Makes 8 to 10 servings.*

Easy Plum Pudding

1 package gingerbread mix
¾ cup cooked prunes, pitted and chopped
¼ cup diced candied citron
1 egg yolk

¼ cup orange juice
½ cup juice from prunes
Foamy Rum Sauce or Rum Hard Sauce

Combine gingerbread mix, prunes, citron, egg yolk, and juices; blend well. Pour batter into 8 buttered Pyrex custard cups. Place cups in large roasting pan; pour boiling water into pan to come halfway up sides of cups. Cover with foil, crimping foil around edge of pan. Bake in oven preheated to 375° F. until center is firm to touch—35 minutes. Remove from oven; leave in cups but do not chill. To reheat for holiday dinner, place cups again in roasting pan and pour boiling water around cups; cover pan tightly with foil; let stand at least 30 minutes. Unmold cups on serving plates. Serve with Foamy Rum Sauce or Rum Hard Sauce. *Makes 8 servings.*

TO HEAT CANNED PLUM PUDDING. Place unopened can in saucepan of boiling water; let stand, covered, 1 hour. Remove from water; open can; turn out on platter.

TO FLAME PLUM PUDDING. Warm rum in small saucepan; spoon warm rum over warm pudding and set aflame with match (let match burn a second to get rid of sulphur fumes).

Peanut Butter Pudding

2 cups cold milk
½ cup chunk-style peanut butter

1 package instant butterscotch or chocolate pudding mix

Combine ingredients in mixing bowl; beat with rotary beater or electric beater at low speed for 1 minute. Pour into custard cups or dessert dishes; let stand in refrigerator at least 5 minutes. *Makes 4 servings.*

Fruit Puddings and Cobblers

Easier than pies, these hearty old-fashioned dessert casseroles are beloved by children and most are quite simple to make.

Apple Crisp

4 cups peeled, sliced apples	nutmeg
1 teaspoon lemon juice	½ cup flour
½ cup sugar	½ cup oatmeal
1 teaspoon grated lemon rind	4 tablespoons butter
¼ to ½ teaspoon cinnamon or	

Sprinkle apples with lemon juice. Combine remaining ingredients; work with fingers into a crumbly mixture. Place apples in pie pan or shallow baking dish; cover with crumb mixture. Cover pan or dish with foil. Bake in oven preheated to 350° F. for 30 minutes; uncover; continue baking until topping is lightly browned. Serve warm with cream or ice cream. *Makes 6 servings.*

CHERRY CRISP. Use 4 cups pitted tart cherries instead of apples; or use 2 1-pound cans sour red pie cherries, drained, and ½ cup of the cherry juice.

PEACH CRISP. Use 4 cups peeled, sliced peaches instead of apples.

RHUBARB CRISP. Use 4 cups diced rhubarb instead of apples; increase sugar to ¾ cup; omit lemon juice.

Apple Brown Betty

3 cups peeled, sliced apples	Pinch of salt
1 cup Grapenuts breakfast cereal*	1 teaspoon grated lemon peel
	1 tablespoon lemon juice
2 tablespoons brown sugar	2 tablespoons butter
½ teaspoon cinnamon	¼ cup hot water

Prepare apples. Mix together remaining ingredients except butter and water. Arrange apples in layers with cereal mixture, ending with cereal mixture on top. Add butter to hot water; pour over top. Bake uncovered in oven preheated to 350° F. until top is browned—35 to 40 minutes. Serve warm with cream, or Hard Sauce. *Makes 6 servings.*

*Instead of breakfast cereal, 1½ cups soft bread crumbs may be used; increase sugar to 1/3 cup.

Apple Pandowdy

4 cups peeled, sliced apples
1 cup light brown sugar
½ teaspoon nutmeg
4 tablespoons butter

½ cup water
1 cup biscuit mix
¼ cup light cream
Heavy cream

Set oven at 425° F. Butter a 1½-quart baking dish; fill with apples. Combine sugar and nutmeg; sprinkle over apples. Dot with 2 tablespoons butter; add water. Add remaining 2 tablespoons butter to biscuit mix, chopping until fine; blend in cream; knead with fingers into smooth ball. Roll out ¼-inch thick on floured board, or press with fingers into shape to cover apples in baking dish. Bake until crust is golden—20 minutes, then remove briefly from oven; cut crust into squares and push down into hot apple juice; return to oven. Lower heat to 375° F.; bake 15 to 20 minutes longer. Serve warm topped with heavy cream. *Makes 4 to 6 servings.*

Blueberry Slump

¾ cup sugar
¾ teaspoon mixed spices
   (nutmeg, cinnamon, cloves)
8 slices firm-textured bread

½ cup melted butter
4 cups fresh blueberries
1 teaspoon lemon juice
½ teaspoon grated lemon peel

Blend sugar with spices. Cut each slice of bread into strips and brush both sides with melted butter. Place a third of bread in bottom of 9 x 5 x 3-inch loaf pan. Sprinkle with 2 tablespoons sugar-spice mixture. Add half the blueberries, previously washed; sprinkle blueberries with half the lemon juice and grated rind and 2 tablespoons sugar-spice mixture. Repeat with bread and berries, sprinkling each layer with spice mixture and berries with lemon. End with bread as top layer. Bake in oven preheated to 375° F. until bread is toasted and blueberry syrup is bubbling. Serve warm with cream or ice cream. *Makes 6 servings.*

RASPBERRY SLUMP. Use 2 10-ounce packages frozen raspberries, defrosted, instead of fresh blueberries; increase sugar to 1 cup. Spices may be omitted. Before baking, press top layer down so that bread is soaked with juice.

Veiled Country Lass (Danish Apple Cake)

This "cake" is surprisingly like apple pie in flavor and texture; it is attractive in appearance and easy to make. The rye bread crumbs give it a delightfully different flavor.

4 cups soft rye bread crumbs	¼ cup raspberry jam
¼ pound (8 tablespoons) butter	¼ cup currant jelly
3 tablespoons sugar	½ cup heavy cream, whipped
1 can (1 pound) applesauce	

Remove crusts from rye bread; break bread into tiny pieces. Melt butter in heavy skillet; add crumbs and 2 tablespoons sugar; stir over high heat until crumbs are crisp and lightly browned. Spoon half of the crumbs over center of dinner plate or small round platter. Spoon thin layer of applesauce over crumbs, then add remaining crumbs and remaining applesauce in layers. With flat side of knife, mold layers into cake shape. Chill for at least 1 hour. Meantime, heat jam and jelly together, stirring constantly until jelly is melted. Remove from heat; cool. After cake has chilled, again press sides with knife or back of spoon to shape. Spread jam mixture over top. Beat cream until stiff; fold in 1 tablespoon sugar; frost sides of cake with whipped cream. *Makes 4 to 6 servings.*

Cherry Dumplings

2 cans (1 pound each) sour red pie cherries in heavy syrup	3 cups biscuit mix
1½ cups sugar	¾ cup milk

Combine fruit and syrup with sugar; bring to a boil; simmer 10 minutes. Blend biscuit mix with milk; drop by spoonfuls into the boiling fruit. Cover; cook 10 minutes longer. To serve, spoon dumplings on individual dessert plates; spoon the cherries and their syrup over the top. Serve warm with ice cream. *Makes 6 servings.*

BLUEBERRY DUMPLINGS. Use 2 1-pound cans blueberries in heavy syrup instead of cherries.

Peach Cobbler

1 large can peach halves in syrup	1 tablespoon sugar
1 tablespoon butter	1/3 cup heavy cream
1 cup biscuit mix	

Place drained peach halves in bottom of 1½-quart baking dish. Spoon half the peach syrup over them. Dot with butter. Combine biscuit mix with sugar and cream; stir with fork until well blended; spoon mixture over top of peaches, spreading to cover. Bake in oven preheated to 375° F. until crust is golden—about 20 minutes. Serve warm topped with hot Lemon Sauce or cream. *Makes 6 servings.*

BLUEBERRY COBBLER. Use 2 1-pound cans blueberries in heavy syrup instead of peach halves.

PURPLE PLUM COBBLER. Drain 1 large can purple plums, saving syrup. Pit the plums; place in baking dish. Add to the syrup 1 teaspoon lemon juice; boil down until syrup is reduced to one half. Pour over plums. Top with biscuit mixture and bake as in basic recipe.

Ice Cream and Other Frozen Desserts

The availability of ice cream in a multitude of flavors has made this finest of desserts almost too ordinary. There are, of course, vast differences in quality among the various commercial ice creams, and differences in price, too.

When buying ice cream, it is best to buy the size container that will be used up at one serving; once the container has been opened, even if the ice cream is returned immediately to the freezer, the texture is adversely affected. A pint makes 3 normal or 4 small servings. A half-gallon (2 quarts) is about right to serve 12 persons.

Ice cream made at home in the freezing tray is not a very satisfactory product. An electrically operated ice cream freezer makes superb ice cream, and is a worthwhile purchase for those who treasure homemade ice cream made with pure cream and milk. Recipes will come with the appliance.

Quite impressive desserts can be made by combining two or more flavors of commercial ice cream, softening the cream enough to shape or mold it, then refreezing it. Baked Alaska is not to be forgotten—and it's easier than it sounds.

For family desserts, ice cream from the carton with fruit, a sauce, or nuts as a topping is fine enough. And ice cream laced with a liqueur can always be offered to company.

Ice Cream Bombe

Buy two flavors of ice cream; let them soften enough to be shaped with a spoon. Line a mold (a melon-shaped mold is attractive) with one flavor; place the second flavor on the inside. Press down to fill mold solidly and completely. Two pints will fill a 1-quart mold, two quarts a 2-quart mold, and so on. To unmold, invert on plate or platter; pat outside with a warm towel, then tap to loosen. Cover with plastic wrap and return to freezer until time to serve. Garnish with a ring of fresh fruit (strawberries, sliced peaches, overlapping slices of banana).

Good flavor-color combinations: chocolate ice cream outside, pineapple sherbet inside; blueberry ice cream outside, peach inside; strawberry outside, lemon sherbet inside; vanilla outside, orange or raspberry ice inside.

Ice Cream Charlotte

A gala offering for a big party. A spring-form mold is best, though a 10-inch tube pan with removable bottom may also be used. You will need a half-gallon container of chocolate ice cream, 3 pints lemon, orange, or pineapple sherbet, and 18 (1½ packages) ladyfingers.

Split ladyfingers and sprinkle them with sherry or brandy. Arrange them around the sides of the mold and in spoke formation over the bottom. Press chocolate ice cream (softened enough for molding) over bottom and up sides. Press sherbet on the inside. (If a tube pan is used, not all the sherbet can be placed inside; keep it frozen until the Charlotte is unmolded.) Freeze until very firm—6 hours.

To unmold, place over platter or cake plate and pat outside with warm towel. It should come out easily. If tube pan was used fill center with sherbet. Return to freezer until time to serve. *Makes 20 servings.*

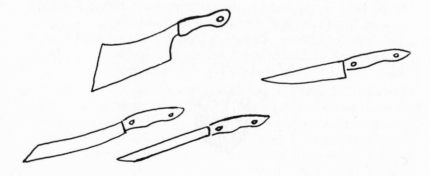

Ice Cream Layer Cake *

Bake 2 9-inch cake layers (white or chocolate). When cool, split each layer in half horizontally to make 4 layers. Soften 2 pints ice cream of contrasting color and flavor to spreading consistency and spread between the cake layers, ½ pint between each layer. Press layers together; place cake on foil-covered cardboard cut to fit; wrap outside with foil or plastic. Freeze. When frozen, frost the outside of cake with whipped cream, flavored with sherry or brandy, if desired; return to freezer. Transfer cake from freezer to refrigerator ½ hour before serving. *Makes 8 to 10 servings.*

Possible combinations: (1) With white cake: black cherry or black raspberry ice cream and pistachio ice cream. (2) With chocolate cake: vanilla and peach ice cream, or pineapple sherbet and coffee ice cream.

Baked Alaska (Basic Recipe)

1 quart (2 pints) ice cream	3 egg whites
1 baked 9-inch cake layer, or 1	¼ cup sugar
8 x 6-inch sponge cake sheet	⅛ teaspoon cream of tartar

Mold the ice cream into a shape that will fit on top of the cake, with a ½-inch margin around the edge: If a 9-inch cake layer is used, the ice cream should be molded in a bowl with a top diameter of 8 inches; if an 8 x 6-inch sponge layer is used, cut brick ice cream into a 7 x 5-inch rectangle.

Refreeze the ice cream after shaping it; it must be very firm. Place the cake on heavy brown paper; cut paper so that it is ½-inch larger than the cake all around; place the paper and the cake on a baking sheet, wooden board, or platter that can go from freezer to oven. Beat the egg whites until stiff; blend in sugar, 2 tablespoons at a time, and cream of tartar. Unmold ice cream over cake. Cover cake and ice cream completely with meringue. Return to freezer until time to bake. Preheat oven to 500° F. Take Alaska from freezer; put into oven immediately and bake until meringue is delicately browned—3 to 5 minutes. Serve immediately. *Makes 6 to 8 servings.*

For 12 to 16 servings, double all ingredients.

INDIVIDUAL BAKED ALASKAS. Buy sponge cake shells, one for each portion. Shape ice cream to fit over top, leaving a ½-inch margin around edges. Cover completely with meringue as in basic recipe. Freeze until time to bake. Preheat oven to 450° F.; bake until meringue is delicately browned—3 to 5 minutes. Serve immediately.

CHOCOLATE ALASKAS. Use chocolate cake for the base; top with vanilla fudge ice cream.

PEACH ALASKAS. Use chocolate cake for the base; top with peach ice cream. Sprinkle chocolate sprinkles over meringue before serving.

Ice Cream Snowballs

Roll scoops of ice cream (of any preferred flavor—chocolate and peppermint are both very good) in shredded coconut; keep in freezer until time to serve. Allow two or three for each serving; serve topped with chocolate sauce. Or try one of the following combinations.

- Roll scoops of vanilla ice cream in coarsely chopped peanuts. Serve with commercial butterscotch sauce.
- Roll strawberry ice cream in coarsely chopped toasted almonds. Serve with fresh strawberries or with marshmallow sauce.

Quickie Ice Cream Combinations

- Serve butter-pecan ice cream topped with butterscotch sauce and ringed with sliced bananas.
- Serve peppermint-stick ice cream with coconut cake.
- Honey dribbled over vanilla ice cream becomes a superb sauce.
- Top each serving of vanilla ice cream with peach jam.
- Damson plum preserves are good as a topping for vanilla ice cream.
- Shredded coconut makes a nice topping for chocolate ice cream.
- Pineapple sherbet is delicious crowned with chocolate sauce.

Biscuit Tortoni

2 egg whites
½ cup confectioners' sugar
1 pint heavy cream
1 teaspoon vanilla, or ¼ tea-
spoon almond extract, or 1 tablespoon sherry
½ cup macaroon crumbs

Beat the egg whites until stiff; gradually beat in ¼ cup of the sugar. Whip the cream until thick but not stiff; fold in remaining ¼ cup sugar, vanilla or other flavoring, and ¼ cup macaroon crumbs. Fill 6 soufflé cups or custard cups, or iisure in freezer until very cold but not hard, then spoon into 6 paper baking cups. Sprinkle remaining macaroon crumbs over top. Freeze until firm. *Makes 6.*

Liqueur-laced Ice Cream

Almost any liqueur can be used as a topping for ice cream, especially for vanilla ice cream. Especially good are Grand Marnier, Curaçao, Tia Maria (especially good on coffee ice cream), Cointreau, Chartreuse, Cherry Heering, kirsch (on peach or cherry ice cream), and blackberry brandy or cordial.

See also Ice Cream Pie; Ice Cream Tartes.

Dessert Sauces

Custard-type sauces are delicious over fresh or canned fruit, pudding, cake, even ice cream. Even easier than the sauces made with eggs are those that use fruit juices and/or brandy or a liqueur and are thickened with cornstarch. Such a sauce served warm over slices of stale cake turns the cake into Cottage Pudding, a truly delicious dessert.

Most of the following sauces will keep well in the refrigerator for up to a week. If a sauce containing egg separates, place it in a blender or the small bowl of an electric mixer and beat until smooth again; serve immediately.

Golden Wine Sauce

½ cup sugar	1 teaspoon lemon juice
½ tablespoon cornstarch	3 egg yolks
Grated rind of ½ lemon	1 cup sweet white wine*

Blend sugar and cornstarch; add grated lemon rind and lemon juice, the slightly beaten egg yolks, and the wine. Pour mixture into heavy saucepan or into saucepan or bowl that will fit over pan containing boiling water and cook over very low heat. Stir constantly or beat with portable electric mixer at low speed until mixture is smooth and thickened. Remove from heat; continue beating about 30 seconds. Chill. *Makes 2 cups sauce.*

*Such as Château La Salle, sherry, or white port. If a dry white wine is used, omit lemon juice.

FOAMY WINE SAUCE. Prepare as in basic recipe, but after chilling sauce add 2 stiffly beaten egg whites just before serving. This increases yield to 3½ cups.

SPICED WINE SAUCE. Use cream sherry for the wine; add ¼ teaspoon cinnamon to the sugar-cornstarch mixture. Add beaten egg whites if a foamy sauce is desired. Especially good over sponge cake.

Foamy Applejack Sauce

2 eggs, separated
½ cup sugar

3 tablespoons applejack brandy

Beat egg yolks and sugar in blender until very light and fluffy; add brandy. Separately beat egg whites until peaks form; fold into yolk mixture. Serve over pudding or cake. *Makes 1½ cups.*

FLUFFY RUM SAUCE. Use dark sweet rum instead of applejack.

RUM CUSTARD SAUCE. Combine 2 egg yolks, ½ cup confectioners' sugar, and ¼ cup light cream; beat over hot water until mixture thickens noticeably. Stir in 1 or 2 tablespoons rum; beat until smooth. Serve this way or fold in 2 stiffly beaten egg whites just before serving.

Pineapple Angel Sauce

2 egg yolks
1/3 cup frozen pineapple juice
concentrate, right from can

1/3 cup milk
½ cup sugar
1/3 cup softened butter

This is easy in a blender. Simply put all ingredients in the blender at once; beat until smooth—about 30 seconds. Pour into saucepan and cook, stirring constantly, over low heat until the sauce coats the spoon. Cool at room temperature. Serve over slices of angel food cake. *Makes 1 cup.*

Orange Cake Sauce

¼ cup softened butter
¼ cup frozen orange juice concentrate, right from can

¼ cup evaporated milk
½ cup brown sugar

Put all ingredients in electric blender; beat until smooth. Serve over cake, ice cream, or thin pancakes. *Makes about 1 cup.*

Raspberry Satin Sauce

1 package vanilla pudding and
pie filling mix
¼ teaspoon salt
1¼ cups water

1 10-ounce package frozen raspberries
2 teaspoons lemon juice
1 tablespoon butter

Combine pudding mix and salt in saucepan; blend in water. Add block of frozen berries (defrost slightly); cook and stir over medium heat until mixture comes to a full boil and is thickened.

Remove from heat. Stir in lemon juice and butter. Serve hot over cake or cold pudding, or chill and serve over Danish Rum Pudding or ice cream. *Makes 2½ cups. To reheat cold sauce,* place in top of double boiler over hot water; stir once or twice until as warm as desired.

Hot Lemon Sauce (Basic Recipe)

½ cup sugar	1 cup boiling water
1 tablespoon cornstarch	2 tablespoons lemon juice

Blend sugar and cornstarch; stir in boiling water, then lemon juice. Bring again to a boil; simmer until thickened—5 or 6 minutes. *Makes 1 cup.*

HOT LEMON-BRANDY SAUCE. Use 1 tablespoon lemon juice and 2 tablespoons brandy.

HOT LEMON-BOURBON SAUCE. Use bourbon instead of brandy.

ORANGE-BRANDY SAUCE. Use the same amount of sugar and cornstarch, but ½ cup water, ½ cup orange juice, and 2 tablespoons brandy.

Orange Syrup

1 seedless orange	1 cup maple-blended syrup
2 tablespoons butter	2 tablespoons Cointreau

Remove outermost peel of orange; cut into thin slivers. Remove and discard all white membranes; dice orange finely. Combine orange, orange peel, butter, and syrup; heat to boiling. Turn off heat and stir in Cointreau. Delicious over dessert pancakes or on puff pancakes for brunch. *Makes 1½ cups.*

Red Fruit Sauce

Combine cherry preserves, red raspberry jam, strawberry preserves, or a mixture of Damson plum preserves and currant jelly, with just enough brandy or sweet (not dry) wine to thin preserves to a saucelike consistency. Many combinations are possible. An excellent cherry sauce is made by adding 2 tablespoons Cherry Kijafa wine to ½ cup cherry preserves. A fine Currant-Cherry Sauce is made by heating together ½ cup currant jelly, ½ cup cherry preserves, and 2 tablespoons brandy or sherry until jelly is melted. Cool but do not chill.

Hard Sauce

2 tablespoons butter, softened   1 to 2 tablespoons rum or brandy
1 cup sifted confectioners' sugar

Cream butter and sugar until smooth and fluffy; beat in rum or brandy. Chill. Cut into small squares to serve over hot pudding. *Makes about ½ cup, or 8 servings.*

Cherry Hard Sauce

1 stick (8 tablespoons) butter,   Grated rind of ½ lemon
  softened   1 tablespoon syrup from cherry
8 tablespoons sifted confection-   preserves
  ers' sugar

Cream butter until fluffy; work in sugar until very smooth. Add grated rind and cherry syrup; blend well. Chill until firm. Delicious over steamed plum pudding, fruit cake (warmed in top of double boiler), or fruit pudding. *Makes A cup, or 8 servings.*

Hot Fudge Sauce

2 squares (2 ounces) unsweet-   1½ cups white corn syrup
  ened chocolate   ⅛ teaspoon salt
½ cup water   1 teaspoon vanilla

Combine in saucepan the chocolate and water; stir over low heat until chocolate is melted and mixture is thickened. Remove from heat; stir in syrup and salt. Return to low heat; simmer 10 minutes, stirring occasionally (take care it does not burn). Stir in vanilla. *Makes 2 cups.*

Quick Fudge Sauce

1 6-ounce package semisweet   ¼ cup light cream
  chocolate chips   3 tablespoons water

Place chocolate chips in blender; heat cream and water to steaming; pour into blender. Beat at high speed 1 minute. *Makes 1 cup sauce.*

Quick Butterscotch Sauce

1 cup brown sugar, firmly   2 tablespoons white corn syrup
  packed   2 tablespoons butter
¼ cup light cream

Combine ingredients in saucepan; bring to a boil; stir until thickened and smooth—3 or 4 minutes. Serve warm over butter-pecan, chocolate, coffee, or vanilla ice cream. *Makes ¾ cup, or 4 servings.*

Chocolate-Peppermint Sauce

Place 1 package (about 20) chocolate-covered peppermints in top of double boiler with 2 tablespoons butter; melt over hot (not boiling) water; stir in enough cream to thin to desired consistency. Excellent over vanilla ice cream or yellow cake. *Makes 1 cup.*

14 RELISHES, MARMALADES, AND CANDIES

The American supermarket and the home freezer together have completely changed the role of pickles and relishes. Forty years ago, August and September were canning months and home kitchens steamed with jams, jellies, and conserves, while fruit and vegetables were neatly fitted into glass jars and processed for hours in kettles of boiling water. All that has changed. Even those who have big kitchen gardens now store the harvest bounty in their freezers. Quickly and with little fuss pickles can be made any time of year for the fun of it, not because there are pecks and bushels of garden stuff demanding to be preserved at once before they rot.

The first step in preparing any of the following relishes, chutneys, or marmalades is to sterilize the jars or jelly glasses: First wash the jars and their lids in soapy water or in the dishwasher, then place them in the largest pan you have. Cover with water and bring the water to a rapid boil. Keep the water boiling 10 minutes; turn off the heat, let the jars remain in the hot water 5 minutes longer, then lift them out with tongs and place them upside down to drain thoroughly. When filled, the jars or jelly glasses should be still warm but dry. Jams and marmalades should be covered with clear paraffin as a preservative; most pickles will be preserved by their brine and therefore an airtight seal is not vitally important if the pickles are used within a reasonable length of time, like 2 months.

Preserves, and candies, too, make fine gifts. Wrap them in decorative paper, tie with pretty ribbons, and carry them to friends and neighbors as a sweet way of expressing "best wishes."

Homemade Chili Sauce

There is no lovelier fragrance than that of this sweet-sour-spicy mixture bubbling away on the stove. It makes a superb sauce for hamburgers, with baked beans, to top scrambled eggs or for a Western omelet, or as a relish with cold cuts.

1 peck (8 quarts) garden-ripe tomatoes	2 teaspoons cinnamon
2 cups chopped green pepper	1 teaspoon ground clove or allspice
2 cups chopped onion	1 teaspoon dry mustard
1 quart cider vinegar	½ teaspoon cayenne
2 cups brown sugar	1 teaspoon freshly ground black pepper
2 tablespoons salt	

Scald the tomatoes to loosen the skins; place them in a large roasting pan; cover completely with boiling water; let stand 5 minutes. Skins should then come off easily if tomatoes are vine-ripened. Chop tomatoes in blender; transfer to clean, dry 10-quart kettle. Chop peppers and onions in blender; add to chopped tomatoes. (Make sure all seeds and all white membrane are removed from peppers.) Add vinegar, sugar, and seasonings. Bring to a boil; lower heat; simmer, uncovered, until mixture is thickened—about 3 hours. Stir occasionally to prevent scorching; if heat cannot be kept low enough, put an asbestos pad under kettle. Taste; add more salt if needed. Ladle into hot, dry jars, filling almost to top. Cover immediately, then twist the cover tight to seal. Store in a cool, dry place. *Makes about 8 pints.*

Bread-and-Butter Pickles

25 medium cucumbers	5 cups sugar
8 large onions, thinly sliced	2 tablespoons mustard seed
½ cup salt	2 tablespoons celery seed
5 cups cider vinegar	1 teaspoon whole cloves

Select firm cucumbers with no trace of mold or decay. Cut off ends; slice about ⅛-inch thick. Arrange layers of cucumbers alternately with layers of onions in large roasting pan; sprinkle with salt. Place ice cubes over the vegetables to keep them crisp. Let stand 3 hours, then drain thoroughly. Place vinegar, sugar, and seasonings in kettle; bring to a boil; boil hard 10 minutes. Add drained cucumbers and onions carefully to avoid breaking up slices. Return to the boil, then turn off heat. Promptly ladle vegetables into hot, sterilized pint or half-pint jars; add the spiced brine to fill to top. Cover at once and tighten to seal. *Makes about 5 pints.*

Pickled Watermelon Rind

This is a fine by-product of a watermelon feast. Use the rind after the red fruit has been eaten and enjoyed.

1 quart diced watermelon rind
2 cups sugar
1 cup vinegar
1 cup water

1 small lemon, thinly sliced, seeds removed
1 stick cinnamon
1 teaspoon whole cloves

Remove and discard all the tough outer green part of the rind and all red fruit. Cut trimmed rind into pieces ¼-inch thick. Soak overnight in salted water (¼ cup salt to 4 cups water). Drain; rinse in cold water; cover with ice-cold water for 1 hour; drain again. Cover with fresh boiling water; return to a boil; cook until barely tender—about 10 minutes; drain again. Meantime, place remaining ingredients in kettle; bring mixture to a boil; simmer 10 minutes. Add drained rind to this syrup; simmer until rind is translucent. Ladle into hot, sterilized jars; add syrup to cover. Seal immediately. *Makes 5 or 6 pints.*

Chow-Chow Pickles

1 pound green or ripe tomatoes
½ pound small white onions, peeled
1 sweet red pepper, seeded, chopped
1 green pepper, seeded, chopped
3 medium cucumbers
1 cup cauliflower broken in small pieces

3 stalks celery, diced
1 cup string beans, sliced diagonally
1 tablespoon mixed pickling spices
1½ tablespoons salt
1 teaspoon whole cloves
1 cup sugar
1 cup cider vinegar

Almost any combination of vegetables may be used, not necessarily those given above. You need a total of 5 cups of vegetables, all cut in small pieces. Tomatoes, onions, and peppers can be chopped in blender. The rest should be cut with sharp knife. Combine vegetables with pickling spices, salt, cloves, sugar, and vinegar in a large kettle; bring to a boil. Boil, uncovered, for 2 minutes. Ladle into sterilized glass jars; cover with the boiling-hot vinegar mixture. Seal immediately. Will keep in cool place for several months.

Sweet Dill Pickles

6 cucumbers
1 large onion, thickly sliced
3 tablespoons minced dill, or 3 sprigs fresh dill

1 cup sugar
1 cup water
2 cups vinegar
1/3 cup salt

Soak whole unpeeled cucumbers in ice water 3 to 4 hours. Drain thoroughly. Slice lengthwise or cut in thick rounds. Place in hot, sterilized jars with onion slices and dill. Heat together sugar, water, vinegar, and salt; bring to a boil; pour boiling hot over pickles; seal at once. Store in a cool, dry place until cucumbers look transparent—about three weeks—before opening. *Makes 3 pints.*

Dilled Beans

5 cups water	2 pounds fresh beans
2 tablespoons salt	¼ cup fresh dill, or 1 tablespoon
3 tablespoons vinegar	ground dill seed
1 tablespoon sugar	2 cloves garlic

Heat water, salt, vinegar, and sugar together just to boiling. Cool. Separately cook beans, which have been sliced diagonally, for 2 or 3 minutes, no longer. Drain beans; place in the brine. Add dill and whole peeled garlic cloves. Keep at room temperature 3 or 4 days, then transfer to sterilized glass jars. Seal tightly. Store in refrigerator or in cool, dry cellar during very hot weather; the rest of time store at room temperature. *Makes 2 pints.*

Peach Chutney

4 quarts (½ peck) peaches, not overripe, free of blemishes	1 teaspoon powdered ginger
	½ teaspoon salt
1 1-pound box light brown sugar	1 12-ounce box raisins
1 quart pineapple vinegar	¼ cup chopped onion (optional)
½ teaspoon powdered mustard	Grated rind and juice of 1 lemon

Peel and stone peaches; chop fine in blender. (You should have 2½ quarts, or 10 cups, chopped peaches.) Combine sugar, vinegar, spices, and salt; bring to a boil; add chopped peaches, raisins, onions, lemon rind and juice. Simmer over low heat until very thick. Cool. Ladle into hot, sterilized jars. Cover tightly. Can be stored at room temperature; once the jar is opened, it should be refrigerated. Excellent with shrimp or chicken curry. *Makes about 6 pints.*

Green Tomato Chutney

6 cups chopped, trimmed green tomatoes
1 clove garlic, minced
2 tablespoons instant minced onion
¾ cup crystallized ginger, chopped
1 12-ounce box raisins, chopped
3 cups cider vinegar
3 cups brown sugar
¼ cup salt
¼ teaspoon cayenne
½ teaspoon mace
½ teaspoon coriander seed

Combine all ingredients in kettle; cook slowly 3 hours. Spoon into hot, sterilized jars and seal immediately. Do not use for at least one month. *Makes about 3 pints.*

Quick Apple Chutney

4 tart apples, peeled, chopped
1 teaspoon salt
1 tablespoon lemon juice
4 medium onions, quartered
1 green pepper, seeded
¼ cup shredded coconut

Sprinkle chopped apples with salt and lemon juice; let stand about 5 minutes; drain well. Chop onions and green pepper in blender; add apples and coconut; blend thoroughly. Keep in refrigerator. Serve as a relish with lamb or beef curry. *Makes about 2 cups.*

Instant Damson Plum Chutney

1 jar Damson plum preserves
½ teaspoon curry powder
1 teaspoon instant minced onion
2 tablespoons vinegar
½ cup chopped canned peaches, well drained

Combine all ingredients; blend well. Let stand 1 hour before serving. Serve as a relish with curry. *Makes about 1½ cups.*

Cranberry Chutney

2 pounds fresh cranberries
2 large yellow onions, quartered
1 cup water
2 cups sugar
1 cup vinegar
1 teaspoon powdered cloves
1 teaspoon cinnamon
½ teaspoon ground allspice
1 teaspoon salt
½ teaspoon freshly ground black pepper

Pick over cranberries; discard any that are blemished. Cook cranberries and onions together in water until soft. Beat in blender until mushy but not puréed—about 30 seconds. Add remaining ingredients; transfer to saucepan; cook until thick—about 8 minutes. Ladle into sterilized jars or glasses;

cover; twist cover to seal. Excellent with roast turkey or with chicken curry. *Makes about 2½ pints.*

Orange-Date Chutney

2 large navel oranges	2 cups granulated or brown sugar
1 pound pitted dates, chopped	1 tablespoon salt
3 medium onions	1 tablespoon curry powder
1 clove garlic, minced	1 teaspoon cumin
1 cup seedless raisins	½ teaspoon powdered ginger
1 quart pineapple vinegar	1 cup chopped walnuts

Carefully peel oranges; cut outer yellow part of rind of 1 orange into fine slivers. Remove white membrane from both oranges. Quarter oranges; chop in blender; add dates, onion, garlic, and raisins to blender. Beat until quite fine by turning on, off, on, off (do not purée).

Combine vinegar, slivers of orange peel, sugar, salt, and spices. Bring to a boil; cook 5 minutes. Add orange mixture and walnuts, continue to cook over lowest heat until reduced and thickened. Cool. Ladle into hot, sterilized jars. Cover; twist tight to seal. Store in cool, dry place; use within 2 months. *Makes about 3 pints.*

Uncooked Cranberry-Orange Relish

The commercial cranberry-orange relish is excellent, but if you want to prepare your own, this is quick, easy, and inexpensive. Be sure to prepare 2 days ahead so it can "season" in refrigerator.

4 cups fresh cranberries	2 cups sugar
1 navel orange	

Pick over cranberries; discard any that are blemished. Feed into blender; beat at medium speed until chopped. Peel orange so that orange part of rind is removed; add rind to blender. Cut away all white membrane, then add orange segments to blender. Add sugar to cranberry-orange mixture. Beat until blended; do not purée. Ladle into jars. Store in refrigerator 2 days before using. *Makes about 4 cups.*

Wild Blackberry Sauce

Carefully pick over and wash blackberries. Add 1 cup sugar to each cup berries. Place in large saucepan; bring slowly to a boil; simmer 5 minutes. Ladle into sterilized jars or glasses; seal. Thinner than jam, this is a marvelous topping for ice cream. *One quart berries makes about 3 cups sauce.*

Blackberry-Lemon Jam

A wonderful use for wild blackberries picked from thickets in the woods or along country roads.

2 quarts blackberries   2 lemons, seeded, chopped
9 cups sugar

Wash and pick over blackberries, removing all hard caps and overripe berries. Arrange in kettle in layers with sugar and chopped lemons (the best way to chop lemons is in blender; they should be cut quite fine). Let mixture stand 1 hour, then slowly bring to the boil; cook until thickened—about 20 minutes. Ladle into hot, sterilized jars. Cool. Pour melted paraffin over tops. Cover with fitted lid. *Makes 4 or 5 pints.*

No-cook Strawberry Jam

One of the miracles of commercial pectin is that it makes it possible to make fresh-fruit jams that require no cooking at all, so that the full fruit flavor is preserved. The only drawback: these jams must be stored in the refrigerator and used within 3 weeks. When jam is set, it may also be stored in freezer.

1 quart fully ripe strawberries   pectin
4 cups sugar   ¾ cup water
1 1¾-ounce package powdered

Sterilize jelly glasses or other glass jars with fitted lids or covers. Pick over strawberries; use only those free from blemish. Wash thoroughly; remove hulls. Place strawberries in large bowl and crush with pestle, or crush in electric blender. Add sugar. Combine pectin and water; bring to a boil; boil 1 minute, stirring constantly. Stir into strawberry mixture; continue stirring until thoroughly dissolved. Ladle into the sterilized glasses; cover glasses. When cooled to room temperature, place in refrigerator. *Makes 5 or 6 cups.*

Tomato Marmalade

Utterly delicious—a real treat for breakfast over English muffins or crisp buttered toast.

2 pounds garden-ripe tomatoes   2 tablespoons preserved ginger
(yellow or red plum or cherry,   2 lemons, thinly sliced, seeded
or regular tomatoes)   2 tablespoons sherry
2 pounds (8 cups) sugar

Scald tomatoes to loosen skins; remove skins. Quarter large tomatoes. Cover with sugar; let stand overnight. Drain off accumulated liquid; place liquid in saucepan with the ginger, shaved very thin, and the thinly sliced lemon. Bring to a boil; add tomatoes; cook until syrup spins a thread and is clear and thick. Skim occasionally. Add sherry. Ladle into hot, sterilized jars with fitted covers. Marmalade that is not to be used within a few weeks should be covered with melted paraffin. *Makes 3 or 4 cups.*

Peach-Orange Marmalade

Use 3 cups peeled, chopped peaches to each cup diced, seeded orange. First select ripe but firm peaches, free of blemishes. Peel, stone, and dice; measure by cupfuls. Place in large saucepan. Carefully remove outer rind from orange. Cut rind into slivers; add to peaches. Remove all white membrane from orange segments; dice and seed oranges and measure by cupful; add to peaches. Add ¾ cup sugar for each cup fruit and orange peel. Bring slowly to a boil; simmer, skimming occasionally, until syrup is thick and clear and spins a thread. Ladle into hot, sterilized jars. If you start with 4 cups of fruit, you will end with *about 3 cups.*

Candies

Making candy is always a good rainy-day occupation for restless children. It is also a fine way to solve the Christmas-gift problem when there are grandparents, aunts, and uncles to whom the little ones want to give gifts. The no-cook candies are best for this purpose. For gifts from adult cooks, the more elaborate and time-consuming candies are more appropriate.

Chocolate-Nut Clusters

1 6- or 8-ounce package semi-sweet chocolate

1½ cups walnut halves or peanuts

Place the chocolate in the top of a double boiler and partially melt over hot water. When about half the chocolate is melted, remove from heat; stir quickly to melt the remainder. Stir the nuts into the chocolate; remove with a spoon and drop onto waxed paper. If using walnut halves, each nut half makes 1 candy. If using peanuts, remove a cluster of 2 or 3 peanuts together. Cool until firm. For a gift, wrap each cluster in plastic or printed foil; twist. Place wrapped candies in tin containers or paper gift boxes. *Makes about 2½ dozen.*

NUT-FRUIT CLUSTERS. Add ½ cup seedless raisins, or use ¾ cup each chopped nuts and raisins.

NUT-MINT CLUSTERS. Add 1/3 cup crushed peppermint stick candy (a good use to make of candy canes that break before they can be hung on the Christmas tree).

PEANUT BRITTLE CLUSTERS. Instead of nuts, crush ½ pound peanut brittle; add to chocolate; drop by teaspoons on waxed paper.

CHOCOLATE-NUT BARS. Instead of dropping in clusters on wax paper, line a 9 x 9-inch pan with wax paper; spread mixture of chopped nuts and raisins over the bottom; pour melted chocolate over mixture, which should be no more than ¼-inch thick. When thoroughly chilled, cut into bars with sharp knife.

No-cook Lemon Fondant

1 6-ounce package lemon chips	Dash of cream of tartar
1 egg white	Walnut halves, or halved maras-
1½ cups sifted confectioners' sugar	chino cherries

Place lemon chips in top of double boiler; melt over hot water. In mixing bowl, combine unbeaten egg white, confectioners' sugar, and cream of tartar; mix thoroughly. Add melted lemon chips, cleaning out every bit from top of double boiler with rubber spatula. Beat mixture until smooth. Take out about a tablespoonful at a time; rub between palms of hands into balls ½ inch in diameter. Place on waxed paper; press a walnut half or half a cherry into the top of each. Let stand at least 3 hours. *Makes about 4 dozen.*

Uncooked Vanilla Fondant

1 egg white	sugar, sifted
2 tablespoons butter, softened	1 teaspoon vanilla
1 1-pound box confectioners'	

Combine all ingredients; beat until well blended, then work with greased fingers until smooth. Form into long rolls; cover with damp cloth and let stand 1 hour. Cut into pieces; roll each with fingers into desired shape.

VARIATIONS. Centers may be filled with nut meats, pieces of preserved ginger, or cherries. Or add chopped nuts to fondant; press into square pan; mark into squares and let ripen 24 hours, then break into pieces.

CHOCOLATE-COATED FONDANT. Melt semisweet chocolate over hot water, stirring until smooth. Then place chocolate over cold water and dip fondants into melted chocolate. Use tines of fork to lift out; drain over edge of pan. Place on waxed paper over wire rack to dry.

RUM FONDANT. Instead of vanilla, add 1 tablespoon rum to butter-sugar mixture. Decorate as desired or dip in chocolate.

Turkish Delight

1 cup applesauce
1 3-ounce package cherry-, strawberry-, or raspberry-flavored gelatin

1 cup sugar
2/3 cup almonds or walnuts, crushed or ground
Confectioners' sugar

Heat applesauce in a saucepan; add the gelatin; stir until dissolved. Add the sugar; stir over low heat to dissolve. Remove from heat; add the nuts (they should be ground almost to powder); stir to distribute thoroughly. Pour into greased 9 x 5 x 3-inch loaf pan. Refrigerate until very firm—about 4 hours. Remove from refrigerator; dip pan in hot water to loosen the jelled mixture; turn out and cut into 1-inch cubes. Roll in confectioners' sugar. Return to the refrigerator for 24 hours. Then roll in confectioners' sugar again. These make colorful holiday gifts. *Makes about 40 pieces.*

Butterscotch Bonbons

2 packages instant butterscotch pudding mix
1 cup chopped pitted dates
½ cup chunk-style peanut butter

½ cup light cream
1 12-ounce package semisweet chocolate bits, melted

Combine all ingredients except chocolate bits; blend well; roll into 1-inch balls. Dip the balls in melted chocolate. Place on rack over baking sheet; chill in refrigerator until firm. (Store in refrigerator; not suitable for mailing.) *Makes about 3 dozen.*

Chocolate Fudge

2 1-ounce squares unsweetened chocolate
¾ cup milk
2 cups sugar

Dash of salt
2 tablespoons butter
1 teaspoon vanilla

Grease a 9 x 5 x 3-inch loaf pan. Add chocolate to milk; place over very low heat until chocolate is melted, stirring occasionally; blend well. Add sugar and salt; cook and stir until sugar is dissolved and a spoonful of mixture can be shaped into a soft ball when dropped into a cup of cold water (candy thermometer registers 234° F.). Stir in butter and vanilla. Remove from heat; cool to lukewarm. Beat until mixture begins to thicken and loses its shiny look. Pour into greased pan. Cool completely before cutting. *Makes about 18 2-inch pieces or 2 pounds of fudge.*

CHOCOLATE-NUT FUDGE. Add 1 cup coarsely chopped nuts to mixture before pouring into pan.

RUM-CHOCOLATE FUDGE. Instead of vanilla, add 1 tablespoon rum. For a richer fudge, use ½ cup evaporated milk plus ¼ cup water instead of ¾ cup whole milk, and use part brown sugar.

Quick Fudge

2 8-ounce packages semisweet chocolate
½ teaspoon salt

2 teaspoons vanilla
1 1/3 cups sweetened condensed milk

Grease an 8 x 8-inch pan. Partially melt chocolate over hot water; remove from heat; stir until completely melted. Add remaining ingredients; blend well. Pour into greased pan, spreading evenly. Chill until firm. Cut into 1-inch squares. *Makes about 50 pieces.*

Popcorn Balls

2 quarts salted, popped corn
½ cup light corn syrup
½ cup molasses

1 teaspoon vinegar
4 tablespoons butter

The easiest way to pop corn is to place it in an electric skillet with 2 tablespoons butter; cover the skillet; set temperature at 350° F. When you can't hear the corn popping any longer, turn off heat and remove cover. Sprinkle salt to taste over the corn. Place popped corn in large mixing bowl.

When the popcorn is ready (not before), place syrup, molasses, and vinegar in deep saucepan; bring to a boil, stirring occasionally, until a candy thermometer registers 240° F., or until a little of the syrup dropped in a cup of cold water forms a soft ball. Now stir constantly until the thermometer registers 270°, or until the syrup instantly hardens when dropped in water. Remove from heat; add butter; stir to blend. Pour syrup over the popcorn; toss to coat quickly. Grease the palms of your hands, then pick up popcorn and shape into balls about 2 or 2½ inches in diameter. *Makes 10 to 12 balls.*

CHRISTMAS BALLS. Add to the popcorn about a cup of chopped glacé cherries, or a mixture of cherries and minced citron.

15 BEVERAGES

"What would you like to drink?" It's the first question asked the arriving guest because something to drink is an instinctive gesture of hospitality. At the table the question is put once more, this time meaning a beverage to be enjoyed with the food. Between meals, a drink may be a pick-up or a slow-down, depending on the pace of work—or play. An eye opener means, to most adult Americans, the first cup of coffee in the morning; a nightcap is the last drink before bedtime.

More milk is consumed per capita in the United States than in any other country in the world. The U.S. also ranks among the top coffee-drinking nations. Americans are the greatest imbibers of cocktails and we probably put away more carbonated beverages than any other people on earth. We are, in fact, a drinking nation, and what we drink, and when, and how much, can make a critical difference in the family food budget.

Coffee

Some people become positively passionate on the subject of how to brew a perfect cup of coffee. Coffee makers in dazzling array are offered for sale in housewares departments. The most popular types are percolators, drip, vacuum, and those which require a paper filter. Espresso machines have become chic but are so costly their use is limited.

Despite all the fuss and the fancy contraptions, more people all the time resort to instant coffee. It's the easiest way, of course, especially when only one or two cups of coffee are wanted. And if made properly, instant coffee is not bad. (I say this warily, knowing that such a sentiment is likely to place me on many a coffee lover's blacklist.)

Whatever the method of brewing coffee, it's important to buy good coffee and to measure it carefully. This is as true of instant coffee as it is of ground coffee. Some like their coffee bitter-black and very strong; others will settle for a far weaker beverage. Determine the proper measure for the strength you like, then be consistent. One can get used to overstrong coffee or too-weak coffee, but not to a constantly changing formula. Also, be sure to buy the right grind for your appliance.

Percolated coffee is the strongest. Two important points: Always clean the pot thoroughly—grease from coffee oils can collect in the corners and cause bitterness and that "dirty" taste. Avoid letting it perk too long—five minutes is optimum.

Drip coffee tends to be weakest in flavor, and unless the lower half of the pot can be kept on the stove, it cools off very quickly. And cold coffee can ruin an otherwise pleasant morning disposition.

Filter and vacuum coffees are excellent, full bodied, and protected against overbrewing, but the filters are a nuisance to change and the glass pots are fragile and complicated to handle.

Instant coffee is best when the coffee powder is placed in a deep pot, *cold* water added, and then brought just to a boil. Do not let it remain boiling; either remove from heat at once or turn heat as low as possible. A deep pot must be used, and water should be added only to the halfway mark to prevent its boiling over. The perfect appliance for this is a thermostatically controlled electric pot or percolator from which the basket may be removed. When the water reaches a boil, the heat automatically decreases to a point that keeps the coffee hot but does not permit it to simmer.

If you must make instant coffee in a cup, use a deep mug. The aroma is retained better in a deep cup or pot.

Freeze-dried coffee is better than powdered instant coffee, but it is also more expensive.

Espresso coffee is available both in pulverized grinds for espresso machines and in an instant powder. The coffee itself is of darker roast (that is, the coffee beans were roasted longer before grinding), and so is stronger in flavor. Espresso coffee may be used in any recipe calling for dark-roasted coffee.

Caffein-free coffee is available in both regular grinds and instant powder. Use in place of regular coffee in any of the following recipes.

Demitasse

The term is generally used to mean black after-dinner coffee served in small cups. Espresso coffee is often used, but regular coffee made stronger than usual will also do. Sugar is always passed; cream may be, too, though it usually isn't. It is nice to have tiny demitasse spoons to serve with the coffee.

Café au Lait

For this use a dark-roasted (espresso) coffee, or make the coffee double strength. Heat milk separately; pour equal quantities of hot milk and hot coffee into each cup. This is the favorite breakfast drink in New Orleans and in most of Western Europe. (The quickest way: Add instant espresso powder to hot milk; stir until dissolved; no water is added.)

Kaffee mit Schlagober

An Austrian specialty. Make strong black coffee; pour into glass tumblers, about two-thirds full. Top with whipped cream. Pass sugar. The whipped cream may be blended in with a spoon, or the coffee may be sipped through the cream.

Cappuccino

Brew espresso coffee; separately heat milk. Combine equal quantities of coffee and milk; stir in sugar and cinnamon to taste, or dust top of each cupful with cinnamon-sugar blend, or use a cinnamon stick to stir the sugar in.

ANOTHER WAY. Combine ½ teaspoon cinnamon with 2 teaspoons sugar and 2 heaping teaspoons instant espresso coffee; add to 2 cups milk; heat milk, stirring, until sugar, cinnamon, and coffee are dissolved. *Makes 3 demitasse servings.*

Spiced Viennese Coffee

4 tablespoons instant coffee powder	¼ cup sugar
7 whole cloves	½ cup whipped cream or heavy cream
1 stick cinnamon	Cinnamon
3½ cups hot water	

Place instant coffee, cloves, cinnamon, hot water, and sugar in saucepan; bring to a boil. Remove from heat; let stand 5 minutes. Remove cloves and cinnamon with slotted spoon. Reheat coffee briefly; pour into cups. Float heavy cream over top of each, or add a dab of whipped cream. Sprinkle cinnamon over top of cream. Delightful to serve to ladies with Lacy Oatmeal Cookies. *Makes 5 servings.*

Caffè Romano

Prepare espresso or extra-strength coffee; serve black in small tumblers with a thin sliver of lemon peel in each. Pass sugar but no milk or cream.

Turkish Coffee

This must be made in a special copper pot for brewing Turkish coffee—no other appliance will work. Use espresso or another dark-roasted coffee, either instant or the finest pulverized grind. Make each individual cup to order: Place a heaping teaspoon of coffee and ½ teaspoon sugar (or to taste) in the pot. Add water to two-thirds from top. Bring three times to a boil; after the third time, let coffee settle a few seconds, then pour into demitasse cup. Only about half the coffee can be drunk—the rest is grounds. Fun with a Greek or Turkish dinner, but it will not satisfy those accustomed to big cups of American coffee.

Russian Chocolate

2 cups extra-strong coffee
2 cups hot milk
½ cup instant cocoa or
  chocolate-flavor mix

¼ teaspoon cinnamon, or 1 teaspoon vanilla
Whipped cream

Combine in large coffee pot the coffee, milk, cocoa mix, and cinnamon or vanilla; heat and stir until dissolved. Serve hot in mugs topped with whipped cream. *Makes 5 or 6 servings.*

MOCHA FLOAT. Prepare as above but omit whipped cream. Place chocolate mixture in blender with 2 scoops vanilla ice cream; beat to blend. Serve cold.

Café Royale

Prepare extra-strong black coffee. Serve in demitasse cups. For each serving, place a cube of sugar in a spoon; add brandy to the sugar. Set brandy aflame; drop sugar into coffee. When flame has died, stir sugar until dissolved.

Irish Coffee

To each serving of strong black coffee, add 2 tablespoons Irish whiskey and sugar to taste. Stir to dissolve sugar. Top each serving with whipped cream.

Café Diable

Long spiral of orange peel	Pinch of allspice
10 whole cloves	6 tablespoons dark sweet rum
2 tablespoons sugar	2½ cups double-strength coffee

Stick orange peel with whole cloves; add sugar and allspice. Heat in blazer or chafing dish until sugar has melted. Add half the rum; continue heating until tiny bubbles appear around the edge, then lift up orange peel with a long-handled fork; pour remaining rum down the peel and set a match to the peel. The sugar-rum mixture will burn, setting remaining rum in bowl aflame. When flame has died out, add coffee; stir to blend; heat until steaming. Ladle steaming coffee into demitasse cups. *Makes 6 demitasse servings.*

Iced Coffee

Prepare double-strength coffee; cool slightly, then pour over ice cubes. Or, make coffee ice cubes (fill freezer tray with cold coffee; freeze); add cubes to regular-strength coffee. Pass cream or milk and sugar.

ITALIAN ICED COFFEE. Crush ice; pass in daiquiri glasses or brandy snifters. Pour strong coffee (cooled to room temperature) over the ice. Pass superfine sugar. Sip through a straw.

Tea

More than half the world's people drink tea every day. There are more than 300 varieties of tea and expert tea blending is both a profession and an art. For those who enjoy experimenting with exotic tastes and aromas, tea offers fascinating variety.

Most teas are classified as either *green* or *black*. This refers to the curing process. The leaves of green teas are steamed, then oven-dried; the leaves of the black teas are first dried, then subjected to a process of fermentation that changes the color to brick-red (the Chinese call these "red teas," not black) and gives the tea a more pungent flavor. A third type is called oolong: The greenish-brown leaves are only partly fermented, making a tea more full-bodied than the green teas but less pungent than the black.

Orange pekoe is not a variety but a grade of tea: The tea is composed of larger leaves. It is not orange-flavored, though once it may have been, just as *jasmine*. a green tea, contains a few blossoms of the jasmine flower.

Earl Grey is a special blend of teas with a very pungent flavor. It is quite popular with the English. *Gunpowder* is the name of still another blend. The best way to find your favorite is to·try a number of different teas. Some you will like, others you may not care for.

In addition to what are still popularly known as the "China teas" (even though very few of those on the American market come from China any longer), there are the *matés*, or herb teas. The number of these is countless. They are found chiefly in health-food stores. Some are considered to be of medicinal value; to soothe one's nerves or calm a stomach upset. They are fun to experiment with, too. Expect the flavor, however, to be completely different from that of the "China teas," either green or black.

HOW TO BREW TEA. Nothing is more horrifying to a tea lover than to be given a cup of hot water containing a tea bag. This is not tea—it's only colored water.

Tea bags have their purpose, but to extract the full tea flavor it is necessary to put the tea bags in a pot, add water that has been brought to a full, rolling boil, and let steep 5 minutes. Stir once before pouring. One American tea bag generally will make 2 cups of tea, though this is a matter of taste. Those who like strong tea may consider it enough for only 1 cup. (Tea bags manufactured in England contain more tea, and 1 bag may make 3 or 4 strong cups of tea.)

Loose tea goes further and makes more full-bodied tea. If made in a proper teapot and well steeped before serving, only a very few of the leaves will come out. Some people insist that the teapot should first be heated by rinsing with boiling water, then the tea placed inside, then the boiling water added. After a lifetime of brewing tea to my taste nearly every day, I have concluded that prewarming is not necessary. If the water is brought to a white-steam boil and allowed to boil that way for 1 minute before pouring onto the tea, the pot will be instantly heated and the tea fragrance instantly released. Three minutes is usually enough time for steeping loose tea but, again, this is a matter of taste. Stir once before pouring. Use 1 teaspoon loose tea per cup and one for the pot.

HOW TO SERVE TEA. Breakfast tea should be a strong brew, made with black tea and served with cold milk. Pour the milk in the cup first; add the steaming-hot tea. The English like afternoon tea served the same way.

For an American tea party, where a choice of milk or lemon is usually offered, the tea is poured first, then a tray containing cold milk (not cream), lemon slices, and cubes of sugar or a sugar bowl is passed. If only one kind of tea is offered, it should be black. When jasmine or another green tea is offered, neither milk nor lemon is necessary—in fact, even sugar is not necessary. This delicate flower-scented tea has a kind of sweetness of its own.

Russian tea is always served in a glass with lemon and sugar. The tea served in Chinese restaurants (and the proper tea to serve with a Chinese dinner) is strong, but not bitter, black tea, served in narrow, deep cups without handles; neither milk nor sugar need be added, although sugar may be passed, of course.

MAKING TEA FOR A CROWD. For a tea party of 25 or more, it is absolutely essential to have both a large teapot and a teakettle in order to make fresh batches of tea without interruption. There is no really satisfactory way to make large quantities of tea in advance. Tea bags should be used because they are so easy to remove and discard when a second potful is to be brewed. Measure the capacity of the pot by cupfuls; place in the pot 1 teabag for each 2 tea cups, or 1 teabag for each 8 ounces of water. After the tea has steeped 5 minutes, remove the teabags. Keep water at a boil in a teakettle so that each time the pot is emptied, another potful can quickly be brewed.

Select the best quality tea; if the tea bags have paper tabs, remove them or see that they are kept outside the pot, for the flavor of paper in tea is ruinous.

Iced Tea

First brew extra-strong tea (for each 4 glasses of tea, use 6 teabags or 4 teaspoons loose tea). Cool to room temperature but do not refrigerate (this will make it cloudy). Add ice cubes to tumblers when time to serve; pour tea over ice. Pass superfine sugar. Garnish glasses with sprigs of fresh mint, if available. If you are sure everyone wants sweetened tea, dissolve sugar in a small amount of boiling water (allow 1 or 2 teaspoons sugar per glass of tea, according to taste); let water cool; add to cooled tea.

Lemon, either sliced or in wedges, is usually offered with iced tea.

ICED TEA FOR A CROWD. For each gallon (20 servings) of iced tea, place 2/3 cup loose tea in a teapot; add as much boiling water as the pot will hold; steep 3 to 5 minutes, stirring once. Strain into a gallon container; add water to fill. (If a thermos jug is used, cool tea first, then add a few ice cubes to the tea concentrate before adding cold water.)

GARNISHES FOR ICED TEA. Besides mint sprigs, fresh pineapple wedges, orange slices, or cinnamon sticks may be placed in the glasses. If a presweetened tea is being prepared, a little powdered cinnamon or cloves may be blended with the sugar. Many people like iced tea blended with frozen lemonade concentrate: Use 1 teaspoon of the frozen concentrate per tall glass. No other sweetening is needed.

TEA AS A BASE FOR PUNCH. Tea is excellent in holiday punches; the tea flavor will not be noticeable but it serves as a catalyst for other flavors and also helps to keep the cost moderate. Make extra-strong tea, as for iced tea; cool to room temperature; do not refrigerate. Blend tea with sugar and fruit juices several hours before serving.

Chocolate and Cocoa

Hot Chocolate Float

6 tablespoons Dutch cocoa mix
1 cup water
20 cinnamon candies

3 cups milk
Vanilla or chocolate ice cream

Combine the cocoa mix, water, and cinnamon candies in saucepan; bring to a boil, stirring to dissolve the mix and the candies. Reduce heat; stir in the milk slowly. Heat until mixture steams (do not boil). Serve in mugs, topping each with a small scoop of ice cream. *Makes 4 servings.*

Viennese Chocolate

1 8-ounce bar (or 2 4-ounce bars) sweet chocolate
6 cups milk

¼ teaspoon powdered cardamon or nutmeg
Whipped cream

Break up the chocolate; place in a 3-quart saucepan with cold milk and spices. Heat slowly, stirring until chocolate is melted. Serve in teacups; top with whipped cream. Sprinkle nutmeg over the cream, if desired. Orange Spritz or fruit cake cookies are delicious with this. *Makes 8 servings.*

Acapulco Chocolate

2 1-ounce squares unsweetened chocolate	3 cups milk
¼ cup sugar	1 teaspoon grated orange rind
Dash of salt	1 teaspoon vanilla
1 cup water	Marshmallows or heavy cream

Place chocolate in saucepan with sugar, salt, and water; stir over low heat until chocolate is melted, then increase heat; bring to a boil, stirring constantly. Heat milk separately. Add the chocolate mixture to milk with the orange rind and vanilla; beat with egg beater until frothy. Serve in cups or mugs. Top with a marshmallow or float a little cream over each. *Makes 5 or 6 servings.*

Chocolat au Rhum

Prepare hot chocolate with Dutch cocoa mix and milk; stir in 1 tablespoon rum for each cup. Float cream over the top.

Birthday-party Cocoa

Prepare sweetened cocoa mix according to package directions. Serve with peppermint-stick stirrers and a marshmallow floating on each cup.

Milk, Eggnogs, and Ice Cream Drinks

Graham Cracker Milk Shake

4 graham crackers	1 scoop vanilla ice cream
1 cup milk	

Soak crackers in milk until soft; add ice cream; beat until smooth. (For extra nutrition, add an egg; this makes it a Graham Cracker Nog.) *Makes 1 serving.*

Frosted Chocolate

2 scoops chocolate ice cream	Dash of cinnamon or nutmeg
1 scoop vanilla ice cream	Whipped topping
2 cups chocolate milk	

If rotary beater is used, let ice cream soften slightly at room temperature, then combine with milk and cinnamon and beat until smooth. If a blender is used, put ice cream right from freezer into blender with milk and cinnamon; beat until smooth. Serve topped with whipped topping. *Makes 2 servings.*

Brown Cow

Place a scoop of vanilla or chocolate ice cream in a tall glass. Pour in root beer and stir briskly with a long-handled spoon until the ice cream is about half melted. (Or place ingredients in an electric blender; beat no more than 30 seconds—too much beating will make it a frappé rather than an ice cream soda.) Drink through a straw.

Strawberry Cow

Place 1 pint of strawberry ice cream in a large mixing bowl, electric mixer bowl, or electric blender. Add 2 cups of milk. Beat until foamy. Pour into tall glasses, filling half full. Add ginger ale; stir briskly. Drink through straws.

Cream and Cola

Place a scoop of vanilla ice cream in a tall glass. Add cola drink; stir briskly until ice cream is partially melted. Drink through a straw.

Pineapple Ice Cream Soda

For each serving, place a scoop of pineapple ice cream or sherbet in a glass; add ½ cup milk; stir briskly, then add ginger ale or club soda and stir until foamy. (Or, use vanilla ice cream, and pineapple juice instead of milk.)

The fortified eggnog is, according to tradition, strictly a Christmas drink. But unfortified, it's the most nutritious of beverages, perfect for youngsters as an "instant breakfast" or an after-school refresher. All the following are nonalcoholic.

For adult holiday eggnogs and related drinks, see pages 795 to 799.

Plain Eggnog

1 egg	1 tablespoon sugar, or to taste
1 cup milk	Dash of nutmeg
½ teaspoon vanilla	

Combine all ingredients in a bowl and beat with rotary beater until foamy; or beat in electric blender for 30 seconds. *Makes 1 serving.*

Fortified Eggnog

1 egg	2/3 cup milk
1/3 cup instant dry milk	½ teaspoon vanilla
1 tablespoon sugar, or to taste	Dash of nutmeg or cinnamon

Place egg, instant milk, sugar, and half the milk in bowl or blender. Beat just to blend. Add remaining milk and vanilla. Beat until foamy. Top with nutmeg or cinnamon. This is a good way to increase milk intake of a child who doesn't care much for milk. *Makes 1 serving.*

Dieter's Eggnog

1 egg
1/3 cup instant dry milk
2/3 cup skimmed milk or water

½ teaspoon vanilla
Noncaloric sweetener or sugar to
 taste

Combine ingredients in bowl or blender; beat until foamy. An excellent "instant breakfast" for the weight conscious. *Makes 1 serving.*

Pineapple Nog

1 cup pineapple juice
1 egg

1 small scoop vanilla ice cream

Combine pineapple juice and egg; beat until foamy; add ice cream and beat just to blend well. *Makes 1 serving.*

Purple Cow Nog

¾ cup (1 6-ounce can) frozen
 grape juice concentrate
1 egg

1 tablespoon sugar
¾ cup milk
¼ teaspoon vanilla

Combine all ingredients (do not add water to grape juice concentrate); beat until foamy. *Makes 2 servings.*

Orange Nog

1 cup orange juice
1 teaspoon sugar
1 egg

¼ teaspoon vanilla
¼ cup milk or light cream
Dash of nutmeg

Combine all ingredients; beat until foamy. *Makes 1 large serving.*

Spicy Christmas Eggnog (nonalcoholic)

8 eggs, separated
1/3 cup sugar
½ teaspoon cinnamon
¼ teaspoon cloves

¼ teaspoon nutmeg
2 teaspoons vanilla
2 quarts milk

Beat together the egg yolks, sugar, spices, and vanilla. Add the milk a cup at a time, beating until foamy. Separately beat the egg whites until stiff. Fold egg whites into the milk-egg mixture. Serve in a punchbowl. *Makes 20 punch-cup servings.*

Nonalcoholic Fruit Drinks and Floats

Raspberry-Lemon Punch

Save the syrup from frozen raspberries. Make lemonade with a 6-ounce can of frozen lemonade concentrate; add ½ cup raspberry syrup (or as much as there is available). Stir to blend well, then pour in contents of a 7-ounce bottle of club soda or lime-lemon carbonated drink. *Makes 6 to 8 servings.*

Pineapple-Lemon Float

Fill tall tumblers a little more than half full with canned pineapple juice. To each glass add a scoop of lemon sherbet. Fill glass with club soda or ginger ale. Add a cherry for garnish.

Peach-Lime-Lemon Float

Add water to frozen lime-lemonade concentrate as directed on container. Pour into glasses or paper cups. Add a scoop of peach ice cream to each; beat with long-handled spoon just enough to partially melt ice cream. Drink through straws.

Ginger Grape

Combine equal parts grape juice (canned or reconstituted frozen) and ginger ale. Serve with ice cubes or add a scoop of vanilla ice cream to each glass.

Orange Spritzer

Fill glasses half full with orange juice. Add ice cubes and spirals of orange peel. Fill glasses with club soda. Very refreshing—grown-ups will like it as well as the youngsters.

Orange-Pineapple Frappé

Reconstitute 1 6-ounce can of orange juice concentrate; add to it 2 scoops pineapple sherbet. Beat until frothy (in an electric blender, if you have one). To serve, pour enough of the frappé mixture into each glass to fill a little more than half full. Add another scoop of the sherbet and top each sherbet scoop with a fresh, ripe strawberry. Serve with straws and ice-tea spoons.

Fruited Summer Pitcher

Reconstitute one can of frozen pineapple-lemon punch; add 2 cups ginger ale, ice cubes, and balls of honeydew melon. Garnish pitcher with mint sprigs. Serve over ice in tall glasses; place a long sliver of honeydew in each glass.

Peach Soda

1½ cups canned peaches with   1 cup vanilla ice cream
  syrup   Ginger ale
2 cups milk

If you have a blender, simply put peaches, milk, and ice cream into it and beat until the mixture is frothy. If you are using an electric mixer or rotary beater, mash the peaches slightly first, then add the other ingredients and beat. Put enough of the frothy mixture into each glass to fill halfway; fill with ginger ale; stir briskly. Drink through straws. *Makes 6 drinks.*

Fruit Punches

Cherry Punch

FROZEN FRUIT RING

1 large bottle maraschino cher-   chunks
  ries   3 cups reconstituted frozen lem-
1 navel orange, thinly sliced   onade
10 to 12 canned pineapple

Make the ring a day before it is needed. Thoroughly drain the cherries, saving syrup for the punch. Thinly slice the orange; cut nicks around the rind to form a jagged edge (see sketch); cut each slice into quarters. Thoroughly drain pineapple; mix fruit together. Pour a third of the lemonade into a 1-quart ring mold; add a third of the fruit. Freeze until partially frozen. Add a third more lemonade and a third more fruit; partially freeze again. Add remaining lemonade and fruit; freeze until solid.

PUNCH

2 6-ounce cans (or 1 12-ounce
  can) frozen lemonade
1 cup pineapple juice
Syrup from maraschino cherries

Sugar
1 quart lemon-lime carbonated
  drink
1 quart ginger ale

Reconstitute frozen lemonade with water (4 parts water to 1 part frozen concentrate), making 1½ quarts. Add pineapple juice, maraschino syrup, and, if needed, sugar to taste. Chill thoroughly. Finish punch at the last minute: Place lemonade mixture in punch bowl; unmold frozen ring and add to bowl. Add the carbonated beverages at the very end. *Makes about 30 punch-cup servings.*

Tea Punch

1 quart hot tea
1 cup superfine sugar
½ cup strained lemon juice
1 quart water or strained orange
  juice
1 quart pineapple juice

1 cup canned apricot nectar
1 navel orange, thinly sliced,
  stuck with cloves
1 or 2 lemons, thinly sliced
1 large bottle club soda or ginger
  ale

Make tea ahead; cool to room temperature. Add remaining ingredients except soda. Shortly before serving, add ice cubes or 1 large block of ice to punch; add the soda or ginger ale. *Makes about 40 servings.*

Wine Punches

The following recipes are very light in alcohol and they are refreshing, delicious, and especially suitable for warm-weather patio parties.

Sangría

2 bottles inexpensive red wine
  (claret type or Spanish Rioja)
½ can frozen lemonade concentrate

1 lemon, thinly sliced
1 or 2 ripe peaches, peeled,
  chopped
1 quart club soda

This may be mixed in a pitcher, if you have one large enough; if your pitcher is small, mix one bottle of wine at a time, adding half the remaining ingredients. Combine all ingredients. Stir just until lemonade concentrate is thawed; crush the peaches slightly. *Makes about 20 servings.*

Sherry-Orange Punch

1 6-ounce can frozen orange
  juice concentrate, reconstituted
1 bottle (fifth) dry sherry
1 pint cranberry juice (optional)

2 small navel oranges, thinly
  sliced
1 large bottle club soda

Reconstitute the orange juice with water; beat briefly in blender; add to sherry and cranberry juice. Chill mixture. Place in 3½-quart bowl; garnish with sliced oranges. Add ice and club soda just before serving. *Makes 25 to 30 punch-cup servings.*

SHERRY-ORANGE PITCHER. Reconstitute orange juice; combine only half the sherry and orange juice at a time. Omit cranberry juice. Use a tall pitcher instead of a punch bowl.

WHITE WINE PUNCH. Combine sherry and orange juice as for Sherry-Orange Punch; omit cranberry juice; instead of orange slices, garnish with a spiral of lemon peel; add 1 bottle (fifth) dry white wine. *Makes 36 to 40 servings.*

SHERRY-PINEAPPLE PUNCH. Instead of orange juice, combine sherry with reconstituted frozen pineapple-lemon punch; add 1 46-ounce can apricot nectar and 1 cup brandy. *Makes 36 to 40 servings.*

Fruit Shrub

½ cup lemon juice
1½ cups orange juice
1 cup canned pineapple juice
1 cup syrup from pickled peaches*
¼ teaspoon cinnamon
Sugar to taste

1 bottle (fifth) Cherry Kijafa
  wine
1 bottle (fifth) dry white wine
½ cup brandy or rum (optional)
Lemon and orange slices for garnish

Combine juices, fruit syrup, cinnamon, and sugar; beat in blender to dissolve sugar. Place in large punch bowl with wines, brandy, and lemon and orange slices; let season 1 or 2 hours before serving. Add ice just before serving. (If desired, add 1 12-ounce bottle club soda to extend the punch.) *Makes 24 to 30 punch-cup servings.*

*Or use syrup from canned peaches; add a teaspoon vinegar, a pinch each of cloves and nutmeg, heat until well blended.
†Or use tawny port.

Vermouth Punch in a Pitcher

1 bottle (fifth) dry vermouth
½ bottle rosé wine

1 ounce (2 tablespoons) Curacao
1 large bottle club soda

Combine vermouth, wine, and Curaçao. Fill pitcher half full with mixture; add ice, then soda to fill. Repeat as needed. A very dry, delightfully delicate punch with champagne-like flavor. *Makes about 20 servings.*

VERMOUTH-RASPBERRY PITCHER. Instead of rosé wine, use 2 cups reconstituted frozen raspberry-lemon punch concentrate or the syrup drained from frozen raspberries combined with lemonade to make 2 cups.

Vermouth-Cassis Punch

2/3 cup cassis or currant syrup
1 bottle (fifth) dry vermouth
2 cups brandy

Long spiral of lemon peel
1 12-ounce bottle ginger ale

Use imported cassis syrup or make currant syrup by heating 1/3 cup currant jelly and 1/3 cup water until jelly is dissolved. Combine cassis with vermouth and brandy; chill. Just before serving, pour over ice; add lemon peel and ginger ale. *Makes 20 to 25 servings.*

Holiday Punches and Bowls

Most of these are much stronger than wine punches, and are meant to be so. Some, however, are delicately lighter in alcoholic content, or are nonalcoholic, for the benefit of those for whom alcoholic spirits are not appropriate.

Traditional Holiday Eggnog

12 eggs, separated
½ cup confectioners' sugar
1 pint heavy cream
6 cups milk

1 quart blended whiskey
½ cup dark sweet rum
Ground nutmeg

Place the egg whites in a large bowl; keep at room temperature until shortly before serving. Beat the egg yolks with the sugar until mixture is thick and lemon-colored. Add cream, milk, whiskey, and rum; blend well. Chill. If possible, chill the punch bowl, too (in cold weather, placing it outside may be enough). Shortly before serving time, beat egg whites until stiff; fold in yolk mixture. Transfer to punch bowl; sprinkle with nutmeg. Serve in punch cups. *Makes about 30 servings.*

KENTUCKY EGGNOG. Use only 1 quart milk; use bourbon instead of blended whiskey and 1 pint brandy instead of rum.

Sack Posset

This makes a pleasant evening drink for a small gathering. For children, teenagers, or nonimbibers, use apple juice; for others, sherry.

2 cups milk	½ cup medium sweet sherry or
2 eggs, separated	apple juice
3 tablespoons sugar, or to taste	Grated nutmeg
Grated rind of ½ lemon	

Combine milk, egg yolks, sugar, and lemon rind. Beat until smooth. Add sherry or apple juice. Chill thoroughly. Just before serving, beat egg whites until stiff; fold into yolk mixture. Sprinkle top with nutmeg. *Makes 8 punch-cup servings.*

HOT POSSET. Combine milk, egg yolks, sugar, and lemon rind as above, pour into chafing dish, heavy pan, or casserole. Heat, stirring constantly, until slightly thickened; stir in sherry, light rum, or apple juice; keep over fire another minute, then serve, dusted with nutmeg, in mugs or punch cups.

CAUDLE. This could be called an eggless eggnog: Heat 1 quart milk with 1½ tablespoons brown sugar, ½ teaspoon nutmeg, and ¼ teaspoon powdered cloves or allspice. Do not allow to boil. Add ½ cup sweet sherry or rum; beat with rotary beater until frothy. Serve warm in mugs. *Makes 6 servings.*

Syllabub

1 quart milk	½ cup lemon juice
1 cup cream	2 cups Rhine wine
2 cups sugar, or to taste	½ cup cream sherry
Grated lemon rind	Nutmeg

Combine milk, cream, and sugar; beat with rotary beater until sugar is dissolved. Grate the lemon rind into the milk. Strain lemon juice; add wine and sherry. Place sweetened milk in mixing bowl; beat with electric mixer, slowly adding the lemon-wine mixture, until frothy and thick. Sprinkle nutmeg over top. Chill. Best if made 24 hours before use; keep in refrigerator. *Makes 20 to 24 servings.*

Wassail Bowl

2 cups brown sugar
½ teaspoon ginger
¼ teaspoon nutmeg
½ teaspoon cinnamon
1 cup water

2 bottles medium dry sherry
1 cup cognac or brandy
6 eggs, separated
8 "lady's apples" or crabapples
  stuck with cloves and baked

Combine sugar with spices and water; bring to a boil; stir until sugar is dissolved; add wine and brandy. Beat egg yolks until very thick and light. Separately beat egg whites until stiff. Stick the apples with cloves; sprinkle with sugar; put into medium oven 1 hour before serving. (They must be hot when added to the Wassail Bowl.) Shortly before serving, heat the spiced wine to steaming (do not boil); beat into the egg yolks; fold in egg whites. Take the "lady's apples" or crabapples from the oven; slip "hissing" into the Wassail Bowl. Serve hot, accompanied by snippets of cinnamon toast or fruit cake. *Makes about 20 punch-cup servings.*

Scandinavian Glögg

The traditional holiday drink throughout Scandinavia, this spicy hot wine punch has an aroma as fragrant as mince pie baking and as warming to the "cockles of the heart" as the spirit of Christmas itself. Each Scandinavian home has its favorite glögg recipe, but basically the drink is always a blend of wine, spirits, spices, and fruit. Usually the drink is flamed just before serving. Served with cheese and fruit, this is a merry way to celebrate Christmas Eve.

Peel of 1 orange
12 to 16 whole cloves
4 cardamom pods
2 sticks cinnamon
½ cup raisins

15 blanched almonds
2 bottles red wine (burgundy-
  type)
½ cup sugar
2 cups brandy

Trim the orange peel carefully, removing every bit of white membrane. Cut peel in sections; stick each section with a clove. Place in bowl; add opened cardamom pods, cinnamon, raisins, almonds, and wine. Marinate overnight. Before serving, heat to steaming (do not boil); add sugar; stir to dissolve. Pour into punch bowl; add brandy; do not stir. Just before serving, set brandy aflame. Serve the glögg hot in punch cups or mugs. *Makes 20 servings.*

ANOTHER WAY. Instead of red burgundy, add port wine or Cherry Kijafa wine. To make it go farther, add 1 quart water. A few raisins and almonds are usually placed in each glass.

Junior Glögg

When grown-ups are enjoying alcoholic drinks during the holiday season, this makes an appetizing hot punch for the younger generation.

1 6-ounce can frozen rasp-   ¼ cup sugar
  berry-lemon punch, reconstitut-   ¼ teaspoon cinnamon
  ed, or 4 cups Hawaiian Punch   Pinch of ground cloves
1 6-ounce can frozen lemonade,   4 cardamom pods, opened
  reconstituted   1 orange, sliced
¼ cup raisins   12 whole cloves

Combine raspberry-lemon punch with lemonade, raisins, sugar, cinnamon, ground cloves, and cardamom pods. Heat to steaming. Serve in a 2-quart bowl. Float orange slices stuck with whole cloves in punch for garnish. *Makes 10 servings.*

Hot Spiced Cider

4 cups sweet cider   Pinch of ground cloves
½ teaspoon cinnamon   1/3 cup brown sugar
¼ teaspoon nutmeg

Combine all ingredients; heat to steaming (do not boil). Serve in mugs. *Makes about 10 servings.*

Pendennis Club Punch

1 bottle (fifth) cognac or brandy   1 tablespoon maple-blended
1 cup Curaçao   syrup
Juice of 2 lemons   1 bottle (fifth) champagne
Spiral or orange peel   1 large bottle club soda

Combine first five ingredients; marinate several hours or overnight. Shortly before serving, pour over block of ice in punch bowl. Add champagne and soda as guests are assembled. *Makes about 30 servings.*

Fish House Punch

This famous punch of revolutionary days, said to have originated in a Philadelphia club in 1732, was a favorite drink of both George Washington and General Lafayette.

2 cups brown sugar   1 bottle (fifth) brandy
2 quarts water   ½ bottle Jamaica rum
Peel and juice of 6 lemons   2 tablespoons peach brandy

Heat sugar and water together until sugar is dissolved. Add lemon peel (cut in spirals with all white membrane removed), lemon juice, and remaining ingredients. Marinate several hours or overnight. Strain over a large block of ice about an hour before serving to chill thoroughly. *Makes about 50 servings.*

Plantation Punch

1½ quarts orange juice
1 bottle (fifth) white wine
1 quart bourbon or Canadian Club

1 teaspoon Angostura bitters
2 lemons, sliced
2 large bottles ginger ale

Combine orange juice, wine, whiskey, bitters, and lemon slices; marinate several hours. Pour over ice in punch bowl just before serving; pour in ginger ale. *Makes about 60 punch-cup servings.*

Hot Winter Cups

Honey and Hot Sherry

Place a teaspoon of honey in each mug; add ¼ cup sherry (medium sweet or dry, according to taste). Fill cup with boiling water; dust with nutmeg. Delightful on a blustery, freezing night.

Hot Buttered Rum

Place in each mug a teaspoon of brown sugar blended with a dash of ground cloves and a teaspoon of butter. Add a 1½-ounce jigger of rum to each; fill with boiling water. Offer cinnamon sticks for stirrers.

Steaming Bishop

Stick a navel orange with whole cloves; roast in a medium oven about 30 minutes. Cut orange in quarters; place in a casserole or chafing dish; add 1 bottle red wine (burgundy-type) and 1 or 2 tablespoons maple-blended syrup. Heat at the table, stirring occasionally, just until wine begins to steam. Ladle into cups. (For a more potent drink, ½ cup brandy may be added.)

Glühwein

A favorite drink of skiers; some people consider it the best of all medicines for a cold when drunk steaming-hot just before bedtime.

1 bottle red wine	½ teaspoon cinnamon
¼ cup brown sugar or honey	Spiral of orange peel
8 whole cloves	

Combine all ingredients in large saucepan; bring to a boil; lower heat; simmer 5 minutes. Serve hot in cups or mugs. *Makes 6 to 8 servings.*

Cocktails

What to serve at cocktail parties is given the complete treatment in Book 5. The following cocktails include both classic mixtures and "fun drinks" for those weary of the same old apéritifs.

MANHATTAN. Combine 2 parts bourbon or rye (blended whiskey) with 1 part sweet (Italian) vermouth and a dash of Angostura bitters (optional). Shake with ice. For a Manhattan on the rocks, serve over ice cubes. Traditionally, a maraschino cherry should be added to each glass.

KIJAFA COCKTAIL. Similar in taste to a Manhattan. Combine 2 parts bourbon and 1 part Cherry Kijafa wine; serve over ice. Add bitters or not, as preferred.

ROB ROY. Make like a Manhattan, but with Scotch whiskey.

OLD-FASHIONED. Place a lump of sugar in an old-fashioned glass; add a dash of Angostura bitters, then a 1½-ounce jigger of whiskey (bourbon or rye). Add ice and, if liked, a bit of soda or branch water.

WHISKEY SOUR. Mix together lemonade and whiskey to taste. Or, combine confectioners' sugar and lemon juice to taste; add whiskey and cracked ice; shake. Usually served in whiskey-sour or parfait glasses.

BRANDY SOUR. Made like a Whiskey Sour, but with brandy instead of whiskey.

DRY MARTINI. Gin and dry vermouth in proportions ranging from 3 to 1 all the way up to 7 to 1. Some hardened martini drinkers add a mere drop of vermouth. Shake with ice briefly, or pour over ice in old-fashioned glasses for martini on the rocks.

VODKA MARTINI. Vodka instead of gin, with dry vermouth in whatever proportions liked.

BLOODY MARY. Add vodka to tomato juice; season to taste with salt, pepper, lemon juice, and Worcestershire sauce.

SCREWDRIVER. Add vodka to orange juice.

MARGARITA. These must be served in cocktail glasses. Moisten rims of glasses; dip each in salt; chill thoroughly. Combine 1 jigger tequila with ½ jigger Triple Sec or Cointreau and 1 jigger lime juice; shake well. Fill glasses with cracked ice; add the tequila mixture. The salt on the edge of the glass is what makes it special.

DAIQUIRI. Mix together the juice of ½ lime and 1 teaspoon confectioners' sugar (or use 1 teaspoon frozen daiquiri mix) for each drink. Add 1½ ounces white rum; shake with ice. (The frozen mix is very good; what isn't used can be put back in the freezer until next time. The mix can also be used with tequila to make a Margarita.)

ABOMINABLE SNOWMAN. Combine 4 parts vodka with 1 part crème de menthe (2 jiggers vodka, ½ jigger crème de menthe). Serve over cracked ice.

PLANTER'S PUNCH. For each drink, combine juice of 1 lime, 1 teaspoon sugar, dash of Angostura bitters or grenadine syrup (as preferred), and 3 ounces Jamaican rum. Place ingredients in tall glass; add shaved or cracked ice. Sip through straw.

CUBA LIBRE. Add to each tall glass 1 jigger medium or dark rum; add ice cubes and cola. A slice of lime or lemon is usually placed in each drink.

BEACHCOMBER. Combine 2 parts pineapple juice with 1 part rum (white or dark, as preferred) and a dash of Angostura bitters; serve over crushed ice with a thin twist of orange peel.

FRANGI-PANGI. For each drink combine 1 jigger vodka, 1 jigger pineapple juice, and ½ jigger lime juice; add sugar to taste; shake with ice or pour over cracked ice in cocktail glass.

ANDALUZ. Combine sherry and orange juice in almost any proportions liked. For a tall drink, use mostly orange juice; add a jigger of sherry. For a cocktail, combine equal parts orange juice and sherry; shake with ice or pour over ice cubes. This is sometimes called a Spanish Screwdriver.

ADONIS. Combine 2 parts very dry Spanish sherry with 1 part sweet vermouth; serve over ice.

GOLDEN ROOSTER. In a cocktail shaker combine 2 ounces medium sherry with the juice of half a lemon, a few dashes each Curaçao and Angostura bitters; shake with ice; strain into a cocktail glass.

WINE SPRITZER. Very dry white wine and club soda over ice. A very fine summer drink.

PINK SPRITZER. Rosé wine and club soda over ice.

PAGO-PAGO. For each drink combine 1 tablespoon lime juice, 1 tablespoon Cointreau, a 1 ½-ounce jigger of gold rum. Serve over ice with a pineapple stick for a stirrer.

BOOK FOUR

Guide to Entertaining

Just four ingredients are required for a successful party:

- •The host and hostess must enjoy it themselves.
- •The atmosphere should be easy, relaxed, free of tension.
- •The guests should be selected with as much care and forethought as the food and drink they are to be served; enough mutual interests to keep conversation rolling on its own bearings, with the wits and ebullient talkers balanced by good listeners, and the stiff shy ones balanced by others who have warm, friendly personalities. Always, if possible, bring in someone new, for when dinner-party guests know each other too well and see one another too often, the conversation is likely to drop to the level of petty gossip or dull small talk.
- •The food should be good and attractively served, but need not be pretentious. The hostess who has worn herself out preparing startling, conversation-making dishes may find she is too exhausted when the guests arrive to spark the party into life. If there is a dish at which you particularly excel, don't be apologetic about serving it often. If it's one your guests are not being

served everywhere else they go, they will probably enjoy coming to your house in anticipation of your specialty.

The skilled, experienced cook may be bold enough to serve something brand-new, attempted that day for the first time, and have successful results. For most people, however, it's better to have a dry run first, and try the new dish on the family or very close friends.

Atmosphere counts a lot. Women are prettier by candlelight, a beautifully set table strikes a note of elegance, flowers in vases and stemware that sparkles in the reflection of candle or fireplace flames help to make the food taste better, the occasion more special. A dinner party is more than food alone; above all, it's people, happy to be together, stimulated by sparkling conversation, relaxed as much by the easy hospitality of the host as by any cocktails offered.

Informality is the keynote in all American entertaining today. Even black-tie dinners may be help-yourself buffet affairs with guests taking as many helpings as they like, wandering to the bar to reorder or even to pour their own drinks. Etiquette has been reduced to one simple criterion: make everyone as comfortable as possible.

Not all entertainment need be planned; in fact, the best parties are often those that just happened. Why postpone asking the new neighbors over until you're in a mood to make it a formal invitation? You will be more relaxed, and probably they will be too, if it's a simple weeknight dinner. When you run into an old friend in the supermarket, why not suggest she come home with you for a pot-luck lunch? Children are always delighted if they can invite their friends to stay to supper; why not make them proud to be part of a hospitable family—and what better way is there to become acquainted with their companions?

Modern Rules of Etiquette

Invitations. The way an invitation is issued should serve as a clue to the type of party to expect.

Obviously, a simple telephone call or an invitation extended across the back fence is enough for an unplanned party. But even an invitation of this kind should be specific regarding hours, and it should contain a clue about dress.

"Come on over about six-thirty," the hostess may say, when inviting neighbors to a patio supper. It will be thoughtful of her to add, "Don't dress up—John will probably be in a sports shirt, and I intend to wear something cool and comfortable in this hot weather."

Or suppose, despite its being a last-minute invitation, the guests are likely to appear dressed up. Then the invitation should subtly suggest this. "This is strictly a spontaneous party," the hostess might explain—but she's used the word "party," which implies dressing up, and she might add, "There are some other very interesting people coming I think you'll enjoy meeting."

Invitations for any *small* gathering may be issued by telephone, even if the party is to be two or three weeks hence. In fact, telephone invitations have the great advantage of determining the guest list quickly. That careful list you have composed, of people with similar interests but different geographical backgrounds, could be thrown completely awry if one very charming person is unable to make it, and you may need to find another equally ebullient guest to spark the gathering.

Always issue telephone invitations tactfully; don't make it a broadside. Start out, "We're having a small dinner party a week from Friday and I wonder if you and your husband could join us?" *Don't* ask bluntly, "What are you doing a week from Friday?" The answer might be embarrassing for both of you. *Be specific about the time.* Americans today tend to be much too casual about arriving an hour or more after the stated dinner hour. It's wise to warn, "We plan to eat at seven-thirty," so the guests will not show up at eight o'clock thinking they are missing only the first of two rounds of cocktails. Or, if they do show up at eight, when you have told them dinner will be at seven-thirty, don't be embarrassed about serving dinner the moment they arrive.

If those you have invited by telephone are coming to your home for the first time, it is courteous to send a follow-up note with specific directions as to how to get there (a map is wise if it's a suburban area and the guests will be driving), and an idea of how long it may take. Also, be sure your telephone number is at the bottom of the note, in case they get lost en route (your directions may not be as clear as you thought).

Written invitations may be formal or informal, and they, too, should provide clues to the nature of the affair. For a big cocktail party or open house, for example, gay commercial "It's a Party" notes may be sent, with the name, address, date (day and month), hours (from when to when) and type of party (such as "for cocktails") filled in on the appropriate lines. Written replies to a cocktail party are not obligatory unless the host has written RSVP on the bottom, but it's courteous nevertheless to mail or phone a reply. Every host likes to have some idea of how many people to expect.

For a formal (black-tie) dinner party, the invitations may be printed or engraved especially for the affair, but today most people write out the invitations in longhand, using the note paper known as "informals." (An indication of how real formality has now all but disappeared.) Such an invitation might read:

Mr. and Mrs. John Smith
request the honor of your company
at dinner, March 10th, 8 P. M.

Black Tie   *18 Sunnybrook Lane*
RSVP   *Westhaven*
Tel.: 330-4649

This tells the ladies receiving the invitation that they are expected to wear dinner dresses to offset their husbands' or escorts' tuxedos. It also warns them that this is going to be a very elegant affair. The reply should be sent by note, but need not be in such formal language. You may write merely, "We'd love to come! Mary and Ed Golden."

Showers, big teas, and semiformal buffet suppers all rate written invitations, and happily greeting-card companies now have special cards for each such affair, which means all you have to do is fill in the blank spaces and write names and addresses on the envelope. An invitation to tea does not require a reply, unless it says so. However, a reply is in order for a buffet supper invitation, and while a reply is not obligatory for a shower, the hostess would certainly like to know.

Arriving on Time. A polite guest times his arrival about fifteen minutes after the hour given by invitation. (If you arrive exactly on time or a little early, you may find the hostess worriedly trying to get her false eyelashes in place or her back zipper pulled up.) To arrive half an hour late is forgivable; to be later than that is putting a strain on the hosts. To show up as much as an hour late is downright rude. If the delay is unavoidable, at least try to let your hosts know what has happened. Phone to explain that the baby sitter has been delayed, or the train broke down, or there was a big traffic jam—or whatever.

Introductions. Even the manner of introducing guests to one another has become less formal. It is quite acceptable to use both first and last names in making introductions, *provided* the guests are more or less of the same age, and are Americans. "Mrs. Crawford—Isabel, I'd like you to meet the Cherniks, Joe and Mary. And this is *Mister* Crawford over here—Fred . . ." However, this abrupt use of first names among strangers shocks many foreign visitors, and displeases some older Americans, especially those of more conventional leanings. In case of doubt, use only the surnames, and find a way of mentioning first names later in the evening, in casual conversation.

An older woman always receives deference. "Mrs. Jones, I would like you to meet my friend Martha Lorenzo," if Martha is obviously much younger. If they are of more or less the same age, or same generation, it would be, "Mrs. Jones, this is Mrs. Lorenzo." Guests, male and female, are introduced to an older woman first; in fact, whatever the age of a woman, men are brought to her, not the other way around.

Because few people remember names when introduced, especially when a lot of new names and faces come all at once, it's thoughtful to establish identities in other ways, to offer a capsule of information which serves both as a conversational gambit and a "place-the-stranger tag."

"Mrs. Jones, may I introduce Mr. Trent. Mr. Trent has just been transferred here from Pittsburgh, and his is such interesting work . . ." Mr. Trent, in turn, is told, "Perhaps you noticed a lovely old colonial house on the corner as you were turning up our street? That's where Mrs. Jones lives, and you should see her *wonderful* collection of antiques!" Even if Mr. Trent abhors antiques, this gives him a clue as to Mrs. Jones's interests.

In today's mobile society, when American business executives and their families are shifted from city to city and country to country every two or three years, acquaintanceship must be telescoped from weeks into minutes, and a social gathering in your home will be far more successful if you help your guests to establish mutual interests as quickly as possible. They will enjoy the food you have prepared far more, too, if they are having a good time, finding acquaintances who offer promise of turning into new friends.

Seating Arrangements. Whenever guests are expected to eat from plates with forks or spoons, you should plan for seats enough and table space enough to make eating comfortable.

Collapsible TV tables, plus cocktail and end tables, are a help. Count the number of guests, tote up the table space, and make sure each person will have a place for putting down a glass while taking up a plate, or vice versa.

If you haven't enough tables or chairs, consider renting them for the evening. The same rental firms can supply punch bowls, glassware, portable bars, coat racks, table linens, dishes, and tableware.

A sit-down dinner, brunch, or lunch not only requires a chair for each guest and sufficient table space to avoid bumping elbows, but serious thought must be given to who shall sit next to whom. Work this out in advance; to help yourself remember, it might be a good idea to draw up a crude chart. Avoid putting husbands and wives next to one another. The most important male guest is seated to the right of the hostess; the most important female guest to the right of the host.

Suppose you have more females than males? Scatter the males among the females as well as you can, be very careful that those ladies seated beside one another, without a man between them, at least have an interesting man on one or the other side, or directly across the table.

It helps if, among the preponderance of women, the "extras" are pretty, attractively dressed, or exceptionally good listeners. The trend toward "unisex" in dress, business competition, and morals has not altered in the least the fact that men consider the most brilliant of all women to be those who listen most attentively.

Having more males than females is a problem few hostesses have to worry about. Should it occur, it offers a good opportunity to ring up one of the divorcees or unmarried business women in your acquaintance and ask them to help you out. Most will jump at the chance.

Even when it's an all-female or all-male gathering, table placement must be considered with an eye to compatibility. The most important guest is always placed to the right of the host or hostess; those who have mutual interests should be close enough to talk together without having to raise their voices above the conversation of others.

How many to invite for a sit-down dinner? Four at table is difficult; when you must get up to change plates or bring on the dessert course, it leaves too few for good conversation—unless it's a spontaneous invitation issued to friends who know one another very well.

Six or eight at table is optimum. When you don't have men enough to balance the table, make it a minimum of six (with at least two men), a maximum of nine. Some men don't mind at all being outnumbered, especially if the extra women are attractive. Their wives might, of course, be uncomfortable, especially if they aren't too sure of their husbands. Determining these personality factors is the ultimate test of a clever hostess.

How do you have a sit-down party of more than eight, when you have only an ordinary dining table in a small dining room?

Rental services could be one answer. Rent enough card tables and chairs to take care of the extras. Have eight at table in the dining room, one or two tables (of four each) in the living room. This makes it possible to have twelve to twenty dinner guests. Rent out matching dinner cloths for the card tables if necessary, and if you don't have enough of your own, order extra dishes and glassware, too. It's wise to have outside domestic help for a dinner of this dimension, so that after the card tables have been cleared, they may be folded up and taken away.

Table Settings: General Rules

Put only those pieces of silverware on the table that will be needed for your meal. This applies whether it's being served buffet style or at table.

For individual table settings, forks always go on the left, knives and spoons on the right. This is a heritage from European custom, for in Europe the fork is always held in the left hand, and there's no switching from left to right hand. The order is determined by which utensil is used first. A soup spoon, for example, is always placed on the far right, even though it's the largest of the spoons at the place setting. If there are two forks, a smaller one for pastry, the smaller one goes next to the plate, because it is used last.

Knives go directly to the right of the plate, even though a butter knife might be picked up before the soup spoon (an exception to the rule).

Napkins are placed to the left of the fork, and may be folded in any way you like. There's no hard and fast rule in this regard. In modern American society, paper napkins are considered suitable for any dinner, even dress-up affairs, especially since some of today's paper napkins are of such fine quality that they feel almost like cloth.

For a buffet setting, the same logic applies: napkins first, forks next, then knives if needed (usually they are not), and finally spoons. Plates come after this. Foods are placed on the buffet in the order in which they would logically be eaten—that is, hors d'oeuvres at one end of the table (the one where guests start), entree and salads at the other end. It's best if the table is pulled out into the center of the room, so that guests may circulate all around it; then coffee cups and glassware may be placed following the salad. Otherwise, these should be placed on a separate table, the one on which the dessert will also be served.

Advance Preparation

It's a golden rule in home entertaining today that everything possible should be prepared in advance. Some super-efficient hostesses with big home freezers even cook all the food a week ahead and store it in the freezer so that it need only be taken from freezer to oven on the day of the party.

Certainly the food and all other supplies should be purchased as far in advance as possible—everything but the fresh vegetables and salad greens, but even these can be bought a day ahead.

First plan the menu, then draw up a complete shopping list. Check all supplies on hand, down to the salt and pepper. Then make a step-by-step timetable of preparation. Study recipes with an eye as to which ones can be prepared hours or even days in advance, and which must be put together within a short time of serving. An hour or so spent this way in the beginning will save many hours of vexation later.

PLANNING THE MENU

Instant Hospitality

Plan for unplanned parties by keeping appropriate emergency foods among your pantry supplies and in the freezer.

For cocktail appetizers, besides the usual crackers and chips, olives and pickles, there are canned herrings in cream, sardines, liver pâté, whole beets (to be served with sour cream as a dip), salted nuts in sealed cans, and all sorts of cheese spreads. Cold cuts in sealed packets will keep for a long time in the refrigerator, ready to wrap around pickles or artichokes (also in cans) for instant hors d'oeuvres.

A quick casserole can be thrown together from leftover meats combined with canned soups (for sauces), frozen vegetables and canned mushrooms, the mixture artfully seasoned with herbs, spices, and a little wine or brandy and topped with crumbs and cheese.

Menus for Instant Hospitality

Spaghetti Dinner
Smoked oysters
Radishes, green olives
Spaghetti Bolognese
(use frozen chopped meat,
canned tomato sauce, instant
onion)
Salad
Brandied canned peaches

Noodle Casserole Dinner
Avocado appetizer
Sharp Cheddar, crackers
Tuna Casserole
(canned tuna, noodle dinner
mix, diced pimiento, pitted
black olives)
Broccoli (frozen)
Beets (canned)
Chocolate éclairs (frozen)

Omelet Dinner
Spanish Tortilla
(with potatoes and onions)
Artichoke hearts (frozen)
cooked in oil
Orange-onion salad
Instant chocolate pudding

After-Theatre Supper
Frozen blintzes with sour cream
Cappuccino coffee

Pancake Supper
Pancakes with sausages, and
Broiled Peaches (canned)
Ice cream with chopped
peanut topping

Quick Company Lunch
Instant Antipasto (pickled beets,
salami, sardines, lettuce)
Crabmeat Bisque
(canned crabmeat, cream of
celery soup)
Corn-in-butter (frozen)
Frenched green beans (frozen)
Compote of canned fruit

Unexpected Reunion
Corned beef hash (canned)
topped with fried eggs
Mexican corn (canned)
Italian beans (frozen)
Coffee ice cream with Tia Maria
liqueur

Drop-in Saturday Supper
Shrimp Spanish Rice
(precooked rice, chopped
pimiento, canned shrimp,
chopped ham)
Double Bean Salad
Canned apricots with crème
de menthe

Additional "unplanned" menus could be built around the following as entrees.

Last-Minute Casseroles

Chicken Hekka (using leftover turkey or
canned chicken)
Chinese Fried Rice (use packaged precooked rice plus any leftovers in the
refrigerator)
Chinese Pork with Eggs

Creamed Eggs in Cheese Sauce (or
   Creamed Ham and Eggs, or Tuna and
   Eggs)
Easy Cheese Soufflé
Ham and Artichokes Madeira
Quick Chicken and Ham Tetrazzini
Quick Bean Bake
Quick Macaroni Lunch
Pastel de Choclo
Tamale Pie

Quick Meat Dishes

Chinese Pepper Steak
Economy Beef Kabobs
Ham Steak à l'Orange
Hamburgers (see Hamburgers 52 Ways)
Hungarian Meatballs
Luncheon Meat Picadillo
Minute Steaks Amontillado
Pork Chops in Cream
Roast Beef Hash (make it with any left-
   over cooked beef)
Scallopini
Steak Diane
Steak Strips Teriyaki

Spur-of-the-Moment Desserts

Ice cream, topped with canned peaches,
   sugared fresh fruit, jam, chopped nuts,
   chocolate sauce, or any liqueur

Fruit bowl

Assorted cheese and crackers

Compote of mixed canned fruit laced with
   brandy, or topped with shredded coconut

Melon, plain, or each serving topped with
   a scoop of ice cream or sherbet (vanilla
   ice cream for cantaloupe, lemon or
   pineapple sherbet for honeydew)

Frozen cake or eclairs (stored in the freezer for emergencies)

Brunch, Lunch for the Ladies, or Showers

All these are planned parties, but in each case the food offered should be light, a bit frivolous, easy to prepare ahead and
serve without outside help.

"Ladies' food" is different from that offered to mixed company. Ironically, while most women these days are very conscious of their figures, what they most want to be served is foods bathed in rich cream or butter sauces followed by desserts lavish with cream, chocolate, or nuts (or all three). Which should one cater to—their expressed or their suppressed desires?

Even if low-calorie, high-protein foods are served, they should be presented beautifully. Sauces may be passed separately, so those who have the courage of their convictions may forgo them if they wish. Salads, aspics, and ramekins, or casseroles containing chopped foods in a creamy sauce, are certain to please. Mixtures served in patty shells always delight female guests, as do rich, gooey pastries artfully garnished.

If brunch is served to mixed company, it's probably wise to include meat in some form in the menu, making it heartier and less frivolous fare.

BRUNCH MENUS

1

Broiled Grapefruit Halves
Shrimp Curry   Rice   Cheese Biscuits
Caffè Romano

Advance Preparation. Curry can be prepared the day before and reheated in a casserole shortly before serving. Cheese should be grated for the biscuits, and added to biscuit mix shortly beforehand.

2

Strawberries in Orange Juice
Scrambled Eggs and Avocado   Grilled Chicken Livers
Toasted English Muffins, black currant jam
Café au Lait

3

Honeydew with Lime

Ham and Eggs sur le Plat
Pineapple Corn Muffins
Viennese Coffee

LADIES' LUNCHEON OR BRIDGE LUNCHEON MENUS

1

Chicken Orientale
(use chicken breasts)
Parsley Rice   radishes, black olives, celery
Buttered Parker House rolls

Chocolate Cherry Chiffon Pie
Tea or Coffee

Advance Preparation. The pie can be baked the preceding
day. The chicken can be prepared in the morning, placed in the
oven in a casserole, kept warm until lunchtime at very low heat.
The rice, too, can be prepared ahead and kept in the oven, in a
covered casserole, until lunch time. Heat rolls in the same oven
shortly before serving.

2

Tomato Bisque (hot, in cups)
Florida Shrimp and Potato Salad
Toasted Garlic Bread
Peach Cheese Tarts
Coffee

Advance Preparation. Prepare both the salad and the tarts the day before. The bread should be brushed with melted garlic butter shortly before guests are due, and placed in foil to be heated in the oven at the last moment. The Tomato Bisque can be prepared quickly on the morning of the luncheon, heated in a saucepan, poured into cups at serving time.

3

Gorgonzola Balls
Pineapple in Prosciutto
(served in living room before lunch)
Shrimp-stuffed Crepes
Orange Nut Compote
Coffee

Advance Preparation. The day before, the dessert and appetizers can both be prepared, kept in refrigerator until time to serve. The crepes can be prepared, too, placed in a casserole, to be reheated and the top glazed under the broiler shortly before serving.

A *shower* usually calls for a decorated cake to be cut ceremoniously, fruit punch (it may be a wine punch if the guests are known to prefer alcoholic drinks), cookies, and dainty "tea sandwiches." Instead of a decorated cake, an imaginative centerpiece may grace the tea table, with favors strung from the centerpiece. If the cake is prepared by the hostess, tiny "fortunes" may be buried in the batter: miniature pieces from a game, such as a tiny shoe (the recipient will be traveling far), a hammer (something is about to break), or a fake gold coin (money in the future).

Teas, large or small, start with similar foods: cake, cookies, small sandwiches. The spread may also include small cream puffs, or Cheese Profiteroles.

Serving tea to a large group. It is considered a mark of honor to be asked to assist at a tea, especially to pour the tea or coffee. All foods should be easy to eat with fingers; spoons should be needed only for stirring coffee or tea.

Set the table so that traffic keeps moving. Assistant hostesses, if it's a large gathering, may pass cookies, sandwiches, or slices of cake to guests later.

Small Dinner Parties

This is the nicest of all ways to entertain. In a small group the hosts have more of an opportunity to mingle in the conversation, and if the menu is well planned, there are fewer things to worry about.

Appetizers served in the living room may be the first course. If soup is the first course, serve a clear soup in cups, and bring these to the living room. Once the company is seated at table, it is awkward for the hostess to get up to clear dishes. If she does so, invariably one of the guests will offer to help, and the relaxed atmosphere immediately becomes disturbed.

Avoid clearing the table by having only one course, or remove dishes from the main course to a tray table or sideboard, then transfer dessert from the sideboard to the dinner table. This keeps the hostess near her guests and makes it all seem so easy that they need not be conscience-ridden about not helping her.

Because of the increasing awareness of obesity, many quite chic people now dispense with a dessert altogether, merely serving coffee and liqueurs in the living room after the main course is finished. A cheese tray may also be brought into the living room, or fruit that can be eaten easily and daintily with fingers (frosted grapes, strawberries arranged around a center of confectioners' sugar, tangerines, or seedless oranges already separated into segments).

Or, offer bonbons or chocolates for those who feel a meal is not complete without something sweet at the end.

It is quite proper to serve even a small number of guests buffet style, if your dining table will not seat them all comfortably. Or, you may put all the food on a buffet and let people help themselves, then come to the table.

The most gracious way, whenever possible, is to have everyone seated at the table, and for the host or hostess to serve main-course foods from serving dishes or platters.

The preceding suggestions are made with the assumption that there will not be any domestic help either before or during the party. Some people prefer to hire outside help for the evening, even for a small dinner party. If the same woman comes repeatedly, and she is therefore familiar with your kitchen and your way of doing things, this may be worthwhile. She can then pass the serving dishes. Outside help is not really necessary, however, if the dinner is carefully planned so that everything is under control from start to finish, and if there is a dishwasher into which most if not all the dishes can be piled the moment the guests leave.

DINNER MENUS FOR 4 TO 6

1

Pickled Mushrooms   Radishes   Shrimp with Guacamole
Tournedos à la Gredos
Cauliflower and carrots   Caesar Salad
Hot rolls
Red wine (full-bodied)
Biscuit Tortoni
Coffee

Advance Preparation. *Day ahead*, prepare pickled mushrooms, cook the shrimp, freeze the Biscuit Tortoni. *Few hours beforehand*, wash, trim, and freshen radishes in salted ice water, then chill, tightly covered, in the refrigerator. Prepare Guacamole; keep covered until time to serve. Cut up carrots and cauliflower, place in saucepan to be cooked at last moment (5 minutes' cooking is enough). Prepare the tournedos so that they are ready to be broiled when guests are having appetizers.

Have all salad ingredients ready to toss together. *During last hour*, put out hors d'oeuvres. Set table, pull everything together. Vegetables will be cooked and tournedos broiled as guests enjoy cocktails in living room.

2

Roquefort-stuffed celery
Taramasalata
Avocado Balls
Chicken and Lobster Costa Brava
Rice   Green Peas
Lettuce and onion salad
Chilled white wine

Linzer Torte or Cherry Pie

Advance preparation. *Day ahead*, bake the torte or the pie. Prepare the taramasalata. *Morning of dinner* (or evening before), prepare Chicken and Lobster Costa Brava, to be reheated. Stuff celery, roll avocado balls in parsley; keep both tightly covered with plastic in refrigerator. Have rice and peas in saucepans ready to cook. *Afternoon*, pull the menu together, get serving dishes ready. Wash salad greens and tear in pieces, place in vegetable crisper to chill. Reheat entree and cook rice and peas shortly before guests are due.

DINNER MENUS FOR 8 OR 9

1

Louisiana Crab Canapés (hot)
Cherry tomatoes   Black olives

Königsberger Klopse
Saltzkartoffeln   Spinach
Winter Salad
Moselle or Rhine wine
Pound Cake with Hot Lemon Brandy Sauce

Advance Preparation. *Morning of dinner*, prepare the meatballs for Königsberger Klopse, doubling the recipe given in this book, and cook in broth. (Sauce will be prepared shortly before guests are due.) Prepare crab canapes, getting ready to place under broiler. Prepare salad; chill in refrigerator. *Afternoon.* Pare potatoes (Saltzkartoffeln), cook; transfer to casserole to reheat in oven later. Wash spinach, have ready to cook. Make sauce for the pound cake (which could come from store or bakery). Complete making sauce for Königsberger Klopse.

2
Bagne Caude with assorted crisp relishes
Poularde Portugaise
Rice   Salad Valenciana
Light red wine
Rum Chiffon Pie

Advance Preparation. *Day ahead*, make the pie. Keep in refrigerator until time to serve. *Morning of dinner*, prepare the chicken (Poularde Portugaise), place in casserole to be reheated. Wash and trim vegetable relishes for the appetizer course, chill these in vegetable crisper. *Afternoon*, cut up orange and onion for salad, marinate in dressing. Wash and chill lettuce for salad. Prepare the Bagne Caude. Put rice in saucepan, ready to be cooked. *Shortly before guests are due*, reheat chicken in oven, cook rice, put cooked rice in covered casserole to be kept warm in oven. Complete salad, put in salad bowl. Take pie from refrigerator.

3
Brie or Camembert with crackers
Radishes
Deviled crab balls (frozen, reheated;
serve with curry mayonnaise as dip)
Bouillabaisse
Tossed salad
Chilled white wine (Chablis type)
Lemon Sponge Custard

Advance Preparation. Prepare the dessert; chill it. Prepare the court-bouillon for the Bouillabaisse, have all fish ingredients ready, but do not cook the fish until after guests have arrived. While they are enjoying cocktails and appetizers, finish the Bouillabaisse.

Larger Dinners or Buffets

All the following could be sit-down dinners, or could be served buffet style. Each is a "serious" menu, and if served buffet, make doubly sure that seating and eating arrangements will be comfortable. Even if tables are set, the food may be served from a buffet help-yourself fashion, then guests take their plates to the tables, searching for place cards to learn where each person is to sit.

DINNER MENUS FOR 10 TO 16

Before preparing any recipes suggested in the following menus, check yields, multiply ingredients according to number of persons to be served. Be sure to write out revised recipes before you begin.

1

Artichoke hearts in smoked salmon
Black olives
Crab-Almond Pâté
Boned Roast Leg of Lamb al Vino
Oven-browned or rissole potatoes
Egg and Green Bean Salad
Red wine (full-bodied)
Baba au Rhum

Advance Preparation. *Day ahead*, prepare the Baba, also the Crab-Almond Pâté. Cook eggs for the salad. *Morning of dinner*, marinate the boned rolled leg of lamb. Make broth with the bones for the gravy. Marinate beans, eggs, and onion for the salad in salad dressing. Wash and chill salad greens so they will be ready to add to marinated beans. Prepare salmon-artichoke heart roll-ups; put these and olives in serving dishes. *Afternoon*, put meat in oven, if you have an oven clock set it to go on so that meat will finish cooking after guests have arrived. Peel potatoes; partially cook, drain. Brush with melted fat or oil and place in pan in oven. See that all foods to be served cold are ready. Pull menu together.

2

Toasted spiced almonds
Sherried Black Olives
Frango al Caril
Assorted curry condiments
Rice
Tossed green salad
Chilled white wine

Flan (individual caramel custards)

Advance Preparation. *At least one day ahead* (or longer), prepare the chicken. (It may be frozen and reheated.) *Day ahead*, toast almonds, marinate olives in sherry. *Morning of dinner*, bake the custards, chill. Prepare salad ingredients; chill. Prepare rice, place in covered casserole to be baked in oven at same time as curry is reheated. *Afternoon*, set out all condiments.

3

Potted Ham   Caponatina
Spicy Cheese Dreams
Ragout of Beef Manhattan
Baked Potatoes   Double Bean Salad
Red wine

Chocolate Bavarian

Advance Preparation. *Day ahead*, prepare the Ragout (or this can be prepared several days ahead, frozen to be reheated). Prepare Potted Ham and Caponatina; chill both. Cook beans for salad. Prepare the Chocolate Bavarian. *Afternoon of dinner*, fix Cheese Dreams ready to place under broiler. Scrub potatoes, place in oven. Assemble ingredients for salad, marinate everything but lettuce. Put Ragout in casserole to reheat in oven. Unmold the Bavarian, return to refrigerator.

Buffet Suppers

The following menus are planned especially to be served buffet style. All the foods should be easy to eat, in small pieces, requiring no knife for cutting. Appetizers should be the finger type. Dessert, too, must be easy to eat. Cookies or cake are best; if ice cream is to be served it should be quite firm, not topped with a sauce, which might dribble.

1

Sardine Hors d'Oeuvre
Picante de Huevos
Dilled carrots
Spaghetti Ham Casserole
Salade Niçoise
Chianti
Ice Cream Charlotte

Advance Preparation. *Day ahead*, prepare the casserole or casseroles, tripling the recipe given in this book. Prepare all the hors d'oeuvres. Prepare the Ice Cream Charlotte and return to freezer. *Afternoon of supper*, put casseroles in oven, set timer (if your stove has an oven clock) to go on shortly before guests are due. Prepare salad, ready to assemble at last moment. Set out appetizers and drinks. (Do not remove Charlotte from freezer until first course is being served.)

2

Shrimp Vinagreta, Yogurt Dip, Corn Chips
Pellão of Pork Indienne,
Avocado and Orange Salad
Chilled white wine or beer
Rum Chocolate Cake

Advance Preparation. Bake the cake several days ahead. *A day ahead*, cook the shrimp, marinate in the sauce. *Morning of dinner*, prepare the Pellão (cook now to be reheated later). Marinate avocado slices and orange segments in salad dressing, so that only lettuce need be added at last moment.

Cocktail Parties

A cocktail party is a before-dinner affair which should end by nine o'clock at the latest. If the hosts want the guests to remain all evening, the affair should be referred to in the invitation as a "cocktail supper" or "cocktail buffet" and foods should be served which are hearty enough for a meal.

Even when the party ends before nine, it is nice to have a few close friends remain for pot-luck supper, friends who won't mind helping to clean up the mess. There should be food in the freezer or refrigerator ready to heat up for such an impromptu meal.

Planning how much and what to serve in the way of drinks (since this is the main business of a cocktail party) is discussed in Book V. The foods for the most part are intended to stimulate thirst, not to satisfy appetites, but if the appetizers as a whole are too rich, the overall effect on the livers of the guests will be just as bad as from too much alcohol. This means a well-balanced cocktail menu: some crisp unadorned foods—the vegetable relishes, for example—to balance the cream dips and cheeses, some hot appetizers to balance all the cold dainties, and at least one substantial food to provide ballast, such as baked ham or roast turkey or meatballs.

If it's a "cocktail supper," the table setting should be much like that of a buffet, but with more emphasis on finger foods, less on casseroles. Sweets should never be offered, not even for a "cocktail supper." Coffee, however, should be prepared as that "one drink for the road."

To keep traffic moving, so that no guests get stuck in a corner without knowing how to extricate themselves, *place foods on several different tables*. This provides a good excuse for guests to get out of a corner, or to gain an introduction to an interesting-looking person on the other side of the room.

Tableware, napkins, and dishes should all be placed on the main table or buffet, along with the main dishes. Foods on other tables should be finger foods, or dips or spreads with crackers.

COCKTAILS FOR 5 TO 7

Russian Chicken Salad Pumpernickel Bread
Parsleyed Avocado Balls Cherry Tomatoes
Grilled Sherried Shrimp (hot)
Salami-Pimiento Roll-ups
Assorted cheeses, crackers

Advance Preparation. *Day ahead*, prepare chicken salad; marinate the shelled shrimp so that they are ready to place under the broiler. *Morning of party*, prepare avocado balls and salami roll-ups. Put out cheese and crackers on cheese board.

SUBURBAN COCKTAILS FOR 6 TO 9

Meatballs Manhattan (hot)
Curried Tuna Pate Cheese-stuffed Ham Roll-ups
Spiced Almonds Herring Salad
Stuffed Eggs with Caviar Hot Dogs in Blankets

Advance Preparation. *Day ahead*, cook meatballs, marinate in sauce overnight. Also prepare Tuna Pâté, Herring Salad, and the Stuffed Eggs. Cover with plastic wrap, store in refrigerator. Roll out pastry for hot dogs (cocktail franks), roll up, ready to bake. *Day of party*, put hot dogs on baking sheet ready for the oven (bake them after guests have arrived). Reheat meatballs, keep warm in chafing dish or casserole.

COCKTAIL BUFFET
Liptauer Cheese Cone, crackers
Oyster-stuffed Cherry Tomatoes   Celery Stuffed with Egg Salad
Cazuela Americana
Vegetable Salad Platter   Garlic Bread

Advance Preparation. *Day ahead,* or morning of party, make up the Cazuela Americana, to be reheated when guests have arrived. Cook the vegetables for the vegetable platter; marinate separately in salad dressing. Prepare Liptauer Cheese Cone. *Day of party,* stuff celery and tomatoes. Brush bread with melted garlic butter, wrap in foil ready to heat in oven.

Semiformal Buffets

These are very elegant, dress-up affairs. For all but the super-efficient hostess, it is wise to have outside help for serving the meal and for cleaning up afterward. Platters of hors d'oeuvres should be passed to the guests as they are having cocktails, and when they have progressed to the entree, a waitress should circulate among them to ask if seconds are wanted, carrying serving dishes on a tray. However, as at all cocktail parties and buffet suppers, guests should be encouraged to help themselves to both food and drink.

HOLIDAY BUFFET DINNER
Molded Shrimp Pâté
Cocktail Sausages in Bourbon (hot)
Cantaloupe with Cheese Dip   Pimiento-Anchovy Canapes
Boned Stuffed Turkey (hot)
Tomato Rice   Molded Perfection Salad
Chilled white or rosé wine
Bourbon Pecan Cake
Coffee   Brandy

Advance Preparation. *Several days ahead*, bake the cake, soak with bourbon. *Day ahead*, stuff the boned turkey, ready for the oven. Prepare Shrimp Pâté; chill. Prepare Perfection Salad, chill. *Day of party*, unmold the pâté and the salad on platters; keep in refrigerator until time to serve. Prepare cantaloupe and dip. Precook sausages, to be reheated in bourbon. Prepare Pimiento-Anchovy Canapes. *Afternoon*, place turkey in oven. Set tables. Pull menu together. Prepare rice to be baked, covered, in oven at same time as turkey (or if there is not space in oven, cook on top of stove in casserole with cover).

RIJSTAFFEL
The true Indonesian Rijstaffel may consist of thirty different dishes, all very highly spiced and served with perhaps thirty different spicy relishes. The following menu is adapted to American realities. Some of the dishes are frankly American with Oriental flavoring. Others come not from Indonesia but from other parts of Southeast Asia. But there are also some Indonesian dishes (the Satay, the Nasi Goreng, and the Indonesian Chicken and Pork Casserole).

Tables should be set with exotic flowers, exotic rum drinks might be served before dinner.

Hot Cocktail Franks with Red Hot Indonesian Dip
Chow-Chow Pickles   Oriental Stuffed Mushrooms
Abalone (canned) in Soy Sherry Sauce
Rumaki (hot)
Beef Satay   Indonesian Chicken and Pork Casserole
Nasi Goreng
Curried Green Beans   Saffron Rice with raw onion rings
Assorted chutneys and condiments
Coffee   Liqueurs

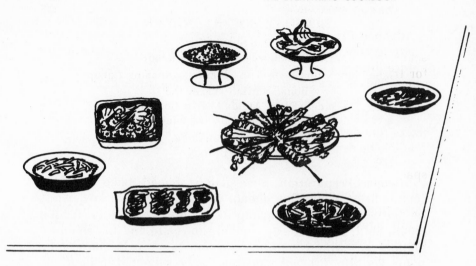

Advance Preparation. The cookies, pickles, and chutneys may be prepared several days ahead. *Day ahead,* prepare the ingredients for the various casseroles and entrees, cutting them up; marinate the beef in its sauce so that it will be ready for the broiler. Also, prepare the sauces, the stuffed mushrooms, and put together the Rumaki ready for the broiler. *Day of party,* complete preparation of the Chicken and Pork Casserole; have the Nasi Goreng ready, either completely cooked to be reheated, or all ingredients lined up ready to be combined in the skillet. This is a big enterprise and requires careful organization.

The best beverages to be served with such a meal are beer and white wine (not too dry). Both should be well chilled. Offer guests a choice.

CHINESE DINNER
Chinese Hot Pot
Shrimp Toasts   Egg Rolls
Pineapple Chunks Rolled in Coconut

Moo Goo Gai Pan
Sweet and Pungent Pork   Chicago Chop Suey
Chinese Pepper Steak   Bacon, Pepper, and Shrimp Fried Rice
Rice

Tea
Fortune cookies (purchased)

Advance Preparation. All ingredients should be prepared, ready to cook, but actual cooking must be done in last hours before dinner. Obviously, this is more than one person can do alone. This is an excellent menu for a cooperative dinner; each of the entrees can be brought by a different person, leaving the hostess with responsibility for only the Hot Pot and other appetizers (the egg rolls could be purchased already made, frozen, ready to be reheated).

SMORGASBORD

This is a complete meal, with everything from appetizers to dessert, and traditionally guests return to the buffet again and again to take as much as they like of everything. The following is a very ambitious menu; many of the dishes could be eliminated for a more simple spread. Serve cocktails with appetizers, red wine or Tuborg beer with the meal. Or the beverage might be Glögg, if the meal is served during the holiday season.

Hot Codfish Balls   Herring Salad with Apples
Smoked Salmon   Sardines   Anchovy-Egg Canapes
Sültze   Assorted Cheeses   Pickled Beets
Limpa (Swedish rye)   Rye-Krisps
Assorted wafers
Swedish Meatballs (hot)   Macaroni and Cheese (hot)
Danish Rum Pudding, Red Fruit Sauce
Coffee   Swedish Punch

Advance Preparation. *Several days ahead,* prepare the Sültze, the Danish Rum Pudding, and the Herring Salad. Keep all refrigerated. *Day ahead,* bake the bread (if homemade), prepare Codfish Balls ready to fry. *Day of party,* prepare meatballs and the macaroni and cheese; place both in oven to keep warm (250° F.) until after guests arrive, then place over candle warmers or hot trays on buffet. The salmon, sardines, pickled beets, and even the anchovy-egg canapes require little more attention than opening cans and arranging the foods attractively on platters.

Holiday Open House

This may be like a cocktail party, but with eggnog and/or Glögg instead of cocktails, and as many sandwiches and appetizers as cookies or cakes. Or, it may be a buffet supper with foods kept warm in casseroles over candle warmers, or hot trays.

The atmosphere is important: the usual Christmas decorations, lights, carols (Christmas music over the stereo if not from wandering church choirs), a trimmed tree, gingerbread men and cut-out cookies hanging on the tree (and available also on platters).

At any party where there is a continual influx and outflow of guests, glassware and dishes become a problem. They should be picked up periodically and carried to the kitchen to be stacked in the dishwasher. You will need a plentiful supply of glasses. Don't hesitate to turn on the dishwasher when it's full; the roar of the dishwasher has become a part of today's living.

Traditionally, "open house" means people will come if they can. This is an exasperating kind of party to give. You may expect only half the number you invited and all will show up; or, conversely, you feel you must be prepared for all forty of those to whom you sent invitations and only twenty come. If this worries you too much, put RSVP on the invitations. Or, plan the kind of food that can be eaten by the family if left over, or can be put away in the freezer for another party next month. Above everything, don't become paranoid if the party is not as noisy nor your home as crowded as you expected it to be. Smaller parties usually turn out to be more fun anyway.

Eggnog (or Glögg)
(Be sure to have both alcoholic and nonalcoholic
versions)
Potted Cheese   Potted Shrimp   Assorted cheeses
Assorted breads and crackers
Baked Ham and/or Escalloped Oysters (hot)
White Fruit Cake   Dresden Stollen
Pfeffernusse Gingerbread men
Coffee

Advance Preparation. Traditionally, the weeks before Christmas are a time when the house is spicy with the fragrance of holiday cakes a-baking; all the sweets can be prepared long ahead. So can the Potted Cheese and Potted Shrimp. The ham may be baked the day ahead to be served cold, or could be put in the oven a few hours before the party, to be still warm when carved. Only the oysters and the drink for the punch bowl require last-minute attention.

Clambakes, Beach Parties, Luaus, and Picnics

Get-togethers such as these require careful organization and a spirit of complete informality, with a return to caveman-style eating, discarding bones and other "kitchen middens" in the still-glowing picnic fire.

Both a New England clambake and a Hawaiian luau require a large pit in which the food is cooked—that is, if these are done in the traditional way. The pits must be dug by the men of the party early in the morning, a big fire started, and the food buried at the proper time, to steam-bake in the pit for hours. This slow moist cooking gives everything wonderful flavor.

New England Clambake. The traditional combination is chicken (quartered or split in halves), whole lobsters (placed still alive in the pit), the clams in their shells, corn in its husks. When the pit is dug, firewood is laid in it, then big stones placed above the wood. When the fire has heated the stones to red-hot, then died down to glowing coals, a thick layer of damp seaweed is placed over the stones, then the food is added in layers, topped by more seaweed. This is covered by gunny sacks, which in turn are covered by beach sand.

When the food is removed cooked from its steaming pit hours later, nothing else is needed for the feast but drawn butter (as a sauce for the lobster and clams and also for corn on the cob), salt for the roast corn, and vegetable relishes (garden-ripe tomatoes, celery, carrot sticks), with melon or other fresh fruit for dessert.

Lacking beach area where a pit can be dug, the food can be cooked in big steamers with seaweed. Lobsters and clams can be ordered by the barrel for this purpose, the seaweed and steamers included. Or, of course, the lobsters and clams could be simply cooked the usual way in water (but separately), and the chicken and corn roasted on a charcoal brazier.

Traditional Hawaiian Luau. The same sort of fire in the same sort of pit is laid, and again stones are heated in the fire. In Hawaii, such a pit is called an *imu*. Suckling pig is the traditional meat, baked in the pit with sweet potatoes, taro and crabs in their shells. The word "luau" means the leaves of the taro plant, which are wrapped around the meat. Instead of an entire suckling pig, pork tenderloin may be wrapped with taro leaves. The food is steam-baked about 4 hours.

The modern version of a luau is quite a different thing, especially what is sometimes called a "backyard Luau." This may be any kind of picnic in the yard, with paper leis thrown around the necks of the arriving guests and a rum punch offered so that everyone will quickly respond to the spirit of the occasion.

The pork is more likely to be barbecued over a charcoal fire. (By whatever method the pork is cooked, whether in the *imu* or over a fire, a meat thermometer should be inserted in the thickest part of the meat to be sure the pork is thoroughly cooked when served.) Sweet potatoes can be cooked in the coals of the fire, and so can bananas, in their skins (the skins are pulled back, the fruit sprinkled with sugar and rum, then the skins replaced and the fruit wrapped in foil). Barbecued chicken and corn on the cob can be cooked in the usual manner.

The traditional appetizer served with rum punch, before the main feasting begins, is Lomi-Lomi, raw salmon "cooked" in a marinade of lime juice, grated onion, and chopped tomatoes. The traditional dessert is fresh pineapple: cut out the fruit so that the shell remains intact; the fruit is sweetened and flavored with rum, then returned to the shell to marinate. This makes a superb dessert at any time.

Texas Barbecue. This, too, once required the digging of a pit in which big fires would be laid, but with whole steers or hogs suspended from big spits above the fire, slowly turned and basted all day long, served with fiery-hot sauces. Today charcoal braziers are used instead, but the same enormous quantities of food are prepared and the spareribs, steaks, chickens, and beef roasts are all liberally brushed with spicy, thick sauces.

Besides corn on the cob (which is in truth *more* American than apple pie), baked beans, chili beans, tamales, and enchiladas are traditional parts of a Texas barbecue. Hot coffee is served *with* the meal, plus beer and soft drinks.

Portable Picnics. Most of the food for today's picnics is prepared at home and carried to the picnic site in insulated hampers. Hot dogs and hamburgers may be grilled over portable braziers set up on the beach, but the baked beans and/or potato salad are prepared at home, as are such standbys as cole slaw and fruit punch (carried in a thermos).

The following recipes, to be found elsewhere in the book, are useful for those planning beach parties and picnics. If the affair is a big "do," food preparation should be divided among the families participating, with one person assigned to make the potato salad, another to prepare the beans, still another to bring the sauces and condiments needed for the meat, chicken, or fish to be cooked in the open.

Hamburgers 52 Ways	Red Kidney Bean Casserole
London Broil	Lentils with Rice
Barbecued Spareribs	Potato Salads
Broiled Chicken Variations	Cole Slaw (and variations)
Shish Kabob	Marinades and Barbecue Sauces
Souvlakia Lefkas	Chicken Lau-Laus (for a luau)
Quick Bean Bake	Fruit Punches

See also Go-withs for Barbecue Meals

Cooperative Dinners or Suppers

If it's an affair sponsored by a church or club group, food preparation will probably be assigned to volunteers, with the overall menu selected after group discussion. Such menus need to be fairly conservative, since they are being prepared for a cross-section of people of varied cultural backgrounds.

If it's an annual dinner for a private social club, or one dreamed up by a group of young people because no one couple can afford to swing such an entertainment alone, the menu may be much more exotic, with international overtones.

Whatever the make-up of the group to be fed, certain practical considerations are important. The food should lend itself to mass production, should be easy to transport and easy to reheat. Cold foods should not require freezer space (ice cream is the exception). The best salads are gelatin molds (no need to worry about the lettuce becoming wilted). The best desserts are cakes and pies. Soup is the best first course, because it's easy to prepare in large quantities and to keep hot, and people can easily help themselves from the tureen.

Wherever the affair is being held, make sure there will be plenty of chairs and table space. Extra dishes, silverware, and glasses may be loaned by a friend to the hostess, though if it's an organizational affair, it is probably better to rent all such appurtenances to avoid blame or resentment for breakage of prized china or beloved stemware.

In nearly all cases, all the food should be set out on a buffet or long table. If the dinner is held in a public place, this might be improvised by putting a row of card tables together, covering them with long cloths or the largest paper lunch cloths. Or, long "barbecue" tables could be rented.

All the following menus are suitable for cooperative preparation. After checking the recipes, examine yields, multiply by the number of persons to be served, and rewrite the recipes before starting the preparation.

To figure out how many pies are needed, remember each pie makes six servings. A layer cake makes approximately ten servings.

CHURCH OR CLUB SUPPER

Cream of Corn Soup

Church Supper Turkey Pie
Cranberry-Orange Relish
Escalloped Potatoes
Golden Glow Salad

Assorted Pies
Coffee   Fruit Punch

SCOUT LEADER'S DINNER

Chicken Rice Soup

Meatloaf   Italian Macaroni Casserole
Jellied Beet Ring
Cottage Cheese

Assorted Cakes   Ice Cream
Coffee

PRIVATE SOCIAL GET-TOGETHER

Shrimp Gumbo

Baked Ham   Rice and Limas
Ribboned Vegetable Salad

Assorted Pies and Pastries

EXOTIC CLUB DINNER

Dolmades   Mixed Seafood Salad
Vegetable Relishes

Turkish Prune Pilaf

Tomato Aspic   Blue Cheese Dressing

Pecan Pie à la Mode

BOOK FIVE

All About Wines and Spirits

"Light the candles . . . pour the wine . . ." What an image of romance and gaiety those words provoke! Any dinner by candlelight does indeed seem more gracious, and the right wine does enhance the food. This is, in fact, the sole reason for serving wine with meals—not to get tipsy, but because wine actually makes the food taste better; it opens the taste buds, as it were. It also helps conversation to sparkle because the guests, relieved of tension and drawn by this elixir into a feeling of camaraderie, think of bright, witty, gay things to say.

Wine is a fascinating subject, but those who are unsure about what to buy find little help on the part of clerks in liquor stores.

"Red wine with meat, white wine with fish, rosé wine with anything." That's the general impression, and like all other oversimplifications, it's erroneous. Rosé wines are *not* good with everything. These are light wines, pleasant, "young," and no host or hostess need apologize for serving them. But, since wine makes food taste better, is is worth learning which wines do most for which foods, and why.

All true wines are made from grapes, though there are beverages light in alcohol made from other fruits or plants which are sometimes called "wines" (cherry wine, dandelion and elderberry wine, and so on).

When wine grapes are harvested, pressed, and poured into vats, fermentation begins almost immediately, because of microscopic enzymes which have attached themselves to the grapes as they ripened. These enzymes convert the grape sugar into alcohol with such rapidity that the vats appear like seething caldrons, the juice or must making a hum like that of angry bees.

Red wine gets its color from the skins of the grapes, which are left in the fermenting vats for varying lengths of time, depending on the grapes themselves and the type of wine being produced. From the skin, *tannin* is imparted to the wine, and this in turn gives red wine a flavor different from that of white wine. Virtually all red wines are dry wines.

Rosé wine is technically a type of red wine, but the skins are left in contact with the must for a very brief time. This means the wine not only is lighter in color, but contains less tannin and therefore is somewhere between a red and a white wine. A few rosés owe their color to a pigmentation in the grape pulp; the skins of these do not go into the fermenting vat and so they resemble white wines even more closely than the others. Rosé wines vary from very dry to moderately sweet.

White wines have had the skins separated from the juice at the outset, at the time the grapes are pressed. This is why they are "white" (in fact the color ranges from pale straw to deep gold). White wines range from very dry through moderately sweet to quite sweet. A very few special white wines are sweeter because the grapes have been picked at the last possible moment, leaving more natural sugar in the grapes, but most are deliberately made sweeter by stopping fermentation before all the grape sugar has been converted to alcohol. Some cheaper wines are sweetened by the addition of sugar, a practice wine makers in general frown upon.

After the fermentation has subsided, the must is drained off and put in huge barrels or cylinders to age. Even a "new" wine must be at least a year old before it is fit to drink. The better wines are not bottled until after two years of aging in the wood, and some not for three or four years, or even longer.

If you are genuinely interested in learning about wines, you should visit a winery, where you will see the giant barrels row upon row, inhale the wonderful aroma that permeates the air, and learn from the men who devote their lives to viniculture of the many steps required in turning the must of the grapes into mature, well-balanced wines. In California, on a weekend, visitors arrive in swarms at small and large wineries alike, take the tour, taste samples of the wines, and buy their selections by the case.

The only way to learn about wines is to drink them, and one need not start with vintage wines. On the contrary, it is best to begin with simple, inexpensive wines, to have these often enough so that one develops favorites. After drinking simple wines frequently it is easier to distinguish different flavors and aromas, to develop what is called a palate. Then the finer wines can be much better appreciated.

What Is a Vintage Wine?

Wine snobs are tiresome people. They prattle of vintages, act as if only boobs bought inexpensive wines, and frighten the uninitiated into feeling they must pay a high price to get a decent wine. On the contrary, the price is not necessarily an indication of excellence.

The vintage means the year of the wine harvest, so that all wines have a vintage, but the phrase "vintage wine" means one selected by the vintners at the time of the harvest as fine enough to be stored after bottling in the vintners' deep wine cellars to mellow and develop special bouquet and pungency and to acquire brilliance of color. A vintage wine is never a blended wine; it is a wine of a specific vineyard or estate. Especially fine vintage wines, from renowned vineyards, are sometimes aged in bottle for twenty or twenty-five years—for as long as fifty or sixty years in the case of a few rare ones.

Not all wines improve with age; some are no good after two or even three years, and even the costly wines of outstanding vintage reach a peak, after which they deteriorate in quality. The wines put away to age after bottling must be sampled periodically to learn how they are maturing. A wine that promised to be superb, from a vintage believed to be outstanding, might begin to turn after five or six years. Another, rated as a secondary wine when it was "laid down" (bottled and placed on racks in the deep underground cellars), may surprise the experts by developing mellowness and character they had not believed it capable of.

How much difference the year of vintage makes depends to a large degree on where the wine was produced. In warm climates, where frost comes late if at all and the summers are long and dry, the wine production is pretty much the same year after year, and it is then more important to learn about wine areas and outstanding vintners than about vintage years. This holds true of California wines and wines from southern Europe. The farther north the vineyards, or the more variable the duration of the rainy season, the more difference the years of vintage make. A season of heavy rains can ruin the wine harvest; so can blight, hail, or unexpectedly early frost.

Yet even in a great vintage year, not all the wines of a given harvest are great. The true connoisseur of wine must not only keep abreast of what years are great and what years have seen poorer harvests, but must know which particular bottlings of the better vintage years are the best buys. In many cases, a blended wine from a renowned estate or château will be better than a vintage wine from a lesser vintner.

The vast majority of us cannot possibly be so well versed, and there's no point in trying. Concentrate on general knowledge, learn to enjoy wines of all kinds, and in time you will find you are more of an expert than you ever expected to be.

Dry Versus Sweet. Dry wines are the opposite of sweet, though wines in this classification may vary from "bone-dry" to moderately sweet. It depends on the grapes themselves and their natural sugar content, also on how much of the grape sugar has been converted to alcohol. (Yet the total alcoholic content of a dry wine is usually *less* than that of a sweet one: most table wines range in alcoholic content between 7 and 12 percent, very few higher than this.)

Those who are just beginning to learn about wine usually prefer the sweeter ones, but the more wine one drinks, the drier becomes the palate. This is another way of saying that educated taste buds prefer the drier wines. Why? Because the drier wines do more to enhance food, to open the taste buds to other flavors. Sweeter wines have more of a cloying effect: one tastes the sweetness of the wine rather than the food flavors. However, if the sweeter table wines please you more, by all means buy them. Wine is meant to be enjoyed.

A good dry wine is not acidic. The educated palate will reject too acid a wine as quickly as one that is too sweet. But it takes a lot of *critical* drinking of wine before one learns to distinguish

these fine differences. One should sip wine slowly, apprecia-
tively, in order to detect subtle nuances of flavor and aroma.

Other Wine Terms You Should Understand

Table wines are all moderately dry to dry wines.

Sweet wines are those containing a larger amount of uncon-
verted sugar (or added sugar, in very cheap sweet wines). Such
wines are best with fruit or dessert, between meals, or after
dinner.

Fortified wines are those that have been blended with brandy during production. Their alcoholic content ranges from 18 to
22 percent. Some are *aperitif wines* (meant to be consumed
before meals); some are *dessert wines* (meant to be served with
sweets, or after dinner).

Blended wines are wines of the same vintage year but from
different vineyards and different grape varieties. The purpose
of the blending is to achieve a well-balanced wine, or to
achieve a uniform product year after year, or to make a poor
wine better. Some blended wines are very fine indeed. Others
are the opposite. It depends on the vintner and the market he is
aiming for. Mass-produced inexpensive wines are blended to
keep the price down.

Château-bottled or *estate-bottled* wines are those from a specific estate or vineyard, bottled at the winery, bearing the name
of the vineyard or the producer. (Most bottling is done at big
central bottling plants.) Presumably only the finest wines are so
bottled; they are samples of which the vintner is very proud.

Pasteurized wines have been heated, then cooled, to kill certain bacteria. Fine wines are never pasteurized, because pas-
teurization prevents the enzyme action which gives wine as it
ages those mellow, pungent, velvety, or aromatic qualities
which are so highly prized. Inexpensive wines, especially
American wines, are pasteurized so that they will keep longer,
and such wines do remain palatable for a longer time after the
bottle is opened. This is another way of saying that a vintage
wine (or any fine blended wine) should be consumed the same
day it is uncorked, but for family or everyday use, when only
half a bottle of wine may be consumed at one meal and the rest
put away to be served several days later, the pasteurized wine
has certain definite advantages.

Bouquet is the aroma given off by the wine. Red wines in
general have more bouquet than the white, which is why red

wines are served at room temperature, so that the volatile fragrance will be released more fully. But both white and red wines have distinctive fragrance to be appreciated, quite as much as the taste; wine must be both sniffed and sipped.

A *full-bodied wine* is one that is robust, with distinctive taste, as different from a wine that is more delicate and lighter in body. As you drink wines critically, you will begin to understand this meaning better than words can describe.

Heavy means the wine is full-bodied, mellow but a "strong" wine. The term is used principally to describe those red wines that are best served with beef and lamb. Red wines of the Burgundy district of France tend to be heavy wines.

Tart means very dry but without acidity.

Soft means the opposite of harsh, suggests delicacy and great mellowness. A very delicate wine may be soft, as may a well-aged, full-bodied wine.

Fruity means a wine with a faint taste or aroma of the grapes from which the wine was pressed (but not in any sense like grape juice). Such a wine is different from those tart light wines that are almost bracing in flavor.

Foxy is a term used to describe some of the American wines produced in the Eastern states which have a distinct grape juice-like flavor (this is not considered good in a wine).

Vin ordinaire is French for "ordinary wine," the kind most Frenchmen drink most of the time.

Generic names refer to types of wine; *varietal* names refer to the grapes used in making the wines (these are terms used primarily in the American wine industry).

Wine regions are those areas where wine making is a major industry, and where differences of soil, climate, and production methods have resulted over the centuries in creating wines of distinctive character.

Sophisticated wines are not wines at all but a phony product of fruit juices blended with alcohol and artificial flavoring. This frightening trend in wine production began in Italy and has spread to other countries. Beware! These may taste palatable to the uninitiated, but they are poor imitations and can be damaging to health.

Wine Tastings

By all means attend any public wine tasting given by wine institutes, importing firms, or large liquor stores. And if there is a liquor store in your town that specializes in wines, you might arrange to give a wine tasting for your friends in your home, instead of a cocktail party or tea. It might be a combined wine and cheese tasting; let the liquor store suggest which wines to offer, and a local cheese merchant tell you (if he can), which wines are best with which cheeses.

The driest white wines are always tasted first, followed by others somewhat less dry. Lighter reds come next, then the heavier, more full-bodied reds. Finally the sweet wines, the sherries, ports, or white dessert wines.

Take only a small amount of each wine; hold the glass up to your nose and sniff; then take a small sip and roll it around your mouth, from front to back. Pretentious? Not at all. This is the way to savor the wine fully; often a wine that seems excessively dry when you first sip it lets you know it has more character and flavor as you roll it around your mouth.

How to Buy and Store Wine

As a beginner, buy several inexpensive wines at a time, try one then another at home in the intimacy of the family or with close friends. When certain wines please you especially, buy these for dinner parties. It's economical to buy favorites by the case, or by the half-gallon. Most liquor stores will give you a 10 percent discount if you buy 12 bottles (fifths) at a time, even though the case is mixed. Only domestic wines are available in half-gallon and gallon jugs.

A single bottle of wine, if not consumed at the first pouring, may be recorked and kept in the refrigerator for several days. Refrigeration will only delay the souring, however. It's best to finish a bottle within two or three days after it has been opened.

Wine bottles should always be stored on their sides, lying flat, so that the cork remains moist. (With capped bottles, it doesn't matter so much.) Wine racks are a help, but not essential. If a case of wine is delivered, simply put the carton on its side, so that the bottles will be in a horizontal position. Or, lay the bottles side by side on a shelf in such a way that they won't roll. Ideally the temperature should be constant and cool, about 60° F., moderately dry (slightly humid but never damp), and the place dark. A dry cool cellar is ideal, provided the wine is well protected from heat sources. If you have no such storage place, at least keep it away from heat and at a steady temperature.

How to determine what is a good buy in wine? There aren't any hard and fast rules. Price is not a criterion, as already explained. Vintage years marked on the bottle are meaningful only if you are well versed in which years are good, which ones less desirable—and with less expensive wines, even this can be deceptive. Then how do you choose the right wine? More or less by trial and error. When you find wines that particularly please you, buy them again and again. Some of the varietal and regional names given on the following pages can serve as a general guide for your experimentation.

How many servings per bottle? A fifth of wine (the standard size) contains 25 ounces, or 8 3-ounce servings. If you fill 8-ounce glasses half full, it will make only 6 servings. How many bottles you need for a dinner party will depend on whether your guests are great wine drinkers or only sip at it. For a dinner party of 6, two bottles is probably right. This might be enough for 8 persons, but to be safe, better have a third bottle in readiness.

How to Serve Wines

In general, serve *white wines*, well chilled, with these foods:

- Seafood of all kinds
- "White" meats (chicken, veal, pork)
- Any foods that are light and delicate in flavor
- Sweet white wines with fruit or cake

Rosé wines should also be well chilled, and can be served with any of the same foods as white wine, though the sweeter rosé wines do not seem to go well with fish.

In general serve *red wines* at room temperature, or (in hot weather or if your house is kept at a high temperature), very slightly chilled, with the following foods:

- Meats, especially beef, lamb, and pork
- Pastas
- Bean dishes and hearty soups (except fish soups)
- Cheese of all kinds
- Chicken

Note that both pork and chicken may be served with white, rosé, or red wines.

Red wine is good with all kinds of cheese, but certain cheeses go very well with certain white wines (generally those not terribly dry). Veal is delicious with a tart, light red wine, equally good with chilled white wine, or with rosé.

In summer, I personally prefer well-chilled white wine with almost everything, even broiled meats. My liking for rosé wine increases in summer, too. Full-bodied red wines are more to be enjoyed in cool or cold weather.

Curried dishes will spoil a good red wine; a well-chilled moderately sweet white table wine is better, and some people feel the best beverage with curry is beer.

How cold is chilled? For white or rosé wine, 1 to 2 hours in the refrigerator is optimum; longer than this may "freeze" the bouquet. If red wine is to be cooled, it should be in the refrigerator no more than half an hour. Red wine should never be actually cold, and I personally prefer red wine at room temperature even when the temperature is in the high 70's. Chilling wine in a champagne bucket is fun, but the ice should be coarsely crushed, not in big cubes, or the bottle will not go down into the ice all the way. For white wine, 20 to 25 minutes in an ice bucket is about right; for red wine (if it is to be cooled), 10 minutes is ample. Turn the bottle frequently; keep bucket covered with a linen napkin or towel. Cheaper red wines are more likely to require cooling than the better ones, for a poor red wine has little bouquet to begin with.

Fine red wines, those that have been aged two years or more in the bottle, should always be uncorked at least 1 hour before serving—preferably 2 hours. Some Bordeaux wines should be opened 3 or 4 hours before serving.

This is because of the tannin in the wine. When the bottle is open, permitting the wine to "breathe," the tannin fumes evaporate.

Beaujolais, one of the most popular of the French red Burgundies, should not be opened more than an hour before dinner (and half an hour is enough). This is a young wine, at its prime when only two years old—there is no such thing as a "vintage" Beaujolais. The same principle holds true of most *vins ordinaires* or moderate-priced domestic wines. A short "breathing" period is recommended, but not too long or the wine will lose too much of its volatility.

Glassware. Simple wines can be enjoyed from any kind of glass or tumbler, but even ordinary wine seems more special in stemware, and fine wines can be fully appreciated only if served in the proper type of glass.

This does not mean investing in an entire set of expensive glasses. A single all-purpose wineglass may be used, the 6- or 8-ounce stemmed tumbler, of clear glass, tulip-shaped.

Never fill any wineglass more than two-thirds full; half full is better, and for any aged red wine, the glass should be only one-third full.

This is because, to savor the wine fully, the bouquet must be captured, and for the bouquet to arise from the wine, there must be space between the top of the wine and the top of the glass. The tulip shape, slightly more narrow at the top than in the bowl, holds the bouquet inside the glass so that it floats up to the nostrils.

If you enjoy the ceremony of serving wine, it's fun to have more than one type of glass. The long-stemmed Rhine wine glasses are elegant for any kind of white wine. Why the difference in the length of the stem? A glass holding red wine should be grasped by the stem with the hand cupped around the bowl, to warm the wine slightly and thus encourage the release of the bouquet. But white wines are not intended to be warmed; they are to be sipped chilled, so the stem is grasped below the level of the bowl.

Champagne is best in a tulip-shaped glass, which helps to retain the bubbles; in the saucer-shaped champagne glass, bubbles disappear too quickly. The elegant champagne glass is the tall tulip, but the all-purpose 6- or 8-ounce tulip glass is also perfectly proper.

Should Water Be Served with Wine? Americans are accustomed to water with meals—ice water no less—and while this may shock the European visitor, those accustomed to chilled water with meals may find that wine alone does not quench their thirst. If you have sufficient glassware to put both wine and water glasses at each place setting, by all means do so; or, if there is only one glass at each place, ask guests whether any prefer water to wine. Some will, especially if cocktails have preceded dinner. And if water is not served with the entree, it should be offered later, with coffee.

OUTSTANDING TABLE WINES OF THE WORLD

The following is not and cannot be an all-inclusive list, but it names most of the best-known and popular wines of the chief wine-producing countries, starting with our own, since most Americans will buy domestic wines most of the time.

These are table wines only. Apéritif and other fortified wines are discussed separately.

California Table Wines

The vintage years 1968 and 1969 were rated by California vintners as among the finest in the history of California wine making. California wines are now being praised by visiting Frenchmen as of superb quality. Many Californians now maintain their own wine cellars, putting away wines of good vintage years to age in the bottle.

For those who have the storage facilities, and can take the time to learn which are good buys, this is worthwhile; wines aged in the bottle in the wineries must be sold for a higher price than those sold soon after bottling. One must be knowledgeable, though, and willing to take the risk that the wines will fulfill their promise.

California wines should be judged on their own merits, not as copies of European types. Even though the wines are made from the same grape varieties as renowned European wines, soil and climate conditions always affect the final product as much as the seedlings from which the grapes grow.

Those in the California wine trade are now putting more emphasis on varietal wines, but regional names are not yet being used, as in Europe, which is rather unfortunate. The best of all American table wines are those from the Napa and Sonoma Valleys of California; the best of these wines are from grapes grown on the higher slopes.

PRINCIPAL WINES OF CALIFORNIA

Generic Name	Varietal Name	Characteristics
Burgundy*	Pinot Noir	Full-bodied, deep red, fragrant
	Gamay	Similar to French Beaujolais; light, fruity
Claret	Cabernet Sauvignon	Considered the finest of all the California red wine varietals. Clear brilliant color, lighter-bodied than the Pinot Noir.
	Zinfandel	Made from a grape that may be native to California; light, tart, sometimes a bit harsh
Chablis	Pinot Chardonnay	Clear, light gold, a very fresh crisp white wine, excellent with seafood
	Chenin Blanc	A light "sprightly" wine without quite as much character as Pinot Chardonnay
Rhine	Riesling	Intended to be similar to the German Rhine wines, but more dry and with less body. Pale green-gold, delicate.
	Traminer	Slightly deeper in color than Riesling, quite dry
	Sylvaner	Soft, light, delicate white wine
Sauterne†	Sauvignon Blanc	Soft white wine with distinctive aroma, ranges from moderately dry to semisweet
	Haut Sauterne	Decidedly sweet, but light. May be served as a table wine but is more suitable with fruits or dessert.

See also Sweet Wines.

*In American terminology, Burgundy refers only to red wines.

†A completely different wine from the sweet white wine the French call Sauternes (with a final s).

New York State Wines

Only 9 percent of the American wine output is from New York State; 85 percent is from California, the rest from other

Eastern states. Table wines produced in the Eastern wineries are labeled with the same generic names as in California: burgundy (more full-bodied red), claret (lighter body, lighter color), Chablis (very dry white) and Rhine (dry white). However, the wines are made from native (indigenous) grape varieties, with some cross-breeding with European grape types. Some of these wines are quite good, judged as ordinary wines. But the best of the Eastern output is found in the champagnes and sherries. The only *varietal* wines of note produced in the east are moderately sweet to sweet white wines (Catawba, Delaware, Scuppernong), which are in a very small supply.

French Wines

So formidable is the French reputation in viniculture that most people believe all French wines are superior to any others. (It's much like the awe with which French cooking is regarded.) When it comes to *great* wines, the French do excel, perhaps above the vintners of any other country in the world, but these are expensive wines, beyond the pocketbooks of most of us. French wines costing under $4 a bottle are not great wines, though some costing around $3 a bottle are very fine indeed, and if one is lucky, those living on the Eastern Seaboard may be able to pick up an excellent French wine for around $2 a bottle, about the same price as a good California wine.

(Shipping costs make French wines more expensive than this on the West Coast, and make California wines more expensive in the East than in California.)

French wines are all named for the places where they are produced, the *region*, such as Bordeaux or Burgundy, the *district* or growth area within the region which is noted for wines of certain characteristics, and, in the case of the finest wines, the *château* (or estate, or specific vineyards) on which the wine was produced and bottled. When a wine label carries the words *appellation controllée*, it means inspection has certified that the wine was produced in the district or estate so named, from grapes of a defined variety, harvested in a specified manner. Every bottle of French wine for export also bears the year of vintage.

If this were done with American wines, all the wines produced in the Napa Valley would be known as Napa wines, and those produced in or near, say, the town of St. Helena would be further classified as St. Helena wines. (Someday, perhaps, we will come to this.)

Most of the French wines reaching American markets come from the *Bordeaux* region. The red Bordeaux wines are what the English call *claret*. There are also excellent white Bordeaux, though the most famous of the white Bordeaux are sweet wines: Sauternes (always spelled with the *s*, even in singular), Barsac, and Graves Supérieur. The best *dry* white Bordeaux wines come from the Graves district, which also produces outstanding red wines.

Equally famous for its wines is the *Burgundy* wine region, though production is considerably smaller than that of Bordeaux. Two of the greatest dry white wines in the world are produced in Burgundy: Chablis and Montrachet. The red wines of Burgundy tend to be more full-bodied and heavier than those of Bordeaux, though there are numerous exceptions.

Beaujolais is actually a wine of the southernmost part of the Burgundy region, but its popularity has become so great all over the world, Beaujolais has now been designated a French wine region rather than a district. The only wines bearing the Beaujolais name are red wines; it is a young, light, fruity red wine, at its peak when two years old. There are white wines produced in the adjoining wine district, Mâconnais, and a few in the defined boundaries of Beaujolais as well, but they must bear a different name.

The following are names worth knowing about so that when you feel like splurging with a fine French wine, you will know what to look for. Be sure to uncork the red wines long before serving.

FAMOUS BORDEAUX REDS

Haut-Médoc. The Médoc is that district in the Bordeaux region where the finest of all red clarets are produced, the "queen" of red wines. The Haut Médoc is the upper part of the Médoc district. The wines are delicate, a brilliant clear red, with a bouquet which has been described as having "the indefinable fragrance of woods in springtime." Some have been known to be still superb after 60 years in the bottle.

Margaux. Part of the Haut-Médoc, the most "feminine" of all the Médoc wines, light-bodied, bracing.

St. Julien. A very popular wine of the Médoc, more full-bodied than Margaux, but lighter than St.-Émilion.

St.-Émilion. The fullest and most pungent of the Bordeaux reds, heavier than those of the Médoc, deep in color, more like the Burgundy reds than any other of the Bordeaux red wines.

Mouton-Rothschild. You probably won't be able to afford this, but it's fun to know about its grandeur when you gaze on the label. A heavy wine, sometimes called "fleshy," almost metallic.

Haut-Brion. One of the greatest of the French red wines, with a distinctive taste all its own. One legend asserts that the vineyard was originally established by an Irishman (O'Brien) but there is no historic basis for this. (A white Haut-Brion is also renowned but quite rare.)

Château Lafite. One of the world's most expensive red wines, and, at its best, supreme. It was a favorite wine of Madame du Barry.

FAMOUS BURGUNDY REDS

Chambertin. In limited supply and great demand and therefore very expensive. A strong wine, deep ruby-red in color, with a pungent bouquet and lingering aftertaste.

Vosne-Romanée. Magnificent full-bodied wines; in top vintage years they are velvety-soft with a long lingering aftertaste.

Côte de Nuits. Not so costly as the previous two, but considered "regal."

FAMOUS WHITE BURGUNDIES

Chablis. The only French wines allowed to carry this name must be produced in the region immediately surrounding the town of Chablis. They are flinty-dry, clear, pale, delicate, probably the most bracing and well-balanced of all the very dry white wines.

Montrachet. Much more full-bodied than Chablis and somewhat sweeter, flowery, rich, deep gold in color. Dumas said one should drink it on one's knees with bowed head.

Mâconnais. Could be called the white counterpart of Beaujolais since this is the district bordering on Beaujolais. The wines in general are fairly light and fairly dry.

Pouilly-Fuissé. A white wine of the Mâconnais district, somewhat between a Chablis and Montrachet in dryness, greenish gold in color, with decided bouquet. Excellent with lobster. One of the best white table wines.

Other fine but lesser French table wines are produced in the Loire and Rhône wine regions. Of the Loire Valley wines, the most popular are **Vouvray**, a light fruity white wine with the essence of springtime, sometimes naturally effervescent (though only the still wine is exported to any extent, and not all of this ships well); and **Anjou Rosé**, one of the nicest of all the rosé wines.

(Rosé wines are produced in all French wine regions but the French consider rosés as *vins ordinaires*. All should be drunk while young, no more than two or three years old.)

Best known of the Rhône wines is **Châteauneuf-du-Pape**, a soft, heavy red wine, so dark in color as to be almost "black."

GERMAN WINES

Two of the greatest white wines in the world are produced in Germany: **Moselle** (or Mosel, in German) and **Rhine** (or Rhein) wines. There are no German red wines of note.

The Mosels are lighter, fruitier, and frequently drier than the Rhein wines which tend to be full-bodied, deep gold in color, ranging from quite dry to very sweet. Sweetest of all are the rare and very expensive wines labeled Trockenbeerenauslese, which are produced from selected grapes so ripe they are ready to fall from the vine, a stage of ripeness called "noble rot." (Don't try to pronounce the name: they sell for prices like $100 a bottle, so you aren't likely to be asking for them often.)

Vintage years are especially important to know about when buying German wines, because the growing season is so short and hazardous. As in France, wines are named for the regions, the districts, and the estates.

German labels tell you everything, if you understand the terminology. First comes the wine district, then the town or village, then the vineyard, and finally the grape type and variety. The vintage year is also given, and some labels even give the number of the vat in which the wines were aged before bottling.

Kabinett means superb, worthy to have a place on display in the owner's cabinet or sideboard. *Auslese* means the wine is from selected bunches of grapes individually picked. *Abfüllung* means much the same as "château-bottled." *Spätlese* means the grapes were not gathered until the last stage of ripeness (these wines are always sweeter than others).

Because the vintage wines are so costly, many blended wines are produced in Germany, and this is the only country in the world where reputable wine producers are permitted to add sugar to the wine while it is fermenting. Such wines are, of course, *vins ordinaires*, but when a season has been very short (early frost), the grapes may have so little sugar that without added sweetening the bulk of the wine production would be undrinkable. Because this practice is so common, many bottles of German wine carry the designation *Natur* or *Naturrein*, meaning the buyer can be assured the wine is pure, without added sweetening.

The name **Liebfraumilch** is utterly meaningless. It is purely a commercial name for a blended wine of dubious worth. A better risk is the wine known as **Schwarze Katz** (black cat), also a blend, but those I have tried have all been quite good.

The following are names worth looking for when you want to serve a very fine German wine.

RHEIN WINES

Markobrunner. Full-bodied, a poem of a wine at its best, beautifully dry. Said to have been Thomas Jefferson's favorite Rhenish wine.

Rudesheimer. Consistently good, though not the greatest of the Rhein wines.

Schloss Johannisberg. A famous name and at its best a superb wine, though not as outstanding as it used to be.

Schloss Vollrads. A heady distinctive wine with great bouquet, generally rated of the world's finest white wines.

MOSEL WINES

Bernkastler Doktor. The most famous of the Mosels. The name "doctor" was bestowed on it in the fourteenth century when the Bishop of Trier claimed the wine cured his near-fatal illness.

Piesporter Goldtropfchen. Piquant, fruity, delicate. Sometimes slightly sweet but always has a dry aftertaste.

Excellent white wines from the same grape varieties, Riesling, Sylvaner, and Traminer, are produced in Alsace and Austria. Switzerland also has several outstandingly good white wines, but most are consumed by the Swiss themselves. **Neuchâtel** white wines are the most widely exported of the Swiss wines; this is a fine wine to serve with a cheese fondue.

Spanish Table Wines

The finest are the **Rioja** wines, currently the best bargain in table wines of any, domestic or imported, available in the East. These are available in reds, whites, and rosés, called *rosadas*, and cost only a little more than $1 a bottle. The chief drawback is that quality is uneven and in the very same case, one bottle may prove to be much better than another. These are light wines with a distinctive taste of their own, made from grape varieties peculiar to Spain. Some, the more expensive ones, are outstandingly good; most can be regarded only as *vins ordinaires*, but on that basis, they are commendable.

Portuguese Table Wines

The light, sometimes bubbly **Vinho Verde** is gaining an increasing audience in the United States, largely because the wine is so reasonable in price, but also because these are pleasant wines, light, tart, very pale in color. The naturally effervescent ones are like a poor man's champagne. The best of the Portuguese red wines are those from the Dão district. Like the Spanish Rioja wines, these are not great, but they are very pleasant and for the price extraordinary. Probably the best known of all Portuguese table wines is Mateus rosé, a moderately sweet table wine which should be served well chilled.

Italian Wines

Everyone knows about **Chianti**, whose attraction lies as much in the charming straw-colored bottles in which the wine is sold as the quality of the wine itself, which is often harsh. Brolio is probably the most reliable in quality of any of the imported Chiantis. (American wines of the same name are now being produced and are seen increasingly in Italian-American restaurants).

There are other Italian wines as good as Chianti—in fact, better—but they are not in wide distribution, and the recent Italian practice of producing "sophisticated wines," which aren't wines at all, is casting doubt on all wines brought in from Italy. It's a shame, for Italian food does seem to need the rough tartness of red wine, and those straw-covered bottles make dinner *a l'Italienne* seem so gay.

Chilean Wines

The white wines are the best; the Chilean Riesling, in fact, is probably the best *inexpensive* white wine for the price to be found in American liquor stores. The red wine sold in the same round bottle is not nearly as good.

Inexpensive and pleasant table wines from Hungary, Yugoslavia, and Algeria are also available in Eastern markets.

SPARKLING WINES

Champagne is probably the only wine which may be served for any occasion, before meals, with meals, or after meals. The bubbles are caused by a second fermentation, induced by the adding of a sugar syrup after the first fermentation has ceased and before the wine is bottled.

There is much more to the production of champagne than this, of course. A fine champagne must start with a fine blend of white wines—always blended; one wine alone is never used. Whether it is to be a sweet champagne, a semidry, dry, or brut, the driest of all, is determined in the blending. The reason French champagnes are the most expensive (the name is for the Champagne wine region of France where the process originated) is that such care is taken in France to ensure a "bubbly" that will be a superb wine, not just a carbonated wine. In France, only wine that lives up to all the various specifications can legally be labeled Champagne.

Today wines called "champagne" are produced in every wine-producing country of the world. Quality varies enormously, as does price, but there is no such thing as a good cheap champagne.

The chief attraction about champagne to most people is the ceremony of popping the cork. Ironically, experts advise that, to savor a fine champagne to the full, the cork should be slipped off gently so that it does not pop, permitting the wine to go cascading over the top.

If champagne is purchased primarily for the cork popping, to be served to people who won't know the difference, a fine French champagne will be wasted. Nor is there any reason to buy good champagne for punch or champagne cocktails. How sweet and how dry a champagne you select also depends on the sophistication of those who will be drinking it. Brut champagne is bone-dry; for the uninitiated, this may seem merely sour; they will be just as happy with a comparatively inexpensive domestic champagne, either semidry or sweet.

Very pleasant American champagnes are being produced in both California and New York State. However, what are called "champagne-type wines," or "carbonated wines," are poor imitations; you might as well mix white wine with club soda.

Sparkling Burgundy is a red wine processed like champagne—that is, with sugar added to induce the second fermentation. It tends to be rather sweet.

Other sparkling wines produced domestically (of the "champagne type") include Sparkling Moselle, Sparkling Sauterne, and Sparkling Muscat. The last is very sweet. So is **Asti Spumante**, an Italian sparkling wine produced from the muscat grape.

How to Buy and Store Champagne. Champagne is available in sizes ranging from a "split" (a small bottle just right for 2 persons), to the standard fifth, from which 6 to 8 servings can be poured (for 3 to 4 persons), and the magnum, approximately 2 quarts, suitable only for big occasions and big crowds. It also comes in 4- and 6-quart sizes.

If purchased some days before it is to be served (or if a gift bottle is to be put away for future use), be sure to lay the bottle on its side in a cool dark place, away from any heat sources. To chill, place in the refrigerator 2 to 3 hours before uncorking, or in an ice bucket 25 to 30 minutes.

SWEET WINES

Most of the sweet wines are fortified and therefore will be discussed in the section that follows. Those that are naturally sweet—that is, produced from grapes very high in natural sugar content—are quite rare, or quite expensive. These include the French Sauternes, the German Rhein and Mosel wines characterized as Spätlese or Beerenauslese, and Hungarian **Tokay**. The latter is one of the world's great wines and should not be confused with the inferior sweet wine of the same name produced domestically.

The Tokay of Hungary owes its unique character to the soil where the vines grow, to a grape variety not grown anywhere else in the world, and to the method of picking the grapes only after snow has fallen, when the grapes are partially dried and oozing with sugar. Some of the wines are more dry than others, but the driest Tokays are sweet wines; all are of legendary renown. The proper pronunciation, incidentally, is To-kie (rhymes with "sky").

Most sweet wines are made that way deliberately, by stopping fermentation or by adding sugar. Some of the cheaper sweet wines are also syrupy. This is true of the purplish Kosher wine made from Concord grapes, Manischewitz, which enjoys extraordinary popularity, and also of all the wines called *muscatel* which are brownish in color, heavy, and cloying. These are not wines to serve to wine lovers.

Among the more pleasant moderately sweet white wines are Château La Salle, a straw-colored California wine, and Catawba, made in New York State of native Catawba grapes, very pale in color with a peculiar wild grape flavor.

Though technically it isn't a wine at all, **Cherry Kijafa** belongs in this category. A Danish import, it has winelike taste but with distinctive cherry flavor and a very slight pleasant bitterness. It is not too sweet to be served as an apéritif and is quite popular with women as a before-lunch drink. It is not a table wine.

Est! Est! Est! is the name of an Italian sweet wine made from muscat grapes which is popular with many Americans.

THE FORTIFIED WINES

All those wines classified as apéritifs are fortified, that is, blended with brandy. Only the vermouths are strictly meant as apéritif wines, the others, sherry, Madeira, and port, are produced in a variety of types ranging from dry to sweet. There are also several fortified wines so sweet that they are only meant to be dessert wines.

Sherry

This is the most wide-ranging and varied of all the fortified wines. True sherry, the only wine that is supposed to be called by this name, is produced in a triangular wine region in southwestern Spain around the "sherry capital," Jerez de la Frontera.

There are three principal types of Spanish sherry: the driest are the *finos*, the medium sweet and medium dry are *amontillados*, and the sweeter types, *olorosos* ("fragrant"). But in all three categories there is a wide range of flavor and sweetness, bouquet, consistency, and aroma. Each sherry *bodega* (winery) has its own prized jealously guarded *referencias*, recipes by which the sherry houses are able to reproduce the same products consistently year after year.

The sherries produced for export are different from the very dry, lightly alcoholic *vino de Jerez* sold in tavernas in Spain.

Sherry is a mysterious wine, different from all others. As the must lies in the vats, some of it becomes covered by a white yeast blanket called the *flor;* some of it remains clear. Why, no one knows. The very same harvest and even the very same grapes develop differently. The wine blanketed with the flor

becomes fino (and amontillado); the rest is classified as oloro-
so.

All sherries are blended and all are fortified. The very driest
dry sherries are not blended with sweet wines, but most sherries called "dry" do contain some proportion of a sweet wine.
The best known of the "bone-dry" sherries is Tio Pepe. Wine
drinkers with a "dry palate" rate this as one of the finest of all
apéritif wines, but it is often too dry for the average person. La
Ina, not quite so dry as Tio Pepe, is one of the most popular of
the finos with Americans. Every sherry bodega produces what
are popularly called "cocktail sherries"; no two are alike.

Amontillados start out as finos, but are blended with a little
more sweet wine and are aged longer than the finos. They are
deeper in color, more of an amber, with a taste sometimes described as "nutty," and a pungent, heady bouquet. All amontillados are so labeled.

Dry sack is a very popular sherry, sweeter than the finos, yet
it is not an amontillado. Dry sack is a favorite before-dinner
sherry.

The sweetest of the olorosos are called "cream sherries."
This name is said to have originated in Bristol, England, where
sherry was once called "Bristol milk" because, according to an
old account, "such wine is the first moisture given to infants in
this city." In the early nineteenth century, a wine dealer named
Harvey, who wanted to introduce a new dessert sherry to his
clients, offered a sample to a lady customer, who exclaimed in
delight, "If your other sherry is milk, this must be cream"
Harvey's Bristol Cream is still the most famous (and one of the
most costly) of all the cream sherries, but there are many others
equally fine, just as smooth and velvety.

One of my favorite olorosos is called Double Century, produced by the Pedro Domecq bodegas. This is moderately sweet,
a deep gold (the cream sherries are deep brown), very mellow.
But there is a Spanish sherry for every taste. The fun is tasting
them to discover your favorite.

Because all sherries are brandy-fortified, their keeping qualities are almost unlimited. Because all are blended, there is no
such thing as a vintage sherry.

There are two other Spanish wines so similar to sherries they
are often considered a form of sherry. One is manzanilla, produced on the coast not far from the sherry vineyards. These are
even drier and saltier than Tio Pepe and also lighter in alcohol

(14 to 16 percent, whereas sherries range from 18 to 22 percent).

The other is *montilla*, produced in the hills above Cordoba, also light in alcohol, very pale in color, bracing and bone dry but not quite as tingling as manzanilla. (Montilla bears no relation at all to the amontillado sherries.)

Many other wine-producing countries including our own have tried to imitate the sherries of Spain. Both California and New York state produce wines called sherries, ranging from "cocktail dry" to "dry," "golden," and "cream." The sweeter golden and cream sherries are the more successful—it is easier to imitate the sweeter wines. But the dry sherries, even though pleasant wines, are not like the dry finos of Spain. Most American sherries are "baked," more like the way Madeira is processed. Only a few wineries follow the solera method.

The traditional glass for sherry is the very narrow tulip with a short stem, holding 6 ounces. This should be filled about half full if the rich pungent sherry bouquet is to be appreciated.

Sherry, whether dry or sweet, should always be chilled before serving. If this has not been done ahead, serving it "on the rocks" is the quickest way to chill the wine. Even in the narrow tulip sherry glasses, small ice cubes may be added, preferably just one at a time. Otherwise, old-fashioned glasses will do. Connoisseurs may be shocked at the idea of diluting sherry this way, especially an imported sherry, but the truth is it makes sherry much more appealing to most Americans; and if only a single small cube is added, the dilution is not that great.

Vermouth

Of all apéritif wines, those in the vermouth category are most popular at the cocktail hour. The two main types are dry ("French") vermouth, and sweet ("Italian") vermouth, though now both sweet and dry vermouth-type drinks are produced in both countries, and a number of American firms produce both types in the very same winery.

Vermouth is an herbed, spiced wine. Each formula is individual and exceedingly complex; often as many as 40 different ingredients are used. This accounts for the wide variations in flavor. The wine used as the base is usually a fairly cheap wine, a white wine for both the dry and the sweet types. (The reddish-brown color of sweet vermouth comes from caramel.) Most sweet vermouth contains a small amount of quinine, which gives the wine its bitter taste. All are fortified.

Because the formulas vary so greatly, the only way to select a vermouth which pleases your taste is to try a number of them in succession. Most are available in half-bottles.

Dry vermouth is an essential ingredient in martinis, sweet vermouth in manhattans. Both are increasingly popular by themselves on the rocks, or with soda. A thin sliver of lemon peel adds piquancy to either type; a sliver of orange peel is good in sweet vermouth.

Other apéritif wines classified as vermouths include Dubonnet (both white and red types are available; both are fairly sweet), Amer Picon, Byrrh, and Campari.

Madeira

In the early days of our country, Madeira was the most popular and fashionable of all wines served at ceremonial dinners, at turtle roasts along the Schuylkill River, and at candlelit barbecues in the South. Today it has fallen greatly in both esteem and demand.

All wines called Madeira are produced on the island of that name, a Portuguese territory lying in the mid-Atlantic in a semi-tropical climate. There are four types of Madeira: the driest is *Sercial* (Thomas Jefferson would not have considered serving turtle soup without it), pale gold, lighter in body than the others, with a powerful bouquet. "Dry" it is called, but in truth it is quite as sweet as an amontillado sherry, sometimes sweeter. *Rainwater* is the name of a Sercial type, pale, very smooth to the tongue. Next in sweetness is *Verdelho*, softer, more amber in color, and a degree sweeter than Sercial. *Bual* is a russet brown, considerably sweeter and richer, while sweetest of all is *Malmsey*.

Madeira is best served between or after meals, a lovely wine to enjoy with cheese in the late afternoon on a terrace or before the fire, or to offer after-dinner guests by itself, or as an accompaniment to cheese or fruitcake. Sercial is promoted as an apéritif wine, but it is almost too sweet to be of interest for more than one drink before dinner. Like sherry, Madeira is best served chilled.

Also like sherry, Madeira has brandy added to the must after fermentation has ceased; it is then racked and stored in an *estufa*, a kind of baking oven where temperature is gradually raised to a peak (over a period of weeks) and then gradually lowered again. The process originated after it was observed that the wine greatly improved in richness and character after it had been rolling in the hold of a ship en route to India, through tropical seas. Many early Madeiras bore the name "East India" as a mark of excellence.

After the wine has been "baked," it is blended and then transferred to great oaken casks, where it undergoes a long period of maturity before being bottled. Madeira is supposed to be one of the longest-keeping of all wines; some are said to have been still fragrant and luscious after 100 years. It is doubtful if today's Madeiras would keep this long.

Port

In the Port Wine Institute in Lisbon, it is claimed that as many as 200 distinctly different ports may be sampled, though I don't know that anyone has ever taken up the challenge. Like Madeira and sherry, the original port wine was a British invention. During a war with France, the English began importing table wine from Portugal, but by comparison with the clarets of Bordeaux, found the Portuguese wines too harsh and young. To please the English palate, the Portuguese wines of the Douro valley were sweetened and fortified with brandy—and immediately became popular.

Tastes in wine have changed greatly in the last twenty-five or thirty years and the demand for port, primarily a dessert wine, is no longer anything like what it used to be. The poets and literati who grew eloquent in its praise are long dead. Even in England, drier apéritif wines now sell better.

To meet these changing tastes, the producers of port now are promoting the "cocktail dry" white ports, some of which are fairly dry, but others are still too sweet for the taste of most cocktail imbibers. The chief market for port wines today is France, where the drier white port is popular with French *boulevardiers*.

Those connoisseurs who can afford it can still be enraptured by a vintage port, perhaps the most superb of all the dessert wines still to be found. These are outstanding wines of outstanding harvests, matured with brandy until the wine has reached the proper "age of decorum," when it is bottled and corked. Only now does its life really begin: years pass as the bottles, laid down in deep cellars, become coated with dust and the wine develops extraordinary mellowness, body, and fragrance. The wine may lie this way ten, fifteen, even twenty years. When it is ready to be opened (a ceremony which makes the popping of champagne corks juvenile), the cork must be gently removed and the wine allowed to "breathe" for perhaps one or two days before it is ready to be served.

Crusted port is also rare and costly. It, too, is aged in the bottle. The name refers to the sediment which gathers inside during the years the wine remains laid down in cellars. Before being opened, the bottle is supposed to remain upright long enough for the sediment to drop to the bottom; when the wine is decanted into a cut-glass decanter, only the clear wine will be drawn off. The only difference between vintage and crusted ports is that the latter is a blend of the finest wines, the former the outstanding wine of an outstanding vintage.

Tawny port is good enough for most of us, if and when we can afford it. It is a blend of fine wines of different vintages, matured in oak casks for years, with the vintners sampling and blending until they feel they have perfected a truly outstanding wine. During this time, the wine becomes golden-brown, rich, aromatic. (Some less expensive tawny ports, created to meet the demands of the market, are simply blends of younger ruby and white ports.)

Ruby is a younger version of tawny port; the color is more red than brown, the wine is not so full-bodied or so smooth and mellow. White port is made from grapes with a white skin; it therefore can't be compared to apéritif wines with a dry white wine base, and the explanation of why many white ports are sweet, not dry, is that the production method is the same as for ruby ports. But to meet the demand for the *dry port*, brandy is not added to the must until all (or nearly all) the grape sugar has been converted.

American producers have copied the names "tawny," "ruby," and "white" for the wines called port, produced in the United States. These are not port, and it is unfortunate that they should be so called. They are very sweet fortified wines; the same is true of muscatel, of the American Tokay, and of a variety of other syrupy sweet wines produced for the pleasure of non-wine drinkers.

Marsala

Much less important than the other major fortified wines, Marsala is produced on the island of Sicily, where it was first developed—you've guessed it—by an Englishman. It was made originally in imitation of sherry. It was wisely given a different name, and so acquired respect. It is not like sherry, any more than Madeira is, or like the American wines called sherry are, but it is a fine sweet wine, nut-brown in color, with a pleasant taste all its own and a lovely bouquet. Like other fortified wines, it is extremely useful in the kitchen.

BRANDIES AND LIQUEURS

Brandies are produced in all the wine-producing countries of the world. The finest and most renowned are produced in the Cognac region of France. Other superb French brandies (distilled from wine) are produced in Armagnac, the Basque or Gascony region of southern France, and *fine champagne* brandies are produced in the. Champagne wine district. The most renowned of the latter is Rémy Martin, which many connoisseurs rate even higher than the brandies of Cognac. In France, it is common to ask for a *fine*, meaning a fine champagne or brandy.

Greek brandy is the heaviest and sweetest. Spanish brandies (made from sherry) are also very heavy, but not sweet.

The name "brandy" is also frequently given to alcoholic beverages distilled from fruits: cherry brandy, apricot brandy, blackberry, and plum brandies. The most famous brandy made from plums is slivovitz, a fiery colorless spirit from Yugoslavia. Applejack is another name for apple brandy; the Calvados of France is a distillate of cider (also therefore apple brandy). Kirsch (or kirschwasser) is a spirit made from cherries in Germany and Switzerland.

Liqueurs are a blend of alcohol with flavoring ingredients, sweetened with syrup. Actually, the fruit brandies are technically liqueurs. Cordials are the same; the words are synonymous.

Brandies and Cognacs may be served at the cocktail hour (Brandy Sour, Brandy and Soda, brandy on the rocks) but primarily they are intended to serve after dinner, with or following coffee.

Liqueurs are strictly for serving after dinner (though they are also quite useful in the kitchen, especially for flavoring desserts).

It is fun to have a selection of brandies and liqueurs to offer dinner guests along with coffee, after or in place of dessert. Only a small amount will be consumed each time (guests rarely want a second liqueur), which means that while the initial cost may be high, the per-serving cost is fairly reasonable. Because of the high alcoholic content, liqueurs will keep indefinitely, in any closet.

The following liqueurs are worth knowing about. Personal taste is the only criterion that matters. If there are certain ones you like, stick to them.

Anisette. Liqueur flavored by anise, licorice-like. Serve in very small glasses; if used in the kitchen, use very sparingly, because the flavor is so penetrating.

Benedictine. A renowned liqueur whose formula is so secret that no one has ever been able to duplicate it (though vast sums of money have been spent trying). B and B is a mixture of half brandy, half Benedictine, preferred by those who find straight Benedictine too sweet. To meet the demand for a less sweet liqueur, the firm now produces DOM, which is less sweet than standard Benedictine.

Chartreuse. There are two types, green and yellow. The former is more potent alcoholicly; both have a spicy, aromatic flavor, both are now made in the area of Tarragona, Spain, though originally they were made by the Carthusian Fathers of the convent of Grande Chartreuse in France.

Cherry Heering. A famous Danish product, made from the black cherries of Denmark.

Cointreau. A Triple Sec-type liqueur; of French origin, but now also made in the United States.

Crème de Cacao. The flavor is of cocoa and vanilla beans; the liqueur originated in Venezuela.

Crème de Cassis. A liqueur flavored by black currants, used primarily to make the drink Vermouth Cassis.

Crème de Menthe. Peppermint-flavored liqueur; now made in the United States.

Drambuie. Made of Scotch whiskey and honey.

Grand Marnier. Another orange-flavored liqueur but of complex formula, more subtle than Curaçao. Now available in two types, one sweeter than the other.

Grenadine. Now a non-alcoholic sweetening syrup; originally a cordial made with the syrup of pomegranate juice.

Kümmel. Flavored with caraway seeds.

Maraschino. A liqueur flavored with the sweet cherries of Dalmatia; originally what we call maraschino cherries were preserved in this liqueur.

Sloe gin. Liqueur flavored with sloe berries (from the black-thorn bush).

Strega. White Italian liqueur, almost colorless, with spicy flavor.

Swedish Punch. National liqueur of Sweden, with licorice flavor.

Tia Maria. A coffee-flavored liqueur made with a rum base, from the West Indies.

Triple Sec. A white Curaçao, stronger in alcohol than orange Curaçao.

Incidentally, *any* liqueur may be blended with an equal part brandy to produce a less sweet drink.

WHISKEYS AND OTHER SPIRITS

A distilled spirit (any distilled·spirit) is produced by converting a fermented beverage into a vapor by the application of heat, which serves to separate the "spirit," the element which caused the beverage to bubble with fermentation, from water. When the vapor is condensed again into liquid form, the spirit is collected separately. The apparatus used to bring about this evaporation, separation, and subsequent condensation is called a still.

Brandy is a spirit distilled from wine. The alcohol used as a base for liqueurs and cordials (and for perfumes, flavoring extracts such as vanilla, and many, many commercial products) may be distilled from fruit juices or from grains. Curaçao, blackberry cordial, and applejack are spirits distilled from fermented fruit juice.

Most of the very potent spirits classified as "hard liquor" are distilled from fermented grain, or mash. This is true of all the whiskeys, and of gin, vodka, schnapps, and aquavit. Rum is distilled from the fermented juice of sugar cane. Tequila is distilled from the fermented sap of a plant that grows in Mexico (pulque, a popular Mexican drink, is the same fermented sap before it is distilled).

Proof is a term used to indicate the alcoholic content of a distilled spirit. Before there were other methods of proving the alcoholic strength, a lighted match was applied to the distilled liquid; if it would burn, this was regarded as proof that it met the classification of "spirit." That was long ago; more precise methods are now used, but the old terminology lingers on. In American usage, the "proof strength" is 50 percent of alcohol by volume; this means 80 proof whiskey is 40 percent alcohol, 100 proof is 50 percent alcohol. There is one very potent rum labeled as 151 proof, which means it is 75.5 percent alcohol.

Whiskeys

The name "whiskey" (or whisky, as it is usually spelled in the United Kingdom and Canada) is derived from the old Irish *uisce bethad*, literally "water of life." **Scotch**, the whiskey produced in Scotland, is made from barley, and the characteristic smoky flavor is due to the way the malted barley is dried over open peat fires before it is placed in the vat for distillation. The kind of water used, and the type of oak casks in which the whiskey is aged, also make a difference in flavor. When freshly made, all whiskeys are completely colorless, like vodka, and very harsh, like "grain alcohol." The golden to amber color is due mainly to the addition of caramel, but also partly to ingredients absorbed from the wooden casks in which it ages. Scotch is often aged in charred oaken casks which were formerly used to age Spanish sherry.

Irish whiskey (spelled with the e) was being made long before the "water of life" was being produced in Scotch stills. It, too, is made chiefly of barley, but the barley is not dried over peat fires so Irish whiskey does not have that smokey flavor. The finest Irish whiskeys are aged in the wood for at least seven years; it used to be that no Irish whiskeys were blended, but time and price competition have forced the manufacturers now to blend some brands. Those labeled straight Irish whiskey are not blended.

Canadian whisky (no e) is made from a malt of rye grown expressly for this purpose, plus corn and barley. It, too, is aged in casks charred on the inside. The slow aging in wood is said to give the Canadian whiskey its distinctively light golden color, but the smooth body is due to strict government control over every step of operation—more stringent than that of any other whisky- (or whiskey-) producing nation.

Bourbon is the finest of American whiskeys (spelled with an e). Produced from corn (a minimum of 51 percent) with other grains, bourbon is aged in new oak barrels which have been slightly charred. If the original distillation is aged at least two years in wood, not blended, it is called *straight bourbon*. If blended only with other bourbons, it is labeled *blended straight bourbon*. If labeled simply *blended bourbon*, it has been mixed with other spirits, either other grain whiskeys or neutral alcohol. This explains the price range. The distinctive flavor of bourbon is due not only to the methods of production but to the water used—lime water from deep underground sources which gives the whiskey its crisp clean flavor.

Sour-mash bourbon is rated superior to others. The term means the grain which is to be fermented into a "mash" is triggered into action by adding the residue from a previous fermentation. Sweet mash whiskeys are made by adding yeasts to the grain, which starts the fermentation much sooner and saves money for the producer.

Rye whiskey today is in very short supply. As the name implies, the grain used is predominantly rye (at least 51 percent). Straight rye is a heavier, sterner whiskey than bourbon, deeper in color. But most of what is called "rye" is really **blended whiskey** which may contain only 20 percent whiskey, the rest neutral grain spirits. About one-fourth of all whiskeys sold on the American market today are blends. These are, of course, much cheaper than straight whiskeys, and the cheaper the blend, the less proportion of real whiskey it contains.

Gin

All gins consist of straight grain spirits flavored with juniper. *London dry* means it is unsweetened (nor necessarily made in England). But few gins are sweetened nowadays, and even fewer are aged. The only aged type is *golden gin* which acquires light color from the wood of the barrel. A few gins contain other flavorings than juniper (fennel, licorice, cardamom orange, sometimes almond), but most are very dry to meet the American taste.

Vodka

A colorless spirit distilled from grains with no flavor whatsoever. The name means "little water" in Russian. It was originally made from a potato mash in Russia, and it was and still is the favorite tipple of most Slavs, who generally drink it neat, tossing it off in one gulp. It is prized for cocktails by Americans *because* it has no flavor, only effect.

There is no earthly reason for paying a high price for vodka. All vodkas are the same; only the labels and brand names are different.

Rum

Nearly all rums on the American market come from the West Indies, where they began life as a by-product of sugar cane or molasses. The darkest and sweetest type is **Jamaica** rum (use in any recipes calling for "dark sweet rum"). This is a very heavy rum with a distinctly molasseslike flavor and slight bitterness.

We used to get the finest light rums from Cuba until Castro took over. Now similar rums, including the inimitable **Bacardi**, a white rum, are being produced in Puerto Rico. The only significant difference between white and gold rums is the amount of caramel added for coloring—that and the care used in distilling and aging the rums, which is a difference of quality. Most rums are a blend of young and old rums; some have been flavored with a small amount of sherry, brandy, or raisins. "Liqueur rums" are very mellow and smooth, like fine brandies, and can be served as brandy is served, after dinner.

Most of the rums, light, gold, or dark, are used as cocktail ingredients, combined with fruit juices (especially lime, lemon, or pineapple) or fruit syrup (such as grenadine), with cola, or bitters and fruit juices (as in Planter's Punch). Rum is also extremely useful in the kitchen.

Lesser Known Spirits

Ouzo. A Greek neutral grain spirit flavored with aniseed; when water is added, it turns milky. The drink is licorice in flavor and slightly sweet, but much more potent than it seems when first sipped.

Schnapps. A colorless spirit, like vodka, popular in Germany and Scandinavia. Often a quick drink of schnapps, tossed off in one gulp, is followed by beer as a chaser.

Akvavit or **aquavit**. The Scandinavian vodka. The word comes from the Latin *aqua vitae*, "water of life."

Tequila. Distilled from the fermented sap of a Mexican plant.

Sake. Technically this is classed as a beer, since it is made from a fermented grain (rice) but not distilled. But it is quite high in alcohol (17 to 18 percent), and its effect is much more like that of a spirit. It is often referred to as "rice wine"; some find its flavor similar to that of a very dry sherry; for this reason, dry sherry is sometimes used in oriental recipes.

How to Buy and Store Spirits. A fifth (25-ounce) bottle of any distilled spirit will make 25 1-ounce drinks, or 17 drinks using

1½ ounces. If 2 ounces is poured in each glass, the fifth will make only 12 to 13 drinks. Most spirits manufactured in the United States are available in both fifth and quart sizes; a quart makes 32 1-ounce servings, or 21 1½-ounce servings. There is no problem of spoilage, because of the high alcoholic content.

Choosing the best buy must be weighed against such factors as what you can afford, and how appreciative those to whom you plan to serve the drinks will be. A straight sour-mash bourbon can be a magnificent drink (it has been called the American Cognac), but it may cost exactly twice as much as a blended whiskey.

Buy the cheapest vodka; the higher-priced ones are that way only because of the brand name and advertising revenues. Some people insist there is a vast difference between gins and that it pays to invest in a higher-priced one. There are slight differences in flavor, and in *distilled gin* the herbs used for flavoring have been added during the distilling process; those labeled *compounded gin* (or not labeled at all) have been flavored with oils, and are basically much the same, for all practical purposes, as what once was called "bathtub gin."

BEERS AND ALES

The history of brewing is as old as that of wine making, which is to say as old as civilization, but the beer of the ancients was an altogether different beverage from the one we know by that name today.

Beer starts with *malt*, the sprouts of barley grains. The barley is encouraged to sprout by being moistened; in the process an enzyme is developed which will later contribute to fermentation. The sprouts are dried, crushed, blended with other starchy cereals (in American beer production, rice and corn), and then "cooked" with water, hops, and sugar to form the *mash*. (It's the hops that give beer its characteristically bitter flavor.)

Yeast is added to the mash, and the quality of the yeast has a great deal to do with the final quality of the beer itself. During fermentation, many times the original amount of yeast is produced—and this will be saved to be used either as the yeast for subsequent brews, or to make such by-products as brewers' yeast, which is such an excellent source of vitamin B, and the dry yeast we use to make homemade breads.

After fermentation has ceased in the vats, the beer is transferred to storage tanks or other vats to mature. **Lager beer** is stored longer, at lower temperatures, than other types, until all sediment has sunk to the bottom. It is then carbonated and bottled.

Draft beer, instead of being bottled, is put into pitch-lined kegs (the purpose of the pitch is to seal the wood, for if oxygen reaches the beer through the wood it will be soured).

Bock beer is a heavy dark brew, sometimes slightly sweet, traditionally consumed in the spring. It used to be made of the dregs or sediment found in the bottom of the vats when they were given their spring cleaning, but today it is deliberately flavored and colored with caramel.

(In France, bock beer is a very light, delicate beer.)

Pilsner is a pale-colored, lightly carbonated beer with a decided hop flavor. The original Pilsner was a beer produced in the city of Pilsen, Czechoslovakia, whose distinctive flavor was due to the extraordinarily fresh pure water of the district. The term is used now, however, to describe a beer type.

Ale used to mean a beer without any hop flavor, but today the term is used to mean a beverage heavier and more bitter than beer, usually higher in alcoholic content.

Besides an ample supply of domestic beers, which can be purchased in supermarkets along with hamburger buns and potato chips, many beers are imported, among them Tuborg and Carlsberg from Denmark, Bohemian Pilsner from Czechoslovakia, Münchner from Munich, and Heineken from Holland. Each has its own special charm for the beer connoisseur.

How to Buy and Store Beer. Most beer is sold in supermarkets in six-packs, canned or bottled. It can be stored either in pantry or refrigerator; the reason for keeping it in the refrigerator is to have it already chilled whenever in demand. Long chilling will do it no harm. Once opened, however, beer goes flat very quickly.

How to Serve Beer. Because it is light in alcohol, beer may be served with meals as wine is served, though it is better with certain foods than others. Beer drinkers like it with spaghetti, hamburgers, sauerkraut, seafood, and sauerbraten. It is also considered the proper beverage with curry and other very highly seasoned dishes. It is not recommended for reducing diets, because of its high carbohydrate content.

Most beer drinkers prefer not to have a big "head" of foam on their glasses. The way to avoid this is to hold the glass at an angle and pour the beer in slowly. The foam will be higher if the beer is not thoroughly chilled; in fact, if the beer is warm when the bottle or can is opened, half of it may foam over and out before it can be poured.

USING WINES AND SPIRITS IN COOKING

Most recipes calling for the use of wine in generous amounts originated in countries where wine is plentiful, comparatively cheap, and taken for granted. In other words, when the pantry or cellar is well stocked with *vins ordinaires*, it's the most natural thing in the world to enrich and glorify a sauce in this way. To buy a bottle of expensive wine simply for use in a recipe is something else.

Gourmet snobs, or those so wealthy they don't have to worry about the price, may use a vintage wine in their Beef Bourguignonne if they like. It is true that the better the wine, the better the sauce. But one must use good judgment.

My criterion is to use in cooking only a wine that I would drink myself. By this I mean *vin ordinaire*, but good *vin ordinaire*. If a wine has started to turn sour, there are only two kitchen uses for it: 1) as a vinegar, and 2) as a marinade.

If it's to become a vinegar, add distilled vinegar to the soured red wine so it will turn thoroughly sour more quickly. If it's to be a marinade, use it only for marinating, not as a sauce; throw it out when the marinating process is finished.

Such a wine gone sour could also be used in making Sauerbraten, in place of the vinegar listed in the recipe, or in any recipe calling for vinegar, including pickles.

What about "cooking sherry"? Try drinking it. If you like the taste as a beverage, perhaps you'll like it in a sauce, too. I wouldn't. The same test should be applied to any very cheap wine a liquor-store clerk may try to sell you for cooking.

There are two basic reasons for using wine in cooking. The first and most important is for flavor. That's why a cheap poor wine is worse than no wine. The second is as a tenderizer and preservative. Meat soaking in a wine marinade for several days will improve in flavor and tenderness and will also remain fresh and usable longer.

Wine loses all its alcoholic content with cooking. Therefore there is no reason for not serving a cooked sauce containing wine to children or to anyone not supposed to touch alcoholic beverages.

The same rule of good sense applies to using brandy, bourbon, rum, or liqueurs in recipes. If you have some already on hand, by all means use it. If you haven't the particular kind the recipe calls for, you may be able to use a substitute with equally good results. Remember, however, that you are adding the spirit for *flavor*, not for alcoholic content. The reason spirits are flamed is not just to make a spectacular dish, but to burn off the alcohol, so that only flavor remains and the flavor will be more concentrated.

Here are some substitutes that I have found to work successfully:

•*Instead of brandy*, use bourbon, or a combination of bourbon and rum, or a moderately sweet sherry.
•*Instead of dry white wine* in some (not all) recipes, dry vermouth may be used; generally about two-thirds as much vermouth as the measure of white wine.
•*Instead of Madeira or Marsala*, sweet sherry can always be used.
•*Instead of Grand Marnier*, use Curaçao or any other orange liqueur.
•*Instead of sherry*, rum can be used, but half the quantity.

The results will *not* be the same; don't expect them to be. But they should be almost as good, and sometimes you even discover that a substitute is better than the original. (I prefer vermouth in Sole Véronique to white wine.) Wine cookery requires experimentation. You must add a little, taste, stir, and cautiously add some more. Remember, the wines (and brandies) themselves differ. One "dry red wine" will be more dry than another. One "dry white wine" may be quite tart, another almost sweet.

A sweet wine is not usually a satisfactory substitute for a dry wine, or vice versa, but it depends on how sweet the wine is. A domestic port, for example, which is a very sweet wine that happens to be red (ruby port, at least, is red), is not a satisfactory substitute for dry red wine in any recipe. Yet I have used Château La Salle, which to my taste buds seems quite sweet, in seafood and chicken recipes which called for "dry white wine," and the results were very pleasant.

Using beer in cooking. Beer has fewer uses in the kitchen

than wine, but it often can be added to a recipe that calls for sherry with good results. Flamande Carbonnade, the Flemish beef stew, is made with beer; some versions of Sauerbraten call for beer as the liquid rather than wine; shrimp may be cooked in beer instead of white wine; beer is excellent as the liquid in a frying batter. Beer can also be used as a marinade; it's especially good for chicken that is to be barbecued. And it's fine blended with cheese for a cheese spread.

HOW MUCH AND WHAT TO BUY FOR A PARTY

Here are general rules to go by when purchasing liquid supplies for any party:

- Count on an average of at least 3 drinks per person.
- Each bottle of hard liquor (whiskey, gin, vodka, or rum) will make (on the average) 15 to 20 drinks.
- Each bottle of wine or vermouth will make 6 to 8 drinks (that is, for 3- or 4-ounce servings. For 2-ounce servings, the total goes up to 12 or 13 drinks.

For a Cocktail Party

Suppose you have sent out invitations to 30 people. If 20 come, it's a good average. For 20 people, you need about 60 drinks (though more than 20 might show up, and some people will put 2 ounces of whiskey in their highballs instead of 1½).

These are friends of yours, so presumably you have some idea of their drinking preferences. The following suggestions should be amended accordingly; they are suggestions only.

Most people at a cocktail party will drink either highballs, on-the-rocks drinks, or cocktails—that's what they've come for. A few will prefer lighter drinks, such as vermouth or sherry. And you should always be prepared for the nondrinkers.

For 20 cocktail guests, you should buy a minimum of 3 quart bottles of hard liquor: one of scotch, one of bourbon or blended whiskey, the third of gin or vodka. To be safe, buy 4 bottles, adding to the previous list a second bottle of whichever spirit is more popular among your friends.

In addition to hard liquor, it's wise to have 2 bottles (one may be a pint) of apéritif wines. These may be sweet and dry vermouth (sweet for manhattans, dry for martinis), or dry vermouth and sherry, or vermouth and another wine. In summer, especially, many people like a wine spritzer made of white wine and soda. Sangría, made with red wine and lemonade, has become very popular. Cherry Kijafa may be offered as an apéritif, too. A manhattan can be made with sherry instead of sweet vermouth; even a martini may be made with a very dry sherry and gin (or vodka); make it 1 part sherry to 5 or more parts gin or vodka.

The larger the party, the more simple should be the "menu" of drinks offered, because mixing esoteric drinks in quantity is all but impossible. Most people today prefer on-the-rocks drinks to either highballs or cocktails. This simplifies service: for two-thirds of the company, old-fashioned glasses will do, using 2 large ice cubes in each glass. Pour over the cubes whiskey and water, or vermouth (dry or sweet as requested), or sherry, or cocktails. Martinis and manhattans on the rocks are now much more in demand than either of these cocktails served in a cocktail glass.

Vodka is popular with hostesses because it is so versatile. Use it instead of gin in martinis, add tomato juice or orange juice to it for, respectively, a Bloody Mary or a Screwdriver (and both tomato juice and orange juice are good beverages to have on hand for nondrinkers). Either frozen lemonade or frozen daiquiri mix may also be added to vodka, or pour Vodka and crême de menthe over crushed ice for an Abominable Snowman (strictly a "ladies' drink").

Other supplies needed for mixing, in the order of their importance:

Club soda	Angostura bitters
Tonic (quinine water)	Sliced oranges for garnish
Lemons (for the slivers of lemon peel)	Cocktail onions for gibsons
Frozen lemonade concentrate	Maraschino cherries for manhattans
Ginger ale	Limes
Martini olives	Cola (for nondrinkers)
Frozen daiquiri mix	Superfine sugar
Frozen orange juice concentrate	

Of these, the first four are the most important. Many people now dispense entirely with what is inelegantly called "the garbage," meaning olives, cherries, onions, or fruit garnishes. The frozen concentrates are good to have on hand, and if not used for the party, will keep in the freezer for other occasions. Cocktail mixes are also available, though the most popular cocktails are very easy to mix, and some people, including some of your guests, may take great pride in their ability to make a very dry martini or a very smooth manhattan.

Glassware. It is quite possible to give a cocktail party today without a single cocktail glass in the house, because of the increasing demand for on-the-rocks drinks. At least half the glasses should be old-fashioneds for this reason (even a highball can be served in an old-fashioned glass). Another one-fourth to one-third of the glasses should be tall tumblers for highballs, but it's best if they are not too tall; the 8-ounce size is best. Taller than this, the drinks are likely to be diluted with too much soda, or the amount of whiskey added may be too generous, or the drink will take so long to consume that it will become flat.

For a large party, it might be wise to rent glassware, for the more people at your party, the easier it is to "lose" glasses—that is, guests put their glasses down, then forget where they are, and meantime take a clean one. This means you could need about half again as many glasses as you have guests.

Bar Equipment. A bar can be set up on any table, though it should be fairly close to the kitchen, for convenience in getting fresh supplies of water and ice. It could be in the kitchen if you don't have outside help for the party and if yours is a kitchen you want to show off. Either a cocktail shaker or a cocktail pitcher will be needed for martinis and/or manhattans, and a long spoon (such as an iced tea spoon) for stirring. You also need a jigger, a bottle opener, and a corkscrew. A strainer is convenient for cocktails, but not essential. An ice bucket is very important.

If you don't have outside help, the bottles of liquor and all apurtenances should be placed conspicuously so that it will be easy for guests to help themselves. If using an ordinary table, cover it with a cloth, then with oilcloth to prevent damage to the wood from spilled water and alcohol.

Consider traffic when setting up the bar. To keep people moving, have appetizers on two or three different tables, the bar somewhere between, but remember the greatest congestion will be around the bar, so there must be ample space for moving past en route to other parts of the room.

Where to Leave Wraps. The usual way is to direct guests to a bedroom, where the coats may be piled on the bed. Few people have coat closets big enough to hold the wraps of all the guests. There is one drawback to the bedroom arrangement: when people are ready to leave, they may have trouble finding their coats under the pile. It is possible to rent a coat rack for the evening, from the same supplier who rents glassware and other cocktail needs.

Drinks for the Nondrinker. For any form of home entertainment, be sure to have nonalcoholic beverages ready to offer. Many of the same supplies you buy for mixing alcoholic drinks can be served straight: tomato juice, orange juice, quinine water, ginger ale, lemonade (Tom Collins without the gin), or a nonalcoholic cocktail of daiquiri mix and pineapple juice.

For Smaller Parties

For before-dinner drinks, you need to offer much the same sort of variety as for a cocktail party. This can be costly if you don't entertain much and don't have much selection on hand in your liquor cabinet (or perhaps don't even have a liquor cabinet). Most hard liquors can be purchased in pint sizes; a pint makes about 10 drinks.

A good way to straddle the issue is to offer a single drink, such as a daiquiri (which may not be anyone's favorite but is likely to be acceptable to all), or to have lemonade ready and offer a choice between Whiskey or Brandy Sour and a Tom Collins (using either gin or vodka), all three of which are made with lemonade.

It's easier to offer fancy drinks for a small cocktail party (8 to 10 guests), than for a large one. If esoteric enough, these might even supplant some of the demand for highballs. A rum drink served from a pineapple shell, for example, makes for conversation, and nearly everyone will want to try the concoction. Or a Frangipangi (vodka, pineapple and lime juice) is fun and refreshing. Offer just one such fancy drink, though; keep the rest simple.

In warm weather, the only before-dinner drink might be Sangria, served from either a punch bowl or a tall pitcher. In warm weather, it's also good to have beer in the refrigerator. Gin and tonic is one of the most popular of all summer drinks. In the winter holiday season, a punch may be served, or eggnog. But whatever the time of year, expect most of your guests to want whiskey. It's the American national drink.

Dinner-Party Beverages

Two rounds of drinks before dinner is normal, and it is proper to offer a choice of two spirits, perhaps whiskey and gin, plus vermouth. Dry vermouth may be used to make martinis, or served on the rocks with a twist of lemon. Quinine, soda water, frozen lemonade concentrate, and prepared cocktail mixes make it easy to amplify the selection.

If wine is being served with the dinner, you will need at least 2 bottles for a dinner party of 6, including yourselves. One bottle (a fifth) of wine will serve 2 persons abundantly, 3 generously; for 4 it is stingy. For a dinner party of 8 to 10 persons, you should purchase 3 bottles.

If you are having seafood as a first course, you might want to offer white wine first, followed by red wine. This is elegant and fun. But since most American dinner parties are reduced to one course at table for easier serving, it's probably best to stick to one wine.

Offering brandy and liqueurs with coffee in the living room after dinner is very chic. But if cocktails or highballs have preceded dinner, and wine has been served with dinner, the after-dinner *digestif*, as the French call Cognac, may serve only to induce a hangover the next day. If the host feels he must offer something more to drink when dinner is finished, a tall drink with a soft drink or just the soft drink alone, is probably a better *digestive*. Or, you might make the coffee a "fun drink," Café Royale, Caffè Romano, or Café Diablo, which makes any further libation unnecessary. The guests by now should be feeling quite happy, and the talk good, and that's the most important part of all.

Index

A-1 Sauce, 74
Abbachio ai Ferri, 309
Abominable Snowman, 801
Acidophilus milk, 43
Adonis Cocktail, 802
Aioli (Ailloli) Sauce, 237
Akvavit, 868
Albondigas, 285
Alcoholic beverages, 865–869
 buying and storing, 868–869
 for parties, 873 ff.
 and weight control, 132
 See also Wine; etc.
Ale, 870
 and weight control, 132
Allspice, 71
Almond(s),
 equivalent measures, 101
 Bread, Lemon-, 641
 Cookies, 718
 Cream Filling, 751
 Meringue, 686
 Pâté, Crab-, 170
 Sandwich, Hot Roquefort, 207
 Stuffing, Rice, 207
Ambrosia, 730
 Jellied, 741
Anchoiade, 199
Anchovy(ies)
 Anchoiade, 199
 and Egg Canapés, 180
 Eggs Stuffed with, 180
 Garlic Dressing, 242
 Pan Bania, 200
 -Pimiento Canapés, 180
Andaluz Cocktail, 802
Angels on Horseback, 188
Anise, 70
Anisette, 864
Antipasto, Instant, 187
Appetizers, 159–210
 and weight control, 128, 129
 Anchoiade, 199
 Anchovy(ies)
  Anchoiade, 199
  and Egg Canapés, 180
  Egg Stuffed with, 180
  Pan Bania, 200
  -Pimiento Canapés, 180
 Angels on Horseback, 188
 Antipasto, Instant, 187
 Artichoke Hearts, 161
  in Ham, 165

Appetizers (*cont.*)
 Aspics, 208–210
 Avocado
  Balls or Cubes, 161
  Guacamole, 168
 Bagne Caude, 174
 Bean Salad, Greek, 179
 Beef
  Chinese Hot Pot, 202–203
  Fondue Bourguignonne, 202
  Piroshki, 195
  Salad, Corned, 176
  Smørrebrød
   Potato, 204
   Tartare, 205
 Beets, 161
 Bourekakia, 183
 Bread Circles, Fried, 178
 Bubbly-Jock, Potted, 170
 Cabagge Piroshki, 195
 Camembert and Onion on Pumpernickel, 207
 Canapés, 180–181
 Caponatina, 173
 Carrot(s)
  Curls, 162
  Dilled, 165
  Slivers, 162
 Cauliflower Buds, 162–163
 Caviar, 186–187
  Greek Red, 175
 Celery
  Curls, 163
  Dilled, 165
  Stuffed, 166
   Shrimp-Cheese, 182
 Cheese, 615
  Balls
   Gorgonzola, 182
   Pecan-Crusted, 182
   Sesame, 182
   Shrimp, 182
  Bourekakia, 184
  Celery with Shrimp and, 182
  Cucumbers with Blue, 167
  Dreams, Spicy, 181
  Fancies, 182–184
  Flan, Swiss, 197
  Fondue, Swiss, 201
  Liptauer, Cone, 172
  Nun's Beads, 183

Appetizers
 Cheese (*cont.*)
  Pizzas, 198
  Petits Chassons au Roquefort, 183
  Potted, 168
  Profiteroles, 184
  Quiche Lorraine, 196
  Rarebit, Welsh, 201
  Rum Tum Diddy, 201
  Sandwiches
   Camembert and Onion, 207
   Grilled, 206
   Ham and, 207
   Pinwheel, 208
   Ribbon, 208
   Roquefort-Nut, Hot, 207
  Smørrebrød, Egg and Danish Blue, 203
  Sticks, Walnut-, 184
  Twists, 183
 Chicken
  Chinese Hot Pot, 202–203
  Karibabyaki, 202
  Livers
   Chopped, 171
   Pu-Pus, 193
   Rumaki, 193
   in Packets, 194
  Pu-Pus, 193
  Salad, Pea and, 176
  Smørrebrød, Shrimp and, 205
 Clam(s)
  Angels on Horseback, 188
  Fingers, Hot, 199
  Glaze, Tomato, 209
  Salad, Caribbean, 176
  Steamed, 188–189
 Cocktail Sauce, 172
 Codfish
  Balls, Baby, 186
  Piroshki, 195
 Conch Salad, 176
 Crab
  Balls, Deviled, 186
  Canapés, Louisiana, 181
  Pâté, Almond-, 170
  Quiche, 196
  Salad, 176
 Croque Monsieur, 207
 Cucumber
  Cubes in Salmon, 166

879